991

THE
Struggle for the Border

U.S.S.R.

Arctic Ocean

GREENLAND

ICELAND

ALASKA

Hudson Bay

CANADA

STRAIT OF
JUAN DE FUCA

UNITED STATES

Pacific Ocean

Atlantic Ocean

MEXICO

Gulf of Mexico

SOUTH AMERICA

THE BORDER
UNITED STATES AND CANADA

THE STRUGGLE
FOR THE BORDER

BY BRUCE HUTCHISON

Maps by James MacDonald

LONGMANS, GREEN & COMPANY
TORONTO   NEW YORK   LONDON

Longmans, Green and Co.,
20 Cranfield Road, Toronto 16

Longmans, Green and Co. Inc.,
55 Fifth Ave., New York 3

Longmans, Green and Co. Ltd.,
6 & 7 Clifford Street, London W. 1

THE STRUGGLE FOR THE BORDER

PUBLISHED SIMULTANEOUSLY IN THE UNITED STATES OF AMERICA
BY LONGMANS GREEN & CO. INC., NEW YORK

First Edition, September, 1955

44,829.

PRINTED AND BOUND IN CANADA
T. H. Best Printing Co., Limited, Toronto

TO

John Owen Wilson

"A FRIENDSHIP AS HAD MASTER'D TIME"

Contents

viii CONTENTS

Introduction

AN INFLUENTIAL SCHOOL OF MODERN HISTORIANS SEEMS TO HOLD that man's affairs are settled by ineluctable, impersonal, and calculable forces to which various convenient labels are given. That may be true. But human beings—uncertain, personal, and incalculable—also have something to do with the course of human events or, if not, we had better leave the future to the Communists, who have everything well arranged and taped up in advance.

This book has little to do with any theory of history but is concerned almost solely with individual men and their private adventures upon the North American earth, from John Smith, at Jamestown, to Dwight Eisenhower, at Washington; from Champlain, at Quebec, to St. Laurent, at Ottawa. If the book has any theory at all it is that, from time to time, at certain fluid moments, men, large and small, in wisdom, passion, or mere accident, made North America what it is, hardly suspecting the issue of their lives.

The historic, constitutional, and economic relationship of the two nations dividing between them most of North America has long been noted and much discussed by historians. Their excellent works on what might be called the rationale of the continent must now fill a vast library. This book is not intended to be an addition to that study, in such learned terms. It deals with people, many of them quite irrational. The writer's modest purpose will be served, therefore, if such a tale interests the reader in the past and future affairs of America, which, he believes, are greatly misunderstood and in urgent need of understanding.

The reader will see at once that, although this book is a joint account of Americans and Canadians in war and peace, in the contest of exploration, diplomacy and commerce, it is written from a Canadian standpoint, as must necessarily be so when the writer is a Canadian. In any case, this approach is deliberate. The writer believes that the American standpoint on the affairs of America has been amply set forth and that a Canadian viewpoint, often quite different, may be of interest—not because it is more valid but because it may set things in better proportion; for assuredly more

proportion is needed in a subject so important to every North
American and too often distorted in our schools, by misguided
patriotism, on both sides of the border.

Some of the opinions herein expressed will not meet with the
approval of many readers and historians. For such opinions the
writer must accept full responsibility as a layman and not as a professional historian. In a book covering so long a time and so wide an
area—more than three centuries and the whole struggle for America
—it is certain that, despite diligent effort, some items of history will
be presented in a fashion which professional historians will dis-
countenance or challenge. But I repeat, this is not a formal book of
history. It is an adventure story of men in action and careless of
what history would record.

The student concerned with abstract historical facts will find
them richly documented in countless better books than this, both
American and Canadian. While I have not attempted to compile a
bibliography out of many years of reading, a few books invaluable
to the student deserve to be mentioned—the works of Parkman, to
begin with, covering America's early history; Edgar W. McInnis's
The Unguarded Frontier; Charles A. Beard's standard works on
American history; John Bartlet Brebner's *North Atlantic Triangle*
and other books on North American affairs; Arthur R. M. Lower's
Colony to Nation and Donald Creighton's *Dominion of the North,*
the best modern Canadian histories; Professor Creighton's biography of Sir John A. Macdonald and John W. Dafoe's biography of
Sir Clifford Sifton, for a study of Canadian politics; the joint work
of F. W. Howay, W. N. Sage and H. F. Angus on *British Columbia
and the United States;* that superb saga of the prairies, Joseph
Kinsey Howard's *Strange Empire* and the essential records of western exploration by Bernard De Voto; George F. G. Stanley's study
of Canadian military history, *Canada's Soldiers;* a fascinating collection of Canadian quotations and phrases (which instantly illuminate
many obscure events of the past) by Robert M. Hamilton; and, of
course, the direct reports of such explorers as Champlain, Captain
James Cook, Alexander Mackenzie, Lewis and Clark, Simon Fraser,
George Simpson, and John McLoughlin.

I am indebted to the Parliamentary Library and Archives of
Ottawa; to the British Columbia Parliamentary Library at Victoria;
and most of all to Jean Ellis for her indefatigable work in organizing
the manuscript.

B. H.

Victoria, B.C.

THE
Struggle for the Border

1

The Odd Neighbors

[1535–1955]

ROM THE CREST OF MOUNT ROYAL, THEN AFLAME IN THE autumnal foliage of 1535, Jacques Cartier surveyed the St. Lawrence and called it the Ready Way to Canada—"*grand, large, et spacieulx*"—flowing from sources so remote that the Indians "had never heard of anyone reaching the head of it."

White men would need 273 years more to discover the western counterpart of the St. Lawrence and, with it, the chance to bisect North America by a political boundary.

In the summer of 1808 Simon Fraser, a dour Scots-Canadian and refugee from the American Revolution, descended an unknown river by canoe, or sometimes on hands and knees along a spiderweb of Indian ladders—"Our situation most precarious . . . as the failure of the line or a false step might have hurled the whole of us into Eternity, a desperate undertaking."

The discovery of the Fraser River, the sight of the Pacific Ocean, and Britain's claim to the northern half of the continent left Fraser heartbroken, in "great disappointment." He had missed his prize, the Columbia, by three degrees of latitude. And three years earlier Lewis and Clark had reached the Columbia's mouth, overland from the Mississippi, to claim America's richer half for President Jefferson's fledgling Republic.

Between the St. Lawrence and Fraser's new-found river lay the continental land mass, a long portage only, as the first explorers judged, on the sea passage to China. The strategic anatomy of this misplaced and inconvenient island was not grasped for nearly two centuries. But from the settlement of Jamestown, in 1607, and Quebec a year later, who could doubt that the continent, at least all of it north of Mexico, ultimately must be one and indivisible, the

1

property of the nation and race strong enough to seize it. Or, if that logic failed, America must be fractured, like Europe, into a congeries of quarrelsome little states.

To reasonable men all the laws of geography, politics, power, economics and common sense, the inexorable mandate of nature itself, seemed to impel a continental union. The countless public and private wars of America were fought to compel it. Though our schoolbooks usually record the process in two separate compartments, American and Canadian, the shifting line of those wars sewed up the history of the continent in one piece.

Champlain's clumsy arquebus, aimed at some Iroquois chiefs, defined the future route of north-south invasion and, with a first murderous shot, announced that America belonged to France. This was in the summer of 1609.

As late as autumn 1871, a pitiable mob of Fenians, thirty-nine in all, made the last armed attempt to capture Canada for the United States and ended in jail. Even in 1903 an American president was waving his Big Stick on the Alaska boundary, threatening to use force if necessary and speaking with "good-humored courtesy in *everything.*"

How comes it, then, that America has been bisected, nature defied, logic rejected, the normal course of human events wrenched out of joint by an experiment without any parallel in the five thousand years of man's recorded follies? What manner of man has described and held an invisible, defenseless line running from the eastern anchor of Cartier's river to the western anchor of Fraser's? Whence the myth that the American and Canadian peoples have been friends throughout most of their lives together when they were implacable enemies until less than a century ago? Whence the submyth that they are of identical character, instinct, and purpose when, in fact, they have always been inherently different and are becoming more unlike with every passing year?

Why, after perfecting the unique political arrangements of America, have these peoples failed so lamentably to perfect their economic arrangements; have integrated their military resources but refused to integrate their industrial resources; have erected an unexampled living standard by their technical skill and yet often managed their common business to the point of lunacy?

Why have they, and the rest of the world, assumed that they understood one another? And why is it that recent mistakes, misfortunes, or accidents have threatened to complicate both political and economic arrangements without for a moment threatening a friendship forged for the most part in violence?

In short, what improbable combination of circumstances, what fertile mother, what prolific womb could bear at once the American Republic, the Canadian monarchy, and the only ideal or almost ideal relationship between any two nations on earth?

They came from the same mother, the same womb, the same dream. Both nations were conceived blindly in the American earth and brought forth by the American Revolution.

To be sure, Washington, in the winter of Valley Forge, Jefferson, appealing to the opinion of mankind from Philadelphia, their opponent, Guy Carleton, then racing to the rescue of Quebec in the disguise of a French-Canadian *habitant*, King George gibbering in London and Dr. Johnson denouncing those disjointed "abortions of folly" pleased to call themselves the United States of America—these men, even the farthest-sighted of them, could not foresee the double fruits of the Revolution. Many North Americans cannot fully comprehend them today.

Yet somehow the continent has overcome its primary continental logic of union and achieved a unique logic of peaceful division. Somehow the United States always managed in the early days to fortify Canada while attempting to destroy it and, for reasons hardly known to itself, has accepted the northern rim of Manifest Destiny nailed down by a handful of Canadians. Somehow the fragile, the invisible and impossible line has held through the jungle of Maine and New Brunswick, along the St. Lawrence and the Great Lakes, across the Pre-Cambrian badlands, the central plains, the Rockies, and the coastal forest to the western sea without a fort or hostile gun on its 3,986.8 miles.

It has not been held by an act of God or, until recently, even by an act of friendship. It was held in the first place mainly by Canadians' abhorrence of the American Revolution. The United States is the affirmation of the revolutionary process; Canada the negation. The second American state began, indeed, as a counterrevolution against the Inalienable Rights of the Philadelphia Congress. This mere negation could not hold the boundary forever. It is now held by an unprecedented act of human intelligence.

But intelligence of itself has not been enough. The boundary of the 49th Parallel, apparently anchored by contract, is really anchored and can be securely anchored only in the conscience of the American people and in the dumb will of the Canadian people to be themselves. No paper document and no military force could sustain such an unlikely design; it is sustained by some 175,000,000 separate human beings in the unconscious course of their daily lives. That is the private miracle of America. No other continent has ever been able to duplicate it.

Like all workable human institutions, the boundary is a paradox. It was created by animosity on both sides but it lives by friendship. It divides two distinct races, nationalities, and living ways but unites them in one neighborhood, all the more durable because it permits diversity. It separates two political entities but it carries back and forth, in ceaseless motion, day and night, the largest freight of goods, travelers, and ideas crossing any frontier in the world.

Action and reaction, trial and error, antithesis and synthesis, hatred and affection have fixed the shape of America's geography, politics, and inner mind. The boundary is like a mighty heart, in systolic and diastolic pulse, nourishing one community of two parts, separate but organically interdependent.

In modern times the heartbeat has been so steady and reliable that the potent body of the continent is hardly aware of it. Though the organism generated by long evolution seems outwardly tough and muscular, inwardly it is as delicate as any human body. The very intimacy of the American-Canadian friendship makes it brittle and supersensitive—as the closest friends will ignore a stranger's offenses but will be wounded by the smallest slight from one another. Thus the border is marked by many secret scars, slowly healed, and by a few recent scratches.

They are hardly surprising when many of the greatest North Americans have resisted the continental division.

An unknown young Virginian officer rides into Fort Le Boeuf, on December 11, 1753, and warns France out of the Ohio country. He has asserted the unlimited power of England and the innate totality of America. After his escape from drowning in the Allegheny River —by a freak of weather which almost appears designed for larger purposes—Washington will soon assert the power of another nation, his own; but, like England, it still hopes to clutch the continent entire.

As if to symbolize that vain hope, a frozen hand reaches through the drifted snow of a Quebec street, on New Year's morning, 1776. It is the hand of another American soldier, Richard Montgomery, dead of Canadian bullets. His reach for the broken dream of a continental republic has exceeded his grasp, or any man's.

Wiser men than Montgomery and his companion, Benedict Arnold, can never bring themselves to abandon the dream. It is articulated by Benjamin Franklin, laboring with pen and printing press in a Montreal cellar and, shortly afterwards, with shrewd horse trader's haggling and bland innocence, in the salons of Paris. Jefferson likewise refuses to reconcile himself to the inevitable and unnatural. He proclaims again, in 1812, the wholeness and indivisibility of America—without providing the means to enforce it. At

Queenston Heights a shattered American army and a dead British general find the answer to this curious equation. Even so, the Republic will not accept the answer, since it affronts nature and the scheme of things. Has not Henry Clay laid down the dictum that the United States should "take the whole continent and ask no favors" for "I wish never to see peace till we do"? Does not the United States, indeed, hold a "mortgage" on every inch of Canadian soil, solemnly filed by Senator Zachariah Chandler, in 1871, to satisfy the Alabama Claims? And even in 1911 is not the Honorable Champ Clark, Speaker of the House of Representatives, affirming that he expects "to see the day when the American flag will float over every square foot of the British North American possessions, clear to the North Pole"?

Those thinkers regard the contrary notion—that America must be sundered by a scrawl of ink on a fictitious map—as a heresy, an aberration from the human norm, a repeal of reason, an insult to self-evident truth, not to be borne by rational men.

Nor were they obliged to bear it, at least in the past century. Grant's Grand Army of the Republic could have taken Canada in an easy march, as an afterthought to the Civil War, and Canadians listened anxiously for the tramp of that third and final invasion. At any time since then the conquest of Canada would have been a fairly simple military operation.

Why was the order not given? Because, some Canadians like to think, the United States never actually wanted the barren wastes of Canada.

No doubt there is a good deal in this theory. It explains the attitude of some Americans in the past and the present. It does not begin to explain the policy of their nation. The United States let Canada alone, after two botched and futile invasions, mainly because a third would confront the power of the British Empire and because the Empire was eager to appease the old enemy at Canada's expense. From the latter decades of the nineteenth century, however, the United States was strong enough to take Canada, so strong, indeed, that it had already nibbled off, by diplomatic pressure, the fringes of Canadian territory considered vital to its eminent domain. But to assume that it saw nothing beyond that line worth taking is to ignore the clear record of the boundary.

Since the days when Franklin affably proposed the cession of Canada as a legitimate dividend on the Revolution and Britain almost agreed, since Lewis and Clark sought a river leading to the rich northern peltries and President Polk propounded a simple proposition called Fifty-four Forty or Fight—since the beginning of the struggle for America the United States suspected and coveted the treasure beside it. Newly revealed, the treasure is more desirable today than never, one of the great and shining temptations of the world.

It has not been seized, in the fashion of other continents, because the United States has long since abandoned the thought of such a crime. The betrayal of a friendly neighbor would betray the United States itself and everything it has stood for in its own mind and in the opinion of mankind, would destroy the world's faith in the American people, their faith in themselves. Canada has been and is the ultimate test of the American conscience—to which a French-Canadian prime minister has lately given public testimony, oddly enough in the capital of India.

What is the simple meaning of these quite incredible events? It is that both nations of America have accepted, as no nations in their circumstances have accepted before, a sensible limitation of national sovereignty.

An agreement of that sort was easy, of course, in the case of the Canadians, since the overwhelming preponderance of power lay with their neighbors. It was not easy in the case of the Americans for precisely the same reason. Nevertheless, the Republic acted as no great power has ever acted, by concluding that it would gain more in the end by the limitation than by the expansion of national power. This conclusion is surely the sovereign lesson which North America now offers a world tortured and bedeviled by the old fetish of sovereignty.

The Republic took a long time to learn the lesson for itself. It probably would not have been learned at all if half the continent had not been inhabited by a stubborn northern breed not rational enough—or perhaps too rational—to admit the obvious continental facts; by such men as John A. Macdonald, for example.

Summoned to his door, half awake, this apprentice lawyer of questionable habits and bibulous look was offered his first brief in 1838—the defense of a gallant Pole and a band of American patriots who had fortified themselves in a stone windmill beside the St. Lawrence to liberate Canada from its British oppressors. Macdonald could not save his clients from the hangman's rope at Kingston, but he had begun slowly but surely that day to build a Canadian nation by toil, political cunning, private tragedy, alcohol, genius, and a deep distrust of the United States.

Or consider, in this unlikely conjunction of continental forces, the case of Macdonald's most notable victim, Louis Riel. A half-breed, a prophet of divine mission and, some said, a madman, Riel briefly bestrode the prairies with a wooden crucifix in his hand while Manifest Destiny invited him to hand the West over to the Republic. Riel's madness could not comprehend any better than Macdonald's sanity the logic of the continent. He was still a Canadian, convicted of treason, when Macdonald's government hanged him (and itself) from a gallows at a town named Pile o' Bones.

Or again, what kind of logic could produce that other Canadian rebel, William Lyon Mackenzie, who fled from the comic battle of Montgomery's Tavern, disguised as an old crone, sought refuge in the United States, almost involved it in a war with Britain, and ended his days as a member of Parliament and loyal subject of the Queen? What incalculable destiny could make the rebel's grandson, Mackenzie King, prime minister of Canada and intimate of Franklin Roosevelt, even though King suspected his friend of secretly coveting the Canadian state?

What unimaginable chance could sprout, in the field of an Ontario bush farmer, Duncan Fife, the only kind of wheat able to survive on the western plains and thereby populate and hold them for Canada?

Let the modern historian, who sees order and rhythm in history, explain the case of Doc Keithley, John Rose, Sandy MacDonald, and George Weaver. These four men, hungry and beaten, were ready to abandon their search for gold in the British Columbia mountains. Their last pan of gravel filled their packs with nuggets and launched the Cariboo rush of the sixties. Canada's empty Pacific littoral suddenly found itself with people enough to resist the northward expansion of Oregon. It also found a man born plain Smith, who changed his name to Amor de Cosmos, the Lover of the World, and persuaded his countrymen, by a narrow margin, to vote against union with the Republic. Then, at the critical moment, the United States provided William Cornelius Van Horne to push a Canadian railway to the Pacific for the sole purpose of preserving his adopted from his native land.

Accidental men of this breed fitted into no pattern until they built a pattern of their own. They knew nothing but a fierce appetite for the Canadian earth. In the darkness of an empty wilderness they had no light but an inner flame, hidden under an arctic silence. Their homemade equipment was sufficient for their wants.

Given the two quarrelsome breeds on either side of the border, the wonder is not that they fought so long but that they halted their struggle short of final conquest. On both sides the advances and retreats, the broken truces, the blunders, deceptions, and crimes were beyond reckoning. So were the heroism, agony, patience, labor, and ingenuity. These peoples threatened continental war because a worthless little ship had been burned and sent flaming over Niagara Falls, and again because an aged pig had been stolen and eaten on a Pacific island. They were so long haunted by the specter of renewed conflict that even a man as sensible as Macdonald, the first Canadian prime minister, was suggesting, on April 9, 1867, that India attack San Francisco to divert the United States when it attacked Canada. The shot fired at Fort Sumter, said Macdonald's colleague, Thomas D'Arcy McGee, warned Canadians "to sleep no more except on their arms."

All those alarms have passed. Soldiers of the United States and Canada are living together in the Canadian arctic to protect a split continent. They sleep on arms that can never be aimed inwards on America. Cartier's river, where Indians and whites fought since unremembered time, is being tamed today by the joint dams and canals of its dual owners; Fraser's river nourishes its salmon hordes under the regulations of an international authority; every drop of water crossing the boundary is controlled by amicable contract.

The great change—little more than half a century old and hardly to be judged decisive until the past two decades—has followed a long and fitful fever. Madness and sanity, greed and generosity, quarrel and reconciliation, sin and forgiveness, loss and gain have welled along the border of America in tidal flow. They have left behind, in firm sedimentary layers, the continent we now inhabit, the only continent surely at peace and divided by agreement.

If human affairs show no parallel to the 49th Parallel of latitude, certainly the feat of human intelligence thus bounded is by no means complete. Nor is the journey, begun by Champlain at Quebec and John Smith at Jamestown, yet safely finished. On the contrary, it is only well started. And its future is far more dangerous than its past.

More dangerous because it must survive in a world on hair trigger; more complex because the power balance of the continent is being steadily revised. The affairs of America were never simple and seldom what they seemed to be in the rhetoric of politicians, in the neat arithmetic of the economic determinists, or in the school history books, written for the most part with malice on both sides. These affairs have grown overnight in intricacy, in subtlety, and in need of greater knowledge. They have been changed by the impact of a world revolution.

The revolution is vast and amorphous beyond human understanding. The past, the present, and, in essentials anyway, the joint future of the two American nations can be understood if we put our minds to it.

That we have hardly begun to do. In the eyes of most Canadians the United States, for all its devices of information, remains a caricature compounded of Broadway, Hollywood, and the dark underside of Washington politics. To most Americans the people of Canada are pioneers on a lonely northern frontier, suburban residents just outside the walls of the Republic, or exiled Englishmen, and in any case good, honest folk, reliable in the pinch, safely to be taken for granted, and indistinguishable from their neighbors, except for their tricks of accent or silence.

The two-sided caricature contains enough truth to make it mischievous. Americans are usually not angry but deeply hurt when Canadians misunderstand and criticize them. Canadians, being even more sensitive under a placid exterior, cannot bear to be taken for granted. So, in an age of mechanical communication the real lifestuff of both peoples fails to come through the radio waves, the television boxes, the speeches, and the printed word.

How many Americans have yet distinguished the hard facts of the border from among the genial myths?

The fact that two peoples, so alike in their outer habits, differ fundamentally because their historic experience is different.

The Americans spiritually whole after cutting their ties in Europe; the Canadians refusing to cut those ties and thus spiritually split by the contrary tugs of their origins overseas and their attachment to their own land.

The Americans confident in their own unequaled power; the Canadians balanced uncomfortably on a transatlantic tightrope of memory, sentiment and interest, forever conscious of their mortal peril if their two friends, the United States and Britain, fall to quarreling.

The Americans devoted to their written doctrines, fixed principles, self-evident truths, ironclad Constitution, and government by laws, not men; the Canadians skeptical of all theory, deliberately pragmatic and inconsistent in great concerns, compelled to live, huggermugger, by compromise in a society of two races, yet grimly attached to their curious institutions, their folkways and their queen, who happens to live in London.

The Americans lively, humorous, articulate, excited, certain of man's essential equality, and truly democratic; the Canadians superficially stolid, apparently humorless, silent, unruffled, yet full of a hot inner pride, always aware of man's inequality, and convinced that democracy has its limitations.

Two peoples, in fact, who have been exposed to the same American environment but see it through divergent angles of refraction.

How many Americans have considered a more obvious and measurable fact: If civilization lasts, the United States must live, half a century hence, beside a nation of something like fifty million people, more powerful than any nation now in Europe?

Or the fact that, even now, the United States could not fight a foreign war without Canadian supplies; that Canada buys more American goods than any other nation and far more than it sells to the United States where industry, comically enough, is afraid of Canadian competition.

The fact—far more important than the hard Canadian dollar, and all Canada's minerals, oil, forests, farms, and other natural resources combined—that a new nationality, race, and human creature have emerged at last north of the border; that the secret watershed of Canadian history has been crossed only in the present generation and the nation finally proved viable.

Above all, the fact that no foreign people on earth has so intimately, persistently, and inevitably affected the course of American history as a few million Canadians who only wished to be let alone.

On the other hand, how many Canadians have grasped the fact that they have built their nation mainly by the consent and cooperation of the United States, despite its occasional gestures to the contrary; that Canada not only began as the child of the American Revolution but is viable today only under American protection; and that if Canada cannot contract out of American power and American mistakes, yet no nation of its size and strength has ever received such generous treatment from a giant on its undefended flank?

Not many Canadians or Americans have grasped those facts of the past, understood the urgent problems of the present, or foreseen the greater problems of the future. A single event of recent times— unimportant, preposterous, but highly revealing—briefly lighted the gulf of cordial misunderstanding which marks the border more clearly than any map.

The United States Senate proposed to transfer its spy investigation, complete with television cameras and partisan politics, to Ottawa. The statesmen of Washington were amazed because the Canadian government refused to permit this obvious affront to its sovereignty. A few days later the Canadian people showed themselves equally ignorant of their neighbors. Lester Pearson, Canadian foreign minister, had been smeared by some obscure American publications, as soft on communism. Probably not one American reader in a thousand had heard of this poisonous nonsense. But the Canadian press blazoned it in hysterical headlines and the Canadian nation writhed in a fury of national outrage. That American senators could so misconstrue the feelings of Canada, that Canadians could so quickly suspect the good sense of the United States, was surely a disturbing thing.

Such absurd incidents, and many more significant, though less noted, have long roots. They come out of an endless adventure, a combination of men, geography, natural forces, and sheer accident— the unbelievable story of the 49th Parallel. It is a story at first dominated by outsiders but essentially the story of two distinct peoples striving to subdue the American environment in their own separate fashions. Though the Bourbons, Pompadours, Richelieus, Mazarins and Napoleons of France, the Tudors, Stuarts, Georges and Norths of England, and all the other innumerable bunglers of Europe attempted to print the Old World's image on the New, the American nations quickly took their own from the earth around them.

When Frontenac gloatingly reported his massacres of New England settlers, when La Salle announced a new empire awaiting France on the Mississippi, and the La Vérendrye brothers mistakenly registered their first sight of the Rockies, they wrote in French. When Mackenzie recorded the white man's first crossing of the continent, when Simpson noted the secrets of the fur trade in his private code, when the Founding Fathers devised the American Constitution, when McLoughlin signed the effective surrender of Oregon and Webster the boundary settlement of Maine, they wrote in English. All of them were thinking, unconsciously, in a language of new meanings. Their minds had taken on an American dimension. They might regard themselves as transplanted Frenchmen or Englishmen, but they had been transformed by the continental environment, by the wilderness and far places, by the spectacle of river, lake, prairie and mountain, by the very air, the fierce sun, the cruel winter, the loneliness of their land—and not least by their struggle to unify or divide it.

2

The Rock

[1608–1635]

I N HIS FORTRESS OF ST. LOUIS THE GREAT MAN OF NORTH AMERICA
lay dying. It was Christmas Day, 1635.
Samuel de Champlain could see from his dank chamber the
rock of Quebec, the frozen glare of the St. Lawrence, the huddle of
shacks beside it. If he knew that the river held the inner secrets of
the continent, all the hopes of the French race in this land, perhaps
even the ultimate hope of a passage to Asia, if he had held the
river for France and the Faith after a life of ceaseless battle, suffering and betrayal, yet he must die without guessing the issue of his
work.

It was larger than he supposed—hardly less than the shape of
civilization in America. With a few musket balls he had launched,
singlehanded, two centuries of struggle for America's possession,
begun its division in two states, and discovered an idea which alone
could enforce that division.

Neither Champlain nor any successor could put a name to the
decisive idea but by the tests of war and peace it would suffice—
the idea of Canada.

The French at home would never grasp it and, in consequence,
must lose their grasp on America forever. The English to the south
must learn it by long experience and much bloodshed, would hardly
understand it for three centuries yet. And least of all could the
English suspect that they themselves were building the northern
nation which they were determined to destroy. Understood or not,
Champlain's discovery could never be suppressed, purchased, or
escaped.

On that Christmas Day the dying man, forgotten in his icy prison,

12

surveyed all the human contents of the nation conceived only in this single mind.

Fewer than three hundred Frenchmen clung to the rock and claimed, with no shadow of power to uphold it, title to all the unknown lands from here to Asia. Such a comical claim could impress only the clerks of Paris, with their amorphous, ever-changing maps. Perhaps, in his spare moments, the tired and rouged Cardinal remembered Champlain, his servant, but Richelieu had larger affairs than Canada to consider these days. He was making France mistress of the world.

The seven thousand English heretics thriving beside the Atlantic coast doubtless had never heard of the man in Quebec. Or if they knew France's continental ambition, their mere presence denied it. England, not France, obviously must possess America, by the force of numbers, by superior virtue, and of course by God's will. Why, it was said that the Royal Governor of Virginia traveled in a coach-and-four when Quebec had just imported its first ox. That lonely animal toiled across the farm of Louis Hébert, the only farm in all Canada. It was clearing a battlefield for Wolfe and Montcalm.

The two embryonic forces already grappling in the first distant encounters of Indian ambush, raid, and fur barter were not only one-sided: they were totally misjudged. Champlain supposed that he had fought for France, the Faith, and Canada against England and the Protestant Reformation. Actually his adversary was, or would soon become, a new state, a new race, and a new system. The English imagined that they were fighting France and popery. They confronted in fact the beginnings of another new state, race, and system which, for better or for worse, they would never conquer or seduce.

A few hundred men in Quebec and a few thousands in the English colonies must unite the continent by arms or divide it in peace. Champlain's arquebus and cold stroke of murder had established the first rough line of cleavage. But where would the final line run?

Along the river certainly, for it was the natural bisection of the continent as far west as white man had penetrated. Could the French hope to hold even the river line? It seemed unlikely and, to anyone less inspired than Champlain, less calculating than Richelieu, impossible.

Only six years earlier England had taken Quebec and, without firing a shot, could have clutched all the lands from the Spanish colonies of Florida to the North Pole. To secure his queen's dowry the English King had given Canada back to France at a future cost beyond reckoning. Another king less idiotic would hardly make that mistake a second time.

The tiny French settlements on the Atlantic coast, called Acadia, had been twice seized and gutted by the English. They now lay defenseless beside their thrusting New England neighbors.

Half a century ago Francis Drake had looted his way northward along the Pacific coast, heavy with the Spanish gold of South America, in search of the Strait of Anian, supposed to cut America in two. He had been turned back by the "frozen nimphes, the thicke mists and most stinking fogges." Twenty years later a Greek seaman called Juan de Fuca said he had sailed from California through a passage leading to the Atlantic or the arctic and located on the 47th degree of latitude—a bold lie but there was a speck of truth in it. De Fuca's imagination had hit by accident on solid geographical fact. A strategic channel did penetrate the western coastline and someday might prove defensible.

The Pacific remained outside the practical politics of Champlain's age. French settlers on the St. Lawrence and English on the Atlantic coast were concerned with the space between the coasts. What lay there in the bourne of an undiscovered country where Frenchmen had left only an occasional moccasin print and Englishmen had never ventured, a country ending apparently not far from China? That was the primary American question. No man would answer it for a long time yet. And when it was answered, what mind could distinguish any tenable frontier to divide French from English power? Not even the spacious mind of Champlain, the soaring mind of Richelieu, or the tortured, hagridden minds of the New England Puritans would ever hit upon the 49th Parallel.

To the French the whole interior down to Mexico, whatever its size and shape, was part of the King's royal peltry. The English did not see far ahead, knew nothing beyond the Atlantic shelf but intended to take any land they needed and, as soon as convenient, to dislodge the troublesome papists on their northern border.

The 49th Parallel thus had no virtue for either side and neither had thought of it. A geographer in London or Paris who chanced to put his finger on that line could not tell where it lay beyond the river, through what unimaginable regions it traveled to the western sea. If such a line were to be anything but a scratch of a pen, man must make it so, for nature and geography disregarded it. If nature, geography, and even common sense were to prevail, there would be no frontier because there would be a single state. Or if, defying those laws, man made two, then only a man-made prodigy could hold the 49th Parallel as a boundary between them.

A larger prodigy would be needed to make the parallel a guardian of peace.

No man in America was wise enough to ponder either possibility. All Americans—English, French, Spanish, and Indians—were pondering delusions sufficient to occupy them fully in the visible future. But invisibly the continental prodigy was under way. Of which the shacks on the St. Lawrence bank and the dying man in his fortress were the symbols and first cause.

The civilized world was too distracted that Christmas to consider, much less to comprehend, such things.

While Christians marked the festival of the Prince of Peace, the Thirty Years' War rolled on, insensate and insatiable, spawning new wars in the strangest places every day, for no cause that men could remember, but all fought in the interests of religion. It rolled over the crushed face of Europe and across the seas into savage lands where the benefits of civilization had never been shared before. It had ground the chief nations of the times into starvation and disease on a scale to be duplicated only after three hundred more years of progress.

The Age of Reason was dawning—an age of philosophers, statesmen and poets, of plunderers, assassins, pirates and royal harlots, an age wherein ancient dynasties lurched toward block and ax, the feudal underpinnings of the Middle Ages cracked silently one by one, the Old World writhed in labor of bearing its offspring and could not see the form of the thing it bore—least of all its twin children of the New. In short, the kind of age which modern man once more inhabits.

The inflexible velvet hand of Cardinal Richelieu held everything in Champlain's homeland of France, deftly manipulating king, queen, nobles, armies, and treasury.

A handsome English sovereign had begun to lose a head over-stuffed with Divine Right, and an obscure squire named Cromwell with "swollen, reddish face," his linen "plain but not clean," brooded on the Rights of Man and would brood on regicide.

First-class passengers on the rival ships of state could not be expected to observe lesser ships, mere cockleshells, bobbing on the Atlantic—within them nameless men who, landing on the American shore with all the racial memories and religious hates of the Old World and a secret cargo more explosive than gunpowder, would sing their psalms, cultivate their fields, slaughter the natives, hang witches, devise a weird new notion called democracy, and hatch they knew not what a marvel.

A world of heroism and horror little noted nor long remembered the fortress on the black rock and its prisoner. Though he had ignited a process more important and far more hopeful than all the brawls of Europe, he must die alone beside his river.

Champlain's enemies were little noted either. But their cramped farms among the swamps of the south and the stones of New England contained a weapon too strong for the first Canadian and all the power of Europe's mightiest state. The English had come to stay while the French had come to trade. Therein, as perhaps he surmised, lay Champlain's tragedy.

Another century must pass before the tragedy would reveal itself. Meanwhile the life of Champlain had established one of the two great facts of the future America. It had planted the life and forecast the character of the Canadian people.

Champlain combined the energy, practicality, loneliness, tough nerves, and inarticulate love of the Canadian earth that would make Canada. He was in himself, despite his unmixed French blood, the microcosm of the future Canadian race. He was also the first man to feel the contrary pulls of geography, sucking Canadians ever deeper into America, and of history, wrenching them back to their sources in the old land. And he was the first to choose between these opposites. The primary national decision had been made when he turned from history to geography and chose to die in Canada.

Of his true place in the North American scheme he could know little and far too little is known of him. We cannot see even the image of his face. All his portraits have vanished. His bones are lost in the ruins of his town. His inner mind, his courage, patience and stern religiosity, his streak of ruthlessness and, at times, the gambler's cool calculation, all speak through his hard, factual and humorless writings.

Nearing the end, he confessed his sins to his chaplain "with sentiments of piety so lofty that he astonished us all." There could have been few to confess. His memories that day were of another sort—boyhood at Brouage as a mariner's son; ten years of fighting against his fellow countrymen in the mud of Brittany; the voyage to the West Indies as the King's geographer, when he proposed a canal across the Isthmus of Panama; the first sight of the St. Lawrence in 1603, the island of Mount Royal, and the rapids of Lachine. There, in that glimpse of a glorious unknown, he had found the true purpose of his life.

Cartier had stood on Mount Royal nearly seventy years before. The fishermen of France, England, and Spain had long fished the Grand Banks, careless of the land beyond them. Raleigh had planted

his Roanoke colony whose 108 inhabitants had disappeared, leaving
only an arrowhead pointing toward the west. The Spanish had
destroyed two great civilizations in Mexico and Peru to build a
third of their own. The French had failed in three attempts to settle
Canada.

All these failures could not discourage the young Champlain once
he had grasped the presence of the river as the vital artery of a
new continent—probably, as he hoped, a water passage to Asia.

The five succeeding years were a restless interruption in his
chosen work of exploration. The gallant de Monts' settlement on the
island of St. Croix, against the western shores of Fundy, where
frozen cider was served in chunks and nearly half the 250 settlers
died of scurvy; next year the building of Port Royal, solid and comfortable in the sheltered basin of Annapolis, with Champlain's gar-
den, his trout ponds and summerhouse; his *Ordre de Bon Temps*—
the ruler of the feast with "wand of office and the collar of the
Order worth more than four crowns"—curing scurvy and boredom
by banquets of moose, caribou, partridge, geese, and delicious
beaver tails; the first theatrical performance in America, "Theatre
of Neptune," contrived by the merry Lescarbot; a cruise down the
coast as far as Cape Cod; a skirmish with the Indians; the fateful
verdict on this land of Norumbega as useless for settlement; its loss
forever to the English—all these labors seemed wasted. Champlain
yearned only for the river.

De Monts lost his charter in 1607 and his settlers abandoned
Port Royal. The first English reached Jamestown the same year.
They had occupied the richer half of the Atlantic coast and faced
the vaster riches behind it.

Champlain forgot the English in the summer of 1608. He had
reached Quebec and seen the thrust of rock looming dark, naked,
and as it seemed, impregnable over the gate of America.

The businessmen of Paris regarded Quebec as a site to control
the river traffic and lure the Indians' wealth of furs into the coffers
of France. Champlain held it as a way point on the road to China.

His backer, the able Pontegravé, had been granted one year's
royal monopoly of the fur trade. Champlain was expected to establish French control of the entire American peltry. Any larger ideas
in his mind were his affair. Paris knew nothing of Canada, cared
less and was interested solely in the hides of beaver to make felt
hats, especially the *castor gras d'hiver,* those rich, winter-trapped
pelts long worn and oiled to fashionable perfection by the sweat of
Indian bodies. For such skins merchants were ready to risk money
and the skins of better men.

The jealousies of rival fur traders followed Champlain to Quebec. He soon discovered that they were planning his assassination. This man of God could strike fast. He seized John Duval, leader of the plot, who was "strangled and hung and his head was put on the end of a pike . . . that he might serve as an example to those who remained, leading them to deport themselves correctly in future."

Champlain's Habitation, rising daily on the river shore, was a lopsided, rambling, crazy structure, as his crude drawing shows. There were three buildings, two stories high, with a gallery around them, a moat and a palisade. The bare timber against the black rock, the wink of light, and puff of smoke made less than a pin's prick on the wilderness.

Imprisoned by winter, the twenty-eight inhabitants ate eels and forest roots, and died slowly the hideous death of scurvy. Far away at Jamestown the first Americans were starving also. John Smith's matter-of-fact record notes: "So great was our famine that when a Savage we slew and buried, the poorer sort took him up againe and eat him."

Champlain's spring census showed that "out of the twenty-eight first forming our company only eight remained and half of them ailing."

Their impatient leader still could not strike out on the open road to China. He had already made the decision which thenceforth must dominate the struggle of France and England in America. He would drive the Iroquois from the St. Lawrence, leaving the friendly Algonquins and Hurons, north of the river, free to bring the furs of the interior to Quebec. All his other plans were set aside as he undertook a brief detour southward with his new allies against their ancient enemy.

The first major war of America led him up the Richelieu to a noble lake marked by his name. He had stumbled into the continental trench. Thenceforth it must carry the French southward and then the English northward, in perpetual march of arrow, musket and cannon, of pitched battles, sieges, advances and retreats, of heresies, Inalienable Rights, Declaration of Independence, Manifest Destiny, and God knew what else, all designed to engulf a people who would never be engulfed.

Now came one of the seminal moments of North American history. The French and their Indians met the Iroquois at Crown Point "advancing at a slow pace towards us, with a dignity and assurance which greatly impressed me." Champlain, and two other Frenchmen, in plumed casques, breastplates and steel cuisses, leveled their massive arquebuses. Each was loaded with four balls for

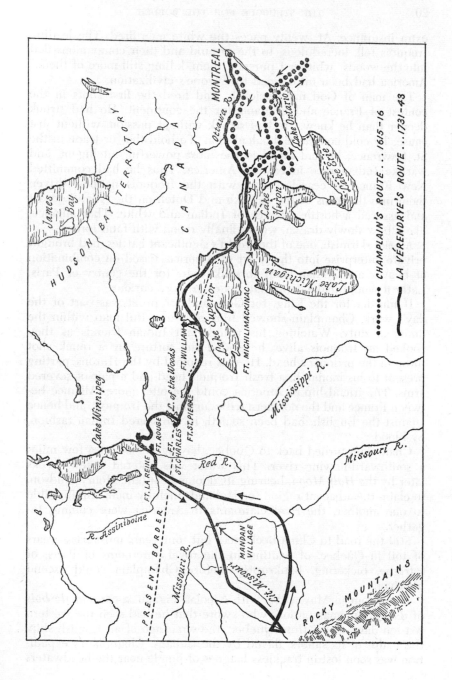

CHAMPLAIN'S ROUTE ... 1615-16

LA VÉRENDRYE'S ROUTE ...1731-43

MONTREAL

Ottawa R.

CANADA

Lake Ontario

Lake Erie

Lake Huron

HUDSON BAY TERRITORY

JAMES BAY

Lake Michigan

Lake Superior

FT. WILLIAM

FT. MICHILIMACKINAC

Mississippi R.

Lake Winnipeg

L. of the Woods

FT. ST. PIERRE

FT. ST. CHARLES

FT. ROUGE

FT. LA REINE

Red R.

Missouri R.

R. Assiniboine

PRESENT BORDER

Missouri R.

MANDAN VILLAGE

Lit. MISSOURI

ROCKY MOUNTAINS

extra insurance. At twenty paces the white men fired. The leading Iroquois fell, incredulous, to the ground and their companions fled into the woods "whither I pursued them, killing still more of them." America had been introduced to Europe's civilization.

The man of God unconsciously had fired the first shots in the contest of France and England for the continent. He had struck deeper than he knew. He had struck without passion, without just cause, by cold commercial calculation. To hold the fur trade in the St. Lawrence, he had attacked the most powerful, intelligent, and warlike Indian race in eastern America. Thus he had committed New France to ceaseless war with the Iroquois nations, driven them into the arms of the English and Dutch on the Atlantic coast and assured a hostile alliance of Indian and white. That alliance, like a bow slowly drawn, would finally recoil with fatal force.

A brief skirmish, one of the world's significant battles, had brought private enterprise into the heart of America, based on combination of beaver and Indian skins to make hats for the gentry of Paris. Later it would make combinations even more curious.

If murder for the King, for God, and for profit was part of the day's work, Champlain showed himself a merciful man within the limits of duty. Watching his triumphant Indian friends as they cooked an Iroquois alive, he ended the torture by a quick shot through the prisoner's head. He was revolted by the Hurons' parting present to his monarch, a fresh Iroquois head and a pair of severed arms. The friendship of America could not offer more. Alliance between France and the northern tribes against the Iroquois, and hence against the English, had been sealed, in the sacred Indian fashion, by blood.

Champlain turned back to Quebec, having missed by a few miles a southward-flowing river. This water was entered a few weeks later by the *Half Moon*, bearing its doomed captain, Henry Hudson, to claim the adjacent region for Holland. Inch by inch, still invisible to one another, the rival claimants to America were coming together.

Still the road to China beckoned, but four years must pass—years of toil in Quebec, of waiting in the royal anterooms of Paris, of intrigue, bickering, bankruptcy—before Champlain could ascend his river.

He set out in May, 1613, with Nicolas Vignau, a *coureur de bois* of dangerous imagination, who swore that he had seen the western sea ten days' travel from Quebec, the wreckage of an English ship, the scalps of its sailors, flayed by the Indians. Champlain's expedition was soon lost in trackless leagues of jungle near the headwaters of the Ottawa. Vignau confessed his lie and Champlain turned back, unable to endure his deceiver "any longer in my presence."

Two years later the desperate Hurons and Algonquins needed help against the western Iroquois. Champlain started up the Ottawa again, entered Lake Nipissing, descended the French River, and beheld Lake Huron in Georgian Bay—a mighty vision but a cruel disappointment. This was only Mer Douce, not the salty western sea.

Champlain had begun to grasp the mainsprings of American geography, but he could not pause to explore or ponder his discovery now or even to see the full sweep of Lake Huron. The maples were in autumn flame, the pumpkins of the Indian villages ripe under the first frosts. There was no time to waste if the Iroquois were to be taught another lesson. He turned south, with eleven French musketeers and a large war party of Indians, crossed Lake Ontario, and attacked the stronghold of the Onondagas.

All his careful planning on that disastrous October day quickly went awry. To carry the thirty-foot palisades he had built a *cavalier* of protected scaffolding, on which he stood to fire down on the defenders while his allies burned the fort. The fort would not burn. The allies would not fight.

After three hours the besiegers were in such confusion that Champlain could not make himself heard above the din. Already wounded in both legs and "seeing that shouting would only burst my head," he allowed himself to be carried out of the battle on an Indian's back. The disorderly retreat northward was, he wrote, a "gehenna" of pain under the first snow of winter. All for nothing. The Iroquois' nest had been little damaged. They buzzed like hornets and prepared to sting again.

Champlain spent the winter in the filthy lodges of his friends. For fear of the Iroquois' revenge they would not let him go. It was not until the next autumn that he could return to Quebec, wondering if he would ever see the country of the lakes a second time. "If ever there was one greatly disheartened it was myself. . . . But realizing that I could not help the matter and that everything depended upon the will of God, I comforted myself."

It was cold comfort. His explorations were finished. Until his death he must spend half his time in twenty-five Atlantic crossings to plead for his king's support, the other half ruling a hamlet of threescore inhabitants and forever watching the Iroquois. Their memories had always been long. Now they possessed the long muskets of the Dutch and English.

Champlain's enemies were not a band of rootless nomads. They

were a people of high intelligence and had built the most successful Indian society in eastern America.

The Long House of their five nations stretched from the Hudson
to Niagara in a close-knit polity. Their central council, the forty-
eight Lords of the Confederacy, elected by all adult men and
women, met under the Tree of the Great Peace at Onondaga. They
were bound together by their Great Immutable Law and by the
legend of Deganawidah and his disciple, Hiawatha, founders of
their far-flung state.

Long before the French or English, the Iroquois established a
working democracy. Their people were all born free and equal.
Even prisoners of war, adopted into the Five Nations, were given
the full rights of citizenship. No aristocracy of birth was tolerated.
A leader must demonstrate his worth. A chief must be elected. The
chastity of women was sacred. The code of honor was violent and
merciless but it was strictly enforced.

These people were usually at war but they looked forward to
the day when all men would share in peace the hunting grounds
of America, governed by the democratic principles of Onondaga.
The Iroquois utopia might appear to a civilized man like Champlain
as a childish dream. Yet civilized man, more than three centuries
later, could devise no better.

Probably some 12,000 to 15,000 Indians were leagued in the Five
Nations and the Sixth, the Tuscaroras, who joined the Confederacy
early in the eighteenth century. They lived mainly by the hunt but
they cultivated, around their villages, crops of corn, pumpkins,
beans, and other vegetables. A crude economic system of trade
among themselves and with other tribes supported them in their
own style of life. They regarded it as quite satisfactory until the
white man offered the larger benefits of guns, metal implements,
and liquor.

Thus organized, and inspired by their myths, the Iroquois were
able not only to resist Champlain's alliance with the more northern
Hurons and Algonquins, and later alliances much more powerful,
but to defend their lands against the English and assert their independence for some hundred and fifty years of one-sided struggle.

Champlain's hold on Quebec, now challenged by the Iroquois,
was weaker than he supposed but it was France's only hold on
America. Without his stubborn faith the Canadian colony would
have quickly perished. It had made no mark on the American
earth save the twelve acres of farm hewed out of the woods on the
far side of the cliff by Hébert, the Parisian apothecary. Nevertheless, the first Quebec farm was a notable mark even if the French

court had heard no rumor of it and the fur traders regarded all cultivation as a crime against their business.

The furrow begun by Hébert and his nameless ox would reach far, finally spanning the prairies and wriggling down to the Pacific shore while the plowmen of Paris, in furrows now stretching across the map of Europe, were sowing crops to be harvested at maturity by Dr. Guillotin's ingenious reaper.

Hébert's farm, extended by more settlers of his tough breed, might save France against the English. The fur trade must ruin it. Already in these first days the fatal pattern was established. The search for fur and quick profit drained the energies of the colony, lured the most active young men into the woods, despite the King's prohibitions, and made Canada a parasite, dependent upon France even for its food.

At least Champlain's religious ambitions were prospering. One Indian soul gathered to Christ, he had written, was of "more value than the conquest of an empire." Souls were gathered in ample harvest by the gray-robed Récollets, to be followed by the black-robed Jesuits, each carrying in his birchbark canoe the vestments, altarcloths, and communion wines of the church, together with an inner thirst for martyrdom, quickly quenched.

Jean de Brébeuf, the bearded giant who had turned from aristocracy to God, the mild Jérôme Lalemant, Isaac Jogues, and Antoine Daniel were to die with more agony than their Master after the Iroquois' refined tortures of red-hot irons, burning belts of pitch, and baptism with boiling water. They perished gladly and all their missions in the Huron country must soon be destroyed. But, like Latimer at the Oxford stake, they had lighted a candle. It could never be snuffed out by pagan Indian or Protestant English.

The distractions of fur, politics, war, and religion left Champlain scant time for the satisfactions of private life. Long ago, at forty-three, he had married a child wife of twelve years, Hélène Boulé, only to find, when she reached Quebec, that she had secretly imbibed the poison of the Huguenots. Poor waif, she was soon rescued for the Faith by her husband, flitted briefly through Canadian history, fled home to France, childless, to enter a convent, and was seen no more. Champlain could do comfortably without her. He had married Canada.

Hidden from his eyrie, a quiet shift in the military, economic, and political gravity of America already was in process. The grand continental strategy had taken its first crude shape in the awkward hands of men who knew not what they did.

Champlain's counterpart, the unshakable John Smith, somehow

held his Jamestown colony together and unwittingly revealed a primary fact in the division of the continent—its southern half had far more agricultural soil and better growing weather than the Canadian north. When John Rolfe married the kidnaped Pocahontas, thus cementing friendship with the Indians; when he learned to cure a native weed; when all Europe was smoking his product in defiance of King James's futile "Counterblast to Tobacco"; and when Raleigh "tooke a pipe before he went to the scaffold," thereby making it fashionable everywhere, a booming new economic system was built solidly on smoke. England could never be driven from America after that except by its own sons.

English settlers crept north from Jamestown, year by year closer to the French. In 1613 they struck their first blow—a feeble blow, cowardly and illegal, but from then on, for 146 years, English and French arms in America would seldom rest.

The original settlements of Acadia, on the Bay of Fundy, were selected for this act of piracy. Jean de Biencourt, Seigneur de Poutrincourt, indefatigable man, had returned to Port Royal after its earlier abandonment, financed in his desperation by the Marquise de Guercheville, a uniquely chaste inmate of the French court, who had steadfastly refused the bed of a king, and by other noble ladies less fastidious. Lacking virtue, they made up for it by a fine frenzy of religion. All they asked of Poutrincourt was the chance to send out the first Jesuits and save the savage souls of the jungle.

They secured from their young friend, King Louis, a grant of all lands from Florida to the St. Lawrence. That was easy, for the gallant French monarchs would never refuse anything, even a continent, to a pretty face. The Pope also agreed to this redivision of America, which a predecessor had granted in its entirety to Spain. So far as French occupation on the Atlantic was concerned there seemed to be little enough to divide. Besides Port Royal two other French settlements, mere hangouts for vagrant fur traders, stood on the west shore of Fundy.

Somehow reports of these establishments reached Sir Thomas Dale, the choleric Governor of Virginia, at Jamestown, and he was outraged. England claimed the entire Atlantic littoral, north of the Spanish lands, by virtue of John Cabot's voyages more than a century before in the service of the thrifty King Henry VII. (Cabot had been paid for a new empire by a pension of £20 a year and £10 in cash.)

To Governor Dale, therefore, England's title was clear and must be enforced against the trespassers of Acadia, even if England and France were at peace. He had at hand a satisfactory instrument.

Samuel Argall, amateur gentleman and professional pirate, had lately turned up at Jamestown in an unlicensed trading vessel to begin a career of many exploits, including the abduction of Pocahontas. As Dale realized, here was the very man—fearless, cunning, unscrupulous—to drive the French out of Acadia. The Governor's faith was well placed.

Sailing up the New England shore "to fish for cod," Argall encountered some Indians whose bowings and scrapings must have been learned from the ceremonious French. He easily spied out the French settlements and seized them. Having picked the locks of their strongboxes, he took the precaution of stealing the French land titles to Acadia and then demanded that the French produce them. No one could find them, since they were in Argall's pocket. He thereupon denounced the settlers as illegal squatters and enemies of England, set fifteen of them adrift in an open boat and carried fourteen back to Jamestown.

There the outraged Governor proposed to hang the lot until Argall, whose word occasionally was good, protested that he had promised their safety on his honor. He finally admitted the theft of the title deeds. The Governor relented but ordered him back to Acadia to complete his congenial work.

Argall systematically burned the French settlements, first stealing all property of value down to the locks on the Port Royal doors. A handful of remaining Frenchmen, left in the woods, lived through the winter on game and roots. For these and other knightly services Argall was knighted by a grateful monarch.

France's hold on the Atlantic coast had been shaken. It could not be broken. The Acadians crept out of the woods and rebuilt their homes. Often attacked, eventually deported, they would always return and could never be dislodged from their beloved tidal acres. But if a pirate and his crew from tiny Jamestown could wreck these colonies in a day or two of easy work, how could they hope to survive larger English colonies, now sprouting a few miles away, in New England? If Quebec itself was vulnerable, as a few more years would show, Acadia looked like the Achilles heel of New France. So it would remain.

Europe's various claims to America, north of the Spaniards, were asserted so far by Jamestown, an outpost of Dutchmen at the mouth of the Hudson, the desolated habitations of the French around Fundy and Champlain's garrison on the St. Lawrence. In 1620, a curious cargo, on its way to Jamestown, was blown 900 miles out of its course upon the shores of Plymouth. America would never be the same again.

The freight of the *Mayflower* included a hundred ardent men and women, some contraband ideas unnoted by the King's customs officers, and a "compact" signed in the dingy cabin. The passengers had bound themselves together as a "civil body politic." Germs of democracy, that most dangerous of diseases, had arrived in the New World.

The English were established fifteen years later in New Hampshire, Massachusetts, Maryland, and Connecticut. Things were going badly in Canada under a French government reputedly the ablest in Europe. They were going well in the English colonies under a government stupid to the point of imminent suicide.

One man had begun to grasp the nature of the approaching contest. To John Winthrop, in Boston, the New France on his northern shoulder was an unclean den of popery. King Charles apparently could not resist the seductions of Rome in England. His wife had her private Catholic chapel regardless of all the laws of the realm to the contrary. Winthrop's New England would repel the Pope's spreading power and perhaps someday exterminate it.

The struggle for America was to be not only military, economic and political, but religious—the Reformation ranged against Catholicism. Europe's exhausting wars of religion had spanned the Atlantic but most of their fire had been blown out in the passage. The New World was to be spared the worst follies of the Old.

It was plain by now, however, that the English colonies, quickly outnumbering the French, were entirely different in kind.

As early as the founding of Port Royal the long reach of French feudalism had paralyzed New France. English feudalism, on the eve of its destruction in civil war, never managed, for all its royal edicts, governors' warrants, regulations and Navigation Acts, to control the free men who poured into New England and Virginia to build a new society as they pleased.

The French of the St. Lawrence would never know even the theory of self-government nor desire it. In 1619, when Champlain's word was law in Quebec and only echoed the word of his king, the first elected colonial assembly met in Virginia. The principle of self-government had been planted—a beginning fatal to the English throne which tolerated it. In the same year the first Negro slaves were imported to tend the tobacco fields. The irony of the coincidence was not appreciated, nor its future price guessed. That price, as finally paid, would touch and threaten the 49th Parallel.

The two rivals in the American contest differed also in their daily lives.

Canadians, except for Hébert, were still engaged almost solely in the fur trade, roaming the wilds with the Indians, begetting a new race of half-breeds and depleting the colony's strength.

The practical-minded English built their houses, plowed their fields, and seldom ventured beyond them.

The Canadians were the great wilderness people of America, the English the stay-at-homes.

Two religions, two political systems, and two separate varieties of creature were now in conflict.

Seen by the retrospective eyes of history, the result of such a race between hare and tortoise could never be in doubt. There was another factor, calculable only in retrospect—the English were not only land but water animals. Their sea power, which already had driven Spain from the North Atlantic in Elizabeth's time, could lay Canada in hopeless siege. None of these results was foreseen in the seventeenth century. Neither side understood the strengths and weaknesses of the other.

The stern Protestant eyes of New England saw the French as the agents of Rome, the greedy monopolists of the fur trade, the conniving friends of the Indians, who constantly raided the English colonies. Canada saw the English as rivals in trade and empire, but not yet serious rivals, since Canadians could travel so much farther and faster, knew the country better, and were far more experienced in jungle war. The English thought of their neighbors, if they thought of them at all, as outlandish heretics, too far away to matter.

Canadian misjudgment of the English was to be one of the chief causes of New France's ruin. There was much more to the English than the French supposed—so much, indeed, of dissent, conflict, soul-searching, doctrinal quarrel, and perversity, yet so much also of thrift, stubbornness, and sheer endurance that no foreigner could hope to understand them.

The English thought for themselves—that was their trouble and their strength. The Canadians left their thinking mostly to a distant government, whose mind was on other things more interesting than the snow and squalor of Canada.

Life in New England presented to the logical French mind of Paris a spectacle of certain failure. The inhabitants had fled from England, as they said, to escape religious persecution; but they had no sooner escaped than they set up their own local inquisitions, compelled everyone to work and to worship in the established fashion, willy-nilly, refused the franchise to all dissenters and persons judged godless, exiled the pious Roger Williams and Anne Hutchinson in the woods of Rhode Island, cut off offenders' ears,

hanged witches, harangued one another in endless sermons to turn
a healthy Catholic stomach, decreed in Plymouth that "there should
be no gameing or reveling in ye streets" and in Connecticut ordered
death for any boy over sixteen who would not obey his mother.
How could such a preposterous society endure?

Notions of government in the English colonies were equally
bizarre. Winthrop had called democracy "the meanest and worst of
all forms of government." John Cotton, the spiritual mentor of
Boston, held that "democracy I do not conceive that ever God
did ordeyne as a fit government either for church or commonwealth." The ideal of Samuel Stone, another eminent cleric, was
"a speaking Aristocracy in the face of a silent Democracy." Yet the
original heresy of Protestantism was breeding a subheresy of politics
proclaimed by Thomas Hooker: "The foundation of authority is
laid in the free consent of the people."

There, to a Frenchman, was the first preachment of anarchy. In
the growing schism of the New England theocracy these quarrelsome, litigious, noisy, and demented colonies surely could never be
united.

Besides their heresies they also nourished a sleek and repulsive
hypocrisy. They equated their profits with the glory of God. They
exploited one another and made indentured white labor a kind of
limited slavery. They defrauded their king by systematic smuggling
—all as part of God's work—while they wrestled in public with their
consciences and their devils.

If they had any sense of humor or enjoyment of life, the foreigner
could not discern it. They preached sexual purity, encouraged bun-
dling, made sex an economic policy by taxing bachelors to compel
them to breed legally, and as in Groton, Massachusetts, were appalled to learn that a third of the local congregation had bred
before marriage. When a ribald band of bachelors, in rebellion
against the Puritan code, settled at Quincy, Massachusetts, in 1627,
remained drunk all winter, lived with squaws and erected the final
horror of a Maypole next spring, Boston was scandalized and suppressed them.

To such a mind as Richelieu's, brooding coldly behind painted
cheeks in Paris, the disordered thought, chaotic government, and
inevitable failure of the English colonies must have offered some
ray of cheer.

The Cardinal had mastered the affairs of France and most of
Europe. Now he found time to master Canada. This systematic
man was disgusted with the endless disputes of the successive fur
monopolies, the mergers, reorganizations, bankruptcies and frauds,

the refusal to bring settlers to Quebec as the royal contracts provided. Champlain had complained that the fur traders cared for nothing "so long as they got 40 per cent on their money," and apparently Champlain was right. So Richelieu organized his own company of One Hundred Associates, backed by the huge capital of 300,000 livres.

Things seemed to be looking up in Canada. Champlain had begun to build the first fort on the rock. The missionaries were garnering an abundant crop of Indian souls. King James had granted the region of Acadia to his friend, Sir William Alexander (calling it Nova Scotia, with its own noble baronets who watched it comfortably from home), but the few French survivors of Argall's raids hung on, almost forgotten, and the expected Scots settlers failed to appear. New France, still containing only some three hundred white inhabitants, was at last taking shape.

It was the wrong shape, a shape which could not endure. As Champlain suspected, as Richelieu could not see from Paris, Canada was wholly dependent on fur and fur was the enemy of settlement. The fur traders knew exactly what they were about. They refused to bring settlers, for settlers would drive out the fur animals and the trappers.

Equally dangerous to Champlain's dream of a new nation was his quarrel with the Iroquois. He must keep them off the St. Lawrence to protect his middlemen, the Hurons and Algonquins. He dared not make a permanent peace with his enemies lest they become the middlemen and take the furs to the Dutch and English. The temporary peace patched up in 1624 was soon broken by his Indian allies and the old war of sudden ambush began again.

Nevertheless, by 1628, Champlain's affairs were in good order, for the moment anyway, and a great convoy of colonists and supplies was on its way from France when a sudden shift in the affairs of Europe ruined everything.

As if there were any lack of troubles at home, King Charles of England embarked on war with France. Canada was the last thing in that royal chowderhead but it had not escaped the attention of the three sailor brothers Kirke—David, Thomas, and Lewis—gentlemen of honor, part English, part French, and part pirate. These adventurers, well equipped for such work, were chosen to open, as a mere annex to the war in Europe, the second and what might well prove the last round in the American struggle.

Bearing letters of marque from Charles and instructions "utterly to drive away and root out the French settlements in Nova Scotia and Canada," the Kirkes set sail in three ships. A few weeks later

Lewis was training his guns on the fort and houses of Quebec. He sent a messenger to Champlain suggesting a "courteous" surrender and promising "all kind of contentment both for your persons and your property which, on the faith I have in Paradise, I will preserve as I would my own." Kirke was always the English gentleman, in part anyway.

Champlain resolved on a bold bluff. He strained his Christian conscience in the interests of his king and retorted with a brazen lie. His fort, he said, was well stocked with food, was armed and ready to fight. In truth it was starving, had sixteen soldiers and fifty pounds of gunpowder to defend it, and would collapse at the first broadside.

The lie succeeded. Kirke had heard of larger game and could afford to leave Champlain safely on ice through the winter. He sailed away without a shot and, rejoining his brothers, waited off Gaspé. There he surprised Richelieu's helpless fleet of eighteen merchantmen, bound with colonists and supplies for Quebec, and captured them all after the first naval battle in North American waters.

This gigantic booty—its loss disastrous to Richelieu's new company and lethal to the starving garrison of Quebec—satisfied the Kirkes, for one season. They had other plans. First they formed, with Alexander, the Anglo-Scotch Company to exploit all Acadia and Canada. Then they set out again next spring to finish the job at Quebec.

Champlain and his villagers were now living on eels, acorns, and seeds gathered one by one from the earth of Hébert's farm. Quebec was abandoned and helpless, Champlain forced to surrender at Kirke's second demand. As the golden lilies of France fell from the flagstaff of the fort and the flag of England replaced them, amid beat of drums and boom of cannons from the English ships, Champlain saw his work finished, Canada lost, the great dream ended.

The surrender was conducted in the best of manners. Champlain spent a pleasant interlude with the Kirkes, shooting birds along the St. Lawrence, and then was taken courteously to London.

Meanwhile the son of Alexander had possessed his father's land of Nova Scotia. He had occupied Port Royal but failed to take the French fort on the southeast tip of the Acadian peninsula. The indestructible La Tour still asserted the claims of France in this region and, after queer adventures, martial and marital, would end his days as a British subject.

Champlain found in London that he had not calculated on the stupidity of King Charles. It was indeed beyond man's calculation. The war already was over. Charles had dismissed Parliament and, unable to collect taxes, had suddenly remembered that the French still owed him most of the dowry of his French wife, Henrietta Maria. For this $140,000 in hand, which Richelieu paid gladly as a dirt-cheap bargain, England returned Quebec and Acadia to France in the spring of 1633. Never had empire been bartered away at such a price. More than a queen's dowry and thousands of better men than Charles must be expended to buy it back.

The issue of America could have been settled then and there at no more cost of blood or treasure. No boundary across the continent might ever have been drawn. The 49th Parallel would have dropped out of history. Instead, France was given a new chance. Champlain set sail from Dieppe as governor of Canada.

He must have wondered, as his ship moved from the harbor, whether he would ever see his native land again. He would not see it again. The pull of geography in the first Canadian had proved too much for history. He was committed to Canada. History, still too strong to be denied, would bring Canadian soldiers into this very harbor of Dieppe 210 years later, almost to the day, in rescue of France.

Two years only were left to Champlain. He needed them. Quebec must be completely rebuilt, for it lay in ashes, the first work of the English in these parts, where they would return three times. By the end of the two years a new town had risen and the fur route of the St. Lawrence had been regained. Champlain lived a celibate life among Jesuits, now the real rulers of a Canadian theocracy, and Catholic soldiers as pious as he. His fortress became almost a monastery.

It was a comfortable life, as secure as any life could be within easy reach of the Iroquois and not far from the colonies of England. The New Englanders had seen Canada fall without a blow, only to be frittered away by a foolish king. They did not want it particularly but they would never sleep sound in their defenseless cabins while French papists and murderous Catholic Indians roamed the woods.

The results of their fears and ambitions were mercifully hidden from the lonely man in the fort. He had little to regret in his own life. Still, the bitter taste of disappointment remained. His private longing, sacrificed to the needs of his colony, had always been to ascend the river, find the passage to China, and unlock the mystery of the continent. Now it was too late.

He heard, near the end, some startling news about the country he would never see, news at once sweet and tantalizing.

Jean Nicolet had pursued the route to China and reached Lake Michigan. There he had been told by the local Indians that the Winnebagos, beyond the lake, lived by "stinking waters." They must surely be the western ocean. The Winnebagos, Nicolet concluded, were probably Chinese. He therefore approached them in a robe of Chinese silk, "all strewn with flowers and birds of many colors," brought with him for such an occasion. The Winnebagos, alas, turned out to be only Indians.

They told Nicolet he was only three days' march from the Big Water. He hurried back to Quebec in time to assure the dying Governor that Asia would soon be reached. Champlain had no time to learn the truth.

In the autumn of 1635 he was sixty-eight years old, his worn-out body paralyzed. He foresaw the end and poured out, with ceaseless tears, his confessions, his fears, and his hopes to the kindly Father Lalemant. The first Canadian died peacefully on Christmas Day.

He was given, says Father Le Jeune, who delivered the funeral oration, "a very honorable burial, the procession being formed of the people, the soldiers, the captains and the churchmen. . . . Those whom he left behind have reason to be well satisfied with him."

They buried him somewhere in the recesses of his rock, white now under the snow, and in the fury of the succeeding years forgot even this lodgment. They buried him scarce knowing what they buried or suspecting the future dimensions of the nation and race he had founded.

Far beyond his rock, beyond his farthest footsteps, in the unknown land up to the leagues of solemn tundra, the buffalo grazed through the snow. The Indians huddled over their smoky fires. Frozen prairies prepared next spring's surge of grass. Dark forests awaited the upward flow of sap. Minerals of men's use lay deep in the rounded, glacial rocks and oil flowed under the foothills of the mountains. The great rivers of America were moving, unseen, to the western sea. And across this unimaginable void lay an imaginary parallel of latitude which no man had marked.

3

The Lost Blueprint

[1665-1672]

TOWARD THE END OF THE 1660's JEAN BAPTISTE COLBERT, FACTOtum to young King Louis XIV of France and the ablest filing clerk in Europe, began to receive disturbing letters from Canada where, for more than thirty years, weaker men had tried to hold Champlain's narrow beachhead.

As Colbert read these messages it is to be supposed that his neat little face, the image of a neat little mind, was rumpled with annoyance, his wide, intelligent eyes opened wider, his woman's lips were pursed in thought, and he scratched the flowing false curls imitated from the "full-bottomed" wife of his monarch. Colbert, justly called the "man of marble," was not easily disturbed. But this latest news shook him.

In 1665 he had sent to Quebec his brightest young man, Jean Talon, with strict instructions and a perfect blueprint of government. Under Talon, as its intendant and real ruler, Canada was to be no longer a foreign mission but a province of France. It was to be organized, regulated, and compressed in the St. Lawrence Valley. Above all, it must cease wasting its money and manpower in the pursuit of fur, exploration, and war.

Talon had understood his instructions when he left Paris, had been thoroughly trained for his job as Canada's first bureaucrat, had learned all Colbert's methods, and in face and mind was almost the exact duplicate of his master. Moreover, he knew the King's will and, so far, had never disobeyed it.

Yet here on paper, before Colbert's incredulous gaze, was the evidence of Talon's sudden aberration. The coolheaded bureaucrat clearly was suffering from euphoria, the same sort of infatuation and lunacy that seemed to afflict everybody in Canada. Instead of

33

building a compact province on the river, he was proposing, quite seriously, to capture New York! In the next line he announced that "nothing can prevent us from carrying the name and arms of His Majesty as far as Florida."

The filing-cabinet soul of Colbert was horrified. Hastily, on the margin of Talon's letter, he scrawled the single word "Wait." Then, on second thought, he seized his pen and wrote a more solemn warning: "It is much better to restrict yourself to an extent of territory which the colony itself will be able to maintain than to embrace much land that eventually a part may have to be abandoned, with some consequent discredit to His Majesty's Crown."

That should have been sufficient to hold the Intendant and prevent a new clash with the English, King Louis's temporary friends. Colbert knew Talon. Unfortunately, with all the apparent facts before him, he did not know Canada, nor the tricks it played with the most sensible men.

To Colbert, Canada was a minor state in Louis's expanding realm. How could he suspect, in the methodical world of Paris, that Canada was in fact a state of mind? Already it was turning the mind of Talon upside down. The wilderness, that age-old siren, had seduced the respectable Intendant, changed him into an adventurer, an empire builder, an amateur *coureur de bois*. In defiance of his orders, he was preparing to push Canada to the Gulf of Mexico, to the Pacific, to the arctic, if possible to China.

What of the English in Virginia and New England? Talon's enlarged blueprint covered their case. They would be hived on their narrow coastal shelf, east of the Appalachians. Dazzled by his dream, drunk with continental distance, Talon could not wait. And inevitably, with the best intentions, he had launched a process which must end in war with the English and the ruin of New France.

That end could not be foreseen by Colbert and Louis or they might have crushed Talon at the beginning. They were not averse to empire building, they were planning the subjugation of Europe, but they were not ready yet to meet England in full collision. Assuredly, though Louis had discovered Canada for himself, was fascinated by its mystery, and intended to make it a subordinate department of his government, he did not propose to let it spread all over America at the cost of war and treasure when America, after all, was of far less value than an inferior province in Europe.

So far all Louis's plans had worked satisfactorily in the competent hands of Colbert. A bright new age had dawned, lit by the rising effulgence of the handsome young Sun King, who was the state entire. The Thirty Years' War had collapsed long since in senseless exhaustion. Cromwell, the disturber of Divine Right, had been buried and dug up for public exhibition and his Puritans driven underground. The Counter Reformation was in full motion, the Catholic Church apparently restored to something like its old power, the cracked foundations of feudalism painted over with royal gilt in the new fashion called rococo. The Christian world had been given a breathing space, shorter than any man supposed. The exhalation of its relief could be heard all the way across the ocean.

Talon, therefore, must wait, in accordance with Colbert's timetable.

So also could England, where a dark and sleek voluptuary, wiser man and worse than his father of the same name, ruled on a single principle—he would not begin his travels and exile again. The first Charles had squandered his throne and head in fighting the people. The energies of the second, remarkable for their promiscuity, were conserved for the safer task of procreation, whence appeared, with brief interruption, nine titled bastards from seven titled concubines, but, alas, no heir. On the very day when Talon landed in Quebec "pretty, witty" and illiterate Nell Gwyn had been given her first role at Drury Lane where, as it was assumed in Paris, she alone held the eye of a harmless sovereign.

Louis and Europe underrated Charles. Canada also had caught that roving eye. Indolent as he always seemed, this king "who never said a foolish thing nor ever did a wise one," nevertheless was beginning to construct, in conspiracy with two of Canada's cleverest rascals, a little-noted northern dam across Talon's plans, while the English colonists were making ready to flow through the southern dam of the Appalachians in irresistible torrent.

At the moment, however, Louis saw no reason to worry about his new Canadian province. It seemed to have survived its time of troubles since Champlain's death, thirty years ago.

They had been worse times than any king in Europe or any backwoodsman in America could imagine.

Champlain's strong hand had been removed for hardly a dozen years when the Iroquois undertook to extinguish New France and came within a scalplock of success. To capture the fur routes of the west and carry its furs to the English and Dutch, they fell upon Huronia, north of Lake Ontario, burned all the Jesuit missions, murdered Fathers Daniel, Brébeuf, and Lalemant with obscene and unspeakable torture, obliterated the Huron nation, left 8,000 of its people to starve, lunged westward to Lake Michigan, threw the whole tribal organization of eastern America into chaos, turned south to wreck the powerful Susquehannas, and joined the English colonies in a permanent alliance which laid down the future imperial strategy of the continent.

New France, with its 3,000 inhabitants, necessarily was the Iroquois' main objective, the western campaign incidental. For New France was drawing from the western tribes the furs that the Iroquois needed to trade for English goods now essential to their life—especially English rum.

Quebec was too well fortified for frontal attack, but the outlying settlements could be picked off one by one. The Iroquois, says a Jesuit dispatch, "approach like foxes, attack like lions and disappear like birds."

Montreal, founded on Cartier's river island of Hochelaga by the pious Maisonneuve and forty-three priests, nuns, and settlers in 1642 "for a testimony," and called Ville Marie, the personal property of the Virgin, lived in siege. The holy women often clutched their crucifixes, knelt in prayer, and prepared to die as the men fought the Iroquois from the palisades and watched them torture their French captives.

To the west the fur route, umbilical cord of New France, had been cut. The colony was dying for lack of nourishment.

Even at Quebec the Iroquois appeared openly around the walls and, insured by the French hostages in their villages, defied the guns of St. Louis. Helplessly the garrison beheld them abduct eighty Huron colonists from the Island of Orleans and heard the Huron chief, Jacques Oachonk, chant Christian hymns while his torturers scalped him, poured hot sand upon his skull, and twisted his ligaments with red-hot gun barrels.

It was a time of brief armistice, broken truce, bribery and treachery on both sides; of solemn conferences in smoky bark lodges; of feasts, orations, and costly presents; of prisoners and torture used by Indian and white alike as instruments of barter and politics; a time of religious ecstasy when nuns saw visions, demons, comets, flying Iroquois canoes, and other portents in the night sky, when priests recorded daily miracles and rejoiced over the burning bodies of Iroquois braves at the torture stake because their pagan souls, absolved by the church, would soon fly to Paradise.

It was a time also of heroism such as the world has seldom witnessed. The Jesuits still entered the Iroquois villages and, without complaint, accepted the martyrdom of fire. During a lull in the war, while the Iroquois were occupied in the west and needed a temporary accommodation with Quebec, fifty-three Frenchmen even founded a hostage settlement among the Onondagas and escaped, the night before their intended execution, by feeding their hosts into unconsciousness.

The Iroquois' pretended friendship was brief. In 1660 they set about the systematic destruction of Montreal and were thwarted only by a marvel of human courage.

Learning that part of the enemy would descend on the town by the old Ottawa River route, Dollard, Sieur des Ormeaux, and sixteen other youths resolved to die in its defense. They received the final sacraments of the church, paddled up the river, and took their stand on the Long Sault with a handful of Algonquins and Hurons.

There 200 Iroquois besieged them in their flimsy wooden stockade and were repelled for eight days. The main Iroquois attacking force of 500, waiting on the Richelieu, was compelled to by-pass Montreal and join the Homeric battle on the Ottawa. Though 700 attackers finally killed the last dozen Frenchmen, torturing four who still breathed, the cost of this victory was too high. After their losses the Iroquois abandoned their attack on Montreal and slunk home in howling shame.

The Canadian Thermopylae was a miracle but the colony could not live on miracles.

It had narrowly survived on the river. It had lost Acadia again to the New Englanders.

A fleet assembled in Boston harbor in 1654 for an attack on the Dutch post of Manhattan. At the last moment a ship from England brought the news of Cromwell's peace with Holland. The thrifty Boston townsfolk could not bear to waste a fleet, which was hard to come by, and bethought them of the papists in Acadia. England and France also were at peace but that small technicality could not prevent Robert Sedgwick and his company from taking defenseless Port Royal without serious resistance, and at the mouth of the St. John they discovered a willing captive in Charles de La Tour.

This man of iron nerves had long conducted a private war with Governor Charnisay of Port Royal and was frequently away from home. Charnisay took advantage of his absence to attack his fort. Madame La Tour defended it for two months until food ran out. She surrendered on Charnisay's guarantee to spare the lives of her little garrison. He hanged everybody before her eyes. She died of horror.

Thus the first chapter of the La Tour epic. The second opened with the opportune drowning of Charnisay. La Tour promptly arranged a cozy settlement of the old feud by marrying his enemy's widow. Then, on the arrival of the New Englanders, he suddenly recalled that he was a British subject with a Scottish title, one of the late King James's baronets of Nova Scotia. The invaders, swallowing his story, appointed him a proprietor to administer their conquests.

The 250 French in Acadia, a breed as flexible as La Tour, paid little heed to conquest or change of government, but two English expeditions had proved that Canada's hold on the Atlantic littoral was feeble and easily broken. Only an accident of an unthinkable sort could prevent New England from pushing permanently northward to the Gulf of St. Lawrence. That accident lay far ahead.

Talon reached Canada in 1665 to find it on the brink of ruin. His blueprints would be needed. Much more reassuring to the Canadians was the giant form of the Marquis de Tracy, who had recently distinguished himself as a soldier in the West Indies and whose face was sallow from its fevers. He brought a thousand well-seasoned French troops, the veteran regiment of Carignan-Salières, in their gray uniforms, wide black hats, and purple stockings. As these experienced warriors landed at Quebec and their commander knelt on the bare pavement to pray, the villagers felt safe for the first time, protected by the only regular military force ever seen in the New World.

The new Governor, Daniel Rémy, Sieur de Courcelle, was too impatient to wait for de Tracy and attempted a winter march on snowshoes southward into the Iroquois country, reached the frontier of the Dutch colonies, lost his way in the snow and retreated, his army of six hundred hungry and half frozen.

In the autumn of 1666, after the priests had preached a holy war against the heathen, de Tracy moved south. Crippled by gout and carried on an Indian's back, he led the Carignan-Salières with their Canadian and Indian guides up the Richelieu and Lake Champlain trench—1,300 men in 300 canoes. The Mohawks fled before an army and navy of unimaginable size and from a safe distance observed their burning villages. This terrible revenge forced the whole Iroquois Confederacy, under a chief called the Flemish bastard, to sue for peace. It was to last more or less for eighteen years.

France had inflicted on its immediate enemy a wound desperate but not mortal. De Tracy's three new forts on the Richelieu pushed its power far south of the St. Lawrence to the outer rim of the English colonies and the New Englanders, seeing their Indian allies crushed, were terrified. Governor Nicolls of New York attempted to rally the other colonies for a joint invasion of Canada. His plan came to nothing.

The French had good reason to assume that the divided, scattered, and penny-pinching English could never unite, perhaps could be obliterated separately at leisure. Meanwhile Talon would reorganize Canada on the Colbertian model.

This genial young man, with his wig of flowing curls, his rather feminine face, wisps of upturned mustache and Cupid-bow mouth, was to be the business executive of Canada. Government was removed from the old fur companies and vested in the Sovereign (later the Superior) Council, of which Governor Courcelle was the titular head and military commander, Talon and Bishop Laval the other two effective members. A dozen Canadians were appointed from time to time to sit with the French triumvirate as a kind of cabinet and supreme court. Talon was instructed to administer the colony in all but military and religious affairs.

His clash with the Bishop began at once. Talon had secret orders to curb the Jesuits. Laval could never accept the new imperial decision to make Canada a secular province of France. It must remain a mission and its primary purpose the salvation of the Indians. Talon, therefore, was his enemy and the enemy of God.

Of the two men the Bishop was the larger and the tougher. François de Laval-Montmorency, first of many Canadian churchmen who would defend the Faith against the apparatus of the state, was the perfect expression of the Counter Reformation. He represented the Pope direct, with the full power of Rome behind him. He stood above kings and earthly law. He was a scholar, aristocrat, and tyrant to his finger tips, a wily politician and yet a mystic. He knelt at prayer half the night in his freezing cathedral, slept in blankets crawling with fleas, and was said to conduct other mortifications of the flesh too revolting for the common ear. His long, horsy face, huge nose, drooping mustache, tiny goatee, and, above all, his heavy-lidded, fanatic eyes were enough to daunt any worldling.

They failed to daunt Talon but they gravely inconvenienced him. Immediately the impact between the two established monopolies, of religion and trade, one aimed at the Indian's soul, the other at his furs, the two irreconcilable ideas of a holy Canada under Laval and worldly prosperity under Talon, split the Sovereign Council and kept official Quebec in a continual state of public quarrel and private cabal, always bitter, sometimes comic. The village on the rock was becoming a fair imitation of a European court.

Despite the Bishop, Talon proceeded to apply his blueprint. His first problem was to increase the population. France, which could spare 10,000 dead in a single European battle, could allow Canada only 500 colonists a year. The fertile breed of Normandy quickly multiplied, with the assistance of the state.

Colbert's instructions to "marry youths at eighteen or nineteen years and girls at fourteen or fifteen" were supported by bonuses to large families and taxes on bachelors. Ships from France brought cargoes of assorted women, the "filles du roi," willing to marry anyone. The village youths lined up to watch them, in cold appraisal, passion, or humor.

"The Vestal Virgins," one of the French soldiers wrote home, "were heaped up in three different Apartments where the Bridegrooms singled out their Brides just as a Butcher do's an Ewe from amongst a Flock of Sheep. In the three Seraglios there were as much variety and change of Diet as could satisfie the most whimsical Appetites; for here were some big, some little, some fair, some brown, some fat and some meagre."

Pitiable and helpless these girls must have seemed as they faced their suitors, the rude hamlet of seventy houses, the dark rock and beyond it emptiness and mystery; but gallant, too, and durable, the sturdy foundation stock of Canada.

With such material, and with the support of the King, who was entranced by his long-distance discovery of the New World, Talon could begin to fashion a new French province. He set the colonists to building houses, to work in field and kitchen, to smoke meat, store grain, and weave cloth. He laid out a model farm of his own to instruct them in agriculture. He built a brewery and protected its products by high taxes on imported French wine. He opened a shipyard, attempted an unsuccessful export trade in the West Indies, investigated copper deposits around Lake Superior, and even reported the discovery of coal deep in the rock below the Governor's residence.

He was seen everywhere, this bustling and efficient young manager, inspecting his little industries; peering into bake ovens; watching the women at their looms; offering himself as godfather to an Indian baby; making sure that the immigrant girls were "free from any natural blemish or anything personally repulsive"; fixing wages and prices; fining profiteers; regulating the number of horses for every farm; ordering all chimneys swept regularly and all dogs locked up at 9:00 p.m.; enforcing Louis's personal edict against profanity on pain of cutting out the offender's tongue; branding one Paul Dupuy with a fleur-de-lis on his cheek because he had whispered that the English were wise to execute King Charles; contriving pageants and frolics for the public; imagining, in his Colbertian illusion, that he could make the sprawling substance of Canada self-contained, state regulated, and automatic from top to bottom by the simple mercantile economics of his master.

All was going well for the indefatigable bureaucrat. The colony took on its first look of permanence. Its population doubled, rising to 6,000 in three years from immigration and copious birth rate. The woodland along the river rang with the sound of axes and felt the first bite of the plow. There had been one horse in all Canada. Talon imported eighty and the same number of sheep. And what a proud day when he could inform Colbert that he was now covered from head to foot in Canadian-made cloth!

So far he had not heard the siren call of the West. He scrupulously obeyed his instruction to concentrate his settlers on the St. Lawrence in a tight and defensible community. He carved the land into narrow farms stretching back from the single highway of the river into the woods and granted it in seigneuries, on the feudal model of France, to worthy citizens, retired officers and hangers-on from Paris, who were elevated into a clumsy Canadian *noblesse*.

Actually feudalism and nobility were little more than names in Canada. The local seigneur could parcel his land out to tenant farmers, receive their oaths of fealty, together with their *cens et rentes* and a gift of poultry on St. Martin's Day; he could never make the tenant into a serf or himself into a nobleman.

"The nobility," a later governor wrote with disgust, "is everything which is most beggarly." Its members were often as poor as their tenants, worked in the fields beside them or, bankrupt, fled to the woods and the illegal fur trade. Revolution, slowly fermenting in France, found no nourishment in Canada. The farms and villages of the old land, the stone houses with massive chimneys and low-hanging eaves, the churches with glistening steeples and carved altars could be reproduced here, but not the hungry French peasant or the rapacious French nobleman. The chemicals of explosion were lacking where any man impatient with authority could easily escape it in the Great Beyond.

Something else, unplanned by Colbert and unsuspected by Talon, was under way—the lineaments of a new race, the French Canadian, had started to emerge. Neither royal authority, foreign invasion, nor military conquest could ever suppress it.

As Governor Denonville noted a little later, "The Canadians are tall, well-made and well set on their legs, robust, vigorous, and accustomed in time of need to live on little. They have intelligence and vivacity, but are wayward, light-minded and inclined to debauchery."

Other observers from France continually remarked on the industry of the peasants, their unequaled skill in woodcraft, travel and war, their reckless bravery and their weakness for liquor. Around the mock court of Quebec, however, the official set was idle, the women were flirtatious, gaudily dressed, and too pretty for men's good. They wore curls and low-necked gowns, forbidden by Laval, and made themselves, said the Bishop, "the instruments and the captives of the fiend." They even indulged in the devil's sport of dancing, though he had denounced it and personally prescribed for the Governor's daughter "modest and moderate dances with persons of her own sex and only in the presence of her mother."

Despite the peasant's vice of alcohol and the light habits of Quebec society, Canada must have been the most pious community in the world. The doctrines of a single church were never questioned. Miracles occurred on all sides and were accepted as commonplace. The Jesuits, curbed by Talon, were still the strongest power in the country and the Bishop its most formidable figure. Priests and nuns lived in holiness and poverty. No one doubted the sanity and everyone praised the virtue of Jeanne Le Ber, a virgin of Montreal, who spent twenty years in a filthy cell, a hairshirt next to her skin, alone except for a swarm of angels.

Far to the southward, behind the barriers of mountain and forest, the American wilderness was producing another breed, equally distinct.

The English had brought with them to New England the inherited character of their island race but it was subtly changed by an environment of unlimited space. A quick disintegration of an all-powerful church and a universal belief already was producing sectarian quarrels, rival panaceas, and the stubborn individualism of the free citizen.

He was not a woodsman, fur trader, soldier, or friend of the Indians. He was a farmer, a sailor, or a fisherman, he hated the Indians and slew them like vermin when he could, he was concerned only with his little plot of land, his fishing boat, or the local government.

Even at this date he was developing dangerous notions about the laws of a distant crown and parliament, which had started to hedge his business around with regulations, Navigation Acts, and taxes, all designed to make him a hewer of wood and drawer of water for the industry of England. He had won some control over his own local laws in elected assemblies, he was still loyal to the King, but if the King's overriding laws did not suit him he broke them without qualms of conscience and the jury of his peers increasingly refused to convict him. The combustibles of revolution, unknown in New France, would not be discerned until too late in New England.

Some men of learning had given the English colonies the seeds of scholarship. Harvard University had been hopefully founded with capital of £400 and an endowment of 260 books, the year after Champlain's death. This first frail intellectual growth soon withered in the frontier labors of survival, but ideas at least were relatively free, the quarreling churches could not prevent secular speculation, a few books circulated before Canada imported its first printing press, and a rudimentary American literature of a godly, dark, and irascible sort had appeared.

The Canadian's joy was in the companionship of family and friends, in life more than in possessions, and for him life on this earth was a fragment of eternity.

The English were generating a ruthless spirit of competition, a ravenous appetite for material wealth, and would soon pronounce them virtues ordained by God for His elect. In their towns a new creature of granitic visage, the American businessman, thrust himself from among the populace and surveyed the earth which he intended to inherit and manage for the common good. In the Virginian plantations the first Southern gentlemen were established on a foundation of slave labor—among them a man named John Washington, at Bridges Creek, whose great-grandson would alter the life of America more than all the kings, soldiers, politicians, and businessmen combined.

A penetrating French traveler thus sums up the contradictory characters of the two breeds: "In New England and the other British colonies there reigns an opulence by which the people seem not to know how to profit; while in New France poverty is hidden under an air of ease which appears entirely natural. The English colonist keeps as much and spends as little as possible; the French colonist enjoys what he has got and often makes a display of what he has not got."

Such were the peoples, antagonistic in their habits, instincts and interests, who must collide in the struggle for America—the French united by church and state, the individualistic and ingrowing English apparently unable to unite even for joint defense.

As the open conflict between them approached, Canada had all the advantages of discipline, experience in jungle fighting, and the leadership of able European generals. The English, with a population of 260,000 against 13,000 Canadians at the end of the seventeenth century, had the advantage of numbers, twenty to one. They also had behind them the power of Britain's navy. It would prove decisive.

In this balance of continental forces perhaps only Laval saw the mortal weakness of Canada, and he saw it dimly.

The fur trade he considered dangerous only because it was the spawning bed of perdition. Its brandy debauched the Indians as fast as the missionaries could convert them. It lured the most vigorous young Frenchmen into the woods to break the laws of government and church, to live like savages and breed with them. Worst of all, not content to debase themselves, the *coureurs de bois* had become the heroes and real *noblesse* of the country, secretly admired and envied by peasant and townsman. When they swarmed into Quebec, Three Rivers, and Montreal for the annual fur fairs, and a Bacchanalia of drink and fornication, they were "prodigal not only in their cloaths but upon women." They appeared naked, greased and painted like Indians, or dressed themselves in the finest silks and laces, carried the most costly swords, and, having squandered their year's fur profits, "e'en sell their Embroidery, their Lace and their Cloaths; this done, they are forc'd to go upon a new Voyage for Subsistence."

While the fair lasted—a barbarous spectacle of buckskin, feathers, bare flesh, Paris fashions, and the sober robes of priest and nun— the prodigals from the *pays en haut* could not be controlled by church or state. They danced, feasted, drank, gambled, and whored as they pleased and laughed at the Bishop's injunctions. "We cannot enjoy ourselves," wrote the great woodsman, Lahontan, "at play or in visiting the Ladies but 'tis presently carried to the Curate's ear, who takes publick notice of it in the Pulpit." But after these orgies the sobering *voyageur* would crawl to the priest for absolution before facing the trail again.

If all Laval's *mandements*, his raging sermons, his orders of excommunication, or Talon's consignment of illegal fur traders to the King's galleys, could not tame the white savage, that was fortunate in the short run, though disastrous in the long. Had the traders ceased to bring the furs to market, the colony would have lost its essential source of income.

Talon had no intention of discouraging the fur business and no means of eliminating the unlicensed bootlegger, but he mollified the Bishop by forbidding the trade in brandy. It was quickly replaced by cheaper and stronger English rum, which threatened to divert the thirsty Indian's furs to New England and his soul to heresy. So the ingenious bureaucrat invented a comical compromise—the Indians might sell their pelts for French brandy but were forbidden to get drunk, on pain of the pillory and a fine of two beaver skins. These the state would be happy to receive.

No compromise could satisfy the Bishop or stop the brandy flowing out of every fur post of the interior. Laval continued to quarrel with drunkenness, licentiousness, and even protocol, insisting that he must receive greater public deference on the street, a higher seat at board than the Governor.

The fur trade was obviously the enemy of religion, its brandy

the poison of Indian life. Neither Laval nor Talon grasped the
larger process stemming from the same cause and now engulfing
the colony. Canada was committed totally to the fur trade, and the
fur trade drove the fur-bearing animals before it, dragged Canada
forever deeper into the West, sapped its strength, erased Colbert's
blueprints, and infallibly assured the victory of the English.

Laval saw this only as a threat to the church. Talon never saw it
at all. Dizzy with sudden dreams of empire, infected with the Canadian disease of distance, gloriously ill of sheer space, he saw only
a chance to carry the glory of France across the continent.

The thrifty Colbert, still patiently planning his concentrated
French province on the St. Lawrence, was staggered at first by
Talon's euphoric dispatches and the probable bill of costs when
his hands were full and his treasury empty under the appetite of
the King for palaces, pleasures, and wars. To his amazement Colbert soon realized that the fur trade had grown faster than agriculture, in denial of his orders. So he scribbled "Wait" on the margin
of Talon's latest letter.

It was no use. The policy of the fur trade and the infatuation of
Canadians with the wilderness, that magnet which no red-blooded
man could resist, quickly expunged Colbert's warning, Anyway, the
man of marble had begun to feel the tug of the magnet himself.
He, too, like the King, was soon dizzy from the western dream, at
second hand, for it was part of the larger dream of French power
throughout the world.

Talon hurried to Paris and explained his vaulting ambitions.
Both Colbert and Louis approved them, gave their local manager a
free hand, and planned their complementary conquest of Europe.

The theatrical pageant of the Sun King had begun. In both thea-
ters, European and American, it was to be brief and ruinous.

Even if there had been no larger European causes to produce it,
Talon's thrust westward, northward, and southward meant even-
tual war with England. It need not touch the English colonies at
first and was designed only to hold them within their coastal shelf,
but it collided immediately with their allies, the Iroquois, who,
though punished by de Tracy, still struggled as middlemen to
possess the western fur trade. Not long hence French expansion
would collide directly with the English, since population rose
steadily in the Atlantic reservoir and must spill through the mountains. The original charters of Virginia, Massachusetts, and Connecticut had given them the lands to the Pacific. So far as they
were concerned, that writ overrode all Louis's titles. The English
planned to seize their own property, as yet undefined.

The Canadians, by the nature of their business and their own adventurous temperament, were far ahead in the western race. Etienne Brulé had reached the junction of Superior and Huron as early as 1623, after the Iroquois had pulled out his beard and some years before the Hurons murdered him. Within four decades other Canadians were nearing the headwaters of the Mississippi and the shores of Hudson Bay. No English colonist would cross the Appalachian dike until 1671 and no English post would be built on the Great Lakes until 1722.

So moved the race of the hare and the tortoise. It could not move long in peace.

In the 1660's the French began to push seriously through the country of the Great Lakes. There they found the tragic human wreckage of the Iroquois wars. The remains of the Hurons, Neutrals, Ottawas, and Salteurs had been driven into refuge west of Lake Michigan and south of Superior. Refugees, in conflict with natives for survival, had upset the entire tribal balance, hunting grounds, and economy of the interior.

As few of the fur-hunting Indians dared to run the gantlet of the Iroquois, French traders increasingly traveled to the source of supply with trade goods of brandy, guns, hatchets, kettles, beads, and gaudy cloth. They carried home the furs by Champlain's route from Georgian Bay down the Ottawa to bypass the Iroquois and the falls of Niagara.

French birchbark canoes were enlarged to the length of six fathoms and a cargo capacity of six tons, the cargo divided into portable 90-pound bales. The tireless *voyageurs* paddled sixteen hours a day, measuring their progress by regular pauses for a pipe of tobacco. They lugged their bales and canoes over countless portages, suffered the misery of mosquitoes and black flies, spread the glory of their king (who personally made the largest kettles, the best guns, the strongest brandy), and by skill, muscle, paddle, birchbark, and sheer endurance devised a transportation system which would finally take them through the Rockies to the Pacific.

Like a busy needle the canoe pierced the substance of a continent. It stretched a thin thread of French power from Quebec to the Lakes and far beyond them, with longer stitches every year.

Historians could explain, in comfortable, armchair retrospect, the political and economic forces propelling this curious odyssey. They meant nothing to the fur trader. He was seeking his own private profit, often illegally, the carefree woodland life, and the mystery of the unknown beyond the next river bend. So, careless of imperial policy, of a remote king, the laws of the church, the regulations of the state and the homebound heretics of New England, the *coureur de bois* burst into the *pays en haut* with swirl of paddle, sweat of portage, crunch of snowshoe, smoke of Indian lodges, and the casual consolation of some dark-skinned bedfellow.

By survival only of the fittest, such a life—lonely, hard, barbarous, and usually short—produced a unique species. It was more Indian in its instincts than white. It retained the white man's cunning but it had absorbed the vices and virtues of the native, the secrecy, callousness, cruelty, and dumb, stoic courage. It imitated the native's cunning and used the arts of civilization to deceive him—as when Nicholas Perrot, in the Michigan country, subdued a hostile tribe by the magic of fire from flint and steel, calmly announcing, "I am the dawn," and then, by superior magic, lit a cup of water after first mixing it with inflammable brandy.

Nothing could halt the march of this species, nothing could prevent the resulting revolution and chaos of the Indian's culture, nothing could save New France from its self-ordained fate. Ignorant of these things, the *coureur de bois* left his bones unburied, unhallowed, and unmarked beside his endless trail, his name unrecorded, his work soon forgotten by the empires, kings, merchants, and millionaires who battened on it.

A few of these jungle creatures are remembered vaguely for exploits superhuman and almost unbelievable—not least the merry partnership of Groseilliers and Radisson.

To their fellows Médard Chouart, Sieur des Groseilliers, and his brother-in-law, Pierre Esprit Radisson, were merely a pair of woodsmen, undistinguished except for their courage, their avarice, and their disregard of the King's rules—reckless rogues but perhaps useful to the government at Quebec when, in four successive years, at the height of the Iroquois wars, no furs came down from the Lakes country and New France obviously was dying. The partners, officially sponsored, set out from Montreal in 1654 to negotiate with the western tribes a resumption of trade. This was a desperate mission but the ambassadors were well trained for it.

Groseilliers had the gift of geography. Radisson had been captured by the Mohawks at the age of fifteen and had watched them burn his companions. His odd French, translated into odder English, tells that story: "They burned a frenchwoman; they pulled out her breasts and took a child out of her belly whch they broyled and made the mother eat of it; so in short died . . . They bourned the soales of my feet and leggs. A souldier run through my foot a swoord red out of the fire and plucked several of my nails . . . They cut off yor stones and the women play wth them."

Radisson escaped death by adoption into a Mohawk family. He knew the jungle from boyhood. At times he hated it: "A strange thing when victualls are wanting, worke whole nights and dayes, lye down on the bare ground and not allwayes that hap, the breech in the water, the feare in ye buttocks, to have the belly empty, the weariness in the bones and drowsiness of ye body by the bad weather that you are to suffer, having nothing to keep you from such calamity." Occasionally this wanderer even thought of "the chimney smoak" and home "when we can kiss our own wives or kisse our neighbour's wife wth ease and delight."

Such pangs were soon forgotten when the partners reached Green Bay, on Lake Michigan. This was not unknown ground. Nicolet had reached it twenty years before, and, striking south-westward, almost reached the sources of the Mississippi. Groseilliers at once suspected that these upper streams led by some unknown river to Mexico. Radisson saw in the central plain of America, "so beautifull and fruitfull," the home of a new nation: "What conquest would that bee att litle or no cost, what laborinth of pleasure should millions of people have, instead that millions complain of misery & poverty!" Two rough *coureurs de bois* had given the world its first true vision of America's largest treasure.

Business came first. By threat, cajolery, and bribe Groseilliers persuaded the Indians to take their furs to Montreal again. The arrival of that cargo in 1656 ended the colony's immediate crisis but the intrepid explorers received small thanks. Having saved New France, they paid a tax of 25 per cent on their profits.

Three years later they went west again to explore the Indians' report of a river leading to Hudson Bay. They paddled the length of Lake Superior, discovered a new empire of fur, met Indians who had never seen a white man, and "were Cesars, being nobody to contradict us . . . the Gods of the earth among these people."

Not for long. In the following winter they lived on dogs and stewed tree bark, "our gutts became very straight . . . we mistook ourselves very often, taking the living for the dead and ye dead for the living." Next spring, guided by a strange nation called the Crees, they moved north, how far they never knew, perhaps to the rim of Hudson Bay. Whether they reached it or not, the ignorant men conceived an inspiration which would bring England into the north and transform the whole strategy of the American struggle.

Groseilliers knew little of the bay's location and size. He knew only that Henry Hudson had entered it in 1610, had been turned adrift in a boat by his mutinous crew, and perished with his young son and eight sailors. The bay, therefore, must be navigable from the Atlantic. Groseilliers's extraordinary sense of geography told him that these waters must penetrate far southward. A ship, there-fore, could take on a cargo of fur, direct from the world's richest peltry, and carry it to France without the long journey, the cruel portages, and the Iroquois ambush of the Montreal route. The American economy would be revolutionized.

The partners returned to Montreal, their canoes heavy with pelts (passing on the Ottawa the unburied bodies of Dollard and his companions of the Long Sault), and vainly offered their plan to the government. No one took it seriously. Governor Argenson was interested only in the King's profits and his own. The discoverers of the far West were rewarded for their labor with taxes and fines for illegal trading, 24,000 livres in all, or 40 per cent of their selling price. Of the grafting Governor, Radisson sourly records: "The Bougre did grease his Chopps."

He had cheated the wrong men. Groseilliers and Radisson sailed angrily for France to seek Louis's support in their mission to Hudson Bay. Dismissed as lunatics, they appeared in London shortly after the second Charles had entered it as king. Charles, for all his idleness, had more sense than Louis. He entertained the Canadians as his personal guests at Oxford and Windsor, listened with growing excitement to their tales, and interested his rich friends in their plans.

In June, 1668, the *Eaglet*, bearing Radisson, and the *Nonsuch*, with Groseilliers, sailed from Gravesend for the bay. The *Eaglet* was turned back by storm but Groseilliers's ship reached the southeastern shore of James Bay. The flag of England was raised to claim the whole tributary drainage basin, an indeterminate region stretching to the Rockies.

New France was now pinched in a continental nutcracker as yet dimly seen. To the south stood the expanding English colonies; to the north Charles's newly organized Governor and Company of Adventurers of England Trading into Hudson's Bay. The bureaucrats of Montreal and Paris had overtaxed and then ignored two humble *coureurs de bois*. They must pay the penalty in the coin of empire.

So lay the new lines of American geography and imperial pressure when Talon began to rebuild the Canadian colony. He soon received heady news from the woodsmen who followed and extended the trail of Groseilliers and Radisson and from Jesuits who had found in the West a limitless preserve of pagan souls ready for salvation.

America expanded every day. New rivers, unseen but reliably reported, were hastily drawn on the maps in Quebec and Paris. The Jesuit explorers concluded that Hudson Bay opened into the long-sought Northwest Passage. A magic word, "Mississippi," had entered the American lexicon. Clearly the great central river, as yet a rumor only, must run into the Vermilion Sea of California (which was now recognized as an island). Champlain's western sea, the mighty inland lake emptying into the Pacific, was only twenty days' march from Lake Superior, and would turn into nothing more than Lake Winnipeg.

All this, vague and contradictory as it was, quickly turned the cool head of the Intendant. Revising his maps, dashing off his letters to Colbert, he prepared his seizure of the West. By the Mississippi he could outflank the Spaniards on the Pacific and doubtless snatch a share of Mexico's golden loot. From Hudson Bay the Northwest Passage might lead France to the edge of China and the Eastern spice islands.

Talon's wild surmise had no boundaries, but the trained bureaucrat was not a man to satisfy himself with dreaming. The Mississippi must be followed to its mouth, the English pushed out of the bay, and France's title nailed down on everything in sight or beyond it.

There was no time to waste. The English colonies had begun to show a disturbing instinct of expansion, they had lately conquered the Dutch colony of New Netherland on the Hudson, they were pushing at their steady tortoise pace toward the St. Lawrence, they held Acadia and presently might trickle through the Appalachians. Anyway, outright war with England could not be far off. King Louis had alarmed his European neighbors and they were coalescing against him.

So Talon, after poring over the latest maps, placed his finger on Sault Ste. Marie where the foaming St. Mary's River joined Superior and Huron. This point, as he rightly guessed, was the nexus of the West and lay, as he wrongly informed Louis, only 3,750 miles from "Tartary, China and Japan."

On June 4, 1671, by Talon's orders, the most formidable assembly ever seen in the American hinterland convened at the Jesuit mission of Ste. Marie to proclaim the future of the continent. Delegates of seventeen western tribes, in ceremonial furs, feathers, buckskin or nakedness, mixed with the black-robed figures of the church and the silken representatives of the French King. The solemn Indian signatures, drawn in shape of beaver, otter, sturgeon or deer, accepted without understanding the King's claim to the Great Lakes and "all other Countries, rivers, lakes and tributaries contiguous and adjacent there unto, as well discovered as to be discovered, which are bounded on one side by the Northern and Western Seas and on the other by the South Sea, including all its length and breadth."

Louis thereby took possession of America, known and unknown. Its ancient owners had given their full consent and transferred the title deeds. The English were perpetually compressed on the Atlantic, the Spaniards within an unmapped strip somewhere north of Mexico. But the Indian givers in fact had surrendered nothing, had merely enjoyed a day of ceremony and feasting. The English and Spaniards had not signed the surrender and would pay no more attention to it than did the signers.

Such was the gaudy gesture of Sault Ste. Marie, the impressive posture of a king who would never see America, the heroic gesticulation of a heroic nation which lacked the power to enforce its boast.

The echoes of that occasion, the clamor of French cheers and Indian war whoops, the musket fire at the crossroads of the continent, did not reach New England. The farmer, fisherman, and embryonic American businessman had never heard of Ste. Marie and cared nothing for Louis, his church or his empire of paper. Let the Indians paint their signatures, let the Jesuits raise their giant cross with its royal *fleur-de-lis* beside the rushing river, let the Sieur de St. Lusson, "Commissioner subdelegate of My Lord the Intendant of New France," in plumed hat, curled wig and lace ruffles, shout Louis's claims "in a louid voice, with public outcry," and raise a sod three times on sword point in symbol of this land's royal ownership, let the feathered tribesmen exhale their approval with "reverent hissing," let Father Allouez announce to this hushed conventicle that Louis was "more terrible than thunder," that "the earth trembles, the air and sea are set on fire by the discharge of his cannon"—let France assert in empty word and strident flourish a claim that only arms could make good. Within three months the English would breach the Appalachian dam as they had already breached the ice floes of the bay. They would pour into Louis's empire, knowing no law but their own, heeding no signature of Frenchman, no picture writing of Indian or writ of French king, inscribing their own clumsy caveat with ax, plow, and musket.

Who among the colonies of New England, who in that French audience beside the river of St. Mary could guess that its waters would bound the two unborn nations of America?

Talon had staked the royal claim at the nerve center of the continent. Colbert had negotiated a return of Acadia to France. The north, however, remained in English hands.

Talon moved to the bay during the summer of the Sault Ste. Marie masquerade. His agents, Paul Denis, Sieur de Saint-Simon, the hardy Jesuit Father Albanel, and a half dozen Frenchmen, ascended the Saguenay out of the St. Lawrence, reached the Rupert River, and by a route almost impossible to Indians reached James Bay in the following June.

King Charles's men-of-all-work, Groseilliers and Radisson, were still there to assert his rights and gather his furs. The French told them in a courteous fashion that the title of King Louis was prior and sovereign. After an exchange of compliments with the two shifty partners, the French discreetly withdrew, leaving the legal ownership of the north as doubtful as ever. Legal ownership mattered little. The practical fact was that the English held the bay, entered and left it as they pleased by ship, took its unequaled pelts to England, and had broken the French fur monopoly forever.

Talon's gestures had extended his original blueprint west and north he knew not how far, but it was far enough. There remained the south and the Mississippi, that easy route to California. It must be explored. He tried to hire a moody young explorer, René Robert Cavelier, Sieur de La Salle, now brooding at his seigneury of La Chine, west of Montreal. La Salle was too busy with his own private visions of the West to work for the Intendant. Louis Jolliet, a seasoned fur trader, and the sickly Jesuit, Father Jacques Marquette, were appointed instead. La Salle's epic and tragedy had been postponed.

Jolliet and Marquette prepared to embark on the great river and complete the new blueprint. Its draughtsman, however, was worn out by his labors, his quarrels with governor and bishop, his impossible dream. Talon set sail for France in November, 1672, broken and sick.

He looked back from his ship on a Quebec rebuilt to his pattern, a colony now numbering 7,000 Christian souls, a spiderweb of fur posts, missions, canoe routes, and portages stretched halfway across America.

All Talon's work was stretched too thin, was likely to break at the first blow and New France with it.

Those facts were hidden from the Intendant, soon happily installed as First Valet of Louis's wardrobe. Hidden also from Louis. The dazzling and dazzled Sun King found no more time for Canada, a distant fragment of his imperial design, for he had just launched his war with Holland and was preparing for the engorgement of Europe.

There now waited in the royal anteroom an unemployed soldier— impatient, arrogant, and poor. He must save Canada and Talon's blueprint, as best he might, singlehanded. Louis de Buade, Comte de Frontenac, asked no fairer chance.

4

The Eagle

[1672–1685]

THE ERRATIC TIDES OF THE THIRTY YEARS' WAR HAD LONG CAR-
ried back and forth across Europe in ceaseless motion a
morsel of living flotsam, unnoted and unsinkable. When at
last it was swept across the Atlantic and lodged in the most unlikely place it remained a gritty and dangerous speck of friction
on the shifting boundary of America. For twenty-six years, with
one brief interval, Louis de Buade, Comte de Frontenac et Palluau,
of himself transformed that boundary, the life, tempo and power
balance of the continent, his tools being war, massacre, diplomacy,
bluff, stage acting, and genius.

His arrival in Canada as governor, on September 12, 1672, caused
no stir in the English colonies. Doubtless one of the last to hear
of him would be an illiterate young ship's carpenter, named William
Phips, twenty-sixth child of a poor Kennebec River woman. He was
now working as an apprentice in Boston, learning to read and
write in his spare time and planning to marry a well-born widow,
to whom he had recklessly promised "a fair brick house" and a
husband in command of a king's ship.

Both promises seemed unlikely to be redeemed. It was improbable that Phips and Frontenac—so much alike in ambition, arrogance and courage, so unlike in everything else, the New England
shipwright and the courtly French soldier—would confront each
other, as the agents of two imperial powers and the rival architects
of the ultimate frontier, at Quebec. Yet so, on this continent of the
impossible, it would turn out.

Frontenac was the older and larger man. At fifteen years of age
he had marched with the armies of France in the Low Countries,
son of a family as distinguished as it was poor. At twenty-six he

53

was a brigadier general, wearing with a swagger the scars of many honorable wounds.

Two years later, with his customary violence, he fell in love with Anne de La Grange-Trianon, than sixteen, a famous beauty at King Louis's court. As her father objected to the match, the couple eloped. The father was reconciled to the bridegroom. The bride soon tired of him.

This was not surprising, for Frontenac proved a hard man to live with, as America would find—vain, domineering, splenetic, "his dress always of patterns invented by himself" and "paraded like a child," while "all who wished to gain his good graces were obliged to admire his horses, which were very indifferent," according to that vivid diarist, Mademoiselle de Montpensier.

Small wonder, then, that the separation of bride and bridegroom was swift and so bitter than when he later approached her at a friend's house she fell into a fainting spell and a priest hurriedly brought "holy water to exorcise her."

After fighting a forlorn hope against the Turks in Crete—the first of many—Frontenac, in his fifty-third year, had nothing but a rolling name, a reputation for bravery and bravura, a wife who refused to live with him, a small income, and massive debts. The career of the unemployed veteran and bankrupt, this hero of "excellent parts, living much in society and completely ruined," appeared to be at an end.

Why Louis chose such a man to govern Canada is unknown. The Duc de Saint-Simon concluded that Frontenac "found it hard to bear the imperious temper of his wife; and he was given the government of Canada to deliver him from her and afford him some means of living." More scandalous gossips held that Madame de Montespan had shown her favor to him, that he had accidentally dropped a love letter to her out of his pocket and the King, on reading it, had packed a suspected rival off to the wilds in a fit of jealousy.

So wagged the loose tongues of Paris as Frontenac set out for Canada and his wife sat for her portrait as Minerva, with plumed helmet, glistening shield, and striking display of bosom. She presently retired into genteel poverty as the companion of the lovely Mademoiselle d'Outrelaise, the pair known as Les Divines, who "demanded incense like goddesses, and it was lavished on them all their lives."

Though man and wife were to be forever parted, the tie between Frontenac and his goddess somehow held to the end. She bore him a son, killed early in war or duel. She promoted his interests at court, where he was always in trouble. She remained his only anchor in Europe, the custodian of his split nature's civilized half, as Canada held the larger barbarous half.

Louis doubtless felt well rid of an uncomfortable hanger-on. Frontenac, a seasoned soldier, could serve well enough against the impotent English colonists and, as something of a savage himself, should get on with the Indians. It was an age of such ignorant adventurers, the age of the Three Musketeers, the original cloak-and-dagger age in which, for example, the Duc d'Epernon had lately punched the Archbishop of Bordeaux in the belly, remarking, without any sense of satire: "If it were not for the respect I bear your office I'd stretch you out on the pavement." In such an age Frontenac would do.

The face of the man who strode up the narrow streets of Quebec in the brisk autumn weather is long forgotten. An imaginary mask constructed by modern painters and sculptors—the flowing curls, pointed mustaches, and Olympian scowl—is as good an integument as any for a character which makes its own image in history. Against the gray walls of the château and the black rock he strutted in his laces, ribbons, and feathers like a gorgeous tropical bird straying by mistake among the drab Canada geese. If the plumage seemed that of the parrot, an eagle inhabited it.

Frontenac found his true mate in the virginal stuff of the Canadian wilderness. That second marriage was indissoluble. The wilderness possessed him utterly, as he possessed it.

Quebec, he announced in his first letter to Louis, "could not be better situated as the future capital of a great empire." Already he had seen Talon's dream. "The colonies of foreign nations," he wrote, "are trembling with fright. . . . The measure we have taken to confine them within narrow limits . . . do not permit them to extend themselves, except at the peril of having war declared against them as usurpers; and this, in fact, is what they seem greatly to fear."

Some of the English may have held such fears. Not men like Phips.

The dimensions of Canada fitted the stature of its governor. Hedged in too long by the battlefields and salons of Europe, he found the elbow room he needed. At once the tired soldier, past middle age, the unsuccessful courtier, the ruined spendthrift, seemed to renew his youth in a passionate love affair with a continent.

His first act was to carry through Talon's plan of exploration on the Mississippi. In the summer of 1673 Louis Jolliet, a Canadian churchman turned woodsman, and Jacques Marquette, an ascetic and dying Jesuit, were crossing the portage south of Lake Michigan and drifting with five *voyageurs* down the great central river.

It was easy going. The Indians stuffed the visitors with feasts of buffalo and corn. The country around, with its lush vegetation and teeming game, was the most fertile they had ever seen. Some seven hundred miles from the river mouth, they turned back in fear of capture by the Spaniards and convinced that the Mississippi led not to California but to the Gulf of Mexico. The largest and most dangerous of all Canada's adventures was beginning.

Jolliet hurried back to Quebec with the news but lost all his papers in an overturned boat a few miles from home. The brave Marquette died soon afterward and was buried on the east shore of Lake Michigan. There his bones were soon disinterred by friendly Indians, reverently washed and carried in a birchbark coffin for reburial at the mission of St. Ignace.

While his explorers were descending the Mississippi, Frontenac had remained restive in Quebec. This man knew only war and would have it. But how? King Charles in London was the obliging pensioner of King Louis in Paris. The Iroquois were quiet temporarily under de Tracy's harsh lesson. Still, there was always the chance of agreeable hazard upriver. Frontenac had gazed on the St. Lawrence and, like all men before him, could not rest until he had followed it to the westward.

He summoned the Iroquois to meet him, swept up the river in a fleet of canoes and two painted barges, camped at Cataraqui near the eastern end of Lake Ontario, and staged his first theatrical performance. In his tent, as in a throne room, he received the old enemies with a combination of firmness, friendliness, and rodomontade which they instantly understood. Surrounded by his little bodyguard (nearly all the soldiers in his colony) and dressed in his finest court silks and gold lace, he delivered purple passages of oratory on the power of his king, with promises of royal protection for the Indians and strong hints of a more disagreeable alternative. He made presents to the Indian women, dandled their babies on his knee, and adopted eight Iroquois children as his own. This purple passenger was the kind of man the Iroquois liked and feared. The legend of the great Onontio, carried by the moccasin telegraph, quickly penetrated the whole interior.

Frontenac, the soldier, did not rely on theatricals. His camp followers quickly built a fort at Cataraqui, the present site of Kingston. It was given Frontenac's name and placed under the seigneurial control of La Salle, whose look of melancholy and brooding power had impressed the Governor at their first meeting. Thus was formed the strange and tragic partnership intended to profit both partners in the fur trade and destined to produce wider results in the politics of America and Europe.

The Iroquois had been flattered and cowed and the fur route defended by the new fort, but at Quebec everything went wrong.

Ruling alone, without bishop or intendant to interfere, Frontenac behaved like a king. He immediately re-created the antique fiction of three estates of the realm: the Jesuit clergy; a *noblesse* of military officers, together with a half dozen *gentilshommes;* the commonality of merchants and citizens. This mockery of a states-general, long suspended in France, met with all the pomp that the creator could contrive, with solemn oaths of allegiance and many rousing speeches. Louis was not impressed. As soon as he heard of these arrangements he abolished them. There must be no organized assembly which might challenge the King's power. What could have been the seed of popular government in Canada, with incalculable effects, was never allowed to sprout.

Frontenac received this first royal rebuke humbly. Others, more serious, were not long delayed.

Like Talon, Frontenac hated the Jesuits as spies and meddlers. By undermining him, they undermined the King's rule and even had the audacity to preach against the legal brandy trade. Quebec was split in two parties, the friends of the Governor and his enemies. The opposition party, led by the Jesuits, was composed of the established merchants and fur traders, who resented the new rivals supported by Frontenac, for his own profit as his enemies alleged.

Most of them he treated with contempt. Those who were worthy of his chastisement soon felt it. The eagle's talons reached far, fastening themselves first on the subgovernor of Montreal, an officer named Perrot. That earnest fur grafter watered brandy "with his own hands" for sale to the Indians and "bartered with one of them his hat, sword, coat, ribbons, shoes and stockings, and boasted that he had made thirty pistoles by the bargain, while the Indian walked about town equipped as Governor." Frontenac ordered Perrot locked up in Quebec. From his barred window the prisoner could observe the body of one of his assistant grafters swinging from a gibbet. Though the chastened Perrot was released ten months later, as one of Colbert's personal friends, his example was not forgotten.

Three years of feud and furious transatlantic correspondence convinced Louis that Frontenac could not be trusted to govern alone. The inflexible Bishop Laval, after an absence in France, was sent to Quebec with a new intendant, Jacques Duchesneau, to watch the Governor. They only deepened the quarrel.

The Bishop opposed Frontenac's policy of western expansion, as he had opposed it in Talon's time, because the fur trade corrupted the Indians. The Intendant opposed it because it cost too much and sapped the agriculture of the colony.

Despite Colbert's patient admonitions, the government was riven and could not be united. It argued with solemn comedy about precedent in church services and public ceremony. It wrangled for weeks without deciding who should preside over the Council, all its business suspended. Frontenac banished three of his local enemies to their country houses. He is said to have beaten Duchesneau's young son and torn the sleeve from his jacket. The terrified Intendant barricaded himself in his home. The Governor's only useful work was the construction of a new château fit for his rank.

This clash of individuals—the strutting Governor, the holy but cast-iron Bishop, and the fussing, timid Intendant—represented superficially the organic schism which had always divided Canada, the contest between a compact colony, as conceived by Colbert, and the imperial expansion launched by Talon.

The Intendant, interested in money, and the Bishop, concerned only with Indian souls, seemed to overcome the Governor. As the supporter of the fur trade, Frontenac was embarrassed by its rising cost of transportation over ever-widening distances and by a sudden surplus of pelts when the fashions of Paris decreed a smaller felt hat. Furs were burned prodigally to keep prices up, by an economic theory still popular three hundred years later. Only 25 canoes, carrying three men each, were licensed to trade in the interior. Under the Bishop's prodding, the sale of brandy was forbidden.

The leading citizens met in the "Brandy Parliament" of 1678 and voted 15 to 5 against this prohibition, since it would turn the Indians' business to the English, to cheap West Indies rum, and to the greater evil of heresy.

In any case, prohibition of furs and brandy was impossible. Only seventy-five traders were licensed, yet poor Duchesneau estimated the illegal *coureurs de bois* at more than five hundred. Nearly everybody, from the Governor down, was doing business in furs, directly or through secret agents, and often smuggling contraband into New York. Besides, the English, having no regard for fair trade, outbid the French, paid the Indians more in cheaply made goods, offered a better kettle of copper and a coarse cloth, dyed red or blue, which no Indian could resist and no French weaver could imitate.

For six years Louis heard nothing from Quebec but Frontenac's charge that Bishop, Jesuits, and Intendant were conspiring against the King, the Bishop's countercharge that Frontenac's trade and brandy ruined the King's Indian subjects, and the Intendant's whining insinuation that Frontenac was grafting in partnership with the outlaw *coureurs de bois.*

Louis's patience ran out. In 1681 he abruptly dismissed the Governor and the Intendant together. Frontenac returned to France in disgrace. His last act was to record in the official register the fact that his rank was higher than Duchesneau's—small comfort to the ruined soldier, old and penniless, who must haunt the outskirts of the court until he died.

Paris and Quebec seemed to be the center of events. Actually they stood on the perimeter. The center had moved west to the Lakes country and that fact of itself proclaimed the victory of Frontenac's policy, now in full motion, even while its author moldered on the fringes of society.

The recall of Frontenac came at the worst possible time for Canada. The Iroquois had recovered from de Tracy's lesson and already were attacking the Illinois and Miami nations, Canada's friends, around Michigan. This minor campaign, starting in 1680, was the true beginning of open continental war between England and France, nine years later.

As usual, the antagonists operated through distant agents. The English had the Iroquois to fight for them. France now rediscovered its bland and treacherous tools, Radisson and Groseilliers. They had tired of high life as Hudson's Bay Company employees in London, had grown dissatisfied with King Charles's "gold Chaine and Meddal" and pensions of £100 a year. So they fled to Paris about the time Frontenac reached it. Their treachery was overlooked because Louis could use them.

In his service they sailed to Hudson Bay again and, by stealth and diplomacy, seized the company's fort, its governor and furs. This rich booty they carried to Quebec. Somewhere in the course of their obscure expedition Groseilliers died. Radisson soon returned to the English, who were glad to have him, regardless of his crimes.

He earned his pay by quietly recapturing for England the fort he had lately captured for France. So long as there was money and danger in it, he would gladly work for anyone and in his own specialty he was an expert without peer. But after his unequaled life which, with Groseilliers's leadership, had changed the face and prospects of America, his end was bitterness and anticlimax. He died in England, with an English wife and children, destitute except for his pension.

The future of the bay, a far-off incident in the main contest, must await even more improbable adventures. France's energies were concentrated in the heart of the continent.

On Frontenac's instructions his agents, La Salle, Daniel Grey-solon, Sieur Dulhut, king of the *coureurs de bois,* Nicholas Perrot, and other men of the same hardy breed, were making peace be-tween the restless western tribes and, by blandishment, presents, threats and sheer nerve, welding them into a confederacy, leagued with Canada. Each of these men made his private epic but only a fragment of their story was appropriated and distorted, in wildest travesty, by the ineffable Father Hennepin, whom Dulhut had res-cued singlehanded from the terrible Sioux. Hennepin repaid his rescuer with a book of sensational lies. Europe received a carica-ture of the West and its discoverers.

That was of passing interest. The fact vital to Canada and dangerous to the English colonies was that the new confederacy, often wavering, somehow held. Canada controlled the West.

Its title was now expanded by an unequaled feat of imagination— the imagination of Frontenac's young, moody and visionary friend, La Salle. He was ready to descend the Mississippi, as he hoped, to the western sea. A mad project, it appeared to his neighbors near Montreal. They called his seigneury La Chine, mocking his attempt to reach China.

He built a ship on Lake Erie, the first to ply the waters above Niagara, took it to Lake Michigan and filled it with furs. It dis-appeared on the return voyage without trace. Unaware of this ruinous accident, La Salle built a line of posts in the Illinois coun-try and then, with his one-armed aide, the indomitable Henry Tonty, and a score of Canadians, reached the mouth of the Missis-sippi without mishap on Thursday, April 9, 1682. A great day for France, the beginning of La Salle's tragedy.

He knew at last that the Mississippi did not lead to the Pacific. Once again the water passage to China, first sought by Cartier and Champlain, had faded into the mapless blank of the West. But La Salle had glimpsed the Great Valley of inner America and immediately named it Louisiana in the King's honor. It included all the unknown drainage basin of the Mississippi. If others did not understand its value, La Salle, a man of Champlain's far-ranging geographic instinct, recognized it as America's most precious treas-ure. This inland kingdom, unlike Canada, could feed itself, com-

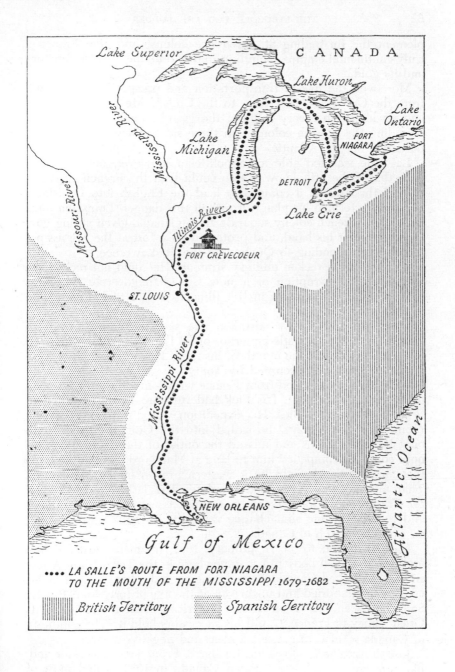

Lake Superior

CANADA

Lake Huron

Lake Ontario

Lake Michigan

FORT NIAGARA

Mississippi River

Missouri River

DETROIT

Lake Erie

Illinois River

FORT CRÈVECOEUR

ST. LOUIS

Mississippi River

Atlantic Ocean

NEW ORLEANS

Gulf of Mexico

•••• LA SALLE'S ROUTE FROM FORT NIAGARA
TO THE MOUTH OF THE MISSISSIPPI 1679-1682

‖‖‖ British Territory   Spanish Territory

plement the fur-trading St. Lawrence colony, and give France a truly continental empire, including in due time the Spanish territory and its gold.

Moreover, the line of transportation and prospective settlement, from the Gulf of St. Lawrence to the Gulf of Mexico, now in fact and no longer in theory fulfilled the grand Canadian strategy by bounding the English colonies on three sides. They were left with no egress but the Atlantic.

La Salle was too able a geopolitician, however, not to see at once that if the little-known Ohio could lead the French eastward toward the English it could also lead the English into Louisiana. He quickly formed his plan to forestall this danger. Louisiana must be made a French colony separate from Canada, given strong government under his hand, and protected by a fort at the Mississippi mouth, corresponding to Quebec on the St. Lawrence.

La Salle could reckon military strategy. He could not reckon the stupidity and corruption of a new Canadian governor who was soon plundering his posts in the Illinois country and driving him to France for redress.

Louis was not always mistaken. He saw the young explorer's worth. La Salle was made governor of all Louisiana and authorized to found a colony at the mouth of his river. His northern posts were restored to him and occupied by Tonty.

In 1684 La Salle sailed from France with four ships and 400 men to begin his settlement. His luck had run out. He nearly died of fever in the West Indies. His expedition was disrupted. Half sick (some said half crazy), he sailed into the Gulf of Mexico with only 180 companions and missed the outlet of the river. His mutinous company compelled him to land at Matagorda Bay in the hope that an inlet there might be a western branch of the Mississippi. That mistake was discovered too late. The last ship had sailed for France. Only forty-five men remained, many sick, all hungry and rebellious. One slim chance was left. La Salle must attempt an overland march to Canada.

He had not far to go. In January, 1687, his men murdered him and left his naked body to rot somewhere in the Texas bush. A few survivors reached Canada. None remembered where a titan of his century lay unburied and unshriven at the age of forty-four. But La Salle had seen the vision of the American interior and given its Great Valley to France. Could his successors hold it? The condition of Canada seemed to present a clear and negative answer.

Joseph Antoine Lefebvre de La Barre, Frontenac's successor and, like him, an old soldier, reached Canada in 1682 to find most of

Quebec in ashes. Beyond the ruins of its recent conflagration sparks more dangerous smoldered in the Iroquois country.

The new Governor settled down comfortably enough and made deals with a group of fur merchants—rivals of the Frontenac group—for a cut in their profits. Thrifty man, he also petitioned the King for a raise in pay.

The old enemy had been released from the threat of Onontio, but was not quite ready to attack the French direct. Instead, urged on by the English, the Iroquois evidently planned to repeat their old western strategy against the Illinois and other French allies of the Lakes country.

La Barre could not understand the continental forces now in flow, the stealthy creep of a few Indians, the swift, silent movement of a few white men who, in the emptiness of America, could grasp or lose territories larger than European states. At least he knew that the fur trade was in danger and, more alarming, that his own profits were at stake; for he and his partners had lately placed large quantities of trade goods at Michilimackinac, between Michigan and Huron, straight in the probable path of the Iroquois.

So, for imperial and personal reasons, he resolved to crush the foe before it could march. This resolve taken, he bristled with gasconade. Louis was assured that his army of 1,200 men would defeat 2,600 Indians and that "I will perish at their head or destroy your enemies."

He did neither. At Montreal he met a delegation of Iroquois chiefs, urged them not to attack the licensed French trade canoes "without permission," and indicated that they might advantageously seize any others—meaning, of course, the canoes of his trade rivals and Frontenac's friends. (This instruction the Iroquois soon followed rather too literally by appropriating two canoes of the Governor's own organization, which he had neglected to license.)

When he asked the Iroquois timidly why they intended to attack the Illinois a chief replied, in fine contempt, "because they deserve to die." La Barre endured this humiliation without a word and even promised to punish La Salle for arming the King's Indian allies. The trained noses of the Iroquois never failed to smell weakness. They surged into the Illinois territory.

Since they were thus engaged in the West, Canada gained a short reprieve. La Barre used it to expand his private trade and to smuggle his furs into New York.

These peculations were disguised, and Louis deceived, by ostentatious preparations for a march against the Iroquois. Boats of war were built on Lake Ontario and used to carry the Governor's furs.

Fort Frontenac was made the entrepôt of his business. In the spring of 1683 he seized La Salle's new fort of St. Louis as the western outpost of his private empire, only to have a raiding party of Senecas and Cayugas steal his canoes, goods, and traders because they were supposed to be the property of La Salle and fair game under the Governor's recent instructions.

This was too much. Now that his own fortunes were in peril, La Barre decided to make good his threats. Setting out from Quebec for Lake Ontario, he informed Louis again that it would be a pleasure to die for His Majesty. "I cannot refuse to your country of Canada and your faithful subjects to throw myself, with unequal force, against the foe."

He had quite overlooked the real target. It was not the Iroquois, it was the English. While the English had their hands full at home and no intention of risking war if it could be avoided, they had long since learned how to use the Iroquois as their shock troops, at a safe distance. And now England had an agent who knew his business.

Thomas Dongan, the able new governor of New York, was an Irishman and a Catholic. He had spent some years in France and knew both its language and its mind. His instructions from London were to provoke no trouble with Canada. He therefore attempted to head off La Barre's attack on the Iroquois by homemade diplomacy.

His first step was to end a series of border quarrels between the Iroquois outposts and the struggling colonies of Maryland and Virginia. To that end a peace conference was called at Albany. The offending Oneidas, Onondagas, and Cayugas promised to cease their raids and thereupon buried their hatchets in a ceremonial hole outside the council house. Lord Howard, of Virginia, and the delegate from Maryland contributed hatchets of their own. The hole was filled and peace signed.

These disagreements satisfactorily settled, Dongan's diplomacy moved into wider territory. The fatuous La Barre had lately advised him of the intended Canadian campaign (thus alerting the Iroquois to their danger) and had implored the English not to arm the enemy. Dongan saw his chance.

In a letter to Quebec he asserted England's sovereignty over all the Iroquois nations and its ownership of all land south of the Great Lakes—asserted, in fact, England's right to half the continent at least. It was a bold gambit so early in the game, obviously too bold to be enforced at present, but presaging the shape of the final contest and even fixing the rough location of the future boundary.

The Iroquois, as always, played the English and French off against each other. Though promised 800 English troops by Dongan, they refused to accept him as anything closer than their "brother," whereas the Governor of Canada was still their "father," albeit a poor substitute for the great Onontio, now languishing in Paris.

Dongan had much to learn about the native mind. La Barre had more. He led a powerful expedition of 130 regular soldiers, 700 Canadians, and 200 Indians up the St. Lawrence to Fort Frontenac and half his men fell sick with fever. His nerve and health thereupon collapsed. The intended attack was abandoned, the Iroquois politely asked to make peace. Their chiefs appeared, led by Big Mouth, a statesman of other large measurements.

La Barre demanded from his armchair—he was too sick to stand— that the Iroquois cease their raids on his western allies and make reparation for their crimes. Big Mouth listened in silence, his eyes on his pipe. He had seen through the Frenchman and his lieutenants had soon discovered the real state of the fever-ridden garrison. After a long pause the chief arose and, pacing up and down before the Governor's armchair, began a classic of Indian eloquence:

"Onontio, when you left Quebec you must have thought that the heat of the sun had burned the forests that make our country inaccessible to the French, or that the lake had overflowed them so that we could not escape from our villages. You must have thought so, Onontio; and curiosity to see such a fire or such a flood must have brought you to this place. Now your eyes are opened; for I and my warriors have come to tell you that the Senecas, Cayugas, Onondagas, Oneidas and Mohawks are alive . . . Listen, Onontio. I am not asleep. My eyes are open; and by the sun that gives me light I see a great captain at the head of a band of soldiers who talks like a man in a dream. He says that he has come to smoke the pipe of peace with the Onondagas; but I see that he came to knock them in the head, if so many Frenchmen were not too weak to fight. I see Onontio raving in a camp of sick men, whose lives the Great Spirit has saved by smiting them with disease."

To confirm this noble insult, Big Mouth flatly refused to offer any reparations for the Iroquois' western raids and announced that "we have the right to go whithersoever we please, to take with us whomever we please and buy and sell of whomever we please."

La Barre swallowed the insult, signed the peace of actual defeat, and limped back to Quebec. He had earned nothing but the contempt of the Iroquois and his own allies. French power in America, built on Indian alliances, was near collapse.

The news soon reached Paris in angry dispatches from Intendant de Meulles. Louis acted promptly. The next ship brought his last letter to the Governor. La Barre was dismissed because "your years do not permit you to support the fatigues inseparable from your office."

The grafter who had once been a soldier returned to France, if not a sadder and wiser, at least a richer man. He left Canada exposed to an Iroquois invasion, its allies disillusioned and restive, its real enemy, in New York, quietly planning, by diplomacy, for war.

In La Barre's place Louis had appointed Jacques René de Brisay, Marquis de Denonville, an aristocrat, a soldier and a pious churchman, brave enough but not big enough for the job. He passed an Atlantic voyage "in prayer and the reading of holy books" and reached Quebec to find conditions worse than he had feared.

The Iroquois still warred on the western tribes. The betrayed French allies seemed likely to join their remorseless enemy. Dongan was even sending traders into the French peltry of the upper Lakes. The English in Hudson Bay monopolized the northern furs. New Englanders freely battened on the Acadian fisheries and frequently raided the Canadian coast.

As Denonville at once advised Louis, Canada must assert itself, teach the Iroquois a final lesson, master the West or lose everything to the English.

Dongan was equally disturbed. For all their weakness, the Canadians were entrenched in the Illinois country, with forts on the Mississippi and a plan to settle at its mouth. Talon's strategy of encirclement was well advanced, despite La Barre's disasters.

Both Denonville and Dongan, chafing in their capitals, were restrained by the orders of their kings. Neither the weak James, newly crowned in London, nor the strong Louis in Paris was ready for more than diplomatic skirmishes. Besides, they were friends and united by a hatred of the people. In their North American representatives they had found two ingenious diplomats, well able to string out the skirmishes indefinitely, short of an open rupture.

5

Letters from New York

[1695–1698]

THE NEW CANADIAN GOVERNOR QUICKLY GRASPED THE CONTINEN-
tal strategy. He knew that the English were the real enemy
and he intended to subdue the Iroquois as their only effective
fighting arm. But he was not ready to move. Nor was Dongan.
These two wily men began a cat-and-mouse game with a ludicrous
correspondence between Quebec and New York.

Dongan welcomed Denonville to America in the French language. Denonville replied as "A man may do who wishes to dis-
simulate and does not feel strong enough to get angry." One series
of letters to Paris begged his king for troops; another, to New York,
tried to divert Dongan with pleasantries. "I should reproach myself
all my life," Denonville assured his enemy, "if I should fail to render
to you all the civility and attention due to a person of so great
rank and merit."

The correspondence suddenly turned astringent when Dongan
learned that Denonville proposed to build a fort at Niagara and
protect Lake Erie. Using blunt English now, and his own curious
spelling, Dongan confessed that "I cannot beleev that a person
that has your reputation in the world . . . be so ill advized by
some interested persons in your Govert. to make disturbances between our Masters subjects in those parts of the world for a little
pelttree."

Denonville set aside his piety to assure Dongan, with a cynical
lie, that he had no intention of fortifying Niagara. He added that
Dongan's rum was turning the Indians "into demons and their
lodges into the counterparts of Hell." To which Dongan replied
tartly that "Certainly our Rum doth as little hurt as your Brandy,
and, in the opinion of Christians, is much more wholesome."

67

This façade of ink and paper could not disguise events now moving fast in the old cockpit of the West. Dongan quietly pushed his traders farther into the French peltry and planned a treaty of trade and military alliance with Canada's Indian friends, whose confidence La Barre had destroyed. Denonville hurriedly ordered the ubiquitous Dulhut to fortify the Strait of Detroit, as a cork in the bottle of the upper Lakes. By a sudden inspiration he urged Louis to end the entire conflict by a simple method. Let France purchase the New York colony, seat of all his troubles.

Louis was not interested. The Governor next reported that "I have a mind to go straight to Albany, storm their fort and burn everything." As he lacked the resources to storm anyone, he continued to write futile warnings to Dongan.

The New Yorker had also received warnings from London to be careful. He could find no support in the other colonies. His letters to Denonville, therefore, resumed their old obsequious tenor, with the promise of punishment for any Iroquois who "doe amisse to any of your Government."

The promise was accompanied by a gift of oranges, "hearing that they are a rarity in your partes." That peace offering failed to impress Denonville. "Monsieur," he retorted rather acidly, "I thank you for your oranges. It is a great pity that they are all rotten."

Their condition symbolized the whole correspondence and the state of the frontier between two peoples.

Louis was not ready to strike at the English but he reinforced Denonville and ordered him to attack the Iroquois. The first blow fell elsewhere, in the one place where no Englishman expected it— the most daring, imaginative, and successful blow yet struck in America.

While France and England remained at peace, Denonville assembled eighty experienced woodsmen at Montreal in the spring of 1686 and instructed them to drive the English out of Hudson Bay. It was an assignment impossible for any ordinary soldiers to execute, perhaps not beyond the skill of the great Charles Le Moyne's sons, the blond giant, Iberville, his brothers, Sainte-Hélène and Maricourt, three musketeers straight out of the pages of Dumas.

Under the leadership of Chevalier de Troyes, they pushed secretly up the Ottawa, labored by land, river and lake across the northern watershed, paddled to the bay on the early summer freshet, and at night, without warning, fell upon the sleeping English in Fort Hayes. The three brothers climbed the palisades. Their comrades broke down the gate with a battering ram. The English were captured, bloodless, in their nightshirts.

Fifteen English were asleep at Fort Rupert when the Canadians burst the walls, dropped grenades down the chimneys, shot five of the garrison, including a woman, and then, for good measure, swarmed upon an English ship nearby to capture it after a brief scuffle with the bewildered governor of the Hudson's Bay Company posts.

The English in their nearby fort of Albany were forewarned and determined to defend themselves. Nothing could stop the ravenous brothers. They blew up the palisades with captured English cannon. The garrison quickly raised a white flag. Honorable surrender was sealed in Spanish wine and toasts all round to Louis and James. Iberville drank deep, never guessing that he would return here not long hence for another, more deadly toast.

If eighty of these incredible Canadians could flit silently across a trackless waste and capture three forts in a short summer's outing, London must recalculate the logistics of America.

The calculation appeared ridiculously lop-sided. Only 10,000 Canadians had undertaken to challenge 200,000 English. The odds were 20 to 1. Such calculations ignored the quality of the 10,000.

A Canadian could leap across half a continent almost before an English farmer could drop his plow handles and load a musket. And the Canadians controlled most of the Indians, the major military force now engaged.

The warriors of Louis's totalitarian state operated by one central plan, under one man's direction, and, given a leader like Frontenac, moved like a single machine. The English, with their queer notions of liberty, seldom took orders from anybody, could hardly unite even within one colony, and needed another century of costly experience to achieve a general union. They would defend their narrow ground on the Atlantic. They could not strike beyond it.

The French hare thus continued to run leagues ahead of the English tortoise and seemed to increase its speed with every passing year, from the Gulf of Mexico to the arctic. The tortoise would learn in time. It possessed not only a hard shell but an extra dimension which the hare would never attain—the sea power of England. Slowly, inexorably, and fatally the English Navy could bottle up Canada and starve it.

The statesmen of England and France—to whom all America was at most a side issue in the wars of Europe—may have understood these calculations, somewhat vaguely. Anyway, Louis wanted peace for the time being and he usually controlled James by bribery. Denonville and Dongan, therefore, were ordered to maintain the highly practical friendship of their masters. At the same time Louis ordered Dongan to delay no longer the attack on the Iroquois.

In the period of official neutrality the succession of wars for America, to last three generations, had begun. The Le Moynes had opened it merrily in Hudson Bay. Denonville proposed to continue it south of Lake Ontario. Dongan sat powerless in New York, able only to write ingratiating letters to his rival. The words doubtless stuck in his irascible Irish throat.

Other personages more illustrious were caught in these complex crosscurrents, already converging in tidal wave. James was rapidly losing the last Stuart throne of England. A prince of Orange, cunning, sickly and invincible, was preparing to cross the Channel, at the invitation of a desperate English nation, and sign a curious document called a Bill of Rights, which would be imitated elsewhere. Louis was driving Europe into coalition against him. The Sun King's reign had passed its noon.

Figures so famous and so fully occupied at the center of events found scant time to waste on the barbarous warfare of their colonies. A few unknown men, as usual, were settling for themselves the future of America, by impossible marches, night raids, conspiracies in Indian lodges, Jesuit sermons and scalping parties, by birchbark, paddle and portage, by diplomatic correspondence, gifts of oranges, and toasts in Spanish wine.

In the summer of 1687—unaware of La Salle's assassination and the loss of Canada's hold on the Gulf of Mexico—Denonville was ready at last to use sharper weapons. Still blandly assuring Dongan that he had no plan of war, the Canadian Governor secretly mobilized his 1,600 French regulars and the Canadian militia. This army of 2,000 reached Fort Frontenac, where some half hundred Christian Iroquois, then being slowly tortured by the Indian allies of New France, were treacherously seized and sent to serve as slaves in Louis's galleys.

Now, to his infinite relief, Denonville was joined by 200 French *coureurs de bois* and 400 Indians of the upper Lakes—proof that Dulhut and the other Canadian agents had managed to hold their tottering western confederacy.

The augmented expedition of 3,000, mightiest ever assembled in America, moved through stifling heat—the commander in his shirt sleeves—against the Senecas south of Lake Ontario and directly into a murderous ambush. The brave old French General brandished his sword, rallied his panic-stricken troops and charged. Realizing that they had ambushed only the advance guard of a vast army, the Senecas fled. The forty corpses left behind were quickly mutilated by Denonville's Christian allies. He was forced to watch them, as he wrote in horror to Paris, "cut the dead bodies into quarters like butcher's meat, to put into their kettles, and opened most of them while still warm to drink the blood."

The enemy had disappeared after setting fire to their town. Denonville's men systematically burned the stores of grain and cut down the growing crops. The victors sickened on feasts of fresh corn and pork but their work of destruction was soon complete and the Iroquois nowhere to be found. The army moved back to Lake Ontario. Denonville paused briefly to carry out his original plan, about which he had lied to Dongan. A fort was built below Niagara to bar the English from Lake Erie.

What had he accomplished in a campaign huge by American experience? He had re-established Canada's lost credit with the western tribes. He had punished the Iroquois and scared the English. It was a temporary gain. The Senecas rebuilt their villages and borrowed food from their confederates. They had lost less than a hundred dead. The remainder, as dangerous as ever and angrier, patiently plotted their revenge. It was to be reaped manyfold two years hence.

On hearing of the Iroquois' defeat, Dongan could contain himself no longer. If James would not protect his Indian subjects, New York must do it alone. The Iroquois chiefs were summoned to Albany and told that they had suffered their just deserts for disobeying Dongan's orders and doing business with the French. Hereafter they must bring all their furs to the English, who would support them.

Dongan accused Denonville of invading "the King my Master's territorys in a hostill manner" and asserted the title of England over the whole Iroquois region. The illegal French claims, he said, were based on the travels of the Jesuits, and he added a final taunt: "The King of China never goes anywhere without two Jesuits with him. I wonder you make not the like pretence to that Kingdome. . . . Your reason is that some rivers or rivolettes of this country run out into the great river of Canada. O just God! What a new farr-fetched and unheard-of pretence is this for a title to a country. The French King may have as good a pretence to all those Countrys that drink claret and Brandy."

King James at last was plucking up his courage, too late to save his crown but perhaps in time to save his colonies. He ordered Dongan to fight the French if they attacked again. With this royal support, Dongan demanded that Denonville return his Iroquois prisoners and a few English traders still in his hands and demolish the new fort at Niagara, English territory.

Denonville had weakened, on instructions from Louis, who

needed an accommodation with James. The Governor was also depressed by the latest news from London. New York, New Jersey, and
New England had been placed under a single government, headed
by Sir Edmond Andros, and Dongan recalled, with honor and rank
of major general. Andros, as Denonville warned Louis, was "more
dangerous by his suppleness and smoothness than the other was by
violence." Also, Andros carried a commission which formally granted
him control of all land from the English colonies to the Pacific—
the boundaries unfixed but expandable at pleasure.

Andros was not the immediate enemy. Disease suddenly desolated the garrisons at Niagara and Frontenac. The Iroquois began
to prowl again. West of Three Rivers the Canadian settlers dared
not venture outside their palisades. No crops were sown. Fur trade
ceased for two years. The bankrupt Intendant, de Meulles, was
paying his bills in playing cards, thriftily cut into quarters, signed
and officially called money.

After one Pyrrhic victory Canada was destitute. "We should suc-
cumb," Denonville reported, "if our cause were not the cause of
God."

His nerves were shattered by diplomacy, calamity, and age. To
reduce his losses he obeyed Andros's command and razed Fort
Niagara.

The Iroquois understood this gesture of desperation. They pressed
their advantage and clamored for the return of their captured
brothers, some of them in Louis's galleys.

Denonville managed one last spasm of courage. He proposed a
double attack on the Iroquois by Lake Ontario and the old Richelieu route, but Louis was too engaged in Europe for distant adventures. Denonville undertook to conciliate the Iroquois. Meeting
Big Mouth at Montreal, he offered to surrender the prisoners.

The oily Indian politician pretended to believe the Governor. He
and his lieutenants retired to their villages for consultation. Their
reply came on the night of August 4, 1689.

A blinding hailstorm hid 1,500 warriors as they surrounded the
sleeping village of La Chine, west of Montreal. They worked fast.
By morning the town had been burned to the ground, 200 inhabitants butchered on the spot and a hundred carried off for refined
torture. Denonville's courage had ebbed out. He refused to pursue
the butchers. His soldiers from Montreal, outraged by his orders,
stood helpless and watched their friends being carved and eaten
on the far shore of the St. Lawrence.

Canada was prostrate before the most terrible disaster it had yet
known. Worse news followed. James had fled England. His successor, William, had formally declared war on France. The Cana-

dians, faced by the full power of England under a fighting king, were left alone to their fate.

No, not quite alone. Denonville had been dismissed. And Frontenac in his seventieth year—with Louis's blessing and little else—was on his way to Quebec. He would never see France or his reluctant goddess again.

"I send you back to Canada where I am sure that you will serve me as well as you did before, and I ask nothing more of you," Louis had told the old Count, their old quarrel conveniently overlooked in the new crisis.

It was asking a lot, in present circumstances probably more than any man could deliver. But there was no alternative to Frontenac. He had been a failure as a governor. His violence of peacetime might well be his virtue as a soldier in war. He had paid for his failures by seven years of futility, idleness, and poverty. Such experience might have broken a weaker man. It only hardened Frontenac. Vindicated and forgiven, he returned to Quebec on October 15, 1689, with all his old arrogance but neither troops, money, nor years to spare.

Quebec welcomed him as its savior. Torchlight parades, fireworks, and orations warmed his wild heart. As nowhere else he was home again in the wild land that fitted his own nature.

The word soon spread for a thousand miles by the moccasin telegraph—Onontio was back. The Canadians and Indians knew what that meant. The New Englanders knew little of their deadly opponent but presently would find out more.

Whether Frontenac's counterpart, in New England, the ambitious Phips, had even heard of his future antagonist by now, the record does not show. Frontenac had been idle. Phips had busily elbowed his way upward in his little world, had discovered a sunken Spanish galleon in the West Indies, quelled his mutinous crew with his own fists, and taken £16,000 as his share of the treasure. He had been knighted by his grateful king.

After such experience, and with the self-esteem built of courage, frontier ingenuity, ignorance and luck, Phips might well be regarded as the only figure in America comparable to Onontio—the newly rich product of New England business, the amateur gentleman, ranged against the French aristocrat of noble birth, now more than half a savage. The collision between these two, each representing forces larger than he could comprehend, was not far off.

Frontenac had come to Quebec with a daring military plan in his pocket, as devised by Denonville, and in the hold of his ship had brought thirteen bedizened Indian prisoners. They formed part of that plan.

A thousand French troops and 600 Canadians were to move down the Lake Champlain route, capture Albany, and descend the Hudson to New York, there meeting two French ships of war. The invaders would burn the wooden town of 200 houses. English Catholics were to be spared, if they swore allegiance to Louis. Protestants would pay ransoms and their lands would be granted in feudal tenure to the French troops while they were banished to New England and Pennsylvania. Then the adjacent New England settlements would be razed and others, more distant, compelled to pay perpetual indemnities to France.

Some eighteen thousand English would thus be ruined and dispersed. The Iroquois would be at the mercy of the French. The fur business would be confined to the St. Lawrence. France would possess the whole interior. The English would occupy a reduced strip on the Atlantic coast and, at a suitable moment, would be finally conquered and attached to the French Empire. Denonville's plan, executed by Frontenac, proposed nothing less than the end of English power and civilization in America.

Conceivably, though it was at best improbable, such a project, for all its risks, could succeed if Louis did his part. Louis was too busy with the larger projects of his new war in Europe. The French men-of-war did not reach Acadia until mid-September when it was too late to attempt a Canadian march southward. The great plan, which might have changed the entire history of the continent by smashing the English or, more likely, exhausting Canada, was never launched.

Frontenac contrived another plan, less formidable, equally brutal.

But it must wait for the present. He hurried to Montreal to find the terrified Denonville living in a state of siege, the ashes of La Chine as the Iroquois had left them, the farmers afraid to till their fields, the fur trade suspended.

What was worse, Denonville had just sent a party of soldiers to blow up Fort Frontenac, named for its founder and always his pet. The angry Governor dispatched messengers to cancel this order but it was too late. The fort already lay in smoking ruins. France had cut its own lifeline to the West. The Iroquois, as if to celebrate Onontio's arrival, launched a new series of raids on the outlying settlements.

The soldier's mind could not be distracted by these disasters on the perimeter of the war. He was aiming at the center, the English colonies. Until he could strike them down the Iroquois somehow must be pacified by diplomacy. Frontenac produced his thirteen Iroquois prisoners, captured years before by Denonville and long chained in Louis's galleys.

These bewildered warriors had been transformed, by the magic of politics, from slaves to noblemen and now appeared about the Château St. Louis clad in the silks, laces, and plumes of the French court as bait for their fellow countrymen. Three of them were dispatched immediately to Onondaga with Frontenac's paternal message of forgiveness: "The great Onontio, whom you all know, has come back again. He does not blame you for what you have done, for he looks upon you as foolish children and blames only the English, who are the cause of your folly and have made you forget your obedience to a father who has always loved and never deceived you." If the Iroquois would repent they could have the remaining prisoners and Onontio's old friendship.

This first gambit was a failure. At the very moment when the great chief Cut Nose, Frontenac's messenger, was advising the Iroquois to accept such generous terms "if you wish to live," a courier arrived from the upper Lakes.

He bore startling news—nine tribes of the interior had signed a treaty with the Iroquois and the English, announcing that "Onontio is drunk . . . we wash our hands of all his actions; neither we nor you must defile ourselves by listening to him."

If that treaty held, the grand strategy of Canada, carefully nourished through eighty years of diplomacy and war, was shattered. The Iroquois council hesitated no longer. Frontenac's offer was rejected. Messengers sped to New York and New England to promise that "we will fight with Onontio . . . but tell us no lies." Another messenger informed Frontenac at Quebec that it would be time enough to talk of peace when all the prisoners had been surrendered. The Iroquois had no intention of making peace anyway. They were planning, with the western tribes and the English, to exterminate the French.

Frontenac made a last attempt at conciliation, but the second emissary to Onondaga was brutally beaten and sent as a prisoner to New York after two of his guides had been burned.

Frontenac might yet rebuild the broken alliance in the West. He sent an embassy to Michilimackinac assuring the Indians there that "the English have deceived and devoured your children, but I am a good father who loves you." The western tribes listened sullenly to promises that they doubted. They were inveigled at the eleventh hour by a ghastly trick.

French messengers had captured an Iroquois hunter on their westward journey and now urged the Hurons and Ottawas to kill him. This treachery should turn all the Iroquois nations against their new friends. The life of a single captive was a small price to pay in a bargain so vital. As the Hurons wavered, a Jesuit missionary, highly practical in his Christianity, urged them in God's name to "put the Iroquois into the kettle."

This chance of free amusement was too good to be lost. The prisoner was tied to a stake and systematic torture begun. It proved disappointing. The Iroquois failed to show a warrior's fortitude and the disgusted torturers scalped and shot him.

His life had saved Canada's position in the West for the time being. The western tribes, realizing that their new allies would not forgive their crime, and persuaded by Frontenac's threats, promises and rich presents, decided not to ratify the pact with the Iroquois. As Frontenac well knew, it could be revived without notice. He held the West by a single scalp. It was pause enough for his immediate purpose. Now he could drive a three-pronged fork into the sluggish body of New England.

In the first snows of winter, 1690, war parties were assembled at Montreal, Three Rivers, and Quebec to lunge southward on snowshoes. Their plan was unknown to the English and, if known, would not have been believed. Only madmen, French, or Indians would attempt it.

The Montreal party of a hundred French and a hundred Indians was headed by the brothers Le Moyne—Iberville, Sainte-Hélène, and Bienville, a trio which had no rivals in the art of jungle war, knew no rules, and was restrained by no scruples. Dragging their provisions on sledges, wallowing in the soft snow of a sudden thaw, half drowned in the flooded swamps, they toiled up the Richelieu, reached the Hudson, abandoned the impossible project of attacking Albany, and in the first days of February descended instead on Schenectady, the last outpost of New York.

The village held only eight militiamen, under the brave but incompetent Lieutenant Talmage. Its affairs were in confusion after a revolution in New York against William of Orange. Its gates hung wide open, guarded by two imitation sentinels of snow. Its Dutch inhabitants were asleep, comfortable in the knowledge that Canada lay far away. Here was a temptation to massacre. The brothers Le Moyne accepted it.

Silently the French and Indians passed through the stockade and with the signal of a war whoop battered down the doors of the houses. Sixty inhabitants, men, women and children, were efficiently butchered in half an hour but thirty Mohawk warriors were spared to show Frontenac's friendship for the Iroquois. A few Dutch escaped to Albany on horseback to raise a general alarm.

When the pious Le Moynes withdrew, their hands red with Protestant blood, they counted only two Canadian dead. But New York had been alerted. It appealed to New England for aid in a joint attack on Canada. The English colonies seemed likely to unite for once.

Frontenac's second war party snowshoed from Three Rivers in January under François Hertel, a grim man who might do much with only fifty Canadians and Indians. He had learned his business as a boy, in the hands of the Iroquois. One of his fingers had been burned off in the bowl of a pipe, a thumb amputated by a tomahawk. This news he had concealed from his aged mother in a letter written on birchbark. Hertel was still fearless, religious, and ruthless in his forty-eighth year, an army in himself. For good reason Canada called him the Hero. The English would call him other names.

Three months of misery brought Hertel and his little band to New Hampshire and the unsuspecting village of Salmon Falls. It was defenseless and, like Schenectady, bewildered by the recent uprising in Boston, which had confined Governor Andros in jail and turned the affairs of the colony into chaos. The frontier garrisons were in mutiny. The fierce Abenakis, with French support, had long ravaged the borders, lately had captured sixteen small forts and massacred the whole town of Dover. The eastern English, bungling, quarreling, and apparently incapable of war, were in straits as bad as the western French.

Hertel therefore found Salmon Falls asleep and ready for his ax. The half hundred skilled butchers tomahawked thirty of the inhabitants in their beds, captured fifty-four women and children, burned the town and surrounding farms, and retreated as quickly as they had come. A party of English militiamen hurried from Portsmouth and caught up to the raiders at the swollen Wooster River. Hertel held a narrow bridge, singlehanded, sword in hand like the Roman Horatius, until his followers had crossed. Then the French faded into the woods. Hertel paid off his Indian braves with a gift of English prisoners, who were tortured too fast for adequate amusement.

The Hero was not finished yet. He hastened northward and in the spring joined Frontenac's third war party from Quebec at the English Fort Loyal, on Casco Bay (Portland). The joint French force, and recruitments of local Indians, numbered nearly five hundred men against hardly a hundred amateur soldiers in the fort, under Captain Sylvanus Davis.

The French undertook a systematic siege, on the European model, by trenches burrowed to the palisades. After some desultory cannonading, Davis surrendered, on the sworn promise of quarter for all his people. As they marched out the Indians fell upon them, killing many and carrying off the rest. The French commanders explained that the English had earned this punishment because they were in rebellion against their lawful king, James.

Three offensives of sudden massacre, on a scale and over distances never known in America before, had succeeded beyond Frontenac's highest hopes. The captured Captain Davis complained to him in Quebec but he repeated, with a straight face, his lieutenants' explanation that the victims of his chastisement were all rebels, that no harm would have befallen them if they had not supported the usurper, William of Orange.

The far-flung victories of snowshoe, tomahawk, and treachery had changed Canada from a beleaguered and tottering garrison into the scourge of the New World. It was all the work of a single man. Nevertheless, Frontenac, entertaining Davis hospitably in broken English, broken promises, and good French wine, had miscalculated the English. Among other things he had ignored or probably had never heard of Phips. Now it was that redoubtable Bostonian's turn.

In New York a congress of the English colonies—faint foreshadow of larger congresses to come—met to concert an attack on Canada, as originally proposed by the wiser Iroquois. Large plans were made on paper—700 men to descend on Montreal by the Richelieu under Fitz-John Winthrop, of Connecticut, a fleet to capture Acadia.

While the Richelieu expedition floundered and wrangled, Phips assembled a little armada of seven ships, 280 sailors, and 500 drafted militiamen. On May 11, 1690, he reached Port Royal. It promptly surrendered.

The going so far had been easy; also profitable to the thrifty Phips. He rifled the fort, sparing the inhabitants when they took an oath of loyalty to King William, and personally seized all the money of the French commander, Meneval, besides "six silver spoons, six silver forks, one silver cup in the shape of a gondola, a pair of pistols, three new wigs, a grey vest, four pairs of silk garters, two dozen shirts, six vests of dimity, four night caps with lace edgeings," plus the pots, pans, and kitchen linen. This booty and sixty-two prisoners accompanied him to Boston.

Governor Bradstreet, an honest man, ordered Phips to restore the stolen goods. Phips gave up Meneval's money and some of the worn-out clothing. The remainder of the loot he kept for himself, to add to his treasure of the Spanish Main. A man of practical mind who evidently could be trusted with larger undertakings, now under way.

Holding not only Port Royal but the other French posts of La Hêve and Chebucto, the English were again in possession of Acadia, their old stamping ground, and ready for an attack on Quebec.

Despite the confusions of the recent rebellion, despite its bankrupt treasury and the refusal of help from England, Massachusetts burned with martial fire, also with Puritan religion. The inhabitants of Boston were called together for a day of repentance and prayer before descending on the papist idolaters.

Since battles, even Puritan battles, were not always won by prayer, and since the frugal townspeople failed to subscribe sufficient funds, the colonial government, against all its principles, finally supplied the sinews of war by borrowing. Thus thirty-two little vessels were collected and the necessary crews conscripted. Phips, their commander, weighed anchor on the ninth of August, dangerously late in the fighting season.

As the fleet sailed confidently toward the St. Lawrence, the overland expedition was falling to pieces from dissension, dysentery, and smallpox on the shores of Lake Champlain.

Frontenac knew nothing of these events. He was occupied in a renewal of his old feuds. Louis could not interfere with the indispensable defender of Canada, so the Governor defied the Jesuits, the unhappy Intendant Champigny, and the entire council, which was compelled to wait upon him humbly at his erratic pleasure. He had saved Canada, wounded the English, cowed the western tribes by his victories, re-established the broken fur trade, and brought Canada its most prosperous times. Who dared to question the changing moods of the indispensable man?

He was rude or genial by turns and at all times impossible to his colleagues. No matter, he got things done. Through the winter and spring he had rebuilt the fortifications of Quebec in case the English should appear but when their sails were sighted in the river he was at Montreal to meet the first western fur cargoes, to promise his Indian allies the conquest of the Iroquois and then, brandishing a tomahawk and whooping like a madman, to join in their dance and their feast of two oxen, six dogs, and a barrel of prunes cooked together. These festivities were interrupted by the news of Quebec's peril. Frontenac hurried back to his fortress.

In the sparkling autumnal air of mid-October Phips beheld the *fleur-de-lis* above the Governor's château, high on the rock. He expected the French flag to be hauled down in easy surrender. Quebec would yield like Port Royal.

An English messenger was landed in the lower town, was blindfolded and conducted by a bewildering route to the château amid crowds cheering and laughing in a game of blind man's buff. He found Frontenac ready for him. The reception had been arranged by a master of stage direction in a scene of crude melodrama, the whole preposterous little court assembled in its bravest finery, bewigged, beribboned and powdered, the old eagle deceptive in parrot's plumage.

A translator read Phips's letter aloud in French to Frontenac, who listened with wooden face. The former ship's carpenter evidently had burned much midnight oil in his cabin to compose a literary masterpiece. Being anxious to avoid "all inhumane and unchristian-like actions," Phips was prepared to accept the surrender of Quebec, "together with . . . all your persons and estates at my dispose; upon the doing whereof, you may expect mercy from me. . . . Your answer positive in an hour returned by your trumpet, with the return of mine, is required upon the peril that will ensue."

To mark the time allowed, the messenger offered his watch to Frontenac. The old man pleaded that his failing eyesight could not read the hour. It was, said the obliging young envoy, just ten o'clock. The Canadians had until eleven to reply with trumpet blast of capitulation. Frontenac's officers burst into growls of indignation but he remained silent. The veteran actor was waiting for his cue.

When he spoke at last it was to deliver a rehearsed and theatrical speech, insolent, a little too long and overdone but imperishable: "Tell your general that I do not recognize King William . . . a usurper who has violated the most sacred laws of blood in attempting to dethrone his father-in-law. I know no King of England but King James."

He continued in this lofty vein for some moments until the trembling messenger asked for an answer in writing. This, for Frontenac, was the final cue line. He spat out his immortal phrase: "No, I will answer your general only by the mouths of my cannon, that he may learn that a man like me is not to be summoned after this fashion. Let him do his best and I will do mine."

The New Englander, speechless with amazement, was blindfolded and led back to his boat. Phips thereupon prepared to launch a clumsy, amateurish plan of assault, apparently with little confidence in it and aware that winter was at hand, his time running out. He had delayed too long. Suddenly he heard a roll of drums and a clamor of shouting on shore. It announced the arrival of 700 regulars and *coureurs de bois* from Montreal. "Ma foi, messieurs," a French prisoner informed the English, "you have lost the game. There is nothing for you now but to pack up and go home."

That sound advice was rejected. Phips wasted two days in councils of war, then landed 1,300 men on the Beauport shore, below the town. A stubborn fight against the French sharpshooters carried the New Englanders up to the St. Charles River, whence they were to rush the walls of Quebec from the rear while Phips attacked from the front.

Too impetuous to wait, he began to cannonade the rock with reckless waste of ammunition. Frontenac's voice, as promised, spoke through his guns. The noisiest bombardment ever heard in America made nothing but a few harmless dents in Quebec's stone walls but the French fire heavily damaged the English ships and a lucky shot broke Phips's flagstaff. The cross of St. George fluttered limply into the river, floated toward the shore, was seized by some daring Canadians in a canoe, and carried triumphantly to Frontenac as a sure omen of victory.

Two days of futile bombardment brought Phips no nearer to Quebec. Most of his powder was gone. His own ship was dismasted and its pierced hull ready to sink. He drifted out of range on the river current, leaving his troops on the St. Charles hungry, without ammunition, and shivering in the first sudden spell of winter.

These brave men still advanced toward the town and drove in Frontenac's skirmishers. One of the three brothers Le Moyne, Sainte-Hélène, fell dead from their bullets. But without Phips's support the attack was hopeless. Frontenac could afford to husband his men and shot. He soon saw the English painfully withdrawing, embarking on boats, and returning to the battered fleet.

Phips called another council of war and a prayer meeting. It was no use. The ferocious Canadian climate decided the issue. In a storm which threatened to destroy him he withdrew to shelter behind the Island of Orleans. There the telescopes of Quebec revealed him plying his old trade of ship's carpenter. As soon as his vessels were seaworthy he disappeared, lucky in his escape.

Yet for Frontenac, with all his confidence, it had been a close thing. His overcrowded town, short of food, could not have endured even a short siege, as its governor well knew while he watched the English flag borne to the cathedral, with bonfires, cheers, the Bishop's thanks for a miracle, and the pealing chant of the Te Deum. If the new English had united, if the old English had given them adequate help, no guns or rhetoric could have saved Canada.

Phips had failed. An abler, or a luckier general, not yet born, might retrieve the failure.

Frontenac wrote at once to Louis, urging an attack by sea on New York and Boston to end the English menace forever. Louis was still too busy in Europe.

During these events on the St. Lawrence the New England overland expedition had slunk home in quarrel, hunger, and smallpox. To make at least a gesture of war, Captain John Schuyler raided the French settlement of La Prairie, near the Richelieu mouth. Some twenty-five farmers, caught in their fields, were killed or captured— a worthless dividend in the bankruptcy of Boston's great plan.

Puritan Massachusetts was crushed "under this awful frown of God" and committed the unspeakable sin of the American business-man. Its tattered troops were paid off in its first issue of paper money.

The allies of the English had not remained idle. As a hungry Canada awaited supplies from France in the spring, the Iroquois struck again in bloody border raids, but they were tired of fighting alone. Their appeals to New York at last rallied an expedition of some three hundred men under Major Peter Schuyler. He struggled down the Richelieu, attacked La Prairie with some damage and, caught in a withering French ambush, boldly fought his way back to Albany.

The English had failed on all fronts but Frontenac knew they might come again. He implored Louis to send more troops for "we are perishing by inches, the people are in the depths of poverty . . . our troops and militia are wasting away."

The Iroquois still skulked upriver and blockaded the fur route for two years. Farmers cowered in their forts. Fields were untilled and soon devastated by a plague of caterpillars. At Verchères, on the St. Lawrence, below Montreal, a heroine of fourteen named Madeleine compelled two soldiers, her two small brothers, and a man of eighty, beleaguered in their blockhouse, to stand off a large band of Iroquois for a week until rescue arrived. Reports that the Bostonnais were sending 10,000 troops to Quebec set even the royal council digging trenches and building palisades. A bounty of twenty crowns was offered to the friendly Indians for white pris-oners or their scalps, though Louis complained bitterly of the cost. A victorious Canada was suffering from the organic weakness of an overstretched colony, unable to support itself. The defeated English lived comfortably enough on their farms and fisheries.

Canada might be prostrate. Its governor, in his middle seventies, seemed to have reached only his prime. He strutted about his tiny court. He feuded with the church. He encouraged his officers to present pageants and even comedies, despite the horror and sermons of Bishop Saint-Vallier. He insulted that unfortunate prelate pub-licly in the streets. And he never ceased to plan the conquest of the English.

The war against them had moved to Acadia. For a decade the English privateers had raided the Canadian fisheries but could never exploit Phips's capture of Fort Royal to occupy the country, or even to hold that ancient post. A thousand Acadians, using the barbarous Abenakis, continuously harassed the closer New England settlements, to push the indeterminate boundary southward. The English just as stubbornly pushed it north.

Phips, appointed governor of Massachusetts for his doubtful exploits, and not quite the fool that Frontenac supposed, built a fort at Pemaquid which so menaced Acadia that Frontenac sent two ships, under the restless Iberville, to reduce it. They were beaten off but nothing could stop Iberville for long. He returned from France with a larger fleet, took Pemaquid and prepared to take Boston, where Frontenac was to join him by marching overland. That plan, like so many others, collapsed, because Louis's supporting ships failed to arrive.

Not to waste a moment of his precious time, Iberville now descended on the English fishing villages of Newfoundland and, in a desperate snowshoe march along the coast, burned them all. Then, in the crowning epic of a career surely without parallel, this red-haired giant of sea and land sailed north to sweep down on the English posts of Hudson Bay.

In the midsummer of 1694 his ship, the *Pelican*, wallowed through the ice floes, its three consorts lost. Iberville nevertheless steered for Fort Nelson, on the west coast of the bay. He was overtaken by three English ships. Outnumbered and outgunned, he instantly attacked and sank the *Hampshire*. Having exchanged a toast in wine with his next victim, he aimed his guns at the *Hudson's Bay*. She soon struck her flag. The *Daring*, despite her name, was chased off and disappeared. A fair day's work even for Iberville.

The sailor now became a soldier again. His own sinking ship was driven ashore. His crew faced starvation in the first autumn snow. He undertook to carry Fort Nelson by land and survive on its provisions. Fortunately at that critical moment the three lost French ships turned up and the fort surrendered.

The northern jaw of the English nutcracker, in the bay, had been broken; Iberville had left his trail, by land and water, from the coast of Maine to the arctic and would shortly extend it to Louisiana.

All this wake of destruction lay along the outer rim of the struggle. At the center Frontenac's hold on the Lakes, the West, and the Mississippi remained brittle under the menace of the Iroquois. Happily they were sickening of the war, were depleted, like the Canadians, by overexpansion and disgusted with their New York allies who offered them words and rum, but no troops.

To gain time they sent ambassadors to their old father, Onontio. He welcomed them with relief, with banquets in his château and costly presents, never for a moment deceived by their pretended friendship.

Somehow the western tribes, lately wavering again, must be rallied. The money-saving orders of Louis were defied and Fort

Frontenac rebuilt. Its founder was ready for his last stroke of war. He led an army of 2,000 on the well-worn trail into the Iroquois villages south of Lake Ontario. Too old to march, he was carried over the portages by the Indians, sometimes in a canoe, sometimes in an armchair. As before, the birds had flown, leaving their oft-burned towns in ashes. Frontenac completed the ruin of the Iroquois fields.

The terrified royal council of New York debated a counterattack, vainly sought the aid of the other colonies but solemnly resolved in the end that "it will be very grievious to take the people from their labor, and there is likewise no money to answer the charge thereof."

Frontenac was soon back in Quebec to dictate more of his lurid dispatches. Louis was given a picture of brilliant Canadian victories, with the discreet suggestion that he might allow his servant to spend a few last years in the comfort of some honorable post in France. The King's reply was the gift of the Military Order of St. Louis and a bitter attack on his governor's extravagance. The whole policy of fur trade and expansion was canceled, the original Colbertian theory of a compact, safe colony resurrected, and the outlying posts closed. All Frontenac's campaigns, Iberville's epic, the heroism of the Canadian people, and the great dream of empire, conceived by Champlain, were to be abandoned by a tired king who, turning religious in his old age, now ruled from the bedroom of Madame de Maintenon.

Louis's surrender had hardly been ordered before it was canceled and the old process of expansion, fatal but irresistible, resumed. It paused on the news that King William's War was over, the peace of Ryswick signed in 1697 by statesmen who thought, with pen and ink, to draw the boundaries of America.

On the whole, the subsequent settlement was a victory for Canada. Frontenac had rescued it at the edge of the abyss. Acadia and all the posts of Hudson Bay, except Albany, were again in Canadian possession. Though Frontenac would not live to hear the news, Iberville would soon found a fort at Biloxi, on the Gulf of Mexico, where La Salle had failed, and anchor the Mississippi line against the westering English. The Iroquois, finally broken, sought peace.

Frontenac's singlehanded work, more than enough for any man's lifetime, a work seldom equaled in North American history, was complete and his age was passing. Phips already had died in London while answering charges against his mismanagement of Massachusetts. Louis, the Sun King, had entered an effulgent and deceptive sunset.

No one knew better than Frontenac the futility of the pens at

Ryswick but, like his king, he was too old to alter the map again. The peace was celebrated at Quebec with a banquet to the English envoys, a toast to Governor Bellomont, of New York, and the sighs of a spent and dying man.

In the early winter of 1698, when the last ships had sailed for France and the Governor was alone on his frozen rock, he had just enough strength left to dictate a will. The meager fortune of a man long suspected of graft was bequeathed to his wife, with his heart in a lead casket—the wife who, after half a century of separation, remained his last link with civilization, his true love, his goddess.

He doubtless thought of her now, as he sat shakily before his fire, of the France he would not see again, of the dead son, of marches, voyages, campfires, councils, sieges, massacres, and victories. He must have thought also of the West and the unknown country beyond his farthest footsteps. What lay there, behind the receding glitter of the Canadian dream? Only more wilderness, animals, and Indians? Or the road to China and a treasury of riches inconceivable? He would never know the answer. But he knew something beyond exploration.

He knew the feeling of this Canadian land. He knew the distance, toil, solitude, and planetary emptiness, the pungent woods, the jut of glacial stone, the glint of hidden lakes, the crash of rivers and breaking ice, the whisper of snow, the chuckle of water against birchbark, the click of paddle, the smoke of Indian lodges, the war cry of the Iroquois, and all the sounds, scents, colors, and fierce weathers that together made the stuff of Canada. He had become a part of all that he had met. He had made himself a Canadian and saved a new breed, overlooked and incalculable in the future of America. And he was ready to depart.

On November 28, in the full odor of sanctity and absolved by a Récollet confessor, that wild spirit found the first peace it had ever known.

Frontenac was buried, by his own instructions, not in the cathedral but in the humble Récollet church. Canada had lost its defender, the Indians a fellow savage, Louis his indispensable man. The English had escaped but would never forget the scourge of America.

If the Iroquois were broken, the English divided and impotent, how long could Onontio's work last? Not long. For nothing had been settled by the pens of Ryswick. The future boundary, from the burned Acadian fishing villages to the Great Lakes and beyond them through the prairies to the western sea, lay fluid and unmarked, awaiting the men who alone could fix or remove it.

6

A Soldier of Virginia

[1698–1755]

IN THE DUSK OF A WINTER EVENING THE CANADIAN GARRISON OF Fort Le Boeuf beheld a horseman emerge from the forest south of Lake Erie. The rider was young, tall, and exhausted. His rain-soaked saddlebags contained a freight then invisible, not to be measured for some time, not fully measured even at the present day, but including among other things a world war, a revolution, two nations and the boundary line between them.

When the weary traveler dismounted, he introduced himself to the sentry as Major George Washington, adjutant general of Virginia's militia. He came on a simple errand—merely to warn Canada out of the Ohio Valley.

The Virginian, a man of lean, muscular body and hard, square face, was twenty-one years old. His century, the eighteenth, that fertile mother of the modern world, had achieved her fifty-fourth year, pregnant with Empire, Rebellion, Enlightenment, and many other wonders new to mankind. Her larger children could be observed in strange places and queer postures, all bent on the theft of neighbors' lands, destruction of existing maps, enslavement of distant peoples. Of which the two American nations—the first discernible but unproclaimed, the second unconceived and unsuspected by Washington or any living man—were to be the chief and only permanent issue.

The first half of the eighteenth century already had undone in America much of the work achieved by the second half of the seventeenth.

Frontenac had saved Canada from the English colonies and the Iroquois. Louis was not long in squandering those victories, as he squandered the treasure and blood of France.

Within two years he observed the empire of Spain falling to pieces as its emperor, Charles, lay dying, all too slowly. The pieces somehow must be redistributed and put together again in a new balance of power, a durable balance, a permanent recomposition of the civilized world, as Louis thought, if he could seize all the pieces for himself.

His treaties with England and Holland forbade such a comfortable arrangement, but trivial technicalities assuredly must not cloud the expiring rays of the Sun King. Therefore, the temptation too great to be resisted, Louis accepted the throne of Spain for his grandson, the infant Bourbon duke, Philip of Anjou, and, bearing that unfortunate child into the court of Versailles, announced to his courtiers: "Messieurs, voici le roi d'Espagne."

Europe's answer was the War of the Spanish Succession, called Queen Anne's War in America.

The coalition against Louis was led by England, and England had found at last in John Churchill, Duke of Marlborough, a soldier of talent and ancestor of an even greater strategist to appear in a greater crisis, 240 years later. Much of Europe felt the devastation of Marlborough's marches, but only a small strip of America was physically touched by Queen Anne's War.

Since the Iroquois remained neutral under Frontenac's recent instruction, Canada could confine its campaigns to the east coast. And since Louis could offer no help under Marlborough's pounding, the Canadian Governor, Philippe de Rigaud, Marquis de Vaudreuil, disguised his weakness by the traditional raids on the borders of Maine, New Hampshire, and western Massachusetts.

They were not as serious as the wars of Frontenac but they lasted for ten dreadful winters and they massacred uncounted settlements, butchered the people of Haverhill and Deerfield (where Pierre Gaultier de Varennes, Sieur de La Vérendrye, one of the great North Americans, participated, unmarked, in the butchery), and came within twenty miles of a terrified Boston. In Newfoundland the French from Placentia sacked the English fishing center of St. John's.

Vainly New England attempted retaliation with an ambitious plan to take Quebec and eliminate Canada forever. Its overland army camped through the whole summer of 1709 at Lake Champlain, awaiting a British fleet in the St. Lawrence. The fleet was sent instead to Portugal. Two years later, when the colonial militia waited in the same place, another fleet was wrecked in the Gulf of St. Lawrence with loss of a thousand sailors and its remains staggered home.

New England had to satisfy itself with its third easy capture of Port Royal, a local victory but vital; for now Acadia was lost to France forever. British power, established on the south of the gulf, enfiladed the entrance to the St. Lawrence. More important, Britain was now committed to the subjugation of Canada at a convenient moment. The American war no longer was a skirmish between colonies. It had become an essential part of the world struggle, centered in Europe.

At the center Louis overreached himself. He was beginning to lose his empire to England's new sea power. His armies depleted, his treasury bare, the Revolution already lighted, like a slow time bomb, he accepted at the peace conference of Utrecht, in 1713, large losses in America to avoid larger in Europe.

The Iroquois were recognized as British subjects, Acadia and Newfoundland permanently surrendered. Equally vital in the grand strategy, the undefined territories of Hudson Bay became British. Canada was hemmed in from the north. Its lifeline to the West was under threat of the British Iroquois. It had been pushed off the Atlantic mainland coast. Its front door was menaced from Acadia, now called Nova Scotia.

Out of this first great defeat, the beginning of the end, Louis had saved one fragment which, he thought, might save the rest. Cape Breton Island, almost touching Nova Scotia on the north, remained French. Here Louis projected the greatest fortress in America to protect the St. Lawrence route, without which Canada could not live.

The fortress of Louisbourg, rising like a mirage from the rocks and mists of Cape Breton, even its stones brought from France (and some of them promptly sold to New England merchants in the customary process of French graft), would be a hard nut for England to crack, but the dominance of English sea power was now established throughout the Atlantic; the age of English imperial expansion had been launched; Utrecht was another short recess in the ripening competition for the world.

If Canada was to survive as the protectorate of France, a land power, it must survive where land power could operate, in the West. It must develop Louisiana, hold the English east of the Alleghenies, maintain the line between the two gulfs, and thrust westward from the Great Lakes.

"Whoever rules the mouth of the Mississippi," La Salle had said, "rules whatever peoples may live in an area of three million square miles." This exaggeration was essentially true.

France built the flooded cypress shacks called New Orleans to defend the outlet of the great river. Its traders—such men as the daring Etienne de Bourgmond—paddled up the Missouri beyond the Platte, terrifying the Spaniards to the southwestward who, like the French, had absurdly underestimated the width of America. Louisiana, astride some of the richest real estate on the continent, might have held the whole hinterland for France if Louis had colonized it, but there, as in Canada, lack of population, coupled with the usual corruption, assured a certain failure.

Advance from the Mississippi was soon barred by the terrible nation of Foxes, west of Lake Michigan, who, in a war of forty years, almost drove the French out of the central interior.

Neither Indians nor the treaties of Europe could long restrain a man like Sieur de La Vérendrye, last of Champlain's breed. As a boy of twelve in Three Rivers, he had joined the militia, watched the massacre of Deerfield, fought against Marlborough at Malplaquet, and come home proudly with the scars of nine wounds. Ignorant of the larger events now convulsing Canada and the Thirteen Colonies, he became commander of the most distant Canadian post at Nipigon, north of Lake Superior. From there he proposed to follow Champlain's dream and reach the Pacific.

It could not be far away. The mighty *coureur de bois*, Dulhut, had reported that the Sioux spoke with a Chinese accent. Indians at Vérendrye's lonely fort excited him with their tales of the western sea, where lived civilized men, bearded, only four feet tall, eyes protruding beyond their noses. Long ago, in 1688, Jacques de Noyon had crossed the watershed west of Lake Superior to discover the continental route from Rainy Lake to the Lake of the Woods and to reach almost the edge of the central plains. Just beyond that farthest white man's trail, Vérendrye thought, must lie the ocean and China.

Though usually broke—money being "always a secondary consideration with me"—he managed by his fur trade to finance a fort on the Lake of the Woods in 1732. Two years later he sent his son, Jean Baptiste, down the fierce white water of Winnipeg River to Lake Winnipeg. Canada had emerged from the lakes, forests, and Pre-Cambrian rocks upon the prairies. Only a flat horizon separated Vérendrye from the Pacific coast and its human prodigies. Skilled Canadian fingers were probing inland to find a western border against the English.

Vérendrye had discovered almost a second America, but the Comte de Maurepas, minister of marine at Paris, was too occupied with conspiracy, flirtation, and his witty tongue to interest himself in these irrelevancies. He refused money to his agent and offered nothing but abuse. Obviously, said Maurepas, Vérendrye was bat-tening on furs or long before now he would have completed the easy fortnight's journey to the Pacific.

How could a Parisian courtier comprehend that the solitary bankrupt of the West—ceaselessly marching from one Indian en-campment to another, dancing and orating, like Frontenac, and sometimes impressing his allies with "the wounds I got at Mal-plaquet, which surprised them"—had hit upon the penultimate secret of the continent, that only the secret of the Rockies remained?

Vérendrye gambled everything on his dash to the sea, even the life of his son. Jean Baptiste was sent on a war party to satisfy the Monsonis, his risks well known, and was decapitated by the Sioux on an island in the Lake of the Woods.

After chafing for seven years, Vérendrye was ready in 1738 for a march, estimated at 750 miles, to the Pacific. He must reach it now or never. Over fifty years of age, he could not long face the long trails and searing blizzards of the prairies.

With two of his sons and an Indian expedition of 300, he left the Red River, paddled up the Assiniboine, and struck southwestward to the Missouri. The Mandans who met him there, and carried him on their shoulders triumphantly to their village, had light skins and the hair of some was reddish. He suspected that they were the half-white offspring of the coastal civilization, that the twisting Missouri emptied into the Pacific, but too far south, in the Spanish lands.

As all his trade goods had been stolen by the hospitable Mandans, he retreated in ghastly winter trek to the Assiniboine. Next spring he sent his son, Louis Joseph, westward again. This remarkable youth, called the Chevalier, hit the Saskatchewan, where the Crees informed him that the river rose in "very lofty mountains," hard by a great lake, "the water of which was undrinkable." The Rockies had been introduced, as a vague rumor only, into the white man's geography. Close behind them lay the ocean.

These reports only confused Vérendrye the more. The whole American map was in worse chaos than ever. But the upper Missouri and the Saskatchewan, the two essential routes to the Rockies, at least had been found, even if no one understood their meaning.

Vérendrye was now too old and too busy surviving the tax col-lectors of Paris to follow his dream. His final purpose had been foiled. Nevertheless, he had seized the farthest known West for Canada. His retreat from the Missouri across the 49th Parallel had unconsciously forecast the future boundary bisecting the continent. His new ring of posts across the prairies had reduced the flow of

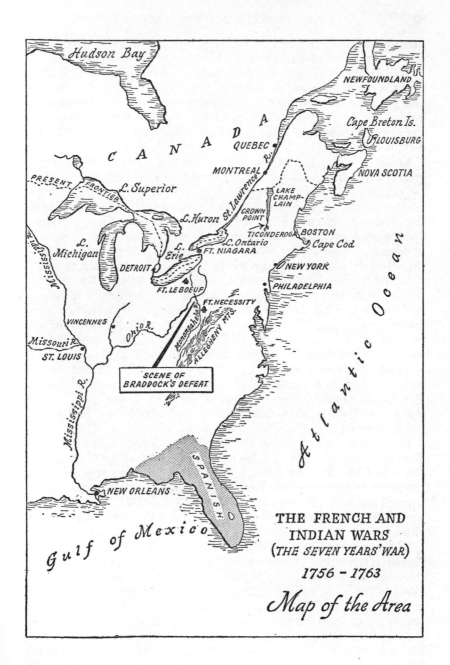

Hudson Bay

NEWFOUNDLAND

Cape Breton Is.

C A N A D A

QUEBEC

MONTREAL

LOUISBURG

NOVA SCOTIA

PRESENT FRONTIER

L. Superior

St. Lawrence R.

LAKE CHAMPLAIN

L. Huron

CROWN POINT

TICONDEROGA

BOSTON

L. Michigan

L. Erie

L. Ontario

FT. NIAGARA

Cape Cod

DETROIT

NEW YORK

Middle R.

FT. LE BOEUF

PHILADELPHIA

FT. NECESSITY

Mississippi R.

VINCENNES

Ohio R.

Monongahela R.

ALLEGHENY MTS.

Missouri R.

ST. LOUIS

SCENE OF BRADDOCK'S DEFEAT

Atlantic Ocean

Mississippi R.

SPANISH

NEW ORLEANS

THE FRENCH AND
INDIAN WARS
(THE SEVEN YEARS' WAR)

1756 – 1763

Gulf of Mexico

Map of the Area

fur into the English posts of Hudson Bay to a trickle, despite the paper settlement of Utrecht.

The Hudson's Bay Company had sat too long, with English phlegm, on the northern seacoast. As early as 1689, however, it had permitted Henry Kelsey, a youngster of nineteen, perhaps the boldest explorer in the West, who had learned his business from the great Radisson, to walk inland and drum up business with the distant tribes.

Kelsey was the first white man to see the barrens, the prairies, grizzly bear, and musk ox. Accompanied by one frightened Indian, he reached the edge of the Rockies, His reports, some of them written in clumsy doggerel beside his campfires, failed to impress the sleepy governors of his company in London. They remained uninterested in poetry or geography, were concerned only with dividends. Kelsey's discoveries were forgotten. The company continued to drowse on the bay while Vérendrye outflanked it.

Maurepas finally dismissed Vérendrye as a failure. The greatest white plainsman returned to Three Rivers, sick and ruined. Two sons of his own mold, Louis Joseph and François, still pressed on their father's work. In 1743 they retraced the old trail southwestward and reached the Black Hills of South Dakota. These, then, were the last mountains and doubtless visible on their far side lay the ocean.

The brothers pushed their horses up the foothills. At that electric moment their Indian guides fled in panic from an imagined enemy. The Canadians were carried along in the rout. Looking back helplessly from their saddles, they told each other that they had missed the final secret of the continent by inches.

It was some compensation to claim everything in sight for France. This they did by burying a lead plate at the junction of the Teton River and the Missouri. The mere shadow of French power now stretched south of the 49th Parallel in the far West, as on the Mississippi. That lead plate would lie buried until 1913, to be dug up accidentally by a schoolgirl of fourteen, called Hattie May Foster, child of a nation called the United States.

The epic of the Vérendrye family was finished and must soon be erased as a political fact by events in the East. An experienced frontiersman, Legardeur de Saint-Pierre, succeeded to command in the West but did not remain there long. He was hurriedly summoned eastward for more important business—a trying interview with a young major from Virginia at Fort Le Boeuf.

Long before this, from the day when the peace was signed, France had attempted to undo the losses of Utrecht. It wrangled over the boundaries of the Hudson Bay territories while Vérendrye disregarded them. It argued, with years of tiresome negotiation, that in Acadia only the peninsula of Nova Scotia and not a mile of the mainland beyond the isthmus of Chignecto had been surrendered. It still occupied the land which would become New Brunswick and it constantly agitated the Acadian farmers against their English masters.

On the St. Lawrence and around the Great Lakes a desperate race of military fortification was launched by both sides. Canada built Fort Frédéric on Lake Champlain to block the old invasion route of the Richelieu. The English of New York struck to the shore of Lake Ontario in 1727 with their fort of Oswego, on land up to now always regarded as French. Canada replied with a new fort at Niagara and a second called Rouillé, on Lake Ontario, to guard the passage around Niagara Falls and prevent the western furs reaching Oswego. Two empires faced each other almost within musket shot.

Canada still held the Mississippi line, strengthened by the new Fort Miami, east of Michigan, and Vincennes on the Wabash. This far-flung trade system, siphoning the western furs into Montreal, gave Canadians an era of unprecedented prosperity. It was to be their last under the French flag.

Prosperity and all the affairs of America remained at the whim of strange incidents.

Who, in Canada or the Thirteen Colonies, had ever heard of Robert Jenkins, captain in the British Navy? Who knew that in 1731 he had set out from the West Indies, in the brig *Rebecca*, wearing both his ears, and that, arriving in London, he wore only one? The other had been cut off by a piratical captain of Spain, who boarded the *Rebecca* and casually performed an amputation of momentous results. A speechless parliamentary committee in London beheld a one-eared servant of the crown. Such an outrage was not to be endured. England went to war with Spain. As usual any spark, or even a seaman's lost ear, served to light the tinderbox of Europe into conflagration.

Besides, the Great Powers had just seen an easy chance to steal the spoils and droppings of an Austrian empire recently inherited by a young empress, the pathetic Maria Theresa, clutching her baby and appealing to her Hungarian nobles for rescue. The appeal aroused the cheering Hungarians but failed to move the chivalrous statesmen of other countries. The War of Jenkins's Ear quickly matured into the general War of the Austrian Succession and became King George's War in America.

The Thirteen Colonies finally saw the chance to repair their past mistakes and acquire Canada on the cheap. After many false starts, this was to be the last contest. And in the new governor of Massachusetts, William Shirley, the colonies had found a man who knew how to win it.

Meanwhile the borders of New England, New York, and Pennsylvania must bleed again under Canadian and Indian lightning raids. Another attempt of the English to invade Canada by the Champlain corridor failed miserably. As Shirley saw it, the central objective, the sovereign prize, was that mirage of stone floating in the mists of Cape Breton Island, the fortress of Louisbourg. When it fell Canada would lose control of the St. Lawrence Gulf and quickly die of starvation.

Louisbourg was impregnable, on the word of the ablest soldiers, sailors, and architects of France. So they assured King Louis XV, who replied that it ought to be after all the money lavished on it for the last twenty-five years. Louisbourg had cost so much, said Louis, that he expected at any moment to look through the window of his swarming bedroom and see those bastions and spires clear across the Atlantic.

The safe enclosure of Capt Breton—two and a half miles of walls thirty feet high and twelve feet thick—housed the silken gallants and their painted women, the pirates, smugglers, Indians, and grafters of Louisbourg. They lived a gay life of balls, theater parties, and dalliance, in a fair imitation of Versailles, supported mainly by illicit trade with their enemies of New England. What if the garrison had mutinied only last autumn? Louisbourg stood impregnable on its stone perch.

Shirley, it appeared, was too stupid to understand that simple fact. He summoned the lawmakers of Massachusetts in sworn secrecy to reveal his impossible plan for the capture of America's strongest fortress. One of the pious legislators, it is said, prayed so loudly for divine guidance in this crisis that the Governor's strategy was overheard in the street below. At all events, everybody soon knew that the Thirteen Colonies were planning a noble enterprise. The Assembly in Boston approved it by a single vote because, as Canada was informed, one of its opponents providentially fell and broke a leg on his way to the meeting.

Shirley quickly recruited a rustic army of 4,000 from Massachusetts, Connecticut, and New Hampshire, each volunteer bringing his own gun and only six able to load a cannon. William Pepperell was given the command, not because this militia colonel understood war but because he was a successful fish merchant and shipbuilder. As it turned out, he was also a better soldier than Shirley.

Thus in the spring of 1745, full of patriotism, Protestantism, ignorance and rum, the madcap armada sailed north after a day of fasting and prayer, its chaplain, Sam Moody, brandishing a hatchet and vowing to chop down the "Catholic idols." At the Nova Scotia port of Canso, recently sacked by the French, the New Englanders were joined by an English fleet of four warships under Commodore Peter Warren.

Dupont du Chambon, governor of Louisbourg, was entertaining at a ball in his citadel as the English neared his harbor and asleep at dawn as they entered it. An officer rushed in his nightshirt to the Governor's chamber, bells were rung and cannon fired, but there was surely no need for alarm. A freakish frost had blocked the harbor with ice. The invaders spent three weeks in awkward drill while absorbing the sermons of Parson Moody and more potent liquid inspiration from the West Indies. Chambon could afford to smile at such clumsy amateurs.

Pepperell ignored Shirley's insane plan of frontal attack and approached the fort from the rear to burn the storehouses with "three rousing cheers." The smoke blew into the French Grand Battery at the harbor mouth. Its garrison fled in panic without even spiking the guns. Chambon smiled no more.

His own guns of the Grand Battery were soon firing on his citadel. The first shot killed fourteen persons. Parson Moody preached next Sunday on an appropriate text: "Enter into His gates with thanksgiving and into His courts with praise."

Then the English, blessed by an ignorance of war, dragged their artillery on sledges through the swamps behind the fort, 200 men for every sledge, and hauled up seven more cannon from the harbor bottom, where the French had sunk them years before. Though these rusty barrels often exploded with heavy damage to the gunners and ammunition was so scarce that the New Englanders were paid a shilling for every retrieved cannon ball, the plight of the French had become still worse. Impregnable Louisbourg began to starve.

Pepperell's next maneuver was disastrously English. He sent 400 volunteers by night in rowboats, with muffled oars, to capture the Island Battery. The attackers again announced their presence with three rousing cheers. Immediately the French guns killed sixty brave and idiotic men, 116 were captured, and the remainder driven off.

It was a temporary disaster. Only forty-nine days of siege pulverized Louisbourg into surrender on June 17. A week later twenty French vessels, arriving too late to rescue the fort, were lured into the harbor by the French flag (which Pepperell had kept flying for that purpose), and captured. The loot provided Commodore Warren with £60,000 and each of his sailors with £250. Pepperell enjoyed the privilege of spending £10,000 out of his own pocket.

The English garrison, already homesick and mutinous, had hardly settled in and suffered 900 deaths by plague before it heard alarming news from Paris. Half the French Navy, sixty-five ships under the Duc d'Anville, sailed from Brest in the summer of 1746 to recapture Louisbourg, avenge the honor of France and, if possible, take Boston.

D'Anville, a lucky nobleman, had risen to high naval rank without bothering to learn seamanship. His luck suddenly deserted him. The armada was wrecked and scattered off the coast of Nova Scotia. Its remnants, desolated by scurvy, found refuge in Chebucto Bay. D'Anville promptly died of humiliation and apoplexy. His successor, d'Estournel, proposed to abandon Louisbourg and return to France. His officers indignantly rejected his advice. Whereupon he retired to his cabin, locked the door, and drove a sword through his heart. His ghost, often seen by the English afterwards, alone remained at Chebucto. The survivors of the French fleet finally sailed home, nourished by a diet of rats. A Canadian and Indian war party managed to reach Acadia overland but failed to take Annapolis Royal and could not risk an attack on Louisbourg.

That "awful frown of God" had been removed from New England. The homemade strategy of a Boston fish merchant had captured the mightiest bastion of America, the Gulf of St. Lawrence was in English control, and Parson Moody's hatchet had chopped down the popish idols. So the fires of rejoicing burned throughout the Thirteen Colonies—too soon.

At Aix-la-Chapelle, England, having fared indifferently in the European campaigns, traded Louisbourg for the French post of Madras in India. The Thirteen Colonies shouted betrayal, as well they might. A distrust of England was sown deep in the minds of Massachusetts, to be tended by sedulous gardeners, yet unknown, and to ripen in the streets of Boston twenty years hence.

If Louisbourg was back in French hands, and control of the gulf with it, Aix-la-Chapelle, like Utrecht, had settled nothing, had failed to provide even a truce in America. And the immediate center of the world struggle had shifted to the lonely Ohio forests, of all places.

The Ohio Company, of Virginia, containing two members of the Washington family, was chartered a year before the peace of Aix-la-Chapelle. It sent its first agents to spy out land for settlers west of the Alleghenies in 1750. English traders already had oozed through the mountain dike and, offering better kettles than their rivals, brighter cloth of red and blue, and cheaper alcohol, distilled from

French West Indies sugar, challenged the old Canadian fur monopoly.

Actually settlement was far more serious than English trade for Canadian and Indian alike. To Canada it would mean the loss of the Mississippi line and the whole West, under weight of sheer numbers. To the Indians it would mean destruction. The settler with his ax and plow, more than the soldier with his musket and sword, must determine the future of America. Most of the western Indians knew it and hastily rediscovered their loyalty to Canada.

No one knew it better than the new Governor of Canada, the tall and scholarly Marquis de La Jonquière, who had led the broken French armada home from Chebucto. He could only thrust a finger here and there into the leaky Ohio dike.

In 1749—a notable year since it also saw the founding of the British stronghold of Halifax at Chebucto under Governor Edward Cornwallis—Jonquière sent Céleron de Blainville with a small company of Canadians and Indians to order the English out of the Ohio Valley. The arms of the French King, engraved on tin plates, were nailed to tree trunks and lead plates, similarly inscribed, buried at the roots. Roving Indians soon found them and melted the lead for bullets. English traders disregarded these warnings. They reappeared as soon as the Canadians had left.

Poor Jonquière worried himself to death at Quebec after first ordering the wax candles removed from his bedside. Cheaper tallow, he said, was good enough to provide his last light in this world— and the last economy ever practiced by a French government in Canada.

Where plates of tin and lead had failed, the Canadians now reverted to their old and reliable weapon of unofficial war in this time of official peace. Charles Langlade led a force of Ottawas and Chippewas against Pickawillany, on the Miami River, main center of English trade and seat of the famous chief called the Demoiselle by the Canadians, Old Britain by the English. He was boiled and eaten for his devotion to England. The fall of Pickawillany returned the Miamis to French allegiance. English traders were driven back to the Alleghenies.

To make sure they stayed there, the new Canadian Governor, Marquis Duquesne, built Fort Le Boeuf, commanding, as he hoped, the strategic forks of the Ohio. If this tiny cork could plug the junction of the Monongahela and the Allegheny, Canada could hold the West. A frail hope.

Thus had the final lines of the American struggle been drawn as a distant annex to Europe's great game of power.

The chief player, William Pitt, had arrived in the nick of time. "We are undone both at home and abroad," groaned the immaculate Lord Chesterfield. "I am sure," Pitt replied, "that I can save this country and that nobody else can."

In truth England looked past saving. Its Elizabethan spirit and the brief energies of the Orange William had sunk into the vinous and gouty stupor of the German Georges. Its politics were ruled, over the gaming tables, by the King's crapulous sons and over-stuffed ministers, those "mountains of roast beef"; its manners by Beau Nash; its morals by the plump court strumpetry; its higher tastes by Horace Walpole, with his monkeys and private printing press at Strawberry Hill; its highways by Dick Turpin's successors; its poor by gin. Only in Dr. Johnson's Club, it almost seemed, the old lamp burned on, rather dimly.

Still, its guttering light was perhaps more reliable than the dazzling and final spurt of flame, with its flutter of suicidal moths, at Paris. Pitt's principal adversary, Madame de Pompadour, born plain Jane Fish, once mistress and now procuress of the bored fifteenth Louis, managed the affairs of the world's greatest state as a boudoir intrigue among a race of half-men in powder and patches, walking on "a carpet of flowers unconscious that it covered an abyss."

Some few men saw the abyss, none more clearly than Voltaire. That skeletal creature, shrunken within his oversized wig, went everywhere and noted everything. He had recently stolen the candle-sticks of his host, Frederick the Great, had left Prussia hurriedly as a result of certain poisonous little forgeries, was now safely installed outside Paris and giving his mind momentarily to America. As he said, America was not worth more than a moment of thought. For what did New France contain? Nothing but a few acres of snow.

Frederick, the third player, was worth watching, was already marked as a future victim of the infuriated Pompadour for some of his obscene verses touching her virtue. He had reached his hour after long training by a father who drilled and caned him, sometimes threw dinner plates at his head, and thus instructed him in the mastery of Europe. But no Prussian, however trained, could master Europe alone. Frederick needed a partner of comparable genius and found him in Pitt. "England," said the admiring young prince, "has been long in labor and at last she has brought forth a man."

A queer man, to be sure, egocentric, theatrical, an alien among the mountains of roast beef, but a man. And with him another, still young, with a caricature of a rabbit's face, a shock of red hair, and a gangling, ill-jointed body. Recently he had written to his father a boyish design for life: "All that I can wish for myself is that I may at all times be ready and firm to meet the fate that we cannot shun, and to die gracefully and properly when the hour comes." A parent of those days must have regarded such a self-imposed debt to society as a little naïve and precious. It would be paid in full. The youth's name was James Wolfe.

In the early murk of the eighteenth century a similar candle had been lighted across the Channel. A French youth of small and delicate mold, round, handsome face and lively, poetic spirit, wrote a simple pledge to his father: "To be an honorable man, of good morals, brave and Christian." It was a doubtful recipe in the current world. Yet the writer, Louis Joseph, Marquis de Montcalm-Gozon de Saint-Véran, would fulfill it according to the motto of his family— "War is the Grave of the Montcalms."

Those two youths, English and French, must meet not long hence in an outlandish spot, the long-tilled upland of Louis Hébert's farm. A third, from Virginia, would not be present, but the three, never seeing one another's faces, would combine unwittingly to produce curious results. The most casual, unexpected, and impossible by-product of that combination would be the second nation of America, created by three men who neither foresaw, liked, felt, nor understood it. Even more curious, the joint death of the Englishman and Frenchman would assure the immortality of the American and, on the border of Canada, his only serious failure—the stubborn border that he could never obliterate.

This obscure triumvirate was unknown to the famous posturers of Europe, though its works must be accepted, for better or for worse. Least known of all the Virginian. At Fort Le Boeuf, on the night of December 11, 1753, the French commander, old Legardeur Saint-Pierre, had never heard Washington's name. Nor could he speak with him, as Washington knew no French. He could not even read the messenger's letter from Lieutenant Governor Dinwiddie, of Williamsburg. While Washington and his six followers were offered dinner and good French wine, Saint-Pierre retired to another room with a translator.

Dinwiddie, it appeared, must require the immediate departure of the Canadian trespassers from the Ohio and "that you would forebear prosecuting a purpose so interruptive of the harmony and good understanding which His Majesty is desirous to continue and cultivate with the Most Christian King."

The veteran Canadian woodsman, fresh from the Indian wars of the farthest West, must have smiled. For he knew that the white man's war, the ultimate war for America, already was under way, however the politicians of Europe might disguise it. So, no doubt, did the young Major from Virginia.

But there were many things that Washington could not yet know, some obvious things that he would have to discover for himself, others that he would never guess.

Would he even know, so early in life, that all men are created equal and endowed by their Creator with Certain Inalienable Rights? Not likely when his family had long been owners of rich lands and Negro slaves, when he himself was a typical Southern aristocrat, in all his instincts an English country gentleman.

Or had he foreseen, had even Ben Franklin of Philadelphia, the first fully formed American and so far the greatest, foreseen the clearest political and military fact of the continent—that France, England's enemy, was England's only real security in America; that if France were driven out of Canada and the old menace removed from the flank of the English colonies, they could risk a break with their mother and her navy, but not otherwise?

Or if any American suspected that, as a few men in England suspected it, could an immature soldier's mind like Washington's, or a mature statesman's mind like Franklin's, discern a still more tenuous fact—namely, that the remote and improbable event of an American Revolution, designed to make one nation, must of itself make two, and then, with blunder and bloodshed, draw the frontier between them?

Finally, why should a healthy man of twenty-one, rested from his hard ride and warmed with French wine, have any reason to expect that within a week he would be saved from sudden death by something like a miracle of nature?

So, mercifully ignorant of his danger, Washington awaited at Fort Le Boeuf an answer to Dinwiddie's ultimatum, an answer which would ignite the Christian world.

The Canadian commander took three days to write a suitable letter. It was a ticklish business for a backwoodsman out of the far West. At last the message was complete and Washington read it with the help of a translator. Doubtless he realized its result.

The Canadian proposed to refer Dinwiddie's demands to the Governor at Quebec. Meanwhile Canada would not abandon the Ohio country. The little garrison would stay put at Le Boeuf.

That answer—since the Ohio was the flash point of the world-wide explosion—must mean nothing but war. Washington could hardly have been surprised. War was assured in any case. Only its timing and outcome remained in question.

The Virginian pocketed Saint-Pierre's letter safely beneath a heavy Indian matchcoat and started back for Williamsburg. His journey must be counted one of the most chancy and momentous in the entire history of America.

As the horses soon tired, Washington left them with his servants and hurried forward on foot, accompanied only by Christopher Gist, his guide. A bullet from the gun of a Canadian Indian at the camp of Murdering Town narrowly missed Washington, but he refused to let Gist kill the attacker. Worse danger lay immediately ahead.

In fear of Indian pursuit, the two men walked through the rain and snow for a night and a day without a break, each carrying a gun and a pack, until they reached the Allegheny. It was not frozen, as they had hoped, but aswirl with broken ice. Somehow the river must be crossed and, without food, they could not wait. A few fragments of rope tied some logs together to make a raft. It bore perhaps the most valuable cargo afloat in the eighteenth century.

Washington used a pole to steer through the ice drift. All went well at first. Then he slipped on the wet logs and plunged into the water, sinking deep under the weight of his pack. Only the eyes of Gist saw him struggle to the surface. The eyes of the world were directed elsewhere, but some of its highest hopes struggled with the drowning man in the Allegheny. Somehow Washington reached the raft.

Its helpless passengers were spun down the main current and tossed upon an island in midstream. They dragged themselves ashore to lie through the night without food, fire, or shelter. Next morning they found the river frozen solid and walked ashore on a bridge miraculously provided by nature. She evidently knew what she was about. Seldom had a whim of weather so altered, in one night, the prospects of the human family.

Of that Washington knew nothing as he and Gist trudged to a trader's house on the Monongahela and finally back to Williamsburg. Europe was obsessed with its own affairs. It had missed the decisive event of the times, on a wild river which had almost drowned and suddenly saved the one essential instrument of America's future.

Dinwiddie prepared for war by ordering his London tailor, Mr. Scott, to cut "a suit of regimentals." He did not "much like gayety in dress," but "conceived this necessary," provided there was no lace on the coat, only "a neat embroidered buttonhole."

It was easy to order a suit, harder to make the cranky Virginian House of Burgesses vote money for the defense of the West. Dinwiddie managed to extract an appropriation of £10,000. With this he was expected to drive the Canadians out of the Ohio country. His only real asset was the Adjutant General.

Washington crossed the mountains again in the spring of 1754 to fortify the strategic forks of the Ohio. A small advance party starting to build a palisade suddenly beheld a fleet of bateaux, with some five hundred men, sweep down the Allegheny. The Canadians took possession of the forks and built their own Fort Duquesne.

This, to Dinwiddie, was an overt act of war, however London might regard it. He undertook to fight the war in his own fashion from Williamsburg, but events were soon out of his hands. The young Adjutant General had taken over.

Washington's force of some 250 men cut a wagon road over the divide, twenty miles in two weeks, and camped at Great Meadows, which the commander pronounced "A charming field for an encounter." He should have stayed there.

Instead, hearing of a Canadian patrol nearby, he marched out impetuously with forty men, fell on the enemy, and killed ten of them. The French called it murder. Washington called it sound strategy. Probably both were wrong. Whatever it was, a young Virginian had fired the first shots of a world war.

He may have suspected that as he retreated to the charming field of Great Meadows and hastily reared a rude fortification. Before it was finished 700 Canadians from Fort Duquesne burst out of the woods.

The plight of the 350 Virginians was hopeless but they fired from their palisade for nine hours on the day of July 3. Both sides were tired then, soaked by torrential rain and out of powder. The Canadians proposed a capitulation. Washington read their letter by a sputtering candle and knew when he was beaten. His deceptive victory had trapped him into disaster. He had committed his first blunder and suffered his first defeat, by no means the last.

Next morning he led his men back on the road to Virginia, the wounded carried in hideous pain by their comrades. Canada held the Ohio. It was the darkest day of Washington's life. It was July 4, a day to remember.

The dullest settler on the Atlantic coast could understand the meaning of Washington's defeat, small in dimensions, incalculably large in future result. After nearly a century and a half of quarrel and isolation, seven of the thirteen colonies met at Albany in 1754 to consider an almost impossible project, their confederation under one government, loyal to the English crown.

Franklin, the first national mind of America, had brought along from Philadelphia what he modestly labeled some "Short Hints," devised between his experiments with electricity, stoves, and journalism. These rough notes contained a detailed plan of colonial union. It must be imposed by a law of the British Parliament so that no colony, on joining the confederation, could ever escape. Franklin considered union essential to repel the totalitarian power of Canada and to carry the English west of the Alleghenies, since

"The English settlements, as they are at present circumscribed, are absolutely at a stand; they are settled to the mountains."

Not only circumscribed and at a stand, but heaving with strange forces; divided between the idea of democracy, first imported on the *Mayflower*, and the privileges of the ruling classes; moving to a struggle between poor and rich; yet driven together for survival against an external danger.

The Albany convention, overture to great conventions later on, was "inflamed with patriotic spirit," its debates "nervous and pathetic," and its decisions, said Attorney General Smith of New York, "might properly be compared to one of the Ancient Greek Conventions." In fact, they represented, though they could not quite manage for the present, the process of union which Greece had failed to achieve and, in failing, had perished.

Franklin's "Short Hints" and the scheme of union evolved from them—including a claim to all lands from Atlantic to Pacific between the 34th and 48th Parallels—also failed at first in the immature colonial assemblies. It was a temporary postponement. Sooner or later Franklin's logic must be faced. The idea of union had been born and would not die. A nation, or the blurred image of it, had appeared for the first time in America.

The corrupt courtiers of the Château St. Louis could not comprehend it, but Canadians no longer faced a rabble of helpless little states. They faced the United States in the gristle, very weak yet but soon to harden, as Burke would say, into the bone. One nation had been forecast in a Short Hint, with long shadows. The last thought in Quebec was the possibility of a second.

Pretenses of peace were elaborately maintained in London and Paris through the winter following the Albany conference. Why, asked London, was France feverishly building warships and assembling troops for Canada? Nothing hostile was intended, Paris answered, while instructing Governor Duquesne to destroy Halifax but to pretend that he was acting without orders. Why, asked Paris, was England massing an army under General Edward Braddock for dispatch to Virginia? There was no intention of offending any power, London insisted, while instructing Braddock to drive the Canadians out of the Ohio Valley.

England was eager to strike quickly. France sought delay to build up its forces. And Braddock, though shielded from the terrors of intelligence, dimly foresaw his fate. He told his actress friend, Anne Bellamy: "Dear Pop, we are sent like sacrifices to the altar."

So it happened in the summer of 1755, last year of official peace, first year of large-scale war.

7

To Hébert's Farm

[1755–1759]

BRADDOCK'S ARMY, MIGHTIEST FORCE EVER ASSEMBLED IN AMERICA
—with wagons hurriedly commandeered by Franklin, with
axmen, cannons and cattle, with everything but leadership—
cut its way through the Alleghenies to the Monongahela. There it
fell headlong into an ambush of Canadians and Indians.

The British General was stupid but fearless. He met like a hero
the fate he had expected. Four horses killed beneath him, he cursed,
threatened, and refused to retreat. His sword hammered the backs
of his men to make them stand in suicidal ranks against 900 invisible
snipers, firing calmly from the underbrush. Three hours of mass
murder shot down the easy red target. The line broke and streamed
homeward. Retreat turned to rout and panic.

Braddock fell from his last horse, a bullet through his arm and
lungs, and was dragged along on a stretcher. "We shall know how
to deal with them better another time," he whispered, practical and
British to the end. They buried him hastily in the middle of the
newly cut road so that the feet of his fleeing soldiery would obliterate his grave against Indian mutilation.

His aide-de-camp, Colonel Washington, four bullet holes in his
uniform but his skin magically untouched, watched that retreat and
knew how to deal with them better another time. He did not suppose
that his enemies would be English, like himself.

The Canadians also retreated, not yet aware that they had destroyed a whole army. Their Indian allies enjoyed the customary
sport of scalping and burning prisoners at leisure.

It was not all panic and rout for England and its colonies that
year. In Nova Scotia the great fort of Halifax balanced Louisbourg
and held the coastline. Fort Lawrence had been built on the isthmus

104

of Chignecto, within sight of the new Canadian forts of Beauséjour and Gaspereau. Two empires stared at each other across the sluggish stream of Missaguash, a queer international boundary.

At Beauséjour the commandant, Captain Duchambon de Vergor, a scrofulous and stuttering creature, contained in himself the ruin of New France. He had been instructed by François Bigot, the Canadian Intendant and another creature like himself, to "profit by your place, my dear Vergor; clip and cut. You are free to do what you please so that you can come home to join me in France and buy an estate near me."

Vergor clipped and cut with rapacious fingers. His own private sale of military stores, while his fortress went short, might be no great matter in a world war. Multiplied a thousandfold by Bigot and the clippers and cutters of Quebec, it had become an incurable disease, and mortal. As if by the inevitable pattern of things and an iron law of history, it would be Vergor in person who must open the doors of Quebec to England.

He first opened the doors of Beauséjour in surrender and gave England control of the entire Atlantic coast, except Cape Breton and the fort of Louisbourg. This success would have satisfied Governor Cornwallis of Halifax (uncle of a nephew whose future lay in Yorktown), were it not for the insoluble problem of the Acadians.

They stubbornly refused to become Englishmen and had long refused even to sign the required oath of allegiance to King George. Cornwallis found their passive resistance baffling. As neither Englishmen nor New Englanders cared to settle Nova Scotia, the only settlers somehow must be made to see British horse sense. But how? The Acadians were peaceable, respectful, and unyielding. They would do everything else the Governor asked. They would not swear an oath to the English heretic lest it destroy their hope of Paradise.

A stout British soldier called the thing inexplicable. He wrote in despair to the government: "You have a secret, I fear an inveterate Enemy praying on your Bowels, masked but rotten at bottom." Shirley still believed that the Acadians could be gently Anglicized, possibly Protestantized and turned into sound citizens of the British Empire. Cornwallis knew now that Shirley was wrong, that the Acadians had become a fifth column which quietly prevented him from controlling Nova Scotia. The Acadians knew only two things— they were Catholic and they owned this land.

The real enemy was not the local settlers, but their friends. Since England's occupation of Nova Scotia the government at Quebec had treated the Acadians less as human beings than as counters in the old diplomatic game. The player in charge, a master, was Abbé Joseph Louis Le Loutre.

This tireless priest and agitator served his king much better than his God. Year after year he terrified the Acadians with threats of God's anger, stirred them up against their new masters, intrigued with the fierce Micmacs, organized raids on the English, and paid 100 livres apiece for English scalps. Le Loutre and his Indians were financed and armed by Bigot, the Intendant, under instructions to "manage the intrigue in such a way as not to appear in it."

Cornwallis was not fooled. He offered £100 for Le Loutre's head, but the wily conspirator hid it successfully in the forest or behind the walls of Beauséjour.

Once that fort fell, the English could wait no longer. Governor Charles Lawrence gave the Acadians a chance to take the oath and, when they refused, herded more than 6,000 of them—the actual numbers were never known—upon his ships. "Praying, singing and crying," many parents separated from their children, the exiles were unloaded in the English colonies, from Massachusetts to Georgia. Some escaped the roundup. Some reached Louisiana and remained there. Others trudged back to their homes in better times. Even an expulsion, generally regarded as the crime of the century, could not destroy them. The breed was indestructible. Actually, the English had treated it far more leniently than the French had ever treated heretics.

Le Loutre, the chief architect of the Acadians' tragedy, was captured at sea as he fled to France. He had eight years to meditate his own crimes in Elizabeth Castle, on the Island of Jersey. Vergor was court-martialed for graft at Quebec but saved, by Bigot's packed court and doctored evidence, for a graver betrayal.

Canada had lost the Atlantic coast. In the last year of the official peace it successfully blocked the Champlain corridor. Old Baron Dieskau, a German commanding the Canadian forces, met at Lake George a colonial army trained on rum and such sermon texts as "Love Your Enemies." He was routed and captured, but the New Englanders were too badly mauled and led to advance on Montreal. An ill-managed expedition under Shirley struck at Niagara and disintegrated at the news of Braddock's defeat.

The Governor of New France, Marquis de Vaudreuil, a native-born Canadian and son of a former governor, was a born conspirator, rogue and bungler, with a woman's face and pretty smiling mouth. He concluded, after the successes of the interior campaign, that he was America's military master. His letters to Paris advised the King that, under Vaudreuil's firm hand, Canada remained safe and New England in terror.

His right-hand man, Bigot—a fat, red-haired, pimply, and ingratiating little rascal, who somehow proved irresistible to women—rested comfortably on the spoils of government contracts and various hospitable beds. He spent his days in clipping and cutting, his nights in venery. He had converted the government into a private purse to nourish his massive estates and prodigious love life by methods crude but effective.

Learning, for example, that the Canadians had advanced against Washington on the Ohio, Bigot smuggled into the freight of the expedition the obliging cuckold husband of his latest mistress, Madame Péan. It was a small affair, easily arranged. Expanded by plunder of the King's supplies, by extortionate prices to the Canadian people in the royal stores (known to everybody as La Frippone, the Cheat), such arrangements in Quebec and Paris were bleeding Canada into defeat, France into revolution.

Canada had lived for 147 years since Champlain's arrival. Only ten thousand immigrants had come from France, but they had produced a population of some sixty thousand, who were expected by their king to hold off the power of about a million English in the Thirteen Colonies. So far they had done it. Now, for the first time, they were growing angry with a master never questioned before, or at least with his grafting servants.

Vaudreuil boasted of his victories, but he soon found the people short of bread, agitated by "seditious libels," and displaying "une indépendance extraordinaire." They were beginning to act, in short, like Canadians. A succession of crop failures deepened the general misery. Bigot, now thoroughly alarmed, reported that the hungry *habitants* would have revolted but for his charity in distributing free grain, a small debit in his personal ledger of peculation.

Canada, in truth, was bankrupt. The accountants of Paris demonstrated, by their annual figures, that it never paid its way in trade with the mother country. Bigot was warned by his king that if he could not change the colony from a perpetual liability to a profitable investment it would be abandoned altogether. The Intendant was shocked, for he had not quite completed his clipping and cutting. He needed a little more time to prepare for his comfortable retirement in France.

Happily, men like ex-Governor Glassonnière, the brave little hunchback, who had seen the potential wealth of Canada, persuaded the court that its loss would be serious to France. He argued that, while France might not be able to defeat an English coalition in

Europe, because it could not control the sea, in Canada and Louisiana and in the old Spanish territory, which it now controlled, France could drain off England's power and checkmate its world-wide designs. The court reluctantly accepted this advice, groaning under the cost.

So far as Canada itself was concerned, there appeared precious little to save. In the West stood forty-four posts, some, like Detroit and Niagara, formidable military centers, most of the others mere cabins behind flimsy wooden walls; at Quebec some noble buildings, about eight thousand people, and a ridiculous court of gallants in laces and powdered ladies in high-heeled shoes; at Montreal four thousand inhabitants within their village palisades; on the St. Lawrence an almost unbroken street of churches and steep-roofed, whitewashed cottages.

The tenants of the local seigneuries were hospitable, courteous, high-spirited, religious, and litigious. Of Quebec they knew little, of France, New England, and England nothing. They were carefully shielded from all outside ideas. That dangerous invention, the printing press, had never been allowed in Canada. After Frontenac's quarrel with Bishop Saint-Vallier over the performance of Molière's *Tartuffe*, Canadians had seen no theatrical show.

Despite this isolation, or rather because of it, a curious and, for France and England, a secret and deadly thing had happened in Canada, not to be discovered for a long time—to the Canadian, France was no longer home. He had escaped entirely the Enlightenment, which was rapidly engulfing France and carrying it toward revolution. And when that revolution exploded in Enlightened godlessness it must cut forever the spiritual link between France and its Canadian children. That was a profound continental fact. England and New England would learn it with difficulty.

The other fact—that the Canadian was now a distinct breed, as indestructible as the Acadians—would take still longer to penetrate the English mind, in England and America, would not penetrate it completely for two centuries, if ever. Shortly, however, the English of England and America would find, to their amazement, that the French Canadian would fight for Canada against anybody, for the only home he knew.

The figures of a million people confronting a twentieth of that number strung along the St. Lawrence must impress the military mind of London and Boston. In military terms there could be only one answer to such a contest. The ever-changing border between the two peoples inevitably would be expunged.

Unknown to the soldier's pat calculations, much more than military terms were involved—much more, indeed, than the ablest brains of English politics could distinguish. Even the brain of a Burke did not realize yet that Canada, like the Thirteen Colonies, was a tough gristle. Given time, it could harden into the bone of nationhood.

When the Seven Years' War of Europe, the French and Indian War of America, became official in 1756, France could hurl 100,000 troops against the alliance of Pitt's England and Frederick's Prussia, and France was backed by Austria, Russia, Sweden, and Saxony. Yet King Louis could spare only 1,200 soldiers for Canada and a little-known commander, Montcalm, age forty-four.

Montcalm's plump face, small stature, delicate manners, and bubbling speech deceived the homespun Canadian Governor. An Indian chief, wiser than Vaudreuil, quickly gauged the true dimensions of the new General: "We wanted to see this famous man who tramples the English under his feet. We thought we should find him so tall that his head would be lost in the clouds. But you are a little man, my father. It is when we look into your eyes that we see the greatness of the pine tree and the fire of the eagle."

Here, then, was the usual divided triumvirate of Quebec—Vaudreuil, holding supreme power and determined in his jealousy and wrong-headed Canadianism to suppress the French General; Bigot, determined on nothing but loot and venery; Montcalm, doomed as their victim from the beginning, another eagle like Frontenac but, unlike him, pinioned between two vultures.

At first sight Montcalm hated Canada because he never saw more than its sordid side. He yearned only for his wife, his ten children, his estate at Candiac, and his olive groves. As he looked across a soil forever alien to him, his cry—"What a country, where rogues grow rich and honest men are ruined!"—was the despairing cry of the Old World. It could not long hold the New.

Montcalm quickly grasped the desperate plight of the colony. Some barren victories had been won. The English colonials, untrained and idiotically led, had been thrown back. Canada's Indian allies were murdering, torturing, and raping at will on the abandoned English frontiers, whence a settler wrote: "It is really very shocking for the husband to see the wife of his bosom, her head cut off, and the children's blood drunk like water by these bloody and cruel savages." But back of the frontier panic stood a million English learning at last the need of unity, and back of them the overwhelming strategic fact of English sea power, able to bottle up and starve Canada.

What strength Montcalm possessed lay largely in geography. The

English could attack Canada only by the St. Lawrence, which Quebec commanded; by the narrow Champlain corridor, which perhaps could be defended; by the difficult Mohawk trail to Lake Ontario, which was separated from Montreal by dangerous rapids; and by Washington's route through Pennsylvania, past the grave of Braddock and into the Ohio watershed, where a road must be cut to carry an army.

The St. Lawrence being safe for the present, Montcalm instantly struck at the Mohawk and Champlain invasion trails to close them. On Lake Ontario he seized Oswego by surprise at night. Its bewildered officers were the first to learn that Canada was led by the ablest soldier yet to appear in America. Then Montcalm hurried to Ticonderoga, on Lake Champlain, to await, with 5,000 men, an attack by 10,000 English under the blustering General Loudon. But Loudon retreated in the autumn without a fight, muttering, as was his custom, "God damn my blood!"

Vaudreuil claimed entire credit for these successes and assured his king that "the hopes of His Britannic Majesty have vanished and will hardly revive again, for I shall take care to crush them in the bud."

Canada, as Montcalm knew, had felt only the enemy's first feeble resistance. He knew also that Vaudreuil was undermining him at Paris while flattering him at Quebec. In the same letter the Governor asked the King how the General "can restrain his officers when he cannot restrain himself?" and yet promised to maintain "the most perfect union and understanding" with the man he was systematically destroying.

Montcalm had no stomach for such intrigue. After the Governor's wife had publicly questioned his strategy at a banquet, the General replied: "Permit me to have the honor to say that ladies ought not to talk of war." Madame Vaudreuil and everybody else in the court circle continued to talk behind his back. From sheer boredom, he threw himself into the winter festivities at Quebec and Montreal, entertained at dinner "three times a week," played cards for high stakes, overspent his salary, and like Frontenac, danced with the Indians.

The family man was sick at heart under this public pose. A constant stream of his disjointed and unpunctuated letters asked his wife for news of his children, his farm, and his olive mill. He requested a shipment of prunes, olives, anchovies, muscat wine, capers, sausages, confectionery, scent bags, perfumed pomatum for presents, and especially a dozen bottles of English lavender to cut the very smell of Canada. He had "no time to occupy myself with

the ladies even if I wished to" but in a letter from Montreal to
Quebec he confessed to a friend that he was glad to be remembered
by "the three ladies in the Rue du Parloir and I am flattered by their
remembrance, especially by that of one of them in whom I find at
certain moments too much wit and too many charms for my
tranquillity."

He perceived, through the brief comedy, the approaching tragedy
of Canada and his own: "I am a general-in-chief subordinated [to
the Governor]; I am esteemed, respected, beloved, envied, hated;
I pass for proud, supple, stiff, yielding, polite, devout, gallant etc.;
and I long for peace." This was the civilized spirit of France, desolate and rootless in the wilderness. It was not the spirit that could
save Canada. If Montcalm was America's ablest soldier, he could
never be a Canadian.

The spring of '57 rang down the curtain on the winter tableau.
England began real war with another siege of Louisbourg, only to
find that the French Navy, for once, was there in time. The great
fortress stood invulnerable and the colonial armies, moved out of
the interior for a siege, were hustled back again—too late.

In their absence Montcalm struck again, as only he could strike.
The helpless garrison of Fort William Henry, at the south end of
Lake George, was surrounded and forced to surrender. Whereupon
Montcalm's Indians fell upon the prisoners as he rushed about vainly
shouting: "Kill me, but spare the English who are under my protection!" No one knows how many English were murdered. The
French said fifty, but six or seven hundred were carried off, of
whom Montcalm rescued some four hundred. He was appalled to
see the Indians forcing some Englishmen to eat their fellows and,
to his protest, a cannibal chief made a classic reply: "You have
French taste. I have Indian. This is good meat for me." The civilized
General was confirmed in his horror of America, sickened by a
victory which the English remembered only as a massacre.

Massacre or victory, it drove England and its thirteen colonies
together. Montcalm in his second winter at Quebec, could see the
jaws of that leisurely beast, the English lion, closing rapidly. "I
don't know," he wrote home, "what to do or say or read or where
to go and I think at the end of the next campaign I shall ask bluntly
blindly for my recall only because I am bored." There was to be no
such easy way out.

Vaudreuil could see nothing. He did nothing but write of his victories and the incompetence of his general. Bigot saw everything
and profited by everything he saw. He inflated the currency, drove
the peasants to starvation and riot, feasted the aristocracy at his

palace (quaintly called the Hermitage), gambled at Madame Péan's bagnio, and dragged his friends by sleigh on the St. Lawrence from Quebec to Montreal, with a ball at every nightly stopping place.

Pitt had finally perfected the amphibious strategy designed to capture Canada entire. His general, Jeffrey Amherst, a stupid, slow, but competent soldier, besieged Louisbourg on the way to Quebec in the summer of '58. The fortress proved more formidable than he had expected. By the time it surrendered under his bombardment the season was too far gone for the intended advance up the river.

Pitt's master plan had failed temporarily under Amherst, but young Wolfe had landed in America, among the first ashore at Louisbourg. He carried no weapon except a wooden cane. Though his tall body in scarlet uniform was a reckless and easy target, the French gunners managed to miss it. He was preserved for another landing the next year. The delay infuriated him. When Amherst refused to attack Quebec, Wolfe threatened to resign, but he was mollified and spent the next winter in England. There he contrived with Pitt a larger plan for '59.

Observing the gaunt and fiery soldier, that eminent political fixer, the Duke of Newcastle, remarked that Pitt's young general was mad. "Mad, is he?" replied the King in a passing moment of intelligence. "Then I hope he will bite some of my other generals."

The fall of Louisbourg threatened to seal Canada on the east. In the same summer the English tried to cut it through the center by the well-worn Champlain corridor. They might have succeeded under the gallant young Lord Howe—a general who washed his own clothes in the brook and entertained his officers on pork and beans—but for a chance bullet. It killed him instantly on his march to Ticonderoga. His witless successor, James Abercromby, hesitated too long and finally threw his force of 20,000 men against Montcalm's 5,000, safe behind their breastwork of fallen trees.

The ensuing battle produced the worst carnage yet witnessed in the New World. A scarlet English army was skewered like game on sharpened stakes, seldom seeing even the white uniforms of the French. Having fought all day in shirt sleeves, Montcalm looked out from his hill upon a shambles, the English in frantic retreat, the lilies of France still serene above the towers of Ticonderoga. He raised a cross bearing a Latin poem of his own composition and sat down on the battlefield to write a letter of triumph to his wife.

It was his greatest and his last triumph and it was overbalanced by defeat elsewhere.

Louisbourg had been surrendered. John Bradstreet's army had reached Lake Ontario and easily captured Fort Frontenac. Montreal and Quebec were isolated from the interior. John Forbes, dying on his stretcher, and quarreling with Washington, had avenged Braddock. His army cut its way through the Alleghenies to Fort Duquesne, which the fleeing Canadians had burned. In its place Forbes built Fort Pitt, the future Pittsburgh. His soldiers buried the bleached bones of Braddock's victim.

Thus the Ohio, where Washington had begun the war, Louisiana, and the West were lost to Canada. It was truncated by land, bottled up by sea. The campaign of '58, as Montcalm realized, had assured the end. He might hope at best to hold Quebec and, with it as a bargaining counter, the diplomats perhaps could salvage something in this wretched country.

Even Vaudreuil's tone had changed. He wrote in despair to Paris, blamed Montcalm for everything and demanded the General's recall for "infamous conduct and indecent talk." A last flicker of sense made Paris refuse.

Montcalm's personal emissary pleaded for help but the desperate colonial minister, surveying the disastrous campaigns of Europe, retorted: "Eh, monsieur, when the house is on fire one cannot occupy one's self with the stable." That reply wrote the true obituary of New France. Old France had tried to make it a stable. As a stable it was allowed to burn. From the stable would issue a surprising species of animals.

So Montcalm awaited through the endless winter the doom he foresaw in the spring. He was helpless to undo the systematic ruin of Vaudreuil and Bigot. He was numb with grief at the vague news of a daughter's death and would never know which of his family he had lost. "Oh, when shall we get out of this country?" It would not be long.

In England, Wolfe waited also, now aged thirty-two, youngest general in the British Army—his earlier promotions purchased by money, according to the usual custom—and the luckiest. Pitt, he wrote, might "dispose of my slight carcass as he pleases. I am in a very bad condition with the gravel and the rheumatism." He arranged for the care of his dogs, "especially my friend Caesar, who has great merit and much good humor." And with small chance of consummation he engaged himself to Katherine Lowther. Her miniature portrait around his neck, he was ready to capture Canada.

. . . .

The flagship *Sutherland* rode at anchor in the St. Lawrence above Quebec on the night of September 12, 1759. In her cabin Wolfe made ready to redeem the promise given to his father long ago. He wrote his final orders in his own hand and, since he expected to die in the morning, took the miniature from his breast and handed it to his friend, John Jervis. It was to be returned to Katherine, set with jewels costing £500. As everything was ready, he recited to his officers Gray's "Elegy." "Gentlemen," he added, "I would rather have written those lines than take Quebec."

The man who had written them, as it happened, was snug in a professor's apartment at Cambridge University, where he had lately stood in his nightcap, shaking at his students' false alarm of fire. Hence a curious juxtaposition for the study of philosophers—the man who defies death in poetry shrieks in terror at a freshmen's prank; the man who reverently recites the poet's lines faces death at first hand, with nothing more than a dull melancholy, in the darkness of an alien river on the other side of the world, yet knows better than the poet that the paths of glory lead only to the grave. Wolfe was no philosopher. But he understood himself as "a man that must necessarily be ruined." Death had been at his side since boyhood. It was welcome.

His scant store of strength had been used up by now. All summer he had lain with Admiral Saunders's fleet and an army of 9,000 men, impotent before the black rock. Below it, on the river's northern bank, his first rash attack had sunk into the mud. His cannons had smashed the town, emptied it of all but 2,000 soldiers and reduced them to a ration of two ounces of bread a day, while Bigot and the court circle feasted as usual. The rock, though almost deserted, seemed through Wolfe's telescope to remain invincible.

And so he writhed with fever in the attic of a farmhouse and saw the summer ebb out. The first autumn frost announced the approach of winter which must soon drive his ships from the river— and, with winter, that other dark visitor, long expected. Quebec must be taken now or Wolfe would not live to take it.

Amherst, the Fabian General, had promised to invade Canada from the south before now but had bogged down on Lake Champlain, dosed his army of 11,000 men on salubrious spruce beer and built unnecessary forts wholesale. Wolfe was alone, the supreme prize of the New World a few yards off, beyond his reach. He made a dozen plans and rejected them. In the end he adopted, without telling even his staff, the most unlikely plan of all.

To climb the heights west of the town and risk battle there with an army possibly twice the size of his own was madness. The Duke of Newcastle had been right for once. Pitt's general, fortunately, was mad and lucky.

He needed only enough physical strength to see his gamble

through. "I know perfectly well," he told his surgeon, "you cannot cure me, but pray make me up so that I may be without pain for a few days and do my duty." He would not return to England without victory, "to be exposed to the censure and reproach of an ignorant populace." Somehow the surgeon made him up.

From the south bank of the river Wolfe turned his telescope for the last time on the steep slopes west of the Quebec citadel. There seemed to be a rough trail leading from a cove on the shore, called the Anse au Foulon, to the flat field above—once Hébert's farm, now the Plains of Maître Abraham Martin, a dead river pilot, whose name would soon be immortal. A few French were camped at the top of the trail—a hundred, in fact, enough to withhold an army on these heights until the arrival of Montcalm from Quebec or the forces of his lieutenant, Bougainville, now marching wearily up and down the river to watch the English ships.

The hundred guards at the Anse au Foulon were commanded by Bigot's old friend, Vergor. That veteran of Beauséjour was still faithfully clipping and cutting. He had sent his soldiers home to harvest their crops and reap his own fields as well. If Wolfe had known that, he would have felt more confident in the cabin of the *Sutherland.*

As it was, he revealed the night's desperate plan to his staff with no assurance of victory, in complete confidence of death. At the turn of the tide two lanterns were hoisted to the *Sutherland*'s shrouds, the signal to his army. It had marched upriver on the south bank, without attracting Bougainville's attention. Now it embarked silently in bateaux and floated downstream on the tide.

Below the town, on the Beauport flats, Montcalm paced the fields that night, too nervous to sleep. He expected another attack there, for the English warships had begun a heavy bombardment. Boats filled with sailors prowled up and down the shore to delude him. Time was all he asked, time for the river to freeze and drive the English home. But he knew that even if winter saved him now the colony was lost by blockade, by the fall of Fort Niagara before Amherst's leisurely assault and by the inevitable loss of Montreal.

Even on the heights above the town—though no general, even an Englishman, could be mad enough to attack them—Montcalm had taken no chances. He had sent a battalion of troops to Anse au Foulon, that fatal dent in the riverbank, and Vaudreuil had returned them to the Beauport lines. Three days later Montcalm had ordered the battalion back and again Vaudreuil had returned it— this a day before Wolfe's assault. Still Montcalm had no reason for alarm in that quarter. A hundred men could easily hold the narrow trail until Bougainville reached them. How could Montcalm imagine that Vergor was asleep in his tent and most of his men gone home? The General himself had not taken off his clothes since the twenty-third of June.

As Montcalm paced the fields, with a sense of imminent danger, Vaudreuil, the indefatigable penman, was comfortably installed in a distant farmhouse, and writing to France that "I shall do the impossible to prevent our enemies from making progress in any direction" and "will fight them with an ardor, and even a fury which so exceeds the range of their ambitious designs." His farmhouse far exceeded the range of the English guns.

Montcalm paced, Vaudreuil wrote, and Wolfe's boats slipped, unseen, down the river. A Canadian sentry sang out: "Qui vive?" Wolfe had prepared for that, on information from Canadian deserters. In perfect French a Highland officer, Simon Fraser, answered quietly: "France!" and added: "Provision boats. Don't make a noise; the English will hear us." The sentries expected provision boats from Montreal that night. They let the English pass.

The clumsy figure of Wolfe, his resplendent new uniform hidden under a massive gray cape, was the first ashore at Anse au Foulon. He looked up the slippery heights and remarked quite cheerfully to his officers: "I don't think we can by any possible means get up there, but, however, we must use our best endeavor."

They slithered up the wet trail, fell upon Vergor in his tent, shot him in the heel as he fled, and captured his handful of soldiers without warning Bougainville, a few miles up the river. By dawn 4,800 English, all Wolfe could muster, stood in a double scarlet line across Maître Abraham's plains. Louis Hébert had sunk the first Canadian plow in this earth. Now it lay under the sword of the invader. The plow would remain when the sword had gone.

Montcalm, at Beauport, had asked Vaudreuil to warn him of any danger in Quebec. Vaudreuil was safe abed and sent no answer. After a sleepless night of cannon fire, Montcalm was suspicious. He called for his horse and rode in the first light toward the town. Even before he reached it he beheld the line of scarlet across the plains. "This," he muttered to his aide, "is a serious business."

More serious than he yet realized. When he galloped through the town and past the St. Louis Gate he found not a raiding party but the British Army. It stood stolid, motionless, in a silence cut only by the squeal of Highland pipes. "There they are," cried Montcalm, "where they have no right to be!"

To defend Quebec's walls or risk everything on a quick attack? Montcalm hesitated for a moment only. Impetuosity had always been his weakness, but up to now it had succeeded. He would attack. First he sent to the town for twenty-five guns. Had they arrived the English, with only two small field pieces, would have been mowed down where they stood. Ramezay, commander of the Quebec garrison, would spare only three cannons. Vaudreuil, in answer to Montcalm's message, refused to send any troops from Beauport. He was waiting, as usual, to claim victory for himself or to blame defeat on his general. So Montcalm must advance with his present force of some five thousand French regulars, Canadians, and Indians before the English landed any more men or starved Quebec into surrender.

He ranged the army before the town walls and moved up and down their lines, a minute figure on a black horse, sword raised, cuirass glinting beneath his dark coat. At nine o'clock the impetuous General could wait no longer. He gave the order to advance. It was the last order he would ever give. He, too, was about to fulfill a promise to his father.

The line moved forward, the white ranks of the French regulars steady in the center, the Indians whooping on the flanks, the Canadians falling to the ground to reload at every shot. It was a ragged line, not what Montcalm had ordered.

Wolfe stood at the right end of his double ranks. His towering figure and scarlet uniform already had proved an attractive target. A bullet shattered his wrist. He wrapped it in a handkerchief without a word. Another pierced his groin, but he gave no sign of pain. The English stood beside him, no muscle moving. Then, at forty paces, they fired as one man and charged with bayonet. Through the smoke the French were seen shattered, in full flight.

Wolfe led the charge. A third bullet passed through his chest. Slowly, with a surprised look, he slumped upon the soil of Canada. His comrades called out for a surgeon. "There's no need," said the factual young man. He had foreseen everything. "It's all over with me."

Just then he heard above the crash of musketry and the shrieks of the Highlanders a soldier shouting: "They run!" He opened his eyes for the last time. "Who run?" "The enemy, sir. Egad, they give way everywhere." "Now God be praised; I'll die in peace." A moment later the parental vow had been redeemed.

Montcalm redeemed his also. Shot in the back, he had been carried by the rout through the St. Louis Gate. The townspeople clamored around his horse. "It's nothing, nothing," he told them. "Don't be troubled for me, my good friends." They took him to the house of Surgeon Arnoux, who pronounced his wound mortal. "So much the better," Montcalm replied. "I am happy that I shall not live to see the surrender of Quebec."

He sent a note to the English, imploring them to be the protectors of the French Canadians "as I have been their father." That done, he refused to give further orders. "I have much business that must be attended to, of greater moment than your ruined garrison and this wretched country."

Thus he died, an exile and an alien, a child of Europe lost with all his kind in America.

A rough box was hastily nailed together to hold his small body. "War is the Grave of the Montcalms," but no Montcalm had found a grave like his. The box was thrust into a shell hole beneath the floor of the Ursuline Convent and covered with rubble.

The town surrendered. A second and ferocious battle of Quebec had yet to be fought. Next spring the dauntless Chevalier de Lévis, Montcalm's second-in-command, a bon vivant, amorist and skillful soldier, descended the river from Montreal, defeated the English under General Murray and drove them helter-skelter behind their walls. The Canadians might have captured the town but for the opportune arrival of an English fleet. That was the end, assured from the beginning. Britain held the sea and the power to starve its enemy. It had mobilized almost as many soldiers as there were people in Canada.

Amherst finally closed in on Montreal and accepted its surrender. Vaudreuil signed the final capitulation of Canada, blaming it, of course, on the dead French General, and somehow was acquited of his own crimes in the courts of France. Bigot was first imprisoned in the Bastille and later banished to live on the savings of his last mistress, the lovely and thrifty Angélique des Meloises.

Thus ended New France, conquered by overpowering numbers, by the sure strangulation of sea power, by the corruption and stupidity of the Bourbons, by the luck or genius of a young invalid. The future of a continent seemed permanently settled by two men, English and French, who had kept their promises to their fathers.

Wolfe and Montcalm had accomplished much, but not that. New France had died in name only, had become Canada in substance.

Apparently North America, between the North Pole and the Spanish territories, was within England's clutch. There was to be, then, no boundary across the middle of the continent. The 49th Parallel would remain an unnoted line on a map of undivided British ownership. A few men guessed otherwise.

As bonfires blazed across the British Isles, as Walpole scribbled hysterically at Strawberry Hill and Dr. Johnson uttered his profundities in the club, down in Boston a farseeing young preacher, Jonathan Mayhew, announced in his next Sunday sermon that the English colonies, freed of the French menace beside them, must become "a mighty Empire."

Mayhew, perhaps, but not many others, vaguely guessed the ultimate meaning of Wolfe's victory. No longer dependent on England for protection against French Canada, the Thirteen Colonies had the chance to decide their own future, in separation from their mother, if necessary. On Hébert's farm, a new crop had been surely sown, would sprout soon and bear the name of the American Revolution.

Another crop likewise was in the ground, but invisible, and would bear no permanent name for more than a hundred years. English soldiers were helping the Canadians to harvest grain in the autumn of 1760 and sharing their scanty rations with the Quebec townsfolk. The kilted and barelegged Highlanders wore woolen drawers knitted by Canadian nuns against the northern cold. In this friendship between two races, neither quite understandable to the other, the second nation of America already was conceived.

8

The English Gentleman

[1763-1775]

AMONG THE ENGLISH GENTLEMEN OF THE OLD SCHOOL WHO HEARD the latest rumblings from the Thirteen Colonies, not the least startled and incredulous was Guy Carleton.

The news was indeed startling and incredible to such a gentleman as Carleton. A Virginian named Patrick Henry—a shambling, shabby and redheaded yokel, as it was reported in London—had introduced in the House of Burgesses a series of outlandish "Resolves" and had cried out: "If this be treason, make the most of it." Sam Adams, in English eyes an even more repulsive character, a mere demagogue, burly, ragged and vulgar, was stirring up the mobs of Boston. Why, even the American gentry seemed to be losing their senses in pursuit of what they were pleased to call liberty—as if they had not secured, by the Seven Years' War, all the liberty that any Englishman could possibly desire.

Carleton had fought in that war. He had supposed that the British victory would settle the future of America for good and to the satisfaction of all sensible men. Hence it was disturbing and painful for a gentleman of the old school to hear that the Thirteen Colonies doubted the result of the war and the wisdom of His Majesty's government, which had saved them from the French of Canada.

Being an English gentleman (though born in Ireland), Carleton rather resembled in character his future enemy, Washington. In appearance also the two men were not unlike. Carleton stood six feet tall, his body was massive and muscular, his face, like Washington's, was square, heavy-jawed, and solid. A young officer in the British Army, he had earned the nickname of "grave Carleton." Two grave men of middle age, one from Virginia and the other from

120

County Tyrone, had some ten years of business to transact between them, none of it pleasant.

Now that Wolfe and Montcalm were gone and France driven from America, who would govern the continent? As it was to happen—against all calculation, all geographic facts, economic laws, and political theories—Washington and Carleton would split the continent and share the government.

If North American history holds any parallel to Washington's career, it is Carleton's. That fact is generally overlooked, but the parallel is close. Nor does either of them suffer from such a comparison.

Only second to Washington, Carleton was to shape the continent's political future, so far as individual men could shape it. For which he received small thanks from the British government, little recognition from the Canadian people whose nation he made possible, and the hatred of the United States because he held it south of the 49th Parallel. Carleton doubtless was not a man to attract thanks or recognition—too grave, too inflexible, too sure of his own virtue, too ignorant of ordinary men, and a trifle pompous. Yet one of North America's major architects.

His career, like Washington's, began in misfortune and mistake. About the time when Washington was driven from Fort Necessity, after a military blunder, Carleton incurred the high dudgeon of King George II by some indiscreet and bitter remarks about the alien Hanoverian dynasty. The King never forgave him.

But Carleton was an able officer, distinguished in battle, and had caught the eyes of Pitt and Amherst. Ordered to capture Louisbourg, Amherst wanted Carleton with him. The King indignantly refused, to Wolfe's "very great grief and disappointment." When Wolfe was ordered next year to capture Quebec, he insisted on Carleton's appointment to his staff. Again the King objected. Three times Pitt himself begged the royal mind to change and finally got a grudging approval, though George was sure no good would come of it.

The King was habitually wrong. Carleton served as quartermaster general at Quebec with outstanding skill, was wounded in the head during the Battle of the Plains, and was willed a thousand pounds by his commander, besides all Wolfe's books and papers. He had become the dead hero's closest friend and nothing more. Between 1759 and 1766 he continued to fight bravely in Britain's wars, being twice wounded, in France and the West Indies.

Meantime, the new British colony of Quebec remained under the gentle military rule of General Murray. That friendly officer loved the quaint ways of the French Canadians but had begun to suspect that they were difficult, if not impossible to Anglicize. More difficult still, and quite impossible, in another fashion, were the immigrants, fur traders, merchants, political agitators, and carpetbaggers who had flocked to Quebec and Montreal from the Thirteen Colonies to exploit a conquered people.

Murray had trouble even with his own army. It actually threatened to mutiny because its pay was cut by the British government. As a result, among all the endless spectacles witnessed at Quebec, none was more remarkable than the redcoats lined up and ordered, as a sign of obedience, to march between two flagpoles, on pain of instant death, the General promising to kill with his own hands the first man who refused. The army marched.

Much larger armies of a deadlier sort were soon marching to the westward, far beyond Murray's control. A struggle for the West had precipitated the Seven Years' War. Soon it would precipitate the American Revolution. The Peace of Paris had hardly been signed in 1763 before the West precipitated the largest and bloodiest Indian war on record.

White statesmen in Paris had understood little about America. In the lodges of the Ottawas, near Detroit, a red statesman named Pontiac understood the peace treaty better than its makers did— understood at least that it meant the destruction of Indian life.

According to its terms, France ceded all of Canada to Britain, which did not want it. Britain would have preferred the West Indian island of Guadeloupe, with its tons of sugar, to Canada, with its acres of snow, but that sweet prize was reluctantly abandoned in generosity to France, in deference to the existing British sugar interests and in compliance with the prejudices of the Thirteen Colonies. They would never tolerate French power on their borders.

Louisiana, west of the Mississippi, was given to Spain. It now controlled a southern and western empire of indeterminate dimensions, creeping slowly up from Mexico along the California coast.

East of the central river, north to the pole, and no one knew how far west in the Hudson's Bay Company territories, Britain's flag could fly undisputed wherever Britons cared to raise it.

The sprawling substance of the first real British Empire, in America and other continents, must be organized somehow, and Britain did not know how to organize it. The ensuing errors assured the dissolution of the first empire and the beginnings of the short-lived second.

In America the fatal error was to subordinate the interests not only of conquered Canada but of the original English colonies to a

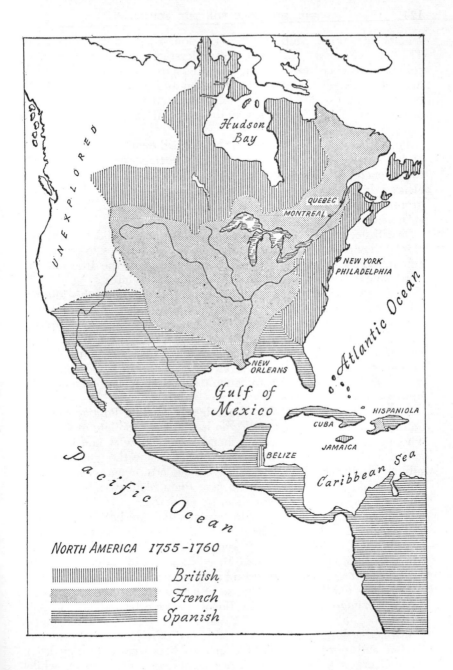

UNEXPLORED

Hudson Bay

QUEBEC
MONTREAL

NEW YORK
PHILADELPHIA

Atlantic Ocean

NEW ORLEANS

Gulf of Mexico

HISPANIOLA

CUBA

JAMAICA

BELIZE

Caribbean Sea

Pacific Ocean

NORTH AMERICA 1755-1760

British
French
Spanish

scheme of empire centralized in London. England misjudged the Thirteen Colonies. It totally misunderstood the new Canadian colony of Quebec, and for that misunderstanding would pay a high price, though not the price of revolution and divorce, to be paid in the case of the United States. But it was not the colonies, English or Canadian, that began to smash the imperial design. The first blow came from the Indians.

Pontiac saw at once that when the English owned the eastern half of Louisiana they would occupy it. The settlers, long contained by the French, would soon pour down the Ohio. Each settler who cleared his spot of soil destroyed some part of the old hunting ground, the habitat of the fur bearers, the basis of the Indians' existence.

The Senecas had grasped the danger as soon as did the Ottawa chief. They sent emissaries to the more western tribes to propose a general confederacy of defense—the old dream of the Iroquois nations—and a war of extermination against the whites.

The Seneca war belts were welcomed throughout the interior where the Indians had listened to their old friends, the Canadian fur traders, remembered Onontio, and expected France to recapture Canada after a temporary defeat. Now, in Pontiac, the Indian race had produced its first political and military giant. He must fail in his own purpose, since his race was doomed. But in his squalid bark house he held the power to launch a civil war large enough to sunder the English race.

The white man could find for a leader against Pontiac nothing better than Amherst, a general who had arrived too late at Quebec, who never bothered to comprehend America, who considered a native uprising "of very little consequence," who thought he could subdue the Indians by refusing them all goods, even essential gunpowder, and proposed instead to give them blankets infected with smallpox and thus annihilate them by epidemic.

Amherst learned better, again too late. Pontiac besieged Detroit and isolated it for six months. Under his influence and the racialist preaching of a Delaware sage known as the Prophet, most of the tribes south of the St. Lawrence rose in a series of sudden coups to spread tomahawk, fire, and torture across the whole western frontier.

One after another, in the course of a few weeks, Mackinac, Sandusky, Venango, Quiatenon, Le Boeuf, Presque Isle, and St. Joseph all fell to assault or treachery. Usually their garrisons, a sergeant's guard and a dozen men, were lured outside the palisades for a conference and murdered. The Mackinac soldiers were entertained, on King George's birthday, by an innocent game of lacrosse, while

the squaws, carrying sawed-off muskets under their blankets, infiltrated the fort and produced these weapons at the right moment
to butcher the inhabitants. Detroit and Pitt were warned by these
disasters, but barely managed to survive their long sieges.

Probably five hundred English soldiers and two thousand settlers
were killed during the summer and autumn of 1763, many of them
boiled and eaten with the usual religious ritual. The English suffered heavier losses from Pontiac's tomahawks than from the French
guns in the victorious campaign of 1759. After ousting France, England seemed likely to lose control of the entire West to its original
owners.

Pontiac's genius, however, could not long contend with the facts
of power, geography, and economics. The far western tribes needed
trade goods, and while they preferred to deal with French Canadians, English traders were better than none. As quickly as it had
arisen, the native conspiracy collapsed. Pontiac buried the hatchet
in Fort Oswego at the feet of Sir William Johnson, the Iroquois'
great friend, received a silver medal and kept his pledge of peace.
A wandering exile, he was soon murdered by his friends in a
drunken brawl.

Nevertheless, he had scared the British government. It hastened
to guarantee the Indians an inviolate reserve between the Alleghenies and the Mississippi, where no white man could settle.

The Proclamation of 1763 thus attempted to clamp down an impossible boundary on Quebec and on the English colonies. Quebec
was bounded on the west by a line drawn from the crossing of the
45th Parallel and the St. Lawrence to Lake Nipissing, roughly the
line of the Ottawa River moved slightly westward. Still more fragile
was the line drawn north and south on the watershed of the Alleghenies to halt the settlers who would never be halted.

Neither the Indians nor the English colonies were fooled by these
arbitrary exercises in geography. The Indians knew the colonists
would move west. The colonists had started the war on the Ohio,
with Washington's guns at Fort Necessity, they had won it, or
thought they had, and were entitled to their reward. The western
land was theirs and they would have it. Quebec, a conquered colony
of France, could hardly complain if it was treated as such and
truncated. The Thirteen Colonies exploded in anger because they
were betrayed. And from England's standpoint the betrayal had
the added disadvantage of being unenforceable.

The attempt to close the West, therefore, became one of the
Intolerable Acts listed in the Thirteen Colonies' bill of particulars
against the British government. It was the first and largest cause

of the Revolution. Without other Intolerable Acts, the closure of the West alone, if seriously maintained, assured the break with England. Again the empty Ohio wilds were disrupting the power balance of the world.

The project of a vast Indian reservation had possibly demonstrated the British government's humanity, or its terror, but its chief motive in practical politics was to preserve the western fur trade from destruction by the settlers of the Thirteen Colonies. England had inherited the complex and delicate anatomy of Talon's trading empire and knew no better than he how to manage it. Like France, England was being sucked into the West and, like France, could not foresee the results.

Though inevitable, they revealed themselves slowly. The Thirteen Colonies were determined to possess the western land and enforce the old charters, running from the Atlantic to the Pacific. They were not yet ready to revolt. Men like Franklin greeted the coronation of the sober young King George III as an assurance that England would do the right thing by its sons overseas. "Faction," he said, "will dissolve and be dissipated like a morning fog before the rising sun." Franklin did not know George or the eminent blockheads around him.

Appointed governor of Quebec by the new monarch—his old affronts to the royal family forgiven—Carleton arrived at his capital in 1766 to find it astir, not for the reasons agitating the Thirteen Colonies and not so angrily, yet with a depressing lack of loyalty to its new king. What, for example, was an English gentleman of the old school to make of the ridiculous affair of Walker's Ear, which had long disturbed Canada as Jenkins's Ear had once disturbed England?

Walker was one of the new English magistrates in Montreal. He and the other immigrants from the Thirteen Colonies resented Murray's softness toward the Canadians and detested his troops for the same reason. When Captain Payne, an English officer, was billeted on a Montreal family, Walker threw him into jail, quite illegally, on the excuse that billeting was prohibited. A posse of masked men, supposedly Canadians, beat up the magistrate and, to mark their displeasure permanently, cut off one of his ears.

That lost ear became the symbol and rallying cry of the British in Canada, the badge of Murray's shameful surrender to the Canadians, a useful piece of propaganda for the agitators of the Thirteen Colonies, already engaged at home in redbaiting the redcoats. Walker's accident also infuriated the British Parliament. But it left the new Canadian Governor as cool and grave as ever.

Carleton saw that much more was involved in Canada than the amputation of a scheming local politician. The important question— far more urgent than he had supposed—was whether Canada would be amputated from Britain and grafted to the rebellious body of the Thirteen Colonies.

Busily stamping down the imperial design upon the Thirteen, the government of England had little time to consider the Four- teenth, in Quebec. Carleton was left alone to grapple with the same design in Canadian terms. He found those terms unworkable but, unlike the conspirators of Boston and Williamsburg, he could quietly change the design in a lonely foreign region, where an alien and conquered people would do whatever he ordered, where England saw little of interest or importance anyway.

Actually, Quebec was the second key to the riddle of America. The first key was being fashioned in Boston and would soon be inserted in the unlikely keyhole of Lexington Common. The second lay in the hands of the Canadian Governor. It was the key to the northern half of the continent.

So far neither Carleton nor anyone else knew how to apply it. An ill-shaped key, designed in England, just would not fit the huge doorway of the Canadian West. England understood no better than France the nature of this country, its geography, its economics, or its people.

The Canadian colonies of Quebec and Nova Scotia, however, had no immediate reason to complain of their conquerors.

Nova Scotia already was a going concern, with its own legislative assembly, granted immediately after the fall of Louisbourg. It was mainly a Yankee concern, peopled by New England immigration from Maine, New Hampshire, and Vermont. It held the northern Atlantic coast for England at such high military expenditure that Edmund Burke groaned out in Parliament: "Good God, what sums the nursing of that ill-thriven, hard-visaged, ill-favored brat have cost this wittol nation!" Yes, but a good investment, as it would soon appear. The hard-visaged Nova Scotians were hard on the inside as well, hard enough to reject the American Revolu- tion.

Quebec was a different proposition. Apart from a small parcel of postwar immigrants from the Thirteen Colonies, its 65,000 people were all French by origin, although (as England had yet to learn) they were no longer French by any other measurement.

At first it was not the native Canadians who undertook to violate and destroy the neat boundary lines of 1763; it was the little coterie of New York and New England merchants who had hurried into

Quebec after the conquest and taken over the old French fur trade. Since the trade had always lived on the great peltry of the West and far down the Mississippi, its English heirs were determined to control the western furs as their predecessors had long controlled them—and their monoply was not to be shared with their fellow countrymen of the Thirteen Colonies.

British Canada was even less able than French Canada had been to hold those regions against the increasing pressures from the Atlantic seaboard. The only practical problem was not whether the Thirteen Colonies would burst the paper dike of 1763 but how far they would flow west and north, how much land they would leave to Quebec—where, in short, the boundary between the fourteenth and the other thirteen colonies would come to rest. No one imagined then that the line, wherever it might lie, would be the boundary of two separate nations.

The local politics of Quebec soon warped the whole impossible design of the British Empire in America and at last received the earnest attention of the British government. What it had heard from its local governor was most confusing. The new Canadians from the Thirteen Colonies were determined to smash the western boundary and revive the old French fur monopoly, and to this end were demanding an elected legislature which their small racial minority would dominate. The native Canadians apparently were not interested in enlightened, elected British institutions.

Still more confusing, the British governors seemed to turn almost into Frenchmen, or at least into Canadians.

Murray had quickly attracted and relished the jolly, carefree nature of the Canadians, so much like his own. He knew they would not change and sooner or later would have their own institutions, regardless of imperial design. Carleton wrote to London that "Barring a catastrophe shocking to think of, this country must to the end of time be peopled by the Canadian race, who have already taken such firm root and got so great a height that any new stock transplanted will be totally hid, except in the towns of Quebec and Montreal."

He was wrong about that because he did not expect an American Revolution to alter the racial balance of Canada. How could he foresee that the French-speaking Canadians of Quebec would soon be a minority in an unimaginable new state? For the present he had only the first known fact to work with—the fact that the Canadians would be themselves—and it was enough to reverse the entire policy of Britain in America.

The original policy was designed to Anglicize the Canadians and, if possible, convert them to Protestantism as part of a homogeneous British and Protestant continent. Carleton had not been in Canada a year before he saw the futility of that hope. Since the Canadians would remain Canadian, if not French, Britain must accept the fact and alter its policies accordingly. Since the other thirteen colonies were growing restive, Britain must consolidate the loyal fourteenth, even if it was not British by race or religion.

This policy must be a poor second-best after the brave hopes of the Seven Years' War and not easily enforced. The Canadians were exposed to the blandishments and democratic heresies of their neighbors. In the event of trouble between America and Britain, France might fish in these troubled waters and try to hook Canada. To avert these two threats the Canadians must be attached to Britain, not on Britain's terms but on their own.

That conclusion was the gauge of Carleton's statesmanship and marked him as one of the decisive figures in North American history. For under his cool management began the great Canadian paradox. It would drastically alter in America the course of human events so complacently laid down and so greatly misunderstood in the Thirteen Colonies.

Anyway, English gentlemen like Murray and Carleton could see great political advantages and a highly congenial social climate in Quebec. There was no democratic nonsense among the peaceable Canadians, none of those instincts of revolt and class warfare now upsetting even the stable society of New England.

A gentleman in Quebec could remain a gentleman. The well-trained, respectful peasants would not question his status, having always been governed by gentlemen; whereas in the Thirteen Colonies persons obviously not gentlemen were uttering the most outrageous notions of sovereignty, equality, human rights, and God alone knew what other seditious libels. Why, then, destroy, by amalgamation, standardization and social debasement, this Canadian island of sanity in the dark and rising ocean of American democracy?

So Carleton began to break the Proclamation of 1763, not outwardly at first but in detail. That document, like so many other imperial designs for America, was soon in tatters.

It had imposed English law in Quebec, but the local courts still followed the law of Paris in civil disputes.

It had promised freehold tenure of land on the English model, but land was still being granted in the French style, *en fief et seigneurie.*

It had abolished the established Catholic Church, but the church still controlled the people and was not only tolerated but encouraged as the most useful implement of government.

It had promised a legislative assembly, but neither Murray nor Carleton ever called one together. Nobody wanted it, save the carpetbaggers from the Thirteen Colonies, who wanted it mainly to nail down their monopoly of the fur trade.

Thus, by another of the queer paradoxes which must always govern Canada, its new English settlers from the Thirteen Colonies were mostly opposed to the English King, the Canadian seigneurs and priests were his ardent supporters, and the peasantry was largely disregarded by its betters. Not, however, by Carleton. To satisfy the ordinary Canadian, he was reducing the proclamation, with its boundaries, to a solemn fiction, more transparent every year.

But for events in the Thirteen Colonies, the British policy might have been left to perish peaceably in stages. As Carleton judged them, those events necessitated a sudden change to end the dying fiction outright and substitute a viable fact, if Britain was to hold Canada.

Patrick Henry's treason—as an English gentleman must view it— had spread far, rephrased in the gaudy language of a former clerk and bankrupt corsetmaker from London named Tom Paine, who considered kings "crowned ruffians" and would soon announce, in a pamphlet oddly entitled *Common Sense*, that America was "an asylum of mankind." In Boston Sam Adams, that master of politics in the raw, was repeating the Virginia Resolves, with the extraordinary proposal that all the colonies must meet right away for common action. The colonists decided to accept the invitation and convene for worse mischief.

Mobs were breaking into the King's New England offices merely because his officers collected a harmless stamp tax to pay a small fraction of the cost of the last war. The colonials, with a lack of gratitude beyond the comprehension of English gentlemen, were boycotting British goods and burning Governor Hutchinson's mansion. Presently the Stamp Act Congress actually declared that only their own legislatures could tax Englishmen living in America. The world of English gentlemen was turning upside down.

Even England seemed not entirely immune to this derangement. A befuddled government might attribute the confusions of the Thirteen Colonies to a few treacherous madmen. To Pitt, the Great Commoner, the colonists were neither treacherous nor mad. They were Englishmen like those of England and equally entitled to their rights.

On January 14, 1766, Pitt, crippled by gout, emaciated, wrapped in clumsy bandages of flannel, the wreckage of the leader who had won the Seven Years' War, had hobbled on crutches into the House of Commons. Those watching him included Franklin, agent of Pennsylvania, seated unruffled in the gallery and thinking his own long thoughts.

Pitt's voice, as he began to speak, was the hollow voice of a ghost but his eyes, glaring beside his sharp hawk's beak, "would cut a diamond" and he had mastered the actor's art, had even coached the peerless Garrick. What would he say about the Thirteen Colonies and the stamp tax?

The House waited uneasily. Franklin "could not divine on which side of the question relating to America he would be." After deliberately keeping his audience in suspense to build up the actor's climax, Pitt suddenly denounced the stamp tax and spat out his imperishable dictum: "The Americans are the sons, not the bastards of England!" This, even from the Great Commoner, was too much. Grenville, who had framed the tax, leaped up to defend it and accuse Pitt of advocating revolution in the colonies. To which Pitt retorted in words like Henry's: "I rejoice that America has resisted!"

If this was treason in Williamsburg, Pitt had made the most of it in London. Lesser men could not resist the power of that ghostly voice. The stamp tax was canceled. Franklin was satisfied. The loyal and cheering crowds of New York erected a statue of King George, with firing of cannon and ringing of bells. A barrel of Madeira was opened at the door of John Hancock, on Boston's exclusive Beacon Hill, so that all passers-by might drink the health of His Majesty and the wise old Parliament of England.

This was all very well for the colonies, but their loyalty had been purchased at substantial cost to the taxpayers of England. Because the Americans (as they would be called henceforth) would not pay their just share of the cost of protecting themselves in the recent war, the taxes must be paid mainly by the English gentry, and they had a profound, highly principled objection to taxes.

Their outburst of rage was more than Pitt could survive as he formed a pro-American ministry. Under the stress of war, illness, and his defense of the colonies he lost his reason. The sanest mind in England went insane at the very moment when it might have saved the first British Empire.

Pitt's successors, led by "Champagne Charley" Townsend, regarded themselves as models of sanity. They proceeded to impose the final insanity on America. There would be no more of Pitt's nonsense, no more truckling to the rabble-rousers like Burke in London or Adams in Boston. The Americans would pay their taxes and, if necessary, the King's army would make them pay. The imperial design must not be sabotaged by a few lunatics in the jungles of the New World. Thus spoke Champagne Charley and the higher lunatics.

Boston crowds seizing one of the King's own revenue cutters; his officials driven into Castle William by Adams's hoodlums; that incorrigible patriot mouthing his sedition from Faneuil Hall, nay, shouting that "if you are men, behave like men . . . let us take arms immediately and be free and seize all the King's officers"; English goods boycotted again; even Franklin, the moderate conciliator, at last "confirmed in opinion that no middle ground can be well maintained"; in King Street, Boston (on the very day when England withdrew the intolerable customs duties), some small boys tossing snowballs at an English sentry, a crowd of idlers assembling, a guard called out, a stone thrown, a soldier firing his musket, five citizens hit, and all the Thirteen Colonies ringing with the tale of the Boston Massacre—this news, quickly carried to Quebec, must set even a cautious man like Carleton thinking furiously.

What, in sober fact, had happened? Though it seemed complex and was generally blurred in the excitements of the moment, it was really very simple. The economic interests of the Thirteen Colonies had collided with the imperial designs of a mercantilist England, which regarded America as a fixed source of raw materials and a protected market for English manufactures, while the colonists intended to do business where and as they pleased. Their demand for practical, bread-and-butter economic rights had now fused with the doctrine of abstract rights imported in the hold of the *Mayflower*. The resulting chemical combination produced explosion.

For a little while it was delayed by England's second retreat from its tax policies. A young American named John Adams was bold enough to defend the Boston Massacre in the courts of Boston. Franklin reoccupied the lost middle ground and thought the crackup of the empire would be a "catastrophe." But the truce would not last long if Sam Adams could break it.

The first manager of machine politics in America, "the master of the puppets," as his enemies called him, and the idol of the little men, was comfortably installed among his Caucus Club, his Mohawks, and Sons of Liberty in a grocer's smoky and rum-flavored backroom, whence poured his endless stream of letters to the underground throughout the colonies, his lampoons, cartoons and handbills, his parades and fireworks, his libels against British officers who, in his imagination, slept with the virtuous womanhood of America. "The foulest and most venomous serpent ever issued from the egg of sedition," Governor Hutchinson now realized, was building revolution by democratic methods, by sheer organization and weight of local votes, to be maintained and perfected by others, for other purposes, in the future.

The chemical combination of commercial interest and abstract human rights was already well mixed in the grocer's backroom. All it needed was a spark to touch it off. That spark emerged, curiously enough, from a cargo of tea in Boston harbor and exploded the first British Empire.

After the Boston Tea Party—$100,000 worth of the East India Company's precious cargo dumped into the harbor lest it damage the American merchants by unfair British competition—no middle ground was left. England closed the port of Boston, threatened the American businessman with ruin and, as Adams had planned it, assured the Revolution.

The hectic young man from Virginia, Patrick Henry, summed up the new posture of things by announcing that "Government is dissolved—we are in a state of nature!" What that might mean neither Henry nor the other revolutionists seemed to know. Certainly it did not mean only revolt against England.

Political separation was but half the Revolution. The other half, within the disunited colonies that called themselves united, was becoming clear, rather late, to all the American businessmen. They might quarrel with England but, having no wish to lose their property and privilege, were appalled to note the rise of the lower classes, the internal social revolution already flowing in strange channels. The propertied classes were getting far more than they had bargained for. Inalienable Rights evidently covered many things besides the right to dissolve the old political bonds of the Atlantic. This two-sided revolution began to look like a Pandora's box from which sprang ugly shapes never mentioned in the noble debates of the Continental Congress. Society, in a state of nature, as the rich observed it, wore the dark habit of anarchy.

Nothing could stop the swelling tide. Somewhat disguised by abstract principles and fine words on paper, it must roll to ends still unknown after almost two more centuries of perpetual motion. Yet men like Washington, the natural leader of the political revolution, were ready to pursue it, whatever the later consequences of social revolution might be.

Treason in Canada had gone to no such lengths, was confined, indeed, to a few agitators like Walker from the rebellious colonies to the south. The Canadians were sullen and disgruntled like any conquered people, heartsick at the loss of their motherland and their fathers' dream, soul-wounded, baffled by a process beyond their comprehension, but they were passive. Under an outer air of submission they hid their passions—deeper, more stubborn and durable than an American revolutionary or an English gentleman could conceive.

Still, grave Carleton saw enough below the calm exterior to confirm his early calculation. He hurried to London with his own revolutionary notions, designed to prevent a revolution in Canada. It took him four years to sell those notions to the British government, which was hardly surprising since they proposed a complete and overt change in the imperial design. At length, when the Thirteen Colonies were clearly on the verge of rebellion, the British government decided that Carleton could be right about his colony after all, that his new plan might insulate Canada from the approaching storm.

So, in 1774, Parliament began a new and unique experiment with the passage of the Quebec Act. It was the first timid and unconscious step in the construction of the second empire and, unknown to its authors, a step toward the third, to be called a commonwealth.

The Quebec Act repealed the Proclamation of 1763 bag, baggage, and boundary. The old French system was virtually re-established in Canada. There was to be no legislative assembly but an appointed gentlemen's government, composed of a few British gentlemen, supported by the Canadian gentlemen who, though Catholic, were legalized and made fit for office by an ingenious new oath. The seigneurial land laws were confirmed. French law was established in civil and English law in criminal cases. The Catholic Church was permitted to collect its old tithes. Far more important for the future of the continent, the country between the Ohio and the Mississippi was restored to the Canadian colony, its original discoverer and owner.

Britain had retreated from the imperial design, so far as Canada was concerned, swallowed its pride, and sacrificed its Anglo-Saxon ideals within eleven years. The Thirteen Colonies, however, saw only a surrender to the French idolaters, whom they had defeated, a brazen theft of their western lands, another absolutely Intolerable Act. Burke called it "squinting at tyranny."

The Ohio, where Washington had started the war, where Braddock had died, where Forbes had beaten the French, was handed back not to France direct but to Frenchmen called Canadians, the old enemies. To suit the political convenience of England in the minor colony of Quebec, the great and victorious colonies of the Atlantic coast were still barred from their destiny in the West.

Nothing could better suit Sam Adams and the hotheads of New England.

If England had made another fatal mistake in the Thirteen Colonies, it had achieved, whether it knew what it was doing or not, a supreme stroke of statecraft in Canada. It had laid the foundations of a loyal British community—not the community it expected or desired, to be sure, but a friendly community perhaps able to abort the whole concept of continentalism and draw a boundary across the continent. A community, in short, which held the first stuff of nationhood.

Carleton, that cold, imperious English gentleman, could not see far through the mists of the latest human events. Who could? Not even a Washington or a Franklin, much less an Adams. For human events were now running wild from New England to Georgia in the first stages of a civil war within the English-speaking family.

9

Blunder at Philadelphia

[1775-1782]

O N THE NIGHT OF APRIL 18, 1775, A LANTERN GLOWED IN THE
steeple of a Boston church, a silversmith named Paul Revere
rode breakneck into the countryside, and next morning,
at Lexington, an angry knot of American farmers fired on English
troops the opening shots of the civil war.

This, then, was the end of something and the beginning of something clse. King George did not guess that yet, but it was clear to a
greater man. Franklin, in London, heard of Lexington from a long
distance. The news shattered his last hopes of reconciliation and
revived his "Short Hints" of the almost forgotten Albany Conference.
On them, perhaps, a new nation might be built, but at the moment
it seemed a doubtful hope in the squabbles of the "united" colonies.
So tears blinded old Franklin's eyes as he read the American newspapers to the great chemist, Joseph Priestley, on his last night in
England.

Carleton did not cry so easily. At times he seemed to have no
emotion in him but a loyalty to the King and his own private code.
However, at the age of forty-eight, while the world reeled and
exploded and the British Parliament was pondering his Quebec
Act, he had yielded to a brief and rather stuffy interlude of romance by proposing marriage to Lady Anne Howard, youthful
enough to be his daughter. She declined the honor and, with
appropriate weeping, admitted to her younger sister, Lady Maria,
that she had "been obliged to refuse the best man on earth."

"The more fool you," Maria retorted. "I only wish he had given
me the chance."

A matchmaking spinster carried that story to the downcast lover.
He immediately accepted the alternative thus offered and married

Maria. She was tiny, with fair hair, blue eyes, and such a delusion of grandeur that the court at Quebec soon became the fussiest in the contemporary world. Carleton humored his child-wife, almost as if he remembered the domestic misfortunes of his predecessors, Champlain and Frontenac. When the bridal pair arrived at Quebec, early in 1775, protocol was of small account. The Continental Congress was preparing to invade and liberate Canada.

Its reasons were sound enough in the strategy of war. Canada was a base from which the British would certainly strike southward, as the French had always done, by the Achilles' heel of the Champlain route. Canada, therefore, must be neutralized. Moreover, the continual irritation of a French and Catholic community at the edge of the Thirteen Colonies could be removed in stages by education, absorption, and Protestant revelation.

To this end the Congress first invited delegates from Quebec to join Canada to the Revolution. As the Canadians paid no attention—the seigneurs and priests saw to that—they must be liberated from their British oppressors by force.

Little force surely would be required. Quebec had been softened up by American agitators, who said the Quebec Act would reimpose the church tithes, institute the barbarous punishments of English criminal law, and unloose a new tyranny. The agents reported to the Congress that Canada was groaning, like its neighbors, under the imperial boot.

Only eleven days after Lexington, some unknown Canadian sons of liberty had defaced the King's statue in Montreal with a necklace of potatoes and a placard proclaiming in French: "Here's the Canadian Pope and English Fool." This was a very hopeful sign. As viewed from Philadelphia, Canada looked ripe for rebellion and needed only a little outside help to throw off its chains. An inexpensive combination of force and persuasion should be enough to drive England out of the north, before its power could be consolidated there, and extend the writ of the Congress to the North Pole.

Carleton, the statesman, reluctantly laid aside his Quebec Act, which had been intended to keep Canada loyal by generous concessions, and became a soldier again. There was no alternative. He found himself in the exact middle of the Empire's civil war. For once, by blind luck, England had the right man in the right place.

While the Congress argued and delayed, Ethan Allen, a towering frontiersman and leader of the Green Mountain Boys, had been conducting a private war with the authorities of New York. Now he took the war against Canada into his own hands.

Across Lake Champlain from Ticonderoga he was joined by a

horse dealer and amateur soldier, Benedict Arnold. They mustered altogether 230 men. The great fortress was held by some forty unsuspecting troops who freely allowed spies to inspect their lack of preparation.

The Americans crossed the lake in the first light of May 10, 1775, the sentry's musket missed fire, the commander was awakened by a knock on his door and the hoarse voice of Allen ordering him to surrender "In the name of the Great Jehovah and the Continental Congress!" Or so Allen told the story afterwards. The commander surrendered in his dressing gown.

Allen's partner, Seth Warner, captured Crown Point and its thirteen surprised soldiers. Arnold seized Fort St. John on the Richelieu in the same bloodless fashion.

The American Revolution controlled the historic invasion corridor at the moment when the Continental Congress was solemnly resolving "That no Expedition or Incursion ought to be undertaken or made, by any Colony or body of Colonies, against or into Canada." Philadelphia changed its mind within a few days and commissioned General Schuyler to "pursue any measures in Canada that may have a tendency to promote the peace and security of these colonies," always providing that "it will not be disagreeable to the Canadians."

By mid-August 1,500 troops and three generals were at Ticonderoga on their way to Canada. As Schuyler fell ill, the supreme command fell to Richard Montgomery, a former captain in the British Army. He was now thirty-eight years old, tall, handsome and dashing, the very image of America in arms. But concerning his army he wrote to his wife: "Such a set of pusillanimous wretches never were collected." Their orders were to take Montreal and besiege Quebec, according to the proved strategy of Amherst and Wolfe.

The right wing of a double assault, under Arnold ("that horse jockey," as Carleton called him), was to strike at Quebec overland from the southeast. In September Arnold's force of 1,100 picked men was dragging its bateaux up the Kennebec. The toiling colonials included some of the crack frontier fighters of the Seven Years' War and an undistinguished character called Aaron Burr, of whom more would be heard.

Canada's old friend, northern winter, caught the expedition on an overgrown, swampy, and almost impassable trail. Three hundred starving men turned back. The dauntless remainder pushed forward, eating dogs and moccasins, shot down the Chaudière by raft and reached Levis, opposite Quebec, on November 8. After one of the most desperate marches on record, Arnold stood where Wolfe had stood and prepared to duplicate his strategy without his resources or his luck.

Beside the river loomed the rock, as Kirke, Phips, and Wolfe had seen it. There was a difference this time. The Canadian *habitants*, who had fought the English invaders for a century and a half, now decided to help them. It was a good omen for the Thirteen Colonies. As always, they were deceived by the outer look of Canada.

Boats and scaling ladders were supplied by the Canadians. Arnold landed at Anse au Foulon in Wolfe's footsteps and marched his bold scarecrow army toward the walls of Quebec. His written demand for surrender was ignored by Colonel Hector Theophilus Cramahé, the Swiss officer commanding the weak town garrison in Carleton's absence at Montreal.

This was not what Arnold had been led to expect by the pundits of the Continental Congress. Inalienable Rights, it now appeared, included one not dreamt of in the philosophy of Philadelphia. The French Canadians and British in Quebec, under a Swiss commander, assumed the right to exclude Canada from the Revolution. Arnold thought that over and wisely marched twenty miles upriver to await the other invasion army of the Richelieu.

Carleton, in Montreal, now faced at first hand the unanswered question of Canada's future—would the French Canadians defend British America? Evidently not. The idiotic government in London had authorized the Governor to raise 6,000 of the King's loyal Canadian subjects, but the Canadians refused to rise even at the exhortation of their seigneurs and priests. Why should they? The civil war among the English was none of their business. The invaders under Montgomery probably would be no worse and might be better than those under Wolfe. A conquered people saw no reason to assist their conquerors.

The sullen and passive *habitants* around Montreal represented the abiding racial problem of the future nation, not yet glimpsed. While they would glimpse it later, almost too late, Carleton had no means of knowing that. A lesser man would have judged the prospects hopeless. With a handful of British and a few Canadian seigneurs he was expected to hold the historic line of the St. Lawrence against the nearly three million people of the Thirteen Colonies. Like France before it, England had left Canada and the few acres of snow to their fate. The prospects were worse than Carleton then knew. He had heard nothing of Arnold's army as he faced the advance guard of Montgomery's.

The advance guard was led by Allen. Disregarding his com-

mander, the chosen instrument of Jehovah and the Congress undertook to seize Montreal almost singlehanded as he had seized Ticonderoga. His 120 men were easily captured or driven off by Carleton's
little force. Allen was handcuffed, angrily protesting this indignity
to a soldier, and later imprisoned in a Cornish castle.

Montgomery easily took the Richelieu forts and advanced on
Montreal. Carleton knew his town could not be defended. Most of
the few Canadian militia who had grudgingly enlisted promptly
deserted. The Indian allies fled. Following Montcalm, in precisely
the same circumstances, Carleton was compelled to fall back on
the citadel of Quebec.

This proved no simple matter. Arnold and Montgomery had
blocked the roads on both sides of the St. Lawrence. Carleton proposed to descend the river by boat, but a northeast gale held him
landlocked in Montreal. The wind shifted on November 11. A single
cannon shot summoned the "whole military establishment" of 130
men, among whom stood Carleton, grave as usual, "wrung to the
soul but firm, unshaken and serene," perhaps aware that half a
continent might well depend on his ability to reach Quebec. The
little company boarded eleven boats and slipped down the river
in the darkness.

Carleton had once been afloat with his lucky friend, Wolfe, on a
similar adventure. Now Wolfe's luck deserted him. Near Sorel the
tiny British fleet stumbled without warning on Arnold's ambush.
Offered honorable surrender, Carleton still refused, staking his
life and probably Canada's on a last wild gamble. Since his fleet
was doomed he withdrew it upstream and left it. He must reach
Quebec alone.

The English gentleman quickly dressed himself as a Canadian
habitant, in a tasseled red bonnet, gray homespun clothes, a gay
sash, and moccasins. Thus disguised, he boarded the whaleboat
of a French-Canadian riverman named Bouchette, better known
for his exploits as the "Wild Pigeon."

The Wild Pigeon knew his business. His crew rowed silently
downriver in the night, oars muffled, and at the narrow passage
between Isle St. Ignace and the Isle du Pas, a few yards from
Arnold's battery, paddled with their hands. Now Wolfe's luck returned to rescue Carleton. The American sentries heard nothing.

Carleton's escape on the St. Lawrence, like Washington's on the
Ohio, was to produce large consequences. Bouchette, the Wild
Pigeon, had played his little part in the course of human events
and, with many other vital players, was forgotten.

"On the 19th," says the diary of Thomas Ainslie, customs collector at Quebec, "to the unspeakable joy of the friends of the Government, and to the utter Dismay of the abettors of Sedition and Rebellion, General Carleton arrived. . . . We saw our Salvation in his Presence."

Arnold captured the Canadian flotilla up the river only to see that his essential British quarry had slipped through his fingers, in the guise of a Canadian.

Carleton found Quebec in grave straits and himself in a singular situation. Only sixteen years earlier he had helped Wolfe capture this town from a French general, now buried in a British shell hole. A British general must take Montcalm's place and defend the town for England against English troops calling themselves Americans. For England? Possibly Carleton alone among his miserable garrison, among the statesmen of England and the philosophers of Philadelphia, dimly suspected that he was defending Quebec for the Canadians.

He was caught in the perennial paradox of Canada and must use the means at hand. They were not much, proportionately about equal to Montcalm's.

His first step was to expel from the town all the able-bodied Canadians who would not fight. That left 5,000 people of doubtful sentiment within the walls, some 350 British regulars, 400 sailors, and 530 Canadian militia. About 1,300 men must face the resources of the Continental Congress, hold Quebec under its fourth siege or, in losing it, probably lose Canada to the Revolution. As so many times before, a scant square mile of rock beside the river contained the destiny of at least half the continent.

Montgomery took Montreal and joined Arnold at Quebec. The two American generals surveyed, in their shrunken army, the tragic military miscalculations of the Continental Congress—and something more, Philadelphia's total miscalculations of the Canadian nature. Desertion and disease had reduced the American force on the Plains of Abraham to about a thousand men. Still Montgomery, knowing war but not Canada, was certain that the Canadians would surrender. He had that on the word of the Philadelphia philosophers, and who could doubt it? Therefore, he would "eat his Christmas dinner in Quebec or in hell." He ate it in his own camp. He would eat only seven more in this world.

A written demand for Quebec's surrender was tied to an arrow and shot over the walls. It informed Carleton that Quebec was "incapable of defence, manned by a motley crew of sailors, the greatest part our friends, or of citizens who wish to see us within their walls and a few of the worst troops who ever styled themselves soldiers." The townspeople were warned that Quebec would soon be a "city in flames, carnage, confusion, plunder, all caused by a General courting ruin to avoid his shame."

There spoke the Continental Congress. It was speaking a lot these days and knew everything. Not enough, however, to save its gallant servant, Montgomery.

Carleton paid no attention to the message by arrow. The Canadians of his garrison appeared to have little wish for liberation. And in their loyalty under siege Canada unwittingly was turning the critical corner of its future.

The futile arrow was followed by mortar shells which "even the woman came to laugh at." The walls were weak but Montgomery lacked artillery to smash them. His troops shivered in their thin captured British uniforms and soon were assailed by a familiar enemy. With smallpox in his camp and Quebec deaf to the counsels of democracy, Montgomery must attack or retreat.

He hesitated for some time, knowing that the odds were against him, decided on a frontal assault from the plains but yielded to his own officers, on the new principles of democratic decision by vote, and accepted a subtler strategy.

Christmas came. His broken promise to eat his dinner in the town, his lack of money, the quarrels between his officers and the well-hated Arnold had changed Montgomery from a gay conqueror to a tired and despondent young man. In the depressed humor of his predecessor, Wolfe, he had almost given up hope of victory. Finally he ordered the two-pronged assault for the night of December 31, a New Year's Eve to be remembered throughout America.

It did not find Carleton unprepared. His garrison was in good order. The Canadian militia stood with unquestioning discipline beside the British regulars—for the first time, but by no means the last. Unity of the two races under arms might mean Quebec's salvation now. It meant much more later. If it could survive this night it might turn the tide of sentiment among the wavering Canadians. Though no one thought of it then, the men of Quebec might begin, for all their puny numbers, to demonstrate the possibility of a biracial state.

On that last bitter night of 1775 their freezing hands clutched sword and musket. They also clutched the conflicting ingredients of a new nation. All that could be lost before another day had passed.

Carleton had no time for such long thoughts. As midnight passed and the world entered a new year of Independence, Inalienable

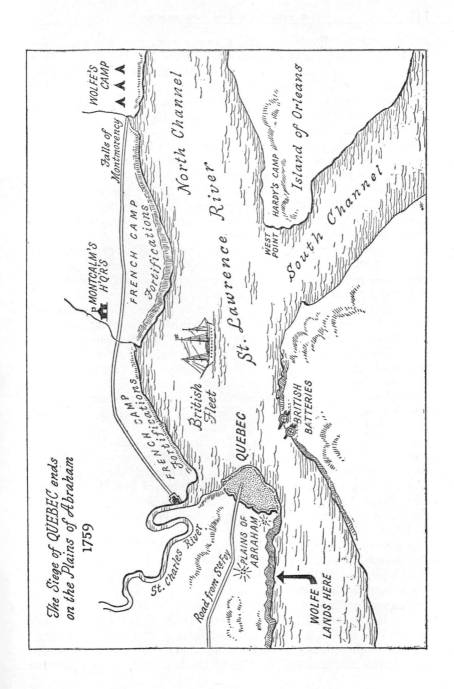

The Siege of QUEBEC ends
on the Plains of Abraham
1759

WOLFE'S CAMP

Falls of Montmorency

MONTCALM'S H'QRS

FRENCH CAMP

Fortifications

North Channel

St. Lawrence River

Island of Orleans

HARDY'S CAMP

WEST POINT

South Channel

FRENCH CAMP

Fortifications

British Fleet

BRITISH BATTERIES

St. Charles River

Road from St. Foy

PLAINS OF ABRAHAM

QUEBEC

WOLFE LANDS HERE

Rights, and Self-Evident Truth, a swirling blizzard hid the Plains of Abraham and the American camp. Then, toward four o'clock, signal fires blazed beside the St. Charles, north of the town. They were answered by two green rockets, arching across the blackness beyond the rock of Cape Diamond. The attack evidently was coming from two sides. Carleton's hour, like Champlain's, Frontenac's and Montcalm's, was coming with it.

The American guns on the plains began to fire against the western walls. Carleton soon surmised that their sound, dulled by the howl of the blizzard, was a feint. He was right. Montgomery intended to round Cape Diamond and attack the lower town from the St. Lawrence bank. Arnold, attacking from the St. Charles on the north, would meet Montgomery and the joint forces would scale the heights to capture the garrison.

Carleton had guarded against all these possibilities. Grave as usual, he stood with his reserves in the Place d'Armes, ready to move where he was needed. Drums, bugles and church bells sounded a general alarm.

Montgomery and 500 men crept out of Wolfe's Cove, by a narrow trail along the river bluffs, in the teeth of a fine, cutting snow. This time no Vergor but an alert guard of fifty British and Canadians, under John Coffin, stood at the barricade of Près-de-Ville with four small guns. They waited in silence and saw nothing but the snow, heard only the guns on the plains.

Suddenly vague figures appeared not twenty yards away. A man crawled forward, looked at the barricade and retreated. Still the guard kept silent in their baited trap.

Now they could see a knot of Americans huddled together in consultation. Montgomery waved his sword and shouted: "Come on, brave lads, Quebec is ours!" As he charged, the trap closed. From a distance of ten yards the four guns of Près-de-Ville fired their single volley of grapeshot. The foremost Americans lay on the snow. No second volley was needed. The surviving attackers had fled.

A man came screaming down the street with the false news that the Americans had burst into the town from the St. Charles. The guard at Près-de-Ville started to bolt in panic. Its commander threatened to shoot the first man who moved. No one moved but the danger had passed. Montgomery would never come back.

The battle had shifted to the north. There Arnold's force of 600, in captured British uniforms, a scrawled slogan, "Liberty or Death," pinned to their hats, was advancing along the road between the St. Charles and the walled cliffs of Quebec. They swept past the outer Canadian lines of snipers with heavy losses and reached the main defense works of Sault-au-Matelot. Their single gun, hauled on a sleigh to smash the barricade, stuck fast in the snow. Arnold paused only a moment before ordering a charge. "Now, boys," he cried, "all together, rush!"

The words were hardly uttered before he fell with a bullet through his leg. He propped himself against a wall with a musket for a crutch but soon fainted from loss of blood and was carried out of gunshot.

Daniel Morgan, leading the charge against the barricade, found himself snared in a dark street, enfiladed by British guns, raked by Canadian muskets from every house window. The cul-de-sac instantly became a shambles of confusing red uniforms on both sides, cannon flashes, grapeshot, and exploding grenades—a few hundred men, cooped up in a few square yards, but fighting one of the world's decisive battles. American soldiers would never fight better or more hopelessly. Such men could make a revolution. They could not capture Quebec against these odds.

Two hours of blind tumult and carnage left a third of the invaders dead in the snow of a mean Canadian alley. When Carleton's reserves sallied out from the Palace Gate and took the Americans in the rear, Morgan perforce surrendered.

The defenders had lost thirty men, killed and wounded. That was the price of saving Quebec. But Quebec was a foothold only of British power in America. Carleton understood the larger forces and dangers in play and was desperately anxious to save the last small chance of reconciliation with the Americans. His prisoners, therefore, were given a good breakfast, warm quarters, and a friendly lecture.

"My lads," said the Governor, "why did you come to disturb an honest man in his government that never did you any harm in his life? Come, my boys, you are in a very painful situation and not able to go home in any comfort. I must provide you with shoes, with stockings and good warm waistcoats. I must give you some victuals to carry you home. Take care, my lads, that you do not come here again, lest I should not treat you so kindly." Sound advice, no doubt, but the Revolution was past its point of no return and, for its leaders, Quebec was only a minor incident.

Search parties were sent out to collect the wounded Americans and bury the dead. They found thirteen rounded humps of snow beside the Près-de-Ville barricade. From one of them a frozen hand protruded. It was the hand of Montgomery.

Carleton and his officers watched the body of that rash and gallant young man lowered into an honorable grave hard by the St. Louis Gate. After all, this was no ordinary war. It was a hateful quarrel within the British family. Montgomery had died because neither he nor the Continental Congress understood the position of Canadians in that quarrel.

Why should they understand it when the Canadians hardly understood it themselves? Even Ben Franklin, wisest of English-speaking North Americans, was baffled by these Americans of older residence and different tongue. Next spring he set up a printing press in the basement of the Château de Ramezay at Montreal, he concentrated the ablest journalistic mind of the continent on persuasive propaganda, he proved beyond the doubt of reasonable men that Canada's place was in the free union of the Thirteen Colonies. Obviously the Canadians were not reasonable men. They listened, unmoved, to Franklin's arguments as they had been equally unmoved by Carleton's.

Up to now most of them had remained neutral in the English family quarrel. When Carleton had saved their beloved Quebec, when the American commissioners paid for supplies in the worthless paper money of the Continental Congress, when the soldiers mocked the Catholic Church, when Franklin's proclamation of liberty began to wear the look of an unwanted alien system, the *habitants* turned sour. Liberation of this sort seemed to be only another invasion of the Canadian homeland under a new name. Militarily and morally it was already the Revolution's first and only permanent defeat.

The survivors of Montgomery's army could maintain the futile siege of Quebec through the winter. Franklin could turn out his tracts, manifestoes, and homespun logic in the Montreal cellar, but the doubtful scales of Canadian sentiment had tilted quietly and forever in favor of England, not because the Canadians loved it more but the Americans and their democracy less. On these humble and invisible scales the political balance of the continent tilted also —and much farther than the British government or the Continental Congress yet supposed. The Revolution had lost its fourteenth state and America's northern half. That decision could be challenged again, thirty-seven years hence, but then it would be too late to shake the French Canadian from the foundation laid by Carleton's Quebec Act and his Quebec victory.

Franklin saw after a fortnight that the land of Canada could not be captured by the small forces sent against it, or its mind by reasonable argument. His reports disappointed the Continental Congress which, however, had more urgent business than the few strategic acres of snow. In the larger strategy now opening, the immediate and highly dubious issue was whether the loose American union could survive at all against the full power of England, aroused at last.

On May 6, 1776, Carleton saw the sails of a British fleet moving up the river. The 800 Americans still camped around Quebec saw them also and ran, leaving their cannon, muskets, and half-cooked dinners.

Almost alone in Philadelphia, John Adams remained as unyielding as Cato. Canada, like Carthage, must be destroyed as a British possession: "The Unanimous Voice of the Continent is Canada must be ours! Quebec must be taken!" Adams could save his energies for more practical tasks. The Congress and Washington were tired of the Canadian problem, for it yielded neither to reason nor to force. They decided to let Quebec alone, temporarily at least, and the Congress contented itself with a resolution inviting the Canadians to join the new union when they came to their senses.

In the early summer of 1776, while Jefferson pondered the Declaration of Independence, the British General, John Burgoyne, was moving into the St. Lawrence with a mighty British force to stamp out the rebels' disrespect for the decent opinions of mankind. Arnold hurriedly extricated the remains of his army and disappeared up the Richelieu to entrench himself at Ticonderoga and Crown Point. Carleton may have been glad to let the invaders escape and was slow in pursuit, perhaps deliberately. He still held the impossible hope of a reconciliation.

It was now October. Carleton must risk a winter campaign, far from his base, or leave the Americans astride the Champlain corridor. He reconnoitered Ticonderoga and retired to Montreal.

George Germain, the British minister responsible for Canadian affairs, was publicly outraged at this retreat and secretly delighted. He hated Carleton for refusing to appoint one of his henchmen to a comfortable job. That offense could now be repaid.

Germain—a sleazy character, who had been cashiered from the British Army in his youth for insubordination, his sentence being read on every British parade ground throughout the world on the King's special instruction, and of whom a colleague said that "there was a general diffidence as to his honor and a general disrespect of his person"—demoted Carleton by restricting his power exclusively to Canada. "Gentleman Johnny" Burgoyne, author of plays, gambler, bon vivant and ardent lady killer, was given full command of next year's expedition, and ordered to cut the Thirteen Colonies in two.

Carleton may have been mistaken in letting the American invaders escape, and in hoping still for a reconciliation, but he had avoided the disaster awaiting Burgoyne. The successful London playwright must now act his own tragedy, written in advance by other hands.

Having saved Quebec and Canada for Britain, and being rewarded by demotion, Carleton at once wrote his resignation to Germain, in a model of restrained and heavy sarcasm, including the hope that his work might be improved by his successor or "at least that the dignity of the Crown may not appear beneath Your Lordship's concern."

His Lordship could not relieve Carleton for another year. In the spring of '77 Burgoyne was launched at the Americans by the Champlain corridor. The great army moving south was to be joined by Lord Howe's forces from New York to bisect and exterminate the Revolution. Unfortunately, in rushing off to a country weekend, Germain forgot to inform Howe of these plans. Howe, therefore, was preparing to take his fleet and army to Philadelphia as Burgoyne advanced against Ticonderoga.

The huge British expedition of 8,000 swept down Lake Champlain in a splendid armada of boats, barges, and canoes. It was led by Indian paddlers, painted and feathered. Behind them came barges, scarlet with British uniforms, and the handsome pinnacles of the field officers. Then the endless impediment of a European campaign, among it two dozen wagons to hold Burgoyne's dress uniforms, silver plate, wine, and other necessities of war. Swarms of camp followers and 2,000 women pursued the advancing host as, with banners flying, drums rolling, and brass bands assaulting the silence of the lake, it approached the battlements of Ticonderoga.

The Americans abandoned the fort at the first sight of an irresistible enemy. Arnold skillfully moved his fleet through the clumsy British armada under cover of darkness, burned all his boats and departed southward. That was enough to remove King George's last passing doubts of his own wisdom. "I have beat them," he cried, "beat all the Americans!"

News of Ticonderoga reached London just as Burgoyne and his army were laboring across the soaked watershed to the Hudson, where Howe was expected at any moment. Howe still had received no contrary instructions from Germain and was blithely sailing for Philadelphia, to the amazement of Washington. No enemy, the American Commander in Chief believed, could be quite that stupid. He had not met Germain.

King George's next news, therefore, was not what he had confidently expected. The British force had shrunk to 5,000. At a remote hamlet called Saratoga it was surrounded by 12,000 Americans, outmaneuvered by Arnold (who "had been drinking freely and behaved like a madman"), divided by sudden wild charges, and hacked to pieces.

Night fell on a scene of havoc but Gentleman Johnny still thought he had won the battle. Next morning, when he saw the pitiable remains of his forces and the Americans ready to complete their work, he surrendered. The surrender probably ended King George's chance to recapture the lost colonies. It brought France into the war against England. Spain followed and then Holland. England had blundered from a colonial revolution to a general war which would soon become the still larger wars of Napoleon, now an unpromising boy in Corsica.

After one siege Quebec was not endangered again and its people were no longer tempted to join the Revolution.

Nova Scotia's position was entirely different. Its people were exposed to attack, were British by blood but divided in interest and loyalty. Its assembly passed rousing addresses of confidence in the King. Secret meetings in the villages pledged support to the Americans. Thus split, and vulnerable from both sides, the Nova Scotians, from Scotland and New England, instinctively reverted to the neutral posture of the original Acadians. They wanted, in the words of a Yarmouth petition, to be "in a peaceable state . . . the only situation in which we with our Wives and Children can be in any tolerable degree safe."

The Americans resented neutrality—the more bitterly when they found it not in natural enemies like the French, but in fellow Americans recently emigrated from New England. American privateers raided the Nova Scotia coast, despite the patrols of the British Navy. In 1776 an expedition from New England attacked but failed to take Fort Cumberland on the Chignecto Isthmus. A larger plan of invasion was repeatedly proposed in Massachusetts, but Washington vetoed it as "unlikely to produce lasting Effects" against British sea power. Britain slowly drove the American raiders out of the Bay of Fundy, preserved Nova Scotia, and pushed down to the mouth of the Penobscot.

Canada's danger was not quite finished. Lafayette, the Americans' new ally, wanted to invade Quebec again and, to prepare the way, eloquently urged the Canadians to fight for their French birthright. Washington vetoed that plan also. If Canada must remain outside his grasp, it would be safer, for the Americans, under Brit-

ish than French control. The Revolution had no desire for a return of France, the old racial enemy, to America.

Encouraged by his own successes, Washington later changed his
mind and considered an advance into Canada. France also had
changed its mind and refused to cooperate. On second thought it
preferred Britain to the United States in Canada. Lacking the northern half of America and close to British power, the new American
Union would be weak enough to depend on French support and
might serve French imperial interests. So reasoned the wise statesmen of Paris, who stood unconsciously on the edge of their revolution.

Thus in the quarrels of its enemies Canada escaped further damage. It had ceased to be an important base of Britain's war against
the Thirteen Colonies, but out of the Lake Ontario country Sir
John Johnson and Colonel John Butler, with their Rangers, and
Joseph Brant, with his Iroquois, ravaged the New York and Pennsylvania border in the old and bloody style of the French and
Indians. Farther west another sort of contest, hardly noted at the
main center of events, was carrying the struggle of the North American boundary toward the Pacific.

British arms staggered from Saratoga to Yorktown and there were
laid down for good, or so it appeared. Lord North's groan, "Oh,
God, it's all over!" echoed throughout England, the King thought
of abdicating, Horace Walpole, almost demented at Strawberry
Hill, wrote feverishly as if this were the end of the world, and
Carleton, the only undefeated British general and the man who
more than any other had saved Canada, was left at home, discredited.

Lord North, according to his invariable custom, had been wrong.
It was not all over. It was only beginning. After two more centuries
it still would not be over. For with the surrender at Yorktown and
the flight of American Loyalists to Nova Scotia and the upper St.
Lawrence, the second sovereign fact of the Revolution already was
emerging, the fact which Britain had never anticipated, which the
Continental Congress was loath to admit, which the American people hardly understand today. The Revolution, designed to create
one nation, had created two. From its womb and from no other
source was issuing, as surely as the United States, the improbable
embryo of Canada.

The diplomats of London and Philadelphia met in Paris to wind
up the family quarrel and there met this stubborn, intractable, and
absurd fact of Canada. What was Canada to be—in race, govern-

ment, boundary, and future? Was the disregarded second child of the Revolution even viable?

The statesmen at Paris, each with his own subtle game to play, hardly understood the questions, much less the answers. One of them at least sensed the ultimate fact of power in America. David Hartley, of Britain, arose to note an "awful and important truth," a truth often forgotten, ignored, or denied in the ensuing years, yet as awful and important today as ever. Concerning the boundary between the United States and Canada, Hartley said: "Our respective territories are in vicinity and therefore we must be inseparable. . . . Political intercourse and interests will obtrude themselves between our two countries because they are the two great powers dividing the Continent of North America."

In vicinity, yes. But where would the line between the two powers lie? How could it be held? The diplomats of Paris obviously did not know. They did not know even American geography. So they began to draw an impossible line on a distorted map. The American and Canadian peoples would have to rectify those mistakes and many others by trial, error, another war, and a full century of wrangle. And if, in the end, any line was to be held across America, only the Canadian people—if such a breed appeared in time—could permanently hold it.

10

The Yankee Horse Traders

[1782]

IN THE SUMMER OF 1782 PARIS BEHELD, THROUGH THE FRONT WIN-
dow of Europe, three of that strange race of men who had
beaten England, now imagined that they could build a nation
in the American wilds, and were ready to draw its boundaries.

Few of the better European minds believed that the nation, if
ever built, would amount to much or last long. It consisted of
thirteen fractious splinters, called itself a confederation, and by no
definition could be called a state. It lacked any effective central
government. It had no general laws. Its money, those torrrents of
paper flowing out of the so-called Congress, were, as the Canadians already had found, "not worth a Continental."

Just the same, its representatives appeared literate, confident,
and smooth. Also, they professed to know all about America and
entertained extraordinary and rather boyish hopes for its future.
Since hardly anyone in the governments of Europe knew anything
about America, the Americans' ignorance of at least half the continent passed unnoted. If they did not even realize that the Congress itself was assuring a second nation in the northern half, if the
peace conference of Paris was about to ratify the unlimited sovereignty of the United States at the very moment when the United
States was limiting its own power, territory and future, all these
dubious affairs were of little interest to Europe.

England may have begun, however, to grasp the huge and bitter
irony of its recent defeat—all the money, people, and genius it had
invested in the southern half of the continent had been used to
drive it into the northern half, the former empire of France. England's own success in the Thirteen Colonies had turned against it.
Having defeated foreigners throughout the world, it could be de-

feated only by its own sons, its own instincts of freedom carried by Englishmen across the Atlantic.

Some men in England also saw dimly beyond this paradox and realized that the American Revolution had been the largest human tragedy of modern times—not because it brought independence to the Americans, who must surely gain it one way or another, sooner or later, but because it had been accomplished by blood and hate when, with better judgment in England, it could have been accomplished by friendly agreement.

Until the eve of Lexington only a minority of Americans and of the Congress had desired a revolution. The blunders of England and a series of sheer accidents had produced the present angry parting, of which the political arrangements were the lesser part. The great, lasting, and tragic loss—not alone to England but to civilization itself—lay not in American independence but in the spiritual schism of the English-speaking peoples. And that schism of the spirit would take incalculable time to repair, with incalculable future costs, risks, and damage to both sides of the unnecessary war.

The American delegates to the Paris peace conference, in the heady days of their triumph, were the last men who could be expected to see these things. They knew all the answers to the immediate questions, supplied them freely, and had few doubts about anything.

Ben Franklin, with his homely, smiling face, his genial and ingratiating manners, his humorous and crackling pen, his way with the ladies, his intimate knowledge of such things as stoves and electricity, had long since found his way through the offices, drawing rooms, and coffeehouses of London, the salons, boudoirs, and intrigues of Paris.

John Jay was a competent New York lawyer, cool, austere, and aristocratic. He had drafted some of the basic documents of the Revolution, had presided over its Congress, and only missed signing the Declaration by an unfortunate absence on other business.

John Adams, of Boston, though inflicted with a dreadful cousin, Sam, appeared to the English as a gentleman learned in the law, handsome, impetuous, vain, and fearless. He regarded the Paris mission as "a difficult errand in diplomacy, demanding wariness and adroitness, if not craft and dissimulation."

The trio of Americans possessed more wisdom, knowledge, and talent than all the experienced diplomats of England, France, and Spain combined, as they at once proceeded to demonstrate. But in the considered opinion of King George (who had decided not to abdicate after all and had yet to lose his sanity) Americans were all "knaves" and must pursue their knavishness with his blessings as a good loser. England's oracle, the omniscient Dr. Johnson, had written off the Americans as a species which "multiplied with the fecundity of their own rattlesnakes," was drunk with "delerious dreams" and pregnant with "abortions of folly." Horace Walpole, wiser than the oracle, "laughed that I may not weep" and wrote to a friend: "We do not yet know the extent of our loss. You would think it very slight if you saw how little impression it makes on a luxurious capital." The hardheaded politicians of France and Spain saw in the conference only a chance of gain. The parody of a nation installed on some obscure roost at Philadelphia seemed certain to provide good pickings when it fell apart.

Three backwoodsmen from the New World, somewhat polished by fortunate contact with the Old, must confront the ablest brains of England or, at all events, the ablest that the existing government could provide.

Lord Shelburne, the new prime minister, was engaged at home in business far more important than a family quarrel overseas and "probably knew less about Canada than about any portion of the British Empire." He cared still less, though Canada remained the Empire's only hold in America. His chief negotiator at Paris, Richard Oswald, was a feeble, vacillating person and had no notion of his responsibilities. Apparently he wished only to make the best of a bad job and get it finished as quickly as possible on any terms.

Canada, the unresolved riddle of the Revolution, was not represented. England's interests alone were to be considered by England, and those carelessly, stupidly, almost blindly. For the contemporary statesmen of England the acres of snow and rattlesnakes could never be more than a minor interest on the fringes of the broken Empire—perhaps might have been better traded for the sugar island of Guadeloupe twenty years before to save all this present fuss.

The dominant fact at Paris thus was not the sagacity of the three Americans, great as it must be reckoned, nor the futility of the English government, equally profound, but the current mood of the English people.

Small wonder—after Wolfe's victory at Quebec, the heavy costs of the Seven Years' War, the ingratitude of its American beneficiaries, the interracial bloodshed, the humiliation of defeat, the whole sorry end of the first empire in the sundering of the English race—that England was disillusioned, sick at heart, wounded in the vitals of its spirit. The motherland had suffered not from ordinary war, which it understood, but from a kind of matricide beyond its experience or understanding. Therefore, the American experiment, from Raleigh's time onward, must be assigned in bankruptcy with no more trouble.

Not only pride but sound business calculation demanded a quick and generous settlement. England had founded colonies, on the Mercantile theory and by the prevailiing philosophy of Rationalism, as sources of raw materials and, above all, as markets. They were a business proposition to be reckoned only on a ledger. The age of Mercantilism and Rationalism was dying already. The mystique of Empire, to be worshiped as a racial dream, and the worship of international trade, almost as a religion, had just begun to appear.

In 1776, while Jefferson was meditating the Declaration, the first light of a new economic philosophy had dawned in *The Wealth of Nations,* written by a revolutionary economist named Adam Smith, who proposed to repeal the wisdom of the ages, all the well-tried restrictions on trade, the entire apparatus of the Mercantile state, substituting therefor the ineluctable, all-wise, and harmonious mechanism of the Market.

As the Paris conference opened, Smith was supposed to have the ear of the Prime Minister, had advised him to abandon political connection with America altogether, to build it up, by the magic of Free Trade, as a larger market for English goods than ever. To the outright economic determinist, half a century ahead of Marx, political boundaries were of relatively small account. Trade, the Market, the natural Division of Labor, the spur of competition, and the unrestricted energies of individual enterprisers offered the true means of greatness, peace, what Jefferson had first called Property, and what the Declaration, as altered in a brilliant flash by Franklin, called the Pursuit of Happiness.

Smith was a little ahead of his time, but not much. In a half century England would fully embrace his theories. So far as the new American nation was concerned, however, Smith had overlooked a disagreeable and essential point. The rebellious Thirteen Colonies would disregard his discoveries. They would soon install the unrestricted, tariff-free Market within their own boundaries. They would not extend it to English goods—or Canadian. England could find other markets. For Canada (if any Canada was left at the end of the peace conference) the plans brought to Paris by Franklin, Jay, and Adams seemed to spell nothing but economic ruin and probably political extinction not long hence.

Smith and Shelburne could not see that far. England's paramount objective at Paris was to part from the Americans as foreigners but, if possible, as friends, to make them good customers and perhaps useful allies against the permanent European enemies. Oswald's assignment, in short, was to cut losses and liquidate a disastrous investment on practically any terms that the Americans proposed. Canada entered the conference vicariously, so far as it entered at all, hamstrung from the beginning.

The Americans, unlike the English, were not tired, frustrated, or disillusioned. They were not dealing with some distant colony, but with their homeland. They were not at the end but at the beginning of things. They alone glimpsed the wealth, the space, the glory of their continent, had only begun to see its possibilities, intended to possess them all, and were aflame with the American Dream. So they know exactly what they wanted.

In a contest of this sort—the English defeated and disgusted, and confused by new economic and political theories, the Americans victorious, confident, overflowing with Life, Liberty, and the Pursuit of Happiness, clutching the world's oyster in their hands—poor Shelburne and Oswald, those fatuous servants of a fatuous king, were no match for the Philadelphia printer, the New York aristocrat, and the impetuous lawyer from Boston.

Before England's follies at Paris are too quickly condemned, as they would always be condemned by hindsight in Canada, consider the known facts of the day. Consider even the little-known map and the unreliable census. They showed something like three million English colonists living between the Alleghenies and the Atlantic; much less than a hundred thousand Canadians, nearly all French by blood, clinging to the St. Lawrence, with weak tentacles stretched southward and westward. Beyond these sparsely settled regions nothing but empty wilderness, buffalo, fur traders, Indians, and cold. The calculations of businessmen and economists like Smith showed that wilderness to be worth little. It produced nothing but a few furs and interminable, bloody border wars.

True, English forts held the whole interior, which the Revolution had never been able to capture. West of the Mississippi lay the barrier of Spanish Louisiana. The Philadelphia confederation, though pleased to call itself a nation, was too weak to resist British power in the West, if it were ever fully exerted by a man like Pitt, as it certainly had never been exerted in the Revolution.

England also possessed unchallengeable control of the world's oceans. (And at that precise moment, by an odd coincidence, its greatest seamen, Horatio Nelson, aged twenty-four, was rowing ashore secretly at Quebec to marry a Miss Simpson, desert the navy and settle down in Canada; from which personal and national catastrophe he was dissuaded in the nick of time and hustled back to his ship.)

England's bargaining position at Paris thus was strong by history, geography, and power. But the interior, including Canada, was hardly worth arguing about, assuredly not worth another civil war. The Americans seemed to prize it for some odd reason, so let them have it, with England's best wishes. Then, perhaps, they would become England's friends again.

For all these queer reasons England's case at Paris—which really meant Canada's—was dissipated in advance, to the secret amazement of Franklin, Jay, and Adams. They went to the conference prepared for a hard fight and a tough bargain. They found a debilitated English government ready to give most of a continent away for nothing but the possible hope of goodwill.

The one-sided bargaining began in denial of all the real facts of power. Strangely enough, there began also the enduring legend that the United States never loses a war or wins a conference. It was not the first time that Paris had settled the future of America. Paris, under its French kings, had split America in the first place. At Paris, France had surrendered Canada in 1763. At Paris, nearly a century and a half hence, Woodrow Wilson would try to settle the future of the world, and his failure would bring Americans back to Paris again within twenty-five years for another attempt. Paris, indeed, had become, with the arrival of the American delegates in 1782, almost the unofficial capital of the New World.

Now that the independence and sovereignty of the Thirteen Colonies must be admitted, the only important problem, it appeared, was to draw their boundaries and wish them well. Since these decisions must forever affect all future occupants of North America—the Americans, the Canadians, the Spanish, the Indians, the unknown Eskimos, and immigrant races without number—they are worth following rather closely.

Franklin, the unequaled horse trader, naturally began the bargain by demanding far more than he expected to receive. Blandly he suggested to Oswald that England hand over Canada entire to the United States as proof of good intentions, as a magnanimous and not very expensive gesture certain to get England and the new nation off to a friendly start. Oswald thought well of the idea and recommended it to Shelburne, who, educated in Smith's new economics, was inclined at first to accept it.

Political and economic calculation could not quite overcome the ancient instincts of England. As Smith had remarked, in grudging concession to human passions, "no nation willingly surrenders territory." Besides, in both military and sentimental terms, England could hardly desert the loyal English colony of Nova Scotia and especially the great naval base at Halifax. In sound economics it must retain the fisheries of the Atlantic coast and especially those of Newfoundland.

Anyway, it soon became clear that no one, not even the Americans, really wanted England out of America altogether. France wanted the United States limited in boundary and power, dependent on French support, for French imperial purposes in the future. So did Spain. The Americans might ask for Canada but if it must remain outside their control, as they expected, certainly it was better to have England beside them than to risk a reviving France astride the St. Lawrence.

Franklin's offer was refused for such reasons as these, though none of them was ever stated. All the motives of England at Paris remained mysterious, *ad hoc,* and varying from day to day. The Americans may well have concluded that an English government which had mismanaged the Revolution was capable of any folly. Nevertheless, beyond the wit of English or American to see, England as usual was blundering through and already creating, quite unconsciously, its second empire. The decision to retain a toe hold in America being reached by the amorphous processes of the English mind—almost in a fit of absent-mindedness, as it would always be said in the future—the first boundaries of the new Empire began to appear.

They appeared first in the jungles of the Atlantic coast. Here was a tricky business for the American delegates. British power had been pushed during the Revolution to the Penobscot. Accordingly, in sound horse trading, the Americans ignored the facts and demanded a boundary well to the north, on the St. John River. That was too crude, even for Oswald and Shelburne.

The Americans then suggested a generous compromise, doubtless planned beforehand. Let the line run by the St. Croix River, south and west of the St. John, on the boundary of Nova Scotia as fixed in 1763. This generosity was immediately accepted by England and the Americans found it difficult to hide their satisfaction.

Of course, no one in Paris knew where the St. Croix lay exactly and no one in England particularly cared. Beyond the unmapped river the line would strike due north, almost to the St. Lawrence, then turn south on the horseshoe of the watershed dividing the tributaries of the St. Lawrence from the streams falling into the Atlantic—again a line unknown to the map. The western half of the horseshoe, at its southern end, would strike the 45th Parallel, which had been given an arbitrary validity, as the boundary of Quebec in 1763 and again in the Quebec Act of 1774. The 45th Parallel to the westward would meet the St. Lawrence about halfway between Montreal and Lake Ontario.

So far agreement had been easy for the Americans when England ignored or was uninterested in the fact that it had cut its Atlantic regions off from their natural connections with central Canada, that if there was to be a Canadian nation its whole geography and sound economic pattern had been grossly warped in advance. That was a minor concern and any bothersome local difficulties discovered by the mapmakers on the unmapped horseshoe would be adjusted by a joint commission later on. England could not foresee that those small concerns would continue to agitate the Canadians and cost them dear for a long time to come.

The more difficult and important problem of the conference remained. Westward from the intersection of the 45th Parallel and the St. Lawrence, where should the boundary lie? Any answer given to that question in Paris must largely fix the future anatomy of the continent. The decision here involved perhaps the greatest stake in the world—the West, for which French Canada had vainly struggled this century and a half, from which the Revolution had first emerged, and in which lay treasures of land, mineral, and forest beyond reckoning. La Salle's dictum of the seventeenth century was still valid in the eighteenth. England overlooked or forgot it.

There was no ostensible reason in practical politics why England should abandon the West, the Ohio country, and all the territory west of the Alleghenies and east of the Mississippi. The Revolution, with its series of raids and marches, had been unable to shake England's hold here. The forts still flew the English flag. However, seeing the English negotiators so pliant and so anxious for the United States' goodwill at any price, the Americans proposed that England retire from the West altogether.

Their first horse-trading gambit was the old western boundary of Quebec, stretching from the intersection of the 45th Parallel and the St. Lawrence, near the present city of Cornwall, and paralleling the Ottawa northwestward to the south end of Lake Nipissing.

That line, if it halted the movement of furs out of the West, must destroy the historic business of Canada, and in any case must leave the colony as a small island of French race in the eastern St. Lawrence Valley. Even the hopeful American delegates must have been secretly dumbfounded when the British Cabinet decided, in August, to accept this bargain and virtually write off any prospect of permanent British power in Canada.

Just as the United States had most of the spoils in its grasp, a delay occurred at Paris and saved the chance of a Canadian nation. Between August and October the British garrison at Gibraltar, under

Spanish siege since 1779, proved, with its newly invented artillery
and red-hot cannon balls, that it could survive Spain's supreme
effort in the form of unsinkable floating batteries made of green
timber. England's power at the gate of the Mediterranean had been
saved. The Empire was not crumbling entirely after all. Englishmen
rejoiced, the imperial mood returned, the nation suddenly summoned up its ancient energies, and the government changed its
mind about America. If Gibraltar was worth holding, so, perhaps,
was Canada.

The English delegates met the Americans again in October.
Franklin, Jay, and Adams found that their original gambit had been
lost. A reviving England not only rejected the Nipissing line, but
intended to retain the whole interior down to the Ohio.

This was staggering news for the Americans. England's possession of the Ohio country would be disastrous to the ambitions of the
United States, for it must have the West, a primary and declared
objective ever since Washington's mission to Fort Le Boeuf.

Now the American delegates were compelled to reassess the
actual facts of power, so far disguised by the earlier weakness of
the English government. In such terms the American position looked
distressingly weak, the position of England incomparably stronger.

An American confederation existed in hopes, ideals, principles,
and Inalienable Rights. A nation did not exist, even in a paper constitution. There was nothing more than a congeries of thirteen states,
each jealous of its own sovereignty. England, though defeated by its
own blunders, was still a leading world power. It held the West by
military occupation. And assuredly the Americans were not ready
for another war to capture the West, if war could be avoided.

England's demand for the Ohio country, therefore, must be met
with diplomacy. When it came to diplomacy the Americans now
discovered that their real position was even more difficult than it
looked on the surface.

The representatives of the Congress had been instructed "to
make the most candid and confidential communications on all subjects to the Ministers of our generous ally, the King of France; to
undertake nothing in the negotiations for peace or truce without
their knowledge or concurrence; and ultimately to govern yourself
by their advice and opinion."

It did not take Jay's shrewd lawyer's mind long to sense the
duplicity of the French. They were playing their own game to keep
the United States so weak that it would remain dependent on
French power. What territorial advantage France hoped to gain
from this double cross, now that it had lost its hold on America,
was never clear, probably even to the French government. But a

weak United States, requiring French support for existence, would tend to strengthen French power and somewhere along the line might come in handy for imperial purposes.

The double cross suited Spain, France's temporary friend and also a great empire. Spain held more land in America and had held it longer than any other European nation. It hoped to push the boundary of Louisiana east of the Mississippi and recover the Floridas. In diplomatic combination, and with appropriate dirty work at the crossroads of the West, French and Spanish power might still keep the Americans behind or near the Alleghenies and Louisiana safe from their pressure.

France had immediate interests apart from territory. It proposed, in secret advances to England, that American fishermen be excluded from the historic waters of Newfoundland to provide more fish for Englishmen and Frenchmen. England, the enemy of the American Revolution, was not prepared to follow the Revolution's allies in double-crossing it. The French proposal was rejected.

Spain then proposed to bound Louisiana on the east by a line running from the western end of Lake Erie to the border of Florida. France countered with a plan for a vast Indian buffer state to hold the Americans at the Alleghenies and indicated that Britain could have all the land north of the Ohio.

These backstage maneuvers of European *réal politique* were rapidly teaching the American delegates the facts of life, which the noble ideals of Philadelphia did not seem to comprehend. Franklin, Jay, and Adams faced a possible combination of power fatal to their nation's future, a combination which could not be resisted, if it was seriously maintained.

Happily the combination never got past the stage of diplomatic whispering. England had the clear chance to grasp the Ohio country and change the whole course of human events in America. It declined to play with France and Spain, for motives both generous and selfish. The Americans must be given justice to settle the family quarrel with a minimum of bitterness and the chance of future friendship; and if they were refused justice they might well be thrown permanently into alliance with France and Spain against England. The Ohio was not worth that risk even in the cold bargaining of power politics. England, in fact, was not so stupid as the king and his former ministers who had provoked the Revolution.

Things thus were moving fast at Paris. On learning of France's overtures to England, Jay and Adams decided to break their instructions and disregard the French government entirely. It would be a serious thing for Congressional delegates to disobey the Congress, but something must be done without delay. They could not wait for new instructions, weeks hence. Franklin objected to his colleagues' daring strategy. He was outvoted. The delegation approached the English negotiators direct and proceeded skillfully to exploit the feuds of the Great Powers. That was the great turning point of the conference, a watershed in American history.

Having demanded most of Canada and then been threatened with the loss of the Ohio country, the Americans proposed a new compromise. It looked generous after their original demands. England could have the north if it would abandon the Ohio claim and support the United States in holding the Mississippi line against Louisiana. Where would the boundary then run between Canada and the United States west of the 45th Parallel at its junction with the St. Lawrence? The Americans were ready with two alternatives, both far more ambitious than American resources could presently enforce.

Britain could have either a straight boundary on the 45th Parallel to the headwaters of the Mississippi or a wriggling line along the course of the St. Lawrence and the Great Lakes, westward to the northwest corner of the Lake of the Woods and thence directly west to the Mississippi.

The second line was geographically impossible, since the Mississippi headwaters lay southwest, not west, of the Lake of the Woods, but no one knew that. Moreover, there was a vast difference between the two alternative lines in territory, natural wealth, and routes of transportation, a difference which must drastically affect the future of Canada, if it had any.

The line of the 45th Parallel would give the United States the rich Niagara peninsula, where Canadian settlement would soon be concentrated, all of Lake Ontario and Lake Erie, half of Lake Huron; but it would give Canada the main artery of travel to the prairies, the northern third of Lake Michigan, all of Lake Superior, much of the farm land of Wisconsin and Minnesota, and the priceless, unknown Minnesota iron field. If the line was ever extended beyond the Mississippi, it would give Canada also North Dakota, Montana, and Washington.

Britain either was unaware of the difference between the two lines or thought it unimportant. What were a few miles north or south between enemies now becoming friends?

Anyway, to the ignorant but practical mind of London the more northern boundary of the St. Lawrence and the Great Lakes looked natural on the map. England accepted it without further argument and surrendered all the country to the south. A stroke of the pen gave away the work of Talon, Jolliet, Marquette, La Salle, and all the old explorers, the fur route, and the interior valley for which innumerable battles had been fought in the wilderness and innumerable men had died. Huge areas, in modern Wisconsin and Minnesota, though no American had ever seen them, were included in the surrender. To make matters worse for Canada, the line across Lake Superior was pushed north of Isle Royale, close to the north shore, and Canadians were almost barred from the lake's western end. As the cynical French statesmen remarked, "England does not make peace, she buys it."

The fur traders of Canada, both English and French Canadian, were the first to realize the extent of that surrender. Their trail to the West had been cut. The canoe passage threaded by the first French *voyageurs*, the portages tramped down by Canadian moccasins for a century, the old peltry, the defending posts of Niagara, Detroit, Mackinac and the others, the control of the Indian fur harvesters, all were handed over to American settlement for the political convenience of England. This was the ultimate betrayal of Canada and it was much larger than the fur traders supposed. Loss of furs would prove to be the least part of the total loss.

English and American negotiators had an easy and false answer to the fur trade and its Indian friends. After all, they said, the political line, a mere scribble on the map, meant little. The important thing for the Canadians was the opportunity to trade with the interior, and this would be protected. England had the assurance of the Americans that Canadian traders would be admitted freely south of the new boundary. It was only on such an understanding that England had consented to the bargain.

If the London government believed that, it would believe anything. Obviously nothing could stop the American businessmen, once they were strong enough, from making the boundary not an imaginary line but a firm wall against Canadian commerce in fur and everything else. The Americans were not undertaking an abstract exercise in Smith's new economics of free trade. They were building a nation and would build it as they pleased.

England failed even to write the proposed system of free trade into a treaty—but not entirely out of neglect or stupidity, as the Canadians might imagine. There were businessmen in London also, as hardheaded as those in Philadelphia. They had been told by the Americans, quite reasonably, that if there was to be freedom of trade in the western wilderness there must be the same kind of freedom elsewhere. English business, built on the theory of mercantilism and protected, discriminatory trade, would not surrender its Navigation Acts and other forms of protection to satisfy a few Canadian fur traders.

The whole problem of trade, therefore, was postponed for later negotiation, the Canadians fobbed off with the promise of a satisfactory commercial treaty at some time in the future. No such treaty would be negotiated for three-quarters of a century and then it would last only ten years. The political boundary drawn in Paris inevitably must bisect not only the territory but the business of North America in pursuit of commercial, political, human and emotional objectives, in denial of all geographic and economic law, in defiance of nature itself.

But a still higher law was operating here, as in all nations—subtle, intangible, illogical, and irresistible. Two different peoples were going their separate ways because they prized their myths more than their treasure.

No one at Paris could yet estimate the full dimensions of myth or treasure.

The Americans certainly had established their myth already. It was written in the Declaration and in the hearts of the people; and because men are always governed in essentials not by fact but by feeling, the myth was more valuable to them and more potent than any map, political system, or economic theory.

The Canadians had a myth also, a French-Canadian myth, but so far inarticulate, and only half the myth necessary to nourish a nation. The Americans, without ever suspecting it, were about to supply the complementary half, already moving into Canada from the new American nation while the Paris conference scrawled its curious line across the map.

It was far too early yet to gauge intangibles far more decisive than the apparent facts. The new map seemed to show only that loyal Canada was imprisoned within a northland barren, poor, and almost worthless beside the rich heritage of the Revolution. Canada had been sold out, not for the first or the last time. Or so it thought.

In their anger the handful of existing Canadians—or those of them interested in the West—overlooked two facts.

The first was the undiscovered fact that north of the new line, in all this mess of Pre-Cambrian rock and stunted trees, lay some of the world's most precious minerals; the sparse prairies, now feeding buffalo and Indian, could grow hard wheat; the foothills of the Rockies covered a lake of oil; and farther west, where no boundary was yet considered, the dark smear of a giant forest ran down to the sea rocks.

The second fact was that a line fixed by power politics, by horse trading and ignorance, by guess and by God, probably was the only line that would stay put in America. It gave the Canadians far less than they deserved, but it also gave the Americans enough to satisfy their appetite. If Britain had pushed the line south to the Ohio, or even to the 45th Parallel, a powerful United States, in due time, would have rolled it back to acquire what the expanding nation needed for its purposes and might have kept rolling to the North Pole.

The southern Canadian boundary, in plain truth, could be held, mainly and perhaps only because the Americans had temporarily lost their appetite for Canada. They seemed to have all the land they knew what to do with on the north. They would somehow secure Louisiana on the west when they got around to it, would cross the Mississippi and reach the Pacific.

In the meantime, winding up their revolution, they were secure south of the natural line of the St. Lawrence and the Great Lakes. West of the lakes, so long as Spain held a Louisiana of indeterminate shape, no boundary between English and American power was needed. Out there the buffalo, the Indians, and the fur traders could continue to cross the 49th Parallel without interruption.

So far, so good for the Americans in the proceedings of the Paris conference. Two other disagreeable matters must be settled.

American fishermen had long fished in English territorial waters along the Atlantic coast. They intended to keep on fishing even if the coast north of the St. Croix lay beyond the boundaries of their new nation. They would land and dry their fish, as usual, on these foreign shores. Franklin called the old fishing rights a *sine qua non* of any peace settlement. The impetuous Adams bluntly threatened another war to keep the fisheries open.

"If," he said, in a sudden outburst of moral indignation, "we were forced off, at three leagues distance, we should smuggle eternally, that their men-of-war might have the glory of sinking now and then a fishing schooner, but this would not prevent a repetition of the crime, it would only inflame and irritate and enkindle a new war, that in seven years we should break through all restraints and conquer from them the island of Newfoundland itself, and Nova Scotia, too."

The threat of war might be a bluff. That the American fishermen would continue to fish and smuggle eternally, beyond England's power to control them, at least without destroying any chance of friendship with the United States, could not be doubted. So England yielded on the fisheries, a business much more valuable than furs. The American fishermen could take fish as they wished in England's territorial waters and could dry them on the shore of its colonies, wherever it was uninhabited. This, too, was surrender on the grand scale. And the sea settlement of the Atlantic would cause more and longer trouble than the land settlement of the West,

The second item of unfinished business at Paris, though it seemed minor, was infinitely more important to the United States and Canada alike than any nice division of land or sea. It contained the great intangible of Canadian nationhood. It housed the essential Canadian myth. It seemed a small item on the Paris agenda, but perhaps more than any other single factor it must settle the future division of America.

The conference was concerned only with the troublesome but apparently practical and businesslike matter of debts owed in the United States to those who had opposed the Revolution. Those debts were substantial. In most of the old Thirteen Colonies, now sovereign states, the lands, homes, and businesses of the Tories had been confiscated. Their owners had been treated roughly, though not so roughly as they doubtless would have been treated in any other nation fighting for its life. A few had been killed as traitors. Some had been tarred, feathered, and ridden out of town on fence rails. The American delegates at Paris could not deny that, in a settlement between future friends, the victims of revolution should be compensated.

Unfortunately, it was difficult to arrange compensation. In the first place, there were so many Tories, as the Americans called them, or United Empire Loyalists as they called themselves. Adams reckoned, indeed, that a third of the people in the Thirteen Colonies had opposed the Revolution. To pay off all who thought themselves injured would be quite beyond the resources of the Continental Congress. The Congress had no power to compensate them anyway. A loose confederation could not compel sovereign states They would deal with the Tories as they chose individually. The Congress could only promise to recommend "earnestly" to the states that the Tories should be treated fairly. As the states had no intention of rewarding treachery to the Revolution, and generally thought that the Tories were lucky to escape with their skins, the promise made at Paris was worthless, its result decisive to the future of Canada.

11

Tragedy at New York

[1782–1787]

WHILE THE CONFERENCE OF PARIS DELIBERATED, THE PEACE NOT yet settled, New York presented one of the strangest spectacles yet witnessed in the New World—also tragic, heart sickening, and of profound consequence to all America.

England had ceased to fight seriously after the fall of Yorktown, but it still held New York. The active Loyalists, who had reason to fear for their safety, flocked behind the English lines. For the second time, in the same man, England found the means of protecting its supporters.

Carleton had been summoned from retirement in his country home and sent posthaste to New York, his quarrel with Germain forgiven. Like King Louis in the case of Frontenac, King George had suddenly realized that he could not do without his reliable old servant.

As the King and government had no clear plans in the present catastrophe, Carleton was given carte blanche along with the command of all English forces in America. He had saved Quebec. Maybe he could save the helpless victims of the Revolution. They were committed to his "tenderest and most honorable care" by the King himself. The government added that "the resources of your mind in the most perplexing and critical situations have been already tried and proved successful. At this perilous moment they give hope to the nation." To Canada they would give the chance of survival.

When Carleton reached New York in May, 1782, it was to find a pitiable and penniless horde of Loyalists seeking immediate evacuation and increasing daily as more exiles poured in from the countryside. The power of England and the United States was represented again, as in 1775, by two grave men whose careers had always run

167

parallel. Carleton at once established a polite correspondence with Washington. They met, as gentlemen of the same mold, with ponderous dignity on both sides but without chance of satisfactory agreement.

Washington, naturally enough, was bitter toward the Loyalists, his enemies. He had been quoted as saying, in an angry moment, that he "could see nothing better for them than to commit suicide." He knew now that his half-formed nation would soon have independence in law as in fact and thus could treat all persons within its bounds as it chose.

Carleton's duty, on the other hand, was to protect the Loyalists, and he still expected a friendly settlement of the war without a political breach. From the beginning, at Quebec and on Lake Champlain, he had sought a reconciliation, had been punished for treating the American invaders too lightly, and in his limited imagination could not conceive of England's total surrender to its erring sons.

Hearing that independence had been granted to the United States, the English gentleman of the old school was outraged. He resigned immediately. The resignation was refused because England could find no substitute. On second thought, Carleton decided to remain at New York and salvage what he could from the wreck.

In April, 1783, he shipped 5,593 Loyalists to the nearest haven of Nova Scotia. The exiles carried little baggage that the Americans could observe but that first ship, like the *Mayflower*, contained in secret freight the missing ingredient of a Canadian nation.

The Americans impatiently demanded their harbor of New York and their last sight of the Tories. Carleton refused to be hurried. He would not withdraw his troops until all the Loyalists had been safely removed.

About a hundred thousand of them left the United States. A third, mostly the English-born, rich and official classes, went to England. Most of the exiles had neither the means nor the desire to leave America. It was their home as much as it was the home of the revolutionists—and that also was a disregarded fact of profound consequence. Some went to the West Indies and Florida. The largest group, probably between forty and fifty thousand—no one ever knew the exact numbers—chose Nova Scotia because it was part of America and close at hand. By the end of November the greatest mass exodus in North American history was complete. And though he could not sense it yet, Carleton's job of salvage had assured a second, but peaceful revolution in the politics of the continent.

Nova Scotia was overwhelmed by the sudden influx, which tripled its population overnight. The Loyalists burst the accommodations of

Halifax and camped around it in a city of tents. They started to build a bigger and better Halifax at Shelburne, on the southwest tip of the peninsula. The former French Port Razoir, corrupted into the English Roseway, then hopefully called New Jerusalem and presently occupied by three fishing families, was now renamed in honor of the English statesman who had just sold out Canada at Paris. To accommodate some eight or ten thousand new residents, the town was divided into wide streets, town lots, and surrounding farms and the gentry were soon giving routs and balls with all the old splendor of silk, crinoline, and silver buckles.

Shelburne was quickly abandoned, having nothing to live on. Other Loyalist settlements in Nova Scotia flourished permanently, despite the return of many of the exiles to the United States. But Nova Scotia never became a truly Loyalist colony. Basically an offshoot of New England, its future population was to be mostly Yankee and Scottish—for a long time more Nova Scotian than Canadian.

The colony, christened "Nova Scarcity" by disillusioned settlers, and the other little colony of Prince Edward Island could not hold the invasion. It poured across the Chignecto Isthmus, peopled St. John, paddled up the St. John River and founded Fredericton, near the ruins of the old French fort of Ste. Anne.

Here the comfortable farmers and tradesmen of the Thirteen Colonies and the disbanded Loyalist regiments confronted a wilderness as naked, cruel, and cold as it had always been since the first days of American settlement. Many of them, accustomed to snug houses, lived through the first winter in tents and bark huts.

The government at distant Halifax could not cope with the demand for land, food, and clothing. There were so many settlers west of Chignecto, so many petitions, so much discontent that the new colony of New Brunswick was established, complete with a legislative assembly at Fredericton like that of Halifax, and Loyalist to the core.

This division of Nova Scotia suited the government at London, then under the impression that the Canadian colonies should be widely separated, kept weak, and prevented from uniting in some new version of a Continental Congress with dangerous notions of freedom.

The first New Brunswick elections showed how ill London had gauged the future of Canada and what it might expect from Canadians, even Loyalists later on. In St. John the working classes of the "Lower Cove" outvoted the gentry of the "Upper Cove" and would have defeated two important officers of the government if a practical sheriff had not saved them by striking out eighty opposition votes. That portent was significant but unobserved.

A few settlers turned back in despair to the United States, after political passions had cooled there. Most of them remained to found an entirely new and distinctive life of their own—not without regret for the easier life left behind. A woman who was to be the grandmother of Leonard Tilley, New Brunswick's great statesman, left a vivid picture of the general homesickness in the first days of St. John when she "climbed to the top of Chapman's Hill and watched the sails disappear in the distance, and such a feeling of loneliness came over me that, although I had not shed a tear through all the war, I sat down on the damp moss with my baby in my lap and cried." But nobody cried for long.

The Loyalists had undertaken one of the true epics of North America and none succeeded better. For all their local differences, the new communities of the Atlantic coast had a basic unity of character and instinct. They were to be the "Maritimes," the home of a unique Canadian breed. It was hard, poor, thrifty, proud, ingenious, indestructible, and forever distinguishable from other Canadians.

The court, the navy, and the military at Halifax, now reinforced by Loyalist aristocrats, gave the Maritimes also a certain elegance and glamour lacking elsewhere. The Duke of Kent, arriving in Halifax a few years after the Loyalists, to live publicly with his mistress, Julie St. Laurent, to build the Citadel and leave his pompous mark permanently on the town, felt quite at home in a Georgian environment. That exuberant young man was quite cast down when he left Nova Scotia, abandoned his faithful paramour to die of heartbreak, and returned to England for the patriotic duty of begetting a much-needed English sovereign named Queen Victoria.

Fewer Loyalists settled in the St. Lawrence colony of Quebec, but strategically and politically they were even more important than the Maritimers.

As early as 1774 the first refugees from the Revolution had trickled into the region around Montreal. Soon after the signing of peace Governor Frederick Haldimand, the able Swiss soldier of fortune at Quebec, had on his hands some seven thousand destitute exiles who had come with "unreasonable expectations."

He housed and fed them in rude camps at government expense and often in wise disregard of his instructions. As soon as the ice thawed in the spring of '84 he moved them up the St. Lawrence in boats and barges piled high with supplies, tools, and cattle.

They were settled along the river west of Montreal, on the north shore of Lake Ontario to Niagara, and on the Detroit River, in racial groups—Yankees from New England, Dutchmen from the Hudson River, Highland soldiers, Hessian mercenaries—among whom those of English race could have been a small majority at most. No matter, they were all Loyalists, they hated the Americans and accepted King George.

Government surveyors hastily and inaccurately surveyed townships in farms of 200 acres, townsites, and streets. The land was distributed to everybody by lots drawn from a hat, officers of the defeated regiments receiving five to ten times as much as ordinary settlers. Even this discrimination failed to satisfy some ambitious officers. Haldimand replied tartly that most of the malcontents were "in fact mechanics, only removed from one situation to practice their trade in another."

Six miles on either side of the Grand River were excluded from the King's sovereignty and given to the loyal Mohawks, who had ravaged the western American borders in some of the bloodiest massacres of the Revolution. Their handsome, well-educated chief, Joseph Brant, settled down in a mansion at Brantford, refused large bribes offered by the American government if he would keep the western tribes peaceful, became the lion of New York and London society, excited James Boswell, refused, as a king, to kiss King George's hand, and on a fancied insult almost tomahawked the Turkish ambassador at a state ball.

Social and racial distinctions counted for little in the Loyalist settlements when nearly all the settlers were destitute. They conducted their business, such as it was, by barter. They depended on the government for food. They were clothed in issues of rough cloth to make trousers and skirts, blankets to make coats. Soon, like their Indian neighbors, they were making their own garments of deerskin.

Each family received an unserviceable ship's ax and a handsaw. A single firelock must serve five families for hunting. A portable gristmill, worked by hand, ground the grain of the whole village. In the "hungry year" of '88, after a crop failure, the Loyalists almost starved. A pound or two of flour could be traded for 200 acres of land. A soupbone might be passed from house to house for successive boilings. Many families ground tree buds and leaves for food.

There were probably ten thousand settlers above Montreal by the end of the eighties. Not all of them could claim to be Loyalists, for every newcomer arriving overland from New York and Pennsylvania by the old route to Niagara, who swore an oath of loyalty to the King, was welcome and given land, no questions asked concerning his part in the Revolution.

It was a poor man's settlement. Many of the settlers were illiterate. A few had managed to lug some pathetic relic of better times across the border—a spinning wheel, a grandfather's clock, a bed or table, to be installed in a log shanty with oiled-paper windows and perhaps no chimney.

If these people lacked money and social background, they held in common an adventure, a hope, and a legend. To preserve these memories, Carleton (now Lord Dorchester on his return to Quebec) proclaimed that as a "Marke of Honour" the United Empire Loyalists were "to be distinguished by the letters U.E. affixed to their names, alluding to their great principle, the unity of the Empire."

That distinction fell out of use, but the Loyalists were drawn together by both memories and necessity. They helped one another at barn raisings and quilting parties. They celebrated at dances, wrestling matches, and drinking bouts. They were further united in demanding their own government, separate from the government of French-speaking Quebec.

Their demand contradicted the whole policy of the Quebec Act, which had confirmed Quebec as a French community without representative institutions. But the Loyalists could not be long resisted, especially when such institutions already had been conferred on the Maritime colonies.

Carleton faced a baffling problem. The Loyalists wanted some kind of elected government. In French Canada all save a small English-speaking minority had no wish to change their old ways and regarded elected government as a device for extorting taxes.

Only about 21,000 of the 130,000 people on the St. Lawrence in 1791 were English-speaking, most of them in the upriver settlements. The colony was split by race, history and custom, but its economic interests were joined by the river highway and by common conditions of life. The government's budget was hopelessly unbalanced and dependent on the British taxpayer; the administration chaotic; the "English judges following English, French judges French law, and some followed no particular laws of any sort whatsoever."

Carleton was old and bewildered and, for the first time, seemed impotent. Tired of his delays, the London government of the younger Pitt decided on its own *ad hoc* solution and cut the colony in two.

The Constitutional Act of 1791, with its subsequent orders in council, created a diminished Quebec, bounded on the west by the convenient line of the Ottawa and now called Lower Canada. The western, English-speaking settlements, of vague dimensions, became Upper Canada.

Both were given governors, appointed executive councils, and parliaments consisting of an appointed Legislative Council corresponding to the House of Lords and an elected Assembly corresponding to the House of Commons.

Lower Canada was allowed to live its own life, to retain its seigneurial land system, support its church, and on the bitter bread of conquest, to become more Canadian than ever.

Upper Canada was expected to reproduce in the wilds the stable, authoritarian system of England under what Pitt called "the very image and transcript of the British constitution." One-seventh of all land was set aside for the support of a privileged but not established Protestant Church. A hereditary nobility was to be created but fortunately was soon forgotten.

Thus with governors who could veto the will of their assemblies and all local laws subject to the approval of the King, England proposed to avoid in Canada the weakness that, in its judgment, had caused the American Revolution. Democratic heresies were to be kept south of the new boundary, Canadians in their places.

Pitt's "image and transcript" at once began to perish, like so many other things of English origin, in the harsh climate of the St. Lawrence Valley.

A unique adventure of racial conflict was under way, an adventure more complicated, difficult, and doubtful than any statesman in London or any settler in Canada yet suspected. Nothing would turn out as planned.

The Loyalist movement looked at first to Englishmen like an act of charity, high in expense, small in result. It cost the English taxpayers probably £6,000,000 altogether in compensation grants, ranging from £10 to the £44,500 awarded to a great landowner like Sir John Johnson. But the Loyalist movement could never be reckoned in money or in numbers. For Canada, for England, for the Anglo-Saxon peoples all over the world it was to prove revolutionary in the following century and a half.

It was revolutionary in Canada from the beginning because it provided an English-speaking population (all the immigrants soon learning to speak that tongue) in which the French Canadians must soon be a minority.

The Loyalists seized the new bridgehead and exploited it so well that larger immigration was continually attracted from the British

Isles and the United States. Before the arrival of the Loyalists few observers in London or Philadelphia could imagine Canada, a tiny French-speaking colony, remaining long within the British Empire. Sooner or later such a vulnerable island must be engulfed by the rising tides of the United States. Now, with a small but substantial and growing population of British stock, the Empire might hold Canada—not, however, on the Empire's existing terms and not for long as a handful of mere colonies.

In the Empire as a whole the Loyalist movement must prove revolutionary for other reasons, not to be understood within a century. Those reasons must also deeply affect the future of the United States—the seed of the world-wide Commonwealth of the twentieth century had been planted on the north shore of the St. Lawrence.

Meanwhile the most conservative elements of North American society had moved out of the United States, some for purely patriotic reasons, more from sheer necessity. The immediate effect of this movement on the society of the United States cannot be estimated. Its immediate effect on Canada can hardly be over-estimated. Its long-term effect on the Empire and on the United States is not clear even to this day. Certain subtle and almost secret changes, much larger than the migration itself and the grafting of a new English-speaking population to the French race of Canada, had occurred in America.

To begin with, the sundering of the British peoples had not been accomplished, as men like Carleton hoped, in goodwill and without spiritual scars. It had been accomplished in anger and agony. It had left a wound on every United Empire Loyalist, to be inherited by his sons, grandsons, and great-grandsons and not to be healed for a hundred years at least, not entirely healed yet. It had made the American and the Canadian not only antipathetic to each other but, in the deepest sense, incomprehensible.

The original French Canadian had seen the United States as an aggressive power, an invader, and a religious heretic. The first English-speaking population of the St. Lawrence remembered the United States only as an enemy, a persecutor, a traitor to the motherland, a political heretic. Such was half the legacy left in Canada by the American Revolution—an incalculable loss to the future spiritual unity of the continent.

The other half, so far as it affected the creation of a Canadian state, was a disguised and negative asset. The Loyalists had fled to Canada hating the Americans. At first, anyway, that hatred, as much as any positive love of England, compelled the new Canadians to create a community of some sort if they were to be safe from American pursuit and annexation. The full power of those joint emotions of hate and love must be fully tested, along with the United States' appetite for Canadian territory, in a war only three decades away.

By these curious means the Revolution had given birth to the future Canadian nation as surely as the American. It had given Canada an English-speaking population, fortified that population with anger and resolve, provided not only the first physical but also the essential and enduring psychic elements of nationhood.

Some of the differences between the American and Canadian communities were obvious enough. The American had some three million people, the Canadian less than a hundred and fifty thousand. The American had established a rudimentary national government and legislature, independent of foreign states, and they would soon be perfected under a Federal Constitution. The Canadian had no central government, except a governor in Quebec with tenuous, theoretical control over the subgovernors of the loose-knit colonies. All of them were governed in great affairs from London. Only a few hopeful men supposed that the mutually suspicious knots of settlement from Halifax to Niagara could ever weld themselves into a nation or prove capable of independent sovereignty.

All that was obvious, so obvious that few Americans realized then, or for a century afterwards, that their revolution of itself had made a second nation possible. Other obscure and little-noted facts were the important ones.

Canada differed entirely from the United States in another respect. Its English-speaking people had refused to cut their roots in England. Its pious Catholic French-speaking people had been betrayed by France at the Conquest of 1759, were finally severed from their motherland by the godlessness of the French Revolution and, therefore, by calculation, though not by emotion, were prepared to accept government from England. The great paradox and ambivalence of the Canadian mind was now established and would endure—a mind split by its love of the Canadian earth and its nostalgia for the Old World, by the vision of England in the English-speaking Canadian, the vision of the lost France in the French Canadian, a mind thus in constant tension and secret conflict between the opposite pulls of geography and history as even Champlain had felt them.

There lay perhaps the deepest difference between the American and the Canadian creature. The United States began spiritually whole. Canada began in division between two races and, within the races, in conflict between two emotions. Finally, the Loyalist tragedy and epic left a permanent tinge on the character and

thought processes of all Canadians, conditioning the weather of
their life thenceforth in a certain conservatism, skepticism, stubborn
silence, and studied outer dullness, all used as a disguise before
foreigners to protect a young, weak nation living always under
siege.

Even that does not tell the whole story. The least suspected fact
of all was that the Loyalists had not been transplanted Englishmen
when they came to Canada, as England supposed. They had been
North Americans. Most of them had been born in America and
were not landed aristocrats, like those of England, but poor mechanics and farmers. All were accustomed to representative government in the assemblies of the Thirteen Colonies. Few had been
entirely satisfied with England's policies; many were angry with
English taxes and eager for reform. They had broken from their
neighbors on the single issue of political separation by civil war.
When they reached Canada they had no intention of accepting
dictatorial government from London.

It was all very well for John Graves Simcoe, the beefy English
Governor of Upper Canada, to declare that "the best Security that
all just Government has for its Existence is founded on the Morality
of the People" and for a successor to promise to "contend against
Democratic principles," but the colonists demanded at least as much
political freedom as they had known in the Thirteen Colonies—
much more, indeed, as they would shortly demonstrate. The germ
of self-government had been introduced in the unworkable Constitutional Act, was fatal to future English control of Canada, and—
most surprising of all—was fatal to the whole British Empire as it
then existed.

In the United States democracy had come as an explosion. In
Canada it would grow slowly, quietly, steadily, illogically, with
roots still spanning the Atlantic. Canada, therefore, was to be the
laboratory of the Empire, in which its future must be worked out
by experiments culminating in a commonwealth of free states, that
supreme Canadian invention.

The United States could not escape either the immediate effects
of a new nation growing up beside it and dividing the continent or
the wider effects of a political organization girdling the world, since
the British peoples must be essential American allies in every future
trial of strength, finally in two world wars. It is hardly too much to
say that the process begun in the American Revolution and carried
into Canada by the Loyalists is the most urgent business of all the
English-speaking peoples in the world of the twentieth century.

Such a process—if anyone sensed it at the end of the eighteenth century—must take time, wisdom, and experience in Canada, in Britain, and in the United States because it represented nothing less than the reconciliation of the English-speaking race after its sundering in the American Revolution. For many years, however, the victors and the victims of the Revolution were too busy to think much of these things.

The sparsely settled, far-flung, and poverty-stricken Canadian colonies somehow survived their first growing pains under political arrangements which could not last and must be altered.

Washington had seen that the existing American system would not serve either, that "something must be done, or the fabric will fall, for it is certainly tottering."

The Philadelphia Convention soon framed the Constitution of the United States. Washington took his oath as president on the balcony of Federal Hall, in New York. The first American nation had a national government at last, seventy-eight years before Canada could achieve it, and seemed to have almost everything that a new nation could desire. No, it still lacked the far West. In pursuit of the West the two nations of America, the older shaped and strong, the younger shapeless and weak, were about to enter a long series of violent collisions. Canada's chance of surviving them appeared small; to most thoughtful Americans, nil.

12

The Mad General

[1787–1794]

B Y THE FIRST DAYS OF 1794 THE YOUNG UNTRIED PEACE OF PARIS
seemed to be dying in its eleventh year. The British Empire
and the new American Republic were on the edge of war. As
usual, the immediate danger lay along the Canadian boundary in
the West, which had bred two world wars already.

A daring American officer, styled "Mad Anthony" Wayne for his
exploits in the Revolution, was advancing from the Ohio country
perilously near to Canada. At Quebec the Canadian Governor
General, Lord Dorchester, who had once been grave Carleton,
evidently had lost all sense of gravity and was about to lose his
head. The Jeffersonian party in the United States Congress was demanding that President Washington retaliate against Britain for
the seizure of American ships at sea. The British government of the
second Pitt had no wish for extra trouble in America, being now at
death grips with revolutionary France on the long road to Waterloo,
but it must maintain its European blockade even against American
shipping.

Known events apparently lay in the hands of distinguished figures
like Washington, Pitt, Jefferson, Dorchester, and Wayne. Unknown
events, in the end more important, were quietly manipulated by unknown men far beyond the existing North American map, in an
empty land of guess and legend, almost to the rim of the Rockies.

These adventurers, some half crazy, most ignorant, and all poor,
included an American guerrilla fighter turned playwright, a frenzied
Irish governor of North Carolina, a killer from New England, a
handsome young Scotsman from the Hebrides, a farm laborer's son
from Yorkshire, a doomed navigator from Denmark, and a company
of Spanish sailors, long dead. Together, in vain pursuit of an ancient
myth, they were giving the civilized world a new dimension.

178

Of these things Dorchester knew little or nothing when he rose— an old man of seventy now, stout, heavy jowled, shaggy and bitterly disillusioned, the very image of John Bull at bay—to address a delegation of Miami chiefs. War between Canada and the United States, he said, was imminent, and then he added his celebrated indiscretion: "You are witness that on our part we have acted in the most peaceable manner and borne the language and conduct of the people of the United States with patience, but I believe that our patience is almost exhausted."

An angry Pitt repudiated this threat as soon as he heard of it, but the repudiation could not reach President Washington by sailing ship for several weeks. Meanwhile the damage had been done. The American war party exploited Dorchester's words for all they were worth and more. Jefferson called them an "unwarrantable outrage."

Perhaps not so unwarrantable as they appeared to Jefferson, for much lay behind them in the West—enough, anyway, to convince Dorchester that the Canada saved by his hands in 1775 was likely to be extinguished by his old enemy in 1794.

The so-called West, between the Alleghenies and the Mississippi, had been a remote suburb of the Revolutionary War, a vacuum where a few men, mostly Indians, marched and countermarched, raided, ambushed, and scalped in the old fashion with little apparent effect on the war's main theater by the Atlantic. Yet large imperial pressures were at work on the frontier.

The Spanish of Louisiana succored American raiding parties with money and ammunition and provided them with sanctuary on the Mississippi when they needed it—not because Spain had the slightest sympathy with the Americans, but because for the moment they were a useful weapon against England. The proposed American Republic, as the Spaniards confidently expected, would exhaust itself in revolution, fall apart, and give Spain all the land west of the Alleghenies. They must be the ultimate boundary of the United States if, by chance, it survived as a nation. The Americans, therefore, must be shored up temporarily until they collapsed later on.

Thus, when young George Rogers Clark, lieutenant colonel of Virginia and a friend of Jefferson, began his daring western raid in 1778, with only 175 guerrilla fighters, all as tough as their leader, he was assured of cooperation from the Spanish at St. Louis.

He quickly conquered the Illinois nation, summoned 4,000 Indians of many tribes to meet him at Cahokia, and there, with oratory as flamboyant as Frontenac's, proposed a general uprising against the Canadians. The western frontier had produced no abler strategist than Clark but continental strategy was against him.

All the vital posts of the Great Lakes system were held by the

Canadians. Skillfully directed by Henry Hamilton from Detroit, Canada's Indian allies stretched their war path all the way to Kentucky and Tennessee and even entered the main war east of the Alleghenies. Canada had always been unequaled in Indian warfare, alliance, and politics. Now it possessed a decisive advantage. It was defending the Indians' peltry and hunting grounds while the Americans intended to settle and destroy them.

Alone in the western vacuum, Clark could not resist Hamilton's march to Vincennes, the key post of the Wabash country, but his counterstroke, like his oratory, was worthy of Frontenac. From Kaskaskia he and his little band of whites and Illinois warriors raced across 180 miles of snow, ice, and mire in February, 1779, to surprise and capture Vincennes from the unsuspecting Canadian garrison. Clark had accomplished his own private epic and not much else. It was a brief hour of glory to be followed by the American hero's bitter end in poverty and betrayal.

The Canadians marched next year on St. Louis and were hurled back. The Americans, with Spanish help, held the Southwest, but the hard fact of Canadian power remained in the vital region of the Great Lakes and the Ohio country. Moreover, Clark's false friends, the Spaniards, were pushing tentatively eastward across the Mississippi; they seized West Florida and awaited the American Republic's inevitable disintegration.

When peace was arranged at Paris in 1783 Britain agreed to abandon the western forts and retire behind the new boundary of the St. Lawrence and the Lakes. The decision had hardly been made and the boundary fixed before the new government of the younger Pitt regretted the follies of the peace settlement. Far too much had been given away to the Americans, quite unnecessarily. Not only had Britain surrendered the best part of the western peltry and the whole French transportation system, but it had exposed itself to another Indian uprising like Pontiac's.

If the English negotiators at Paris had not understood the meaning of the boundary, the Indians knew at once that it meant American settlement and their own destruction. Most of them had fought for Britain in the Revolution. Now Britain had betrayed them for their pains. In rising against the American settlers, they probably would rise against the Canadian colonists as well. Or, if the Canadians supported the Indians, Britain would be involved in renewed conflict with the Americans. Britain could not afford another war of any sort after its recent disaster.

For all these reasons, commercial and political, Pitt's government thought that perhaps a bargain made in Paris at haste might be repealed, or whittled down, at leisure. Interpreted by skillful politicians, the promise to surrender the forts of Detroit, Mackinac, Niagara, Oswego, Oswegatchie, and Dutchman's Point "with all convenient speed" could be strung out indefinitely. Britain was in no hurry. And it could make out a colorable case for delay, since the American courts were slow in implementing the other clauses of the peace treaty, which had promised just compensation for the Loyalists' losses in the Revolution.

Washington sent von Steuben to Quebec to demand the surrender of the forts. Governor Haldimand replied that he was powerless without instructions from London. The soldier's eye of Washington saw through this transparent evasion, saw that British power bestrode the West and showed no sign of retreating where it belonged, north of the St. Lawrence and the Lakes.

Britain hoped at first only to delay its withdrawal for a few more years. Every additional fur harvest would put money into the pockets of the Canadian traders. Trouble with the Indians at least would be postponed. More important, the possession of the forts could be used as a formidable bargaining counter in the proposed trade treaty with the United States, discussed but left in obeyance at Paris. As the years went by and the Canadian garrisons still held the forts, beyond the power of the United States to dislodge them, Britain began to hope that the boundary of 1783 could be swerved southward, perhaps toward the Ohio, certainly far enough to give Canada the crucial Grand Portage from Lake Superior to the Rainy River.

Pitt had good reason to count on American weakness. The loose confederation of the thirteen sovereign states, yet lacking a central constitution, showed increasing strains along the Atlantic coast. In the Southwest to the edge of the Mississippi, the new American settlements were falling under the influence of the Spanish at New Orleans. The wayward state of Vermont had proclaimed its independence. It wanted to use the Richelieu as a trade artery to the St. Lawrence. Ethan Allen—his jail sentence in England forgiven—appeared ready to repent of Ticonderoga and, once more under Jehovah, might bring his state back into the British Empire. An officer of the Revolutionary War, Daniel Shays, had conducted a rebellion in Massachusetts against a local government of property and privilege. "There are," said Washington, "combustibles in every state which a spark might set fire to."

Britain was gratified by those words from the man who had managed the Revolution. Like Madrid, London began to hope that the flimsy agglomeration of American colonies which somehow had won the war might dissolve before a national state could be erected. All such hopes were false. Britain still did not and perhaps never would understand the nature of Americans or Canadians, but the obvious policy for the Micawbers of London was to hold the forts and wait for something to turn up. Any day now somebody might ignite the combustibles. A resulting explosion should blow the West back into the Empire.

Governor Haldimand, that practical Swiss, had invented the project of an Indian buffer state in the Ohio country, where no white man would be allowed to settle but Canadians and Americans could trade freely. Dorchester proposed to expand the boundaries of this preserve eastward to Lake Champlain. The Pitt government warmly endorsed such an easy way out of the stalemate.

Pitt soon found that he was not dealing with the quarrelsome Continental Congress. The Americans had constructed their constitution and nation at Philadelphia. The new nation-state intended to possess its own territory and was governed by the ablest group of statesmen in modern times. The United States government could settle the problem of the Loyalists' compensation and the old excuse of nonpayment, which had long served London's policy of delay, could serve no more. President Washington could raise his own troops, regardless of the individual states, and if necessary capture the western forts.

Finally Britain was now engaged in the ultimate struggle for America on the far and little-known Pacific coast. It faced there the prospect of war with Spain for possession of vague coastal territories and a newly discovered treasure, the hides of certain curious sea mammals. War with Spain might ally the Americans with the Spaniards of Louisiana. Anyway, such a war was no part of Pitt's program. He had his hands full in Europe. France had begun its revolution and was about to elevate a disagreeable little artillery-man into the menace of the age.

Thus complicated, the policy of holding the western forts looked more and more like a losing proposition for Britain. There was still another complication. The western Indians were struggling for their existence against American settlement. Agents of the United States negotiated with them interminably and made treaties with a few tribes, but the Indians as a whole repudiated these surrenders as invalid. The land, they said, belonged to the Indian race collectively. Only a Pontiac was lacking to raise another general Indian war. And an Indian war could hardly fail to involve Britain.

The government of the United States, despairing of negotiation, decided to use force in the West. Americans had beaten the British

Empire. An Indian campaign should be a comparatively small affair.

In 1790 General Josiah Harmar and a small force marched into the western country to teach the Indians a lesson. The invaders were hurled back by a sudden assault. When General Arthur St. Clair advanced from Cincinnati the next year he was ambushed and most of his little army was destroyed in a minor repetition of Braddock's fatal mistake.

Encouraged by these victories, the Indians increased their territorial demands to include most of the present state of Ohio. The Iroquois under Brant attempted to arrange a settlement but failed at a great convention in Sandusky. The Americans blamed Britain for stirring up the tribes. That no doubt was true of the Canadian fur traders, but Britain wanted a settlement genuinely enough to avoid any chance of war with the United States, especially because it found itself, in January, 1793, at war with France.

War with the Americans was difficult to avoid once the British Navy began to seize American ships in the blockade of Europe. That parting in friendship, for which Britain had paid such a high price at Paris, had turned decidedly sour.

Dorchester suffered other troubles at Quebec, troubles deeply rooted in the split racial stuff of Canada. The French-Canadian *habitant* had yet to realize that the Revolution in his motherland was anticlerical and atheistic. In its first stages it promised the emancipation of the common man. And the Revolution, for all its distractions at home, found time and means, with American assistance, to incite the Quebec *habitant* against Britain and Britain's sorely tried old governor.

A weird character, Edmond Charles Genêt, arrived at Charleston in the spring of '93 as France's minister to the United States, aroused the slaveowning planters of the South to passionate defense of the Rights of Man (liberty caps designed in Paris becoming an overnight fashion), proceeded in triumph to Philadelphia, and explained that the French Revolution was the sequel and blood brother of the American. He then organized an underground among the French Canadians. They were guaranteed a new birth of freedom, the end of church tithes, abolition of seigneurial taxes or anything else they could desire if they would only join the Americans in driving the British out of Canada.

A proclamation from "The Free French to their Canadian Brothers" was furtively distributed and even read at the doors of country churches. The old ghosts of Wolfe's conquest walked again beside the St. Lawrence. As in 1775, Dorchester found the French

Canadians bitter, bewildered and wavering between stable British institutions and the boundless promises of the French and American Revolutions combined.

After their betrayal by monarchical France in '59, small wonder that the *habitants* wanted to be on the right side of a war between Britain and a republican France leagued with the Republican United States. "Nothing," Dorchester wrote home, "is too absurd for them to believe."

So once again he strengthened the defenses of Quebec, rushed through his assembly an Alien Act to suspend habeas corpus, and rounded up suspected French and American agents.

Vermont was the center of these intrigues. It conducted them with the skill of long experience.

Ethan Allen had tried to capture Canada singlehanded in '75, had failed in his later scheme to make Vermont a British province and had died, irreconcilable to the last.

His brother, Ira, now proposed to recoup Ethan's failure with another invasion of Canada and was in France collecting 20,000 muskets. They were to be used, he explained, in the harmless drill of the Vermont militia. Unfortunately for his plan, and fortunately for the peace of nations, a British man-of-war captured him and his muskets in a ship oddly named the *Olive Branch*, off Ostend. That was the end of the long adventure begun by Ethan at Ticonderoga.

In any case Washington was tired of the French conspiracy in America. He knew it might drive his struggling young nation into the war desired by the Jeffersonian hotheads and firmly opposed by the Hamiltonian Federalists. Genêt had gone too far by arming French privateers in American harbors and seizing English vessels. Washington quickly repudiated him. Damning the American President, the Congress and even Jefferson, Genêt retired to private life, but not to France, where his own government also was tired of him. He became an American citizen. Adet, his successor, pursued the intrigue more discreetly.

Dorchester, however, saw only that his peasantry were restive and that a new and well-trained American army was poised on the edge of the West, apparently ready to capture the forts along the Lakes. He had every reason for alarm.

After the disasters of Harmar and St. Clair among the western Indians, Washington at last had found a competent general in Wayne. To be sure, he was not exactly the sort of man Washington admired, being, in the President's opinion, "open to flattery, vain, easily imposed upon and liable to be drawn into scraps," and "whether sober or a little addicted to the bottle I know not." Anyway, he could fight, as he had proved in the Revolution by leading his troops over the walls of Stony Point. Washington had high hopes for Mad Anthony. "Time, reflection and good advice and, above all, a due sense of the importance of the trust which is committed to him, will correct his foibles or cast a shade over him." The President's opinion was soon to be justified.

The London government had an even higher opinion of Washington's new general. He was, according to the British ambassador to the United States, "The most active, vigilant and enterprising officer in the American services."

At Cincinnati, Wayne drilled, organized, and equipped his army, despite the irritations of fraudulent contractors and the customary conspiracies of his second-in-command, the unspeakable James Wilkinson, who had long been on Spain's payroll. The new American force was ready to invade the Indian country of the Ohio in 1793.

The weary and futile negotiations with the western tribes delayed him, but Wayne used his time well. An advanced post, hopefully called Fort Recovery to expunge the former American defeats, was built at Greenville, north of Cincinnati. There, in the autumn of '93, Wayne learned that the negotiations had finally failed. He decided to move northward in the first days of spring.

To Dorchester it appeared probable that Mad Anthony would never stop until he had captured the Canadian forts. Lieutenant Governor Simcoe, of Upper Canada, who was building a grubby little capital at Toronto, now renamed York, regarded himself almost as an independent sovereign and the chosen savior of all British America. He bristled with martial indignation, strategic plans, and undisguised impatience at Dorchester's delays.

These pressures—French intrigue, threats from Vermont, Simcoe's disobedience, Wayne's northward march, and an abiding distrust of Americans first learned at the siege of Quebec—cracked Carleton's nerves. He delivered his reckless speech to the Miamis, ordered Simcoe to occupy Fort Miami, an abandoned post on the Maumee, fifteen miles south of Lake Erie, and prepared to protect the approaches to Detroit against Wayne's expected advance.

Even Simcoe, certainly no peacemaker, was a little shocked. The possession of the Maumee fort, he wrote, "will be construed into hostility" by the Americans. But he hurried to Detroit and sent a small body of troops to the Maumee, directly in Wayne's path.

The Indians had twice defeated the Americans. Now they began to realize that Wayne was no Harmar or St. Clair. Little Turtle, war chief of the Miamis, warned his people that they now faced a soldier "who never sleeps, night and day are alike to him. Notwithstanding the watchfulness of our young men, we have never been able to surprise him."

An Indian attack on Fort Recovery failed. When Wayne marched north, Little Turtle rallied the wavering Miamis for a final defense of the ancestral hunting grounds. His braves were gathered for battle at Fallen Timbers, within musket sound of the little Canadian garrison on the Maumee.

On August 20 Major Campbell, the unhappy Canadian commander, heard the first shots of Wayne's attack. Forty minutes later the Americans' single bayonet charge had scattered the Indians. They fled toward the palisades of Fort Miami, but Campbell locked his gates and preserved his neutrality. Would Mad Anthony also remain neutral in the heady moment of his triumph?

He was by no means as mad as his reputation. While torn between his instructions to avoid a clash and the temptation to capture the fort and drive the Canadians from American soil he paused on the brink of war with Britain. Since Campbell had closed the fort to the United States' Indian enemies, there was no excuse for an American attack. Wayne had been cheated of his great chance.

He camped close to the fort for a week, overawing it from a convenient hill and burning the adjacent cornfields. If these gestures were designed to provoke Campbell, they failed. The coolheaded Canadian sent a messenger to Wayne to ask politely what his intentions might be. Wayne replied that Campbell was lucky not to be captured already, that the Canadians' presence was a hostile act against the American Republic, and that they had better go back to Canada while they had the chance. Campbell was unshaken. He said he would defend himself, according to his orders, and leave the great issues of international politics to the politicians.

For a few more days the two hostile powers of North America, the larger represented by a victorious army and the smaller by a helpless corporal's guard, held the prospects of war or peace in precarious balance around a ramshackle fort in the western wilderness. Then Wayne cooled off and retired, his mission accomplished.

Next year he negotiated the Treaty of Greenville, by which the whole Indian country was opened to settlement and its original owners doomed. The Battle of Fallen Timbers had brought the American Republic to the Mississippi. But Canada still held the chain of forts along the Great Lakes. The boundary fixed on paper at Paris had not been applied to the Canadian earth.

Happily, at this dangerous moment the American government had heard nothing of Campbell's advance to Fort Miami. That news might well have cast the die for war. Ignorant also of events at

Fallen Timbers, Washington's government persuaded the Senate to send Jay off to London in a final attempt at a peaceful settlement. He was to negotiate about everything—the disputed forts, the troubles at sea, and the future conduct of trade.

The news of Wayne's victory followed Jay across the Atlantic and then the news of the Indians' final surrender at Greenville. Without the Indians, Britain could hardly hope to hold the forts; it had no excuse for holding them, now that the Americans were paying their debts to the Loyalists, and to hold them probably meant war. The British government therefore ended more than ten years of controversy by promising to retire to the agreed boundary on June 1, 1796, at latest.

Even then the boundary was not fixed. For Canadian explorers had discovered, since the Paris conference, that the proposed line from the Lake of the Woods westward did not reach the Mississippi. Free navigation of the great river had been promised in the treaty of 1783 but the river's northernmost sources lay well south of the boundary. Thet diplomats of London, who had surrendered whole-sale at Paris, were not quite out of ideas. To let Canadians reach the navigable water of the Mississippi it was now proposed that the boundary be curved southward, below the Falls of St. Anthony.

This ingenious afterthought came too late. The United States refused to alter the Paris line by an inch. Britain had been offered the 45th Parallel and had refused it. The chance was lost forever. Canada must live as best it might under the Paris surrender.

Since the boundary could not run as intended from the Lake of the Woods to the Mississippi, the London conference agreed to conduct joint surveys with a view to final negotiations later.

Before that work could be completed, the affairs of the continent would be revolutionized again by the United States' purchase of Louisiana and the need of a new boundary all the way to the Pacific.

The principle of boundary arbitration—destined to play a great part in the future of the two American states—was introduced at the London conference by the establishment of a joint commission to survey the unmapped St. Croix River and fix the eastern boundary.

Canada gained in Jay's Treaty free access to the western fur trade—the issue evaded at Paris—but that freedom was to prove brief and increasingly fictitious.

Altogether Jay had won a momentous diplomatic victory, capping the earlier victory of Paris. Because he could get no concessions for American shipping in the European blockade or in the rich trade of the West Indies, his treaty was almost defeated in the Senate and for a time he became the most unpopular figure in his nation. The judgment of time would correct the Americans' first false impression.

As it turned out, however, the next war of North America had been merely postponed and the border exposed to another generation of struggle. The border remained, as always, in the hands of frontiersman. Reckless of war and peace, ignorant of government, knowing nothing but the wilderness and its profits, they were moving, in continental leapfrog, across the interior to the western sea.

Their course, though aimed at the Pacific, did not lie straight west, It swung by a vast arc from the Great Lakes northwestward to the edge of the arctic, then southwestward to hit the coast not far south of Alaska. The arc was never described in any neat or single line, was not planned in advance or, at first, even understood. It just happened as the fur traders pushed against the points of minimum resistance and maximum profit in any direction, or found some new peltry which dragged them farther on the long voyage begun in Champlain's canoes.

That voyage had continued for a century and a half, in war and peace, in pestilence and disaster, in profit and bankruptcy, by geographic calculation and blind chance. And always in pursuit of the irresistible old will-o'-the-wisp, a Northwest Passage.

13

Beyond the Shining Mountains

[1750–1793]

T HE ABSENCE OF A NORTHWEST PASSAGE FROM THE AMERICAN
map should have been proved long since to any sensible man
but, in the middle of the eighteenth century, it was expropri-
ated and revived by Englishmen of the Thirteen Colonies. That
dream of Champlain, Hudson, Drake, and the other early explorers
was too well established and compelling to be abandoned at the
command of mere facts.

Robert Rogers, the resourceful Ranger and the scourge of the
Canadian border in the Seven Years' War, went to Detroit at the
war's end to receive the French surrender of the western forts.
There this Easterner looked beyond the Great Lakes and conceived
his own vision of the farthest West with all the appetite, imagination, and egomania that would bring him to eminence and finally
to destruction.

He moved to the American South and came under the influence
of Arthur Dobbs, erratic British governor of North Carolina. Dobbs
had long lived, moved, and had his being in one fixed and fallacious
idea which nothing could shake—there was a Northwest Passage,
despite all evidence to the contrary, and it must be found.

Out of old Spanish records, misshapen maps, and forgotten diaries
Dobbs had constructed in his Irish imagination a passage running
from Hudson Bay to the Pacific. He had sent two expeditions to
the bay and when they proved once again that there was no
passage, he refused to believe their reports. The Hudson's Bay Company, he said, was suppressing the facts and intimidating honest
witnesses for its own purposes of commercial monopoly in the north.
At last, in his old age, he persuaded the Admiralty to offer a reward

of £20,000 for the discovery of the secret. The passage must be there because Dobbs and six generations of explorers had said so.

He easily convinced Rogers. After fighting briefly in Pontiac's war, the restless Ranger carried Dobbs's theories to London. There Rogers was briefly a man of fashion, author of a play called *Ponteach,* and the familiar of the great. Failing to secure help from the government or his rich friends, he accepted the post of governor at Mackinac and proposed to finance the final push to the Pacific out of his own pocket.

A new map of America had now emerged, the imagined composite of a hundred rumors, legends, Indian tales, and sheer invention. It was presented in numerous versions but all agreed on the general shape of the continent.

The continental spine and watershed ran north from Mexico, just west of the Mississippi, to a point south of Lake Winnipeg. Thus had the "shining mountains" of Vérendrye's day (probably the Turtle Hills of southern Manitoba) grown into a nonexistent range, drained on the east by the Mississippi's tributaries.

West of the central divide the land was flat to the Pacific, except for a small range along the seashore. Across the western plain and emptying into the western sea flowed an imaginary river called the Oregon, the Great River of the West, which had obsessed Champlain and all his successors. The Northwest Passage, north of the Oregon, began in Hudson Bay and ran southwestward, as a strait of varying width, depending on the mapmaker. The Oregon entered this strait on some maps. On others its mouth lay south of the strait's Pacific entrance.

The Northwest Passage, thus refined and definitely located, was only the old Strait of Anian, where the sirens had been singing since Drake's time.

Rogers had heard their song in distant North Carolina, as echoed by Dobbs, and he intended to travel westward, by what he called the "Ouragan" River, to hit the passage at its Pacific end. Unfortunately, as all his time was occupied at Mackinac, the job was turned over to James Tute and Jonathan Carver, former officers in Rogers's Rangers.

In 1766–67 Tute and Carver advanced to the western end of Lake Superior, far short of the French Canadians' westernmost penetration. The expedition was cut short by the ruin of its sponsor. Rogers had gone bankrupt and would soon be accused of treason. But Carver produced an important book on western travel and rightly assumed that the Pacific lay some two thousand miles west of the Lakes, not just over the prairie horizon.

Long before, the Americans of the Revolution, now the loyal English of Montreal, had learned to master the West, mainly because they had the good sense to use their experienced French-Canadian servants. The English conqueror had won title to the western fur. He could never reap the harvest without the *voyageurs*.

These unique wilderness creatures, in crews of eight to fourteen, could propel a canoe of thirty-five or forty feet, with a five-foot beam, to Grand Portage, carrying four tons of trade goods; lug this cargo in bales of ninety pounds—two bales per man—across the 10-day portage of nine miles; transfer them to the 25-foot craft of the smaller western waterways; paddle across the prairies in crews of five to eight; repair the ever-leaking birchbark with thread of juniper root and cement of pine gum every day; guide it through white water where the touch of a rock would puncture this paper-thin hide; and, after six months of ceaseless movement from dawn to dark at six miles an hour—sometimes a daily log of seventy miles —could bring back the furs safely to Montreal.

Not always safely. Countless *voyageurs*, few of them able to swim, were drowned along the first continental transportation system, with nothing left to mark their furious passage but the familiar wooden crosses beside the rapids.

Only the *voyageurs* knew the canoe, the wilderness, and the Indians by a century and a half of experience. Only they possessed the complex, far-flung, and brittle organization which could conduct the trade. Their peculiarities therefore—their aversion to cleanliness, their occasional debauches, their Indian concubines, their appalling superstitions and ridiculous ritual at every great portage, their unceasing chatter and paddle songs—must be endured. No one else could do their work and no Englishman would willingly attempt it for perhaps two hundred shillings per season and a diet of dried corn, buffalo grease, wild rice, frozen fish, and West Indies rum.

The intricate techniques of the fur trade, America's first large-scale industry, thus remained unchanged after the conquest of Canada, but both private management and state regulation had changed. In fact, regulation, as enforced by the French government, largely disappeared when the English traders of Montreal applied free enterprise to the West, with oceans of rum, price cutting, chiseling, violence, and finally massacre.

It was not a pretty business, it was frowned on by the sedentary Hudson's Bay Company, but in the hands of the Pedlars from Montreal it was making money, it was opening up the far West, every year it was moving closer to the Rockies, and, in defiance of politics and geography, in the most unlikely places and by the most unlikely methods, was building the future boundary of America.

By the seventies the English Pedlars and their Canadian *voyageurs* were following the footsteps of Vérendrye's sons up the two Saskatchewan Rivers and, like them, siphoning off the best furs before they could reach the bay, where the Gentlemen Adventurers of England still drowsed in their century-old slumber.

Even the Hudson's Bay Company awoke at last. It sent Samuel Hearne inland, to build posts and drum up Indian business. Ultimately that insatiable explorer, among the most daring of his breed, reached the Coppermine River, on the arctic shore, and there witnessed one of America's notable atrocities. Deaf to Hearne's protests and tears, his Indian guides butchered a village of sleeping Eskimos, a young girl dying at his feet and "twining around their spears like an eel." He had proved pretty conclusively, by reaching the arctic, that no Northwest Passage divided the continent.

For all its money and political power in London, the company could never keep up with the Pedlars because the Pedlars' business was carried by the incomparable *voyageurs*. The company's imported Orkneymen knew the sea but, in their newly invented York boats, rowed by clumsy oars, were no match for the Canadians' paddle and birchbark.

Soon the Pedlars broke out of the plains into the northern forests and lakes, until their round trip between Montreal and the trade posts took two full seasons. The drive to the Pacific surged with quickening fury across a flat prairie land of infinite weariness; of sluggish, labyrinthine rivers, of swamps, gullies, endless horizons, gaudy sunsets, and shattering dawns; of teeming buffalo, deer, grizzly bear and fish, of waterfowl darkening the sky; of searing heat, ferocious wind, and man-killing blizzard; of black flies, mosquitoes and daily torture on the portage; of Indians in filthy hide wigwams practicing barbarities, sexual rites, emasculations and murder by bullet, arrow, knife, bare hands or teeth, all minutely recorded in many a trader's diary but unprintable; of loneliness, pestilence, and sudden death; of Indian ghosts, demons, and the windigo wailing under the winter moon; of one reliable medicine, cure-all, political weapon, and legal coinage called rum.

-Yet civilization of a sort and a crude culture unlike any seen before in the world were sprouting like wild weeds from the prairie earth. They lived in uncounted little trade posts from the Great Lakes to the foothills of the Rockies, in educated Englishmen and Scots who might cohabit with squaws but would snowshoe a hundred miles to the nearest white neighbor for the chance of company, a year-old newspaper, or a tattered book. They lived most distinctly in a new race, bred of French Canadians and Indians and now appearing as the Métis. These buffalo hunters would contrive, in due time, two rebellions, their own brief republic, and extraordinary political consequences still unsettled in the twentieth century.

The Indian, his life revolutionized by the spread of the Spanish horse out of Mexico, the trader in his sod shanty, busy all summer with the trappers, laboring all winter to cut wood for next year's fires, finding occasional release from dead monotony in dances, shooting matches, drinking parties, and brutal fights, could not place themselves in continental space, in time, or in international politics. They lived—that was achievement enough. But, living, the white man and his *voyageurs* had carried their civilization, or some fragments of it, farther west than it had ever gone before, north of Mexico.

They had outflanked Louisiana and left the Americans half a continent behind. They had grasped all but the last contents of a sea-to-sea nation while their rivals were still poised on the east bank of the Mississippi. They had added to the two basic ingredients of the Canadian chemistry—the original French and the United Empire Loyalists—a third element, the prairie creature, forever distinguishable from his fellows. They had built a new world on fur, never suspecting that their neglected earth could grow wheat, that the rim of Pre-Cambrian rock around it contained even more precious treasure, or that beneath the prairies lay oil, civilization's future fuel. They had produced a special breed which might accomplish the final leap to the sea and hold what it found there for Canada.

Their business had become as costly as it was barbarous. They were busily cutting the throat of the Hudson's Bay Company and their own by excess of private enterprise. Even the superior furs of the far West, bringing extra prices in Europe, even the discovery of a cheap, convenient, and nonperishable diet called pemmican, of sun-dried and pulverized buffalo meat mixed with melted fat and often with wild berries, could not support the cost of hauling trade goods and furs across three-quarters of the continent when the individual trader continually raised his buying prices to the Indians and reduced his selling prices to the Montreal merchants. So the Pedlars began to experiment with combines.

The first successful combine was founded by Thomas and Joseph Frobisher, Alexander Henry, and Peter Pond, just before the American Revolution. Unaware of events at Philadelphia, these men from the Thirteen Colonies, who considered themselves still British, pooled their resources and struck beyond all their competitors, from the upper Saskatchewan to the Churchill, to Lake Isle-à-la-Crosse, Methye Portage, the Clearwater River, and into the Athabaska.

Pond reached this Ultima Thule in 1778 and found there more and better furs than he had ever imagined. Athabaska soon became the fur traders' paradise. Once the Pedlars had formed their final combine, the powerful North West Company, its partners of the Athabaska Department were established as an elite, with extra profits, a private base at Rainy Lake, Gargantuan summer revels, and then the hurried return to the northwest before the rivers froze. From Lake Athabaska they pushed on to Slave Lake, Great Slave Lake, and the Peace River. They had touched the halfway point on the north-south arc and the last barrier between known America and the Pacific.

Pond, a clever, pushing, uneducated, and unscrupulous Yankee, with a quenchless thirst for geography, now became, without knowing it, one of America's most important figures. Only the fur traders and Indians had heard of him, he was alone in his distant post, far outside the knowledge of statesmen who pretended to shape the continent's future, and he was slowly discovering its real shape.

Some wandering Indians told him of another great river, perhaps the Great River of legend, which fell out of a high mountain range into the western sea. Brooding on these stories and many others in his hut beside Lake Athabaska, Pond revised his maps, drew new ones of his own invention, came to believe in his wild guesses, and resolved to follow them to the unknown.

He was too old for that at fifty. Besides, he had lately incurred the displeasure of his more respectable partners by his alleged part in two killings. Just when his unequaled experience would have been most valuable he was compelled to leave the West. But he had with him at Lake Athabaska a young Scot, Alexander Mackenzie, whom he had long plied with his own geographical lore.

Though Mackenzie, a gentleman of education and social background, regarded his ignorant boss with contempt, he listened. When Pond retired, Mackenzie was ready to attempt the last bound to the Pacific—in the wrong direction.

Mackenzie had startling news to ponder at the last outpost of the moccasin telegraph. English sailors, said the long-delayed dispatches from London, had beaten the Canadian *voyageurs* to the coast and discovered the sea otter. Now that the value of a doomed creature was realized, an incidental contest for the Pacific coast of America had opened with five contenders—Spain, Russia, Britain, the newly-formed United States, and Canada. The great empires might regard the coast as no more than an extra dividend on their world-wide investments. It was essential to the United States and Canada. Without it they could not possess the continent, probably could not amass enough power to survive.

Spain long ago had solemnly declared the Pacific a "closed sea" from which all other nations were excluded. Since Drake had rioted up the west coast of South America in 1579, looting Spanish galleons until his *Golden Hind* was half sunk under its cargo of stolen treasure, Spain had been left undisturbed on its private lake.

In the seventies of the eighteenth century its energetic new king, Charles III, began to worry about the Northwest Passage—a splendid vision to others, to him a menace. If there was such a passage, what was to prevent enemy ships from using it to pass from the Atlantic to the Pacific, and then to descend upon the coast of California, upon Mexico itself, upon the silver mines of New Mexico?

King Charles was not needlessly disturbed. Spain had felt the presence of a strong and unexpected competitor in the Pacific.

Czar Peter of Russia, called the Great, had studied the methods of modern sea power as a carpenter in the shipyards of Holland, he had looked for additional territory only to find most of the known world already parceled out among the Western powers and he saw no chance of extending his own empire—already vast enough to satisfy anyone but a Russian—except on the Pacific.

As all the legends agreed, the undiscovered continent of Gamaland lay between Asia and America. It must become Russian. To claim it, Peter chose Vitus Bering, a competent Danish navigator, and ordered him across Siberia in 1725. Bering had barely started this prodigious journey when Peter died, a remorseful maniac screaming in his palace at the ghosts of his victims.

Bering struggled for three years overland to Kamchatka and built ships there. He soon proved that there was no Gamaland, found his strait into the arctic, and came home disgusted. The Russian government ordered him back again. Surely the Pacific must contain a Gamaland somewhere, or at least some real estate which the land-poor czars could use.

For the second time Bering marched across the 6,000 miles of Asia, with 4,000 pack horses, 600 companions, and the weirdest collection of botanists, artists, monks, physicians, soldiers, and assorted lunatics ever gathered in one company. This menagerie of freaks built two ships in Kamchatka, explored the Alaska coast, and added it to the Russian Empire. One ship returned safely. The other, commanded by Bering—now half crazed by the lunacies of the government's experts, dying of scurvy, and helpless in his bunk—was pounded to pieces on a reef. Some of the crew reached a nearby island, dug pits against the cold, and survived the winter. In one of those icy holes Bering died.

Next year a few survivors somehow reached the Russian coast by raft. Their nakedness was covered with the thickly furred hides of animals. Where had this superb fur come from? It had come from an animal about six feet long, with a catlike face and a short beaver's tail, which swarmed in myriads around the rocks and kelp beds of the Aleutian Islands, and was so stupid that any man could kill it with a club. The merchants of Russia and China would pay almost any price for this creature's pelt. It was ebony-black on the surface, gray close to the skin, and of incomparable richness. Such was the sea otter, the beaver of the Pacific and, like the beaver, it was fated to set the empires of the world in violent motion.

Russia plunged into the sea otter business, using vodka instead of rum to trade with the Aleutian natives; slaughtering them wholesale with their animals in one of history's most repulsive crimes; suffering massacre in return; extending its empire to America along the coast of Alaska; unconsciously adding a final complication to the struggle of the Canadian-American boundary; and assuring a Pacific struggle which would continue, with few interruptions, from the time of Peter the Great to that of Molotov, the Hammer.

With Russia in the north Pacific, where it had no right to be, Spain could afford to rest no longer in the sunny harbors of Mexico. Its navigators were ordered to follow the coastline northward wherever it might lead, find the Northwest Passage, and arrange to hold its Pacific entrance. That base should keep England out of the Spanish lake. It might keep the Russians harmless in the far north.

Juan Perez reached the Queen Charlotte Islands in 1773 and, turning back, anchored in a wooded inlet, soon to bear the name of Nootka Sound, seat of remarkable adventures a few years later. Bodega y Cuadra crossed the 58th Parallel in 1775 and claimed Alaska for Spain. Later the same year Bruno Heceta discovered the mouth of a river which later navigators would christen the Columbia. It was not quite the Great River of the old myth, but it was a great river nevertheless and pregnant with the future politics of America.

Spain could now claim, by right of discovery, the entire coast from Cape Horn to Alaska. To claim it was a very different thing from holding it. In London a British Admiralty had no intention of being excluded from the Spanish lake. The job of repealing the Spanish title was given to the ablest navigator of the age, one with few equals in any age.

James Cook was born in the year of Bering's first voyage, son of a Yorkshire farm hand. He was apprenticed to a haberdasher, went to sea in a merchant ship, joined the Royal Navy, and worked his way up by sheer merit against a frozen caste system. At thirty-one he sounded the St. Lawrence channel for Wolfe's fleet.

Attracting the navy's attention by his studies of mathematics and astronomy, he was assigned to explore the South Pacific and discover the great unknown continent supposed to exist there. Two voyages took him around the coasts of Australia and New Zealand, among many of the southern islands, and into the antarctic. He was now established as Britain's chief authority on the Pacific, but the rank of captain was considered sufficient reward for a man of humble birth.

The Admiralty became interested again in the Northwest Passage after the Russians had found the sea otter and the Spaniards had sailed almost to the arctic. The passage, if it existed, would offer Britain a short cut to its new possessions in India.

When Cook was asked who could best lead an expedition to the Pacific coast of America, he replied, with unquestionable truth, that he was himself the man. The Admiralty agreed and passed a special regulation permitting him, though a servant of the King, to win the standing reward of £20,000 if he found Drake's Strait of Anian.

Cook started from England for the Cape of Good Hope in the *Resolution* on July 12, 1776, without knowledge of a certain Declaration signed in Philadelphia eight days before, or any thought of his own effect on the future of the United States and Canada.

In his forty-ninth year he was an athletic figure with handsome, chiseled face, a scholar's learning, and an inquisitive mind. Already he had learned to prevent scurvy by forcing his crews to eat fresh vegetables, while the navigators of Spain were more damaged by this malady than by weather. He got on well with strange races, though in the end he would find a ghastly death among them. He had recorded his world-wide observations minutely and added a large installment to the world's store of information. In short, though born otherwise, he was the very perfect gentleman of the British Navy.

On March 7, 1778, still ignorant of affairs on the other side of the continent, Cook touched the coast of Oregon, Drake's New Albion, and nosed his way north, poking into many bays and inlets, but missing many others in Drake's "stinking fogges." He overlooked the

strait leading to Puget Sound, which was to prove the most important break in the whole coastline, the boundary of the two American
states. He wrote down, indeed, his firm opinion that there could not
possibly be any strait in this vicinity, despite an interesting bend in
the shore and the legends of that discredited old Greek pilot, Juan
de Fuca. The headland at this point, because it might fool a less
experienced seaman, was therefore christened Cape Flattery, monument to Cook's most notable mistake.

Believing that he was still off the mainland coast, Cook reached
Nootka, only to find that the Spanish had been there five years
ahead of him. A few roving Spaniards could not disturb a stolid
English captain with the whole power of his empire behind him.
He paused at Nootka to examine and record the queer customs of
the natives.

They were a noisy, evil-looking, clever breed, flat-faced and Ori-
ental, quite unlike the Indians he had known along the St. Lawrence. Hideous in carved wooden masks, colored hats of basket-
work, and robes of fur or plaited cedar bark, they paddled their
dugout canoes around Cook's ship, greeting him with loud incanta-
tions and gestures of friendship. What chiefly interested Cook and
his sailors were their fur robes, richer than any they had ever seen
before.

The sea otter now entered the commerce of England. For kettles,
buttons, candlesticks, rusty nails, or anything made of metal the
Nootka Indians eagerly disrobed and handed their greasy clothes
over to the ship's company. Cook's observant eye noted something
else—the Indians already possessed a few metal objects. Where had
they come from? He guessed, correctly, that they had traveled all
the way across Canada by the trade system of the Montreal Pedlars.

Soon there were too many Indians about and they began to look
hostile under their outer show of friendship. Cook headed up the
coast.

It was unlikely, as he well knew, that the passage would be found.
Hearne's trip to the Coppermine had proved at least that if there
was a channel it must lie far to the north and west. But if there was
even a strait between Asia and America, as Bering reported, it
would lead to the arctic and the arctic might be navigable.

Everything turned out as Cook must have expected. All the promising curves of the serrated coastline ended in mountain bluffs. The
large inlet to which he gave his name seemed to hold the mouth of
an important river—possibly the Great River—but nothing more.
He followed the shore of Alaska, found Bering's Strait and entered
it. Walls of ice turned him back. He decided to winter in the Sand-

wich Islands, where he had touched on his outward voyage, and to attempt the last push into the arctic next summer.

After visiting the Aleutian Islands and talking in sign language to some drunken Russian fur traders, he landed on Hawaii, his crew fell into debauch and quarrel with the natives, an outraged warrior's dagger was driven between his shoulder blades and his body chopped into small pieces. They were collected by his officers and buried in his natural home, the sea.

Among all its great sons in that age of greatness—the two Pitts, Wolfe, Clive, Wellington, Nelson—Britain had lost none greater than Cook. He had died obscenely on a remote island on the far side of the world, but not before he had opened the Pacific to his empire and—strangest result of all—had precipitated the ultimate contest of Canada and the United States for the western coast of America.

Cook's successor, Captain James Clerke, faithfully carried out his leader's plan by penetrating Bering's Strait in 1779. Again the British ship was obstructed by ice. There could be, then, no passage. The fable of nearly three centuries had finally been proved false. Clerke turned about reluctantly, sold his half-rotten sea otter skins from Nootka to the traders of the Chinese coast, for fabulous prices, and sailed home to England with the news of Cook's murder.

That news traveled fast and far. It was read by Mackenzie at Lake Athabaska, by the Spaniards of California, and nowhere more eagerly than in the United States.

The Americans now owned the fastest fleet in the world. They knew how to sail it, were at home on every ocean. The sea otter fitted their book perfectly. Furs from the Pacific coast could be sold for tea in China, where a large trade already was under way.

But much more than the profits of Yankee merchants was involved in Cook's discoveries. Britain was on the Pacific coast and might remain there. If it pushed a weak Spain out of the closed lake, British power would lie directly behind the Spanish power of Louisiana and athwart the United States' inevitable westward march. The Amercians must lose no time in joining the drive to the western sea.

On October 1, 1787, two American vessels, the *Columbia*, Captain John Kendrick, and the *Lady Washington*, Captain Robert Gray, sailed from Boston and stood off the Pacific coast in the following August. Their commanders observed signs of a great river, perhaps the Great River, but on landing were driven off by hostile Indians.

A few days later Gray's log noted a wide inlet and expressed the opinion "that the Straits of Juan de Fuca do exist; for the coast takes a great bend here." Cook had missed but Gray had seen the future continental boundary. It meant little to him at the moment, for he was in search of sea otter.

At Nootka he found that the English had beaten him to the center of trade. Captain James Meares and William Douglas had settled down comfortably in a palisaded fort, had even built a 30-ton schooner called the *North-West America,* the first ever built in these regions, and were about to launch it with cannon fire and appropriate libation.

The English captains entertained Gray royally but lied like gentlemen and patriots about the fur trade. There were no furs hereabouts, they said, and Gray might as well go on to China for a cargo of tea. Besides, Meares had bought Nootka and the surrounding territory from the Indians for two pistols and a hunk of copper. The English, under Captain William Barkley, had explored Juan de Fuca's Strait. As for the Great River, which Gray had suspected farther south, it was, said Meares, an illusion. The coast, as Gray was told politely but firmly, could offer little interest to the latecoming Americans.

Gray, the skeptical Yankee, was not to be fooled by smooth English manners. He would make his own inquiries. Kendrick, in the *Columbia,* now joined his partner and the two American ships remained all winter at Nootka. Trade in fur was struck up with the Indians, who quickly corrected the Englishmen's depressing story. In the spring, after examining Juan de Fuca's Strait for themselves, the Americans prepared to sail for China with a valuable cargo of sea otter.

At that precise moment Spain made its last grand gesture in the closed lake. While the English and American captains gaped, incredulous, Don Joseph Martinez sailed into Nootka on a mighty ship, twenty cannons pointed straight at the fort of the interlopers. The Americans were allowed to depart in peace, being Britain's supposed enemies, with Martinez's compliments and gifts of Spanish wine. The English were ejected from Nootka in an international incident of dangerous possibilities. Their fort was torn down and replaced by a new one on Hog Island nearby. To make sure that Britain behaved herself in future, Martinez held one of the English ships as security—a final outrage which British pride could not endure.

Spain and Britain seemed to be on the verge of war as Gray's *Columbia* returned triumphantly to Boston from a voyage of 50,000 miles. She was back in the Pacific by the summer of '91 and was joined again by the *Lady Washington.* Things obviously being too hot at Nootka, between Britain and Spain, Gray and Kendrick wisely avoided the trouble spot. They coasted as far north as the Portland Canal; then, turning back, built a post called Fort Defence and a schooner, the *Adventure,* at Clayoquot Sound, safely south of the quarreling powers.

So far Spain claimed everything in sight. Its navigators, despite scurvy, leaky ships, and official negligence, were penetrating the treacherous inlets of Vancouver Island (yet to be so named), were looking into Juan de Fuca's Strait and talked of another great river apparently flowing into these waters. As they arrived one by one, the British trading ships *Argonaut, Iphigenia,* and *Princess Royal* were seized by the Spaniards at Nootka. Spain was taking no nonsense from its rival.

Gray and Kendrick had troubles of their own. At Clayoquot they suddenly discovered that their tiny fort was surrounded by 2,000 warlike Indians, who may have been encouraged by the Spaniards. The Americans' plight was grave. The *Columbia* lay dismantled on the beach. The fort could not be defended.

Gray decided to escape in the night. His sailors waded neck-deep in the rising tide to launch the *Columbia* and clean her hull of barnacles. In the morning she was floated just as an Indian chief came aboard with offers of sea otter skins. Gray slapped his face and sailed south. Nothing could daunt the Yankee skipper. He was determined to find Bruno Heceta's Great River.

The *Columbia* now moved toward this target, sighted by Gray on his previous voyage, and off the Oregon coast encountered two British ships, the *Discovery* and the *Chatham.* They were commanded by Captain George Vancouver, one of Cook's former midshipmen and now a staid man with a long, horsy face and a strong belief in his own talents. He had come to accept the ceremonial surrender of Nootka from a Spanish government unwilling to risk a war with Britain.

Vancouver sent one of his officers, Lieutenant Puget, aboard the *Columbia.* Gray said candidly that he had seen the indications of a river hereabouts, but Vancouver doubted the report. It was the same old story, first told by the Spaniards. Captain Meares had checked it and concluded that "we can now with safety assert that no such river . . . exists as laid down in the Spanish charts." The word of Meares, an English gentlemen, was good enough for Vancouver.

In any case Vancouver had studied the shore for himself, had seen the evidence of a few minor streams falling into an inlet, and

had considered "this opening not worthy of more attention." So he
sailed north and left the hopeful Yankee to pursue his illusion.

Gray was delayed by a brief shooting scrape with some Indians
in a bay thenceforth known as Gray's Harbor, but soon sighted the
breakers of a huge river bar. This, though he could not guess it, was
a decisive moment in American history. Before him lay a mighty
river, perhaps the river of the old continental dream. Could he
reach it across its turbulent bar? He decided to take the chance. On
May 12, 1792, he drove through the breakers and entered fresh
water. The Columbia had been discovered and claimed for the
United States.

Between it and the distant Republic lay no one knew what, west
of the known barrier of Louisiana. But the American government
had a claim to both coasts and, if the Republic could endure, would
surely join them one way or another. The future anatomy of the
nation had appeared. It would not be fleshed without years of
diplomacy and war with Canada.

Having missed the first great river of the coast, Vancouver proceeded northward to miss the second. He poked into Juan de Fuca's
Strait, explored Puget Sound, and turned into the Strait of Georgia,
where the Fraser enters the sea with a vast gout of brown water,
visible for miles. A Spaniard named Narvaez, in a leaky schooner,
with a crew of thirty starving Mexican peons, is said to have located
the Fraser's mouth a few months earlier. Vancouver passed it, unnoticed, in another of Drake's stinking fogs.

Farther north he met two Spanish ships, whose commanders told
him that Don Bodega y Cuadra awaited him at Nootka for the surrender of Spain's possessions there. The British ship completed the
circumnavigation of the island which bears Vancouver's name and
arrived in Nootka at the end of summer.

Spain's surrender of the north Pacific coast was carried out with
Latin glamour. Cuadra's guns thundered a welcome to Vancouver.
The British officers were entertained at breakfast and in return
gave an elaborate dinner to the Spaniards. The fumes of celebration
had no sooner cleared than Cuadra explained that he was sur-
rendering only his fort. Vancouver claimed the whole contiguous
countryside. The two rivals, bearing the load of empire lightly,
agreed to disagree. Both left Nootka, Cuadra for California, Vancouver for the unlikely river mentioned by the deluded Yankee,
Gray.

The river was there, all right. Vancouver saw it for himself and
had little difficulty in concluding that white men had never seen it
before. "No other civilized nation or state," he wrote, "had ever

entered this river . . . it does not appear that Mr. Gray either saw or was ever within five leagues of the entrance." Therefore, the Columbia region belonged to Britain, its discoverer. As usual, the British underestimated the Yankees. For which, not long hence, the price would be paid by Canada, as usual.

While Spain thus claimed everything south of the Columbia, Russia the far north, Britain and the United States the intervening coast, Canada was about to cut its own way to the Pacific, the most improbable and dangerous way of all.

At his desolate post in the Athabaska country young Alexander Mackenzie dreamed Pond's dream of an overland dash to the sea. His dreams, as he wrote home to Scotland, sometimes terrified him. A Scot from the Hebrides, he wore a cold, deceptive surface. His face was stolid and strikingly handsome, his hair curly, his cheeks bristling with sideburns, his chin deeply cleft. Only his piercing eyes revealed an inner Scottish fire.

Someone, sometime, must paddle or walk across the continent. Now that Pond was gone, Mackenzie resolved to be that man.

His motives were ostensibly commercial. The North West Company was stretched too thin from Montreal to the edge of the Rockies, it had beaten all its competitors westward but under its high costs of transportation it was going broke. It must reach the far western fur country by a short cut to the Pacific and, incidentally, take its share of the sea otter.

These economic calculations could not explain the quiet passion of the young Scot. Driven by his private demon, he must be the vessel chosen by fortune to carry the white man's burden to the sea.

Pond's instructions, before his departure from Athabaska, were beautifully clear. Mackenzie was to follow a river emptying out of Great Slave Lake. It would lead him to the Pacific coast after curving around the northernmost flank of the Rockies. It was, in fact, the Great River of the myth. On reaching the coast, Mackenzie, by means of his own devising—for this was no concern of Pond's—was to cross the ocean and walk through Russia to England.

The assignment was even more insane than most in those days of splendid geographical lunacy, but Mackenzie's demon compelled him to follow it.

On June 3, 1789, when he was twenty-five years old, he started down Pond's Great River. His canoe carried, besides himself, five French-Canadian *voyageurs*, an Indian, and two squaws. A second canoe was loaded with supplies and manned by Indians. This unpromising expedition descended the Slave River out of Lake Athabaska to Great Slave Lake and there was swept by a mighty current upon the boundless realm of Pond's fantasy.

The unknown river, on which no white man had floated before, took an encouraging westward twist and then seemed to flow straight north. This was disturbing to Mackenzie, but doubtless the current would turn west in good time as Pond had promised. Day after day Mackenzie watched its course with increasing alarm. Always it lay northward. Now he noted to his horror a range of high mountains on his left. Was there a gap in them? He must find out soon, for the northern summer would be brief.

He pushed on furiously. His crew saw for the first time the vehement flame burning within the young Scot. The *voyageurs* strained at their paddles to complete this mad journey and escape the terrifying loneliness of the barrens.

No gap appeared in the mountains. Ahead lay only endless desolation.

On June 12 the canoes burst into the Arctic Ocean. Mackenzie had traversed the river now bearing his own name. It was another of America's great rivers, by any reckoning, but not the Great River, not the route to the Pacific. He named it Disappointment and, after three days spent in observing the arctic tides, turned back, tantalized, baffled, and heartbroken.

On his way south he met Indians who informed him that just west of the mountains a river ran to the sea, only a short distance away, that along this river lived giants with wings, and that its mouth was occupied by white men in a large fort.

Mackenzie's dream soared again. It would take him some time to explore the real western river. Meanwhile he reported the Disappointment to his partners of the North West Company. They were not impressed by Mackenzie's worthless northern detour, ending nowhere. Their only interest lay in fur and a short cut to the Pacific.

He was embittered but more determined than ever. Neither the company nor the Rockies could stop him.

Thinking these things over in his Athabaska post, he realized his deficiencies as an explorer. What he needed, after his first mistakes, was more education and some accurate instruments. With Scottish thoroughness this painstaking young man paddled all the way to Montreal, sailed for England, and spent a winter studying astronomy and navigation.

London hardly noticed the youngster who had added a giant to the world's river system and carried Britain's flag to the arctic. Everybody was talking of Cook's murder, Vancouver's new expedition to the Pacific, and the chances of war with Spain. Mackenzie cared little for this neglect. His demon was still beside him.

The spring of 1792 found him back at his post and ready for the last adventure. He planned carefully, as always. Since the leap across the Rockies might be too long for one year, he paddled out of Lake Athabaska in October and up the Peace River to its junction with the Smoky. There he wintered.

Seven o'clock in the evening of Thursday, May 9, 1793, was a notable hour in the record of North America and, like most notable hours, overlooked until long afterwards.

A canoe "twenty-five feet long within, exclusive of the curves of stem and stern, twenty-six inches hold, and four feet, nine inches beam, at the same time . . . so light that two men might carry her on a good road three or four miles without resting" (so reads Mackenzie's meticulous record) glided into the current of the Peace. The watchers on shore "shed tears on the reflection of those dangers which we might encounter." Mackenzie, Alexander McKay as his lieutenant, two veterans of the arctic voyage, four *voyageurs,* two Indian hunters, and a dog faded into the sunset. The single canoe was aimed westward at the Rockies and the Pacific. Its commander had passed his point of no return.

The ten men and their dog soon entered the outer defiles of the mountains and the demented waters of Peace River Canyon. Mackenzie leaped ashore, a rope fastened to his shoulders. He tried to haul the canoe through this caldron but the rope broke, the canoe danced into the rapids and for a moment everything seemed lost. Then a freakish current carried the light craft to the shore, where the *voyageurs* pulled it out upon the rocks.

These experienced men had seen no water like the Peace. They would go no farther. A "regale" of rum made them think better of it. The canoe was carried over a nine-mile portage at a speed of some two miles a day. Calmer water above led through a dark jungle of spruce and jackpine to the wide junction of the Finlay and the Parsnip. Here some Indians told Mackenzie of a western river flowing to the "stinking waters," and to white men who wore armor "from head to heel" and sailed in "huge canoes with sails like the clouds."

Where lay that river? Should Mackenzie turn north on the Finlay or south on the Parsnip? It was a terrible decision for the young Scot. By lucky guess he turned south, ascended the Parsnip, reached a rise at its headwaters and, after a portage of only 817 paces, crossed from the arctic to the Pacific watershed, embarking on the Bad River.

The canoe was immediately swamped in fierce rapids but, before it could sink, was tossed upon a sand bar. Seeing their canoe broken and all the supplies and ammunition soaked, the *voyageurs* said they would go no farther. Mackenzie did not argue with them. Alone he began to repair the canoe with resin and oilcloth. His determination impressed his followers. They agreed to take one more chance.

On June 17 they were carried into a current so wide that Mackenzie took it for the river of his dream. Later it would be called the Fraser, after another Scot. Nameless now, unknown and appalling in its sheer canyons of clay, it bore north, turned south, and never seemed to turn west. Was it to be Mackenzie's second Disappointment? Where did it reach the Pacific? Perhaps not north of Spanish Mexico? He was bewildered, all his newly acquired knowledge of navigation turned upside down.

The Carriers, a ferocious tribe whose widows carried their husbands' cremated ashes on their bodies, at first attacked the white men with arrows; later, seeing the glitter of trinkets spread invitingly on the riverbank, they gathered to parley. Their chief drew a map in the sand. By this rough diagram the river seemed to move forever southward, beyond the Indians' experience, and as they indicated with alarming gurgles in their throats, plunged through an impassable canyon they knew not where. However, they said in sign language, there was an easy trail straight west to the sea.

Again a moment of terrible decision for Mackenzie. To follow the river or abandon it and strike overland on the word of a few garrulous natives? As before, Mackenzie's guess was lucky.

He called his crew together and "after passing a warm eulogium on their fortitude, patience and perseverance, I stated the difficulties that threatened our continuing to navigate the river. . . . I then proceeded for the foregoing reasons to propose a shorter route, by trying the overland road to the sea. . . . I declared my resolution not to attempt it unless they would engage, if we could not after all proceed overland, to return with me, and continue our voyage to the discharge of the waters, whatever the distance might be. At all events, I declared in the most solemn manner that I would not abandon my design of reaching the sea, if I made the attempt alone, and that I did not despair of returning in safety to my friends."

If necessary, he would march to the Pacific accompanied only by his demon. North American exploration had produced few equals of that scene on the Fraser's bank—the alternative perils of river or wilderness, the doubtful crew, the young Scot of quiet fury who would reach the sea or perish.

The *voyageurs* discussed their commander's ultimatum around their campfire. Reluctantly they agreed to follow him.

A Carrier guided the company westward up the Blackwater to the last portage of the continent. Now they struggled through a thick coastal forest, soaked with rain, hungry, and hardly able to walk in their weakness. The guide attempted to desert and Mackenzie had to sleep beside this verminous creature, stinking of fish oil.

Still, after two weeks' march, there was no sign of the sea. In the middle of July the exhausted travelers beheld the Dean River, forded it and reached the Bella Coola. Here they found Indians with white men's goods. The sea could be only a few miles distant.

Mackenzie hired dugout canoes from the Indians and, with his companions, paddled down the river. Suddenly they smelled the welcome flavor of salt water. They entered it in North Bentinck Arm, pushed westward into Burke Channel, and on July 22 looked out upon the glittering waters of the Pacific.

Mackenzie mixed Indian red ocher and bear's grease to make a crude paint. With his own hand he wrote his testimony in neat letters across a slab of sea rock: "Alexander Mackenzie, from Canada, by land, the twenty-second day of July, one thousand seven hundred and ninety-three. Lat. 52° 20' 48" N."

That was all. No flourishes. No postures. Only the cold fact. But what a fact! The first white man had paddled and walked across the whole bulk of the continent. Canada had reached the Pacific. And though Mackenzie retraced his steps, almost losing his life in an Indian ambush, and retired to his native Scotland, his lifework done, though his words upon the sea rocks were soon expunged by wind and weather, Canada was on the Pacific to stay. If a Canadian nation could be built, it would be transcontinental. It would share America, east and west, with the United States.

14

Race to the Sea

[1793–1808]

WHILE MACKENZIE LIVED THE LEISURELY BUT SHORT LIFE OF A Scottish gentleman, nothing could repress the forces unloosed by his western adventure. The resulting race across America engaged a new generation of adventurers, among them two daring young Americans, a heroic Indian squaw and her suckling infant, a Canadian of homely face and dumb, plodding courage, a philosopher, inventor, and statesman from Virginia, an emperor from Corsica, a French prince accounted the most devious intellect of the age, and a host of nameless men whose canoes and moccasins must now fix the final boundary of a continent and split its riches.

A moment of continental decision, for which all the past had been only a prelude, was now approaching. The race moved with sudden momentum by two separate courses—from the Mississippi to the mouth of the Columbia, where no white man had walked before; and from Montreal to the Pacific, in Mackenzie's footsteps and by an unsuspected new river.

It was a race between an American republic, constitutionally whole but geographically scarce half made up, and a loose congeries of British colonies known as Canada but a lifetime distant from nationhood. A blind, groping, and bungled race for the most part, neither competitor knowing the presence of the other, yet always sure of its objectives, the highest stakes in the world. Such a race could not long move in peace. Soon it must quicken into war, a war designed to extinguish the northern competitor forever.

In British and Canadian eyes the river discovered by Mackenzie formed the natural boundary between Canada and the United States. It was the same river, no doubt, which Vancouver had sighted, which Gray, on Vancouver's testimony, had only pretended to enter. It was, of course, the Columbia. By a tragic mistake—so thought the North West Company partners in Montreal and the government in London—Mackenzie had failed to descend the Columbia to the sea and thus to anchor the boundary before the Americans could infringe it.

Fortunately the Americans seemed locked behind the Mississippi by Spanish Louisiana. Canada could take its time in completing the job begun by Mackenzie's mismanaged expedition. The British and Canadians had not reckoned on Napoleon Bonaparte and Thomas Jefferson.

Having rescued the French Revolution from the democrats and amateurs, Napoleon had turned his attention to America. American democrats and amateurs were as repulsive to him as the French variety, but they possessed real estate of value. Besides, France and the United States had been getting on badly for some time now.

During the first stages of the wars between France and Britain it was Britain which had mainly angered the Americans by seizing neutral ships in the blockade of Europe. Jay's Treaty had eased these tensions and, therefore, angered France. From 1798 onward France was the chief violator of neutral rights on the Atlantic. If the United States must fight someone to keep its commerce afloat, France seemed to be the obvious enemy. The two nations already lived in a state of undeclared war.

Jefferson, the great theorist of government, confronted some hard facts of a highly practical nature on taking office in 1801. The United States' overseas commerce was being despoiled in the quarrels of Europe. The Canadians clung stubbornly to the bulk of the western fur trade—were, indeed, the only white men who seemed able to penetrate the peltry. The Spaniards still held the line of Louisiana, sat astride the Mississippi and thus, from New Orleans, controlled the water route to the American interior. And now, without warning, came the news that Spain had ceded Louisiana to France, the present aggressor of the Old World, the potential aggressor of the New.

Jefferson instantly understood the meaning of that news. "The day that France takes possession of New Orleans," he cried, "fixes the date which is to restrain the United States forever within her low-water mark. . . . From that moment we must marry ourselves to the British fleet and nation."

It would take the United States more than a century to contract an uneasy marriage by gradual and secret stages. Meanwhile Napoleon's ambitions were not confined to New Orleans or the Mississippi. He, too, had glimpsed the dream of America and a new French empire to replace that lost to Wolfe at Quebec. The heir to the French Revolution must revive and extend the project begun by La Salle and abandoned by the blundering French kings. France was back on its old lifeline between the Gulf of Mexico and the St. Lawrence. As Jefferson well knew, it might become the deathline of the United States.

Napoleon approached America by way of Haiti, where France's Negro slaves had rebelled. The crack French Army sent out to subdue them would be available shortly for more promising work in Louisiana. Napoleon's genius and his seasoned troops—10,000 of them, twice as many as all the forces of the United States and Canada combined—might carry the American empire of France westward from the Mississippi, or northward to Canada, or eastward against Jefferson's Republic. No one could tell where the ubiquitous tyrant of Europe would stop.

The United States had reached the first international crisis of its brief national life. This, then, was no time for theories, constitutional niceties, or any hobgoblins of consistency. Jefferson, the theorist and constitutionalist, prepared, if necessary, to stretch the American Constitution out of joint by purchasing New Orleans, and possibly the Floridas, from their new owners without the approval of the Congress.

Robert R. Livingston, the American ambassador to Paris, was a man of large ideas. Going far beyond Jefferson's instructions, he inquired blandly of Prince Talleyrand, the French foreign minister, if Louisiana, at least north of the Arkansas River, was for sale. Talleyrand, whose poker face deceived everyone, sometimes even himself, was not ready to answer. At this point Jefferson's friend, James Monroe, arrived in Paris with the President's secret assurance that "Something sensible has become necessary . . . on the event of this mission depend the destinies of the Republic."

The Republic now encountered an unbelievable break of luck, not the first nor the last. Monroe had reached Paris at precisely the right moment. At any other his mission might well have failed and the destinies of the Republic thereby been compressed within the southeastern quarter of America.

He found Napoleon distracted by the war with Britain and disgusted by the news from America. His dream of a new dominion in Louisiana had turned to nightmare in the swamps of Haiti. His armies were destroyed by weather, disease, and hordes of furious Negro slaves. He was damning "sugar, coffee and colonies." He had written off the New World. And, brooding in his bathtub, he decided to sell France's Mississippi empire.

Ushered into the presence of Talleyrand, that indestructible cynic who would survive the ruin of his master and nation, Monroe was amazed by what he found. He had proposed the purchase of New Orleans and, if possible, the Floridas. Talleyrand now asked what the United States would pay for the whole of Louisiana. Then, in perhaps the outstanding understatement of his career, he suggested that this territory might be worth $60,000,000.

Talleyrand was dealing with seasoned American horse traders from away back. As horse traders they at once called the price ridiculously high and the empire unattractive. When they left in April, 1803, they had beaten the toughest horse trader of Europe down to $15,000,000. With incidental interest charges, the price came to $27,267,622, or about four cents per acre.

The Republic now owned—except for the Floridas, to be acquired shortly—everything from the Atlantic coast to the Pacific, north of the ill-defined Mexican boundary and as far north in Canada as it could exert its power. Events would soon show that it intended, later on, to possess Canada entire.

Jefferson's speculation in real estate alarmed Spain more than Canada. The Spanish government protested that it had given Louisiana to France in the first place to "interpose a strong dyke" between Spanish Mexico and the United States. Now Napoleon had broken his pledge by alienating the Mississippi colony. The door to the whole West was open to the insatiable Americans. Spain was quite right. Jefferson's purpose had been to open that door.

The proposed marriage to the British fleet and nation was indefinitely postponed, though never quite abandoned. Napoleon for his part was satisfied that the United States, secured on its west flank, would soon fight Britain and Canada. Anyway, a republic would fall apart sooner or later.

These questions could wait. For the present Jefferson, the constitutionalist, was explaining, with little difficulty, his rather loose interpretation of the presidential power. If he had stretched or broken the Constitution by the Louisiana Purchase, he had completed a bargain without parallel. He had bought something like a quarter of a continent for a song. But no one knew quite what he had bought.

Jefferson had formed his own shrewd ideas after reading Mackenzie's alarming book, published in 1801. Mackenzie insisted that the Canadian-American boundary should be pushed south to the 45th Parallel, at least in the far West, to embrace the Columbia. This, said Jefferson, would never do. He had constructed on paper an entirely new division of the continent.

It was now known that the Northwest Angle of the Lake of the

Woods did not lie on the 49th Parallel, as the 1783 settlement supposed. It lay some distance to the north. No matter—Jefferson was
determined that the boundary must start at the angle, continue to
the 49th Parallel, and then westward by that line to his newly purchased Louisiana. He did not know the extent of those lands. No
one did. To make sure they extended far enough north, he construed
their sweep as including the whole drainage basin of the Missouri
River, wherever it lay, and even if it lay north of 49°. Thus in his
mind the unfixed border between the United States and Canada
would not necessarily follow any straight line of latitude but
would curve northward as required to protect the Republic's vital
interests. As a minimum he intended to hold the lower reaches of
the Columbia. This was, after all, Gray's river, not Vancouver's or
Mackenzie's.

Jefferson's ambitions actually soared far beyond the 49th Parallel
and the Columbia. "However our present interests may restrain us
within our own limits," he wrote, "it is impossible not to look forward to distant times when our rapid multiplication will expand
itself beyond those limits & cover the whole northern if not the
southern continent with a people speaking the same language governed in similar forms & similar laws."

It was not certain what he meant exactly, for at times he projected several American republics, but at all events he meant the
end of Canada as a British nation. He had learned many things,
from music to Inalienable Rights. He had not learned the nature
of Canada.

He preferred to keep his intentions obscure, perhaps because
they were not clear even to him. "It may be as well to leave the
boundary of 49° indefinite, as was done on the former occasion."
So it was left for nearly half a century, in which time Jefferson's
theories were to be drastically overhauled by the uncooperative
Canadians and by war.

The first step after the Louisiana Purchase was obviously the exploration of the new American territory and the acquisition of the
Columbia.

The Spaniards knew remarkably little about the land they had
secured from a French king and given back to an upstart emperor.
How did Spanish California, for example, fit into it? Had Spain
any claim to the Columbia's mouth? What about the confused
status of Vancouver's Island after the absurd Nootka affair?

Spanish expeditions westward from the Mississippi had produced
only disordered maps and strange rumors—including Indians descended from Welsh ancestors. That old legend, lately revived, had

deeply stirred the people of Wales and sent a young Welshman, John Evans, hurrying to the Mandan country. There he raised the Spanish flag and preached Christianity to the local Indians. The ill-starred prophet found no Welshmen and failed to reach the Pacific by ascending the Missouri, but he painted an exciting picture of the West which Jefferson now proposed to examine in detail.

The President launched the transcontinental race in a secret message to the Congress, dated January 18, 1803, and asking money for a thorough exploration of the new American West. The Congress agreed. Jefferson chose for this task his close friend and assistant, Meriwether Lewis, and William Clark, brother of the famous Ranger, George Rogers. It proved a perfect choice.

Lewis, then twenty-nine years old, had made himself an expert soldier, bushman, and administrator. He was a lonely and moody character of powerful but tortured mind. His life would be short and closed mysteriously five years hence by suicide or murder.

Clark aged thirty-three, complemented his partner with a happy, gregarious disposition, the simplicity of the born frontiersman, an intuitive sense of geography, and a way with the Indians, who called him the Redheaded Chief. He was accompanied by his faithful Negro slave, York.

The two youthful explorers, among the ablest and certainly the most systematic ever seen in America, "hoisted Sail and Set out in high Spirits" up the Missouri on May 14, 1804, confident that the river would lead them, with an easy overland portage, to the Pacific. The United States had always lagged far behind French and British Canada throughout the West but the Lewis and Clark Expedition was making up for lost time.

Mackenzie, nine men, and a dog had crossed the continent in a canoe and on foot by a series of wild guesses. The American party—forty-five men and Clark's shaggy Newfoundland pup—traveled in a large keelboat, armed with swivel guns, and two pirogues. Slowly, efficiently, and irresistibly it sailed, rowed, and dragged its boats through the shifting channel of the Missouri; met and overawed the terrible Sioux, who had long barred the river; noted tributary rivers from the north that must provide connection with the "Suskashawan" or "Athebaskay" and hence a ready road into Canada; informed the tribes along the way that Jefferson was now their father; and reached the Mandan country in the autumn.

Here a lively winter was spent in Indian politics, hunting, feasting, dancing, and the preparation of reports to the President. When a Frenchman named Toussaint Charbonneau, long a familiar of the Indians, volunteered to act as interpreter, he was promptly hired. He brought with him his Indian wife, Sacajawea, who was probably seventeen years old and carried at her breast an infant, Baptiste, aged two months. She soon proved herself one of the most remarkable women in American history. A daughter of the Snakes, she had been born west of the mountains and abducted in childhood by some wandering raiders from the prairies.

The American cottonwood fort among the Mandans was visited that winter by many strange tribes. They were urged to make peace among themselves and establish that kind of stable, all-American fur trade route now managed by the Nor' Westers in Canada. A few of these Canadians also appeared and were treated kindly, though they had trespassed and traded on American territory. It was explained to them that Louisiana extended to the Qu'Appelle River, a tributary of the Assiniboine, well beyond 49°, for Lewis had decided, by a mistaken calculation, that the legal boundary of Canada ran north of the junction of the Red and Assiniboine, where Winnipeg now stands.

Lewis and Clark intended to drive the trespassers northward by American competition. The United States inevitably must possess the desirable parts of Canada at the proper time. The Americans constantly sought from the Indians news of the Missouri tributaries which would carry Manifest Destiny into the rich northern peltries and outflank the Canadian traders.

In the spring, as a boatload of dispatches, botanical specimens, furs, and the bones of animals started eastward for Jefferson's information, the expedition headed west beyond the bounds of white man's knowledge, still bewildered by a jigsaw puzzle of contradictory Indian maps, still ignorant of that final barrier, the Rockies, and still hoping to hit a westward-flowing river, probably Mackenzie's, to take them comfortably to the Pacific.

The keelboat had been abandoned as too large for the upper Missouri. Thirty-three persons, including Sacajawea's baby, filled the two pirogues and six awkward cottonwood dugouts. Though they often waded the cold spring water, the Americans' journey so far was much simpler than Mackenzie's had been in the raging canyons and trackless forests of the northwest. Unlike Mackenzie, they were never short of food in a land of teeming game. Sacajawea quickly showed herself as strong as any of the men and more useful than most of them. She tanned buckskin for clothes and moccasins, dug up edible roots, cooked the food, nursed her child, and unable to speak a word to anyone but her husband, dreamed of her home beyond the mountains.

What of those mountains? Were they Indian rumor only? Did

they stand beside the sea? Were they low and easy of passage like the familiar Alleghenies?

On a radiant June day Lewis and Clark looked across the plains to behold a line of glittering peaks and to realize, with a start, that all the white man's assumptions about western America were false. They saw but had yet to measure the dimensions of the continental divide.

The expedition pushed on toward the barricade. It seemed to rise higher, in unbelievable elevation, as they approached. Soon, like Mackenzie at the junction of the Finlay and the Parsnip, Lewis and Clark faced a fork in the Missouri and a moment of irrevocable decision. Should they follow the muddy north or the clear south branch? If they chose wrongly they could not hope to reach the ocean that year. With supplies already running short, they might be forced to retreat, their work half done.

Clark moved up the south fork and Lewis the north to reconnoiter. They chose the south because, in its cleanliness, it seemed to flow out of the mountains. Lewis remained fascinated by the notion that the north fork rose above the 49th Parallel in Canada and might lead to the northern trapping grounds. His penetrating prophecy noted that fur must become "an object of contention between the great powers of America with *rispect* to the adjustment of the North-westwardly boundary of the former." A satisfactory fur route, with rivers in the right place, would sever the body of any transcontinental Canadian state.

All their seasoned followers opposed the decision to ascend the difficult south fork, but the guess of Lewis and Clark, like Mackenzie's, was right. A little farther on, however, they heard the distant murmur of the Missouri's falls, boiling in five separate drops out of the Rockies, and knew they must surmount an almost impossible obstruction. They left their boats behind, built crude wagons, and dragged their canoes around the steaming falls by an 18-mile portage.

That work took them a full month, in an agony of heat, mosquitoes, piercing cactus, and mud. Ahead loomed the daunting line of the mountains, growing in height and bulk at every step. Beyond them, what? Lewis and Clark knew only that there could be no return to the East that year. They would be lucky to reach the coast before winter. And winter in the mountains would probably destroy them.

At the Missouri's headwaters they entered a ramifying chaos of tributaries. Which one would carry them to the Columbia over that easy, one-day portage promised by the Indians? They stuck to the

Missouri, poling through a hideous gorge, the Gate of the Rockies, and inching toward the divide.

Now they were in Sacajawea's country, the hunting grounds of the Snakes, but none of those Indians, or their expected horses, could be found. The Missouri, which had carried the expedition from the Mississippi, split into three channels. Again the awful choice.

They chose the north fork and christened it the Jefferson in tribute to their sponsor. On August 12, a memorable day in the life of the young nation, Lewis saw a tiny trickle of water flowing westward. It was Columbia water. The Republic had crossed the divide.

A few days later they met a band of Snakes who, by an incredible coincidence, were headed by Sacajawea's brother. The brave and his sister embraced in tears.

The Snakes provided horses and the expedition's speed increased. But autumn was at hand. Could the coast be reached before winter engulfed the travelers? Their only hope was to press on and escape this mountain labyrinth.

An easy, one-day portage had turned into a terrifying welter of cliffs, canyons, and narrow ledges. The pack horses slipped and rolled into the dizzy ravines. Autumn gales brought drenching rain, sleet, frost, and eight inches of snow. Yet among those exhausted men the young squaw carried her baby, fed it from her breast, and uttered no word of complaint.

Thus suffering Mackenzie's full miseries for the first time, the Americans somehow rounded a semicircle from the headwaters of the Missouri southward and then north through the Bitterroot Valley to turn west by the Lolo Pass. At last, guided by an aged Indian named Toby, they hit the upper Clearwater in mid-September.

They were weak from dysentery. Their food was almost gone. No game could be found. They began to shoot coyotes and eat their horses. But the worst was over. When some Indians of the intelligent Nez Percé nation brought them dried salmon, they knew they could not be far from the ocean.

After a pause to build dugouts of pine, they embarked on the Clearwater. It bore them quickly to the Snake and then into the Columbia, amid a coastal jungle, a smell of salt water, and a horde of strange Indians in painted wooden canoes. By November they were camped just south of the Columbia's mouth on the sandy shore of the Pacific. They called their fort Clatsop. It sheltered them through an interminable winter of rain, gale, and loneliness.

Lewis and Clark had spanned a continent and roughly described the bounds of the Republic, but they remained insatiable for in-

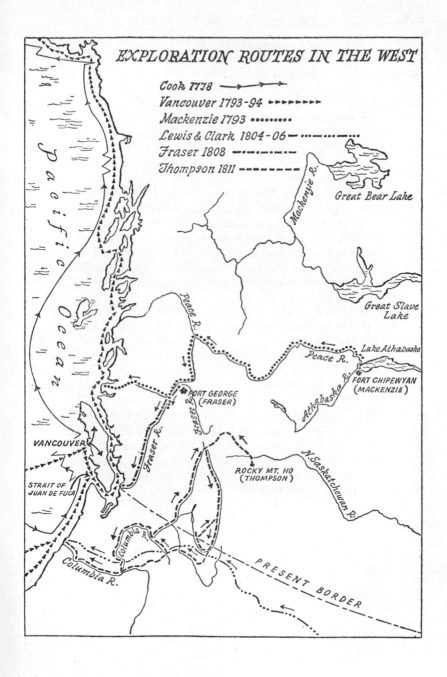

EXPLORATION ROUTES IN THE WEST

Cook 1778 →
Vancouver 1793-94 ►►►►►►►
Mackenzie 1793 •••••••••
Lewis & Clark 1804-06 —••—••—
Fraser 1808 —•—•—•—
Thompson 1811 —————

Pacific Ocean

Mackenzie R.

Great Bear Lake

Great Slave Lake

Peace R.

Peace R.   Lake Athabaska

Athabaska R.   FORT CHIPEWYAN
                  (MACKENZIE)

Fraser R.

FORT GEORGE
(FRASER)

VANCOUVER

ROCKY MT. HO
(THOMPSON)

N. Saskatchewan R.

STRAIT OF
JUAN DE FUCA

Fraser R.

Columbia R.

PRESENT BORDER

Columbia R.

formation. Starting homeward on March 23, 1806, they split the expedition into two parties to travel by different routes through the mountains. Clark hacked out a canoe and rode the Yellowstone. Lewis moved north, following his obsession, a river to the Canadian north. The Marias, one of the four streams which, he hoped, would lead to the Saskatchewan or Athabaska, soon petered out. He drove off a night raid by the Blackfeet, but was wounded in the thigh by one of his own men while hunting deer.

In August the two parties met at their rendezvous on the Missouri and drifted easily down to the Mississippi. One man had died and one deserted. No North American explorers had gone farther than Lewis and Clark, none had succeeded better, and none had ever amassed in one expedition a comparable store of knowledge. Two young soldiers, a band of frontiersmen, a squaw and her infant, and a Newfoundland dog had confirmed the bargain of Louisiana, stretched the Republic from sea to sea, beaten the Canadians to the Columbia mouth, and roughed out the ultimate cleavage of the continent.

There was much work yet to be done. The United States had not penetrated the western peltry north of 49°. The attempt to conquer all of Canada by arms was not yet conceived. Moreover, if the Columbia mouth had been reached, and if Gray's original discovery had established American rights there, the Canadians, under Mackenzie's successors, were now reported—quite erroneously—again on the river's upper reaches.

The Spaniards, Cook, Gray, and Vancouver had begun the struggle for Oregon. Lewis and Clark had merely touched it and, after one winter, departed. The Canadians would possess it. And even while Lewis and Clark were toiling through the Rockies a Canadian named Simon Fraser had reached an unknown river to revolutionize the map of America once more.

15

The Black Canyon

[1808]

FRASER, NOW CONTENDING WITH LEWIS AND CLARK IN THE CON-
tinental race, was as much American by descent as his rivals.
His grandparents had come from Culbochie, Scotland, and
settled at Bennington, Vermont. By an interesting conjunction, this
opponent of American expansion in the West was born in 1776 when
Jefferson was writing the Declaration of Independence. The statesman and the explorer, unknown to each other, were to engage in a
continental competition throughout their lives.

The Frasers chose the losing side of the Revolution. Simon's father
was a captain in Burgoyne's doomed army, was captured by the
revolutionists and apparently died as their prisoner in Albany. (The
son always believed, however, that he had perished at sea on a
ship carrying away the British soldiers after the war.) The widow,
left destitute with four sons and five daughters, was caught up in
the Loyalist migration to Canada and settled at St. Andrews, near
the Ottawa River.

There was nothing to distinguish this family of refugees from
many others, except the character of Simon. His mother, evidently
suspecting his qualities, managed to send him to school briefly in
Montreal. In 1792—as Mackenzie was preparing to descend the
river that would bear Fraser's name—the youth of sixteen was arti-
cled as a clerk to the North West Company. That irrepressible
organization had always owned more talent than money. Its choice
of men amounted to something like genius. The talents of young
Fraser, therefore, were quickly noted. By 1802 he was a "bourgeois,"
or full partner, and the company had picked him as Mackenzie's
successor in the West.

Apart from their courage and their hunger for the wilderness, the two men were as unlike as men could be. Mackenzie was handsome, educated, refined, and imaginative; Fraser homely, with a bullet head, sloping forehead, lank hair, grizzled eyebrows, harsh, protuberant chin—a cold man and stubborn, hiding with difficulty a fierce inner pride and an envy of his famous predecessor. In short, the kind of laborious, systematic, and glum Scot who largely controlled the Canadian West already, was building a nation and soon would dominate its government.

While bitterly disappointed by Mackenzie's failure to descend his river, supposedly the Columbia, the North West Company was slow to repair this blunder. There seemed to be no immediate hurry. The Americans had never been a match for the Canadians in the continental race. Not until 1805, when Lewis and Clark were nearing the Pacific coast, did Fraser start on his march across Canada. He had heard nothing of the American expedition. So far as he was aware, he faced no competition in the race.

Following Mackenzie's trail, he pushed up the Peace and the Parsnip and, in the autumn, built a post at a lake named for his friend, Archibald Norman McLeod. It was the first Canadian post west of the Rockies. There he left his lieutenant, James McDougall, for the winter and turned back to his base camp on the Peace, Rocky Mountain Portage.

When Fraser returned to Fort McLeod in the spring of 1806 he found that McDougall had spent the winter in a thrust to Mackenzie's river and up its first important tributary, the Nechako, which flowed in from the west just below the big bend.

Fraser decided to pursue McDougall's discoveries before starting down the main river. It gratified his vanity and perhaps a rooted inferiority complex to observe that Mackenzie had missed the Nechako entirely and had been careless in some of his observations.

Thus Fraser's rather spiteful diary: "Trout Lake is a considerable large and navigable river in all seasons. It does not appear to have been noticed by Sir A.M.K. [Mackenzie] as he used to indulge himself in a little sleep. Likely he did not see it and I can account for many other omissions in no other manner than his being asleep at the time he pretends to have been very exact; but was I qualified to make observations and inclined to find fault with him, I could prove he seldom or ever paid the attention he pretends to have done, and that many of his remarks were not made of himself but communicated by his men. . . . Sir A.M.K. appears to have been very inaccurate in the courses or there must have been a vast difference in the compass he made use of and the one we had. . . ."

After thus asserting his own superior methods, Fraser abruptly

laid aside his diary on July 18, probably being otherwise occupied
in the ascent of the Nechako to the lovely region of mountain lakes
at its source. He christened the first lake Stuart after one of his aides,
built on its shore Fort St. James and, delighted by this verdant
country, named it New Caledonia, for his grandfather's homeland.
Another post was built on a lake to the south which Fraser marked
with his own name. Three centers of trade west of the mountains
now stretched the business of the North West Company from Montreal almost to the Pacific.

Lewis and Clark had twice crossed the continent by now, but
Fraser still saw no reason to hurry. He returned in the autumn to
his post on the Peace and wintered there. Meanwhile, in Montreal,
the North West Company partners had heard of the Americans'
expedition to the Columbia. They wrote Fraser in some panic, urging him to descend that river without more delay. The necessary
supplies did not reach him, at Fort St. James, until the autumn of
1807, too late for travel that year.

Roused by the news from Montreal, Fraser returned next spring
to Mackenzie's river and, at the mouth of the Nechako, built Fort
George. On May 22, 1808, at five in the morning four canoes floated
into the swirl of the main current. One of America's largest adventures had begun.

Fraser was accompanied by John Stuart and Jules Quesnel as his
lieutenants, nineteen paddlers, and two Indians. The two dozen men
unwittingly were headed into the worst water of the continent.

They wallowed through a dangerous clay canyon, passed the
mouth of a substantial river on their left, named for Quesnel, and
there overlooked one of America's richest hordes of gold. Presently
they saw Indians gathered on both banks and gesticulating wildly.
Fraser decided to confer with them. His broken diary records the
conference of sign language and its bad news:

According to the accounts we received here, the river below is but a
succession of falls and cascades which we would find impossible to pass,
not only on account of the difficulties of the channel but from the extreme
ruggedness and the mountainous character of the surrounding country.
Their opinion, therefore, was that we should discontinue our journey and
remain with them. I remarked that our determination of going was fixed;
they then informed us that at the next camp the Great Chief of the
Atnaugh nation had a slave who had been to the sea and which he might
probably give us as a guide.

It was the same sound advice received near the same point by
Mackenzie, and it had persuaded him to strike westward overland.
Fraser would not leave the river until he had reached the sea. The

Indians produced the guide next day but his information only added to the white men's confusion. They spread an oilcloth on the ground and asked the expert to draw a map of the river's lower channel.

This he readily undertook, but his endeavours soon convinced me that his stock of knowledge was very slender indeed, for his lines were entirely directed by an elderly man, a relation of the chief, who stood by him. We could, however, plainly see in his sketch a confirmation of what had been told us of the difficulties of navigation and thereby the necessity of leaving our canoes with as much of our baggage as we could spare in order to continue our journey by land.

They were south of Mackenzie's turning-off point. No white man had seen this part of the river. No one could imagine the perils ahead. And they were on the wrong river. Nevertheless, Fraser decided to descend it.

On June 1 he launched one canoe experimentally upon an "immense body of water, passing through this narrow space in a turbulent manner, forming numerous gulfs and cascades and making a tremendous noise and of an awful forbidding appearance." The canoe split on a rock. Its five paddlers clung to the slippery bank.

Fraser's diary pictures with Scottish phlegm the first of many accidents:

During this distressing scene we were on shore looking on and anxiously concerned; seeing our poor fellows once more safe afforded us as much satisfaction as to themselves and we hastened to their assistance, but their situation rendered our approach perilous and difficult. The bank was extremely high and steep and we had to plunge our daggers at intervals into the ground to check our speed, as otherwise we were exposed to slide into the river. We cut steps in the declivity, fastened a line to the front of the canoe, with which some of the men ascended in order to haul it up, while others supported it upon their arms. In this manner our situation was most precarious; our lives hung, as it were, upon a thread, as the failure of the line or a false step by any one of the men might have hurled the whole of us into Eternity. However, we fortunately cleared the bank before dark.

Again the Indians warned Fraser to turn back, or at least to travel well away from the river, by horse, over the rolling clay plateau. He refused. "Going to the sea by an indirect way was not the object of this undertaking; I therefore would not deviate and continued our route according to our original intention."

Several hard but brief portages and a "desperate undertaking" in some wild rapids brought him to impassable water. Reluctantly he cached his canoes and the party continued on foot along the jagged and almost vertical bank.

Again, between the dull lines of the diary, one can read this man's recklessness. When one of his companions became wedged in a crevice, "Seeing this poor fellow in such an awkward and dangerous predicament I crawled, not without great risk, to his assistance and saved his life by causing his load to drop from his back over the precipice into the river. This carrying place, two miles long, so shattered our shoes that our feet became quite sore and full of blisters."

On June 19 they reached the mouth of a great river flowing in from the eastward and mingling its emerald-green waters with the brown of its parent. Fraser named it for his friend, David Thompson, who, he wrongly supposed, was then exploring its upper waters among the Rockies. Thompson would be remembered for a river he never saw.

The junction of these two river valleys provided a natural nexus of travel and nourished a formidable Indian village called Camchin. Here Fraser discovered white men's goods. He had touched the ancient Indian route of commerce between the coast and the interior. Already the profits of the sea otter business, in barter between Indian, Spaniard, Briton, American and Russian, were moving far inland.

The intelligent Indians of Camchin told Fraser that no canoe could live in the river a few miles beyond this point. As Fraser insisted on embarking again, the Great Chief, or "Little Fellow," accompanied him. The Indians' warning was soon proved accurate.

Below Camchin the river suddenly closed into a black canyon. Its huge body, constricted to a narrow gut, writhed in deafening paroxysm between sheer walls of stone, churned through endless slimy chasms, and at the final horror of Hell's Gate rose and fell in rhythmic pulsation of brown foam.

Not a moment too soon the canoes were dragged ashore. Now began perhaps the most dreadful march ever undertaken by white men in the West.

The Indians had mastered the canyon long ago. Their trail ran zigzag up the slippery cliffs, clung to every damp ledge and reached the ledge above by a clumsy ladder of tree trunks and withes. Ninety pounds on each man's back, Fraser and his followers crawled like spiders up this monstrous vinegrowth. The diary again:

Here we were obliged to carry among loose stones in the face of a steep hill between two precipices. Near the top, where the ascent was perfectly perpendicular, one of the Indians climbed up to the summit and by means of a long rope drew us up one after another. This work took three hours, and then we continued our course up and down the hills and along the steep declivities of mountains where hanging rocks and projecting cliffs, at the edge of the bank of the river, made the passage so small as to render it, at times, difficult even for one person sideways. Many of the natives from the last camp who accompanied us were of the greatest use on this intricate occasion. They went on boldly with heavy loads in places where we were obliged to hand our guns from one to another, and where the greatest precaution was required in order to pass even singly and free from cumbrance.

I have been for a long period in the Rocky Mountains but have never seen anything like this country. It is so wild that I cannot find words to describe our situation at times. We had to pass where no human beings should venture; yet in those places there is a regular footpath impressed, or rather indented upon the very rocks by frequent travelling. Besides this, steps which are formed like a ladder or the shrouds of a ship, by poles hanging to one another and crossed at certain distances with twigs, the whole suspended from the top to the foot of the deep precipices and fastened at both extremities to stones and trees, furnish a safe and convenient passage to the natives; but we, who had not had the advantage of their education and experience, were often in imminent danger when obliged to follow their example.

On the Indians' fragile web they pursued this river of nightmare as it turned abruptly westward and bored its way through the last mountain range of the continent. At last, in final spasm, it burst from its dark prison and oozed, oily and peaceful, through a rank coastal forest.

Fraser was able to buy some dugout canoes from the local Indians and travel comfortably again. But a gnawing suspicion had gripped this systematic man. His reckoning showed the mouth of the Columbia far to the south and this river was now moving straight west.

Soon he noted its water flooding and ebbing in regular tides, saw the first seagulls and felt the tang of salt air. He could deny his fears no longer—this was not the Columbia. Mackenzie had been wrong. All the mapmakers of the East had been wrong. The whole supposed geography of western America was wrong. Mackenzie had found and Fraser had explored a river unknown before. This was Fraser's own river, to be known thenceforward by his name.

Where the Fraser threads its flat delta and enters the sea by a series of separate channels, he measured its latitude on July 2 as 49° "very nearly"—about three degrees north of the Columbia. His mission had failed. "This river is, therefore, not the Columbia. If I had been convinced of this when I left my canoes I would certainly have returned."

That would have been hopeless. He could hardly have reached the Columbia overland from the Fraser that year, with his diminished supplies, even if he had known the way. And, unknown to

him, Lewis and Clark had driven the Republic's stakes into the soil
of Oregon three years earlier.

Fraser could not see the Pacific, for it was hidden by the whale's
back of Vancouver's Island. "I must acknowledge my great disappointment at not seeing the main ocean, having gone so far as to
be almost within view." Yet he had seen enough to alter the entire
prospects of Canada.

If the Americans could hold Oregon, against all reason and expectation, Fraser had located a natural barrier to their northward
expansion. He had found, in fact, the western Canadian mate to
the St. Lawrence on the east coast. Though he did not suspect it, his
river contained within its sand bars certain yellow flecks which, in
just half a century, would people this region and later join it, by
railway, with the eastern colonies to make a second transcontinental
state.

Fraser turned back with his heartbreak but little time for regret.
Most of the Indians of the canyon had been friendly. A few had
fired arrows at the white men and rolled stones upon them, but the
hostile tribes saw no reason to exert themselves since the strangers
doubtless would perish before they could return. Now, when they
appeared in the lower reaches of the canyon again, they met an
organized and determined attack. Day and night they were harassed
by arrow and stone until Fraser found his men breaking under the
strain, planning to desert, and talking madly of a dash straight eastward through the mountains where winter assuredly would annihilate them. There had been difficulties enough before. This was the
moment of Fraser's supreme peril and it called from him a supreme
act of leadership:

Considering this scheme as a desperate undertaking I debarked and
endeavoured to persuade the delinquents of their infatuation; but two of
them declared in their own names and in the names of the others that
their plan was fixed and that they saw no other way by which they
could save themselves from immediate destruction than by flying out of
the way of danger; for, said they, continuing by water, surrounded by
hostile nations, who watched every opportunity to attack and torment
them, created in their mind a state of suspicion worse than death. I
remonstrated and threatened by turns, the other gentlemen joined me
in my endeavours to expose the folly of their undertaking and the advantages that would accrue to us all by remaining as we had hitherto been
in perfect union for our common safety. After much debate on both
sides, they yielded and we all shook hands, resolved not to separate
during the voyage.

In that scene—two dozen men, hungry, tattered, maddened by

unseen enemies, and lost on a strange river at the far edge of a continent—the quality of Fraser shines through the inarticulate diary. As he had mastered the river, he mastered his followers. They raised their hands and shouted an oath of loyalty above the thunder of the canyon: "I solemnly swear before Almighty God that I shall sooner perish than forsake in distress any of our crew during the present voyage."

Then they climbed the Indians' crazy ladders again, found their cached canoes and were back at Fort George, without a single casualty, on August 5, just thirty-four days from the sea. The downward journey with the current had taken thirty-five. Against obstacles and dangers far worse than any experienced by Lewis and Clark, the dogged American-Canadian Scot had fulfilled his schedule. But he had missed the Columbia.

The first Canadian to see, or rather to recognize, it was Fraser's friend, David Thompson. A half-breed, Jaco Finlay, had reached it from the South Saskatchewan in 1806, by Howse Pass through the Rockies but one more of many rivers meant nothing to this bold, ignorant man, who was only a year behind Lewis and Clark. Thompson needed half a dozen more years to catch up to the trail of Finlay, his servant. The famous surveyor and astronomer of the North West Company had been wandering since 1799 among the swamps, plains, and western foothills of the prairies and even into Fraser's New Caledonia, never able to find the illusive prize. In the summer of 1807, as Fraser was awaiting supplies to descend Mackenzie's river, Thompson was ready for a final attempt.

He struck west from the plains into the Rockies, by Finlay's trail, and discovered a river apparently moving to the Pacific. "May God give me," he wrote, "to see where its waters flow into the ocean." It led him to a larger stream which flowed northward. This was the Columbia, but Thompson failed to identify it.

Greatly confused, he wintered on a lake now called Windermere. By their longitude these waters could be no part of Mackenzie's river. In the following spring, therefore, Thompson crossed a portage of a mile and found yet another river. Surely it must be the Columbia. He followed it southward to the rim of the Lewis-Clark discoveries in the country of the Flathead Indians, who shaped the skulls of their young with bandages and stones. Then this river, too, (the Kootenay) turned north. Geography again was out of joint.

The first Canadian to cross the 49th Parallel west of the Rockies, Thompson penetrated northern Idaho and Montana, reached the Pend Oreille River and missed its junction with the Columbia by half a day's travel—a costly mishap. After all these disappointments he retreated to the prairies, more puzzled than ever, and apparently went on to Montreal for instructions.

The North West Company was now thoroughly alarmed. On the heels of Lewis and Clark other Americans were about to descend on Oregon. Where Mackenzie and Fraser had failed, Thompson must find the Columbia without more loitering and claim its mouth.

Since the route into the Rockies from the North Saskatchewan was held by the hostile Piegans, Thompson struggled up the Athabaska in the autumn of 1810, nearly lost his life by snow and starvation but, packing his supplies on four exhausted horses and two dogs, crossed the divide and finally hit the Columbia toward the end of January, 1811, at the northern tip of its big bend. There he wintered.

Next spring, for unknown reasons, he ascended the current instead of following it downstream and struck overland to the Spokane River. He rode it to a larger stream. After a dozen years of futile roving, he had found the prize—apparently too late.

At the mouth of the Snake he planted a pole, raised the Union Jack, and claimed the surrounding territory for Britain and the North West Company. But when he paddled on down the Columbia to the sea on July 15 it was to find there a post of newly cut logs. John Jacob Astor's Pacific Fur Company, under Jefferson's patronage, had built Fort Astoria. Arriving by sea around the Horn, the Americans had beaten Thompson to the Columbia's mouth by a scant four months.

He met at Astoria several of his old friends from the North West Company, veteran traders whom Astor had shrewdly hired to manage his fur business. These men greeted Thompson boisterously, dined him on salmon, duck and partridge, toasted his overland journey in the wines of Europe. It was a touching reunion, but Thompson had lost the race.

Still there was reason to believe that Astor's venture might fail. His men, especially the Canadians, were grumbling already. They had been dumped on the Oregon shore from a ship, inadequately provisioned, and deserted. They still waited for reinforcements, now toiling across the continent on the route of Lewis and Clark. Such men perhaps could be lured back to the North West Company.

Unknown to them, Astor's concern had recently suffered a major disaster.

Its ship, the *Tonquin,* having dropped its party of traders at the Columbia and lost eight lives by drowning, sailed on up the coast to Vancouver's Island in search of sea otter pelts. The commander, Jonathan Thorn, a retired naval officer, was ignorant and contemptuous of Indians. He would not listen to the advice of Alexander

Mackay, one of the West's ablest explorers, who had accompanied Mackenzie to the sea. Mackay was now alarmed to find the Indians at Clayoquot swarming aboard the *Tonquin* in pretended friendship but obviously armed and hostile.

Thorn scoffed at Mackay's warnings. The Indians suddenly attacked the unsuspecting crew, hacked the captain to small pieces, and threw Mackay overboard among the canoes. The squaws speared him like a fish. Five men escaped from the deck and defended themselves from the cabin until the Indians withdrew. Four of the five made off in a lifeboat. The ship's clerk, Lewis, crippled by a knife wound in the back and perhaps demented, refused to leave the ship. He waved a welcome to the Clayoquots. As they swarmed to the deck he crawled below and fired the powder magazine. The *Tonquin*, Lewis, and the Indians were shattered in the explosion.

Thompson was ignorant of the murder of his friend, Mackay, when he started back up the Columbia after a week's rest. A year later he reached Fort William to report the arrival of the Astorians on the Columbia. This was shocking news to the Nor' Westers. Their three great servants, Mackenzie, Fraser and Thompson, all had failed.

That disappointment was short-lived. The struggle for the great river of the West soon merged into a war for the whole continent.

16

The Man in Scarlet

[1812–1814]

O N THE MORNING OF OCTOBER 13, 1812, A HANDFUL OF AMER-
ican soldiers looked down from Queenston Heights upon the
zigzag of the Niagara River and, beyond it, the metallic shim-
mer of Lake Ontario. They had invaded Canada easily enough and
seemed likely to stay there, since they were backed by eight million
people and opposed by a sixteenth as many. The possibility of a
Canadian nation might well have ended that day but for a tiny
speck of red, now seen moving along the river road.

General Isaac Brock, a giant with curly, fair hair, narrow face
and long, knife-blade nose, was galloping alone from Fort George
on his gray charger, Alfred. He wore a tunic of scarlet and gold,
white breeches, and about his waist an Indian sash, bright with
woven arrows, the gift of another warrior named Tecumseh. In such
a costume he would make an easy mark for any American musket
and within two hours he would be dead.

Those two hours would see the future prospects of North America
reversed, and mainly by Brock's single hand. His ride was short,
his own prospects brief. But the giant on the winded horse might
accomplish more in the seven miles between Fort George and
Queenston Heights than most of the Canadians who had crossed
the continent. All the land they had staked out for Canada, all the
work begun by Champlain and carried on by eight generations of
Canadians now lay at the feet of the American invaders and could
be lost by nightfall if Brock arrived too late at the heights.

Ahead he saw only the reddening autumn maples on the river
slope. His simple soldier's mind—and the abler mind of Washington
—could hardly suspect that the heights would soon mean as much
to Canadians as Lexington had meant to the Americans, that if

Canada was to have any birthplace as a nation it would be this hill beside the Niagara.

So he rode, knowing little of the ultimate continental war now under way, less of its causes across the Atlantic. In his forty-three years Brock had learned only his trade and his duty. The Americans were here again, for the second time, where they had no right to be. Brock's duty was to dislodge and hurl them back across the river—a doubtful task, by all sound military calculation impossible, and the man in scarlet would not live to see its issue.

The causes of the tragic and useless War of 1812 went a long way back, were so complex and immeasurable that, a century and a half later, historians would still be debating them.

Partly they expressed the nature of the continent, the same continental forces that had brought the Kirkes, Phips, Wolfe, and Montgomery to Quebec, the perpetual attempt to make North America, or most of it, a single state. The British had achieved this unification in the Seven Years' War and seen it collapse in the American Revolution. Now the Americans, after the failure of their first feeble Canadian invasion in 1775, were attempting to repeat the strategy of Britain.

Apparently it would be easy this time. Had not Jefferson, the purchaser of Louisiana, announced that "The acquisition of Canada this year, as far as the neighborhood of Quebec, will be a mere matter of marching" across the defenseless border?

Andrew Jackson, a backwoods soldier, judge and duelist, still smarting from a boyhood British saber cut, summed up the inevitable conquest of a neighbor's land in a single complacent phrase: "How pleasing the prospect that would open up to the young volunteer while performing a military promenade in a distant country!"

Henry Clay, speaker of the new House of Representatives and leader of the western War Hawks, had assured his countrymen that "It is absurd to suppose that we will not succeed in our enterprise against the enemy's Provinces. I am not for stopping at Quebec or anywhere else; but I would take the whole continent from them, and ask no favors. I wish never to see peace till we do. God has given us the power and the means. We are to blame if we do not use them."

And William Eustis, secretary of war, in his total ignorance of that art, had informed his government officially that "We can take Canada without soldiers. We have only to send officers into the Provinces, and the people, disaffected towards their own Government, will rally round our standard."

The Americans, therefore, had marched to unify the continent by the laws of geography and power, to free it of an unnatural division, to delete, in a matter of weeks at most, an intolerable boundary line, to repeal for all time the failure of 1775 and the impossible peace settlement of 1783.

Already the groundwork of this invasion had been laid far to the south in the Indiana Territory, where two of America's greatest Indians, Tecumseh and his brother, the Prophet, after years of labor had successfully revived Pontiac's dream of an Indian confederacy to save the ancestral hunting grounds from American settlement. General William Henry Harrison had accused Canada of fomenting the tribes (which was untrue), had attacked the Prophet's town of Tippecanoe in Tecumseh's absence, destroyed the confederacy, driven Tecumseh to the Great Lakes country, and ended all serious Indian opposition east of the Mississippi. Now the western War Hawks of the American Congress, led by Clay and John C. Calhoun, were determined to finish the job by seizing Canada.

There was much more to the War of 1812 than these old continental forces. A large part of the American people, indeed, had rejected the whole theory of continentalism, wanted no part of the war, and were horrified to find themselves on the side of Napoleon, the tyrant of Europe, against Britain and their peaceable neighbors in Canada. New England, fearing the new power of the West and interested mainly in maritime trade, was talking openly of secession to escape the War Hawks' adventures and soon would be suspected of treason. But, as always, America could not escape the quarrels of Europe and they were the immediate cause of the Republic's march across the Niagara River.

France had begun the trouble more than a dozen years before by seizing American ships in the perpetual wars with Britain. Napoleon had lost his navy at Trafalgar and Britain could rule the Atlantic by blockading Europe. Britain's seizure of neutral American shipping and its abduction of seasoned American sailors, needed in His Majesty's shorthanded fleet, naturally enraged the United States, even though American business along the Atlantic coast was fattening on contraband trade and a ravenous war market.

President Jefferson, who knew nearly everything but war, had denounced the "ruinous folly of an American navy," had built a useless collection of gunboats (called "Jeffs" by the contemptuous American sailors), and now could wield only the double-edged weapon of embargo on American exports, which gravely damaged the New England exporter but did little harm to Britain. For all his foresight on land, Jefferson was hopelessly adrift at sea. The commerce of his country was soon facing ruin. More serious, the Republic was split on the issue of war and peace when it needed its united strength to occupy the Louisiana Purchase and hold the Pacific coast.

Jefferson's pupil and successor, Madison—a delicate, wizened, and able man who lacked his great mentor's genius but, said Clay, had more common sense—ended this impossible state of suspense by asking the Congress, in a message of June 1, 1812, to declare war on Britain.

A divided Congress reflected a divided people. The Senate carried the war declaration by 19 votes to 13; the House of Representatives by 79 to 49—this on June 23, five days after Britain had repealed the offending orders in council of the European blockade in a final gesture of peace that reached Washington by ship too late; this also at the exact moment when Napoleon's Grand Army was crossing the frontier of Russia to complete the conquest of the Old World. Odd it might seem to many Americans of the New, and immoral to some, that the American Revolution of Inalienable Rights was now striking Britain, the defender of freedom in Europe, but into this illogical position the Republic had been forced by the logic of events.

The parting in bad blood after the American Revolution, the Americans' lingering distrust of their departed mother, their hunger for Canadian land and furs, their fear of Indians and British power on their flank, the endless haggle over the boundary, the wishful notion that the Canadians only awaited liberation from their overseas masters, and finally Britain's outrageous seizure of American ships and citizens at sea—all this complex of good motives and bad, of anger and ambition, of deliberate design and sheer accident produced the final war for control of North America.

Authorized in complacency, the United States' attack on Canada opened in scandalous mismanagement. No nation could have been less prepared for Jackson's pleasant promenade toward the welcoming arms of Canada. The army, on paper, consisted of 35,000 men but hardly a quarter of them were trained. Before the war's end the United States would raise 575,000—as many soldiers as there were people in Canada—against 125,000 employed by the enemy, but only 56,000 American regulars could be recruited, no general would ever command more than 7,000 in any battle, and the state militia would usually go home after a brief term of service.

As they looked to men like Jefferson, Madison, Jackson, Clay, and Eustis, the odds from the beginning were ridiculously, almost pathetically balanced against Canada. The odds, in fact, were what they usually had been—about sixteen to one. Eight million Americans faced half a million Canadians. The Canadian regular soldiers numbered 4,000. There was an equal number of British troops in the colonies. The ill-trained or untrained militia totaled 100,000 in theory. A few thousand Indians probably could be raised, in changing and unreliable numbers.

A quarter of the English-speaking Canadians in Upper Canada were newly arrived immigrants from the United States and their sympathies lay mainly with their homeland. Two-thirds of all Canadians were of French blood, were only fifty-three years from their conquest by Britain, and were still restive under their conquerors. Would these people fight for Britain? No, they would not. But, as Jefferson failed to understand, they would fight for Canada. And, in fighting, they would answer the question posed by the conquest—whether there could ever be a nation-state north of the St. Lawrence.

This war, though it would occupy 700,000 men at one time or another, could be only a diversion from the United States' continental march; for Canada it was to prove the supreme national watershed.

And so—lamentable, mismanaged, unnecessary, and futile—it began with General Henry Dearborn confined to his headquarters in Greenbush yet promising to "operate with effect, at the same moment, against Niagara, Kingston and Montreal"; the American armies of the West based on Detroit under the hopeless command of General William Hull, who had forgotten what he had learned in the Revolution; and all Canadian forces under Governor General Sir George Prevost, a professional British soldier who equaled the martial idiocy of the prospective invaders. In all that dim galaxy of talent there was only one general competent in his trade.

Isaac Brock had been born of military folk in 1769, the birth year of Napoleon and Wellington, had fought well in Europe, and with Nelson at Copenhagen had learned to turn a blind eye to the signals of stupid superiors. Appointed lieutenant governor of Upper Canada in 1811, he had tried desperately to prepare his little colony for defense but was unable, against the opposition of recent American immigrants, to get a military appropriation from his Assembly at York until two months after war had been declared. The United Empire Loyalist majority finally carried the vote, proclaiming, with excessive hope, that "By unanimity and dispatch in our councils and by vigor in operations we may teach the enemy this lesson: That a country defended by free men, enthusiastically devoted to the cause of their King and Constitution, can never be conquered."

As a piece of literature this was a poor substitute for the Declaration of Independence, but as a statement of fact it was just as true. At all events, it must serve Brock as he learned that Hull had crossed from Detroit into Canada on July 11 and, in the gasconade learned as governor of Michigan, had issued to the Canadian people another declaration, somewhat inferior to the original, in these terms:

The United States are sufficiently powerful to afford you every security consistent with their rights and your expectations. I tender you the invaluable blessings of Civil, Political and Religious Liberty. . . . The arrival of an army of Friends must be hailed by you with a cordial welcome. You will be emancipated from Tyranny and Oppression and restored to the dignified station of Freemen. . . . If contrary to your interest and the just expectations of my country, you should take part in the approaching contest you will be considered and treated as enemies and the horrors and calamities of war will Stalk before you. If the barbarous and Savage policy of Great Britain be pursued, and the savages let loose to murder our Citizens and butcher our women and children, this war will be a war of extermination. The first stroke with the Tomahawk, the first attempt with the Scalping Knife, will be the Signal for one indiscriminate Scene of desolation. No white man found fighting by the Side of an Indian will be taken prisoner. Instant destruction will be his Lot.

This lofty language was designed to impress the Canadians with their weakness; Hull was not much impressed with his own strength.

He might be incompetent himself but he realized that Eustis, the Secretary of War, was a fool, that Dearborn had failed to concert any useful strategy, that the first obvious step was to gain control of Lakes Erie and Ontario, thus cutting Canada in two, and that nothing of the sort had been attempted. Moreover, the daring Provincial Marines of Upper Canada had managed to seize, near Detroit, an American schooner bearing Hull's secret campaign plans. He had never sought this military command, he was tired of it already, and the Canadians, against all the promises of the statesmen in Washington, refused to embrace the invader.

Nevertheless, he ferried 2,500 men from Detroit to the Canadian village of Sandwich and found only 600 Canadians, most of them raw militia and Indians, at Fort Malden nearby. He tried to take the fort but was stopped by a few Indians under an abler general, Tecumseh, at a creek appropriately called Rivière aux Canards. These, then, were the savages who must bring down the full horrors of the "war of extermination." Poor Hull was in no position to exterminate even the tiny Canadian force before him.

Now he learned of a disaster in his rear. On Brock's orders the garrison at St. Joseph's Island, between Huron and Superior, 45 regulars and 180 French-Canadian *voyageurs*, with 400 Indians, had taken the American post of Mackinac without a drop of bloodshed. This was a small but highly significant affair. It had carried the Canadians across the border, rallied the Indians as of old, showed that French Canadians were willing to fight, and given Canada command of the main lanes of travel to the far West.

The second item of news was equally depressing. Hull had ordered the evacuation of Fort Dearborn (Chicago) and half of its garrison of sixty-one had been massacred by Indians, drunk with the fort's liquor, which should have been destroyed. The tomahawk and the scalping knife were loose again. Hull forgot his declaration to the Canadian people and retreated to Detroit, following a month's wasted promenade.

A few hours after he had pushed his war budget through the York legislature, Brock hurried by water to Amherstburg, at the western end of Lake Erie. He arrived just after midnight, August 14, with 300 reinforcements. His operations were small, even in Canadian terms, but they marked him at once as a soldier of imagination. Studying Hull's captured plans by candlelight, he ordered an immediate attack on Detroit. Upper Canada, a colony of 100,000 people, proposed to invade a nation of 8,000,000.

Among those at the midnight council was Tecumseh, of whom Brock remarked later that "a more sagacious or a more gallant warrior does not, I believe, exist." The great Shawnee was nearly six feet tall, hard, lithe, and as nervous as a woods animal. His skin was "light copper, his countenance oval, with bright hazel eyes beaming cheerfulness, energy and decision. Three small crowns or coronets were suspended from the lower cartilage of his aquiline nose."

The blond English general and the dark master of wilderness war met and instantly became as brothers. Tecumseh turned to his thirty followers and pronounced his verdict: "Ho-o-o-e, this is a man!" The chief then unrolled a strip of elm bark and, with his much-used scalping knife, drew a detailed map of the country surrounding Detroit. On this map a plan of attack was quickly devised.

Next day Brock surveyed his 1,500 troops and demanded Detroit's surrender. Hull refused. He had 2,500 men altogether but some 500 of them had been foolishly ordered out of the fort into the country, a march of two or three days. Still Detroit should be easily defended.

That night Tecumseh—whose name had begun to rally the tribes —silently crossed the river with 600 followers and encircled Hull's fort without alerting him. Brock crossed in the morning with 700 men, half of them raw militia, while his battery of five field guns pounded Detroit from the Canadian side. He now learned for the first time that the absent American troops were returning from the south. He was caught between them and the fort. A lesser general would have retreated. Brock ordered an instant advance. Resplendent in scarlet, he rode his gray charger, with Tecumseh beside him on a pony. At this reckless show of strength Hull's martial courage oozed out. He raised a white flag and surrendered not only Detroit but the territory of Michigan.

As the Union Jack was raised over the fort, Brock presented his sash and pistols to Tecumseh, who gave a gaudy Indian sash, spangled with arrows, to his new friend. Brock wore it for the remainder of his short span. Tecumseh bestowed Brock's present on Roundhead, chief of the Wyandots, "an older and more valiant chief."

The news from Detroit sobered the politicians at Washington. Apparently the wrongheaded Canadians had no appetite for liberation and would fight their liberators. The contest was not to be a mere matter of marching, after all. Hull had not launched a war of liberation. He had conducted a comedy.

Brock moved to Niagara, where he rightly expected the main American blow to fall, attempted to forestall it with an attack on Sackets Harbor but found that the wavering Governor General Prevost had arranged an armistice with Dearborn in the hope that the war somehow might be called off. Thus protected from Brock, the Americans rapidly massed along the Niagara and when the armistice ended on September 7 nearly seven thousand of them faced 1,700 Canadians across the river.

As a soldier Brock knew the strategy which the enemy must follow if he was to conquer Canada. Had he the brains to use it?

The essential strategy was as old as the first wars of America. Britain, lacking an army in Canada, must rely on its old weapon, the navy, to blockade the United States' commerce. The United States, lacking a navy, must move by land and move fast before British reinforcements could cross the Atlantic.

In order of priority the historic American objectives were, or should be, Quebec, Montreal, Kingston, Niagara, and the Detroit River. Quebec could not be taken, had never been taken without naval power, but Montreal was vulnerable by the old Champlain corridor. Its capture, or the capture of the Niagara peninsula, would split Canada, cutting off its French- from its English-speaking people. Yet the Americans made no serious attempt on Montreal, the central objective, throughout the war. They aimed at Niagara, a second-best strategy, but for the most part wasted their strength in bungling raids on the Canadian perimeter.

Brock could hardly credit the enemy with such ignorance of the first principles of North American war, an enemy which had recently beaten the British Empire but now found no successors to Washington, or even to Wayne. Sure of early attack, not knowing where he must meet it, and outnumbered four to one, Brock waited impatiently in Fort George, at the mouth of the Niagara River and directly opposite the American Fort Niagara.

An American council of war decided to attack Fort George and Queenston Heights, a hill rising 345 feet above the river, seven miles to the southward, simultaneously. General Smyth, commanding above Niagara Falls, refused to participate. Lacking his support, General Stephen Van Rensselaer proposed to feint at Fort George and take the heights. On October 10 his attack failed even to cross the river. The first boats, carrying all the available oars, were seized by the Canadians. The American Army waited all night in the rain and returned to camp for breakfast.

Van Rensselaer was in despair. A rich and honorable Federalist, he had doubted the wisdom of the war, he had no wish for a command, but had been placed at the head of the New York State militia by the Democratic Governor Tompkins, so that possible defeat could not be blamed on the Democratic Party. Fortunately the American General's cousin, Solomon Van Rensselaer, a trained soldier, was on his staff. After the opening fiasco, Solomon concentrated the army at Lewiston, opposite Queenston, under the cover of the woods, and prepared another assault. This time, taking no chances, he resolved to lead the advance himself.

At half past three in the chilly morning of October 13 he landed at Queenston village with 225 regulars. The rest of the 4,000 American troops were to follow him before dawn. Only 300 Canadians held Queenston, but they poured a well-aimed volley at the first invaders and gravely wounded Van Rensselaer, who was carried back across the river. The Americans had lost their only experienced leader. His successor, Captain Wool, proved an ingenious substitute. He abandoned the frontal attack on Queenston and led a party of 300 by an obscure path up the river to approach the heights from the rear.

Brock, at Fort George, had heard no word of the American landing. He heard only the American guns of Lewiston firing at Queenston. Soon the guns of Fort Niagara started to bombard his own fort. Which target did the enemy intend to attack? Perhaps both at once?

Brock could hope to defend only one point. So he waited, husbanding his scanty reserves.

A messenger rode into Fort George with the news that the Americans had crossed the river in force. Still Brock could not be sure that the attack was aimed at Queenston. It might be a feint to draw him out of his fort. He called for his charger, Alfred, and galloped up the river road.

Ahead, through a drenching rain, he could see the flash of cannon fire—two Canadian guns against twenty-four American—then the figure of a horseman approaching hell-for-leather from the south. Brock did not even slacken his pace as this man, wheeling and riding beside Alfred, shouted that the Americans were swarming up the heights. Brock ordered the messenger on to Fort George. He was to bring all the soldiers to Queenston.

Thus after the comedy of Detroit, after all the distant quarrels of Europe, the duel at sea, the whole long history of struggle on the Canadian border, the continental issue was joined at last. And for Canada the issue that day was nothing less than survival.

On those flaming autumn heights Brock could not hope to win the war of survival or decide whether North America was to contain one nation or two. Repulsed now, the Americans would surely return. But, with luck, he might buy time for his people when only a few more minutes were left to him. If Queenston could be held, the first American attack broken, Canadians of both races might be rallied. If Queenston was lost and Canada split, the whole war doubtless would be lost also. The boundary, which the French had surrendered under Montcalm, which the Canadians had saved under Carleton, would be erased forever.

Brock foresaw all the consequences of his seven-mile ride as he leaned over the neck of Alfred, Tecumseh's sash streaming in the wind. Would he reach the heights in time?

Alfred, nostrils red and flanks heaving, pounded through Queenston village in the first light of dawn. Brock paused only for a moment to order the handful of soldiers there to follow him, then spurred his horse up the heights. At the summit he found eight Canadian gunners. A single 18-pound gun fired on the Americans beside the river.

Apparently Brock had arrived in time. He did not know of Wool's detour around the heights. Suddenly he heard shouts behind him and beheld 300 Americans charging straight at the gun pit. Defense, with only eight men, was hopeless. Brock had just told his gunners to "try a longer fuse." He added in the same breath, "Spike the guns and follow me!" The gunners drove in their spike and scrambled down the hill. Brock had no chance to mount. He led his horse behind him as he ran.

Back at Queenston, he gathered a hundred men and, not daring to await reinforcements, prepared to retake the heights before the Americans could dig in. The Canadians were led out of the village at a run but halted at the foot of the hill. "Take breath, boys," Brock cried, "you'll need it presently!" He stroked Alfred's quivering neck and apologized for pushing him so hard. It was the last farewell between soldier and horse.

After a moment's pause, Brock drew his sword and started up the heights on foot, by a curve inland, to take the Americans in the rear. Wool was ready for him on the crest. A hundred panting Canadians faced a solid American line three times their number. It was no time to measure the odds. Brock's sword led the charge at the American center. It gave way and the Canadians leaped into the gun pit. A few yards off, in the woods, a cool American took careful aim at an easy target. As he fired, Brock dropped without a sound. An instant later a dead soldier sprawled across his general's body. Nerves shattered by their leader's death, the Canadians fled. They carried Brock with them and laid him in a Queenston cottage.

The heights had been lost for the second time. There seemed to be no chance of retaking them.

Colonel John Macdonell, who succeeded Brock, was a man of the same mold. He resolved to avenge his dead commander. Two hundred men were collected and Macdonell led them up the heights. Again the Americans were driven back, the gun recaptured. Again the Canadian commander fell, mortally wounded. And again the Americans drove the Canadians down the hill.

Now the Stars and Stripes floated confidently over the gun pit. Sixteen hundred Americans had crossed the river. Canada's lifeline apparently was severed. General Van Rensselaer sent mounted messengers to Albany, announcing the decisive victory, and made ready to accept the Canadian surrender. In this moment of triumph everything went wrong.

The garrison of Fort George, having silenced the guns of Niagara, at last had reached Queenston. A party of 150 Canadians, with a few Indians, was marching down the river from the falls. This outnumbered force scaled the heights from the south into what should have been a baited trap. But at the sound of Indian war whoops the Americans fell into panic. Some of them ran down to the river and rowed across. Van Rensselaer stamped through his disordered ranks on the Canadian side, ordering, cursing, pleading. It was no use. His army melted before his eyes.

The Americans across the river refused to move. They had been terrified by the rumor of a great British Army approaching from somewhere and "the name of an Indian, or the sight of the wounded or the Devil, or something petrified them," as a survivor testified.

On the heights the gallant Colonel Winfield Scott tried to form a line as the Canadians from Queenston and Niagara Falls joined in a bayonet charge. The line broke and plunged downward to the river. A few men managed to swim the current. The remainder waited for their comrades on the far side to rescue them. When no rescue came, they surrendered. Scott raised a white handkerchief on his sword point.

The Army of the United States, in its first serious promenade, had lost about a hundred dead, 200 wounded, and 1,000 prisoners. Canada's casualties, though only 150 all told, included its greatest soldier, now lying in a Queenston cottage. He had not died in vain. Canada held the heights. The Americans had been driven back across the boundary.

Such a skirmish was a small incident in the affairs of the Republic. It was the turning point of Canadian history. For in death Brock was stronger than in life. The embryo nation of Canada had lacked, until that morning at Queenston, the essential nutriment of its growth—a myth shared by all its people. Now it had the myth, carried by a scarlet figure on a gray horse. Brock had proved that even at hopeless odds Canada could fight and win. If it fought on, it might yet be a nation in fact. Such was the legacy left by the young General, who had died in apparent defeat before he could see his victory.

The Republic must pay more than brief humiliation and a few casualties as the price of rout on Queenston Heights. The larger and longer price was its neighbor's hatred, first lighted in the Loyalists, now corroborated, inflamed, and deepened by invasion. Perhaps that mattered little to a nation which no foreign hatred could ever quench. It meant more to Canada, not yet a nation, than any foreigner would ever understand. To North America it meant that the continental boundary was permanent—if the Canadians could hold it. The Americans had assaulted the boundary and by their assault confirmed it in the mind of Canada.

One little victory at Queenston transformed the Canadian mind but of itself it could have no great effect on the course of the war. The victors must endure the grinding attrition of a long, one-sided struggle, for the losers must surely have learned from their blunders at Detroit and Niagara, must reorganize their forces, revive the historic strategy of invasion, and crush Canada in the end. Strangely enough, they did nothing of the sort.

General Smyth, succeeding Van Rensselaer, blustered on the safe side of the river, launched a few futile raids, planned a great attack, canceled it, and in reply to protests from the Committee of Patriotic Citizens observed that "The affair at Queenston is a caution against relying on crowds who go to the banks of the Niagara to look at a battle as on a theatrical performance." Dearborn sent a small raiding party to St. Regis, on the St. Lawrence, west of Montreal. The Americans were soon sent scurrying home. So the American Army hibernated at Plattsburg, on Lake Champlain.

By land 1812 had been a year of unbroken disaster for the United States, the result of military incompetence in the field and divided councils at home. Madison's government evidently had bitten off more than it could chew. Its first sensible act of the war was to dismiss Eustis and Hull. American troops, under new commanders, should conquer Canada handily in 1813.

By sea the unequaled American sailors had preyed like darting hawks upon Britain's far-flung commerce. They lacked heavy warships of the line, but a score of their "damned frigates," as Wellington was calling them, and 526 privateers had begun to accumulate their amazing tally of 1,344 prizes. The Republic was teaching its maritime mother the art of naval war.

Britain needed its navy on the coasts of Europe. In any case, it was playing a shrewd game. Since New England was against the war, Britain refrained from interfering too much with its commerce or raiding its coast, in the hope that the family quarrel of the Republic would ripen. At the proper moment the navy could contain the whole American littoral and even invade it.

Canada had no navy and only forty-four privateers, the famous Bluenose schooners of the Atlantic colonies. They managed to capture 200 American ships before the war was over.

It was not at sea, but on the fresh waters of the Great Lakes, that the major naval battles would be fought. It was on land that Canada could be conquered despite Britain's sea power.

The new American commander in the West, General William Henry Harrison, who had established his reputation at Tippecanoe, soon found that the Canadians were harder to fight than Indians. His winter advance on the American post of Frenchtown, at the west end of Lake Erie, previously captured by the Canadians and now held by a garrison of fifty whites and a hundred Indians, added another item to the lenghtening list of failure. A Canadian force of 1,000, half whites, and half Indians, crossed the Detroit River on the ice, drove off the Americans, and captured General Winchester. There followed an old-time Indian butchery. In the same winter 500 Canadians crossed the St. Lawrence from Prescott and burned the American fort at Ogdensburg.

In the spring of 1813 the war began at last to go against Canada. A Canadian siege of Fort Meigs (Toledo) collapsed when the militia were ordered home to plow their fields and feed Upper Canada. A summer attack on Fort Stephenson, on Lake Erie, also failed. Meanwhile Dearborn, who should have been taking Montreal, managed a successful amphibious expedition out of Sackets Harbor against York and found the Canadian defenses there in total confusion, many new guns not even mounted. The Canadians fought a brief battle and retreated. A few minutes later 200 Americans were killed by an exploding battery which the Americans took for a time bomb. In revenge they burned the parliament buildings and looted a few houses. Some stolen books and silver plate were later restored by the scrupulous American naval commander, Commodore Chauncey.

From York, Dearborn and Chauncey, with 6,000 troops, moved on Fort George. The Canadian garrison of 1,400 retreated northward along the shore of Lake Ontario to avoid annihilation. The United States had repealed the defeat of Queenston. It had seized the Niagara frontier. One more stroke could divide Upper from Lower Canada. That lethal stroke was never executed.

While the Canadian fleet on Lake Ontario raided Sackets Harbor and might have destroyed it if the egregious Prevost had not ordered a sudden retreat, the Americans under Dearborn pursued the Canadians from Fort George along the lake shore and camped, on June 5, at Stoney Creek to prepare for a decisive battle. The pause proved ruinous.

A small Canadian force under Colonel Harvey raided the dozing American camp at night and drove the invaders back to Fort George. The Canadians advanced cautiously to Beaver Dams, behind Queenston Heights, their Indians continuing to harass the Americans into exasperation. Six hundred picked men were ordered to take Beaver Dams and end the nuisance; at which moment a new Canadian heroine, successor to Madeleine de Verchères, emerged with a cow and a milk pail.

Laura Secord was the wife of a Canadian who had been wounded at Queenston. A poor woman, of little learning, she possessed the hard common sense and tough fiber of the wilderness.

As she set out to milk her cow one morning, she overheard the talk of some American soldiers near Fort George. They spoke of a surprise attack on Beaver Dams. Laura knew at once that somehow she must carry the news to her countrymen. It would not be easy to pass the American sentries but the cow solved that problem. Quietly prodded by its owner, it roamed into the forest. The sentries paid no attention as Laura followed it. Once concealed among the trees, she dropped her milk pail and started on a walk of twenty miles to the Canadian camp—twenty miles of thick brambles, swollen creeks, and stifling heat.

She was exhausted and her clothes in ribbons when she fell into the hands of Canadian scouts, only to find that they knew already of the impending American attack. But, like Brock, she had created a Canadian legend.

The Americans advanced, according to plan, on Beaver Dams and were mowed down by an Indian ambush. Such was their fear of massacre and torture that they surrenderd to white soldiers who had not fired a single shot. Thus ended, for the time being, the threat to the Canadian lifeline. The Republic had been repulsed by its own blunders, by Indian war whoops, a weak ambush, a brave farm wife, and a nameless milk cow.

American strategy of a sort was concerted outside the Niagara theater. The infamous General Wilkinson had been rewarded for his treason in the Mississippi country by command of the troops at Sackets Harbor. He was to take Kingston, descend the St. Lawrence, and join a force from Lake Champlain for the long-postponed attack on Montreal. The Canadians foresaw this danger and thwarted it by a lightning raid which drove the Americans out of Plattsburg and prevented any thrust at Montreal until the autumn.

On Lake Erie the Republic at last had found a naval commander to redeem its generals' fiasco on land. Captain Oliver Perry, aged twenty-eight, was hastily building a flotilla at Presque Isle in the hope of dominating the lake and opening the way to the recapture of Detroit and an invasion from the west. He fitted out nine trim vessels but this formidable fleet was bottled up in shallow water by the six Canadian warships based on Amherstburg under Captain Robert Barclay, a veteran of Trafalgar who, like Nelson, had lost an arm in battle.

While Barclay was absent, scouring the lake for provisions, Perry deftly floated his new ships over the seven-foot harbor bar with the use of air tanks. Barclay was taken completely by surprise. He saw that he must fight these superior forces at once, since the Canadians at Amherstburg, with Tecumseh's Indians, were close to starvation. They could not be fed if Perry controlled the lake. Barclay, therefore, launched the largest Canadian vessel, the *Detroit*, half

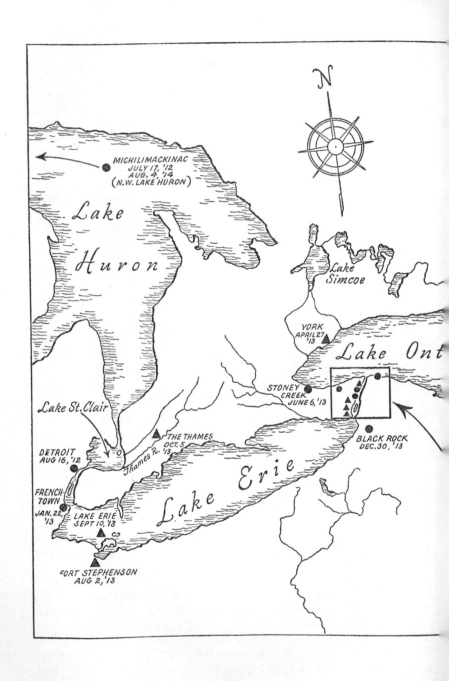

N

MICHILIMACKINAC
JULY 17, '12
AUG. 4, '14
(N.W. LAKE HURON)

Lake

Huron

Lake
Simcoe

YORK
APRIL 27
'13

Lake Ont

Lake St. Clair

STONEY
CREEK
JUNE 6, '13

THE THAMES
OCT. 5
'13

BLACK ROCK
DEC. 30, '13

DETROIT
AUG 16, '12

Thames R. '13

FRENCH-
TOWN
JAN. 22,
'13

LAKE ERIE
SEPT 10, '13

Lake Erie

FORT STEPHENSON
AUG 2, '13

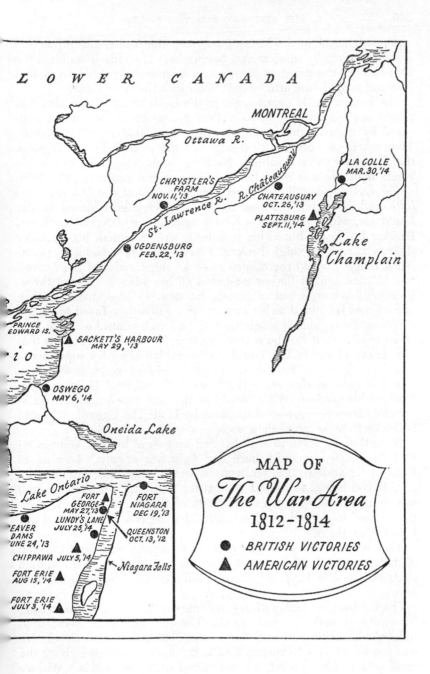

LOWER CANADA

MONTREAL

Ottawa R.

LA COLLE
MAR. 30, '14

CHRYSTLER'S
FARM
NOV. 11, '13

R. Châteauguay

CHATEAUGUAY
OCT. 26, '13

St. Lawrence R.

PLATTSBURG
SEPT. 11, '14

OGDENSBURG
FEB. 22, '13

Lake
Champlain

PRINCE
EDWARD IS.

SACKETT'S HARBOUR
MAY 29, '13

...io

OSWEGO
MAY 6, '14

Oneida Lake

Lake Ontario

FORT
GEORGE
MAY 27, '13

FORT
NIAGARA
DEC 19, '13

EAVER
DAMS
UNE 24, '13

LUNDY'S LANE
JULY 25, '14

QUEENSTON
OCT. 13, '12

CHIPPAWA JULY 5, '14

Niagara Falls

FORT ERIE
AUG 15, '14

FORT ERIE
JULY 3, '14

MAP OF
The War Area
1812–1814
● BRITISH VICTORIES
▲ AMERICAN VICTORIES

equipped, armed with clumsy guns from the Amherstburg fort and manned mostly by soldiers and landlubbers. Tecumseh watched the fleet sail on the night of September 9, promising his braves that "our father with one arm" would soon sink the Americans.

The largest battle ever fought in the fresh water of America was joined next day at Put in Bay. Two miniature fleets were maneuvered by trained commanders in the classic pattern of naval war. They raked each other with deadly broadsides until Perry's flagship, the *Lawrence*, was disabled. Nothing could stop this unsinkable young man. He was rowed to the *Niagara* and continued the fight.

The *Detroit*, equally damaged, had run foul of the *Queen Charlotte* and offered a helpless target. As Perry bore down in the *Lawrence*, with the dash of a Nelson against one of Nelson's officers, Barclay lay in his bunk, his remaining arm crippled, his shoulder shattered, and his thigh broken. Perry's final broadside, at point-blank range, mauled the other Canadian ships, reduced the *Detroit* to a helpless hulk, killed or wounded all her officers, and put three-fourths of her crew out of action. Barclay perforce struck his flag and offered his sword to his enemy, who gallantly refused to accept it. Young Perry, almost singlehanded, had won control of Lake Erie and would hold it for the rest of the war. It was no fault of his that the victory of Put in Bay could not be exploited by his superiors.

Colonel Proctor, an indifferent and hesitant commander, now found himself in desperate straits at Amherstburg. There was no food for his garrison. With control of the lake, the Americans could certainly launch a powerful invasion by land. The Canadians would be lucky to make good their escape.

Nevertheless, Tecumseh, in the last oration of his life, announced that "we wish to remain here and fight our enemy." Turning to Proctor, he added: "Father, you have the arms and ammunition. . . . If you intend to retreat, give them to us and you may go, and welcome. Our lives are in the hands of the Great Spirit. We are determined to defend our lands and, if it be His will, to leave our bones upon them."

That wish would soon be granted. Tecumseh was near the end of his long trail. If he must die, the old dream of an Indian confederacy, the Iroquois' dream and Pontiac's, would die with him.

Proctor burned Amherstburg and moved inland, after promising Tecumseh to make a stand on the Thames. Tecumseh decided to follow, reluctantly and with little hope. He had trusted Brock. He was too wise to trust Proctor. Beside the flames of Amherstburg the chief said to Blue Jacket, his old friend of many battles: "We are now going to follow the British and I feel well assured we shall never return."

The garrisons of Amherstburg and Detroit (also abandoned and burned) retreated slowly eastward up the Thames, Harrison and 4,000 Americans close on their heels. The race ended at Moravian-town where Proctor decided, faintheartedly, to make a stand.

Tecumseh made up his mind to die if his white allies fled. He had beheld in dreams his death and the end of that greater dream. "Brother warriors," he told his fellows, "we are now about to enter an engagement from which I shall never come out. My body will remain on the field of battle." He handed his sword to the Potawa-tomi chief, Shaubena. "When my son becomes a noted warrior," he said, "give him this."

Proctor ranged his 400 exhausted and hungry soldiers between the Thames on the left and a swamp on the right. Tecumseh placed his 1,000 Indians behind the swamp for an enfilading attack on the Americans' left. Dressed in buckskin, his head draped in a scarlet handkerchief and surmounted by a white feather, a silver tomahawk in his belt, he visited Proctor to say good-bye. "Father," he said, "have a big heart." But Proctor, on horseback, had placed himself well to the rear of his troops and, as Tecumseh noticed, seemed ready for quick flight.

Harrison's first wild cavalry charge broke and demoralized the Canadian line. Only fifty men escaped through the woods. The rest were killed or captured. Proctor and his staff galloped off before the enemy could reach them.

Tecumseh had waited in silence behind the swamp until the cavalry were within easy range. Then his volley annihilated the first line. He had picked out the American commander, Colonel Johnson, as his own target and ran at him, the silver tomahawk raised high for the throw. Johnson reeled from his wounds but fired his pistol as he fell, unconscious, to the ground. The pistol had been well aimed. A few yards from Johnson lay Tecumseh, the tomahawk beside his body. The Indians saw their chief's end, re-membered his presentiment of defeat, and bolted.

Harrison camped that night on the battlefield of the Republic's first decisive victory by land. His work of Tippecanoe was com-plete but he never saw his old enemy again. While the Americans slept, Tecumseh's warriors crept into the camp, carried his body into the woods and buried it without a stone to mark the grave of the last great chief in eastern America, where the Indians would never rise again.

The victory of Moraviantown was too far from the center of

events to matter much. By the last days of October, however, Wilkinson, with 7,000 men, was ready to advance from Sackets Harbor on the essential objective of Montreal. He was to be joined by General Hampton and an equal force from Lake Champlain. These converging armies posed for Canada the supreme question of its existence—would the French Canadians fight? The Americans doubted it, as they had doubted at Quebec in 1775.

Marching confidently down the Châteauguay toward the St. Lawrence and expecting no serious resistance, Hampton stumbled upon the fearless Charles de Salaberry and his French Canadians, who proposed to fight at La Fourche, only thirty-five miles southwest of Montreal. They were opportunely joined by another French-Canadian detachment under "Red George" Macdonell. It had arrived by river boat and a forced night march from Kingston. De Salaberry now had 1,600 men, nearly all of the French race and all well trained, to oppose Hampton's 7,000.

The Canadian commander was not only a brave man but an instinctive strategist. He disposed his left on a narrow stream, his right on the adjoining woods, and waited. Hampton planned to crush him from front and rear. Five thousand Americans would attack frontally while 1,500 waded the stream in the darkness behind the Canadians. It was a good plan but failed to work. At dawn the two American forces, separated and out of communication, each expected the other to begin the assault. De Salaberry climbed a dead tree and imediately saw his chance.

He left a handful of men to distract the main American force and wheeled suddenly on the lost Americans at his back, while his little band of Indians whooped and his bugles blared on all sides. The Americans, panic-stricken at this sudden show of strength, stampeded into the woods and shot at one another. Hampton halted his attack and retreated.

His defeat was perhaps of no great concern to the United States, being one of many, but Châteauguay was vital to Canada, for it had complemented Queenston by proving that the two Canadian races could stand together in defense of their country. The French Canadians already had established many myths of their own. Now they shared the joint myth of a united Canada. Grave Carleton's work at Quebec had survived its test. The opposite American myth of a divided people only awaiting liberation should have died at Châteauguay yet would persist half a century longer, with strange results.

Wilkinson learned that lesson the hard way as he moved down the St. Lawrence to join Hampton. He was harassed by Canadian patrols of both races and stopped cold by a stubborn skirmish at Chrysler's Farm. Hampton having limped back to Lake Champlain, Wilkinson, though still vastly outnumbering the Canadians, abandoned the attack on Montreal. Canada's center was safe. The Americans also withdrew from Fort George across the Niagara in December, after burning the village of Newark and turning 400 women and children into the snow.

The new Canadian field commander, General Gordon Drummond, was fresh from the wars of Europe. He closely resembled Brock— tall, handsome, with a narrow, hard face. Like Brock, he was reckless in attack.

Drummond crossed the Niagara River by night, only six days behind the Americans, and without firing a shot routed the garrison at Fort Niagara by a single stealthy bayonet charge. Advancing up the river, he systematically burned Lewiston, Fort Schlosser, Black Rock, and Buffalo.

The year of 1813, which had opened so badly for Canada on Lake Erie and in the West, ended with the Americans all south of the border and the Canadians holding the American side of the Niagara line.

Madison's government had begun to realize that a war against an overwhelming British Navy, now ruling the Atlantic, and a small Canadian Army able to move with disconcerting speed, was a highly questionable investment. The United States may have begun to suspect the truth, already taught to Britain by the Thirteen Colonies, that a few men fighting for their homes outnumbered a host of foreign invaders. It had learned that weak American generalship alone could not explain this long series of defeats, that the United States, with overwhelming manpower, simply was unable or unwilling to use it for foreign conquest.

Certainly the theory of continentalism, of one state between Mexico and the North Pole, was dying in the spring of 1814. But it was not yet dead. Though already seeking peace, the American government resolved on a supreme attempt to smash the border.

Its spring campaign made a discouraging start. The Canadians raided westward out of Mackinac, captured Prairie du Chien and even a vessel on the Mississippi. Seven hundred Americans sailed up the Great Lakes to retake Mackinac but 200 Canadians drove them back to their boats. Canada thus held Superior, Michigan, and Huron. It could not dislodge the Americans from Erie, after Perry's victory, and they raided inland at will.

Since Montreal, the essential target, seemed beyond its reach, the Republic decided to seize the Niagara frontier again. This theater was now held by Drummond's 4,000 troops, strung out on a weak line from Lake Erie along the Niagara River and Lake Ontario almost to York. The new American invasion was commanded by the able General Brown, who had succeeded Wilkinson.

Brown moved out of Buffalo on July 3 with about four thousand men, crossed the Niagara, defeated 2,000 Canadians near Chippawa and advanced diagonally across the Niagara peninsula on Drummond's base of Burlington, west of York. He had just passed the falls when he lurched, without warning, into 1,000 Canadians on a country crossroad known as Lundy's Lane.

Neither side was prepared for this encounter. The Canadians had marched southward, up the river, unaware of Brown's approach. The Americans had marched north, expecting no resistance. The two forces rounded a curve in the road to behold each other at short musket range.

Brown hesitated, exaggerating the enemy's probable force. The Canadians, knowing themselves outnumbered, began an orderly retreat. At that moment the massive figure of General Drummond galloped up the road, in almost exact reproduction of Brock's ride at Queenston. He ordered his troops to stand until he could bring up reinforcements from Fort George.

The Americans, under Winfield Scott, attacked in the sweltering dusk of July 25 and opened one of the most desperate battles ever fought in America.

Throughout the night 4,000 Americans and 3,000 Canadians reeled up and down the knoll where Drummond's seven field guns were captured, recaptured, and captured again by either side until both armies lay down, helpless, around their silent cannons. It was not over yet. The Americans suddenly came to life and prepared to deliver the knockout blow.

Drummond had lost nearly a third of his force. About twelve hundred effective Canadians faced twice as many Americans. Canada was beaten unless more reinforcements arrived soon. They arrived, 1,200 of them, after a weary march from Fort George, just as the Americans began their final attack.

The struggle around the seven cannons was resumed in the darkness. Again and again the Americans took the knoll and were hurled back as both sides reeled drunkenly in the carnage of hand-to-hand fighting. After six hours of this blind slaughter, the Americans slowly staggered back to Chippawa. The Canadians lay down beside their broken guns. In the sudden silence of dawn they heard the thunder of Niagara Falls.

That was Lundy's Lane. Who had won? Both sides claimed a

victory and both shared a common glory. The retrospective opinion of professional soldiers was of little importance to Canada. What mattered was that the American advance had been repulsed, the Niagara line was safe, and Lundy's Lane had entered, with Queenston and Châteauguay, the new myth of the infant nation.

For the rest of the summer the western war was confined to a series of desultory raids and counterraids, until 6,000 Americans, advancing again in the Niagara sector, met 3,000 Canadians under Drummond at Chippawa and withdrew after a brief skirmish. The Canadian lifeline still held.

Both sides had built ships furiously on Lake Ontario, though neither would risk battle. The Canadians took Oswego on May 6 but their small raiding party was destroyed between there and Sackets Harbor.

The Champlain corridor came to life in March. Wilkinson, as if he had not tasted enough defeat already, marched down the Richelieu with 4,000 men, was halted by 500 Canadians at La Colle, four miles inside the Canadian border, and retired once more.

While the land war thus presented the tedious spectacle of advance, retreat, blunder and heroism, the British Navy had systematically sealed up the Atlantic coast, despite the miraculous feats of the Yankee skippers, and ruined the United States' maritime commerce. Quebec and Halifax boomed. The American ports lay idle.

The navy next attacked the Maine shore. Its helpless inhabitants surrendered a vague territory and the border of 1783. At Halifax Britain proclaimed its possession of the coast south to the Penobscot. If this was a temporary gain, won by arms and soon to be surrendered by diplomacy, it showed the Republic's peril against naval power and cooled the early enthusiasm of the war party, the mere marchers and promenaders of Washington. They had learned a first lesson in amphibious warfare.

Britain now undertook to teach a harsher one. An amphibious expedition launched against Washington, in curious contrast to the British bungles of the Revolutionary War, was carried through without a hitch on August 24.

The new American capital, still a village on a steaming sandbank, was defended by Commodore Barney, a brave and resourceful privateersman, who had taken eleven British ships in ten days, and by General Winder, who had been captured by the Canadians at Stoney Creek in the previous year. The government, so eager for war in 1812, departed hastily at the sight of a British squadron on the Potomac. Madison and his plump, comely wife regretfully abandoned the presidential mansion.

Probably no government in history had so completely botched the defense of its capital. Barney had 400 sailors, Winder 400 regular troops and 5,000 militia—this out of a reputed military force of 93,000 in the Washington area. The British fleet brought 4,000 troops to avenge, as the London government explained, not very convincingly, the destruction of York.

Barney was compelled to burn his boats and retreat from the river to join Winder. Some six thousand Americans stood at Bladensburg, north of the town, with Madison and his Cabinet surveying the scene of expected victory from horseback, at a safe distance. The British advanced, eight Americans were killed and eleven wounded in the first volley, and the 5,000 militia promptly fled, leaving the regulars hopelessly outnumbered but boldly standing their ground. They were soon overpowered. Among the captives was the wounded Barney, whom the British rightly treated as a hero.

Britain had captured, with a few shots, the capital of the nation which had defeated it in the Revolution, but this was a raid only, a gesture and a lesson. However inexcusable and unnecessary the lesson might appear, it must have convinced the American Cabinet, then retreating on horseback, that the old motherland was still the most powerful state in the world when it could fight Napoleon and the Republic at the same time—too powerful, perhaps, for such unseemly gestures.

The questionable work of avenging York was completed with efficiency. In the evening the government's buildings, among them the unfinished Capitol, were partially burned, the presidential mansion seriously enough to require a complete new coat of paint to make it the White House. As the raiders departed in good order to their ships, the flames beside the Potomac wrote Britain's garish signature upon this exploit—or crime, as the Americans considered it—and informed the American government of a fact which had escaped Jefferson and Madison in the first place—that no other nation could win a war on the Atlantic while Britannia ruled the waves.

The British also learned something from the raid. Their attack on Baltimore was quickly repulsed while Francis Scott Key was composing "The Star-Spangled Banner." They sailed on to New Orleans and found defeat awaiting them in the person of an American general known as Old Hickory.

But the war had turned decisively in Britain's favor, especially now that Napoleon had been banished to Elba and Wellington could spare trained troops for the defense of Canada.

Canadians soon proved that they could be as reckless as Americans. Prevost, the fatuous Governor General, had prepared the final blow of the land war by an advance down the Richelieu and Lake Champlain, the fatal path of Burgoyne to Saratoga. Prevost had 11,000 troops, the largest army of the war, mostly reinforcements from Wellington's veterans of Europe. For the first time the odds were heavily with Canada.

The immediate objective was the American base at Plattsburg and the proper strategy was obvious enough to anyone but Prevost. Plattsburg, defended by 1,500 Americans, should have been taken and the Canadian guns then trained on the American lake flotilla nearby. Instead, by the highest idiocy of an idiotic war, Prevost forced his own ill-equipped little fleet into action against the American ships in Plattsburg Bay, promising a simultaneous land attack on the American fort.

The doomed Canadian ships, under the dauntless young Captain Downie, sailed into the ambush prepared by the American Commodore Macdonough, who soon proved himself as able as Perry. Prevost made no move on shore. For two hours the fleets fought at close quarters until one Canadian ship ran aground, another drifted helplessly into the American line. It was shot down like a sitting duck, seven of the eleven gunboats scurried away, and Downie hauled down the flag of his sinking *Confiance*. Watching this disaster calmly from the shore, Prevost gave his only comprehensible order of the day. He ordered his idle army to eat its dinner. On second thoughts, he ordered a general retreat.

The Americans had seen their capital burned, had lost the northern coast of Maine, could not seriously dent the Canadian lifeline but at least had blocked the Champlain invasion route. Cooler minds in Washington had realized the futility of the war as early as the previous winter, after two profitless campaigns. An offer of mediation by the Czar of Russia was quickly accepted by Madison in the autumn of 1813. Britain rejected outside intervention but was ready to negotiate direct with the Americans. Madison grasped this chance. The negotiations began early in 1814, while more men died uselessly on both sides, and were completed by the Treaty of Ghent on Christmas Eve, a fortnight before General Jackson routed the British attack on New Orleans.

Again, like that of 1783, the peace, as a French wit remarked, was the peace that passeth understanding. Britain had predominant bargaining power. It held Canada. It had bottled up the Atlantic. It had strangled American trade. It had occupied the northern coast of Maine. It had burned Washington as a crude reminder of its power. And as soon as it finished with Napoleon it could bring its victorious armies to America. Yet Britain refused to use its power. It left everything along the Canadian border in *status quo,* giving American diplomacy its second great victory.

This had not been Britain's original intention. To rectify the boundary mistakes of 1783, its secret plans included an Indian buffer state south of the Great Lakes; British possession of all islands in Passamaquoddy Bay; a "solid land connection" between New Brunswick and Lower Canada, carved out of Maine; the cession of a strip on the American side of the Niagara River; possession of Mackinac, the key to Lake Michigan and the far West; a border westward straight from the Lake of the Woods to the Mississippi; in the far West a border giving Britain possession of the Columbia and the Oregon country; and finally the prohibition of American fishing and curing on the shores of the Canadian Atlantic colonies.

In three respects that plan was quite impossible. The United States might have been defeated in the war (though defeat was never admitted) but it would fight again to hold the Niagara line and Mackinac or to prevent the surrender of the Ohio country west of the Wabash to the Indians.

Why Britain dropped these and all its other demands has never been explained. So far as the North American boundary was concerned, the operations of British diplomacy had always been past understanding. Anyway, the more Britain's position improved in Europe and America the more it diluted its terms of peace with the Americans, whose amateur negotiators, as usual, outguessed and outmaneuvered the professionals of London. In the result it might almost be said, contrary to the later legend, that the United States had lost a war and won a conference.

Britain wanted no more trouble with its rebellious child, the American Republic, and was influenced by the belief that any small advantage wrung from it by bargaining would cost too high a price in American resentment. That calculation does not fully account for the diplomatic defeat of Ghent. It was due mainly to the Duke of Wellington's sudden intervention, in November, 1814.

The great soldier, who was to prove such a failure in politics, solemnly advised the British government, at the critical moment, that it had no leg to stand on by the honorable traditions of war. To his soldierly mind the thing was simple and obvious—Britain had not conquered any of the enemy's territory (he forgot the occupation of northern Maine) and had been unable even to clear all the Americans out of the Lake Erie region. Therefore, Britain could not demand the cession of any American territory. If Britain wished to change the prewar boundary then, in the inflexible code of the Iron Duke, it must be prepared to carry the war to final victory.

No one in London had any stomach for that solution. If the Duke said so, all Britain's claims must be surrendered, and they were.

The war had begun ostensibly because the Republic would not tolerate the seizure of its ships and seamen, because it demanded freedom of the seas and the right to fish off the Canadian coast, and also because the American West intended to possess Canada. No word about these causes of the war was included in the peace treaty that ended it. The *status quo* was left undisturbed in every particular. The Americans might conveniently forget their lost causes. Canada would never forget its victory.

Actually the Treaty of Ghent was an armistice and the details of peace were worked out in various subsequent agreements.

Most notable of these, a new experiment in human affairs and the beginning of permanent peace on the border, was the Rush-Bagot agreement of 1817, by which the Great Lakes system was disarmed. Each nation was allowed four naval vessels of 100 tons on Lakes Champlain and Ontario, and two on the upper lakes. No mention was made of forts, but they were soon dismantled or turned into historical museums. Thus ended the long contest of the St. Lawrence Valley, begun with Champlain's fateful raid on the Iroquois. However, the Rush-Bagot agreement, one of humanity's most hopeful documents, should not be attributed to idealism on either side. Britain knew that the United States could always maintain superior naval forces on the Lakes. The Americans knew that disarmament would save them much unnecessary expense, now that they had abandoned the conquest of Canada.

When Britain withdrew its demand for a change in the boundary, the old line of the 49th Parallel, from the Lake of the Woods to the Rockies, was accepted, in 1818, as final. Britain also withdrew its claim for the right to navigate the Mississippi. The Americans lost the right to fish and cure along the Nova Scotia coast but, as a generous compromise, were allowed to use certain other Atlantic shores. This vague arrangement was to trouble the relations between Canada and its neighbor for nearly a hundred years.

More troublesome and far more important was the boundary in the far West, left unsettled because agreement was impossible. Astor's fur company had sold Astoria to the North West Company, knowing that it would probably be captured in the war, and the defenseless little trading post was occupied by a British naval detachment. As a result, said the American government, Astoria fell under the provisions of the Ghent Treaty and must be returned to its former owners along with all other occupied territory. An American expedition ceremoniously reoccupied it.

That piece of logic was too much for even Britain to swallow. Since Britain refused to accept the boundary of the 49th Parallel west of the Rockies and claimed the Columbia, since the United States refused to give up the claims established by Gray, Lewis and Clark, the whole undefined area called Oregon was to be occupied jointly for ten years, beginning in 1818.

Canadian fur traders, now reinstalled at Astoria, perhaps guessed the end of the dispute. The United States had discovered the Columbia mouth; it had sent Lewis and Clark overland to the Pacific; it intended to own everything south of Fuca's strait, especially the valuable harbors of Puget Sound, and in due time would have the power to enforce its claims. The practical question was whether Canada could hold its neighbor south of Fraser's newly discovered river, whether it could remain on the Pacific coast at all.

What had the United States gained by three years of promenading? Albert Gallatin, the brilliant Swiss immigrant boy, who was now secretary of the treasury, answered that "The war has renewed the national feelings and character which the Revolution had given and which were daily lessening. The people are now more American. They feel and act more as a nation. And I hope the permanency of the Union is thereby secured." Anyway, the American people's eyes were turned from Europe to their own West. A vigorous new nationalism and the long illusion of possible isolation from Europe's quarrels had begun.

Canada felt the same centripetal forces. It had been sucked into the war by extraneous affairs on the Atlantic as a loose and sprawling group of colonies, with only half a million people and fearful that the French Canadians would not fight. It had fought in unity, both races cheerfully sharing the cost in money and blood. Against a nation sixteen times as numerous it had held its border. It could not have stood alone without the support of British sea power, British regulars, and British generals like Brock and Drummond; but without a united people, without the Secords, Tecumsehs, and the nameless farm boys who had swarmed up Queenston Heights, reeled through the hot summer night of Lundy's Lane, and beaten the Americans at Châteauguay, Canada certainly would have been conquered. That it was not conquered, against the existing odds, is one of the miracles of war in America, half due to the fury of an invaded people and half to the follies and divisions of the invaders. No people could go through such a trial and ever forget it.

Who had won the war? The history books of Canada and the

United States would long give opposite versions. Canadians would think of Queenston Heights, a minor skirmish, as a great battle. Americans would exaggerate the naval fight of Put in Bay into something like a second Trafalgar. But so far as Canada was concerned there could be no doubt about the victory. Canada had survived the full power of the United States, and survival was a victory almost unimaginable in military calculation, certainly unimagined by the American statesmen who launched the war.

Military calculation and legal boundaries could not begin to reckon the deeper results among the Canadian people. In the disordered lines of battle the lineaments of a new creature, the Canadian, neither British nor French, had first appeared in America—a young face yet, blurred in infancy, indistinguishable to foreigners but slowly setting into harder lines. The original lines, which would change, were lines of hatred. Canadians had hated republicanism in the Revolution. After invasion of their soil they hated Americans. And obviously, if they were to resist an American nation, they must create one of their own.

It would take them another half century to write a constitution but in the War of 1812 they had discovered the essential contents of a nation. Those contents, little noted at the time, had been supplied by the Americans in the first place through the Revolution, the Loyalist migrations, the attack on Quebec. Now they had been revealed to all Canadians by the same unwitting instructor. Nothing henceforth could suppress them.

The boundary fixed at Ghent might be unfair to Canada, yet after this final test of war it was a durable boundary because the Americans at last had accepted it—accepted it dimly, still without understanding the fact that Canadians were determined to be Canadian. In what was truly Canada's war of liberation—though not the liberation planned by its neighbor—North America had been permanently divided, continentalism had died, and after two hundred years of ceaseless bloodshed a unique experiment in peaceful neighborly relations had begun.

Brock died young, by a casual bullet, on a little hill beside the Niagara. He left the kind of myth on which all nations are built.

17

Emperor and King

[1811–1824]

THOMAS DOUGLAS, FIFTH EARL OF SELKIRK, WAS EXPOSED WHILE
young to dangerous notions of romance, which must finally
destroy him.

In 1778, when he was seven years old, his father's manor house
on St. Mary's Isle, off the west coast of Scotland, was invaded by a
privateersman of the American Revolution and already the scourge
of the north Atlantic. John Paul Jones, also a native Scot, planned
to abduct the elder Selkirk as a prize of war. According to local
gossips, Jones also had personal reasons for this visit, believed himself to be the Scottish nobleman's natural son, and was determined
to establish his parentage. Unfortunately the intended victim was
absent from home at the time and Jones's crew had to satisfy
themselves with a few bags of household plate. Jones later returned
the loot to its owners and did not trouble them again. But young
Thomas Douglas never forgot his first distant brush with the New
World.

A few years afterward he listened to Robert Burns, enlivened
with hot toddy, shout Highland poems around the family fireplace,
among them "Scots wha hae wi' Wallace bled," composed in a
thunder storm the previous night. At college Douglas became a
fast friend of Walter Scott and an admirer of radical economists like
the retired Adam Smith. When he entered the world and assumed
the title Selkirk he was a youth with reddish locks, long, ascetic
face, and heavy-lidded eyes—a romantic, a radical, and an empire
builder.

St. Mary's Isle lay a long way from the West and the quarrels
of the American border. Yet Selkirk had fallen in love vicariously
with the New World on reading the voyages of his fellow country-
man, Alexander Mackenzie. He had drunk deep in the annual was-
sail of the Beaver Club at Montreal, eaten bear, venison and buffalo

258

tongue and, wielding a poker like a paddle, had knelt on the floor
with the tipsy partners of the North West Company to perform the
sacred canoe ritual to the chorus of a *voyageur*'s song. From then
on the young Earl's life had only one purpose. He must colonize
the Canadian West with the destitute Scottish crofters who lately
had been driven from their farms by greedy landlords.

If his soul was filled with romance, charity, and such stuff as
dreams are made of, Selkirk had a Scottish gift for business. To
support his western settlement he quietly bought in a third of the
Hudson's Bay Company's depressed stock at bargain prices. As
part of the deal the company granted him for ten shillings an area
of 116,000 square miles, stretching from Lake Winnipeg south across
the 49th Parallel to the headwaters of the Mississippi, and from the
Lake of the Woods west to the forks of the Red and Assiniboine.

In 1811 he sent out his first three shiploads of some seventy settlers. They were dumped that autumn on the west shore of Hudson
Bay, wintered there, fell to quarreling, and next spring toiled up
the Hayes River and Lake Winnipeg with bagpipes playing to end
their voyage, in August, 1812, on the muddy bank of the Red River,
hard by the North West Company's Fort Gibraltar. The war with
the United States was just beginning back east but it was no concern
of the Red River settlers, for they faced drought, frost, starvation,
and a local war of their own.

The hunger of two winters drove them south across the unmarked
border to hunt buffalo along the Pembina River. Twice the Nor'
Westers of Fort Gibraltar, fearing settlement as the destroyer of
the fur trade and essential pemmican, raided the settlement, which
answered with a single cannon and cut chain for bullets. The settlers finally were driven at musket point into the northern wilderness
and all their belongings were burned behind them. Reinforced by
Selkirk's second contingent, they returned to build their own Fort
Douglas, to destroy Fort Gibraltar and use its stockade to make
their houses.

After four years of misery and terror, they were reaping a rich
crop despite drought, cold, and locusts on the bottomless black
muck of the Red River valley. They had proved that wheat would
grow in the northern prairie; they had begun, with a few plowed
acres, to convert a buffalo pasture into an unbroken farm between
the Lakes and the Rockies; they had placed the first stable speck of
Canadian population on the empty western border.

But Canada's feeble little thrust into the Red River valley moved
far outside the huge tide of American settlement, now pouring west
over the broken dike of Louisiana. Happily for Canada, after the
War of 1812, this mighty current did not turn north. It headed
straight west and would never stop until it reached the Pacific.

By 1820 two and a half million land-hungry Americans, a quarter of the Republic's population had settled beyond the Alleghenies. Gripped by "Ohio fever," the farmers and townsmen of the Eastern states still loaded their wagons, piled their goods and cattle on leaky riverboats and crazy rafts, rowed through the mountains, swarmed across the plains, and overnight destroyed the old power balance of the nation.

It was now a nation of three distinct and hostile segments—the manufacturing North, where Eli Whitney had invented the cotton gin and discovered mass production in making muskets for the recent war; the South of cotton, soil depletion, and slavery; the West of free men in debt to the Eastern banks, discontented, seething with political radicalism and soon to produce the only American who could save the divided Union.

Already the original Union born at Philadelphia had become a museum piece and belonged to the ages.

The South had mortgaged its economic future to Negro labor and intended to spread its peculiar institution into the virgin West.

In the North the industrial revolution, with its thin upper crust of newly rich manufacturers, its city slums, its women and children toiling in the mills, was a travesty of Life, Liberty, and the Pursuit of Happiness as Jefferson conceived them. His dream of a society controlled by enlightened farmers was sinking into his nightmare of an urban proletariat. Hamilton's opposite theory of centralized government by the wise, the rich, and the good was in the saddle, but it too was challenged and terrified by the growing frontier population and dangerous egalitarian instincts of the West. And the issue of slavery challenged the existence of the Union itself while a gangling backwoods boy named Lincoln, who would test whether such a union could long endure, was helping his shiftless father to hack down the forest of Indiana.

Thus the War of 1812 was hardly finished before Canada faced a gigantic new neighbor, appalling in his energy, ambition, and wealth. He had joined the old lands and the new by carving the Erie Canal from Lake Erie to the Hudson; he was shuttling farm stuffs eastward and manufactures westward, spawning the metropolis of New York, assaulting the nostrils of Old Man River with the smoke of steamboats, soon laying roads of steel, and everywhere bursting in ceaseless explosion through all the known boundaries of human experience.

He was too busy with his own affairs to burst the political boundary of the 49th Parallel. However, in 1823 the Republic had proclaimed the Monroe Doctrine (an Americanized British invention, backed by the implicit power of the British Navy) and forbidden

European nations to colonize the Western Hemisphere, but the doctrine apparently did not compel the Canadian colonies to break their ties with Britain. The next year produced Henry Clay's American system of protective tariffs and economic self-containment, the organ voice of Daniel Webster fulminating against the "Tariff Abomination" and defending it with equal eloquence four years later. This restraint on trade across the border hardly touched Canada yet because its markets, protected by tariff preference and Navigation Acts, still lay in Britain, the American system, nevertheless, was the beginning of a tariff struggle on the North American boundary still under way in the middle of the twentieth century.

Finally, when the election of 1828 swept a lank and grizzled Westerner into the White House and even the Old Hickory of Jackson was almost crushed to suffocation in the inaugural reception, to be rescued from thirsty admirers through a broken window, the United States had taken on the third dimension of the West, along with a new version of Jefferson's democracy. So far Canada remained three minute and seemingly static blobs of settlement beside the Atlantic coast, the St. Lawrence, and the Red River.

That appearance was deceptive. The Canadians had begun to create a character quite different from their neighbor's; they did not seethe so easily; they were little given to slogans, processions, and written constitutions; they would never tolerate a flamboyant leader like Jackson and, for the most part, were content to lead a quiet life. They were not as quiet as they looked beside the restless Americans. Rebellion was brewing on the St. Lawrence. Civil war of a sort had broken out on the Red River.

In the summer of 1816 the North West Company, unable to dislodge Selkirk's settlers by bribery or threat, meditated a crushing act of terrorism. Who actually planned it, who was responsible for its bloody outcome, will never be known. All that the Red River farmers knew on June 19 was that a band of about seventy halfbreeds, French Canadians, and Indians decked out in feathers and war paint was riding toward the Red River from the west. The partners of the North West Company had discreetly absented themselves and left the job of butchery in the willing hands of Cuthbert Grant, a half-breed of "great nerve and resolution" but addicted (said the leading diarist of the day) to "ardent spirits and thinks nothing of a Bottle of Rum at a Sitting."

About five o'clock in the afternoon a boy stationed on the bastion of Fort Douglas saw Grant's party moving across the prairies. Governor Robert Semple recklessly led twenty men out of his fort and stood waiting in a grove called Seven Oaks.

The horsemen quickly surrounded the helpless settlers, who tried to surrender and begged for mercy. They were shot down in a single volley. As the killers closed in they found only six of the settlers alive, among them Semple, his hip shattered. Grant promised him protection but a moment later an Indian shot him to death.

Eleven more men hastened from the fort to the rescue of their comrades. They too were massacred. Grant counted twenty-three bodies in the grove of Seven Oaks and he had lost only one man killed and one wounded.

By his order—signed as a representative of the North West Company—the whole Red River settlement was to be abandoned. The settlers were herded into flatboats and headed down the Red River to the bay. Grant's half-breeds at Fort Douglas stripped naked to celebrate their triumph with a memorable orgy.

The Nor' Westers had underestimated the romantic young Earl from St. Mary's Isle. He had been warned in advance and was now moving west from Montreal with about a hundred veterans of the recent war, well trained and armed, to save his colony.

It was not until this expedition reached Lake Superior in July that Selkirk learned from a fleeing survivor the news of the massacre. Heartbroken and furious, he and his little army swept down on Fort William, the Nor' Westers' headquarters, seized it without a blow, arrested nine of the company's partners, charged them with complicity in the Seven Oaks murders, and sent them eastward under guard for trial in York.

Selkirk moved westward in the spring. His men scaled the walls of Fort Douglas in the night and announced the restoration of the colony. The settlers, who had wintered north of Lake Winnipeg, returned to receive the welcome of Selkirk in person. He had saved Canada's only western settlement. He had ruined himself.

In arresting nine North West Company partners at Fort William, he had not been dealing with half-breed assassins like Cuthbert Grant. His prisoners were some of the most powerful men in Canada and included the great explorer, Simon Fraser, William McGillivray, the Montreal capitalist, and a younger, unknown man, John McLoughlin, not to be unknown much longer.

The prisoners started eastward in three canoes. Storm overtook them in Whitefish Bay, one canoe foundered, nine men, but none of the partners, were drowned, and McLoughlin was dragged, half dead, from the water. Selkirk must pay high for this accident.

After seeing his colony set to rights, he paddled back to York at leisure, confident that the courts of Canada would confirm his acts of justice and punish his enemies. Instead, he found himself indicted for the seizure of Fort William and fined £2,000. All his charges against the Nor' Westers were dismissed. His fortune melting in the lawyers' bills of endless litigation, his spirit and health exhausted, the romantic hopes of his youth broken by the reality of the frontier, he died in Europe two years later, hardly realizing that the plows of his Red River colony, in lengthening furrows along the border, had opened to Canada the granary of the western plains.

McLoughlin meanwhile had survived the icy waters of Lake Superior and begun a fabulous career. It would lead him to the Pacific coast, to the ultimate boundary struggle with the United States, to dictatorship, feud, violence and Christian charity, eventually to American citizenship.

This unique and apocalyptic creature had been born at Rivière du Loup, Quebec, in 1874. His father, a bush farmer of mixed French-Canadian, Irish and Scottish blood, was of little account, but the boy's rich maternal relations educated him. He emerged from a sketchy two-year course in medicine as a giant of six feet four inches, with a mane of black hair falling to his shoulders, a face already hardening into the graven lines of an Old Testament prophet, and a lust for the wilderness.

The young doctor joined the North West Company, was soon one of its chief traders, and having fathered a son by some Indian woman, married a pretty half-breed lady, widow of Alexander McKay, who had accompanied Mackenzie to the Pacific and been murdered by the Indians of Vancouver Island.

The escape from drowning as Selkirk's prisoner did not satisfy the honor of McLoughlin. He set out immediately after the accident for York Factory, where he demanded trial on Selkirk's baseless charge of murder at Seven Oaks. The jury promptly acquitted him. He was ready for the incredible work of his life.

The long fur war, culminating in Grant's massacre, had brought the Hudson's Bay and North West Companies close to bankruptcy. Both were ready for peace. In the London negotiations leading to their merger of 1821 McLoughlin was one of the chief negotiators. He proved himself a subtle politician, a tough bargainer, and a gaudy figure in black clerical tailcoat, a gold-headed cane in his hand, the wild mane of hair now almost white.

The enlarged Hudson's Bay Company was the legal government of an empire rolling from the Red River to the mouth of the Columbia. Its own inner government had become a complex hierarchy of Hudson's Bay men and Nor' Westers. Its Little Emperor, as all men called him, was George Simpson, and his like had never been seen before in the fur trade of America.

Born a bastard in Scotland, this systematic, cunning, and potent man, with his barrel-shaped body, his shiny, cannon-ball head and round, florid face, had quickly elbowed his way through life and risen in the Hudson's Bay Company solely by his own merit. Few men, if any, had ever traveled so far, back and forth across America, or at such speed. He moved with an emperor's procession of singing *voyageurs,* kilted Highland pipers, feasts, balls, rousing orations, and secret conferences at every post from Montreal to Astoria.

The fur trade had found in him a strategist, fighter, diplomat, and general manager. He knew the smallest detail of its business, could stand any hardship on the trail, was at home in a London drawing room or an Indian camp. Business, profit, and power were his life but in his ceaseless wanderings he found time to beget unnumbered half-breed bastards, whose mothers he always supported generously and ordered his colleagues to do the same for their casual offspring. He was not only an autocrat, businessman, and amorist, he was also a penetrating historian, though a pompous and clumsy writer. Every night, by campfire or the candle of some remote post, he scrupulously recorded the day's events in a minute diary. His frank and canny opinion of every company official was locked away in a secret box. For double secrecy no name was attached to any of these dossiers but each was numbered by the writer's private code for future reference.

Thus Simpson, after his first meeting with McLoughlin on the western trail: "He was such a figure as I should not like to meet on a dark night in one of the bye lanes in the neighborhood of London, dressed in clothes that had once been fashionable, but now covered with a thousand patches of different colors, his beard would do honour to the chin of a Grizzly Bear, his face and hands evidently show that he had not lost much time at his *Toilette,* loaded with Arms and his own herculean dimensions forming a *tout ensemble* that would convey a good idea of the highwaymen of former Days . . . Wanting in system and regularity but a man of strict honour and integrity . . . ungovernable violent temper and turbulent disposition."

In Simpson and McLoughlin two primitive and irreconcilable forces had met. The whole American West was not large enough to contain them both. In the beginning, however, they got along well enough, each measuring the strength and doubting the purposes of the other.

Simpson picked McLoughlin for the key post of Astoria, now renamed Fort George, and instructed him to hold Oregon, at least north of the Columbia, for the Empire. McLoughlin started west as fast as his *voyageurs* could paddle him. Simpson was to follow some weeks later from York Factory and, to demonstrate the superior speed of the Emperor, overtook his lieutenant by racing from the shores of Hudson Bay to the Columbia in eighty-four days, a new transcontinental speed record.

In 1824 the two men, so far friendly but hastening to inevitable quarrel, wintered on the Pacific and in their lonely fur post discussed the chance of repelling the tide of American settlement. It was hardly a trickle yet. Only a few independent fur traders had ventured into Oregon but they could be bought off or driven out by cutthroat competition among the Indians. Still, Simpson, the practical man of business, was not deceived. He knew what was coming and wrote his opinion in the locked diary (meanwhile gallantly resisting the efforts of the Indian Princess Chowie to bribe him into marriage with a dowry of a hundred beaver skins).

The principal western depot of his company, Simpson noted, "should be situated North of this place, about Two or Three Degrees, at the mouth of Fraser's River." Such a post might hold the international boundary at or near that river, if Oregon was lost to the Americans, and it could launch Simpson's favorite project of transpacific trade with the fur markets of China.

That suggestion of a more northern fort was only a shot in the dark then, but a sure shot. As Simpson surmised, the Fraser, not the Columbia, was the river of Canadian destiny, and it contained more in gold, adventure, and politics than he or any man could guess. McLoughlin at once opposed the projected second line of defense. Oregon, he said, was the supreme prize and Oregon must be held.

Simpson told him to hold it if he could. The fort of Astoria, accordingly, was moved to a better site, ninety miles up the Columbia. Simpson raised the Union Jack, broke a bottle of rum on the flagpole and named the new post Vancouver, as a gesture of British power, after the captain who had wrongly claimed the river's discovery. Then the Emperor started eastward. To him Fort Vancouver was a brief stopping place in his perpetual roamings, a depot of trade and a doubtful gamble in international power. To McLoughlin it was the New Jerusalem.

He was now installed under the Emperor as king of a kingdom lying between the Rockies and the sea, from Russian Alaska to Spanish California—the last king in America and perhaps the most successful. His court was a massive banquet hall where no woman was ever allowed to enter; his attendants Scottish pipers playing behind the throne; his subjects a handful of traders and 80,000 Indians; his methods Spartan discipline mixed with devout religion and prodigal generosity to everyone. But no kingdom could long resist the western thrust of the Republic.

18

Creatures Large and Tiny

[1837–1898]

RRIVING AT YORK AS LIEUTENANT GOVERNOR IN 1806, SIR FRANCIS Gore, a retired British cavalryman with a wealth of ignorance and prejudice, announced that "I have had the King's interest only at Heart, and I have and ever will contend against Democratic Principles." He would never learn that he was contending against the nature of North America. Least of all could he discern the approaching shape of rebellion. Americans had challenged Britain's hold on empty Oregon. Its hold on the settled St. Lawrence Valley was now to be challenged by Canadians.

What Gore, the British government, and its agents in Canada failed to see was an obvious and inescapable fact—that the Canadian people were North Americans and not transplanted Englishmen or Frenchmen. The French Canadians had been North Americans and nothing else for two hundred years. The Loyalists who fled the American Revolution were Americans also. For the most part their people had spent several generations in the New World. The subsequent immigrants to Canada were either citizens of the American Republic or Britons who soon took on the local coloration, the thoughtways and the democratic habits of the frontier.

All this Britain could not understand and could not be made to understand short of rebellion. It had erected in Canada Pitt's perfect counterpart of the British Constitution but that was a fraud. The British people, though few of them yet voted, were represented by a Parliament which could make and unmake governments and had unmade two Stuart kings. The Canadian colonies were governed by the governors sent out from London, by executive councils, and by appointed legislative councils which had power to veto the legislation of the elected assemblies.

There was no room under the Canadian Constitution for Gore's nightmare of democratic principles and no chance—or so Britain thought—for a second republican eruption in America.

In the soil of this cozy system there soon flourished at Quebec a "Château Clique" and an "Aristocracy of Shopkeepers," at York a tight-knit group of court sycophants, salaried officials, land jobbers, privileged gentry, and political heelers called the Family Compact. Family and breeding had little to do with membership, but government certainly was compact. Inevitably it produced a counterpressure in a Reform movement. Driven too far, it could become a movement of revolution.

This counterpressure was nearing the explosion point by the first decade of the nineteenth century.

In the York Assembly the elected Reformers were discovering irregularities in the public accounts.

William Weeks, an Irishman, who had learned law in the New York office of Aaron Burr and, moving to Canada, had become one of the founders of the Reform Party, challenged William Dickson, a kept lawyer of the Family Compact, to a duel after a courtroom argument and was shot to death in this affair of honor on the American side of the Niagara River.

Bartimus Ferguson, another Reformer, dared to criticize the Governor and was put in stocks daily for a month.

Robert Gourlay suggested that the Family Compact, for all its devotion to the crown, had learned to turn a pretty penny in land graft. He was promptly jailed.

John Galt, a Scottish poet who was patriotically promoting the immigration of his countrymen to Upper Canada, called York "one of the worst blue-devil haunts on the face of the earth."

The authentic face of rebellion appeared first in a Dundee draper and amateur journalist, William Lyon Mackenzie. He would be the Sam Adams of a revolution lacking a Washington and apparently a comic failure, yet powerful enough to revolutionize the British Empire.

Mackenzie was a squat and crabbed man with bulging forehead, a cadaverous face, a bristling fringe of white side whisker, and a burning, fanatic eye. The new Lieutenant Governor, Sir Francis Bond Head, recorded his impression of the Canadian agitator with British condescension: "Afraid to look me in the face, he sat, with his feet not reaching the ground, and with his countenance averted from me, at an angle of about seventy degrees; while, with the eccentricity, the volubility and indeed the appearance of a madman, the Tiny Creature raved about grievances here and grievances there."

It was impossible for a man like Head to understand a man like

Mackenzie. "You see," the Prime Minister, Lord Melbourne, had once remarked to Head over his shaving mug, "you're such a damned odd fellow!" The gossips of London said, indeed, that Head had been appointed governor by mistake for another man of the same name, but doubtless he would do to govern Canada. In the Damned Odd Fellow and the Tiny Creature were posed again those fundamental forces of Old World and New that had exploded in the American Revolution.

Elected to the York Assembly, hurled out by the scruff of the neck and frequently re-elected, Mackenzie soon made himself the leader of reform and, after its constant rejection, began to meditate rebellion.

A loyalist mob threw the press of his newspaper, the *Colonial Advocate,* into Lake Ontario for publishing such phrases as "Not to gain the wealth of the Indies would I now cringe to the funguses I have beheld in this country, more pestilential in the Town of York than the marshes and quagmires with which it is environed."

Mackenzie sued for damages, was awarded £625, and continued, as a popular hero, to distill his corroding editorials. The Family Compact revenged itself by tearing down the first fourteen feet of Brock's hideous new monument on Queenston Heights because it contained in its cornerstone, among other papers, some issues of the *Colonial Advocate.*

The Tiny Creature had his own political machine, meeting at Elliott's Tavern and, more secretly, in John Doel's brewery where, on July 31, 1837, was issued the Canadian version of the Declaration of Independence, somewhat awkwardly modeled on the original. It declared that "Government is founded on the authority, and is instituted for the benefit of a people; when, therefore, any Government long and systematically ceases to answer the great ends of its foundation, the people have a natural right given them by their Creator to seek after and establish such institutions as will yield the greatest quantity of happiness to the greatest number."

Here the latest doctrines of Bentham were united with Locke's Natural Rights. Mackenzie proposed to combine them in a new republic north of the St. Lawrence.

In every speech he grow bolder and presently was asking: "Is then the country under the control of a lawless band of sworn villains? If so, the citizens will have to form not only political unions but armed associations for mutual self-defence . . . Sir Francis may find that an opinion is gaining ground that deeds are doing among us, which will have to be answered by an appeal to cold steel."

Loyalists broke up his meetings but they could not stop Mackenzie and the Patriots. They were drilling in the forest by night, learning to shoot at wild pigeons, forging pikes at village smithies, organizing in companies with secret passwords. They had drafted a constitution for an independent Canadian state, in strict imitation of the Philadelphia document. And if they decided to strike with cold steel, to destroy British government in Canada and establish their republic, they must certainly involve the great Republic across the river.

Mackenzie's Patriots worked in collaboration with the *Patriotes* of Lower Canada. The French Canadians also had thrown up a leader in Louis Joseph Papineau who, though himself a grand seigneur, had embraced in rather dilettante fashion, the democracy of the United States. This confused man—regal in stature, superbly handsome, with noble Gallic face and plume of curling hair—had the natural orator's mortal defect. He could rouse himself and the people. He never knew for what purpose. The moment of crisis must leave him impotent.

In any case there was no base for rebellion. As in 1775, the church stood solidly with the government. The *habitants* might be temporarily hypnotized by the great orator but few of these well-disciplined folk, unshaken by war, conquest, and every kind of disaster, could be persuaded to attack established authority. Rebellion, if it came, must be only a superficial disturbance on the deep current of Quebec's feudal history, a passing aberration in its nature.

Outwardly, however, the agitation in French Canada resembled more closely than Mackenzie's the theories and tactics of the American Revolution, though few French Canadians admired or understood it. The *Patriotes* called themselves *"Fils de la Liberté"* after the American "Sons of Liberty." They even tried to revive the old American economic weapon by refusing to wear British cloth and their leaders appeared before the Assembly dressed in outlandish, bulging garments of Quebec *étoffe du pays.*

Papineau, a master of parliamentary maneuver, was not so much concerned as Mackenzie with man's economic rights but he burned with political rights, he blockaded the Governor's legislation and money appropriations in the Assembly, he brought government almost to a standstill, with matchless eloquence he paraded the ghosts of the Conquest and, on every village platform, he ignited the French Canadians' old hatred of the English conquerors.

America's cruel depression of 1837 supplied the spark for this tinder. All the grievances of unemployment, poverty, and business failure could now be blamed on the royal governors, whose governments were soon close to bankruptcy. Mackenzie and Papineau, euphoric in their sense of mob power, were carried beyond their depth into what they seemed to consider a reproduction of the American Revolution.

Even then Head was assuring the British government that the Tiny Creature could do no harm. "First," the Governor reported of Mackenzie, "he wrote, and then he printed, and then he rode and then he spoke, stamped, foamed, wiped his seditious little mouth and then spoke again; and thus, like a squirrel in a cage, he continued with astonishing assiduity the centre of a revolutionary career." But, said Head, there was no need to worry.

Unfortunately Head was a better writer than governor. In the autumn he sent all the regular troops from York to Kingston, under the impression that they might be needed by the Governor General, Sir John Colborne, to suppress a rebellion in Lower Canada. Several thousand rifles were left unprotected in the York City Hall. The temptation thus provided was too much for Mackenzie. He summoned his lieutenants to Doel's brewery and ordered the revolution.

Still the Damned Odd Fellow in Government House was unmoved. He had been informed of Mackenzie's plans by James Hogg, of Hogg's Hollow, one of Mackenzie's frightened followers, but dismissed the warning with contempt. He did not "apprehend a rebellion in Upper Canada."

This worst-managed of rebellions began almost accidentally on November 6, when the loyal Doric Club drove a mob of *Patriotes* through the streets of Montreal into the suburbs. Papineau fled and the Governor General wrongly concluded that he would raise the countryside. Warrants issued for the arrest of Papineau and his lieutenants accomplished precisely this result.

The inhabitants of the Richelieu valley gathered in the villages of St. Denis and St. Charles, planted Trees of Liberty, surmounted by Liberty's cap, and swore their solemn oaths of freedom. A detachment of Colborne's soldiers was met with rusty muskets at St. Denis and driven off, but two days later the Governor's troops easily captured St. Charles. Papineau, having roused the rebellion with no clear purpose and no military plan, decamped hurriedly to the United States. The skirmish of the Richelieu was finished.

A bolder rebel, J. O. Chenier, and a mysterious foreigner, Amaury Girod, assembled five hundred followers in the village of St. Eustache, eighteen miles northwest of Montreal, armed only with muskets and alcohol, and casually awaited the soldiers' approach. At Colborne's appearance with 2,000 soldiers, Girod fled and soon blew his brains out. Chenier and 200 villagers, locking themselves in the church, bravely withstood a brief siege until they were smoked out, killed, or overwhelmed.

Unaware that the rebellion was collapsing in Lower Canada, Mackenzie had altered the timetable of Doel's brewery to strike simultaneously with Papineau.

December 5, the chosen day of freedom, found at Montgomery's Tavern, four miles north of York, the most improbable army in the history of revolution—some seven or eight hundred Patriots with blunderbuss and pike, with banners demanding "Liberty or Death!"; the Tiny Creature mounted on a white farm horse in absurd imitation of George Washington and shouting contradictory orders; his lieutenants already quarreling and his followers bewildered, cold, and hungry.

The attackers were hardly more frightened than the defenders. At York the Damned Odd Fellow had been roused from his bed in the middle of the night and now stood with double-barreled gun in hand and three pistols stuffed in his belt, obediently drilling with the Chief Justice and other leaders of the Family Compact under the instructions of a nameless sergeant.

Thus at York the wavering front against the deep damnation of Democratic Principles, the young Queen's imperial interests, and the highly practical interests of the Compact in loyal combination but unhappily without the soldiers, who had been sent where they were least needed.

At Montgomery's Tavern the depressing news of the *Patriotes'* defeat in the Richelieu country—counsels of caution—scared Patriots proposing to go home—the only soldier among them, Anthony Anderson, dead in a chance skirmish with a loyalist—Mackenzie, half crazy by now, declaring that it was too late to turn back, offering to lead the attack himself, mounting his horse again, his meager body lost in the folds of a vast overcoat, and finally giving the order to advance.

Then a disorderly march down Yonge Street to Gallows Hill—a pause to parley with government agents under a white flag—offer of amnesty by the quaking Governor—contemptuous rejection by Mackenzie—sudden hesitation among the rebels—refusal to advance and, instead of Liberty or Death, demand for dinner. At which Mackenzie's mind cracked and, says the diary of a participant, "he went on like a lunatic. Once or twice I thought he was going to have a fit."

Such a fit now afflicted him. While rations were being served on Gallows Hill, he leaped from his horse, rushed to a house beside the road and set it afire with his own hands. The rabble gaped at this lunacy and all confidence in their leader oozed out. They began to stream back to Montgomery's Tavern.

If he could not fight, Mackenzie could talk. His raging eloquence throughout the afternoon revived the rebellion. Again it was Liberty or Death. At dusk the rebels marched upon the town. Then followed one of the most comical and decisive moments in the record of the British peoples.

Some thirty loyalists under Sheriff Jarvis stood guard by their barricade on the town's outskirts. They fired at the approaching mob and scampered off for their lives. The first rebels returned the fire and dropped to the ground as they reloaded their muskets. Whereupon the remainder, thinking all their comrades shot down, turned and ran. Mackenzie on his horse was swept back in the wild procession to Montgomery's Tavern.

Then more conferences, more quarrels, more oratory. To attack again or await promised reinforcements from the Niagara country? The next day passed in fruitless wrangle, speeches by Mackenzie, reports from spies in York, shortages of food and ammunition, increasing derangement.

As the revolutionary capital of Montgomery's Tavern thus reeled in oratory and doubt, Colonel James FitzGibbon, a veteran of Brock's army, had managed to convert York into some semblance of order. On December 7 he marched out of the town with 1,100 ill-trained troops, to the music of two bands and the cheers of the populace, the Governor urging him on but remaining discreetly in the rear.

Two hundred rebels met the attack but, outnumbered and out-flanked, quickly scattered. Soon cannon balls were ripping through the frail walls of the tavern. Its occupants ran for the woods. The rebellion had been crushed in fifteen minutes with only one man killed, a rebel.

Now that all danger was past, the Governor took full charge, offered pardons wholesale to his prisoners and then, changing his mind, arrested them for treason and burned down the tavern to "mark and record, by some act of stern vengeance, the important victory." After burning down another house over FitzGibbon's protest and turning a woman and four children into the road, Head marched back to York with a flush of martial glory and the assurance that the British Empire, in such hands as his, would go serenely on its way. That was the one sure thing that could never happen.

Mackenzie had escaped from the tavern, horseless, hopeless, and half naked. He scurried through Hogg's Hollow, waded the icy winter streams, hid in frozen ditches while the Governor's soldiers passed a few feet away, slept in haystacks or found refuge in the attics of his friends until he came at last to the Niagara River, disguised as an old woman, with formidable growth of whisker. There he found a boat and rowed to the American shore, followed by the baffled shouts of his pursuers.

He had left behind eleven lieutenants to be executed for treason, ninety-two to be exiled in Van Diemen's Land, and political consequences past reckoning.

The Rebellion of 1837 was now ended, in the opinion of the Damned Odd Fellow. His career at least was ended. The young Queen Victoria, awakened a few months before to learn of her ascension to the throne, saw her empire facing another quarrel in America. Advised by Lord Melbourne, she did not propose to repeat her grandfather's mistake.

Britain appointed a dictator to reform the whole government of Canada and dismissed Bond Head, who thought it wise to retire to England through the United States, garbed for safety as a valet. He was discovered sitting pensively on a wheelbarrow in an innyard at Watertown, invited to breakfast by a whimsical band of refugee Patriots, and sent on his way with cheers. With him went the Second British Empire, begun at Yorktown and ended at York.

The events launched by the affair of Montgomery's Tavern would take longer to settle than the affair of Lexington and would have consequences hardly less important. The Rebellion had failed as a military coup, partly because it had been bungled from the beginning but mostly because a small minority of Canadians in Upper or Lower Canada supported it. As a political movement it would succeed beyond the imagination of Mackenzie, Bond Head, the British government, or the interested spectators of the United States. The Third British Empire—an empire by no recognizable definition—would require more than a century of gestation, but it had been conceived at the barricades of York and nothing could prevent its birth.

At the beginning of this slow process the Rebellion almost caused a third war between Britain and the United States.

Safe on the territory of the Republic and welcomed, at first, by admiring American republicans, Mackenzie undertook at once to foment this war. His snarling speeches, his prophetic look, his devotion to American principles, his promise to make Canada a republic or part of the United States soon gathered a band of some thousand Canadian refugees and American sympathizers on Navy Island, within the Canadian boundary on the Niagara River.

Here great plans for an invasion of Canada were hastily concerted. Mackenzie formed the provisional government of the new republic, issued his own money and raised his own flag with the two stars of Upper and Lower Canada. Americans smuggled muskets out of the U.S. arsenal at Buffalo and produced a government cannon "to shoot wild ducks."

The Canadian authorities, feeling unable to dislodge the mock government of Navy Island, decided to cut off its sources of supply, carried daily from the American shore by the little American steamer *Caroline*. On the night of December 29 a Canadian party crossed the river to reach the *Caroline*, then berthed at Schlosser. The raiders leaped upon her decks and hurled her crew and passengers ashore. One man was killed in the melee. The ship was sent in flames over Niagara Falls.

An overt act of war had been committed against the United States. An American citizen, Amos Durfee, had been killed. A Jefferson, Madison, or Jackson might have reacted differently but the new American President, Martin Van Buren, had no intention of embroiling himself in a border quarrel when he was grappling, or refusing to grapple, with a depression at home.

"Little Van" or the "Little Magician," as he was called, a person of delicate features, luxuriant curls, and immaculate lawyer's language—a piece of Dresden china after the Hickory of Jackson—had assured the Americans, in his inaugural address, that they enjoyed "an aggregate of human prosperity surely not elsewhere to be found" and within two months the banking system came crashing down around his ears. The unemployed laborers and bankrupt farmers of the Atlantic coast swarmed westward for survival.

After eight years of abundant Jacksonian Democracy, the nation was prostrate.

Van Buren could only advise the public, in neat lawyer's circumlocutions, that it was no business of the government to interfere. It was even whispered in Washington that he had departed so far from the principles of his mentor as to buy gold spoons for the White House.

If the Little Magician could not conjure with the enemy of American depression, he was determined at least to avoid a British enemy across the St. Lawrence. He might be gratified to learn that Jacksonian Democracy had spread abroad through such men as Mackenzie, but that also was no business of Van Buren's government. Why should it be concerned when the obvious course of American expansion lay in the Southwest, when Canada no longer was feared as a British base of invasion, and when the immediate problem was economic collapse?

Certainly some sensible Americans, in addition to the armed liberators of Navy Island, were still talking of Manifest Destiny's future advance to the North Pole. This, they thought, would come about not by conquest but by the laws of geography and nature. No European power—so the unanswerable logic went—could retain its colonies in the New World for long. In due time, therefore, Canada would detach itself from the Empire and fall, like a ripe plum, into the waiting lap of its neighbor.

The first half of this proposition was true—Canada could not be held as a British colony. The second half was wishful thinking. The Americans did not imagine, nor did the Canadians, because the thing was unimaginable, that there could be another kind of connection between Britain and Canada in a new kind of empire already conceived but yet to be brought forth.

Though the *Caroline*, in its flaming descent of Niagara Falls, had lighted the border again, the liberators of Canada need expect no help from Van Buren—or serious interference either. This renewal of the old conflict, only twenty-four years after the War of 1812, had gone far beyond the control of its instigator. Mackenzie's republic quickly decamped from Navy Island and later he was arrested by the American government under its Neutrality Act.

The disillusioned rebel spent eleven months in jail at Rochester and then, supporting himself by hack writing for the American press, often saw his wife and family without food after he had sold the gold medal presented to him by the Patriots of York.

His exile of itself symbolized the process now beginning to revolutionize the Empire. In the United States his wife bore a daughter who, some thirty years later, would bear a son named William Lyon Mackenzie King, the future Prime Minister of a completely independent Canada; and in the house of the rebel's grandson, displayed with pride, would always hang a copy of Bond Head's proclamation offering a reward of £1,000 for Mackenzie's capture.

The rebel eventually returned to Canada, fully pardoned, was elected to Parliament, and ended his days as a loyal subject of the Queen. Meanwhile the fire he had lighted on the border was driving the Empire and Republic toward war.

War certainly would have resulted if Van Buren's government had shared any of Jefferson's illusions about the nature of Canada, if the old War Hawks had controlled the Congress, if the British government had not been determined to save the peace at almost any price, despite irritating provocations.

The United States could maintain a meticulous neutrality in the troubles of its neighbor. Its neutral policy was supported by the great majority of the nation. It could not control the border states. They had never been reconciled to the Treaty of Ghent, still believed that Canadians desired liberation, and saw in Mackenzie's Rebellion the proof of their theory.

Thus with the tacit connivance of state authorities and against the mild protests of the Federal government, the border spawned a network of secret societies, usually organized with Masonic ritual— the Canadian Refugees Association, the Sons of Liberty, the Hunters and Chasers of the Eastern Frontier—recruited among passionate republicans, the unemployed, and some thrifty Americans who were promised a cash bounty and a grant of land in a Canadian republic. As always, patriotism, avarice, secrecy, and folly—folly most of all— were linked in the latest assault against the boundary.

After a few minor raids out of Vermont and Detroit had been easily repelled, the Hunters and Chasers, now supposed to number 50,000 secret members from Vermont to Michigan, and from Canada to the Southern states, assembled in convention at Cleveland, in September, 1838, to establish a republican government for Upper Canada, to issue paper money, and to plan a new invasion in force.

The Van Buren government protested, the British minister at Washington denounced the "vast hordes of banditti and assassins maturing plans for the desolation and ruin of a British territory," General Winfield Scott was sent to the border, where he had learned his first lesson under Brock's instructions at Queenston Heights, but the state authorities winked at these preparations as two great powers edged uncomfortably close to an open clash.

The untrained militia of Canada stood awkwardly to arms along the St. Lawrence (among them a gawky youth who presently would bestride Canada like a genial colossus). The Van Buren government continued to protest. The statesmen of London warned their young queen that she might inherit the war of her grandfather. General Scott argued with the Northern state governors. Nevertheless, the Hunters and Chasers were ready to strike in the late autumn.

They had massed about a thousand men at Ogdensburg, opposite the Ontario village of Prescott, ready for the final coup which would unite North America forever. On November 11, the steamer *United States* moved quietly down the St. Lawrence from Oswego to Ogdensburg, picking up at every stopping place knots of tough-looking passengers and bales of heavy, clanking freight.

Like Mackenzie, the American liberators had botched everything. When the *United States* headed for Prescott, no one apparently was in command. A river pirate named Bill Johnston, styling himself "Commodore of the Navy of the Canadian Republic," his belt crammed with pistols and bowie knives, discovered at the last moment that he was bound by his duty to remain with his "fleet." John W. Birge, "General" of the invasion, finding his sword and flashy uniform oppressive, retired to his cabin with a severe bellyache. But among those motley passengers there was one man ready to offer his life for his illusions.

Nils Szoltevcky Von Schoultz, son of a distinguished Swedish family long settled in Poland, had come to the United States with dreams of freedom, had been attracted to the Hunters' cause and assumed that Canadians suffered under an oppressive government as did the serfs of Poland. He had embarked on the *United States* with selfless motives and no notion of the plans under way. Suddenly dumped on the Canadian shore a few miles below Prescott, he had found himself casually elected leader of an armed invasion.

This tall, swarthy, and gentle young man looked over a diminished army of some two hundred as dazed as himself and then observed, not far from the river, a stone windmill. He had little knowledge of war but the windmill seemed to offer a possible fortress. He quartered his followers within its sturdy walls. The defenders had hardly aimed their muskets through the windows before a small force of Canadian soldiers marched across the fields from Prescott. Schoultz ordered his men to fire. They aimed so well that the attackers were beaten off.

The Canadians reinforced themselves and began a systematic siege. Their cannon balls bounded harmlessly off the windmill for five days. The Americans fought bravely but their food had run out, there was no ammunition for their single cannon and they crammed it with nails, hinges, and buckles from their belts while Schoultz waited vainly for the Hunters' promised reinforcements. The *United States* had disappeared, the Canadian farmers failed to rise against their oppressors, the windmill was surrounded and its garrison mad with thirst. So Schoultz surrendered.

He and his men were herded upon a riverboat, carried to Kingston, their arms roped together, and marched through the streets by torchlight, among crowds of gawking townsmen.

One Canadian at least who witnessed that dismal march would never forget it. A Kingston lawyer named John Alexander Macdonald, twenty-three years old and as yet unknown, watched the tall, stoic figure of Schoultz, expressionless and unafraid, his shirt torn from his back, his arms tied, his handsome head held high. As an old man Macdonald, the first prime minister of Canada and its defender against another invasion of this sort, could still remember the face of Schoultz, serene in the torchlights of Kingston.

A few mornings later Macdonald was roused from bed at his boardinghouse. The American prisoners, now locked in Fort Henry, could find no other lawyer willing to defend them. They had fallen back upon the briefless youngster who had just been called to the bar, had distinguished himself only by a courtroom fist fight with a colleague and had never conducted an important case.

Macdonald had been born in Glasgow in 1815 and brought to Canada, at the age of five, by his father, a Micawber with a weakness for liquor and speculation. He had spent five years altogether in school, had joined the Kingston militia, had stood guard, without a chance to fire a shot, against Mackenzie's Rebellion and the expected American invasion. Though he was a loyalist, whose most famous phrase would be "A British subject I was born, a British subject I will die," he was also a lawyer, a man of generous heart, and in his way, a genius.

In the tall, loose-jointed and half-clad figure summoned to the door at dawn, in the gaunt, quizzical face and gigantic, bulbous nose, there appeared that morning one of the great actors in the long drama of the boundary. Yes, Macdonald would take the American prisoners' case and, taking it, was embarked on a tide which would carry him and Canada to fortune.

The young lawyer dressed in his fashionable stovepipe hat, frock coat, and checked trousers and hastened to Fort Henry. The case of his clients, as he well knew, was indefensible. They had been caught as invaders in the Prescott windmill and three of their companions had turned queen's evidence against them. In a military court-martial Macdonald could not even argue or examine witnesses. He could only whisper questions and let the prisoners put them to the court. Those questions showed the hard, practical qualities of the ablest political mind produced by Canada in the nineteenth century. The prosecution must prove that the prisoners had joined with rebellious British subjects in making war on the Queen. The point was narrow and technical, since no Canadians had joined Schoultz at Prescott and he had been accompanied by only three or four ex-Canadians from the United States. However, the charge was soon established to the satisfaction of the court and two men were condemned to hang.

Schoultz would not even employ Macdonald, insisted on pleading guilty, awaited the verdict of death, and received it without a change of expression. The gentle features of the doomed Swedish immigrant, dying uncomplainingly for his illusions, were graven deep in the memory of the young lawyer, and with them an abiding distrust of Americans. Later that suspicion would alter the prospects of the continent.

Schoultz, in his only statement to the court, scorned any defense of his own crime against Canada. He spoke solely to deny, and with convincing truth, that he had been responsible for the mutilation of a dead Canadian at the Battle of the Windmill. His honor satisfied, he asked Macdonald to prepare his will. It bequeathed his money to the new widows of Canadian soldiers, dead by his folly, and informed his sister: "My last wish to the Americans is that they may not think of avenging my death. Let no further blood be shed; and believe me, from what I have seen, that all the stories that were told about the sufferings of the Canadian people were untrue."

The final testament of a fearless young Swede summed up, better than any state document, the nature of Canada and the boundary problem. Had Schoultz's words been noted and believed in the United States, much future mischief would have been avoided. They were little noted, long remembered, or widely understood.

Schoultz bade farewell to his adviser and offered him a hundred dollars for his work. Macdonald refused to take a cent. He had admired Schoultz but detested the Canadian rebels and the American invaders. In such a case, involving his country, he said he could accept no reward. His ultimate reward was to be larger than he imagined. His name as a lawyer had been made when he dared to defend the invaders; he would go on from there to become the father of his country.

The Canadian government hanged eleven men at Kingston but it had no stomach for this work and soon released the remainder under a British policy designed to placate the United States. A policy of conciliation prevailed also in Washington.

The Hunters and Chasers conducted a few more futile raids. A rabble of 200 men from Detroit was easily repulsed at Windsor. Their leader, "General" Bierce, chose to lead from behind. Bill Johnston, who had deserted Schoultz at Prescott, and a band of Americans with blackened faces boarded the Canadian steamer *Sir Robert Peel* on the St. Lawrence and burned her in revenge for the *Caroline*. The British government disregarded the Rush-Bagot agreement by arming a few extra ships on the Great Lakes. But the will to agreement between London and Washington was unbroken.

19

The Titan from New England

[1838–1846]

JUST AS THE TWO GOVERNMENTS SEEMED ABOUT TO LIQUIDATE A dangerous mess which neither had provoked, a meddling Canadian agent named Alexander McLeod suddenly relighted the flames of the *Caroline* affair.

That notable craft, its hulk lying somewhere on the bottom of the Niagara River, could be written off as a casualty of Mackenzie's Rebellion and American interference. The name of Amos Durfee, killed by Canadians in the American town of Fort Schlosser, was not so easily forgotten. The American government was determined to find the killers and it suspected McLeod among others.

As a Canadian government deputy sheriff, he was zealously seeking evidence against various Canadian rebels now in the United States. The American authorities twice arrested him for complicity in Durfee's death and twice released him for lack of proof. Later, emboldened by his escape and primed with liquor in an American bar, he announced to a crowd of hangers-on that he personally had killed Durfee. He was arrested again while a mob tried to lynch him, and charged with murder. Here was serious trouble for the North American neighbors.

Lord Palmerston, as British Foreign Secretary, was well launched on his ferocious career of imperialism and to him McLeod was a sacred subject of the Queen. The question of his guilt or innocence did not concern Palmerston. If McLeod had participated in the *Caroline* raid, it was under the orders of the Queen's government. It could not be bullied by American mobs, statesmen, or courts. Palmerston would not even apologize for the outrage against American property. He demanded that McLeod be freed without trial.

The politics of the United States had long since produced an opponent worthy of Palmerston. In the State Department of President Harrison, hero of Tippecanoe, now loomed the massive figure of Daniel Webster, called "the mount that burned"—an inexhaustible volcano erupting perpetually by the shores of his native New England. This man was about to play his surprising part in the boundary struggle and, by his own methods, to prevent another war.

All the greatness and accumulated experience of New England shone in the seamed face, the luminous eye, and the gorgeous eloquence of the farm boy who somehow had made himself the very image of the American Dream and given it a voice.

Already the moss of legend had grown thick about him—as when, pleading a case for Dartmouth College, he remarked, with his moving power of restraint, that it was "a small college and yet there are those who love it," and the face of the presiding judge wrinkled in pain, "his eyes suffused with tears."

Legendary, too, Webster's Gargantuan appetite for food and liquor, the hospitality of his two great farms, the bottomless debts (of which it was said that he could manage the business of a nation but would never keep any private accounts), his hypnotic control of juries, his ambition for the Presidency which would always elude him and fall to lesser men, his own verdict: "I have done absolutely nothing. At thirty Alexander had conquered the world; and I am forty."

Still more legends would gather about this titanic person, some whispers of corruption angrily disproved and the scars of domestic tragedy. Yet in all the violent cavalcade of a life which made him the American Republic incarnate his work on the boundary would be his only intrinsic and enduring feat of statecraft. Perhaps it was enough for one lifetime. It would protect the interests and assuage the passions of Webster's beloved New England. It would forestall the madness of another continental war.

Webster was the one man ideally fitted to solve such a problem. As a New Englander he had opposed the War of 1812, but taken no part in the somewhat treasonous Hartford Convention. Above all, he was a lawyer who could rise above the split hairs of the law, see the relations of the two American peoples whole and distill out of his opponents' debating points the common sense of the Constitution—was, indeed, the Constitution itself walking on two legs— that document he had first read as a child, printed on a cotton handkerchief.

But it was not of the boundary and his part in its settlement that Webster would think at the end as he lay staring dimly past the shore at the Stars and Stripes, hung on his little yacht and lighted at night so that he might see them with his dying eyes.

He was thinking then of a thousand smaller things that seemed larger than the boundary, of his triumphs in courtroom and council, of orations, caucuses, victories and defeats, of the great prize that had passed him by. And after delivering his last delirious oration on the subject of religion, he looked up to those around him and asked: "Have I, on this occasion, said anything unworthy of Daniel Webster?" Reassured that he had not, he died as he had lived, the supreme actor, orator, and egoist of his race.

History could be left to judge his work. Assuredly in the case of the boundary he did nothing unworthy of Daniel Webster.

At the beginning of the struggle with Palmerston, Webster saw that the burned steamship, the murdered Durfee, and the wretched McLeod combined were not worth another war, though he was denounced in the angry Congress for truckling under to the old British enemy. Even the master of law could not reason with Palmerston (who could?) and was powerless to release McLeod, for he had been charged with murder and arson under the state laws of New York. Governor Seward agreed with Webster that the miserable little dispute should be patched up but he, too, was the captive of political circumstance. To rescue McLeod from the hangman might well be political suicide for the rescuer.

As the case dragged on in the New York courts Palmerston suddenly announced that McLeod's execution would result in war. That ultimatum could not be ignored. Palmerston was a terrifying personality. He actually might mean what he said.

The Secretary of State, not always noted for patience, patiently sought some legal method of getting the troublesome prisoner out of jail. The Supreme Court of New York was asked for a ruling and answered that the state laws applied. McLeod must stand trial. Webster proposed to carry the case to the Supreme Court of the United States, but it was taken out of his hands. McLeod, weary of imprisonment, insisted on trial without more delay.

Fortunately for the peace of nations, Palmerston left the Foreign Office at that point and was replaced by Lord Aberdeen, a less belligerent minister. London's warlike gestures were toned down. The prisoner, however, still stood before a jury as a dangerous symbol of the ancient quarrel.

Then occurred a happy legal accident, which the British government was inclined to attribute to the good management of Webster and the New York authorities. Two of the prosecution's chief witnesses mysteriously disappeared before the trial opened. Without them, the jury acquitted McLeod.

If one speck of friction had been removed and the *Caroline* affair formally deleted from the British-American agenda, much worse frictions, involving more than old crimes, involving territory, money and national honor, had developed on the long-disputed boundary of Maine and New Brunswick. This was a clash of real substance. It might well undo all Webster's work of peace.

The Treaty of Ghent had deliberately left unsettled large sectors of the boundary. Out west there was Oregon, jointly occupied for the time being and actually ruled by McLoughlin. In the East no one knew, no one had ever known from the settlement of 1783 onward, where the line of division lay between Maine and New Brunswick. The settlement of 1783 had been drawn arbitrarily on the map by men who had never seen the land thus divided. Since then traders, loggers, and settlers from Canada and the United States had penetrated these unknown regions and begun to fill in the blank spaces of the map. They intended to stay where they were, however governments might define the arrangements negotiated by Britain and the United States at the close of the Revolution.

The starting point of current argument was the St. Croix River. The boundary was supposed to follow that stream "from its mouth in the Bay of Fundy to its source," and strike due north from there to "the highlands which divide those rivers that empty themselves into the river St. Lawrence from those which fall into the Atlantic Ocean, to the north-westernmost head of the Connecticut River, then down the middle of that river to the forty-fifth parallel of north latitude."

After thus rounding a northern horseshoe, the boundary would follow the Connecticut southward to the 45th Parallel and westward by that line to the St. Lawrence. As no one could even identify the St. Croix from several possible rivers, much less locate its headwaters and the source of the Connecticut, the boundary lay for thirty years where any local settler cared to place it.

In 1798 Britain and the United States had referred the mystery of the St. Croix to a commission of inquiry under Jay's Treaty. The commissioners rejected the Magaguadavic, as urged by the United States, and chose the Schoodic, farther to the west. That meant more land for New Brunswick and less for Maine. The commission drew a straight line north from the St. Croix's presumed source, west of the St. John River, to Maine's disappointment.

How far north did this line extend before reaching the imaginary "highlands" and the north arc of the horseshoe? The British said it ran for only forty miles, ended at Mars Hill, in Aroostook County, fell far short of the St. John, and thus gave the upper reaches of that river and the country south of it to New Brunswick. The Americans insisted that the line ran farther north by 143 miles and beyond the Restigouche. Some twelve thousand square miles of land remained in dispute until after the War of 1812.

Again a joint commission pondered the map, the politics behind the map, and the position of the people within the disputed area. The commissioners managed to divide the islands of Passamaquoddy Bay satisfactorily between the two contenders but, after four more years of work, they abandoned, in 1822, the attempt to fix the boundary from the St. Croix to the St. Lawrence. The problem was handed back to the British and American governments.

Five more years were spent in arranging an arbitration, as permitted under the Treaty of Ghent, neither side willing to accept the arbitrator suggested by the other. In the end both agreed to the King of the Netherlands. That puzzled monarch could find only that the task, as presented to him, was "inexplicable and impractical."

Accordingly, he disregarded the strict definitions of the 1783 settlement and attempted a reasonable compromise by a line along the St. John and St. Francis Rivers. This gave roughly the northern third of the questionable land to New Brunswick and the remainder to Maine. Britain accepted the award. The American government, the Congress, and especially the people of Maine exploded in wrath at what appeared to be a sell-out of their just claims.

Now the United States opportunely discovered that the arbitrator was no longer competent to render any decision. He had been appointed as King of the Netherlands and since the Belgian revolution of 1830 he was only King of Holland—a preposterous argument but, lacking better, it must serve.

The American government threw up its hands in the face of this mounting confusion and sought the advice of the Senate. It rejected the King's findings. Britain and the United States were back where they had started in 1783. That was nowhere in particular.

Arbitrators, diplomats, and mapmakers might abandon the problem as insoluble, but men from Maine and New Brunswick were moving into the unsettled border country, cutting down trees, plowing the earth, claiming them for both countries and constantly colliding. The authorities of New Brunswick were granting valuable timber licenses to Canadians within the area claimed by Maine. Maine was granting similar licenses within the area claimed by New Brunswick. The lumberman's busy ax disregarded the border until New Brunswick seized cut timber within Maine, or what the

Americans called Maine, and Maine did the same in what Britain called New Brunswick. The victims of the seizures on both sides at once demanded redress from their governments.

Soon settlers were following the lumbermen and cultivating the cutover valleys. Farmers from Maine moved into the Madawaska country of the upper St. John, where Canadians already were settled and where New Brunswick asserted its jurisdiction. There followed ten years of seizures, arrests, and litigation while the temper of Maine rose and its governor told the Federal government that "Maine has a right to know fully and explicitly whether she is to be protected or left to struggle alone and unaided."

Maine did not wait for the Federal government to intervene. In 1839 it sent two hundred men to remove the New Brunswick loggers from the Aroostook valley. This raid, like so many others of recent years, was a ridiculous failure. Agents of New Brunswick surprised the Americans by night and carried off fifty of them to the jail in Woodstock. The townsmen of Woodstock, inspired by this victory, broke into the local arsenal, armed themselves, and marched into the Aroostook country as if to repel an invasion.

That was more than Governor Harvey, of New Brunswick, had bargained for. He ordered the Woodstock volunteers back home but informed the government of Maine that, if necessary, he would defend Aroostook with Canadian troops. Maine voted money for an army of its own, Congress authorized the recruitment of 50,000 men; the British and American governments warned each other against provoking a war of incalculable consequence.

The little valley of Aroostook, a pocket of lumbermen and bush farmers, had suddenly become the focal point of world politics. At a distance of a few yards armed Americans and Canadians watched one another, spoiling for a fight. Those few yards proved enough to restrain another continental disaster. For actually neither side wanted a war and nobody started shooting.

The American government now bethought itself of that reliable soldier and pacificator, Winfield Scott. Hurrying to the Aroostock front, he persuaded both sides to release their prisoners and withdraw their forces before the fatal shot could be fired. By tacit arrangement Maine was given control of Aroostock and New Brunswick of Madawaska.

The border lay quiet at the moment when the McLeod case, now nearing its queer anticlimax, was straining British-American relations to the breaking point. Once McLeod was out of the way and the "Aroostook War" halted, it was obviously time for London and Washington to cease this nonsense and arrange a general settlement.

Britain had found in Lord Ashburton a negotiator well trained to deal with the Americans. His financial firm of Baring had large interests in the United States and he had spent much time there, had married the daughter of an American senator, and had helped to finance the Louisiana Purchase. Also, he had met Webster when the American was selling Massachusetts stock in London and trying to re-establish the damaged financial credit of the Republic.

The able British negotiator first tried to make sure that there would be no more McLeod cases. His arguments and pressure from the State Department persuaded the Congress to pass a law enabling the Federal government to remove from state to federal courts prisoners who had acted under the orders of a foreign government. In return for this concession Ashburton wound up the *Caroline* affair by the apology long demanded in Washington and refused by Palmerston. It was a restrained apology, regretting only "the hurried execution of the necessary service" but it was enough to satisfy the United States' honor. Next an extradition agreement (excluding political exiles) was negotiated to cover the criminals of Canada and the United States who continually fled across the border.

These were details. Ashburton's primary assignment was to fix the Maine-New Brunswick boundary and, as a practical man of business, he did not propose to allow either technicalities, historic formulae, or local interests to stand in his way. He told the Canadian Governor General bluntly: "No slight advantage to be derived from contrivance & cunning can for a moment be placed in comparison with those to be derived from having as a result of my negotiations a reciprocal feeling of respect & harmony." Those words laid down the only practical operative principle on which the future boundary could be managed. They deserved to be remembered, would often be forgotten, but could never be denied.

Ashburton found that he could do business with Webster, who was as eager as he for a durable settlement, even if it cost a few square miles of supposedly American territory. As New England's greatest living son, Webster undertook to smooth the temper of Maine and prepare it for the loss of some of its claims.

The London businessman was free of these local politics. Britain, as always, was not consulting the wishes or interests of Canadians but settling an imperial problem to suit its own imperial convenience. It was little worried now by the problem of defending New Brunswick from Maine. Its concern was to leave a corridor between New Brunswick and the St. Lawrence so that troops could be moved from St. John to Quebec for the defense of Upper and Lower Canada when the river was frozen.

Webster was equally concerned with the defense of the historic British invasion route southward by the Richelieu and Lake Champlain. To cork this dangerous bottle the United States already had built a fort at Rouses Point, only to find when final surveys were made that it lay a quarter of a mile within Canada. The British government saw Rouses Point as a useful bargaining counter.

The bargain finally offered by Ashburton to Webster provided a boundary between Maine and New Brunswick on the upper St. John. In return, Canada would leave Rouses Point in American possession. This seemed reasonable but did not satisfy Maine. It still demanded the islands at the mouth of the St. Croix, a slight alteration in the St. John line, and navigation rights on that river.

Ashburton had gone as far as he could. His position was strengthened at this point by an interesting discovery in the dusty archives of Paris, where some diligent clerk produced a map defining the old boundaries of French Acadia as conforming to the British description of New Brunswick. This map also seemed to correspond too closely for the comfort of the American negotiators to a map drawn by Franklin in describing the settlement of 1783.

The Washington government ceased to look for more old records and the government at London quietly suppressed a map found in the British Museum which seemed to support the American case. Webster warned the authorities of Maine and Massachusetts that the maps were against them. He offered each state a subsidy of $150,000 if it would agree to Ashburton's offer. And so the deal was made.

Britain got the boundary it wanted north of the St. John, the United States the boundary it wanted west of the Connecticut, together with Rouses Point, and Maine got the right to use the St. John to carry its logs to the sea. Webster reckoned that he had secured seven-twelfths of the disputed area and four-fifths of its total value. Ashburton thought he had made "greater sacrifices than the thing is worth" because "the whole territory we were wrangling about was worth nothing." New Brunswick thought it valuable and would not quickly forgive its surrender.

Probably Ashburton could not have forced a better bargain short of war. He and Webster seemed to have reached the best compromise available in practical politics if not in theoretical justice. They might not have succeeded were it not that Britain and the United States both needed each other's markets and the United States needed British capital. For Canada, however, the long northern nose of Maine, thrust almost to the edge of the St. Lawrence, was a wedge driven between its interior and its Atlantic coast, a barrier to transportation and a serious economic problem for the future.

The international boundary now ran, unquestioned, from the Atlantic to the Rockies. An agreement of 1818 had settled the old dispute arising out of the 1783 settlement and its impossible line drawn directly west from the Lake of the Woods to the headwaters of the Mississippi. After it was found that the river lay far south of the 49th Parallel, Britain had proposed to swing the agreed boundary southward but the United States Senate rejected this claim and it was not seriously pressed. Britain thus surrendered also its right of free navigation on the Mississippi. By the 1818 convention the line started from the Lake of the Woods and ran straight west by the 49th Parallel as far as the Rockies. Both nations claimed Oregon, occupied it jointly, and left it under the patriarchal rule of McLoughlin.

He was now established as a monarch without constitution or local competitor, the ostensible servant but actually the rival of Simpson, the "White Headed Eagle" of the Indians, the ally of Comcomly, that able one-eyed chief who had been converted to British principles by a gift of a Union Jack, a gaudy tunic, cocked hat, and heavy sword.

Wherever he went the splendid figure of McLoughlin, with his silver mane, his flowing cloak, and gold-headed walking stick was reverenced by the northwest tribes only this side idolatry. As "Dr. John," he treated their diseases with extract of dogwood root, labored night and day through their plague of 1829, watched them leap, crazed with fever, into the Columbia, and wept over their dead. Everyone, Indian or white, was welcome under his sprawling roof and many curious men turned up at Vancouver from the ends of the earth.

One of them was David Douglas, botanist of the Royal Horticultural Society of London. The natives held him in awe for his mysterious power over the creatures of the forest—a fiction invented by McLoughlin. Often Douglas went short of clothing so that he might carry paper for his records and sketches as he added over a thousand strange plants to the science of botany and named the giant Douglas fir, containing within its wrinkled trunk the economic future of the Pacific coast.

Another guest at Vancouver was the British sea captain, Aemelius Simpson. He always wore kid gloves and, pulling them from his pocket one day, discovered some forgotten apple seeds presented to him by a lady in London for planting in the soil of Oregon. They were planted by the fort's gardener, Robert Bruce, their seedling shoots were eagerly watched by McLoughlin, and their first apple was handed around so that all could taste it. That was the beginning of Oregon's great fruit industry.

Not all visitors were welcome. Herbert Beaver, a repulsive character who came as a missionary from England, sent home reports suggesting that McLoughlin's marriage was not quite legal. Hearing of this, McLoughlin caned his guest publicly in the yard of the fort but apologized next day. Beaver rejected the apology, preferring to return to London and spread more slanders.

Least welcome of all were the occasional American fur traders. None was molested, some were bought off, others driven out by cutthroat price competition. When Jedediah Smith, the famous trader and "praying man" of Salt Lake, was attacked by Indians on the coast, McLoughlin rescued him, recaptured his stolen furs, and entertained him all winter. The two became fast friends, but by his presence in the fort Smith, quite innocently, was undermining his host's kingdom.

Smith's reports to Washington warned the government that McLoughlin's influence over the Indians was "decisive" and described in minute detail his flourishing fields of grain, his cattle, apples, and grapes. In thus whetting the American appetite for the rich coastal soil Smith was too honest to hide his ambitions from his friend. The Americans, he said, would surely colonize Oregon. A few years later the Comanches murdered Smith on the Cimarron. McLoughlin grieved deeply.

Perhaps unconsciously his mind already was reconciling itself to Smith's prophecy. So far, however, he had never admitted to himself, much less to Simpson, that Oregon could be lost to Britain. He was constantly expanding his domain with a sawmill on the Willamette River, new posts in the mountains, a farming community on Puget Sound, a depot in Spain's San Francisco Bay, an agency in the Hawaiian Islands to sell his lumber and salmon, and, on the far northern coast, Fort Stikine, to trade in furs with the Russians of Alaska. Vancouver's sphere of influence now stretched from California to the latitude of 54°, a parallel soon to enter international politics and the folklore of the American people.

George Simpson watched this expansion with distrust. McLoughlin had been instructed to build an empire of fur. He seemed to be building something like a colony which, in the end, might prove fatal to the fur trade and actually was building the foundations of the American Republic on the Pacific. In any case, the Little Emperor could tolerate no rival. He was secretly jealous of McLoughlin's power and contemptuous of his openhanded ways with the American competitors.

McLoughlin had indeed grown a little dizzy with success. His salary of £2,900 a year was kingly. His word was law. No one in his great dining hall ventured to interrupt his oracular pronouncements on business, politics, philosophy, religion, and the virtues of Napoleon Bonaparte. On a canoe journey across Canada to England in 1838 he regaled the startled Hudson's Bay factors of the prairies with praises of Papineau, the newly exiled rebel. Where would all this end? As the subtle mind of Simpson may have suspected, it would end in tragedy.

If he was too easygoing with the competitors and too prodigal with the company's money to suit Simpson, McLoughlin could be ruthless. The Clallam tribe having killed five of his traders, he punished them by destroying their village and massacring twenty-five inhabitants.

The King's rule was absolute but at the heyday of his power the tragedy of McLoughlin had begun. He appointed his worthless son, John, to command the Stikine fort and there the youth was murdered by a mutinous crew in a drunken riot. The father was wild with grief and then with anger on learning that Simpson had released the confessed murderer. The quarrel between McLoughlin and Simpson, long growing out of business disputes but mostly out of their egocentric and incompatible natures, was now past curing. McLoughlin's furious letters to the company's headquarters in London attacked Simpson's policies, methods, and lavish sexual morals.

Still, the business of the company must go on. Simpson foresaw the future more clearly, or at least admitted it more frankly, than McLoughlin. In Simpson's mind the original guess that the Columbia line could not be held, that the company must establish itself on the defensible line of the Fraser, had been confirmed by the American pressure on Oregon.

He had ordered the construction of Fort Langley, near the Fraser's mouth, in 1827. A single stake driven there did not satisfy him. Cruising up the coast on the company's steamship *Beaver*, he was struck by the possibilities of Vancouver Island, for it thrust well southward of the 49th Parallel into the Strait of Juan de Fuca. Its southern extremity and a safe harbor would make an ideal site for a fort to hold the island and, if necessary, a boundary through the strait. This was to prove Simpson's most important inspiration. It would largely determine in the end the western division of the continent.

The man who would thus anchor the boundary had lately arrived at Vancouver. He was a towering Scot of mysterious origin, swarthy skin, courtly manners, hard mind, and glacial cold. Young James Douglas had learned the fur trade in Fraser's New Caledonia and narrowly escaped with his life from the Indians there. He immediately took over the management of McLoughlin's business and became his silent alter ego. The two men, with their lively half-breed wives and numerous children, lived apart as a remote aristocracy. McLoughlin and "Black" Douglas dined with visitors in the central hall while their women were forbidden any company.

This comfortable life could not continue. The exotic little growth planted by McLoughlin on the Columbia must perish in the storm of imperial power now sweeping across America or become part of the larger growth of the American Republic, of which the first portents were a few destitute and starving missionaries from Boston. They had crossed the plains by covered wagon, with ghastly hardship, and slid down the river on rafts.

In 1834 McLoughlin had confronted the visage of Manifest Destiny in the person of Jason Lee, a lanky young Methodist minister "with strong nerve and indomitable will." Lee had been moved by a delegation of Flathead Indians, seeking the word of God at St. Louis, and felt called to duty among them.

The little band of missionaries was guided across the plains and mountains by Nathaniel Wyeth, an enterprising merchant, whom McLoughlin liked at first sight. His own Christianity rising above the interests of his company, McLoughlin warmly welcomed the tattered travelers but discreetly directed Lee to the Willamette valley, south of the Columbia, that essential line of British power.

Wyeth was not to be diverted so easily. He decided, against McLoughlin's honest advice, to build his own trade post on Sauvé Island directly west of Vancouver. It saddened McLoughlin to ruin his new friend but, in loyalty to the company, the menace of the Sauvé post must be removed. The Indians, accordingly, were persuaded to boycott the American trader. Within two years he was bankrupt.

This kind of interference could not retard the westering tide of American settlement now rising east of the Rockies and fed by missionary fervor, land hunger, and the chance of commercial profit.

Soon there arrived at Vancouver, via Mexico, the "penniless and ill-clad" figure of Hall J. Kelley, the ardent Boston schoolteacher who had long preached the American colonization of Oregon. McLoughlin recognized him as the archenemy. Kelley, he noted, was garbed in "a white slouched hat, blanket capote, leather pants with a red stripe down the seam—rather *outré* even for Vancouver," and besides, he was a horse thief. This charge, made against Kelley and his guide, Ewing Young, in Mexico, was untrue, but McLoughlin believed it and treated the two Americans coldly. After being housed, fed, and ignored all winter, Kelley went home hating McLoughlin as a "prosecuting monster" and continued his crusade for an all-American Oregon.

Next came Samuel Parker, "the plug-hat missionary" in torn clerical clothes, to spy out the land for his eastern followers. Then, in 1936, Dr. Marcus Whitman and his bride, the lovely Narcissa, on an odd coast-to-coast honeymoon by wagon. They were accompanied by Henry Spalding, a missionary, and his wife, these two women being the first to cross the Rockies.

The American missions, dauntless among the tribes of the coast and interior, and highly practical in their business management, were now firmly established. They asked the protection of Congress for their lands. Lee went east to raise money by lectures on the religious needs and natural riches of the West. The American public was excited by his news, the government disturbed by McLoughlin's hold on Oregon. It was time to find out what had happened to a joint occupation which apparently had turned into a British monopoly.

Captain William A. Slacum was, therefore, sent to Vancouver by sea as "a private gentleman." The disguise failed to deceive McLoughlin, but Slacum was royally entertained and the business affairs of the company opened to him.

His report to the government repaid McLoughlin's kindness by the false charge that the company enforced slavery among the Indians. Slacum's findings were to prove vital in the future of the Pacific coast. They urged the government to demand the 49th Parallel as the international boundary and rightly insisted that the Puget Sound country, providing the only secure harbors north of San Francisco, was too valuable a prize to be lost. The government began to think increasingly of Oregon, where the United States had planted a few men of God and a handful of godless traders but no settlement.

McLoughlin also had been thinking his own thoughts. He had long realized that settlement could not be avoided south of the Columbia and had quietly encouraged it there to prevent its spreading north of the river.

The case of Louis Labonte, a French-Canadian servant of the company, had plainly indicated years before the future of this fertile soil. Labonte had finished his term of service, had secured his discharge, and proposed to farm in the Willamette valley.

Alarmed at this first prospect of settlement, McLoughlin sent Labonte home to Montreal, according to the strict letter of his contract. This determined man paddled back across the continent and cleared his farm. A French Canadian from the St. Lawrence had begun the private settlement of Oregon—a small beginning, a few acres. Nothing thenceforth could suppress it.

McLoughlin made no serious attempt to stop other settlers and constantly twisted the company's regulations to help them. The minute but spreading farms on the Willamette, little known to the statesmen of Washington and London, were perhaps the most significant speck of land at the moment in America. If crops would grow in Oregon, the land-hungry Americans, now halfway across the dry plains, would certainly try to possess this abundant and well-watered earth. The Hudson's Bay empire was doomed by such unnoted men as Louis Labonte with his lonely plow. And, though he did not know it yet, even McLoughlin, the Canadian from Rivière du Loup, the empire's defender, the King of Oregon, was being sucked day by day into the Republic.

In 1841—the year before Elijah White's first immigrant caravan rolled over the Oregon trail—Simpson's erratic travels brought him to Vancouver. He and McLoughlin agreed that the final crisis of Oregon was at hand. They masked their quarrel and, outwardly polite, conferred on strategy.

It was essential, said Simpson, that Britain escape without more delay from the long-standing temporary arrangements and assert its control of Oregon before the Americans could occupy it. The crafty Scot, knowing the ways of politicians in London, suspected that they would surrender in the pinch. Therefore, his original project of a second line in the vicinity of the Fraser, with an anchoring fort on Vancouver Island, could be postponed no longer. McLoughlin approved. He saw his kingdom slipping from him.

Who should be selected for the task of holding the future boundary in the Strait of Juan de Fuca? The choice was obvious. Black Douglas, the silent man who had long been the King's prime minister in Oregon, was sent north in 1843 and built the new post of Camosun, soon to be called Victoria. It stood on the east side of a snug harbor, safe from the Songeesh Indians' village on the western side; it fronted on Fuca's Strait and, though it was only a palisade and a few whitewashed buildings, it must soon become a vital strategic point in the North American struggle.

Douglas, without knowing it, held in his competent hands the future of Canada as a transcontinental state. And far away, on the other side of the continent, in the town of Kingston, Douglas's unseen partner, John A. Macdonald, was still practicing law, learning politics, drinking too much whisky, and little supposing that he would carry Canada to the Pacific some thirty years hence.

In London meanwhile the Hudson's Bay Company was bestirring itself. Governor John Henry Pelly had read with alarm Simpson's urgent dispatches from Oregon. The agreement of joint occupancy and free trade had ended in 1828 and had been renewed indefinitely, either side free to abrogate it with a year's notice. Britain and the United States still could not agree on a permanent settlement. Pelly continually urged Foreign Secretary Canning to prepare his final bargaining terms.

Britain's position looked strong. The American movement into Oregon so far was only a trickle. Washington statesmen seemed little interested in this distant territory, being much more concerned with the Spanish possessions of the Southwest. Britain, said Pelly, should propose a boundary from the 49th Parallel at the Rockies southward on the height of land to a point where Lewis and Clark had crossed the mountains, at about 46°, then westerly along "Lewis' River" until it fell into the Columbia, thence straight to the sea.

This settlement, Pelly thought, would be generous to the Americans—so generous that when McLoughlin first heard of it by delayed dispatches he was outraged. Invaluable fur areas, he protested, would be cut out of his kingdom south of the Columbia and Vancouver's trade ruined.

Already he had seen such Yankee skippers as Captain William McNeill sailing into the Columbia, offering ridiculous prices for furs, and delighting the Indians with the new temptations of toys, whistles, wooden soldiers, jumping jacks and other gimcracks from New England.

The company, after its experience of nearly two centuries, thought it knew best. It proposed that Canning demand far more than he could hope to get. He should insist at the beginning on a boundary well south of the Columbia so that, in the ultimate division, he could offer large concessions to the Americans and, feigning surrender, could retreat to the river line.

All this subtle strategy of the last ten years was now obsolete and McLoughlin knew it when, in 1843, Douglas was building Fort Victoria and 900 Americans of the "Great Migration" reached the Willamette valley. A trickle became a flood. The company had brought in a few Canadian farmers from the Red River colony but their numbers only proved that in the contest of settlement Canada must lose. It lacked the population for such a struggle, while the Republic was bursting with eager immigrants.

The private surrender of McLoughlin also had begun. At first he gave the American settlers credit at his store, contrary to the company's instructions, to keep them alive, though he knew that many of these debts would never be repaid. The flood still rose. The Indians having assembled around Vancouver for a general massacre and announced that "It's good for us to kill these Bostons," McLoughlin rushed among them, brandishing his cane, and forestalled what might easily have turned into a general Indian war and another familiar clash between Britain and the United States.

Under this kind of pressure the aging man suffered a fierce struggle of conscience. He had recently returned to his mother's religion, taken the communion of the Roman Catholic Church, and ratified by solemn rites the secular marriage of the Canadian frontier. As his mind mellowed, the American settlers began to look less like enemies than friends, the American Republic more congenial than the rule of a distant London and its hateful agent, the Little Emperor.

Simpson's worst suspicions would have been confirmed if he had seen McLoughlin board a visiting American ship of war and salute the Stars and Stripes. By this gesture the King of Oregon showed the first outward sign of his conversion.

The increasing settlers of the Willamette—as is the nature of all North Americans—were demanding self-government at their town of Oregon City. McLoughlin was able to postpone this movement briefly by his influence over the French Canadians, his own people. On May 2, 1843, however, an open-air meeting resolved by a majority of two votes to establish a local administration forthwith. Those two votes came from French Canadians who resented Canada's treatment of Papineau. Even Oregon felt the backwash of the Canadian Rebellion.

McLoughlin abandoned his attempt to control the settlers. They were passing their own laws, levying taxes, and seeking admission to the Union. One-man rule west of the Rockies had closed. McLoughlin faced the supreme decision of his life.

Actually the decision had been taken out of his hands. More immigrants were pouring in, 1,400 in 1844. Without British military power behind him, probably without a continental war, McLoughlin could not hold the Columbia line against such numbers. His appeals to London, his hint that he might be elected to lead an independent state of Oregon, went unheeded. He was too old, too tired by his prodigal life, too disillusioned with the company to fight any more.

Next year the settlers elected George Abernethy as their governor. McLoughlin knew this was the end. He formally agreed, on August

15, 1845, to "support the Organic Laws of the Provisional Government of Oregon." His resignation went to London. The King had abdicated. His retreat to Oregon City with his family was a king's voluntary exile. It had been his own manifest destiny from the beginning. And when he built a huge house for himself there and applied for American citizenship the long adventure of the boy from Rivière du Loup was complete. There would never be its like again.

He lived eleven years in exile, more as a legend than a man. The Americans eventually granted him citizenship, they observed the giant stooped figure in old-fashioned clothes moving about the streets, but he had no influence in a bustling little community which become a territory of the United States in 1848.

He was suspect as a former Briton, a retired dictator, and a Catholic. His private land claim was stolen from him by endless litigation, a bitter quarrel with the Methodist Church, and some high-class finagling in Congressional politics. He was compelled to recoup the Hudson's Bay Company out of his own pocket for all the credits extended to the American settlers, who now refused to honor their debts and treated their benefactor almost as an outcast. Sometimes the old man would fall to sobbing over his old account books, the lost assets, the unpaid debts, the memories of better times.

"By British demagogues," he wrote in his final testament, "I have been represented as a traitor. What for? Because I acted as a Christian, saved American citizens, men, women and children, from the Indian tomahawk . . . American demagogues have been base enough to assert that I had caused American citizens to be massacred by hundreds of savages—I who saved all I could . . . I founded this settlement and prevented a war."

He got no thanks for this in life. Americans of Oregon had yet to recognize the father of their state. The Republic little noted the broken man who, more than any other, had carried it, as a British subject, to the Pacific coast. On his deathbed—looking, as a Washington visitor observed, "the picture of General Jackson"—he said he would have been better shot forty years ago. He had now reverted to the French language of his youth on the St. Lawrence. "Comment allez-vous?" asked his doctor and nephew, Henri de Chesne. "A Dieu," murmured the deposed King of Oregon and passed into American history. In good time it would vindicate him. With McLoughlin passed the infancy of the West.

The quickening clash of imperial powers could not pause to observe the tragedy of the man whose arrival in Oregon had precipi-

tated it in the first place. All the long wrangle between London
and Washington had failed to settle the boundary. Britain had proposed in 1826 to hold Oregon but offered the United States a harbor
on Fuca's Strait. The United States refused to surrender Oregon
but offered Britain free navigation on the Columbia. Both offers
were rejected. The uneasy joint occupation continued, each side
still free to end it with one year's notice.

By the eighteen-forties it was plain that the Americans intended
to end the stalemate somehow. For in fact the settlers and not the
Hudson's Bay Company possessed and governed Oregon, whatever
international agreement might say. It remained only to assert this
ownership.

The presidential election of 1844 presented in the Democratic
candidate, a dark horse named James Knox Polk, from the mountains of Tennessee, the man who evidently proposed to say the final
word. Polk's campaign indicated that, if elected, he would have
Oregon and probably would have Texas as well. His policy was
uttered in an alarming slogan meaning little or much—"Fifty-four
Forty or Fight!"

With Polk's election the statesmen of London asked themselves if
this man, grim-faced, angry and subtle, intended to enforce his
slogan literally and expand the Republic all the way up the Pacific
coast to the edge of Russian Alaska. A British warship cruised ostentatiously through the Strait of Juan de Fuca. London proposed an
attempt at mediation. Polk refused, gave legal notice ending the
joint occupation, and undertook public preparations for war.

To all appearances the third British-American war for the boundary was on the way. These appearances were deceptive. As Britain
guessed, Polk's real interest lay in the Southwest and California.
While acquiring the lands of Spain, he desired no more than Britain
a contest in the north.

Following the necessary gestures of power, therefore, Polk offered at the proper moment to accept the line of the 49th Parallel,
cutting straight across Vancouver Island, though he recognized
Douglas's Fort Victoria as a free port. Britain, while ready to surrender Oregon and avoid war, rejected Polk's formula. It had
determined to hold the island and, as a last resort, to accept a
boundary through the Gulf of Georgia and Fuca's Strait. That compromise satisfied Polk, since it gave the United States far more
than it had expected to obtain without a war and left American
energies free to deal with Spain in the Southwest.

Thus the bargain was sealed by the treaty of June 15, 1846, and,
save for a disturbing little clash concerning certain islands in the

Gulf of Georgia, the North American border was fixed from Atlantic to Pacific. The division of a continent, begun at Jamestown and Quebec, had been completed after 238 years of wars innumerable and the labors of countless men now forgotten.

The boundary was fixed on paper. It was backed by the covenant of Britain, the world's leading power, and of the United States, a growing power of the second class. Britain had often surrendered the vital interests of Canada before now, as it had surrendered the rich territory of Oregon, leaving the poorer northern lands to its colonists. Would there be another surrender?

Two men still unknown to each other were thinking of these things at opposite sides of the continent. In Fort Victoria, Douglas held the British far West with a corporal's guard and in a dozen years must meet a new American invasion, peaceful but dangerous. In Kingston, Macdonald was entering his life of politics, as yet youthful, naïve and confused, but behind his convivial manners, the homely face, and the famous nose, already reddening with alcohol, there burned a vehement flame. The murk of politics, the years of private anguish, dissipation, and titanic labor could never extinguish that flame. By its secret light Macdonald had seen the vision of a nation from coast to coast. And he also, in due time, must meet the final thrust of Manifest Destiny on the border.

20

The Dictator and His Disciples

[1838-1849]

I N THE FOOTSTEPS OF CHAMPLAIN, FRONTENAC, PHIPS, MONTCALM, Wolfe, Montgomery, and the others who had worn smooth the cobblestones or battered down the walls of Quebec for more than two centuries, there arrived, on May 29, 1838, an egregious personage, who would have perhaps a larger effect on Canada, the United States, and the world then any of his predecessors. That date, if any can be fixed in an evolution so long and amorphous, will serve as well as any other for the beginning of the Third British Empire, later called a Commonwealth.

When a white charger bore the gaudy, gold-braided figure up to the Château St. Louis, John George Lambton, Earl of Durham, appeared to the eager Canadians as their savior from rebellion, business collapse, and anarchy. He had come from London as a dictator to investigate the Mackenzie-Papineau uprising and, if possible, to invent a new system of government for Canada. His assignment and powers were practically unlimited and quite unprecedented.

Much more depended on him than the young Queen Victoria and her government supposed. They knew only that the bewildered Canadians, even the loyal ones, were dissatisfied with their present system and yet clung to the Empire. What did they want? Maybe Durham could make some sense of this outlandish country. In any case, the easygoing British Prime Minister, Lord Melbourne, had found Durham a prickly companion in Parliament and his voyage at least would keep him out of the way for a while. He was instructed to save Canada from a rebellion which had been suppressed but might recur. Actually he was undertaking to save the Empire, though few men saw that its future was in imminent peril.

Durham's work, failing or succeeding, must forever affect the

299

future of the American public as well. If he failed, the weak, disjointed, and chaotic Canadian colonies would certainly lapse, one
by one or all together, into the United States. If he succeeded,
there might be a Canadian nation on the flank of the Republic and,
later on, other similar nations in Africa, Asia, and the South Pacific.
If a new kind of empire could be invented—a project hardly considered in Britain so far—it might endure as a permanent friend
and ally of the Republic. Not otherwise.

The shoulders on which this heavy and incalculable burden had
been placed were young but powerful. Durham was forty-six years
old. The chiseled face, almost theatrical in its beauty, was crowned
with an aura of glistening curls, the eye luminous and hypnotic.
A brilliant mind and a febrile energy were marred only by frail
health.

This darling of a fickle fortune had come from an ancient county
family so distinguished that his father had scorned a title. After
college and three years in the army, the son had quickly revealed a
certain fashionable Byronic ardor by running off with an heiress
for a somewhat scandalous Gretna Green marriage, had fought a
duel to settle an election argument, had supported the great Reform
Bill with his father-in-law, Earl Grey, and on entering Parliament
had won the name of "Radical Jack."

His radicalism was entirely abstract and intellectual. At heart he
was an arrogant, brittle and moody aristocrat, who traveled across
the Atlantic with his own private band, his family plate, his racing
trophies, and other baggage requiring two days to unload. So
delicate were his tastes, so sensitive his nostrils, that he forbade
anyone on his ship to smoke and, sniffing tobacco one night, rushed
from his cabin in a rage to find Vice-Admiral Sir Charles Paget
crouched with a secret cigar in the lee of a lifeboat.

Conditions in America, as Durham judged them, were much
worse than he or his government had believed. Of Lower Canada
he said in his most memorable phrase: "I expected to find a contest
between a government and a people; I found two nations warring
in the bosom of a single state."

Canada, Upper and Lower, was prostrate with depression—public works suspended, government unable to pay its bills, the people
desperate or apathetic, many farmers emigrating in despair to the
United States. The border still smoldered in the fires of the recent
rebellion. The Canadian steamer *Sir Robert Peel* was burned by a
black-faced gang of American pirates on the St. Lawrence a few
days after the dictator's arrival. The Hunters' raids were being
planned but had yet to come.

One of Durham's first acts was to offer a reward of £1,000 for the conviction in the American courts of any person who had committed a crime against Canada. By this gesture he told the American government plainly that the Canadian rebellion and its aftermath had become an international concern, that he expected Washington to enforce its own laws against pirates and raiders. He then sent his brother-in-law, Colonel Grey, to see President Van Buren and demand an end of American interference.

Next he solved the problem of the hundreds of rebels in the overcrowded Quebec jails by releasing all of them save eight ringleaders, who were mercifully exiled to Bermuda, since no Quebec jury would convict them anyway. That was the fatal step of Durham's career and would soon end it.

Ignorant of the conspiracy now under way against him in London, he set feverishly to work, examined witnesses, questioned delegations, read mountains of documents, dashed about the country by boat, carriage or horseback, and began to compile the famous Durham Report.

It has been called, with some justice, the greatest state paper in the history of the British peoples. Certainly it was to have an effect on their affairs comparable to that of Magna Carta or the Bill of Rights. It was to be, indeed, the starting point of the future Commonwealth, even if few students in Britain, Canada, or the United States seem to have realized its importance at the time.

Who actually wrote the report has never been clear. Durham had brought with him an odd brain trust which reflected his contempt of convention. Thomas Turton, after drafting the Reform Bill of 1832, had acquired a soiled reputation in a disagreeable divorce case. Charles Buller was an able secretary but practiced a sharp wit, wounding to Canadians. Gibbon Wakefield, not a member of Durham's official staff, worked closely with him and undoubtedly wrote some part of his findings. This notorious man had been in jail recently for abducting an heiress. Altogether it was a somewhat gamey group of men to represent the virgin Queen.

Durham's enemy, Lord Brougham, meeting the historian, Macaulay, in a London street, said of the report and its authors: "The matter came from a felon, the style from a coxcomb and the Dictator furnished only six letters, D-u-r-h-a-m." That rather shabby aphorism was typical of Brougham, the prince of cads, who would be remembered chiefly as the inventor of a new kind of carriage. Durham would be remembered for the unconscious invention of the Third British Empire.

No single hand could possibly have written the report in the available time, but it was essentially Durham's work and could hardly have been implemented without his prestige behind it.

There was nothing new in its two principal recommendations. A legislative union of Upper and Lower Canada in one colony had long been discussed by Canadians, had been proposed by the British government a few years earlier but abandoned in the face of Quebec's protest. There was nothing new either in Durham's proposal to give a united Canada and the other Canadian colonies of the Atlantic coast responsible government. That revolutionary reform, which might have prevented the American Revolution sixty years before, had been urged on Durham in York by a Canadian, Robert Baldwin.

In accepting it, Durham proposed to alter the whole course of the Empire's business. Once responsible government had been granted to the Canadian colonies, the process could not be halted. It must be the watershed of the Second Empire leading to the Third and to the modern Commonwealth. If a colonial government was to be made responsible to an elected legislature, the legislature's powers could never be limited. A colony could even contract, when it felt strong enough, out of the Empire.

Moreover, as a dubious British government immediately objected, if a British governor in Canada must accept the advice of his ministers, if that advice conflicted with his instructions from London, if it imperiled imperial interests, which authority should he obey— the will of Canada or of Britain? Durham could not answer that question. It could not be answered by logic or precedent. It must be answered, like so many others, without logic or precedent, in the loose, flexible, and entirely pragmatic methods of the British system, a system only in name.

Durham had seen the first fact of Canada clear and whole—Canadians must be allowed to govern themselves or they would finally leave the Empire, as the Americans had left it for the same reason. The issue, as he accurately concluded, was self-government, more rebellion, or annexation to the United States.

His second conclusion was totally, almost comically, erroneous. He believed that if the French Canadians of Lower Canada were joined in legislative union with the English-speaking Canadians of Upper Canada they would be quietly engulfed and Anglicized. Their separate language, church, and culture would gradually disappear. One can hardly understand why a man so intelligent could not see that once the French Canadians were given the power of self-government they would use it primarily to protect their separate life. So it was to turn out.

These things lay some distance ahead. As Durham was starting work on his report at Quebec he read in a New York newspaper the news of his betrayal at home. Brougham, always malignant and remorseless, had attacked him in Parliament for exceeding his authority in the banishment of the eight rebels to Bermuda, a colony outside his jurisdiction.

The power of Brougham, who might have been the most notable British figure of his age if he had possessed virtue equal to his talent, was too much for Durham's fair-weather friends. Melbourne yielded to the pressure and disallowed Durham's ordinance. The lucky prisoners of Bermuda, as guilty as men could be of treason, were released. Durham instantly resigned. After only five months of office in Canada, he boarded his ship with another ceremonial procession and sailed for England. Quebec townsmen burned Brougham in effigy.

The deposed dictator reached Plymouth in November. Hastening his work with the ruin of his health, he pushed his report into print by early February. About a year later he died of exhaustion, first of four British governors who would go the same way. His last words—"Canada will one day do justice to my memory"—were an understatement. His countrymen built a Greek temple over his grave. His proper monument is the modern Commonwealth.

Durham was dead but he had left a time bomb in the politics of Britain.

The practical politicians of London asked themselves whether his proposed experiment would work, whether it should be allowed to work at the risk of smashing the centralized Empire. That question was hardly less important to Americans than to Canadians. If the experiment worked, it must produce a second American nation not long hence and only such a nation could permanently secure the boundary, still unfixed in Maine and Oregon and no more than a geographical expression from the Great Lakes to the Rockies.

If the Canadian colonies could not learn to govern themselves and join together as a nation, the fate of annexation to the Republic, prepared for them by the statesmen of the Continental Congress, by Jefferson, and by the present American liberators, must ultimately ensue. Canada could not endure in separate, quarreling fragments.

On the other hand, if the colonies governed themselves and decided to unite, how could they be compelled to serve the interests of Britain? What kind of empire would it be if its several members could go their own separate ways in great affairs? Obviously it would be no kind of empire ever known before.

304 THE STRUGGLE FOR THE BORDER

Faced with this apparently insuperable dilemma of logic, the British government instructed its new governor to mark time and feel out the Canadian situation. Responsible government was indefinitely delayed. Only legislative union of the two colonies was to go ahead for the present.

Durham's successor, Charles Poulett Thomson, a timber merchant and candlestick maker of middle-class origin but as able, as handsome, and as sickly as the dictator, had to secure the assent of Upper and Lower Canada to a joint government and legislature.

They were acceptable to Upper Canada because with its smaller population it would have equal representation with Lower Canada in an assembly of eighty-four members and, by combining with the English-speaking members from Lower Canada, could form an English-speaking majority, as Durham intended. Lower Canada opposed the union on those grounds but could not reject it. The Assembly there had been suspended after the rebellion and replaced by Durham's appointed council. So union was formally approved and enacted by the British Parliament in 1840.

That for Governor Thomson, now established at his shabby little capital of Kingston, was only the beginning. Britain's rejection of responsible government in form, as early as 1837, was gradually dissolving in fact. Thomson must try to get on with the Canadians, must accept the advice of his appointed council so long as it did not damage British interests and, in that case, refuse it.

He thus became his own prime minister. He lobbied his legislation through the Assembly. He began to erect a political party in his own support among politicians who had each been a party unto himself, joining with others in brief, shifting combinations, and having no fixed policy save an insatiable appetite for political patronage.

The Governor, Prime Minister, and party leader charmed the backwoods politicians with his Old World manners, his pretty feminine face, his intellectual power, and his deceptive courage. Though too sick to live long, he rode about the country (often with voluntary escorts of settlers on their farm horses), studied every local problem, and finally appeased the sulking Assembly by securing British subsidies to finance the suspended work on roads and the St. Lawrence canals.

The depression began to lift, orderly but not self-government had been established, and Thomson, like Durham, was worn out. Just as he was about to address his queer parliament for the last time and return home, he was thrown from his horse, his broken leg would not mend, and within a few days he knew he was dying of tetanus.

Yet he completed his speech, ending with a prayer for the blessings of Providence on his colony. When they buried him at Kingston the prayer seemed unlikely of fulfillment.

The next Governor, Sir Charles Bagot, an English gentleman of the old school, and negotiator of the Rush-Bagot Treaty, found Canada almost impossible to govern. At least he discovered the cardinal and permanent fact of Canadian politics—this country could not be governed at all "without the French."

Would French Canadians ever accept British institutions and work with their English-speaking compatriots? Would Upper Canada ever abandon Durham's hope and accept a dual society of two distinct races?

Bagot was too old and tired to hazard an answer. He soon encountered the only Canadian who seemed to know it. Robert Baldwin, a Reformer but a moderate of lofty, cold mind and a contempt of demagogues, had urged responsible government on Durham and now urged it on Bagot. The British government's instructions forbade that final grant of power. Bagot escaped the dilemma by death.

His successor, Sir Charles Metcalfe, an able but stuffy and literal-minded civilian administrator from India, regarded Canadians as subject to the same imperial rules as Indians. His attempt to enforce them produced the first serious test of responsible government.

Baldwin had entered Metcalfe's council, still hoping that freedom was broadening slowly down from precedent to precedent. He was backed by a Reform majority in the Assembly and had formed a working partnership with the first powerful French Canadian prepared to accept a dual state. Louis Hippolyte Lafontaine had sympathized with the 1837 rebellion, had fled to France after it failed, had there been noted by Napoleon's veterans as the exact physical image of the Emperor, had returned to replace Papineau as the leader of his race, and had taken office with Baldwin. The cooperation between these men of different races established the only pattern by which Durham's experiment could possibly work, then or later.

Metcalfe challenged these men and repudiated their theory of responsible government by making an appointment without consulting them. They instantly resigned to prove that responsible government did not exist. The destruction of a majority administration failed to halt Metcalfe's private counterrevolution. He made himself the leader of a loyalist party, compaigned throughout the country in an election of fury and riot, and managed to return a legislative majority favorable to him.

His victory was a brief back-eddy in the current now flowing.

Metcalfe went home to die. He was replaced by the greatest governor since Frontenac, the man who would establish responsible government, inaugurate the Third Empire, and almost singlehanded introduce a novel sanity into the joint affairs of Canada and the United States.

James Bruce, Earl of Elgin and Kincardine, was the son of a famous father who had carried the Elgin marbles out of Athens and set them up in England. He had been well educated in government and he nourished a devout Christian's faith in humanity. His square John Bull's face shone with noble sentiments, his manners were disarming, his methods mild, but he could manipulate even the senators of Washington and he turned out to be one of the toughest men ever sent across the Atlantic.

He needed all those qualities. A man less idealistic or less tough might well have smashed the great experiment, ended the chance of an independent Canadian state, and assured the disruption of the Empire.

No American, observing the extraordinary events of 1849, could imagine for a moment that a nation, or rather the deranged elements of a future nation, conceived in vague theory and apparently dedicated to chaos, could endure much longer. Its politics had erupted again in mob violence. Its economic foundations had crumbled overnight. The most optimistic prophecies of the Jeffersons, Jacksons, and Clays seemed to be wholly confirmed.

That view failed to take account of events in London. Britain was embarked on its own revolution. Politically this process was called Reform; economically, the Industrial Revolution.

Reform had brought the Whigs back to office under Lord John Russell and the third Earl Grey, brother-in-law of Durham, to the Colonial Office. The Tories had been broken by Peel in the repeal of the Corn Laws. His successors were ready to enforce the Durham theory of responsible government in Canada.

To the leaders of economic revolution, guided by the Free Trade theories of Adam Smith, Canada no longer looked like an asset. The tariff preferences on its exports to Britain raised the cost of British manufactures. The continual deficits of local governments were a charge on the British taxpayer. Schoolmen of the new religion had long debated how many angels could dance on the point of the Free Trade needle but the better minds seemed agreed that this company did not include the colonies. The eminent oracles of the *Edinburgh Review* had declared that "Every man of sense, whether in the Cabinet or out of it, knows that Canada must at no distant period be merged in the American Republic."

That opinion was widely shared in the new priestcraft of Free Trade, for it regarded all past human experience as a temporary aberration, it worshiped the Market as a divine revelation, and it almost regarded God as the Founder of the Manchester School.

Still, a British government moving steadily into Free Trade and doubtful about its colonial liabilities, was not quite ready to implement an economic faith by an irrevocable imperial sacrifice. Instead, it finally yielded to Durham's recommendation and accepted a dubious trial of self-government. Elgin was sent to Canada with instructions to follow the advice of his local advisers, at least to the point where they might seriously damage Britain. The danger point was not defined and, with luck, might not be reached.

At the same time, the old colonial system was obviously falling to pieces on the Atlantic coast also. In Nova Scotia, Joseph Howe, a man of burly frame and square granite face, a graduate printer, an editor who wrote classic English, a poet who wrote inferior jingles, a coarse raconteur in the back concessions, a platform orator of magnetic eloquence, a politician loyal to Britain but implacable in his demand for self-government, now emerged as the chosen tribune of his people. He had fought a duel, had driven two governors home in disgrace to England, and in his control of Nova Scotia could no longer be resisted. The new Governor at Halifax, Sir John Harvey, was instructed, like Governor General Elgin, to accept the advice of his councilors.

Thus quietly, by secret instructions and official hints, almost by osmosis, the British government had ended the Second Empire, in theory anyway. In practical politics the ending was not to be easy or peaceful.

When Elgin arrived in Montreal, the new Canadian capital, it was to find much more than two races warring in the bosom of a single state. The old racial split remained unhealed and newer sores had developed.

Quebec, under the surface of politics, had changed little since the Conquest but the English-speaking community was divided between Tories and Reformers by the apparent disaster of British free trade and the loss of Canada's essential markets, by the struggle for responsible government and by ferocious sectarian feuds among the Loyalist Church of England, the Methodists, the Presbyterians, and many minor communions. A sudden flood of starving and plague-stricken immigrants from Ireland—dying like flies on the Montreal docks and spreading cholera along the St. Lawrence—had introduced the ancient Irish hatreds of Orangemen and Catholics into religion and a new violence into politics.

Weakened by absentee government, by inability to erect a working government of its own, by internal strain, and by the loss of overseas trade, Canada had fallen far behind its neighbor, economically, politically, and spiritually. Its meager population of less than two and a half millions was frustrated, splintered, and poor while the Republic had burst into the Southwest, now owned Oregon, was about to find gold in California, and with its new railways was building a continental economy of unprecedented wealth.

What was a Christian gentleman out of London's genteel politics to think of such a country? What could be made of a parliament in which the shameless figure of Papineau had reappeared, after his treason, exile, and long indoctrination in the radical notions of Paris, actually demanding his back pay as a former speaker of the Lower Canada Assembly? Elgin, for all his faith in human progress, was appalled.

"Property, especially in the capital," he reported, "has fallen fifty per cent. in value within the last three years. Three-fourths of the commercial men are bankrupt, owing to Free Trade; a large proportion of the exportable produce of Canada is obliged to seek a market in the United States. It pays a duty of twenty per cent. on the frontier. How long can such a state of things be expected to endure?"

Not long, it appeared. "No matter what the subject of complaint," Elgin added, "or what the party complaining, whether it be alleged that the French are oppressing the British, or the British the French—that the Upper Canada debt presses on Lower Canada or Lower Canadian claims on Upper—whether merchants be bankrupt, stocks depreciated, roads bad, or seasons unfavorable—Annexation is invoked as the remedy for all ills, imaginary or real."

Annexation, then, was the overriding issue and it must settle Canada's future one way or the other, soon and forever. The turning point, long foreseen, had been reached. There would be a self-governing nation or no nation at all, and the outcome depended at the moment more on Elgin than on any other man. "To render Annexation by violence impossible and by other means as improbable as may be," he wrote, "is the polar star of my policy."

The catalyst of all these forces—political, racial, religious, and economic—appeared overnight in a piece of legislation called the Rebellion Losses Bill and designed to award generous compensation to the victims of the 1837 disorders. While convicted traitors were excluded from its benefits, many persons who had participated in the rebellion would be paid handsomely for their treason. Such was the Baldwin-Lafontaine compromise between the two races that must compromise or fight.

The loyalists of Upper Canada indignantly rejected the compromise as an outrage and petitioned Elgin to disallow the hateful legislation. He listened but refused to commit himself, waiting for the boil to ripen. As he knew, this was the absolute test of the great experiment. The Rebellion Losses Bill had been passed by a 2-to-1 Reform majority in the Assembly. It was recommended by his chief advisers. If it was disallowed, responsible government would become a farce.

On the other hand, by approving the advice of his council and the decision of the Assembly, Elgin must face the fury of the loyalists, who would accuse him of betraying them and the Queen. By disapproving he probably would foment a new rebellion among the French Canadians and Upper Canada Reformers. The war of words might well become a war of muskets and pikes again—or, more likely, Canada's voluntary annexation by the United States. The issue had become stark clear. Either Canada must manage its own affairs, however foolishly, accept the management of the crown through its agent, or seek escape from the Empire. The birth hour of this Third Empire had arrived. So Elgin, knowing everything, waited and said nothing.

No one else in all Canada seemed to be silent. The introduction of the indemnity bill had revived all the passions of the rebellion. "No pay to rebels!" shouted the Tories and attacked the French Canadians as "Aliens and rebels." W. H. Blake, Solicitor General for Upper Canada, retorted in the Assembly that the Tories were "Rebels to their constitution and country." At which Sir Allan Mac-Nab, an old soldier and deep-dyed loyalist, leaped up to give Blake "the lie with circumstance." The two men rushed at each other, were pulled apart by the sergeant-at-arms and taken into custody until they cooled off. Early use of MacNab's famous silver-mounted dueling pistols was expected but the struggle was too big for settlement on the field of honor.

The country writhed in speeches, demonstrations, parades, and riots. Baldwin, Blake, and William Lyon Mackenzie were burned in effigy. A reporter of the New York *Herald* viewed this spreading anarchy with satisfaction and predicted "a complete and perfect separation of those provinces from the rule of England."

This was a well-worn prediction and as unsound as it had always been. In his lonely residence of "Monklands," outside Montreal, Elgin was watching not the death of the Canadian colonies but a new state and a new empire in their first labor pangs.

His mind was made up: "If I had dissolved Parliament I might have produced a rebellion, but assuredly I should not have produced a change of ministry." The alternative of "reserving" the indemnity bill and leaving the British government to approve or reject it he considered cowardly. The responsibility "rests and ought, I think, to rest on my shoulders. If I pass the Bill, whatever mischief ensues may possibly be repaired, if the worst comes to the worst, by the sacrifice of me. Whereas if the case be referred to England, it is not impossible that Her Majesty may have before her the alternative of provoking a rebellion in Lower Canada . . . or of wounding the susceptibilities of some of the best subjects she has in the province."

The ice of the St. Lawrence broke early in the spring of 1849 and with it the brittle substance of Canadian society. The first ship was sighted in the river on April 25. The Assembly having passed a new tariff act, little noted in the larger excitement, the government proposed to apply it to the cargo of this approaching vessel. Francis Hincks, the treasurer, drove hurriedly out to "Monklands" and asked Elgin to appear in Montreal and approve the new customs duties. At the same time he could sign the Rebellion Losses Bill.

Elgin, expecting trouble, was staggered by his reception in the city. A restive crowd watched him approach the remodeled market building that housed the Assembly. There he signed all the legislation laid before him. The news passed swiftly to the townsmen waiting outside. Elgin left the parliament buildings to be greeted, in his own words, "with mingled cheers and hootings from a crowd by no means numerous. . . . A small knot of individuals, consisting, it has since been ascertained, of persons of a respectable class in society, pelted the carriage with missiles which they must have brought with them for the purpose."

The missiles included a rotten egg, smashed against the cheek of the Queen's representative. He drove on without turning his head. One rotten egg would be a small price to pay for responsible government. It was only the first installment.

That night Canadian democracy took leave of its senses—clanging firebells; streets filled with mobs and flaming torches; on the Champ de Mars a riotous multitude, hoarse orators screaming "Tyranny!"; then the shout, "To the parliament buildings!"; mobs surging into town, smashing Hincks's newspaper plant on the way, breaking into the Assembly, driving out the members, splintering the furniture: "a man with a broken nose" in the speaker's chair declaring: "I dissolve this House!"

It was in truth dissolved. Was Canadian democracy dissolved with it?

The mob had no time for these abstractions. It was lighting balls of paper and tossing them about the wrecked Assembly hall. In a moment the center of responsible government was aflame. Firemen turned back by the rioters, the seventy-two city policemen helpless, the militia called out too late, the buildings soon a smoking ruin, all official records burned, the Queen's portrait carried through the flames by some intrepid young man—thus had responsible government achieved its agonizing birth.

But not quite born yet. Next day there were attacks on the Reform leaders' houses; arrest of ringleaders by Lafontaine; destruction of his home and stables; a thousand special constables, armed with pistols and cutlasses, and regiments of militia patrolling the streets; four days of civic revolution.

The Assembly, though homeless, was unafraid. It drew up an address protesting its loyalty to the Queen and Elgin and decided to present it to him not secretly and safely in rural "Monklands" but publicly, despite the risk, in the heart of the city. For this ceremony it ostentatiously chose the Château de Ramezay, once the residence of the French governors and headquarters of Montgomery and Franklin in '75. The story of this notable building was to have another violent chapter.

Elgin had been assaulted once with rotten eggs. He was warned that on a second visit to Montreal he might be murdered. It did not occur to him to avoid this danger. On April 30 he drove into town again, escorted by a troop of dragoons and looking straight ahead, motionless and cool, when the stones began to fly. A howling crowd tried to block his entry into the château. His dragoons shouldered a narrow passage for him.

The Christian gentleman had not lost his sense of humor. He entered the château carrying in his hand a two-pound rock which had fallen into his carriage.

The address of loyalty was read and accepted. Elgin started home again by a back street. The mob soon discovered him and followed in "cabs, calèches and everything that would run . . . the carriage was bitterly assailed in the main street of the St. Lawrence suburbs. The good and rapid driving of his postillions enabled him to clear the desperate mob, but not till the head of his brother, Colonel Bruce, had been cut, injuries inflicted on the chief of police and on Captain Jones, commanding the escort, and every panel of the carriage driven in."

The loyalist counterrevolution had demonstrated its loyalty to queen and empire by hounding their representative out of the Canadian capital. He escaped into the protection of "Monklands" within an inch of his life. But Elgin had won. By refusing to meet violence with violence, rejecting the use of martial law, sitting quiet in his house and writing his cold, factual dispatches to London, he had at last established responsible government. Could the Canadians manage it? That was the only question remaining.

The counterrevolution, failing by violence, now attempted to destroy Canada by lawful means.

A lunatic fringe of Canadian Toryism had imitated the left-wing lunatics of '37 in riot, had assaulted the Queen's deputy, burned the center of government, and compelled the Assembly to move the Canadian capital from Montreal to Quebec and Toronto, which would be occupied alternately. All this it had done in loyalty to the Queen, in defense of the Empire, and in punishment of the former rebels.

And what had been the loyalists' reward? They had been betrayed by a British governor when he signed the Rebellion Losses Bill. They had been betrayed by a British government when it introduced free trade. The poison of betrayal turned the Montreal Tories sour and a little mad. They swallowed their past, their principles, and their pride by proposing that Canada be annexed forthwith to the United States.

If Canada could not be saved for the Empire in their way it was not worth saving. If it could not provide Montreal with the satisfactory profits of preferential trade, the businessmen must forget all their battles of the border, all their martial memories, and if necessary their sacred honor. They must follow, like the Tories of Britain, the new god called the Market and find that deity in the Republic even though they had been resisting it since Carleton's time.

The Annexation Manifesto issued in the autumn of 1849 was the work of embittered loyalists and desperate businessmen. It argued, with economic determinism worthy of Adam Smith, that annexation was Canada's natural future (a fact oddly overlooked before) and that Britain desired it (a slander instantly denied by the British government, which called the Manifesto a document "scarcely short of treason").

Over a thousand merchants and politicians, some of them the leading figures of Montreal, signed the Manifesto and soon wished they hadn't, for it was to become in the Canadian mind a register of infamy. Outside Montreal the plan of national suicide received no serious support. Quebec would never approve annexation because it would assuredly mean the destruction of the French-Canadian race and culture. The radical English-speaking elements had listened to Mackenzie's republican ideas sympathetically twelve years before but were now pacified by the grant of responsible government. Most Tories refused to trade the British connection for a chance of business in the United States. Few Canadians in any party believed that annexation would be profitable even commercially.

In this test, as in all others previously and afterwards, the Canadian instinct was clear and overwhelming—these people somehow, sometime, would build a nation of their own. Thus the Manifesto, exciting for the moment and humiliating in retrospect, failed to reverse and only swelled the tide of Canadian independence. The work of Carleton at Quebec and Brock at Queenston was confirmed again.

The United States, having twice fought vainly for Canada, showed little interest in acquiring it by consent. Politics in Washington were concerned with the new territories secured by the Mexican War, with the gold discoveries of California, and above all, with the developing conflict between North and South.

The American government made no response to the offer from Montreal. Vermont and New York passed resolutions of approval in their legislatures but nothing came of them. The Republic as a whole saw no reason to take over Canada against its evident wishes when, no doubt, it would be clamoring unanimously for admission a little latter.

Montreal's Manifesto thus proved a brief sensation and total fiasco, but its early death did not kill the idea behind it. Annexation would remain a kind of dark upper attic in the Canadian mind, a possible retreat if all else failed; in the American mind, a long hope for the future. Always thenceforth it would stand dimly in the background of every great Canadian decision and twice it would enter again the foreground of practical politics with continental consequences.

21

Days of Goodwill

[1849–1862]

O NE OF THE LOYAL TORIES WHO HAD KEPT HIS HEAD THROUGH
the frenzied days of 1849 was the young Kingston lawyer,
John A. Macdonald. He had been elected to the Assembly
in opposition to Reform, had found in politics his natural element,
and for all his convivial habits and lighthearted manners, was beginning to attract the notice of older men. "Our fellows," he said of
the Manifesto, "lost their heads." He refused to sign it and, instead,
proposed the formation of the British America League as a "safety
valve" for the Tory Party. The league defended the British connection, began to advocate the confederation of all the Canadian
colonies, and found in Macdonald the final architect of that union.

The same period of reappraisal also produced Macdonald's implacable and lifelong enemy, George Brown, a Toronto editor of
huge frame, bristling whisker, and dry, powerful intellect. This
leader of the Clear Grits—the future Liberal Party—was a man
utterly antipathetic to Macdonald in his logic, his lack of humor,
and his hatreds, especially his hatred of French Canada and the
Catholic Church. Thus began a struggle of men and ideas that
would bring Canada to nationhood, Macdonald to pre-eminence and
Brown almost to the stature of martyrdom after his murder by a
disgruntled employee.

Elgin discerned the true nature of Canada's problem in 1849 more
clearly than most of his Canadian advisers. "Depend upon it," he
wrote to London, "our commercial embarrassments are our real
difficulty. Political discontent, properly so called, there is none . . .
I am confident I could carry Canada unscathed through all these
evils of transition and place the [British] connection on a surer
foundation than ever if I could only tell the people of the province

314

that, as regards the conditions of material prosperity, they would be raised to a level with their [American] neighbors. But if this be not achieved, if free navigation and reciprocal trade with the Union be not secured for us, the worst, I fear, will come, and that at no distant date."

There, in a British mouth, spoke the logic of North American geography. It had failed in the attempt to join the two American communities politically. It might succeed in joining them economically. And, as Elgin foresaw, the commercial union would prevent the political.

An American market was, for the Canadian colonies, the only available alternative to the diminished markets of Free Trade Britain. Until now Canada had sold little south of the border but it was beginning to find opportunities for its wheat and lumber in the growing American cities. As early as 1846 an enterprising Canadian businessman, William Hamilton Merritt, seeing his grain mills and canal works threatened by the prospect of free trade in Britain, had advocated the removal of tariffs from the North American boundary. His insistent agitation finally persuaded the Canadian Assembly to petition London for a reciprocity treaty. London was agreeable to a plan fitting its own commercial theories and likely to cure the perpetual problem of Canada.

When approached in 1849, however, the American government was cool, though the Congress already had considered legislation to permit the free entry of some Canadian products, if Canada treated American imports likewise. This project failed in the Congress, but Canada adopted it.

Reciprocity remained merely a slogan for the next two years and seemed unlikely to become anything else. Strong protectionist industries in the American North were opposed to the competition of Canadian imports. The South saw in reciprocity the first stage of Canadian annexation and the addition of several new anti-slave states to the Union. Suddenly reciprocity was rescued by a curious agent, the codfish of the Atlantic coast.

American fishermen had been excluded from most of the territorial waters of the Canadian colonies since 1818. What were territorial waters? According to Britain, the three-mile limit ran from headland to headland on the sinuous coastline. According to the United States, it followed the curves of the shore and thus allowed Americans into many teeming bays and inlets regarded by the Canadian fishermen as their exclusive preserves.

Aroused by the Canadians' growing resentment of foreign poachers, the British government announced that its navy would protect the three-mile limit as Britain defined it. The American government dispatched a warship to the disputed waters. These gestures alarmed both sides, for neither wanted another war, and compelled them to consider a peaceful settlement, not only of the fisheries but of all commercial problems. So Elgin's project of reciprocity was revived and he was chosen to negotiate it.

No better choice could have been made. Elgin had proved himself a strong governor in Montreal. He proved himself a smooth diplomat in Washington. American senators found his charm irresistible, his dinners opulent, his wine impeccable. It would be written in the Canadian apocrypha that his reciprocity treaty was "floated through on champagne" but actually it required much judicious pressure.

Elgin fortunately understood the art of pressure and soon procured a useful instrument to exert it in a mysterious person, Israel deWolfe Andrews, the first big-time American public relations counsel.

Andrews had been hired previously by the American government to report on conditions in Canada; he had served many generous Canadian employers who desired reciprocity and he had taken "such measures as the circumstances of the case require . . . to keep the public mind in a quiet state." Those measures were costly, but Andrews had no difficulty in raising campaign funds on both sides of the border.

Elgin immediately hired this genius—first of a long line—who held that statesmanship is no substitute for money judiciously spent in the right places. Andrews's bill for such donations to ninety persons in Washington totaled $118,000. A reciprocity agreement, as Elgin knew, would be cheap at the price.

Negotiations, oiled by Andrews and floated in champagne, slid forward with surprising speed. The American government was determined to keep its fishermen close to the Atlantic shores of the Canadian colonies and would pay for those rights by encouraging the importation of Canadian goods. The North as a whole seemed satisfied, because reciprocity ultimately would mean annexation. The South was quietly persuaded that reciprocity would prevent annexation by giving Canadians prosperity and contentment within the British Empire—an argument, sedulously cultivated by Elgin, which had the added advantage of being true.

With Elgin's charm and logic, Andrews's labors of public relations, the unsound assumptions of the North and the sound assumptions of the South, the Reciprocity Treaty of June, 1854, passed without difficulty through the Congress. The only serious opposition came from the legislature of Nova Scotia. It saw its fisheries frittered away without adequate compensation but, after a brief argument in Halifax, the treaty was ratified by all the colonial Assemblies.

American fishermen secured access to the inshore waters of the Atlantic colonies, where the catch was rich; and the Canadians to the American waters, above Florida, where it was poor. However, the free entry of the Canadians' catch into the American market was a substantial benefit to Nova Scotia and New Brunswick.

For Canada, Upper and Lower, the great prize won by Elgin was the abolition of customs duties on nearly all Canadian natural products. The price paid for it, in addition to fishing rights, was reasonable. Canadian tariffs were removed from turpentine, rice, and unmanufactured tobacco to satisfy the South and on many other products to satisfy the North. The United States was given free navigation of the entire St. Lawrence, Canadian ships being admitted to Lake Michigan.

Elgin's Treaty was to last for ten years, after which it could be denounced by either side. In those days of increasing goodwill and dawning economic sense reciprocity seemed likely to be permanent. It had the sanction of both parties to the bargain. It had also the sanction of geography. It recognized the obvious fact of continental economics—that the United States and the Canadian colonies could profit most by producing and swapping the goods which each could produce most efficiently.

The treaty, in short, introduced almost the first ray of sanity in the long and usually insensate struggle of the border by proposing that two peoples living apart politically should prosper by cooperation commercially.

The sanction of geography, economics, and sanity was not enough. Reciprocity would soon encounter much harder facts, the facts of nationality, racial pride, old prejudice, and sheer accident. It could not hope to survive such primitive forces.

The new arrangements had hardly been signed before the survival of Canada itself began to appear questionable again.

A rising young Tory politician like Macdonald, for example, or his radical competitor, Brown, could see already, above the bitter and shifting struggle of politics at Toronto and Quebec, much larger affairs out west that might well doom all their hopes.

Growing reciprocal trade, together with rapid canal and railway construction, had lifted Canada out of depression into an unprecedented boom, had quite overcome the disaster of British free trade, but the boom was narrowly based on the St. Lawrence Valley.

Once across the Alleghenies, the Americans found the rich plains of the Middle West awaiting them. The Canadians' movement out of the St. Lawrence Valley was barred by the badlands, the lakes, rock, and stunted trees of the Pre-Cambrian shield.

Many settlers, discouraged by the shortage of fertile land in Upper Canada or the difficulty of acquiring it from rapacious land jobbers, emigrated to the United States. The Maritime colonies of the Atlantic, their lumber markets in Britain curtailed, their fisheries open to Americans, began to export their young men to New England. The Republic would remain a strong magnet for the human failures of Canada and for those seeking quick success. A tide of immigration, which had flowed northward until the War of 1812, was reversed.

Halfway through the century the United States had built the skeleton of a transcontinental economy, was fleshing it with political organization, had proved its ability to govern and develop the whole land mass between the Atlantic and the newly won state of California.

This westward march passed by, almost without a glance, the vast and empty Canadian plains. When the Americans had occupied and exploited all their own land south of the border, would the pressure of growing population turn them northward? The case of Oregon had proved that population could be irresistible and population was Canada's fatal lack.

The Colonial Office in London admitted that it had never been able to restrain that pressure in America or other continents and "The Government of the United States will be equally unable to prevent such an occurrence." An imaginary, unmarked boundary line of itself would not hold the Canadian West if the Americans wanted it. The hidden fact, as yet unknown to either side, was that the Americans did not want it enough to take it.

No British or Canadian government could operate on that doubtful assumption. If the West was to be surely held it could be held only by settlement and in the eighteen-fifties time obviously was running out.

Between the St. Lawrence and the Pacific Canadian settlement on the prairies was confined to Selkirk's Red River colony, nourishing some five thousand Scots and French-Canadian half-breeds, whose main contact with the outside world was through Minnesota. They were powerfully attracted to the booming American country close at hand and did little business with Canada. American immigrants from Minnesota continually agitated among the Red River folk for annexation and won some converts. Here was a potentially dangerous southward pull in the geographical center of a future transcontinental Canadian state.

From the Red River to the Pacific lived a few fur traders, the Indians, and the buffalo. And beyond the appalling barrier of the Rockies, on the southern tip of Vancouver Island, stood a minute crown colony managed by the Hudson's Bay Company.

Governor James Douglas's little Fort Victoria appeared the weakest of the British colonies and the most likely to fall. As a settlement it had made no progress. The company had agreed to promote colonization, Douglas was as anxious as the British government to hold the boundary of Fuca's Strait, but colonization was the fur trade's natural enemy.

In 1856, therefore, Victoria slumbered as a peaceful trade post with a few acres of surrounding farm lands, ignorant of the imperial currents already threatening it. The cold and swarthy Governor was not asleep. He had been startled by sudden news from the tributaries of the Fraser River.

A prospector named James Huston had crossed the border by the old fur route to the Okanagan valley and moved northward to hit the Thompson River at the Hudson's Bay post of Fort Kamloops. There he had sampled the gravel of Tranquille Creek and found his gold pan full of nuggets. It was filled also with incalculable consequences for the British Empire, Canada, and the United States.

Douglas guessed at once what the discovery of gold would mean. "It appears," he wrote hurriedly to London in 1857, "that the auriferous character is becoming daily more extensively developed, through the exertions of the native Indian tribes who, having tasted the sweets of gold mining, are devoting much of their time and attention to that pursuit. The reported wealth of the . . . mines is causing much excitement among the population of the United States territory of Washington and Oregon, and I have no doubt that a great number of the people from those territories will be attracted thither with the return of fine weather in the spring."

The Fraser's secret was out. It soon reached the restless miners of California, where the great rush of '49 was on the ebb. The original Argonauts surged north to the new El Dorado. They crammed the steamboats, sleeping in shifts on the decks. They came by sailboat, rowboat, and canoe. In the spring of '58 Douglas found his fort besieged by 20,000 men, all bound for the Fraser. This overnight invasion by an army of rough-looking and probably lawless treasure hunters, mostly Americans, appeared more dangerous than the peaceful settlement which had driven Douglas out of

Oregon. He soon saw, however, that the invaders were not so law-less as they looked.

"They are represented as being, with some exceptions," he re-ported, "a specimen of the worst of the population of San Francisco; the very dregs, in fact, of society. Their conduct here would have led me to form a very different opinion."

The American miners, unlike the settlers of Oregon, had little interest in land, government, or Manifest Destiny. They sought nothing but gold. Having bought $2,000,000 worth of supplies from Douglas, they left Victoria as rapidly as they had come and pushed up the Fraser.

Soon they were joined by an overland rush out of Oregon. The coal mines and sawmills of Puget Sound closed for lack of workers. Farmers abandoned their spring plowing. Soldiers deserted the forts. It seemed likely to Douglas that he must confront most of the population of the Pacific coast and he had learned, in the tragedy of McLoughlin, that an American population inevitably would demand its own government.

Douglas, a tougher man, did not intend to repeat that tragedy. During the first year of the rush Britain's power in the West hung almost entirely on this one man, who lacked any official authority over the Fraser River country. His commission covered only Van-couver Island, but that technical flaw did not deter him for a mo-ment. As there was no time to secure new authority from London, he acted without it.

A fee of $6 was charged for every rowboat and canoe entering the Fraser and $12 for a decked vessel. No one could pan a shovelful of gravel without a miner's license of 10 and later 21 shillings a month. These deliberate gestures of sovereignty informed the for-eigner that he was on British territory only at the Queen's pleasure and must obey her laws.

So far Douglas lacked not only authority but any power to en-force laws not yet written. He had no army or police force. He was running a bold bluff. What if the bluff was called? What if the American miners clashed with the Indians and appealed to Wash-ington for protection? How could Douglas resist official American intervention? As he could not resist it, he must prevent it by strict enforcement of the law, quite illegally, and for this purpose he needed a judge.

In answer to his frantic plea, the British government selected the most unlikely judge available. His name was Matthew Baillie Begbie, already a failure in the legal profession of London and re-duced to the humble job of reporting the courts for the *Law Times*.

No established lawyer had any wish to be judge of a wilderness at £800 a year. Begbie—especially after his brother had stolen his girl—was glad to escape from England on any terms.

Though he knew no law worth mentioning, he appeared, in the words of the Colonial Secretary, Edward Bulwer-Lytton, a writer of colorful fiction, as a man "who could truss a murderer and hang him to the nearest tree." It was not the first time the British government, by mere chance, had picked exactly the right man.

Douglas could hardly have suspected that when he beheld the flashy figure of Begbie descending the gangplank at Victoria in November, 1858. The new judge was just under forty years old, a giant in stature, with the waxed mustaches, the pointed beard, and the arrogant eye of Mephistopheles. Douglas surveyed this histrionic creature skeptically but thought he might do.

They sailed immediately for the mainland to introduce the law officially in the gold fields. At Fort Langley, Douglas swore in the judge. The judge then swore in Douglas as governor of the new mainland colony of British Columbia. The law was legal and government established from the Rockies to the sea.

Begbie set out on horseback; he heard the disputes over mining claims and scribbled his judgments in the saddle; he empaneled juries to try criminals, acting as judge, prosecutor, and defense counsel; he screeched and raved in his nasal voice at jurors who returned the wrong verdict; he was threatened with assassination and, overhearing the plotters from his hotel room, contemptuously emptied a chamber pot on their heads; he jailed a newspaper editor for contempt, was himself accused of corruption, and spent years disproving the charge.

He became, in fact, the Queen's law on horseback, her writ carried in his saddlebags—a builder of empire, a tyrant in public, a prodigal philanthropist and humble Christian in private, who had his grave marked only with the words: "Lord, be merciful to me a sinner." The American miners understood, feared, and obeyed the "Hanging Judge."

This unique partnership of the silent Douglas and the garrulous Begbie had not been formed a moment too soon. At the end of '58 some thirty-three thousand miners were washing the sand bars of the black Fraser Canyon. Douglas now heard the news he had expected from the beginning. The Indians were on the warpath. White men's bodies came floating down the river. A series of massacres, the number of their victims never known, was quickly suppressed by the miners' vigilance committees but they were what Douglas most feared—the miners were taking the law into their own

322   THE STRUGGLE FOR THE BORDER

hands. Latest dispatches indicated that they might take British Columbia as well.

At Yale, the head of Fraser navigation, Ned McGowan, a disgraced judge and desperado from California, had quarreled with the local magistrate, arrested him for "contempt of court" and, with a junta of twenty kindred spirits, had fined him $50. McGowan apparently was setting up a government of his own. While it was only a barroom posse, it could quickly grow into something more serious. It might well be, like the first settlers' government of Oregon, another unplanned eruption of Manifest Destiny.

Here, then, was a clear test of British sovereignty. Douglas loaded a hundred British sailors from a visiting warship, some hundred and fifty newly arrived Royal Engineers, Judge Begbie, and a cannon on Tom Wright's stern-wheeler. As that overburdened little craft paddled slowly up the river and headed into the bank at Yale, McGowan blustered and threatened to resist the government, then quickly changed his mind when he saw the troops and the cannon. The absurd rebellion ended with its leader paying a public apology and a fine and giving a champagne dinner at Hill's Bar for the officers who had arrested him.

It was a small affair, a mere comedy, and no blood or tears had been shed, yet precisely the sort of spontaneous incident which, countless times before, had grown into large affairs along the boundary. Douglas's prompt demonstration of force, Begbie's law, invented in his own head and enforced on horseback, the miners' generally good behavior and their lack of interest in anything except gold held the Fraser, that natural line of power long ago identified by Simpson.

The immediate possibility of crisis passed. The miners gutted the river bars and pronounced the Fraser a "humbug." Within a year the tide of invasion drained back to California and Oregon, the river towns were deserted, and the bankrupt merchants of Fort Victoria "could only stand by their doors and project idle spittle into the streets."

Douglas and his forgotten capital lived once more in peace. They had not heard of four ragged men who, in the autumn of '60, struggled eastward from the Fraser, reached Quesnel Lake, and followed an unmapped creek northward into the mountains. Their names were Doc Keithley, John Rose, Sandy MacDonald, and George Weaver.

One bitter night—food gone on the eve of winter, the trail behind soon to be blocked by snow, the creeks empty of gold—the desperate partners sat down by their campfire to debate a question of life and

death. Should they push on or retreat while there was yet
time?

They slept on that question and in the morning awakened to see,
across an upland valley, the glitter of a little stream. If it yielded
nothing, they agreed that they would walk back to the coast.

The first pan of gravel from the creek contained a quarter of a
pound of nuggets. Four crazy men washed gravel all that day, filled
their pockets with gold, and lay down, exhausted, in the darkness.
They awoke under a foot of snow. And now the great Cariboo gold
rush was on.

It brought madmen from every corner of the world—the returning
Argonauts from California, planters from the deep South, gamblers
from New York, workmen from New England, clerks from London,
painted dance-hall girls from Germany (the memorable Hurdy-
Gurdies), yellow men from Asia, and even caravans of lunatics from
Upper Canada, who crossed the continent by ox train, slid down the
upper Fraser on rafts, lost many lives in the current, and never
found a single speck of gold.

This, for the Hudson's Bay Company, was the end of fur monopoly and the good old days. Douglas no longer faced an invasion of
miners but a permanent population.

The weird town of Barkerville—named for Billy Barker, first miner
to dig down through the blue clay and reach the dazzling bedrock,
only to end in an old man's home—sprang up beside Williams Creek
in a single muddy street of saloons, stores, hotels, dance halls, and a
roaring opera house.

The new army of all nations burst through the narrow gut of the
Fraser Canyon by the Indians' old trail in Fraser's footsteps; it built
a detour, at ten miles a day, through the swampy jungles of Harrison
Lake; it pushed stern-wheelers halfway to the Rockies; drove ox
trains and pack mules to death and even imported twenty-one
camels to carry a thousand pounds apiece until the fetid stench of
these animals scared every ox and mule off the trail.

No trail could serve this massive migration and resulting settlement. Douglas saw now that the game of fur was finished. He surrendered all his old hopes in the decision to build a wagon road
from the head of navigation on the river to Barkerville on the
western flank of the Rockies.

As usual, he lacked both money and authority. No matter, the
road must be built or the uncounted thousands of miners in the gold
fields would starve for lack of supplies. Moreover, a road was essential to govern this swarming territory and hold it for the crown.

The shocked British government therefore read a dispatch from its governor, dated October 24, 1861, announcing that he would build a road "to reduce the cost of transport, thereby securing the whole trade of the colony for Fraser's river and defeating all attempts at competition from Oregon." Thus spoke a natural geopolitician. How would he pay for his road? "I have in these circumstances come to the resolution of meeting the contingency and raising the necessary funds by effecting a loan of fifteen or twenty thousand pounds in this country."

Again he had exceeded his powers. But on money borrowed from the Victoria banks and with the labor of a few Royal Engineers, some Chinese, and any idle miners he could find, Douglas undertook the most extraordinary feat of construction yet attempted in America.

Two years later he had finished a road 385 miles long and 18 feet wide, at a cost of $1,250,000. And what a road! It clung like a gossamer to the blank cliffs of the Fraser Canyon; it was bored through solid rock or propped on fragile toothpicks; it crossed the river on a suspension bridge by cables woven on the spot; it wound through the upland jack pine forest, was broken by a steamboat service on the Upper Fraser and finally, across the gravel tailings of the Williams Creek claims, it ended in the muddy street of Barkerville.

Conquered at last, the turbulent Fraser of the far West had complemented the peaceful St. Lawrence of the East. Both of them had carried Canadians into the interior. Both had given the future Canadian nation an essential line of power. The gold of Cariboo, like the furs of eastern Canada, had brought in a permanent population and altered all the prospects of British America. It was no longer a group of colonies on the Atlantic and the St. Lawrence. It had leapfrogged the prairies and landed on the Pacific slope. It finally possessed the ingredients of a transcontinental state.

The ingredients only. Unless the eastern and western settlements could be joined and the empty center filled, there could be no such state.

22

Old Tomorrow

[1860–1866]

THE SOVEREIGN FACT OF THE EMPTY WEST WAS UNDERSTOOD BY A few men in the politics of Canada, now reeling toward new chaos or final paralysis. Brown, leader of the Upper Canada Reformers, saw the West as Canada's only escape from the strait-jacket of the St. Lawrence economy. "We can beat the United States," he wrote in his Toronto *Globe*, "if we start at once. It is an empire we have in view."

Brown could solve any problem in theory. In the practice of poli-tics his doctrinaire approach, his hysterical rages, and his quarrels with his French-Canadian colleagues made him an unequaled critic, an impossible leader.

Macdonald, the patient and durable man (called Old Tomorrow for his habit of deliberate delay), the plodding, indispensable mechanic of the groaning political machine, could see as far as Brown in terms of geography. In terms of politics he knew that the machine must first be repaired and made to work before any prac-tical problem like the acquisition of the West, or indeed the survival of Canada itself, could be solved.

The machine was not working as Durham had hoped, as Elgin had planned. It was hardly working at all. The union of Upper and Lower Canada was legal but no more. The decision to give both the old colonies equal representation in Parliament, regardless of popu-lation, had produced recurring deadlock between the English-speaking and French races.

Two flimsy political parties, in constant shift and realignment, attempted to span this old gulf.

The old Tories, lately calling themselves the Liberal-Conservative Party and dominated by Macdonald in Upper Canada, had formed an alliance with the conservative Roman Catholics of Quebec, under Georges Etienne Cartier who had once followed Papineau but now sought a reconciliation with the Protestant English. This conservative combination of Macdonald and Cartier had constructed, on the Reform foundation laid by Baldwin and Lafontaine, the only kind of national party that could possibly govern such a split community.

In Cartier, a brisk man of business with a terrier face, Quebec accepted the fact that the French Canadians were a minority and could not hope to be anything else. He had strong support in the church for, after the European revolutions of 1848, it held liberalism in horror. And he knew how to win elections.

In Macdonald, English-speaking Canada, or a large part of it, accepted the fact that the French-Canadian minority would never be absorbed, as Durham had expected, that Canada must always be a dual society. Treat the French Canadians as a nation, Macdonald said, "and they will act as a free people usually do—generously. Treat them as a faction and they become factious." Refusing to "ride the Protestant horse," Brown's reliable steed, in Upper Canada and enduring heavy short-run electoral losses in the hope of long-run gains, Macdonald was basing his future for the moment mainly on Quebec. While Brown plied his editorial scalpel, Macdonald had learned the inner anatomy of Canada, not by dissection but by instinct and practical experience with votes.

The Reform Party, soon to be called Liberals, was a loose partnership of the Upper Canada Clear Grits under Brown and Antoine Aimé Dorion's Quebec *Parti Rouge,* a movement deriving its democracy and anticlericalism from the European revolutions. This brittle union suffered grievously in Quebec and the Macdonald-Cartier party increased its strength from Brown's feverish attacks on Catholicism and his demand for parliamentary representation by population ("Rep. by Pop."), meaning domination of Parliament by Upper Canada.

The deepening racial deadlock and the conflict between these loose groups were driving the parliamentary system toward complete breakdown. Governments rose and fell in fluid, short-lived coalitions. Lesser men, like Etienne Taché from Lower and Sandfield Macdonald from Upper Canada, attained titular office now and then but the only permanent parcels of power were in the hands of John A. Macdonald, Cartier, and Brown, all of whom held the title of first minister at one time or another. So far, however, no man and no party commanded enough power to give the country stable government, a consistent policy of any sort, or the energy needed to possess the West.

Men like Alexander Tilloch Galt, a daring railway builder of Lower Canada, who had supported annexation in 1849 but had later become the leading advocate of an all-Canadian political and economic system, had seen the only possible cure for parliamentary paralysis—the divided colony of Canada must be merged in federal union with the colonies of the Atlantic coast and the gold-rush colonies of the Pacific.

The political crisis of 1858, when government seemed to be on the point of collapse, forced Galt, a disillusioned *Rouge,* to join the Conservative cabinet as finance minister on condition that it support a general confederation of all the colonies. Brown's Reformers countered with a more modest plan for a federal union between Upper and Lower Canada and a larger union to come, perhaps, later; or, failing this, a complete dissolution of the existing union.

The project of a Canadian federation was not new. Guy Carleton had vainly urged it on the British government in 1791. William Lyon Mackenzie had proposed it before plunging into the idiotic Rebellion of 1837. Durham had regarded the union of Upper and Lower Canada as the beginning of a general union. Howe had advocated it in Nova Scotia. It had supporters on both sides of politics in Upper and Lower Canada.

But the obstacles appeared insuperable—the unpeopled wilderness between Canada and the Atlantic colonies; the barrier of the Pre-Cambrian shield to the westward; the vacuum of the prairies; then the Rockies, behind which the tiny settlement of Vancouver Island seemed to lie on the other side of the world; and, above all, the impossible cost of linking these distant fragments of population by railway.

For all the talk of politicians and businessmen, the colonies remained almost completely isolated from one another, with separate constitutions, tariffs, and currencies, while the Americans, a few miles away, having passed that infant state and built a nation, were about to test its endurance in a civil war.

No apparent progress was made in any scheme of union, and the maneuvers of political managers, frantic governments, and angry oppositions presented a record of almost unbelievable outward confusion in the eighteen-fifties and early sixties. Still, they reflected deep movements that must make a Canadian nation of the disjointed colonies or carry them eventually into the United States.

Commercial interests favored a confederation strong enough to exploit the West. They were outgrowing the colonial phase when Canada was solely a producer of raw materials for Britain and the United States. They already had begun to push up the tariff on manufactured goods and were devising the embryo of a national in place of an international economic system.

All the great plans of the railway builders, all the chances of profits in the West, and all the economic arguments would never suffice to solve the problem of Canada's future. It could be solved, if solved at all, only by the force of an abstract idea, the sort of idea that had inspired the Philadelphia Congress. That idea—the dream of an independent state from sea to sea—was growing steadily beneath the outer confusion of politics. The greatness of Macdonald's mind, beside the otherwise abler and better-educated mind of Brown, lay in its ability to grasp the abstraction and make it concrete in the political process.

Macdonald had been only a practical politician, none too respectable in his methods and sometimes disreputable in his habits. At moments of crisis he was likely to be absent and drunk. Yet few men could resist him, drunk or sober.

The Governor General's aide-de-camp, in search of the missing Attorney General, once found him in bed with a French novel and a decanter of his favorite sherry. "If," Macdonald told the trembling messenger, "you are here in your official capacity, give my compliments to the Governor General and tell him to go to hell. If you're here as a private individual you can go there yourself."

Another governor general addressed a university in Greek. Macdonald told the newspapers that "His Lordship spoke in the purest ancient Greek without mispronouncing a word or making the slightest grammatical solecism." Asked by a surprised colleague if he knew any Greek, Macdonald replied: "No, but I know a little about politics."

Attacked by Brown for intemperance, Macdonald replied on the public platform: "I know the electors of Canada would rather any day have John A. drunk than George Brown sober." That was true.

"I want," he once said, "men who will support me when I'm wrong," but added wistfully, "Send me better men to deal with, and I will be a better man." Meanwhile he worked with the material at hand and supplied his candidates with what he called, in a famous letter, "Good bunkum arguments."

Under that patient, lined face, with its twisted, humorous mouth, its bulbous red nose and quizzical eye, Old Tomorrow often seethed —as when he shook his fist at Oliver Mowat, his former law clerk, across the aisle of Parliament and screamed, "You damned pup, I'll slap your chops for you!" At sixty he fought an opposing candidate with his fists on the platform. At sixty-three he leaped from the government benches at the opposition, shouting, "I can lick you quicker than hell can scorch a feather!" and was with difficulty restrained from doing it. He was later arrested by the sergeant at arms to prevent him challenging a Liberal to a duel. But to humbler friends whom he had offended in his cups he apologized and begged forgiveness.

He seldom knew or cared to know any detailed facts. His assistants dug them up and briefed him, he scrawled a few notes on an envelope (usually losing it), and then this man who had spent only five years in school could hold Parliament all night with what appeared to be a prepared thesis on any subject. If he suffered from a hang-over on such occasions he supported himself with innocent-looking glasses of water, laced by his friends with gin.

The jaunty dress, the battered face between the disordered mop of curls, the swollen whisky nose, the sly winks and grimaces, the stream of jokes and reminiscences, the bouts of liquor, all hid the lifelong anguish of this many-sided being. As a boy of seven he had seen his brother beaten to death by a drunken servant. His first son died from a fall at the age of two. Then for years the young lawyer and politician had neglected his career to sit night after night beside the bed of his wife and watch her die. His second marriage produced a daughter whose mind never grew out of infancy and whom he treated tenderly as a child when she was a woman of middle age. Toward the end of his days his wife discovered in his room a box filled with the toys of his dead son. The wounds had never healed. He hid them with drink, raillery, and the work of building a nation.

That work seemed hopelessly stalled, the proposed Canadian union was still only a theme of academic discussion when the Confederate guns fired at Fort Sumter on April 12, 1861. At least one Canadian suspected their meaning north of the border.

Thomas D'Arcy McGee, an Irishman and the darling of Canadian politics, at once warned the Assembly that the Civil War would change the quarrelsome life of Canada. "That shot," he said, "had a message for the north as for the south . . . the signal gun of a new epoch for North America, which told the people of Canada, more plainly than human speech can express it, to sleep no more except on their arms."

The shot meant more than even McGee or any other Canadian yet imagined. It might mean a war with the United States. It must mean a Canadian confederation or the end of Canada.

The muskets of Lexington had split Canadians from Americans and assured Canada of an English-speaking population. The muskets of Queenston had convinced Canadians that they could defend that separation. Now the bombardment of Fort Sumter, like the ticking of a clock, told Canadians that their time was short. As from the beginning, Canada must be made or unmade largely by neighbors who cared little one way or the other. Born of the American Revolution, was Canada to die in the overflow of an American civil war?

That fear obsessed many Canadians as long as the war lasted. It outlasted the war in the mind of Macdonald.

There was the obvious danger of a clash between Britain and the United States, involving Canada. Less obvious but equally dangerous was the possibility that the United States, having mobilized huge armies for its own purposes, would use them to repair the failure of 1812. Or there might be a renewal of casual raids like those of 1838. In any case, it was soon clear that the profitable new commercial relations between the United States and Canada would be disrupted, perhaps forever.

Canadians generally sided with the North. They hated slavery. Canada had long been the terminus of the Underground Railway, had defied the Fugitive Slave Law and protected escaped slaves from extradition. Besides, a quick victory for the North, now a major Canadian market, should be good for business, if the Reciprocity Treaty survived.

A minority of Canadians, especially the Tories—including Macdonald, who had stood at arms against the raids of the Hunters and Chasers—nourished an abiding suspicion of the Northern states as the historic base of aggression, whereas the South looked distant and harmless. The Tory press made no secret of its hope that the war would enfeeble or even smash the American Union, and these utterances, though they did not represent general Canadian opinion, inflamed the Northern press.

Even a radical like Brown, who detested the South's Peculiar Institution, was moved to exclaim in his Toronto *Globe* that the tone of the American newspapers was unbearable: "It is not in human nature long to maintain cordial sympathy toward those who are pouring insult continuously upon us."

The slavery issue and commercial interest made most Canadians pro-North, but the war had not been under way long before they felt the historic tug of Britain, always in conflict with the tug of North America.

Like Canada, Britain was divided on the war. The instincts of its people were strongly opposed to slavery. Many of its most powerful leaders, however, men like Palmerston, Russell and Gladstone, sided with the South, and for the South the position of Britain was vital. If the South was to secure the desired recognition of its Confederacy in Europe, Britain must lead the way.

Louis Napoleon, the adventurer who now ruled France and who, on a youthful visit to the United States, had appeared a little insane to the discerning Gallatin, was eager to recognize the South for his own purposes, but dared not act without British support. The British government almost accepted the French adventurer's advice, for the old quarrels were not forgotten, the diplomatic defeats of the Oregon and Maine boundaries were fresh and rankling, while, on the other hand, the North, with memories stretching back to Lexington, still seemed to regard Britain as the Union's natural enemy.

Two men of unequal stature but equal goodwill, the larger in the White House, the lesser in a London palace, understood the madness of another transatlantic war. Lincoln, with the earthy wisdom of the Illinois prairies, and Albert, Queen Victoria's dominant consort, from the perspective of an ancient royal history in Europe, were both determined in their own ways to prevent that calamity. For Lincoln one war at a time was more than enough. For Albert war of any sort was folly in an age of enlightenment and inevitable human progress.

Such men—Lincoln, with all the power of his character and the Presidency, Albert, with only the power of the Queen's shadow—were at the mercy of other unknown men and of sheer accident.

On November 8, 1861, the American ship *San Jacinto* halted the British mail packet *Trent* on its way to England and forcibly removed two Confederate agents, James Murray Mason and John Slidell. The British government, well charged with high explosives in the person of Prime Minister Palmerston, exploded in rage.

The official note of protest to the United States, written by Earl Russell, the Foreign Secretary, was violent enough to drive an American government, perhaps even the cautious government of Lincoln, into war. It came to the twin desks of Queen Victoria and her husband at a time when they were conducting a long feud with Palmerston and seemed to regard foreign policy as their exclusive prerogative.

Albert was dying from a long illness and the immediate effects of a chill caught at Cambridge, where he had gone to discipline his amorous son, the future King Edward VII. The invalid had just time and energy enough to tone down Russell's draft before he died.

In the final version the note was still sufficiently vigorous to irritate the American government and public—especially as they were so obviously in the wrong—but not to the point of war. Lincoln would not be distracted by a second war from his task of saving the

332   THE STRUGGLE FOR THE BORDER

Union. Nevertheless, the North did not forget. The captured Confederate agents were reluctantly released and the *Trent* affair colored all the relations between the United States and Britain during the remainder of the Civil War and beyond it.

Canada, being the nearest British possession, the historic base of British attack on the Republic, was to feel, as usual, the results of an incident beyond its control.

Galt met Lincoln on December 4, at the height of the crisis, to discuss matters of trade. The President's obvious good sense reassured and his droll stories delighted the dour Canadian minister. He reported Lincoln as hinting that the public belligerence of the American government must not be taken too seriously in Canada. The *Trent* business must be "gotten along with," though "we must say something to satisfy the people."

The evident passion of the people sent Galt home in a state of alarm. His report only confirmed Macdonald's old suspicions. The Canadian government hastily attempted to rebuild the frail defenses of the colony with British help. Britain rushed some fifteen thousand troops across the Atlantic and, the St. Lawrence being frozen, marched them overland through the snow from New Brunswick to Canada.

The flash point of war was uncomfortably close that winter and was safely passed only when the United States released the Confederate agents seized by the *San Jacinto*. Canada's fears did not pass. Should the North, after its victory, decide to revenge itself on Britain, now the friend of the South, Canada would be the obvious avenue of attack.

The newly created Canadian Department of Militia, Macdonald in charge, decided on a substantial mobilization. Though the crisis had eased by this time, in the larger commotion of the Civil War, Macdonald's Militia Bill of 1862 provided for an active military force of 50,000 and a reserve of the same number, with the use of conscription if necessary. The annual cost of $480,000 staggered Parliament and people.

Here was an issue on which the opposition could hope to wreck the government. Mostly for reasons of local politics, having nothing to do with defense, it went enthusiastically to work. It had caught the Macdonald-Cartier administration off guard, Macdonald hard up, sick, disgusted with the ceaseless betrayal of politics, tired of carrying the load day in and day out while others came and went and voted as they pleased, anxious to retire, and at the moment on a prolonged drinking bout.

He did not appear for two weeks in the Assembly while the

opposition attack mounted against his Militia Bill. When the vote came at last a few French-Canadian supporters abandoned the government and defeated the bill by 61 to 54. That was the end of the government and, temporarily, of the defense plan, but for Macdonald it was a merciful release. "I am at last free, thank God!" he wrote home. "I have longed for this hour."

The hour was not to last long. At the age of forty-seven Macdonald thought he was finished with public life; he watched with cynical amusement the erection of a Reform government under Sandfield Macdonald (Brown being temporarily out of politics) but there was to be no easy escape for the indispensable man. A few months' idleness in opposition convinced him and his followers that he alone could save the Liberal-Conservative Party. Choosing his own time, he defeated the new government and in the election of 1863 was marching again with bands, banners, and torchlights. The march would end only on his deathbed.

These sham battles of party war did nothing to protect the country from a possible war with the United States, once the North had leisure to consider Canada after crushing the South.

Despite the confusions of politics, a formidable military force, British and Canadian, soon stood on the border, awaiting an American blow; and behind the soldiers stood the power of Britain, restrained by a hair trigger. The nervous finger of Palmerston fondled that congenial weapon.

Canada's official behavior, if irritating to the North, had been strictly correct up to 1863. Now, less by bad will than by bad management, Canadians found themselves involved directly in the American struggle. The involvement fortunately was slight—a series of clumsy blunders which the Canadian government failed to prevent.

The South, in its desperation, remembered the ancient strategy of North America and proposed to make Canada the base of diversionary attacks on the North. It was useless at this stage to expect the overt assistance of the Canadian or British government, but the South hoped at least for tolerance in Canada.

The first test came with the seizure of the Northern ship *Chesapeake,* between New York and Portland, by a band of fourteen Confederates. Unable to think of a better plan, they finally put into Nova Scotia, abandoned their prize, and asked for asylum.

The *Chesapeake* was immediately returned by the Nova Scotia authorities to her owners. Her crew could not be disposed of so easily. The United States demanded their extradition as pirates, but Nova Scotia did not propose to facilitate the hanging of men regarded as political refugees. They were conveniently released by habeas corpus, and when a new warrant was issued for their arrest the police somehow failed to find them. After further American protests the incident was officially forgotten.

More dangerous was the case of Jacob Thompson. This remarkable man had been a member of President Buchanan's Cabinet, had later been appointed an assistant to Jefferson Davis, and in July, 1864, had arrived in Toronto with mysterious instructions from the Confederate government. He was to act "in such manner as shall seem most likely to conduce to the furtherance of the interests of the Confederate States of America."

Thompson's own ideas appeared extremely vague. He proposed as a start to burn St. Louis, Cincinnati and New York, for which purposes professional incendiaries were hired. Then he thought of releasing the Confederate prisoners near Sandusky and Chicago.

As he meditated some method of eliminating the *Michigan*, the United States' only armed vessel on the Great Lakes, a man named Charles H. Cole arrived with an admirably simple plan. He said he was a lieutenant in the Confederate Navy, the friend and drinking companion of the *Michigan's* officers. It would be simple for Cole to engage the ship's company in a debauch while Thompson and a raiding party captured her.

Thompson bought another steamer, the *Philo Parsons*, and filled her at Canadian ports with Confederate agents in the disguise of tourists. She proceeded to Sandusky, where the *Michigan* was moored, pausing only to scuttle a harmless lake boat on the way.

At Sandusky, however, the feckless Cole had spent a subsidy of $4,000 to intoxicate himself instead of the *Michigan's* crew, had babbled in his cups and warned the American authorities of the crackbrained plot. Thompson, therefore, found the *Michigan* bristling with fourteen guns aimed accurately at the *Philo Parsons*. He returned in haste to Canada and scuttled his own ship. Even that simple job was botched. The *Philo Parsons* sank in such shallow water that she was soon salvaged.

Thompson's next project was an uprising in Chicago. The Sons of Liberty, disguised as delegates to the Democratic Convention, would seize the city and release the Confederate prisoners at Camp Douglas nearby. A few agents proceeded hopefully from Canada to Chicago. Their plan was discovered by the American police and suppressed.

The Canadian government at last had bestirred itself. The American government was given all available information on Confederate activities and Thompson kept under close watch until he disappeared in despair. He had accomplished nothing but the waste of the Confederacy's funds and the irritation of the North against Canada.

If Lincoln could have peered inside the Canadian government, he would have realized that it was too weak and convulsed to offer the slightest danger to any country but its own. The United States was rent with civil war but would soon be reunited. Canada, after years of futile talk, was split by political war and seemed to have little prospect of union, then or ever.

Lincoln, the politician writ large, would have been the first to understand the Canadian problem and to understand also that its solution, one way or another, must vitally affect the future of the United States. As he was solving the bloody stalemate of war, the colony of Canada had finally encountered political stalemate and impotence.

23

Back to Quebec

[1864–1866]

MACDONALD AND HIS FRIENDS WERE IN OFFICE AGAIN, BY A majority of a few unreliable votes. They could not govern. Neither could the Reformers. While Macdonald brooded, schemed, and drank but could find no way out of the dead end devised by Durham's constitution, Brown was beginning to rise above his partisan passions and the implacable hatred of his rival.

His sudden hints of reconciliation were quickly carried to Macdonald, who instantly grasped them. With Galt as a buffer, he met Brown ceremoniously at the St. Louis Hotel, Quebec, on June 17, 1864, a memorable date in continental history. The two men had not spoken in recent years, except formally across the floor of Parliament. Now their patriotism compelled them to get down to practical bargaining and save the country.

Brown still favored a federal union of Upper and Lower Canada only, based on representation of the two provinces by population, as a first stage in the confederation of all the colonies. He abandoned that plan on Macdonald's insistence that the whole work must be done at once.

Macdonald had favored a centralized, legislative union, he still believed in it but agreed to a federal constitution as the only system that the colonies would accept.

To this end a coalition government, including Brown and two other Reformers, was erected overnight, the stalemate ended, and the work of building a nation-state begun.

The necessary conferences had taken six days only but the new government and the project of confederation were in reality the product of more than twenty years' trial and error in the iron lung of the existing constitution, of all Canada's experience since the

Conquest. The rivals had been reconciled temporarily by forces larger than their personal quarrel or any wrangle of local politics— by the breakdown of government, by the old haunting fear of the United States, which had created the Canadian colonies in the first place, by the commercial attractions of the West, and most of all by an intangible as old as Champlain—the blind will to build a Canadian community across the northern slope of America.

The deranged Canadian Assembly beheld that old dream again when the new coalition government presented its confederation policy. Reformers cheered Macdonald, their old enemy. Tories cheered Brown. "An excitable, elderly little French member" rushed across the floor in tears to fling his arms around the Reform leader's neck and "hang several seconds there suspended, to the visible consternation of Mr. Brown and to the infinite joy of all beholders."

Confederation, thus announced, was a mighty dream and a dream only. Could it ever be reduced from mere emotion to a written constitution and a living nation? Could the colony of Canada, on the St. Lawrence, and the Atlantic colonies of New Brunswick, Nova Scotia, Prince Edward Island, and perhaps even distant Newfoundland, be united strongly enough to hold the border against a nation presently dismembered but already the largest military power in the world? And what of the West, with its little gold-rush colonies of Vancouver Island and British Columbia?

The speeches, the shouting, and the tears in the Parliament at Quebec were gratifying to Macdonald, the secret sentimentalist. They counted for little with the practical politicians. Yet from now on confederation must be the work of politics on the most practical terms.

By a happy coincidence the Atlantic colonies were then about to meet at Charlottetown, Prince Edward Island, to discuss a union among themselves. Their conference offered a chance to strike while the iron was hot. Accordingly, Macdonald, Cartier, Brown, Galt, four junior ministers, and three secretaries, an impressive delegation, sailed for Charlottetown at the end of August in the hope of selling a continental union to the Maritimes.

Their first reception was damp and discouraging. The little *Queen Victoria* steamed into Charlottetown harbor but no welcoming committee appeared to greet the distinguished visitors. Nearly everybody, including the delegates to the Maritime conference, had left town to see a traveling circus, clearly more interesting than the birth of a nation. Only one man, W. H. Pope, a member of the Prince Edward Island government, took any notice of the Canadian statesmen or the blueprint of the new nation in their pockets. Pope found a skiff and rowed alone out to the *Queen Victoria*. There was lodging ashore for only four Canadians, he admitted with embarrassment, and not even a carriage or wagon to carry their luggage. Macdonald and most of the Canadian delegation therefore remained on the ship.

So began, about as inauspiciously as possible, a circus on shore and a handful of dubious men anchored in the harbor—the Canadian equivalent of the first Continental Congress. But at Charlottetown, as at Philadelphia, a new state was surely in gestation.

Once the circus had closed, things moved fast. The Maritime delegates proved surprisingly receptive to the strangers from Canada. They postponed their own scheme of Maritime union to consider the larger scheme.

This conference presented the supreme crisis of Macdonald's career so far, and he knew it. Keeping strictly sober and for once preparing his speech with meticulous care, he held the delegates all morning with quiet unanswerable argument—the danger of American invasion, the urgency of joint defense, the necessity of building a strong, centralized union, free of those constitutional weaknesses which, he said, had split the American Union in civil war.

The conference was impressed by its first sight of the greatest man in British America. The delegates adjourned to luncheon on the *Queen Victoria* and drank toasts until late at night. One watershed had been crossed.

A lavish banquet on shore, a ball, and an evening of champagne so enlivened the conference that it decided to carry its work and good news to Halifax. There more speeches, celebrations, and champagne revealed that Maritime union already was obsolete, that the colonies would frame a continental union or nothing. At another brave dinner party Macdonald reiterated his former warning—the colonies must "avoid the mistakes of our neighbors" and found a strong central government.

That result seemed assured in the first flush of expectation and wine. It was to be speedily completed at a final conference in Quebec, on October 10.

Macdonald, a very tired man, knew that the really dangerous obstacles lay ahead. Would the British government, though favorable to the confederation project, really accept the beginnings of a new nation in place of its obedient colonies, possibly a restive and truculent nation when it matured? Would the colonies themselves agree on confederation when they faced, in place of easy generalities, the hard facts of national constitution and the essential surrender of local powers to a national government and legislature?

There was little time to prepare for the Quebec conference, though it would make or break confederation, since it must be carried through, if possible, before the first enthusiasm ebbed. On October 10, therefore, the delegates of Canada, New Brunswick, Nova Scotia, Prince Edward Island, and Newfoundland met in a bleak and chilly building constructed as a post office, and used by the Canadian Assembly after its original quarters burned ten years before—hardly the edifice for such an occasion, but larger than Carpenters' Hall, Philadelphia, meeting place of the first Continental Congress. And from the edge of the great rock the Canadian delegates looked down, as so many Canadians had looked before, upon the sleek current of the St. Lawrence, the ancient bearer of their people's life.

Unhappily the river was blurred by rain, yet through the first autumn haze the dullest eye could hardly fail to see the invisible company of this place. Cartier in his icebound ship, Champlain in his first Habitation, Frontenac in his lonely castle, Montcalm looking from his decayed walls upon the British fleet, Carleton waiting for the Americans in a New Year's blizzard, and countless other passengers, brought to Quebec by the broad avenue of the river, all had played their parts, large or small, in the process now nearing its consummation.

Quebec had been the first spiritual center of Canadian life. The long circumference stretched now from Newfoundland to the arctic and the Pacific, enclosing an almost empty circle. Everything had begun in the town built by Champlain. Here, if anywhere, more than a century and a half of toil, agony, and bloodshed could be completed. Canadians instinctively had returned to their original home, driven there mainly by their dangerous neighbors.

If Quebec was to be Canada's Philadelphia and if the problems of the two American unions were similar in many ways, in others they differed radically.

The Republic had burst out of a revolution against Britain, with revolutionary passion sufficient to carry it across the Alleghenies, the plains, and the Rockies to the western sea.

The Canadian Confederation, a peaceful evolution, lacked any such violent momentum from overseas. Its outer propulsion came from the Republic, its inner from quiet men with little of the anger, the scholarship, the confidence, or the philosophic theories of the men who had written the American Constitution in heat and genius. Philadelphia had writhed in anger, inspiration, and noble oratory. The Quebec conference was cold, pedestrian, and dull. For all that, it knew precisely what it wanted.

The Americans had devised an entirely new experiment in government and codified it in rigid law. The Canadians intended to adopt the federal device of that invention, since they could not hope to unite on any other basis, but otherwise their government would be a strict imitation of the well-tried British parliamentary system and would be linked to it through the monarchy.

Economic, physical, and racial circumstances of the two peoples also were different. The Americans claimed the richer half of the continent, the Canadians the poorer, and even that claim, asserted by some three million people, was frail and doubtful. The Thirteen American Colonies had been mostly of one race, culture, language, and tradition. The Canadians were split between two races which would not merge. The American society could be single, united, and homogeneous; the Canadian must be dual, conjugate, and viable only by an almost impossible feat of compromise and concession.

In short, the Americans had come to Philadelphia illuminated by a dazzling vision and expected it to illuminate mankind. The Canadians, all but a very few, saw hardly beyond the immediate problems of a political accommodation and asked only to be left alone to make it work.

Though the Macdonalds, Browns, Galts, and Cartiers could not speak and write like the Washingtons, Jeffersons, Franklins, and Hamiltons of Philadelphia, they had their own dream. It was nebulous, inarticulate, perhaps beyond their grasp, and now half hidden by the St. Lawrence mists. Still it was their own, it was native, it was as valid as the dream of their neighbors.

Thus Philadelphia nearly ninety years before, in the first heady days, the splendid illusions and the written guarantees of the Enlightenment, when the world was clearly embarked on its Great Age; and thus Quebec in the stolid respectability, the automatic progress, the newer illusions of Queen Victoria's deathless *Pax Britannica*. Thus the silks, ruffles, knee breeches, silver buckles, and boundless hopes of the eighteenth century; and thus the sober, bearded men in the top hats, tailcoats, and equal innocence of the nineteenth.

Thus also the sharp distinction between the characters of two peoples—the self-sufficient Americans, their Old World roots suddenly severed, the New World their oyster, and the past disinherited by law; the confused and pragmatic Canadians, half rooted overseas, clinging to their mother, and satisfied to take one tentative step at a time.

Would the next essential step now be taken? Macdonald, hiding his dream and his doubts under a cheerful, bustling air and buoying

up the delegates' spirits by a ceaseless round of parties and unlimited supplies of stimulants (at a cost of $1,000 when the best
French brandy sold for $1.25 a pint) could not foresee the outcome.

As titular head of the Canadian government, Taché, with his
handsome face and halo of white hair, presided at the conference.
Macdonald was its manager and factotum. His long apprenticeship
in grass-roots politics, his knowledge of men high and low, his
capacity as an extraordinary man to feel and reflect the ordinary life
of the Canadian folk, indeed his very weaknesses almost as much
as his inner strength had equipped him perfectly—as formal education could not—for this work, which seemed to be a work of law and
constitution but was actually a work of human nature. Brown might
explain the dry details of the proposed constitution, Cartier the law,
and Galt the problems of finance; Macdonald was the spirit of confederation incarnate, the mirror of Canadian life.

He saw and mollified everybody. He treated Brown not only as
an equal but almost as a superior, referring respectfully to him
(though he was five years younger) as the "old chap." He sensed
instinctively where opposition lay and turned all his playful charm
on the objectors. He was always ready with formulae, adjustments,
and accommodations. Most of the future constitution was written in
his own hand on slips of paper that, one by one, became the 72
Resolutions of the conference.

It was prospering, but the weary, laughing factotum knew that
confederation remained at the mercy of any little private quarrel or
any piqued colonial government. As he rose on the second day of
the conference to deliver his greatest speech he still could not count
on final agreement. The array of bearded faces around him looked
grim and skeptical. Their first ardor had passed. These men must
now be convinced by facts.

Most of them knew little of Canada and less of Macdonald, were
parochial politicians and nothing more. Apart from his unconscious
allies in the United States, he had only two sure supporters outside
his own government—Charles Tupper, the moon-faced and resourceful doctor who had beaten Joe Howe and made himself premier of
Nova Scotia, the dapper little Samuel Leonard Tilley, premier of
New Brunswick, who wanted confederation but was in serious political trouble at home.

Macdonald's immediate task was to swing the four votes of the
Maritime delegation. He was sure of Canada's two. At the end of his
speech he was sure of all. His motion in favor of confederation
carried unanimously, not so much by his argument as by his vision
of a national state. The apprenticeship of public labor and private

pain had not been wasted. The immigrant boy from Scotland, the ill-schooled lawyer from Kingston, had mastered his trade and, in home-spun phrases, articulated his vision.

Now began the hard bargaining on details, the process that had almost smashed the Philadelphia Congress after the Revolution. The Quebec conference lacked a Washington. Luckily, in Macdonald it had found its Franklin. With infinite patience, compromise, strategic retreat, and immovable obstinacy on essentials, he sought to reconcile the conflicting pressures between the more populous colony of the St. Lawrence and the weaker colonies of the Atlantic.

Representation in the elected chamber of the new Parliament must be on a basis of population. The Maritimes, therefore, demanded more than their numerical share in the upper, appointed chamber, corresponding to the British House of Lords, and for this purpose they could point to the American Senate, where population was disregarded in favor of equal representation for every state. The Maritimes asked more than Canada could possibly grant, on the false assumption that the upper chamber would become an equal partner in legislation with the lower. In fact, it was to become little more than a peaceful asylum for the aged and tired supporters of the ruling party.

Long wrangles, much lobbying, many banquets, the unstinted flow of liquor, and Macdonald's stage management gradually revealed the lines of disagreement and possible agreement. Ten days after the conference opened it was obvious that Newfoundland would not enter confederation, that Prince Edward Island's adhesion was unlikely, that Canada and the governments, though not necessarily the people, of New Brunswick and Nova Scotia could agree on representation in the new Parliament.

Then came the division of powers between the central and provincial governments. There was room for dickering and compromise but on one point Macdonald was obdurate—confederation must avoid the Republic's mistake of giving too much power to its states, and the test was the disposition of residual powers not definitely assigned to the central or provincial legislatures.

The Americans, said Macdonald, had made a fatal error in leaving those powers to the states. Confederation must leave them with the central government. He would not yield an inch on that principle, for otherwise, he said, "it would ruin us in the eyes of the civilized world." Again his combination of firmness and geniality carried his principle unanimously.

By October 27, after fourteen working days, a constitution had been roughly drawn. The new state was to be an amalgam of monarchy and federalism. Its apex would be the crown of Britain, represented by a governor general in Canada; its base, an elected assembly and an appointed upper chamber of second thought; its executive, a cabinet, sitting in the legislature and responsible to it.

The projected Canadian state thus was an exact duplication of the British parliamentary system, with the addition of provincial legislatures and governments sovereign in their own prescribed fields of power like the states of the Republic. Where the central and provincial powers began and ended was not quite clear, would be constantly blurred and altered by judicial interpretation for a long time to come, but in general the Fathers of Confederation believed that they were giving their central government more power than that of the Republic.

On the other hand, the constitution of Canada was to be an act of the British Parliament and could not be changed by Canada alone—at least in theory. It did not take a prophet, however, to foresee that if a Canadian nation emerged from the Quebec blueprint it would soon control its constitution in fact, if not in name. Likewise, foreign affairs remained in the control of London. There again that control must become a fiction once Canada was strong enough to make its own foreign policy. Finally, the new union was not to be confined to the St. Lawrence and the Maritimes, it was to be open to the colonies of the Pacific coast and any communities sprouting from the empty soil of the prairies.

Macdonald had been watching the westernmost colonies of Vancouver Island and British Columbia anxiously, knowing that they might elect to enter the United States and bar Canada forever from the Pacific. They must be joined to Canada at any cost. The cost would be even higher than he expected. It would include the one nearly fatal disaster of his career.

All that trouble and much more lay down the years. As he left the Quebec conference, Macdonald carried in his battered valise the 72 Resolutions, most of them in his own handwriting, the anatomy of the new state.

The womb of Quebec, in fitful gestation since 1608, apparently had borne its child. But the child had come into the world scarce half made up. All the Resolutions, proposing a second British nation and, inevitably, a new form of empire unknown before in human affairs, had yet to receive Britain's approval. Still more doubtful was the approval of the Maritime legislatures.

The Quebec delegates now moved on in triumph to Ottawa, the former settlement of Bytown, which Queen Victoria had lately chosen as the permanent capital of the existing colony of Canada, thus, in the words of Goldwin Smith, the eminent English historian, converting "a sub-arctic lumber-village by royal mandate into a political cockpit."

The new parliament buildings rose, stark and unfinished, a jungle of Gothic towers, from the noble hill above the river first sighted by Champlain. They had already the look of a national capital and they appalled the economical mind of Brown.

"The buildings," he wrote, "were magnificent; style, extent, site and workmanship surprisingly fine . . . just five hundred years in advance of the time; it would cost half the revenue of the province to light and heat and keep them clean. Such monstrous folly was never perpetrated before." Folly—that was the word for confederation in financial reckoning. Happily Macdonald was never much of a hand with figures.

Among the littered stone and lumber the Quebec delegates ate a ceremonious luncheon designed to symbolize the adoption of Ottawa as the center of the prospective transcontinental nation. Macdonald's skill and pertinacity had mainly brought confederation this far and completely exhausted him. He was cold sober when he rose to speak but he could not utter a word. Galt took his place in the embarrassed silence. Macdonald was only forty-nine years old. He did not appear that day as a man strong enough, or with enough years left, to lead his nation.

A brief rest in Kingston returned him to his usual gay, bantering, and salty self. That was fortunate. The Canadian government, in the midst of its domestic labors, had been plunged into a new foreign incident wearing a very ugly look. The North American border was again in eruption; or at least the Republic seemed to think it was.

A first feverish telegram from Governor Gregory Smith, of Vermont, in the autumn of 1863, suggested that his state was being massively invaded by Canadians. It turned out, after the hysteria simmered down, that some months earlier a Confederate agent, Bennett H. Young, had arrived in Lower Canada with credentials attesting "his sincerity as a man and his piety as a Christian." His pious assignment was to burn and loot New England. Crossing the border into the Vermont village of St. Albans, on the night of October 19, Young and twenty-five followers in civilian clothes robbed a bank of $200,000, set fire to some buildings, wounded two men, one fatally, and hurried back to Canada with their booty.

The St. Albans raid was a small affair, a sorry fiasco beside the many border battles of the past, and not to be compared to the American raids of 1838, but it had occurred at the worst possible moment, three weeks before a presidential election and after three years of friction between the United States and Britain.

The American politicians made the most of it. Hustings and press rang with the old familiar cries. General John A. Dix ordered his soldiers to follow the raiders into Canada. Secretary of State Seward notified the British government that the United States considered itself free to abrogate the Rush-Bagot agreement and arm ships on the Great Lakes. He also warned the British ambassador that "it would be impossible to resist the pressure which would be put upon the Government to abrogate the Reciprocity Treaty also, if these invasions from Canada continued."

"Invasions"—the word must have made Macdonald smile. He was accustomed to the hysteria and hyperbole of election campaigns, having often used these weapons himself. In one way, the Canadian government found these latest troubles disturbing at the crisis of the confederation scheme. In another, they confirmed the necessity of confederation as a defense measure and were calculated to still the doubts of the Maritimes. As usual, the angry Republic had acted at exactly the right moment—almost, it seemed, by a law of continental nature—to unite its Canadian neighbors.

Those historic forces must take their course. Meanwhile it was essential to satisfy the United States that Canada had played no part in the St. Albans raid and was determined to punish the raiders.

Thirteen of them were promptly arrested, despite their claim for treatment as soldiers engaged in lawful war. They were, indeed, in precisely the same position as that of the notorious Alexander McLeod of the *Caroline* affair. Britain had insisted, on threat of war, that McLeod could not be tried in American courts because he had boarded the *Caroline* on the orders of the Canadian authorities. The St. Albans raiders demanded similar protection. Washington replied that they were criminals and must be extradited at once.

The Canadian government promised to deliver them as soon as their guilt had been sufficiently proved to meet the terms of the extradition treaty. On this assurance Washington's anger seemed to subside, the British government, more alarmed than the Canadian, felt a welcome relief, and Lincoln, the man of tolerance, was re-elected.

A curious state paper of the British Colonial Office noted, however: "If McClellan had carried the Presidency and peace had been made on Southern and pro-slavery conditions, which was a sufficiently possible contingency not to be excluded from our view, the immediate danger to our small force in Canada might have been considerable. That hazard does not seem so great now."

The Colonial Office and the Canadian government had not anticipated the stupidity of Charles Joseph Coursol, a magistrate of Montreal, before whom the St. Albans raiders were arraigned. Quite casually he announced that, through certain obscure defects in the law, he lacked any jurisdiction in this case. Therefore, he could not consider the central issue—whether the prisoners were criminals, subject to extradition, or soldiers of a belligerent nation. The thirteen Confederates were released, some of the stolen money from the St. Albans bank still in their pockets.

Macdonald realized that this had become a serious business. Coursol, he wrote, would be regarded in the United States as a responsible judge though he was only a foolish local magistrate who "altogether mistook his duty." American resentment was even stronger than Macdonald expected.

The Northern press resumed its bitter denunciation of Canada and proposed that when General Grant and the Grand Army of the Republic had finished with the South they could profitably turn north and conquer Canada in a few days' easy march. The American government, urged on by the anger of the Congress, ordered all Canadians to carry passports when they entered the United States. As passports had never been required before, this order, from a president as friendly as Lincoln, sounded ominous.

It was a relief in Canada to hear that the President had canceled General Dix's plan to pursue the Confederates across the border. At the same time it became obvious that the Congress intended to cancel the Reciprocity Treaty at the earliest possible moment and deliver a crushing blow on the Canadian economy.

The half-made confederation of Quebec assuredly was being born into a troubled continent. Macdonald stayed calm. "We must perform our duty," he said, "irrespective of the smiles or frowns of any foreign body and will never be hurried into extra exertions by proclamations like these of General Dix, or prevented by any feeling of indignation from carrying our laws into full force."

They were not easy to enforce. The prisoners had been quickly rearrested after Coursol's judgment but there seemed to be something in the magistrate's reasoning. Under existing law, the government could not secure a conviction. The case dragged on while Parliament sought to amend the law.

These delays brought American public opinion to a final sense of outrage. The wildest rumors circulated in the Northern cities—Confederate forces were being organized in Canada, ships were being armed on the Great Lakes, a rusty ornamental gun had disappeared from a Guelph lawn and doubtless was part of a general conspiracy. Ottawa strove to pacify Washington by hastily forbidding the export of armaments.

The man in the White House, with only a few weeks more to live, had remained serene throughout this turmoil. His doctrine of malice toward none and charity for all evidently included even foreigners north of the border. Lincoln's annual message noted the "insecurity of life and property in the region adjacent to the Canadian border" but assured the Congress that the Canadian government would "take necessary measures to prevent new incursions." The immediate alarms subsided and were soon engulfed in the larger excitement of Northern victories.

Just the same, the Canadian government stationed some two thousand militia volunteers on the boundary to prevent more Confederate crimes and Macdonald organized a secret detective force to advise him of possible raids in the opposite direction. His crude espionage net would be needed within two years.

The desperate Canadian railways, their traffic hard hit by the American passport regulation, urged Macdonald to seek its removal by friendly representations to Washington. He flatly refused: "It would be extremely impolitic . . . if the Canadian Government went on its knees to the United States Government for the purpose of procuring a revocation of the late order. It would give Mr. Seward an exaggerated idea of the inconvenience and the loss sustained by Canada and would be kept up as a means of punishment or for purposes of coercion. The true way to succeed is for the Canadian Government to assume an indifferent tone in the matter, leaving it to the Western States and private solicitation to effect the purpose."

A false air of indifference was maintained on the border and soon the passport regulation was dropped. The threatened abrogation of the Rush-Bagot Treaty also was quietly forgotten. The Reciprocity Treaty, however, was clearly doomed.

Macdonald could feign indifference to a foreign people. His own were quite another matter, for it had begun to appear that the politicians of the Maritimes intended to stifle confederation in its cradle.

Newfoundland and Prince Edward Island definitely rejected the proposed union. Tilley, its sedulous nurse in New Brunswick, faced a revolt among his supporters. He had foolishly promised to call a new election before asking approval of the Quebec Resolutions and he might well lose it. Tupper, who had been so optimistic at Quebec, began to doubt that he could carry the Resolutions through the Assembly of Nova Scotia.

There a Homeric battle had been joined between two local

giants. Joe Howe had once painted the picture of a transcontinental state in lofty orations. Lately he had retired from politics into a safe, insignificant job and a comfortable salary as the British government's fishery commissioner. Now he emerged like an angry bear from hibernation to denounce any scheme of union but his own.

Since confederation had been shaped by other hands in his absence, Howe would have none of it. His glory as the greatest Nova Scotian could not be shared with Tupper, whom he had once contemptuously called "the little doctor." He would not, he said, "play second fiddle to that damned Tupper!" So Howe's unequaled editorial pen and golden voice were turned from fishery reports to the more congenial task of attacking confederation as a "Botheration Scheme" ruinous to the Maritimes, of value only to Canada.

No one could argue with this triumphant and yet tragic man. No one could stop him. The tortures of his megalomania were legible in his coarsened face and brutal language; and in his insatiable vanity, his frustration as a humble observer of codfish, his eloquence and elemental power. Confederation faced a dangerous enemy. Macdonald watched and wondered if Howe's virtues, buried under the rubble of wasted talent and lost years, could ever be excavated for future use. At the right moment the expert human excavator of Ottawa would go to work, but the time was not yet.

The first months of 1865 found Macdonald sick but able to put the Quebec Resolution through the Canadian Assembly; the British government suddenly doubtful about the cost of fortifying and defending Canada; the Americans still incensed by the St. Albans raid and raw from the costly victories of the Civil War; Tupper dizzy from Howe's attacks; and now Tilley defeated at the polls, in the first direct test of public opinion, by a combination of anticonfederationists and American railway interests had hoped to link New Brunswick, by rail, with the business of the Northeastern states.

A weaker man would have retreated before these swinging blows. Macdonald decided to advance. The government, he announced, would confer immediately with Britain on confederation, on the expected loss of American markets, and above all on a Canadian defense plan.

He was more than ever obsessed with the American danger that spring as General Grant swept down upon the Court House of Appomattox and, after defeating the South, would quickly be able to turn the Grand Army of the Republic northward and overrun all the Canadian colonies, if the Lincoln government decided to end the long quarrel by an obvious and quick solution.

The British government's delay in devising a Canadian defense plan, its meager appropriation of £50,000 a year, embittered Macdonald and had not, he said, "Diminished the dread of forced annexation and abandonment by Great Britain. . . . If England can do nothing better for us than vote £50,000 a year for four years to fortify Quebec, we may give up the idea of resistance as hopeless."

On April 15 he learned of Lincoln's assassination. It could hardly have occurred to the harassed Canadian politician that someday his countrymen would regard him with something like the American people's reverence for their martyred president. All he knew then was that the simple, kindly man, with malice toward none. had gone from the White House, that the only sure stabilizing force in American politics had been removed, that the Republic's foreign policy was in new, untried, and perhaps reckless hands, with the world's largest army at their bidding.

Thus, under the usual disguise of careless jest, it was a heartsick Canadian who sailed for England on April 20. The company of the irascible Brown made the voyage no easier. Macdonald put on his most disarming act and Brown seemed to relax for once over cards and wine, suspending his vow to have nothing but "parliamentary intercourse" with his old enemy and temporary colleague. To all appearances they were friends when they reached England. The appearances were to be brief, but might last just long enough to save confederation, if it was not past saving.

The Canadian delegation—Macdonald, Brown, Galt, and Cartier—found the British government surprisingly complacent about the North American border after its alarm two years earlier. "I frankly own my entire inability," said the economy-minded Gladstone, "to comprehend the feverish impatience of the Deputation, and their repeated declarations that the spring of 1866 is the crisis of their danger."

Britain evidently had no intention of financing any defense plan until confederation had been established. The Canadians must satisfy themselves with Britain's pledge to use all its resources in support of Canada in case of war. No real defense plan without confederation and no confederation without a change in the mean little local politics of the Maritimes—it was enough to drive Macdonald to despair.

Instead, he drove out to Epsom for the Derby, naturally picked the winner, won a handsome bet, enjoyed royal refreshments, solid and liquid, and on the five-hour drive back to London amused himself by attacking the holiday crowds with a peashooter and paper bags of flour, even Brown joining for the moment in a sport which would have horrified his Clear Grits in Upper Canada.

What had been accomplished by the London conference? Very little. At least the British government was wholeheartedly behind confederation, if the Canadians could only persuade the Maritimes; it had taken Macdonald's measure as a leader; and it thought the Canadians "all able men with unlimited powers of consuming champagne."

Macdonald reached Canada at midsummer to face still more trouble. Confederation was at a standstill. Old Taché, titular head of the government, was dying. The Governor General asked Macdonald, long the real leader, to accept the formal title. That was too much for Brown to swallow. He would serve temporarily with Macdonald as an equal. He would not accept his rival as a superior.

Finally, to save the coalition and the chance of confederation, Macdonald devised a polite fiction. A minor politician, Sir Narcisse Belleau, became the first minister in name and the ostensibly equal partnership of Macdonald, Brown, and Cartier continued.

These were minor matters beside the daunting look of the Republic. True, the Grand Army was dissolving peacefully. President Johnson was fully occupied with the problems of Reconstruction. But the American Congress was demanding huge damages from Britain for the wartime activities of the cruiser *Alabama*, built for the Confederacy in a British shipyard, and some politicians blandly suggested that Canada might be handed over to satisfy those claims. This could hardly be considered a serious proposal, though Seward had considered it and later sounded out the British ambassador. It indicated, however, the state of the American mind.

Anyway, Galt returned from Washington to report that the Reciprocity Treaty was certainly dead and Canada's vital exports of raw materials must shortly meet a ruinous tariff wall. Something still more sinister was afoot. Macdonald's detective force reported plans for another unofficial American invasion. Once again, as so many times before, Canada was caught in the perpetual feuds of the Old World.

24

Wild Irishmen

[1858–1866]

THE FENIAN BROTHERHOOD HAD BEEN FORMED IN 1858, WITH strong support from Irish Americans, to liberate Ireland from British rule. Its first attempt landed a shipload of invaders from the United States in an English jail.

After this burlesque, a rebel American wing of the movement, led by W. R. Roberts and R. W. Sweeney, proposed to invade Canada and make it the base of later attacks on Ireland. A convention in Chicago in 1863 solemnly wrote the constitution of a Canadian republic, appointed a cabinet to govern it, and organized secret regiments, largely recruited from unemployed veterans of the Civil War. Substantial campaign funds were raised by subscriptions all over the United States and by the sale of Irish Republic bonds.

"General" Sweeney, as secretary of war, strutting at his New York headquarters in gorgeous uniform of green and gold, drafted a detailed invasion plan to be carried out by 30,000 men at a cost of $15,000,000. In two weeks, according to Sweeney's neat timetable, the invaders would hold the western St. Lawrence and secure Lakes Ontario, Erie, and Huron with Republican navies. Then they would strike eastward at Montreal while a fleet from San Francisco "will carry Vancouver Island and the Fraser River country." When Canada fell, it would be officially recognized by the United States as the independent nation of New Ireland.

All this, Sweeney assured his followers and campaign fund contributors, would be easy: "The population of the British provinces is little above two and a half millions and the military resources of the united provinces fall far short of sixty thousand men. Of these nearly ten thousand are of Irish birth or descent. By the tempting offer of a surrender of Canada to the United States, Mr. Seward,

351

it is hoped, will wink at connivance between American citizens and the Fenian Conquerors." The Canadian conquest complete, the Fenians would take Ireland at leisure.

And so, totally misjudging both Seward and Canada, the little band of Irish patriots and American adventurers drilled without interference in the towns of the United States to the rousing strains of their war song:

> We are a Fenian Brotherhood, skilled in the arts of war,
> And we're going to fight for Ireland, the land that we adore.
> Many battles have we won, along with the boys in blue,
> And we'll go and capture Canada for we've nothing else to do.

The American government turned a tolerant eye on these strange pursuits. As an Irishman, Mr. Dooley, would later remark of the Supreme Court, the White House and Congress were watching the election returns and the Irish vote. Britain's international manners in the Civil War had proved intolerable to the Republic. Now the Republic applied the same sort of free-and-easy code to Britain's Canadian colonies.

Macdonald, as minister of militia in his spare time, learned all the Fenians' plans from his private espionage system. In any case, the secret brotherhood could not keep a secret overnight. The invasion apparently was scheduled for the appropriate date of St. Patrick's Day, 1866. By design or disagreement in the high command, this schedule was not carried through. Canadian militia waited vainly along the St. Lawrence on March 17. Nothing happened. Was it all a false alarm?

Macdonald thought not. His agents told him that large numbers of Fenians in plain clothes, and substantial stores of weapons in innocent-looking parcels, were being massed along the border. In April the first blow was struck, not where it was expected but on the Atlantic coast.

A Fenian vessel, ordered to capture the island of Campobello, at the mouth of the St. Croix River, was seized by American officials in Eastport, Maine. The American government was not living up to Sweeney's expectations.

April and May passed without further incident, and most Canadians assumed that the danger had passed also. Macdonald's agents knew better. They reported increasing concentrations of Fenians at St. Albans, Vermont, and at Malone, Ogdensburg, Oswego, Buffalo, and Rochester, New York. As in 1812, the Niagara frontier was regarded as the open door to Canada. Once it had been captured, Sweeney, in personal command at Ogdensburg, would take

Prescott, directly across the river, and the combined forces would begin their march to Montreal.

On the night of May 31 groups of furtive strangers moved out of Buffalo to the Niagara River. The intended breach of the United States' Neutrality Act was obvious but the local authorities did not appear to observe it even when the invaders embarked at Pratt's Iron Furnace Dock on two hired tugs and two canalboats.

The dawn of June 1 revealed some fifteen hundred men on Lower Ferry Dock, a mile below the Canadian village of Fort Erie, where the green Fenian flag, with its gold crown and harp, was unfurled with cheers. General John O'Neill, the well-meaning patriot in charge of this insane adventure, was, according to a Canadian witness, "a gentlemanly man, medium-sized, slightly built, of fair complexion and one whom I should take to be a dry goods clerk rather than the general of a marauding expedition." He was dressed in civilian clothes, with "a small felt hat," and wore no badge or other distinguishing mark, but he was experienced in war. His followers included "old men and some boys of fifteen with muskets and bayonets." Some had come for reasons of Irish patriotism, others on the promise of a good Canadian farm if they succeeded.

By nightfall O'Neill had 2,000 men entrenched in the orchard of a farmer named Newbigging, near Frenchman's Creek. His scouts mistook a few Canadian farmers on horseback for cavalry, fired at them, and retreated. As O'Neill soon discovered, there were no Canadian troops within twenty-five miles.

He, therefore, had time to distribute to Canadians around his camp a ringing proclamation from General Sweeney. This document had a familiar sound to anyone who remembered Hull's invasion of 1812. "We have," it announced, "no issue with the people of these Provinces and wish to have none but the most friendly relations." The Fenians' weapons were aimed only at the British "oppressors of Ireland," and to destroy them "We have registered our oaths upon the altar of our country in the full view of Heaven and sent up our vows to the throne of Him who inspired them." Canada was offered "the olive branch of peace and the honest grasp of friendship," but if they were refused the Canadians could expect "the restraints and relations imposed by civilized warfare."

The Canadian country folk seemed strangely unimpressed. The ten thousand Fenian reinforcements expected from Buffalo failed to appear, having prudently decided to await the news of victory from O'Neill. That unfortunate general, isolated in a strange country very different from Sweeney's blueprints, was compelled to burn hundreds of surplus rifles and large stocks of ammunition because his army could not carry them.

Learning that a Canadian force about the size of his own had marched from Port Colborne, he decided to meet it on a well-chosen position known as Limestone Ridge. The Canadians advanced in ignorance of the Fenians' movements and with the assurance of reinforcements from Chippawa, which were late in arriving, as a result of their commanders' mismanagement.

Everything, indeed, was mismanaged in Canada. The church bells rang in all the river towns. The volunteers poured in, more than the militia could accommodate in their force of 20,000. The troops marched off, under a scorching sun, in stifling padded uniforms intended for winter use. Most of them had no food or even water bottles. They were fed by farmers' wives, drank at roadside creeks, but with parched mouths sang their brave marching song:

> Tramp, tramp, tramp, our boys are marching,
> Cheer up, let the Fenians come!
> For beneath the Union Jack we'll drive the rabble back
> And we'll fight for our beloved Canadian home.

There was no lack of patriotism. There was lack of all other essentials, especially leadership. The Port Colborne troops, still expecting reinforcements, staggered without warning into the ambush of Limestone Ridge.

O'Neill's Fenians met them with a withering musket fire. A few men fell wounded at the first volley. Some nameless farm woman and her little girl brought them water until the child cried: "The pail is leaking!" It was leaking through bullet holes.

The attackers pushed up the hill so resolutely that O'Neill took them for British regulars and prepared to retreat. At that moment some lost Fenians rode out of the woods on stolen horses, whereupon the terrifying cry of "Cavalry!" swept through the Canadian lines. The raw militia were hastily formed into a red square to meet a cavalry charge, thus providing a perfect target for the enemy snipers. But the square held until one company was ordered to retire from an advanced position on the flank. The sitting ducks in the square supposed that a general retreat was under way. They broke and ran. O'Neill pursued them down a choked lane as far as Ridgeway and saw them board a train for Port Colborne.

Such was the strange little battle of Limestone Ridge. Was it the beginning or the end of the invasion? O'Neill did not know. He had won a Pyrrhic victory, killed nine Canadians, and wounded thirty-seven, but what next? In a few hours, he guessed, the whole country would be aroused and his army overwhelmed unless he secured aid from Buffalo. He ordered a retreat to Fort Erie and the escape route of the river.

There he found the town occupied by seventy-six confused Canadians who had been brought by steamer from Port Colborne to await the main army. The Fenians charged down the street with bayonets, drove the Canadians behind a pile of cordwood on the riverbank, and captured most of them in the sight of hundreds of cheering spectators on the American shore. The spectators cheered and that was all. No reinforcements crossed the river.

Too late, O'Neill, like so many former invaders, saw that everything had gone wrong. A large Canadian force was advancing at last from Chippawa. The Fenians at Fort Erie were tired, hungry, and despondent. As night came, but no reinforcements, they began to slip across the river in any boats they could find. Some paddled on planks or swam. A few drowned. Retreat turned into panic. O'Neill shaved off his whiskers to disguise himself and prepared for flight. The two hired tugs and two canalboats arrived from the American side to remove the rest of the marooned army and were promptly taken in tow by the U.S. warship *Michigan*.

After some delay the American government was enforcing its Neutrality Act with energy. Its troops guarded the river. Some eight thousand Fenians massed in Buffalo could not leave the city, were soon living on public charity, and finally were conveyed to their homes at government expense.

O'Neill and the other invaders captured by the *Michigan* were released on bail of $500 each but never brought to trial. Canadians might be indignant at this clemency after what appeared to be not a military action but an organized murder. The British government was glad to see the prisoners escape. It had trouble enough with the United States already.

Two days of incompetence on both sides cleared Canada of Fenians by June 3, General George Meade was in full control of the American boundary, and M. W. Burns, "Brig. General commanding Irish Army at Buffalo," issued a farewell address admitting that "I had hoped to lead you against the common enemy of human freedom, viz. England, and could have done so had not the extreme vigilance of the United States Government frustrated our plans. . . . Be firm in your determination to renew the contest when duty calls you forth."

The failure at Niagara had prevented any attack from Ogdensburg and the other towns of the St. Lawrence. Farther east a final bootless outrage was committed. Some eighteen hundred Fenians from St. Albans crossed the Canadian boundary on June 4 and made their headquarters at Pigeon Hill, where their energetic looting was watched, from a discreet distance, by a hundred frightened Canadian volunteers.

This raid, like all the others, was hopeless. The United States Army had seized the Fenian stores in Vermont. No reinforcements could reach the army of Pigeon Hill. Its officers weeping from mortification, the invaders tramped back across the line. Sixteen of them were captured by a party of Canadians and a few shot. The remainder were arrested by the American authorities.

So ended not the last but certainly the most absurd American attack on Canada. It had tested Canadian defenses and proved them, as Macdonald had feared, sadly inadequate in case of actual war. It had also tested the temper of the American government, which was correct and diligent after some early fumbles and so disappointing to the Fenians that their General Michael Heffernan complained bitterly to Meade: "We have been lured by the Cabinet and used for the purpose of Mr. Seward. . . . They encouraged us on to this." Governor General Monck, with sarcasm rare in diplomacy, thanked Seward for faithfully enforcing the neutrality law "after the invasion of Canada had actually taken place."

Heffernan promised to resume the liberation of Canada at the first chance. William H. Roberts, president of the Fenian Brotherhood, arrested for conspiracy to break the Neutrality Act, issued yet another proclamation from his cell: "Stand by the cause. . . . The struggle must not be abandoned even though our soldiers should be compelled through the over-zeal of the United States to abandon the present campaign. There is no turning back for us, my countrymen."

Many other Fenian leaders found themselves in American jails. Some sympathetic politicians pleaded their cause in Congress and Congressman Ancona, of Pennsylvania, proposed the repeal of the Neutrality Act as a gesture against Britain for its behavior in the Civil War. President Johnson's government was unmoved by this clamor but intimated to Britain that the forty Fenians imprisoned in Canada should be treated with leniency.

Canadian law took its course. Twenty-two prisoners were sentenced to death. When justice and public passion had been sufficiently satisfied, all the condemned men were released after short terms of imprisonment. In the pinch the United States and Canada had shown that, for all their public gestures, they could act with moderation.

25

The Road to Ottawa

[1866–1872]

HAD ALL THE RECENT AMERICAN THREATS BEEN HOLLOW? HAD Canada's alarms throughout the Civil War been groundless? Was the border permanently safe?

Macdonald still doubted it. True, the Fenians had proved unwittingly the need of Canadian defense and thus the need of confederation. They had transferred the problem of union from the abstractions of the Quebec conference to the concrete evidence of Limestone Ridge. They had arrived just in time to decide a vital election in New Brunswick. But Macdonald was thinking longer thoughts.

He was calculating the chance of holding the West against forces much more formidable than a few disgruntled Irishmen. Assuredly the West would not be held without confederation, a railway to the Pacific, and a Canadian population beside it. The vacuum would be filled from one side of the boundary or the other. Confederation, despite the Quebec Resolutions, remained itself a vacuum. Then the climate suddenly changed.

While Tupper was still marking time in Nova Scotia and watching the anticonfederationists of New Brunswick, they found, on defeating Tilley and taking office, that they had no alternative policy of their own. By opposing the link with the St. Lawrence colony they hoped to link New Brunswick with the economy of the Northeastern states by a railway known as Western Extension. The New Brunswick government could not finance this project, could not find any private capitalist to finance it, and realized now that it was useless anyway.

The impending collapse of reciprocity and the resulting loss of potential railway traffic across the border destroyed the economic base of the anticonfederation policy so far as the business of New Brunswick was concerned. When a delegation from the Canadian colonies went to Washington, in a last desperate effort to save reciprocity, a Congressional committe offered, in return for the in-shore fisheries of the Maritimes, to exempt from American customs duties rags, firewood, unfinished millstones, grindstones, and unground gypsum or plaster. This offer was either a joke or an insult. The Canadians went home, even the New Brunswickers convinced that the American market would be hermeticaly sealed if tariffs could seal it. So it was, with the end of reciprocity in March, 1866.

Under these reverses, conveniently delivered by the United States, the anticonfederation government of New Brunswick began to fall to pieces. It lost a decisive by-election, the opposition candidate being financed by Macdonald and his friends, the government candidate, so it was alleged, by American railway interests. One of the joint cabinet leaders, R. D. Wilmot, announced his conversion to Canadian union. The government resigned in the course of a confused ministerial crisis and was replaced by Tilley's confedera-tionists, but Tilley was on shaky ground. He faced a doubtful elec-torate, a dangerous election, and an empty campaign fund coffer.

Macdonald's friends scraped up some $50,000 and carried it secretly to Tilley's treasurer in the safe neutral ground of Port-land, Maine. Even the scrupulous Brown contributed $500 per-sonally to the cause and promised more, if needed. The great silent partner of confederation, however—far more potent than campaign funds—was the United States, which had yet to realize what con-federation was about.

Everything now depended on the disordered politics of the queer little capital in Fredericton, and Macdonald's time was running out. Brown had resigned from the Canadian government, in which he had never been happy, still supported its basic policy but in-sisted that Macdonald make good his original promise to achieve confederation or to form a federal state of Upper and Lower Can-ada, on the principle of representation by population. If confedera-tion was not achieved meanwhile, Macdonald would have to abandon it and accept the second-best when his Parliament met in the summer of 1866.

Thus from his new house in the half-built town of Ottawa he waited with a cheerful front and inward agony the news from Fredericton, from Halifax, and from his agents among the Amer-ican Fenians.

The darkness of that dreadful spring was broken first by the unexpected approval of confederation, despite Howe's philippics, in the Nova Scotia Assembly. Little Dr. Tupper apparently had cured his fitful patient. Then the mobilization of the Fenians, almost as if it had been timed for this purpose, alarmed the people of New Brunswick, turned them against the pro-American policy of the anticonfederationists, and greatly strengthened Tilley in his election. Again an American pressure was driving the Canadian colonies together, this time for good.

That was the old story, beginning in 1775, and often repeated. Now on a small scale—judiciously exploited by Tilley and his friends—the foreign danger had recurred at the moment when confederation hung in the balance.

Well, after this year of perpetual disappointment, Macdonald could do with some luck. Perhaps, on hearing of Tilley's overwhelming victory at the polls, a week after the Fenian raid, Macdonald's private gratitude included the raiders. Certainly they had served Canada well.

The colonies, except Newfoundland and Prince Edward Island, had voted for union, but the timetable remained tight and tricky. Union must be approved by legislation in London before Tupper had to meet again an electorate which might repudiate him next spring under the influence of the furious Howe. The Whig government of Britain, long Macdonald's backer in the confederation scheme, had fallen. Would its Tory successor maintain its policy? And, as Parliament in London would soon adjourn, what chance was there of enacting the confederation statute before Tupper's deadline?

Tupper and Tilley, too impatient to wait longer, set off immediately for London and demanded that Macdonald follow them. He hung on grimly at Ottawa, for he was certain that Britain would not act before the new year and was now disturbed by rumors of a second Fenian invasion. He did not take them very seriously though they spread alarm along the St. Lawrence and caused the new British government to assemble transports and mobilize troops for the defense of Canada. It was no time for Macdonald to be out of the country.

The Maritime delegates chafed vainly in London. Howe was busy there also with speeches, pamphlets, and finally slanders against confederation and its chief architect.

Brown, all his old hatred and envy spilling over, had begun a personal attack on Macdonald's character in the vicious editorial columns of the Toronto *Globe*. Macdonald, said the *Globe,* was a drunkard, he had been drunk when he should have been repelling the Fenian raid, he had been drunk in the Assembly, his "utterance so thick as to be almost incomprehensible," he had been so reeling drunk that he had clung to his desk for support, and his drunkenness made him incapable of performing his duties at a time of national danger.

To Howe the latest copies of the *Globe* were precious ammunition for his fight to kill confederation in the British Parliament by killing Macdonald's reputation. It was Howe's solemn duty to convey privately to the Colonial Secretary the truth about the Canadian leader, the "impropriety and peril" of placing the defense of the Maritimes in the hands of a man "whose habits and gross neglect of important public duties have thus been rendered notorious by the Canadian and English Press."

Driving this shameful dagger home, Howe noted that Macdonald was said to have written most of the Quebec Resolutions and he added: "Assuming the statement to be accurate, the undersigned, while charitably attributing to the inveterate habits referred to the incoherent and defective character of the whole [confederation] scheme, would respectfully submit to Her Majesty's Government whether the knowledge of its paternity is likely to make it more acceptable to the people of the Maritime Provinces, whose institutions it is proposed to disturb." That blow was low, even for Howe in the worst days of his megalomania. Only a man like Macdonald could ever forgive it.

On November 14, satisfied that winter would prevent any new Fenian movement before spring, Macdonald sailed for London. Five delegates from Nova Scotia, five from New Brunswick, and six from Canada assembled in the Westminster Palace Hotel under Macdonald's chairmanship and, with the aid of British government draughtsmen, begun to whip the Quebec Resolutions into the British North America Act, the constitution of a Canadian state.

The work was briefly interrupted. Macdonald fell asleep one night leaving a newspaper against the flame of his candle and set the New Westminster Palace Hotel on fire. He was badly burned in the shoulder but, aided by Galt and Cartier in their nightshirts, extinguished the flames with jugs of water. The burns gave him "a merry Xmas in my own room with my dinner of tea and toast."

He was soon around again, the constitution was approved, and he decided to complete his labors by a second marriage in his fifty-third year. After nine years of widowerhood he had recently met on Bond Street a handsome, middle-aged lady and an old family friend, Susan Agnes Bernard, of Ottawa. His mind was instantly made up. He proposed marriage a few weeks later and it was solemnized before eminent witnesses in St. George's Church, Hanover Square. A honeymoon of two days at Oxford began a happy and lifelong partnership.

The bridegroom still had to await, amid the convulsions of a British political crisis, the passage of the British North America Act.

There remained as well the choice of a name for the new state. Macdonald, having envisaged "a great Kingdom in connection with the British monarchy and under the British flag," proposed to call the state the "Kingdom of Canada" and it was so written into the constitution. The Earl of Derby, leader of the government (who, according to Disraeli, lived "in a region of perpetual funk"), was terrified lest the touchy American Republic object to even the title of an outright monarchy on its border.

Possibly he had some ground for his alarm. The British ambassador in Washington reported that the proposed "Kingdom of Canada" had produced "much remark of an unfriendly nature in the United States." A conscientious republican, Representative H. J. Raymond, of New York, introduced a resolution in the Congress asking the President whether he had protested against the "consolidation of all the British North American Provinces into a single confederation under the imperial rule of an English prince."

The Congress paid little attention to Raymond's inquiry but still, in Derby's mind, there was no point in taking chances. So the Westminster Palace Hotel conference devised as a compromise the title "Dominion of Canada," little suspecting that the word "dominion" would be deplored and abandoned some eighty years hence by a Canadian prime minister as a semantic vestige of colonialism.

The Dominion of Canada it was to be and when Lord Carnarvon, the young Colonial Secretary, brought the British North America Act into Parliament he permitted himself a pretty optimistic forecast of the Dominion's future: "We are laying the foundations of a great State—perhaps one which at a future day may even overshadow this country. But come what may, we shall rejoice that we have shown neither indifference to their wishes nor jealousy of their aspirations, but that we honestly and sincerely, to the utmost of our power and knowledge, fostered the growth, recognizing in it the conditions of our own greatness."

The foundations of a new state, yes. Perhaps a great state of the future. But something much larger—the foundations of a commonwealth of independent states containing many races, colors, creeds, and diverse interests. There could be no turning back now from the first steps taken in Canada. The unprecedented, amorphous, almost unbelievable structure of politics thus begun, and soon to cover white men and black over a large part of the earth's surface, had been invented—or blindly conceived—and pushed toward its illogical yet curiously logical end by a handful of groping Canadians along the St. Lawrence, always with the decisive help of their American neighbors.

Carleton's work at Quebec in the winter of 1775 was almost completed at London in the spring of 1867, but not quite. The Dominion of Canada was still under the dominion of an English queen. Her government would manage its foreign affairs, often very badly. London even had power to disallow Ottawa's statutes. Anyone could see, however, that within measurable time those last vestiges of the old colonial system would become mere antiquities and historical relics, would quietly atrophy and finally disappear.

The forms of Canada's inferior status must remain for the present. Macdonald knelt to kiss the plump hand of Queen Victoria, to thank her for the British North America Act, and to assure her: "We have desired in this measure to declare in the most solemn and emphatic manner our resolve to be under the sovereignty of Your Majesty and your family forever." Canadians' permanent feelings toward the royal family, as a symbol, were thus accurately expressed. Macdonald knew, however, none better, that the sovereignty of Canada would rest, sooner or later, with Canada alone.

What were the prospects of the Confederation which, so far, stretched barely across half a continent? Macdonald thus judged them in his own earthy style: "By the exercise of common sense and a limited amount of that patriotism which goes by the name of self interest, I have no doubt that the Union will be for the common weal."

Most people in the united colonies seemed to agree with him now that the great decision had been made. Much intricate and some sordid work of politics had yet to be done behind the scenes before a national government could begin to function. Macdonald inevitably had been chosen to head it as the first Prime Minister of Canada. It was easy to accept the appointment from the Queen, no one expected any other choice, but to organize a durable ministry before any elections had been held suddenly appeared an almost impossible task.

Macdonald proposed to continue the Conservative-Liberal coalition, maker of the union. Brown at once vetoed this project. He returned to politics, all his old fury ablaze again, and in a shattering speech to the electors of the new province of Ontario announced that he would not permit the "degradation" of the Liberal Party by any further association with the Conservatives. "Go into the same Government with Mr. John A. Macdonald?" he cried. (Cries of

"Never! Never!" from the faithful.) "It was the happiest day of my life when I got out of that concern."

Brown's veto failed. Other Liberals, enough for Macdonald's purpose, remained in the concern.

Its manager was rapidly learning how difficult it would always be to manage. Not only every province but the two main races, the two main religions, and the various economic pressure groups must somehow be satisfied by representation in the Cabinet. Geographical claims must often supersede the claims of real ability. Great men like Tupper and McGee must generously step aside to admit inferiors who came from the right place or professed the right religion. Sometimes despairing of agreement, almost ready at one point to retire altogether, Macdonald knocked together a Cabinet at last, not a moment too soon. Cartier was in it, of course, and Galt and Tilley and nine others, whose names would not be long remembered.

These disagreeable chores of political housekeeping had barely been finished on July 1, 1867, when the Queen's Proclamation, the flags, bands, cannons, parades, speeches, bonfires, fireworks, laughter and tears, in every village from Halifax to the rim of the Pre-Cambrian rock, announced the birthday of North America's second nation.

In Ottawa the birthday party did not go well among the Fathers of Confederation. The crowds cheered, the soldiers marched, but in the new Privy Council Chamber Governor General Monck (he had not bothered even to change his traveling clothes after arriving by boat from Montreal) faced a scene of ghastly embarrassment. His announcement that the Queen had been graciously pleased to make Macdonald a Knight Commander of the Bath was expected and well received by everybody. The second announcement of only a Companionship of the same order for Cartier, Galt, Tilley, Tupper, and a few others was greeted with a painful silence.

Cartier and Galt, regarding themselves as Macdonald's equals in the work of confederation, indignantly refused this second-class honor. Cartier considered the French race insulted. The moody Galt wanted no royal honors. If he had to take them they must be as high as any other Canadian's.

Monck, a well-meaning but gauche man, whose advice involved the Queen in this unpleasant little quarrel, had failed to consult Macdonald in advance. The harm had been done and the old physician must patch it up somehow. In the end he got a baronetcy for Cartier and a knighthood for Galt, the latter accepting it only after he had bluntly warned the Queen that "I regard the Confederation of the British North American Provinces as a measure which must ultimately lead to their separation from Great Britain."

No thought of separation marred the night of July 1 as the gaping crowds of Ottawa saw the new Parliament Buildings illuminated for the first time. No such thoughts had ever entered Macdonald's mind either, but he still had his troubles with the teething pains of the infant state.

There was a general election, to begin with, and in one alarming respect it turned out badly. Ontario, Quebec, and New Brunswick sustained the Macdonald government and confederation by large majorities. Nova Scotia, under Howe's persistent campaign of sabotage, voted decisively the other way and elected no confederationist but Tupper.

This looked decidedly like the beginning of a secession movement. It quickly came into the open. Howe appeared again at London, as the newly elected tribune of his people, and demanded Nova Scotia's exemption from the "Botheration Scheme." The dauntless Tupper followed him to argue the nation's case.

Tupper did not need to argue with the British government, for it would not hear of secession. It was essential to convert Howe lest Nova Scotia, pushing his course to its inevitable end, should finally clamor for annexation to the United States and find willing collaborators there. Somehow these sparks must be extinguished before they ignited the Maritimes.

Tupper tracked the old bear to his lair in a London hotel room and the lifelong enemies met face to face. "I can't say I'm glad to see you," Howe growled, "but we must make the best of it."

Tupper made the best of it. He said he would not insult Howe by asking him to abandon his mission but when he failed, as he must, "it is important for you to consider the next step."

Howe blustered and threatened. He had 800 men in every Nova Scotia county sworn never to pay a cent of taxation to the Canadian government and he defied it to enforce confederation. Very well, said Tupper, the national government would withhold its promised subsidies to Nova Scotia, the province would be bankrupt, and its people would curse the man who had brought them to ruin.

That shook even the great egotist. Perhaps he knew already that the game was up. If Nova Scotia could not secede legally, it must either remain in Canada or join the United States, and no man was more devoted than Howe to the British connection. In the long and wrenching struggle which had torn his soul between vanity and patriotism the larger half of Howe emerged to subdue the lesser. He saw that Tupper's argument was unanswerable, and he saw in the bulldog face of the man he had once called "the little doctor" a force as great as his own.

Tupper finally offered him, in Macdonald's name, a place in the Canadian Cabinet. The old man was "completely staggered."

Well he might be. He had reviled Macdonald from Halifax to London. He had denounced him as a drunkard to the British government. He had exhausted all his adjectives, eloquence, and venom upon the man who now tendered him forgiveness and honor. It was a hard choice. To join the government was to swallow his whole past, quarrel with all his friends, and admit that Joe Howe could be wrong.

Nonetheless, Howe made that choice after he came home and found Nova Scotia talking openly of secession and annexation, the cockatrice hatched by him. Confronted by Macdonald in all his roguish charm, Howe joined the national government.

It was a greater victory than his friends or enemies suspected. Howe had conquered himself. Tired, sick, discredited, cut on the street by his friends, jeered at and hissed by a people who had worshiped him, the broken figure staggered from platform to platform, noble in its ruin, still magical in its power. Howe and Tupper carried their province, all but one constituency, for the Conservative Party and confederation in 1872. When Howe died as lieutenant governor of Nova Scotia, his people had forgiven their greatest son and accepted the nation of Canada.

A nation, yes, in form, in constitution, in natural wealth, in sprawling geography, but not in fact. It could not be in fact until it had leaped the Pre-Cambrian shield, settled the prairies, tunneled through the Rockies, and grasped the Pacific coast.

26

The Five-Ring Circus

[1869–1870]

O N OCTOBER 11, 1869, A PARTY OF CANADIAN GOVERNMENT SUR-veyors was running a line across the Red River farm of André Nault, a French-Canadian half-breed. Sixteen horse-men suddenly circled the surveyors and reined in their horses. A young man leaped to the ground and placed his moccasin firmly on the survey chain. He said in a quiet voice: "You go no further." The Canadian government's control of the West had been challenged. The surveyors went no further.

Thus emerged upon the crowded continental scene one of its most bizarre and tragic actors. Louis Riel had begun his adventure. It would lead him inevitably to the gibbet. It would also halt the last northern thrust of Manifest Destiny, nail down Canada's control in the West, and drive Macdonald's Liberal-Conservative Party into the wilderness for some half a century.

The agent of these events had barely reached manhood when he launched them. He was a youth of striking looks—brown, curly hair, pale skin, drooping mustache, and disquieting, hypnotic eyes. Mac-donald had never heard of him.

Two years after Canada's national birthday Old Tomorrow's skilled hands were full enough without a rebellion on the prairies. He had long been a tightrope walker in a three-ring circus stretch-ing between Ottawa, Washington, and London. A fourth ring had been added on the coast of British Columbia, where the inhabitants talked candidly of joining the United States. A fifth was now added by Riel beside the Red River.

Finally a side show of mysterious contents was under way in the far north. Seward, having recovered from the wounds of the assassin ring which murdered Lincoln, had purchased Alaska from Russia and now observed, with a fine impartiality, that all North America must soon become the property of the Republic; though he was kind enough to add that Canada had built some useful and thrifty provinces well deserving the chance of statehood in the Union. Like many eminent predecessors, Seward was mistaken. But, between south and north, he had pinched Canada in a giant nutcracker.

Things were moving too fast even for the nimble mind of Macdonald. What was one to think of an American government which demanded some of Canada's most valuable resources without paying for them; of a British government apparently ready to give the Americans all they asked, at Canada's expense?

And what could any sensible man make of the wild and frantic figures now loose on the frontier—a prairie rebel who evidently considered himself a king or perhaps a deity; a legless American who rode the plains on horseback and fomented annexation; a Canadian governor who obviously had lost his mind in the wide-open spaces was forging Queen Victoria's name to official proclamations and reading them by lanternlight, outdoors, to a half dozen shivering witnesses, in the teeth of a western blizzard; a Fenian youth busily organizing a vast army of invasion which, when ordered to march, included exactly thirty-nine men; and, to complete this gallery of freaks, the dominant leader of British Columbia, named Smith, who, tiring of commonplace English, signed himself Amor de Cosmos, the Lover of the World?

Such assorted lunacy, threatening the life of a Canada hardly two years old, was almost too much for Old Tomorrow when he must perform in all the five circus rings simultaneously today. For the moment the master of equilibrium lost his balance in the western ring. As Macdonald faltered, Riel took charge of the prairies and for ten unbelievable months bestrode the continental boundary in his moccasins.

This most deadly and improbable of enemies in Macdonald's life of perpetual alarms was like all the great figures of the boundary, an accident—the accident of a personality part genius, part madman, part statesmen and part mystic, and yet altogether a patriot by his own strange lights. If he was an accident, the forces that produced him had been implicit in the life of the West since the first French Canadian burst out of the Pre-Cambrian badlands into the empty plains. Riel made those forces explicit, organized them, set them in sudden motion, and on the way to his own ruin, preserved the keystone of the continental Canadian arch.

His race called themselves the Métis, or the *Bois-Brulés*, the men with skins of singed wood. They had been bred, since Vérendrye's time, by the union between the *voyageurs* of Quebec, the Scottish settlers, and the Indians. Some thirty thousand of these people lived north and south of a boundary. They completely disregarded this unmarked line while farming their narrow plots along the Red River, hunting buffalo, trapping fur and smuggling it, in defiance of the Hudson's Bay Company, to the Yankee market of "Pig's Eye" Parent's grubby town, St. Paul.

Their chief settlement was Pembina, just south of the boundary, and they had begun to regard it as the capital of a new nation. The Métis were, indeed, almost a nation, more numerous and powerful than many Indian nations of the past—a nation of mixed but distinctive blood, of religious unity under the Catholic Church, of common nomadic ways, a language combining French, English and Indian, and a living racial myth.

That myth of nationhood had begun with the massacre of Seven Oaks. The half-breed Métis had there drawn white man's blood and driven Selkirk's settlers back to Hudson Bay. In the flush of their victory and its barbarous celebration they had learned the lesson long taught by the empires and republics of the world—that no little nation could endure unless it was strong, wary, and ruthless.

The Métis were hopelessly weak against the strength of the British Empire and the American Republic but they were not helpless, for they alone occupied and controlled the most flexible, vulnerable, and strategic area in the final contest for the continent—the central and weakest link of Macdonald's proposed transcontinental state, the half-open gate through which the United States might enter the north and seal Canada off at the Great Lakes.

The Hudson's Bay Company, ruling Rupert's Land for Britain in King Charles's broad fief, from the Lakes to the western sea, had never been able to tame the Métis. They wandered, hunted, trapped, smuggled as they pleased.

On the established smugglers' roads from Fort Garry to Pembina and St. Paul the screeching wooden axles of their Red River carts, heavily loaded with contraband fur, could be heard for miles. It was a hideous, ear-splitting, and important sound. It announced to those who grasped the geopolitics of America that the central Canadian West had become an economic and might well become a political suburb of the United States.

Red River had no connection with Canada except the old appalling route of canoe and portage. It had direct access by oxcart to the neighboring American Territory of Minnesota and, after 1869, to the new transcontinental line of the Union Pacific Railway. The land of the Métis thus offered attractive pickings to the American annexationists. They had failed in the St. Lawrence Valley after a century of effort. They saw their last and best chance in the valley of the Red. This time they would avoid their earlier mistakes. And in Riel they thought they had found a perfect instrument against Canada.

They had misjudged the Métis nation and its prophet but they had good apparent reason to trust Riel. He was bred, as it appeared, for their purposes. His father, a man of strong character, was educated for the priesthood in Quebec, returned to his native land and, across the Red River from Fort Garry, near the Catholic mission of St. Boniface, built a flour mill. There he watched the operations of the Hudson's Bay monopoly and learned to detest it.

In 1849 the company arrested four men for smuggling pelts across the line. Riel the elder led a grim, well-armed crowd of Métis into the courtroom of Fort Garry and threatened to remove the prisoners by force. The prisoners were released. After that the company made no attempt to stop the illegal fur trade and the name of Riel was marked for leadership from Red River to the Rockies.

The miller's son, one-eighth Indian and grandson of the first white woman to spend her life on the Canadian prairies, was sent to Montreal for education as a priest. He impressed his teachers by his piety, his handsome looks and brooding eyes, his loneliness, his long silences and sudden passionate outpourings of speech. Though devout, he was happy to leave the seminary and return to his widowed mother at St. Boniface. He found his people on the verge of explosion.

In dealing with them the Macdonald government had bungled everything. It was purchasing Rupert's Land from the company—$1,500,000 for something like a quarter of a continent. The Gentlemen Adventurers had grown weary of their long epic and judged that Canada's plan to settle the West would "sequester our very Taproot." On December 1, 1869, the new Dominion would hold title to all land between the Atlantic and the vague boundaries of British Columbia, which was expected to enter confederation in a year or two. Macdonald, a master of men, had quite overlooked the men of Red River. They thought of themselves as a distinctive race. Wholly ignorant of the West, Macdonald called them "those miserable half-breeds." That was a dangerous, almost a fatal mistake.

The mistake began when the Canadian government, months before the legal transfer of Rupert's Land, dispatched surveyors to lay out townships along the Red River in preparation for large-scale Canadian settlement. As supervisor of this work it chose almost the worst possible agent, Colonel John Stoughton Dennis. He had made a wretched mess of his command against the Fenian raid at Fort Erie and had been cleared of cowardice, at his own demand, by a very doubtful court-martial.

The government was capable of a worse error. To the vital office of lieutenant governor in charge of Rupert's Land it appointed William McDougall, minister of public works in the Macdonald Cabinet and a man destined to prove the most comic and pitiable figure of the western boundary.

The impetuous McDougall set out for Red River while it was still outside Canadian jurisdiction. He was preceded by Dennis, who immediately began his surveys. The Métis, Dennis reported, were sullen and suspicious. They had been given no voice in the London negotiations transferring Rupert's Land—their land—from the company to Canada. No attempt was made to explain the deal to them. Nor had they been given any assurance that their land titles were safe. When they saw the surveyors striding with compass and chain across their farms they concluded that the alien authorities of Ottawa intended to destroy their way of life.

The Métis' narrow holdings, running from the river back for two miles, in the fashion inherited from their French-Canadian ancestors of Quebec, had been used mostly for pasturing cattle while the owners hunted and trapped. Now, it appeared, the rich black muck of the Red River valley was to be redivided, by the American system of rectangular townships, among new immigrants. Like their Indian ancestors, the natives would be pushed aside by the march of the white men. But they were not Indians. They were not squatters or mendicants. In their own eyes they were a nation with a history of a hundred years on this land and must be treated as such by the nation of Canada.

The one man who could express the fierce, confused, and hopeless instincts of these people was Riel. Only twenty-four years old, he already seemed to possess the maturity of age. He was well educated. He spoke French, English, Indian dialects, and the Métis patois derived from them. His orations were attuned to the ears of his folk. He could write constitutional documents of impressive sound. His private talk, as he paced nervously back and forth, had a ring of action. The brooding eyes held a mystery. The saturnine presence summoned up the old memories of the *voyageurs'* canoes, the Indians' campfires, the buffalo hunts, the far horizons of Métis life.

Such a man might do much and go far. Rupert's Land was without any legal government. The company had surrendered its power. Canada, under the casual arrangements of London and Ottawa, had

yet to receive any authority west of Ontario. During the inter-
regnum—complicated by the old quarrel between the Métis and the
English-speaking settlers, between Catholic and Protestant, between
company and smuggler, and now irritated by the Métis' fear of
Canada—even Dennis saw the need of conciliating the Red River
people. His reports were disregarded. So were the pleas of Bishop
Taché from St. Boniface. The Canadian government made no effort
to reassure the Métis or explain its policies, though Joe Howe had
visited Fort Garry and, with experienced nose, smelled trouble.

Driving homeward through the United States, Howe met Mc-
Dougall and warned him that until the transfer of the West to
Canadian control, timed for December 1, 1869, the new governor
lacked any legal power. Mere warnings and footling legal technicalities would not stop McDougall. He moved northward from St. Paul
in October with a train of sixty wagons, carrying his baggage and
300 rifles. All the way he was watched by Métis scouts.

Meanwhile the Métis at Fort Garry had formed a National Committee and chosen Riel as its secretary. Its first decision was communicated to McDougall by letter on the trail. He was ordered not
to enter "the Territory of the Northwest" without the permission of
the committee. That order carried the authority of 500 armed sharpshooters north of the boundary.

McDougall was too dense a man to understand that the committee was not proposing a rebellion but simply did not recognize Canadian authority, for it had yet to be legally proclaimed. The Métis
had not even forbidden McDougall to enter Rupert's Land. They
said only that he must not enter without the consent of the people
who were ready to negotiate with him and with Canada.

McDougall disregarded this message as the pretentious hairsplit-
ting of ignorant half-breed sea lawyers and moved on toward the
boundary.

Captain D. R. Cameron, of the Royal Canadian Artillery, recklessly drove ahead with his wife and two servants. Nine miles south
of Fort Garry he found a barrier across the road, beside it nine
silent Métis. Without a sound or any sign of violence they turned
his horses around and started them southward. When McDougall
appeared next day he was met by an armed Métis guard. It gave
him until nightfall to leave Rupert's Land. He was enraged but he
obeyed. Back in Pembina he and his viceregal entourage settled
down in any log cabins they could find.

The Canadian government had been defied, its representative
humiliated. American newspapers jubilantly announced that the
Métis would set up their own government or join the Union. Enos

Stutsman, of Pembina, a lawyer and journalist, who had been born without legs but on crutches and horseback constantly shuttled across the boundary and had made himself the Métis' trusted adviser, reported that the chances of Manifest Destiny in Red River were ripening fast. James Wickes Taylor, an annexationist, later an American government secret agent but always a man of peace, persuaded the St. Paul Chamber of Commerce to pass a resolution declaring that the new nation of Canada must end at the Great Lakes. All the rest of the continent must belong, by common justice, to the United States.

After reading the memorial from St. Paul, the Senate asked the State Department to ascertain whether the United States could buy the old Hudson's Bay empire. A price of $10,000,000 was suggested as against the Canadian price of $1,500,000, already accepted. This proposal might appear insolent in Ottawa but was milder than General N. P. Banks's bill, introduced in the House of Representatives two years before and suggesting the annexation of Canada entire—a proposal quietly dropped, in the face of strong Canadian protests.

The situation at Red River was now out of Washington's hands, and Ottawa's. On November 2, the day of McDougall's retreat to Pembina, Riel and 120 armed men marched through the open gates of Fort Garry, found the Hudson's Bay factor, William Mactavish, in bed with tuberculosis and seized the capital of Rupert's Land. The Métis nation now had its own capital, 390 new rifles, and thirteen little cannons. Mactavish protested but without enthusiasm. He liked the Métis, he hated the company for selling out its faithful servants, and he regarded McDougall with contempt. Anyway, he was dying.

So far everything had been easy for the young man of twenty-four years. Riel could claim, with some color of legitimacy, dominion over a region larger than many of the world's great nations. His armed men patrolled the muddy streets of the Red River town. He made them take an oath of temperance. He censored all outgoing mail. And to prove that his government was not only legal but democratic, he created a legislative assembly.

The Métis elected twelve delegates and, surprisingly enough, the English-speaking settlers did the same. On November 16 this strange parliament met in the fort with a salute of cannon and drafted a Bill of Rights. This was not the act of rebels but of men who asked only for the right of responsible provincial government within Canada, fair representation in the Canadian Parliament, and the ownership of their own land.

The Métis delegates proposed to negotiate with McDougall. The British objected that McDougall was not legally in office and could not negotiate for Canada. President Riel, strutting in starched white shirt, frock coat, black trousers, and beaded moccasins, found his parliament deadlocked. But there had been no rebellion. The Union Jack flew over Fort Garry.

To the hotter heads of Pembina, St. Paul, and Washington—misinformed by a well-organized espionage net—the puzzled assembly of Fort Garry took on the hopeful look of a Philadelphia Congress. The indefatigable Stutsman wrote President Grant urging "instant and decisive action" of a sort unspecified.

Though misinformed, Washington knew more about events at Red River than did the floundering government of Canada, which heard little, heard it late, and could not understand it. Still, Macdonald's Cabinet could understand at least that it had made a botch of its triumphal entry into the West, that McDougall, its representative, was denned up in a Pembina shack, that Riel's parliament was passing laws apparently obeyed by the Red River people, and that somehow, very late, they must be placated.

Macdonald did not fear any overt act by the American government, only the same sort of unofficial raids that had endangered the boundary in 1838 and again in 1866. They had been easily repelled on the St. Lawrence because the Canadian people were united against them. What would happen in Red River, where there were no Canadian soldiers, where the people might well support the raiders, and where overnight Canada might be faced with a local *fait accompli*, accepted and ratified in Washington?

This seemed a very real possibility. Donald Smith, head of the Hudson's Bay Company in Montreal and one of the shrewdest minds in Canada, told Macdonald that the annexationists of Minnesota were ready to finance such raids and could recruit among the rootless "border banditti," camp followers of the American railway builders, thousands of men quite capable of seizing Fort Garry.

Congressman Ignatius Donnelly had assured his St. Paul constituents in a public speech that, within a few months, they would see the Stars and Stripes waving over the whole territory from Red River to the Pacific. American newspapers heralded the natural unification of the continent, already ordained (as the St. Paul press announced) by God. The Senate asked the State Department for a report on McDougall's purposes at Pembina, remarking with virtuous horror that he apparently planned to take over Red River against the wishes of its inhabitants.

These were mere gestures and not frightening to Macdonald. He had been through the process before. More serious was the proposal of Senator Alexander Ramsey, of Minnesota, for a northern railway to the border at Pembina—a lure which the Métis could hardly resist. At last grasping all the possibilities that he should have grasped before, Old Tomorrow was thoroughly roused. The Americans, he wrote, would do anything "short of war" to secure the West, "and we must take immediate and vigorous steps to counteract them." The vigorous steps were the appointment of a delegation to pacify the Métis and the postponement, if necessary, of the Rupert's Land transfer.

Even Macdonald, for all his skepticism of human nature, had yet to realize the unplumbed depths of McDougall's stupidity. After fuming for some days in his squalid hut, that furious empire builder had conceived his own insane *coup d'état*. He took pen in hand and sat down to compose a lengthy proclamation in which Queen Victoria announced that, reposing complete confidence in her well-loved servant, she herewith authorized McDougall to annex Rupert's Land. The author forged the signature of his sovereign.

Copies of the proclamation were smuggled to Fort Garry and pasted by McDougall's agents on the walls of the fort. Riel denounced them as a fraud. Erratic as he was himself, Riel could not conceive McDougall's next move.

On the night of December 1, the date fixed by McDougall in the Queen's name for his assumption of power, few men in the West ventured outside their doors. The thermometer stood at 20° below zero and a blizzard rumbled down from Hudson Bay. The people of Pembina, crouched around their fires, did not see McDougall and six companions harness a team of horses and drive into the darkness, followed by two faithful pointer dogs. The self-authorized servant of the Queen advanced, half frozen, into his kingdom, but not far.

At an abandoned Hudson's Bay fort just north of the boundary he hitched his horses to an empty building and there performed the highest act of comedy in the record of the North American struggle. The pocket of his overcoat yielded a little Union Jack, which one of his companions held up, flapping wildly in the wind. He fumbled in his pocket again and produced his forged proclamation, written on parchment. While another man held a guttering lantern overhead, the lieutenant governor of Rupert's Land read aloud the words inserted in the mouth of his queen. None of the six men around McDougall could hear his voice. Its sound was whipped from his lips by the gale. The two dogs, only sensible members of the expedition, cowered in the lee of a wall. No, there was one man of judgment present. He took shelter behind a building and drank a quart of whisky.

Having performed his duty and shouted his sovereignty into the blizzard, McDougall crawled into his carriage and drove back to his log cabin in Pembina. The American telegraph lines carried that fascinating news next day to Washington and Ottawa. McDougall's comedy became the jest of the English-speaking world. The Métis at Fort Garry composed a merry song to celebrate the retreat of the bogus governor. And a horrified Macdonald fired him.

It was not all comedy, however. McDougall had commissioned Dennis as his "Lieutenant and Conservator of Peace," with orders to put down an imaginary rebellion. Dennis thereupon seized the idle stone fort of Lower Fort Garry, twenty miles down the river from Riel's capital, and, unable to recruit white men, began to assemble a band of Indians. The annexationist press of St. Paul, instantly arousing the Americans' oldest border memories, accused Dennis of fomenting a new Indian war.

Actually he was powerless in his stone fort, and Riel knew it. But Dennis, his handful of Indians, a little band of loyal Canadians arming themselves at Portage la Prairie, west of Fort Garry, and the extreme Canadian party in Fort Garry itself might provoke Riel to desperate action. He could subdue his own local rebels. He was powerless to defy for long the power of Canada—if it could be transported to the prairies—but he could invite the Americans to come and rescue him when he was pressed too far.

Such was exactly the course that the American agitators at Fort Garry were urging. They offered Riel both blandishments and bribes. They promised liberty and justice for his people under the American Constitution. What was he waiting for?

Riel, under his outward bluster, his postures and orations, had become a very confused young man. He could not foresee his next step but he remained sure about one thing—he was a subject of the Queen. On him, the odd fulcrum of the continental balance, the Americans had counted without knowing their man. They had made the same mistake many times before.

However he might regard the large international affairs temporarily in his hands, Riel had made his word law in Rupert's Land.

On December 7, Dr. John Christian Schultz, the burly and vociferous leader of the Canadian party at Fort Garry, barricaded himself with forty-five companions in his house and defied Riel to arrest him. A force of 300 Métis, armed with rifles and two cannons,

promptly surrounded the insurgents. Riel read McDougall's proclamation and stamped it scornfully into the snow. He gave Schultz
fifteen minutes to surrender. Schultz surrendered. The forty-six
prisoners were marched to the fort.

Dennis, Conservator of Peace, urged the "Loyal Party" to "cease
further action," slipped out of his stronghold in the Lower Fort,
and fled to Pembina.

As master of Red River, Riel posted a proclamation announcing
that the Métis had been abandoned by their lawful government,
were "exempt from allegiance" to it, refused to recognize the authority of the "despotic" government of Canada, and would repel "all
invasions from whatsoever quarters they may come." Probably by
the inspiration of his American friends, Riel's Declaration of Independence pledged "Our lives, our fortunes and our sacred honor."
Nevertheless, he was ready to negotiate with Canada for "the good
government and prosperity of this people." It was not to be that
easy.

True, the Canadian government had been forced to negotiate.
The American annexationists apparently were poised ready to
answer Riel's beckoning finger. Senator Ramsey was asking Grant
for $25,000, which the Métis would use to continue their defiance
of Canada. Grant refused and Riel's finger did not beckon. When
he printed his own newspaper, the *New Nation*, and its editor proposed union with the United States, Riel dismissed him. Everything
at Fort Garry appeared in good order.

Now the Canadian government tacitly admitted Riel's authority
by sending as ambassadors to him the grizzled Donald Smith,
Lieutenant Colonel de Salaberry, and Vicar-General Thibault, a
Roman Catholic cleric of Montreal. They were to seek an amicable
agreement and their instructions repudiated Canada's former "acts
of folly and indiscretion."

It was a heady moment for Riel as he called a mass meeting of
his people on January 19 in the open field outside the fort and from
the platform beheld a thousand Métis, stamping in the snow and
huddling around bonfires to keep warm in a temperature of 20°
below zero. Beside him sat the wily Smith, a master of small intrigues and big business, who noted Riel's own flag, a fleur-de-lis
on a white field, over the fort.

Riel translating his words into the Métis dialect, Smith appealed
for peace, offered to resign from the Hudson's Bay Company if that
would help, and talked so long that the benumbed listeners finally
adjourned in the icy dusk to reassemble on the morrow.

Another and larger meeting followed and, six days later, a convention of forty elected delegates to consider Smith's offer of union with Canada.

Riel appeared confident before the delegates but he was having trouble with his government. It had split between those who sought admission to Canada and those, led by a young Fenian, William O'Donoghue, who demanded annexation to the United States. Riel proposed that Red River enter confederation as a full-fledged province, not a territory. Voted down, he angrily denounced his opponents as traitors. Smith intervened to propose a compromise. Let the Métis send representatives to Ottawa and negotiate a satisfactory settlement.

Riel at once seized on this official admission that his own government was legal. He asked the convention to give him a vote of confidence and create a permanent legislature. The convention agreed. That night the formal establishment of a cabinet, with Riel as its president, was celebrated by a peal of cannon and the discharge of rockets, long hoarded by the Canadian party for appropriate celebration. The Red River delegates started the long journey to Ottawa.

If Riel could have stopped there, at the peaceful summit of his power, he might have become a Canadian hero. He could not stop. He would never stop until he reached the gallows.

His downfall began with a series of small, deceptive accidents.

The dauntless Schultz, a prisoner in an upper room of the fort, had received a penknife, smuggled to him by his wife. He cut a buffalo hide into strips and wove them into a rope. On a night of blinding blizzard, when the guards hugged their fires indoors, he fastened the rope with a gimlet and crawled through the window. The strands of hide parted and dropped him two stories into the snow. He lay unnoticed for some time, fainting from the agony of a twisted leg, then managed to drag himself four miles down the river to the house of a friend. There he lay secreted while Riel's troopers scoured the countryside, with orders to shoot him on sight. Finally he escaped to the United States by dogteam through the worst of the winter cold and, arrived in Ontario, preached a crusade against the "rebels."

The resulting anger in Canada was serious for Riel and it was only the beginning.

Major C. W. Boulton had assembled at Portage a hundred men of the Canadian party. They began to clamor for the chance to assault Fort Garry and release Riel's prisoners. Boulton knew this to be madness against the Métis sharpshooters but his counsel of caution was impatiently rejected. Since he could not stop them, he led his reckless followers through a blizzard on the trail to the fort. The company included a young man named Thomas Scott. This chattering, volatile Orangeman from Ontario, who had been arrested by the Métis and had later escaped, was to be the martyr of the rebellion and the ruin of Riel.

As it moved slowly eastward with a single cannon, dragged by oxen, the Portage expedition was swelled by recruits along the way to the number of 500. They were ill armed and no match for Riel's 600 riflemen. Their spirits cooled by the march, they decided not to attack the fort on learning that Riel had released all his prisoners as a gesture of peace.

Close to their camp, north of the fort, a half-witted and terrified Métis boy fled from the white men. On his way he shot a Scots settler. Boulton's men captured this youth and chopped him to death. It was a familiar story of casual killing, repeated a thousand times on the plains. Now it was destined to have continental consequences.

Forty-eight of the Portage party started homeward without firing a shot, and foolishly passed within sight of the fort. The Métis, suspecting an attack, rode down on these men and captured them. Thereupon the taut brain of Riel snapped.

Boulton must die for killing the half-wit and committing the first bloodshed of a peaceful revolution. This verdict terrified even the president's friends but they protested in vain. Riel coldly rejected the pleas of the Canadians, the Catholic clergy, and Donald Smith, until he beheld on her knees before him the mother of the Scots settler slain by the Métis boy. At this sight Riel broke down in tears and reprieved Boulton.

One danger had passed only to be succeeded by another.

Scott had been arrested with Boulton and, always talkative, abusive and profane, had been cursing Riel, denouncing his jailers, and promising vengeance. When the president visited the prison one day Scott leaped upon him and was dislodged with difficulty by the guards. This was too much. Riel called a court-martial. Acting himself as prosecutor, he secured a conviction by a narrow vote of four to three.

Scott was led into the courtyard next morning, blindfolded, and ordered to kneel in the snow. The six Métis marksmen facing him were well fortified with liquor against their ordeal. Three of their rifles had been secretly loaded with bullets, three with blank cartridges, so that no man would ever know who fired the killing shots.

A single explosion crackled in the cold dawn. Scott slumped forward, wounded but still alive. A revolver was quickly fired point-blank at his head.

Such was Scott's end and the beginning of Riel's—an obscure killing in a remote prairie fort hundreds of miles from anywhere, the gesture of a frightened dictator, the act of a burlesque government; yet few more decisive shots had ever been fired in Canada. Riel had killed only one man in ten months of power. His four bullets had killed the Métis nation.

Not since the Rebellion of 1837 had Ontario boiled in such a passion. An innocent Canadian, an Orangeman, a Protestant, and a patriot had been murdered by a half-breed Catholic madman in Red River. As the tale traveled along the St. Lawrence to the distant homesteads, Scott became a national martyr, almost a saint. Old Tomorrow's delays had caught up with him.

There was nothing for it, then, but a display of military force, with all the risk of bloodshed, a Métis appeal to the United States, and American intervention. Twelve thousand soldiers were mobilized under Colonel Garnet Wolseley, a British officer of future fame. Since the United States, in its present temper, would not allow Canadian troops to pass through its territory or even through the Sault Ste. Marie locks, Wolseley's expedition struggled overland by the old *voyageurs'* trail and the half-built Dawson Road, westward from the Lake of the Woods—the largest force ever seen in the West, one of the hardest marches in American history.

While ostentatiously exhibiting its force, the Macdonald government prepared to meet the Métis delegates in friendly fashion. Senator Zachariah Chandler demanded that the United States recognize Riel's government and invite it into the Republic. That government continued to function peacefully, ignorant of the Ontario storm. Riel had even lowered his own flag and unfurled the Union Jack in its place, at which his dashing young Fenian lieutenant and treasurer, O'Donoghue, raised a second pole to bear the fleur-de-lis.

So they fluttered together in the icy wind as the Métis delegation—at first arrested by the zealous Ontario police and quickly released on Macdonald's orders—met the Ottawa Cabinet and quickly negotiated an agreement. Red River was to enter confederation under the name of Manitoba. This, the delegates explained, meant "the God that speaks." The Bill of Rights drafted at Fort Garry was substantially accepted. Riel was to govern until a lieutenant governor arrived to establish the new province.

Moreover, Riel's representatives understood definitely from Cartier, acting in Macdonald's absence, that there would be a complete amnesty for everyone concerned in the recent troubles.

These terms, as drafted by Riel and approved in Ottawa, were confirmed by the government and legislature of Fort Garry. The Métis apparently had won their struggle.

Appearances, however, were misleading. The struggle would not end for fifteen years or without a second and this time a bloody rebellion, fatal to the Métis, ruinous to Macdonald's government and party.

Riel waited confidently for the arrival of Wolseley's army. It was coming in peace, and with his approval. Soon his scouts, watching the soldiers wallow in misery through rivers, swamps, and hordes of mosquitoes, brought back disquieting news. Only fifty men in this army were French Canadians. The others talked around their campfires of congenial fighting at Fort Garry, vengeance for the murder of Scott, and the hanging of Riel. What of the promised amnesty? No one seemed to know whether Cartier's word was good or bad.

Riel's hotheads and the American agitators urged him to ambush Wolseley in the jungle and destroy him before he reached the open land of the prairies. Riel refused. He was still a subject of the Queen. Wolseley would be welcomed in peace to Fort Garry.

After forty-seven portages and ninety-six days of marching from dawn to dark, Wolseley's army coasted down the Winnipeg River in its heavy boats, emerged upon Lake Winnipeg, and staggered toward the fort in the clinging gumbo of an August rainstorm. Canadian power had reached the West at last. Nothing would dislodge it now. But Wolseley found no scene of war, no sign of rebellion. He was greeted only by "a half-naked Indian, very drunk," and did not know yet that the Métis government had collapsed in quarrel and terror.

Riel stood out to the last for union with Canada. Many of his followers, doubting Canada's good faith and the assurance of amnesty, were determined to fight. Some of them, led by O'Donoghue, still demanded annexation to the United States. In this schism the government melted and disappeared overnight. As the army lurched up the muddy riverbank, only Riel and O'Donoghue stood watching it, from a window in the empty fort. The brave dream was finished. Another little North American nation had found, as the Indians had in their time, that it could not resist the Manifest Destiny of the white man's empires.

The first soldiers had reached the wall of the fort when Riel and

O'Donoghue slipped out the gate, tied some fence posts together with their belts, and rafted across the Assiniboine. They heard from its southern bank the cannons of their lost capital booming the triumph of Canada.

Fort Garry endured a few days of excitement, a little looting, much drinking, and the informal killing of a few Métis leaders. Then Wolseley's army started eastward again, leaving a hundred men to guard the West.

Riel was safely across the American boundary. He had become, as he told a friend who fed him on the trail, "a homeless wanderer with nothing to eat but two dried fish." The immediate game of this talented megalomaniac was not quite played out and a larger game was to follow. At this time few Canadians, perhaps not even Macdonald, realized that already, for all his arrogance, delusion and postures, he had served his country well. His refusal to surrender to the Americans may well have saved the West for Canada. A few weeks hence Canada would need him again.

There had been far more violence and bloodletting at Fort Garry in the first few days of Wolseley's occupation than in Riel's ten months of government, which had killed only one man. But Adams Archibald, first Canadian lieutenant governor of Manitoba, and a man of sense and humanity, immediately won the respect of the Métis.

Riel was now in St. Joseph's, O'Donoghue in Pembina, thirty miles to the east. Riel was beaten, heartbroken, and quiescent. O'Donoghue, the lean, gangling friend of Irish freedom, still lived in his Fenian fantasies, was cocky, ambitious, and full of great plans. First he intended to seize from Riel the leadership of the American Métis. Later he would arouse the Fenian Brotherhood to its ultimate invasion of Canada.

Riel was not to be easily pushed aside. A Métis convention at St. Norbert supported him and rejected O'Donoghue's resolution urging the United States to annex Rupert's Land. As a compromise, the convention asked President Grant to examine the betrayal of the Métis by the Canadian government. Riel opposed even this gesture. Canada, he said, would treat Manitoba justly. The convention adjourned and, Riel safely out of the way, the O'Donoghue faction quietly changed the agreed formula and petitioned Grant to make sure that the Métis secured a government of their own choice or, failing that, union with the Republic.

O'Donoghue discussed this proposal directly with Grant and found the President disappointingly unimpressed. After his rebuff in Washington O'Donoghue carried his plan of Canadian invasion to the Fenian Brotherhood in New York. Still reeling from its recent disasters, it could offer him only "its prayers." These, combined with a few resolute invaders and a Métis uprising in Red River, would be sufficient for O'Donoghue's purposes.

He was joined now by the dauntless O'Neill, recently released from an American jail. The two undertook a speaking tour in Minnesota, raised a little money, but found few followers ready to accompany them across the border. Riel advised his friends to avoid this hopeless adventure and he assured Bishop Taché that "we detest the Fenians."

Governor Archibald was a worried man. With only a hundred troops at his command, he knew that a Fenian invasion, joined to a Métis uprising, could take his province, at least temporarily. He therefore guaranteed in writing an amnesty for any Métis rebel who helped him to repel the expected raid.

This danger had begun to look formidable. It was said that the Fenian army numbered 2,000 men. A few days later it had grown to 3,500 and was still growing. If these numbers were accurate, Archibald judged his position critical.

He found an unexpected ally in Riel. The exile urged his people in Canada to resist the Fenians. Two hundred armed Métis presented themselves at Fort Garry and offered to fight. Archibald inspected this motley little contingent as if it had been a picked guard of honor. His eyes traveled along the line and fastened on a handsome sallow-faced young man with dark, brooding eyes. He knew Riel at a glance, but neither registered any recognition. The exile's service in arms, though welcome, could not be admitted publicly. What would Ontario say if it heard that a Canadian governor was employing the rebel, the murderer of Scott? Riel was solemnly introduced to Archibald without a name, merely as the man chosen by the Métis to lead them. Riel's tragedy had turned for the moment into a rather solemn farce.

Afterwards Archibald confessed that if the Métis had been hostile, and if the Fenians had mobilized an effective raid, he could easily have lost Manitoba. As it turned out, he had no reason for alarm and no use for Riel's sharpshooters.

The Fenian invasion was launched on October 5. It consisted of O'Donoghue, O'Neill, and thirty-seven followers. The oddest army ever seen in America had hardly walked across the border before it was pursued and surrounded by a single company of United States soldiers. The Fenian designs on Canada ended forever in Pembina's crowded jail.

O'Donoghue soon escaped. The Métis captured and handed him

back to the American authorities. Brave, intelligent, and deluded young man, he settled down as a schoolteacher, to die young.

Riel had some fifteen more years and a final tragedy before him. At present he was a grave political liability to Macdonald. If the French-Canadian rebel were punished, Quebec would be outraged. If he were allowed to remain in Manitoba, Ontario would explode. Either way the cost in votes at the next election would be ruinous to the government.

Always a practical man, Macdonald arranged to pay Riel $1,000 out of a secret fund, provided the exile remained in the United States. For once Riel was practical also. He said quite truthfully that the sum was not enough to support him, his lieutenant, Maxime Lepine, and their abandoned families at Red River. Smith—a campaign fund expert who soon would be operating on a much larger scale—raised £600 from the treasury of the Hudson's Bay Company, to be repaid by the government on a less conspicuous occasion. His offer was accepted. Riel and Lepine retired to obscurity south of the border.

The rebellion of Red River—or so it would be called by the Canadian people—had ended. Not its leader. Riel had acquired the most dangerous asset that such a man could possess. He had become a racial myth.

27

The World's Lover

[1867–1871]

IF MACDONALD HAD FIRST MISJUDGED EVENTS IN THE WEST AND THEN settled them more by good luck than good management, it was not surprising in his circumstances. For Red River provided only one ring in his swarming political circus. The Washington ring appeared much more alarming and presently would compel him to execute the most painful performance of his life, an almost impossible balancing act, followed by a humiliating somersault. Meanwhile the central arch of the transcontinental state had been saved, but its far western pier was not even in Canada's possession and seemed likely to slip by natural gravity into the United States.

Vancouver Island and the Pacific mainland, now joined in the single colony of British Columbia, contained some ten thousand white inhabitants, a thin sedimentary layer of permanent population left by the receding tide of the gold rush.

By every logical calculation their future lay with the thriving American territories beside them. They had no links of trade, geography, or transportation with Canada, which lay on the other side of a continent behind the Rockies, the prairies and the Pre-Cambrian dike; no links of memory, or sentiment either, and little interest in the doubtful experiment called confederation. Moreover, they were now sandwiched, by Seward's purchase, between American Alaska to the north and the Pacific territories and states to the south. British Columbia lay on the continental map as the obvious corridor joining the Pacific possessions of the Republic.

Naturally enough, practical men in the tiny colonial capital of Victoria saw no future for themselves except within the United States, for it surely must soon join the remote limb of Alaska with the body of the Union if it did not secure the whole continent.

Besides, the Americans now possessed a transcontinental railway

384

while there was not even a wagon road from British Columbia to
Canada. A short northern spur from the American line would give
British Columbia access to the great markets of the Eastern cities
and Victoria could become a large entrepot of American business,
a major port on the Pacific. Finally—so the formidable argument
ran among the annexationists of Victoria—the United States, in taking over British Columbia, would also take over the alarming
colonial debt of $1,500,000.

Thus, as Elgin had found in Canada, annexation obsessed many
British Columbians as the solution to every problem. It had become
a crudely organized movement even in the days of the Cariboo
rush. It was now supported not only by Americans who had come
to find gold and had remained as residents but by hardheaded
British settlers whose nostalgia for Britain was outweighed by their
British instinct for profitable business.

They did not lack friends in the United States. American newspapers were generously suggesting that the cession of British Columbia might compensate the Republic for the Alabama Claims. A bill
introduced in the Congress proposed that the Pacific colony be
admitted to the Union as a territory, to become in due time a
prosperous state.

The Victoria annexationists could argue pretty convincingly that
Britain no longer cared whether British Columbia remained in the
Empire or withdrew. Had not the London *Times*—a Homer who
sometimes nodded—recently announced, doubtless with official inspiration, that nothing should be done to prevent annexation?

The annexationist argument seemed airtight and unanswerable
in practical politics. Accordingly, it was presented to the Colonial
Office by a group of British Columbians in 1867, the year of confederation. Since London was unmoved by this suggestion, the annexationists turned directly to the United States with a second petition
asking President Grant to arrange British Columbia's admission to
the Union. The American government, while willing to countenance
unofficial penetration, was unwilling to risk official acts possibly
involving a serious quarrel with Britain.

The down-at-heel colonial government at Victoria made no serious effort to discourage this agitation. Its officials received their pay
from London but it was depressingly small, hardly enough to support
them in genteel poverty, and doubtless would never increase so
long as the miserable colony was isolated by an artificial line from
the booming United States.

Governor Seymour complained to London that his dilapidated
mansion overlooking Fuca's Strait needed furniture and "the walls
have no paper to hide the cracks which the settlement of the older

parts of the building have entailed upon them." London was brutally unsympathetic. It advised Seymour to pay more attention to his depleted sinking funds and less to his sinking residence.

In the listless and sickly person of the Governor, Macdonald realized that confederation was supported by a broken reed. "It is quite clear," the Canadian Prime Minister wrote to the Colonial Office, "that no time should be lost . . . in putting the screws on Vancouver Island, and the first thing to do is to recall Governor Seymour, if his time is not yet out. We shall then have to fight only the Yankee adventurers and the annexation party proper, which there will be no difficulty in doing if we have a good man at the helm."

Macdonald's judgment proved better in British Columbia than in Red River. The annexation movement on the Pacific, as on the Atlantic, was producing the historic Canadian reaction and a powerful new continental figure to lead it. He had been born plain Smith but such a name could not long satisfy a man of his soaring ambition, high abilities, and cosmic dreams. To proclaim his true dimensions before mankind he legally acquired the signature of Amor de Cosmos.

The self-styled Lover of the World had a prophetic look worthy of his title. His face was long, narrow, lengthened by a black spade of whisker, and strikingly handsome. His eyes burned with frenzy, his tongue was never still, his restless pen scribbled ferocious editorials in his queer little newspaper, the *British Colonist*, and he had his teeth into an issue that his readers could understand. It was the oldest issue in North American life, common to Canadians and Americans alike—the issue of Responsible Government.

De Cosmos had conducted a lengthy and bitter feud with the official oligarchy first established by Douglas and inherited by Seymour. In the *British Colonist* and in de Cosmos's perpetual orations on public platforms or at Victoria's street corners, the western counterpart of the eastern Family Compact was charged with despotism, mismanagement, and financial sharp practice.

This was the old fight of York, Quebec, and Halifax all over again, the same fight waged by Sam Adams in Boston, Jefferson in Virginia, and countless North Americans from Jamestown and Plymouth onward. De Cosmos and his ardent little coterie had replaced, upon a small but strategically vital stage, such actors as William Lyon Mackenzie, Papineau, Baldwin, and Riel.

The Lover of the World, though violent in speech, was a man of peace. He counted on the intelligence of the people at the ballot box. And, against all apparent logic, he viewed British Columbia as the final and decisive ingredient of the Canadian state.

Such was Macdonald's erratic, theatrical, but brilliant ally in the struggle to complete confederation. The older master of Canadian politics heard with approval that de Cosmos, scorned by the Governor, had organized the Confederation League and was stumping the country. Then he had called a convention at Yale, on the Fraser, roused the handful of delegates with his antique style of eloquence, and formed a Confederation Party. Seymour died at this opportune moment and a successor could be appointed to "tighten the screws."

The official recommended by Macdonald for this essential work was Anthony Musgrave, a genial fellow, quiet but firm, with a hard eye, a walrus mustache, and a bare, pugnacious chin. Evidently, in appointing Musgrave, London had made up its wavering mind at last in favor of holding the Pacific colony.

The new Governor's instructions put in more discreet terms the screw-tightening policy urged in Macdonald's more candid dispatches: "Her Majesty's Government anticipate that the interests of every province of British North America would be more advanced by enabling the wealth, credit and intelligence of the whole to be brought to bear on every part than by encouraging each in the constricted policy of taking care of itself, possibly at the expense of its neighbor." In plain terms, Musgrave was to push British Columbia into confederation without further delay.

He quickly plied his screw driver. His Legislative Council was assembled in the preposterous red wooden pagodas of Victoria (known locally as the Bird Cages) to be acquainted with the policy of the British government. Unhappily, at this great turning point of 1870, the Governor could not appear personally with his message from London, having fallen from his horse and broken his leg. He lay in his cracked and moldering mansion while his speech was read to the Council and excited galleries by the Colonial Secretary, Philip Rankin.

The breathless Lover of the World and his friends found the speech anticlimactic. It did not grant responsible government as they had hoped but promised merely to add two elected members to the Governor's Council. The stingy concession was greeted by the Confederation Party in "stony silence." But when the Governor proposed that British Columbia join the new Dominion the fragile Bird Cages shook with applause.

As Macdonald had always suspected, the annexationists were a minority in British Columbia, as in Canada. The majority needed only leadership and a reasonable offer from Ottawa.

Terms of union proposed by Musgrave had been written by the Canadian government but now issued as the official recommendation of London. Canada would take over the colonial debt; would subsidize the colonists at the rate of 80 cents a year per head; pension off the local officials who opposed confederation lest it destroy their jobs; and, unbelievably, would start building a railway to the Pacific coast within three years, meanwhile finishing a wagon road. These were brave terms, almost incredible to the fluttering Bird Cages, perhaps too generous for Canada's resources, and altogether better than de Cosmos and his friends had any right to expect.

By promising a railway across the Pre-Cambrian wastes, the empty prairies, the Rockies, and the Pacific jungle, Old Tomorrow had staked the future of Canada on the wildest gamble since the American Revolution. It would make or break the new nation. Within three years it would break Macdonald's government.

Even a railway could not impress the annexationists of Victoria. They crammed the bursting Bird Cages—grim men, hardheaded, stubborn, and all unknown to the busy Republic twenty miles across the strait. Yet their victory or defeat must prove decisive to the future of Manifest Destiny, for it would determine the final division of the continent—if the continent could be permanently divided, which the annexationists doubted.

Dr. J. S. Helmcken, the annexationist leader, put the Confederation issue in a nutshell of geopolitics: "However we are in favor of consolidating British interests, our own interests come first. Imperial interests can afford to wait. Whatever may be the result of the present vote, it is impossible to deny the probability of the less being absorbed by the greater, and it cannot be regarded as impossible that ultimately not only this colony, but the whole Dominion of Canada may well be absorbed by the United States."

"No! No!" cried de Cosmos, but who could deny this plain continental logic? "It is dangerous," Helmcken retorted, callously rubbing in the facts, "to place ourselves at the disposal of superior numbers, who must necessarily legislate for the greater number, the people of the Atlantic provinces. No union on account of love need be looked for."

"No! No!" de Cosmos cried again, but before he had time to observe that the Americans offered no union of love either, and would also legislate for the greater number, W. T. Drake leaped up to reveal the ultimate horror of confederation: "We should be transferred from the rule of statesmen at Downing Street to that of politicians at Ottawa!" What kind of rulers he expected to find in Washington was not clear.

These were the last despairing shrieks of the colonial mind, of the economic determinists, the faint hearts, men of the same sort who had signed the Annexation Manifesto of 1849. They must lean on some outside power, either British or American.

As the Bird Cages fluttered anew, Canada found its voice in John

Robson, lieutenant to de Cosmos and a mainland newspaper editor
of hawk's face and cutting pen, who had once been jailed by Judge
Begbie for contempt of court and thus became a popular hero.
British Columbia, said Robson, could not always cling to Britain's
skirts "like a mendicant's child." Better annexation to the Sandwich
Islands or Hindustan than the present dismal plight of a colony
whose "progress has been like that of the crab—backwards." The
hopeless colony must become an exploited appendage of the Republic or a prosperous, manly province of Canada.

The Lover of the World had waited impatiently for his chance,
and now it had come. Standing on this watershed of Canada's life
and his own, the prophetic, whiskered figure surveyed his work and
found it good. "I have assisted," he said, "to make history and this is
a page of it! . . . We are here laying the cornerstone of a great
nation on the Pacific coast!" It was no time for false modesty. When
he had finished his ponderous and able speech the decision of the
Bird Cages had been made. Confederation was approved almost
unanimously by the same assembly which had opposed it only a
year before.

Eloquence, however, and a few votes cast in a wooden shack
beside the Pacific, would not build a railway across a continent. If
the railway was not built, British Columbia must soon tire of confederation and accept the only alternative—annexation.

No one knew that better than the government of Canada as it met
the delegates of British Columbia in Ottawa.

Cartier (Macdonald being ill) quickly accepted the terms of
union proposed by London through Musgrave and already cleared
at Ottawa, and managed to improve them in detail. The railway
would be started within two years, not three, and finished within
ten. That night the delegates sent a triumphant telegram to Victoria: "Terms agreed upon. The delegates are satisfied. Canada is
favorable to immediate union and guarantees the railway." The
telegram itself bore witness to the Canadian crisis. It was carried
westward by American wires.

On the twentieth day of July, 1871, British Columbia entered
confederation by unanimous vote of its assembly. Canada stretched
from ocean to ocean. Its completed boundary described the northern rim of Manifest Destiny. But the boundary was still only a line
on a map. Old Tomorrow had yet to transform it into hard railway
steel and all his energies were otherwise engaged. He was hurrying
toward an unforeseen crisis, the deepest of his life.

28

Defeat on the Potomac

[1871–1875]

I N THE SPRING OF 1871 MACDONALD FOUND HIMSELF ABOARD A
yacht on the Potomac River, listening with feigned interest to
the homely wife of an American senator. She had taken the
genial stranger for one of her own people and felt safe in repeating
their folklore. The unfortunate Canadians, she said, were governed
by a "perfect rascal" named Macdonald.

"Yes," said the stranger imperturbably, "he is a perfect rascal."

"Why," she asked, "do they keep such a man in power?"

"Well," said Macdonald, "they can't seem to get on without him."

At that moment the lady's husband appeared and introduced her
to the Prime Minister of Canada. After enjoying her confusion for
a moment, Macdonald added, "Don't apologize. All you've said is
perfectly true and well known at home."

This sort of badinage would do for a weekend yachting party.
Grave matters had brought Macdonald to Washington and would
send him home a sadder and a wiser man.

His personal crisis was two years off and inconceivable, but he
had long foreseen a new crisis in Canadian-American affairs. As
early as April 9, 1867, he had written to a friend in Calcutta
(whether seriously or in fun, no one ever knew): "War will come
some day between England and the United States, and India can
do us yeoman's service by sending an army of Sikhs, Ghoorkas and
Belochees &c, &c, across the Pacific to San Francisco and holding
that beautiful and immoral city with the surrounding California as
security for Montreal and Canada."

He had been worried increasingly of late by what one of his colleagues called "the pacific hostility of the United States, a judicious
alternation of bullying and coaxing." This process was tidal, rising

390

and falling with events and reaching its highwater mark in the sixties and early seventies.

Confederation at first had alarmed some Americans but now seemed to be grudgingly welcomed as a sure sign that Canada was drawing away from Britain and, without its old overseas support, would fall the sooner into the American orbit. Nevertheless, in many horrendous speeches a minority of Congressional politicians continued to protest that an embryonic Canadian nation was, in the words of Governor Chamberlain, of Maine, "a part of the great conspiracy against liberty on this youthful continent" when, of course, it was an attempt to protect the liberty of Canadians from both the United States and Britain.

The American government had not resisted confederation openly; it rejected all the urgings of Fenians and other annexationists to interfere openly in Canadian affairs, but in day-to-day matters of commerce it expressed, at every chance, the lingering resentments of the Civil War years.

Now that the Civil War was over, the reunited, bustling, self-confident nation emerging from it looked more dangerous in Canadian eyes than ever, and in some American eyes the absorption of Canada appeared to be the natural sequel of the victory over the South. This calculation, like many before it, was fallacious. The first sproutings of Canadian nationalism already were too strong to be suppressed except by naked force, which the United States had no intention of using.

Coaxing had recently replaced bullying, but Macdonald found it equally perilous. Secretary of State Hamilton Fish, for example, had suggested, perhaps seriously, that Canada might hold a plebiscite on annexation. President Grant apparently had considered this project and dismissed it as desirable but hopeless. Anyway, despite all the speeches of the Congress and the short-lived bills permitting Canada to enter the Union, the American people as a whole had little interest in their neighbors, except at a few specific points of friction. It was these that had brought Macdonald to Washington.

The current trouble centered in trade across the border.

The collapse of the Reciprocity Treaty at first had seemed a blow at the primitive Canadian economy more severe than the loss of the protected British market, yet even against high customs duties Canadian goods still moved into the American market. The impending commercial disaster had been exaggerated. As in the case of the passport dispute, Macdonald refused to seek American concessions, concealed the alarm of his government, and waited for the United States to change its mind.

In 1869 the State Department had suggested a new trade agreement with reduced tariffs all round. It could not convert either the Grant government or the Congress.

Canada still held a few of the blue chips in this large gamble. It owned the St. Lawrence canals, needed by American shipping, and the best of the Atlantic coastal fisheries, needed by American fishermen.

The American shippers and fishermen had lost free access to both on the repeal of reciprocity. They were eager to recover their old privileges by a new treaty. The protectionists and annexationists, on the other hand, had originally hoped that reciprocity would lure Canada into the United States and, that failing, now hoped that the lack of reciprocity would drive Canada toward the same refuge.

So far the Congressional protectionists were in the saddle and riding high. Without understanding it, they had now encountered one of the basic facts of American life—Canadians, often disputing among themselves, would always choose the tariff policy which, regardless of immediate cost, appeared most likely to prevent political union.

In the first days of confederation they played the only trump card in their hands by gently discouraging American fishermen in the waters of the Maritime provinces, within the three-mile limit, by imposing a charge of 50 cents a ton on all foreign fish boats. The charge was later doubled and finally raised so high that the Americans began to evade it. Canada then forbade Americans to buy bait or to land their catch in Canadian ports for quick shipment to the American market.

This was a grave blow to the American fishing industry. It was followed in 1870 by the dispatch of six Canadian cruisers to enforce the new regulations. Four hundred American vessels were seized in three months.

As expected, overt pressure brought a quick response from Washington. Turning an angry soldier's eye on Canada, President Grant told the Congress: "This semi-independent but irresponsible agent has exercised its delegated powers in an unfriendly way." Strong words from a friendly power. Grant proposed to buttress them by the cancellation of the bonding privileges enjoyed by Canadian goods in transit through the United States and by closure of American ports to Canadian ships.

The codfish of the Canadian coast, long the prize of international quarrels, had launched the old anti-British sentiment of the United States into full cry again. It found a braying voice in General Benjamin Franklin Butler, a former general of the Northern Army,

somewhat tattered in reputation and remembered mainly for his
famous order in New Orleans, where he had instructed his occupation troops to treat any female showing contempt of Union arms
"as a woman of the town plying her avocation." Butler's attacks on
Canada and Britain were expressed in similar terms of violence.
They found no echo in the American government, though they might
be useful for bargaining purposes.

Actually the government, behind all the alarming gestures of the
Congress, was determined to settle the fisheries question before the
fishing season of 1871 led to more serious trouble. Washington had
come at last to the conclusion that all the postwar issues standing
between it and the British Empire should be settled on a friendly
basis. Thus the inarticulate codfish, more successfully than the
garrulous statesmen like Butler, had introduced a sense of sanity
into the affairs of the English-speaking world.

The agenda of any settlement would be crowded.

To begin with, there were the Alabama Claims—a resounding
phrase of great semantic power, loosely embracing all the United
States' grievances against Britain. Having built that unprofitable
cruiser for the South, Britain must pay through the nose for deliberately joining a revolt against the lawful American government; to
which Lord John Russell had made the typically righteous reply of
the stiff British upper lip: "Her Majesty's Government are the sole
guardians of their own honor." No breach of neutrality was admitted
in London. Britain was anxious, however, to make a deal and, if
possible, end a lingering transatlantic ill-will now a hundred years
old.

President Johnson was agreeable. He had negotiated an agreement by which a joint commission would consider, and an arbitration board would settle, all disputes arising out of the Civil War.
The Senate, of course, would never approve anything likely to bring
credit on Lincoln's lonely heir. Apparently the futile Johnson project had only widened the field of argument to almost comic proportions. Britain, said Senator Sumner, had not merely helped to
arm the South; it had doubled the length of the war and, therefore,
should pay half the cost, or two billion dollars.

Such figures might appear ridiculous in London but Sumner was
not to be brushed off by mere calculations of arithmetic. Before the
Civil War this courageous opponent of slavery had been attacked
in the Senate chamber by an enemy, knocked unconscious to the
floor and confined to his bed for three years, but nothing could daunt
a man who said of himself: "The slave of principles, I call no party
master."

If the Grant government was to settle the Alabama Claims, Sumner somehow must be undermined since he could not be tamed. He was, therefore, deposed as chairman of the Senate Foreign Relations Committee. His demand for two billion dollars of compensation was not to be taken seriously in practical politics. What he and the men around him really wanted, of course, was not cash but territory. Sumner was prepared, with openhanded generosity, to accept Canada as the full price of the Alabama Claims—a modest price, he seemed to think, taking no account of the people who would pay it, the people of Canada.

Senator Zachariah Chandler followed Sumner with a more candid proposition. He proposed that the United States negotiate with Britain for the cession of Canada and added a striking purple patch of eloquence: "I put on file a mortgage on the British North American provinces for the whole amount, and that mortgage is recorded and the security is good . . ." Not as good as Chandler supposed. He, too, had overlooked the Canadians. They recognized no mortgage incurred in Britain.

On second thoughts, Sumner put the case more specifically in a memorandum to the government, noting that the "greatest trouble, if not peril" was Fenianism, and Fenianism was aroused by "the proximity of the British flag in Canada." The solution was beautiful in its simplicity: "The withdrawal of the British flag cannot be abandoned as a condition or preliminary of such a settlement as is now proposed."

In short, Canada, the infant state, was to inherit the sins of its parent and pay the wages in full.

Next in the American bill of particulars was an irritating little wrangle over the far western boundary, as fixed by the Oregon Treaty, from the mainland, at the 49th Parallel, southward through the Strait of Georgia and thence through the Strait of Juan de Fuca to the Pacific.

The prolonged and sometimes absurd San Juan Island dispute, as it was called, had arisen from an ignorance of geography in London and Washington. According to the Oregon Treaty, the boundary, on leaving the mainland, would lie in "the middle of the channel which separates the continent from Vancouver's Island." It was easy to determine the middle of the Strait of Georgia but, to the surprise of American and British statesmen, the line thus drawn cut through a swarming archipelago and its islands suddenly seemed desirable to both parties. Who was to possess them?

They were separated by three natural channels—Haro Strait, nearest to Vancouver Island; San Juan Channel and Middle Channel, splitting the archipelago roughly in half; and Rosario Strait, hugging the mainland American shore.

The United States naturally favored the westernmost passage and claimed all the islands east of it. They contained about 170 square miles of questionable economic value but, in current military judgment, were strategically important as a cork in the bottle of the inland passage leading on the north to the mouth of the Fraser, on the south to Puget Sound.

The largest island, San Juan, had been occupied by the Hudson's Bay Company in 1845 and British possession reinforced by some shepherds and a herd of sheep. Ten years later the United States asserted its rights through the enterprising sheriff of Whatcom County, who, failing to collect taxes from the Hudson's Bay men, seized thirty-four breeding rams before the shepherds arrived to stop him. The British government claimed damages from the American Treasury. After some solemn exchanges, both nations agreed to avoid any more clashes on San Juan until the boundary was finally determined.

The Joint Boundary Commission of 1856 could not agree on the line through the Strait of Georgia. However, the British representative, Captain James C. Prevost, R.N., insisted, with a weather eye turned on the American Navy, that Britain must hold San Juan lest its surrender "prove fatal to Her Majesty's possessions in this quarter of the globe."

While the Great Powers exchanged their interminable memoranda, an American squatter on the island, finding himself in need of meat on June 15, 1859, shot a pig belonging to the Hudson's Bay Company. The value of the single pig in those days was not high but high enough to provoke the stern anger of Governor Douglas, at Victoria. He ordered a magistrate, John Fitzroy de Courcy, to San Juan, transporting him ostentatiously on the British corvette *Satellite*.

That same day the United States landed sixty soldiers on the island, under command of Captain G. E. Pickett, who had been dispatched by Brigadier General William S. Harney, the overzealous commander of the Department of Oregon. Harney blandly informed his government that San Juan was a vital steppingstone to Vancouver Island, which, being "as important to the Pacific States as Cuba is to those on the Atlantic," must eventually fall into American hands.

As soon as he heard of Pickett's arrival, the wrathy Douglas sent a British ship of war, the *Tribune*, to San Juan with orders to prevent any further landings. His ardor cooled when he saw that the Americans were in earnest. Nevertheless, he proposed a joint military occupation until the boundary was fixed and was angry when the British naval officers refused to bite off more than they could chew. Britain, they said, would be sure to surrender the island, as it had surrendered Oregon, and there was no use making trouble in the meantime. So the Canadian civilians and the American soldiers on San Juan were left alone and seemed to get along amicably, the dead pig eaten and forgotten.

Still, President Buchanan, already worried by the threatened split of the American Union, was further alarmed by the prospect of a quarrel with Britain. To prevent it, he sent the ubiquitous General Winfield Scott to Washington Territory. Scott's instructions were to preserve the peace and, if he thought wise, to seek a joint military occupation. This was arranged in correspondence between Scott and Douglas. Two corporals' guards of American and British soldiers settled down to enjoy the fishing, hunting, and leisure of the pleasant little island.

Scott had seen too much of the boundary to feel sure of avoiding an incident, too much of General Harney to count on his discretion. If the joint occupation "does not lead to a collision of arms," Scott wrote to Washington, "it will again be due to the forbearance of the British authorities; for I found both Brigadier-General Harney and Captain Pickett proud of their *conquest* of the island and quite jealous of any interference therewith on the part of higher authority."

Buchanan took the hint. Harney was recalled before he could provoke a collision. Pickett replaced him and lived on friendly terms with the British officers.

After refusing Britain's offers of arbitration, the United States forgot about San Juan throughout the Civil War. In 1869 the American government signed an arbitration treaty with Britain, but the Senate refused to ratify it. The boundary between Vancouver Island and the American mainland remained unsettled, like so many other of North America's affairs.

Thus Chandler's mortgage was a comprehensive document, its terms including the Alabama Claims, San Juan Island, free entry of American fishermen into Canadian waters, and free use of Canadian canals on the St. Lawrence by American shipping.

The bill of costs looked awesome to the virgin Canadian government and it seemed to grow with every speech in Washington. Surely this perpetual inflation could not continue much longer. The time had come to forget impossible demands, Congressional rhetoric, Fenian raids, heroic postures on a Pacific island, the dead pig, the imaginary diversion by Indian troops at San Francisco, and imperial gestures from London.

In September, 1869, Fish got down to cases by sounding out the British ambassador on the possibility of an omnibus settlement. Fish's terms were simple: the United States would arbitrate the San Juan boundary if Britain would arbitrate the Alabama Claims; the United States might reduce its tariffs on Canadian goods if Americans were permitted to fish freely in Canadian waters and use Canadian canals. Britain accepted that offer as a basis of negotiation and both sides met at Washington for a full-dress conference early in 1871.

Macdonald had come to Washington not as the direct representative of Canada, since his government still had no right to conduct foreign affairs, but as a member of the British delegation. British statesmen of the more thoughtful sort may have realized then that after this thin opening wedge had been driven into a centralized British Empire foreign policy, directed by London, Canada eventually would conduct its own business with other states. For the moment it could speak only through Macdonald and the other plenipotentiaries of Britain.

The position of the Canadian Prime Minister was, therefore, difficult, almost impossible. He could not control the terms of the prospective Washington Treaty, even where it touched only Canadian interests, yet he must defend it before his own government, parliament, and people. His balancing act on the imperial tightrope had never required such skill before and the master of the equilibrium had no illusions about his peril or, as he told the senator's wife, about himself. No illusions about the British negotiators either. As usual, he expected them to sacrifice Canada's interests to serve their own.

Now from Toronto, in the thundering voice of Brown's *Globe*, he received a plain warning against any surrender at the expense of Canada to British politicians "triumphantly ignorant of almost anything connected with this continent and so ready to believe that a few million acres here or there do not matter much."

Macdonald occupied the hottest seat at the bargaining table. He had responsibility but no corresponding power. He must do a man's job while his nation still lived in the swaddling clothes of national infancy. And he confronted in Washington at first hand the basic and recurring facts of life in the triangular North Atlantic world— somehow the affairs of Britain and the United States must be reconciled; Canada must always stand in the middle of them as the only North American nation linked with Britain yet linked geographically and economically with the United States; and thus inevitably it was threatened with destruction by the quarrels of the two great powers. Thus also, at the Washington Conference, Macdonald began in a tentative fashion to assume the inevitable Canadian role or burden as an anxious interpreter between those powers.

The costs of that ambivalent status would always be heavy. Some he was not ready to pay. He appeared exceedingly stubborn about the fisheries and instantly collided with Lord de Grey, leader of the British delegation, who was compelled, as he advised the British government, to speak "pretty plainly" to the Canadian. If, he said, Macdonald wrecked the conference over the wretched codfish and if "difficulties with the United States resulted therefrom, the Canadians will find very little inclination in England to help them get out of the troubles they had created for themselves." The immigrant boy from Kingston had been given his first brutal lesson in power politics, as practiced by a British expert.

Actually Macdonald had neither wish nor power to be unreasonable. He had never expected to bar American fishermen permanently from Canadian waters. Fishing rights, however, and free navigation of the St. Lawrence canals were the only cards in his hand. They must be played close to his vest. He would yield them only for a downward revision of the American tariff.

The direct pressure came not from the Americans but from the British. Lord de Grey kept assuring Macdonald that Canadian concessions would surely put the United States in a generous frame of mind. Though he could not guarantee any American tariff concessions, he pressed so hard for the surrender of the fisheries that, at one point, Macdonald was ready to resign from the delegation and go home.

The Americans, for their part, were simply baffled by the Canadian's obstinacy. Since the United States had undeniable claims on Britain and Britain was anxious to pay them as an honorable debtor, why should Canada make itself the dog in the manger? Still, in candor, Macdonald must admit that the Americans—having won all previous conferences when bargaining power lay against them— might well have proved much tougher now when they held nearly all the winning cards and must satisfy an insatiable Congress with its mortgage over Canada.

The two pressures now joined against him made these days of the Washington Conference the worst in Macdonald's life so far. Worse were to follow. Meanwhile he tried to manage his suspicious cabinet in Ottawa and hide his troubles under the persiflage of yachting parties on the Potomac.

It proved easy to agree on the arbitration of the Alabama Claims and the San Juan boundary. The fisheries remained the real sticking point of the conference, for Canada would not surrender them without a new tariff deal which the American government could not promise and which the protectionists of the Congress would doubtless reject. Instead, the United States offered to pay Canada a million dollars for perpetual admission to the fishing grounds and vaguely suggested reduced tariffs on coal, salt, and fish.

Macdonald refused that offer. To strengthen himself in the face of increasing British and American pressure he asked his cabinet, in secret code, for vigorous instructions. The Cabinet obediently ordered him to stand firm. His Fabian tactics of studied delay threatened to smash the conference.

Then the Canadian Cabinet began to lose its nerve. Obdurate in public, it privately urged its chief to take the best terms he could get, lest Canada get nothing but blame for preventing agreement between Britain and the United States. This advice, he replied, had placed him in the most disagreeable position of his career (which was saying a lot) but "the work has to be done and I am resolved to do it."

Even though Fish had withdrawn his earlier offer to Canada and the conference stood deadlocked by mid-April, its net, covering such a wide sea of problems, was elastic enough to provide a chance of compromise. That chance appeared in a new offer from Fish. He hinted that if Britain would agree to a reasonable over-all settlement, the United States might modify its demands in the Strait of Georgia. And perhaps, he added, the value of American fishing rights on the Atlantic coast of Canada might be arbitrated?

Britain grasped eagerly at this proposal, provided that the United States removed its duties on fish caught by Canadians. As Britain and the United States agreed on this formula, Macdonald was effectively isolated. His position was now worse than ever, for his mercurial cabinet apparently had changed its mind again and warned him to refuse any surrender of Canadian interests. Ottawa had advised London direct that a fishery deal imposed without Canadian consent would be "a breach of faith and an indignity never before offered to a great British possession."

This blunt warning began a process not to be completed for exactly sixty years, but in the meantime Canadian interests were ground fine between the millstones of the two great powers.

To them the genial Canadian with the whisky nose and disarming manners still appeared as a stubborn, brittle, and purely negative objector. Actually he was a man of rubber, as he must be in his state of weakness. He stretched but he would not break, and his very flexibility made him all the more difficult to deal with.

The British negotiators asked themselves if a mere colonial was to stand in the way of transatlantic reconciliation after the original parting in bad blood and the century of quarrel.

The Americans asked why Britain could not discipline her wayward child, the colony of Canada.

Perhaps the better minds of London already realized that this child, as it continued to grow, would soon become quite unmanageable. What kind of empire, then, had been hatched by the Canadian Confederation if the Queen and her government, who obviously knew best, could not have their own way with their overseas dependencies? Truly, the Canadians were a baffling breed.

Despite the backstage maneuvering of Washington, none of the suggested compromises seemed to prosper. Somehow, if the conference was to be saved, a new rabbit must be pulled out of the hat. It now appeared, a Fenian rabbit.

Macdonald had always claimed compensation from the United States for the damage of the Fenian raids. The United States demanded compensation from Britain on precisely the same grounds, in the Alabama Claims, but denied it to Canada. This was a nice point, ready made for the skilled diplomats of London, who probably wondered why they had not thought of it before. At the eleventh hour they received a sudden inspiration and produced a pretty formula: Since the United States would not pay for the Fenians' damage in Canada, Britain would assume this debt of honor— provided, of course, that Canada would be sensible about the fisheries.

Macdonald had been driven back step by step to this last ditch. It was impossible to refuse the final offer from London without alienating British power essential to Canada. He regarded the new formula as unfair because it provided no reduction in the American tariff. His objections were recorded in a message to London but he knew when he was beaten and accepted the one-sided deal. He refused, however, to put his name on the proposed agreement as a representative of Canada, signing only as one of the commissioners of Britain. It was a fine distinction, possibly just enough to mollify the Canadian Parliament.

Thus in the Treaty of Washington the deal was made at Canada's expense. The United States and Britain were to make a fresh start and undertake a general housecleaning of their old grievances.

As the treaty spelled out the settlement, American fishermen could fish in Canadian waters for ten years; Americans and Canadians would enjoy reciprocal bonding privileges in both countries; American shipping was freely admitted to the St. Lawrence canals; Canadians (by a somewhat fictitious concession) could navigate the rivers of Alaska, where they appeared to have no interest; the American government would recommend to the various states that their canals be opened to Canadian vessels; the Alabama Claims, the San Juan boundary dispute, and the cash value of the American fishermen's rights in Canada would be arbitrated.

However these arrangements might be glossed over in shiny official language and however useful they might be in curing the transatlantic quarrel, only two facts mattered to Canadians: the American tariff was left unchanged (except for the free admission of Canadian fish) and Britain had put its own interests far above those of its colony. From now on those facts would never lie far below the surface of politics in Ottawa and would drastically affect the future of the British Empire. Macdonald had learned his lesson in power politics at Washington. He could never hope to play in the big league, but he was not quite powerless. Canada controlled its own tariff and he was getting set to use that weapon.

The United States Senate naturally ratified a lucrative bargain. All Macdonald's resources of public argument and secret wirepulling were required to ram the Washington agreement through the Parliament.

The outcome of the three arbitrations did little to mollify Canadian opinion.

In the end the Emperor of Germany (who knew nothing of American geography and apparently was expected to exercise the impartiality of ignorance) was chosen as arbitrator of the Pacific boundary dispute. He fully endorsed the American claim to San Juan Island and fixed the line west of it, in Haro Strait. The future nation of Canada had forfeited another spot of territory. It was not to be the last.

Canada finally received $5,500,000 from the United States for the opening of the fisheries.

The United States received $15,500,000 from Britain to settle the Alabama Claims, a handsome price but somewhat short of Sumner's bill for two billions.

Where did Canada stand after the bewildering events of the last two years—rebellion, so called, on the prairies; British Columbia's entry into confederation, soon followed by Prince Edward Island; betrayal, as it seemed, in London; defeat in Washington; and an ugly political situation in Ottawa?

Canada stood facing the first great decision of national life. Eco-

nomically and politically it could pursue, in Macdonald's judgment
and his people's, only one policy, a policy of outright nationalism.

Since the chance of a continental economy, with trade moving
freely across the border, had been rejected by the United States,
despite its long campaign for continentalism, Canada must exploit
any foreign markets it could find but build up its own by protectionist tariffs. And since it had already assumed the almost impossible task of building a transcontinental state, it must link its
remote segments not merely by bonds of sentiment but by rails of
steel. The great decision, in fact, had been made already by the
promise to British Columbia of a railway from the St. Lawrence to
the Pacific coast.

In a nation of four million people, all but a handful of them east
of the Great Lakes, that promise might appear to an impartial outsider as preposterous. So it appeared to Macdonald's enemies at
home. He was resolved to redeem it just the same, believing that the
railway would make, as its lack would break, the half-formed nation.
He did not foresee that the railway would break him and his government.

Thus mercifully unconscious of the catastrophe ahead, he under-
took a project without precedent, considering Canada's immediate
resources, in the record of nations. Fainter hearts warned him to
build his railway on the cheap, to bypass the daunting and costly
Pre-Cambrian dike north of the Lakes by a detour through the level
American states. The Grand Trunk Railway—already serving the
St. Lawrence Valley, with an auxiliary network running down to
Portland—offered to strike westward to the Pacific through Chicago.
Macdonald would have nothing but an all-Canadian route, for the
whole Canadian future, military, political and economic, depended
on what he would soon be calling a National Policy.

His government offered $30,000,000 and 50,000,000 acres of land
to any company willing to build the transcontinental railway. Sir
Hugh Allan, a Scots-Canadian who had made his fortune in Atlantic
shipping, organized the Canadian Pacific Railway Company on these
terms and agreed, as well, to finance the re-election of the Macdonald government in 1872. His generosity was unlimited and
lethal.

Macdonald, of course, had never supposed that elections were won
with prayers. He knew, as he said in a wry phrase, that many men
could be bought but that few were honest enough to stay bought.
Anyway, in its first test of power after the Confederation election,
the government must have money and, by the rules of the game,
expected Allan to supply it.

On July 30, 1872, Cartier was indiscreet enough to commit these matters to paper in a "private and confidential" letter. "The friends of the Government," he told Allan, "will expect to be assisted with funds in the pending elections and any amount which you or your company will advance for that purpose shall be recouped to you. A memorandum of immediate requirements is below."

The memorandum put down Macdonald for $35,000, Cartier for $50,000, and Sir Hector Langevin, the Quebec party boss, for $25,000. Macdonald was in urgent need of campaign funds but he deprecated letters that could be produced as evidence. As he later told the Governor General, Lord Dufferin, he had been "quite unaware of the extent to which Cartier had committed himself in Montreal. . . . Not until after his death were any of his colleagues aware of his insane course."

Yet Macdonald, too, in a reckless moment proved quite as indiscreet as Cartier. On August 26, a few days before the election, he telegraphed to J. J. C. Abbott, Allan's lawyer, the plea of a desperate man: "I must have another ten thousand. Will be last time of calling. Do not fail. Answer today." He got the money. The government was triumphantly elected.

Its triumph proved brief. Through a traitor in Allan's paper railway empire, the Liberal politicians secured the ruinous evidence of Cartier's letter and Macdonald's telegram. A few weeks of ferreting proved that the Conservative Party had received at least $350,000 from the men who had been awarded the supposedly opulent railway contract. Such was the Pacific Scandal, which burst suddenly upon the virtuous Canadian Parliament, could not be denied, and forced Macdonald's resignation in November, 1873. To all appearances his career was finished, his policies dead.

He offered at once to resign his party leadership, but his followers had sense enough to vote him confidence—with little hope, however. How could this shattered leader ever rebuild a shattered party? "If ever there was a man in low water," wrote a friendly member of Parliament, "it was Sir John as I saw him in the winter of 1875, coming out of the House into the bitter air, dressed in a Red River sash and coat and the old historic mink-skin cap, tottering down the hill to the East Gate alone, others passing him with a wide sweep."

For the first time since his boyhood in Kingston he was alone, he was broke, and he owned little now but an invisible leper's bell. His obvious poverty in the big lonely house beside the river was the best proof that he had never received a cent of personal graft. He had financed his party by the accepted method and apparently ruined himself, financially and politically.

So it was the end of Old Tomorrow. The Reformers, now called the Liberal Party, had no doubts on that score when they assumed office and easily won a national election. Unfortunately the new government, though full of virtue, was not gifted with imagination.

It had chosen as its leader a former Scots stonemason, Alexander Mackenzie, a man of unquestioned probity, granite features, and a literal, stonemason's mind. The genius of the party remained in the erratic mind of Brown, that scolding oracle of liberalism who was out of active politics but, through his *Globe*, seemed to assume the proprietorship of the government, and in the brilliant, remote mind of Edward Blake, Mackenzie's chief colleague.

Both the dour Scots instincts of Mackenzie and the mathematical calculations of Blake were staggered by the prospects of a transcontinental railway. This impossible scheme had broken Macdonald. It would break Canada. The new government might build it in time, but certainly would not be hurried, especially when the country was entering the first stages of a continental depression.

Mackenzie called the railway "a piece of madness," an "insane act," "a piece of deliberate treachery." The cost must bankrupt Canada, and Mackenzie, the Scot, had a strong prejudice against bankruptcy. So had Blake. As Canada's leading lawyer he was ready to break the legal bargain with British Columbia and see it leave confederation before he would fulfill Macdonald's prodigal promise to complete the railway in ten years.

The work, therefore, would be done gradually, in convenient segments. The West must be satisfied at present with a series of separate lines, joined by lake and river steamboats. Macdonald regarded this policy as wasteful, useless, and absurd but was in no position to offer serious criticism. He remained alone with his minkskin hat, his Red River sash, and his leper's bell. Yet he had friends, more than he realized, and Mackenzie was rallying them behind him.

29

Railway and Rebellion

[1875–1885]

A S ALWAYS, SINCE THE FIRST DAYS OF QUEBEC, THE COMFORTABLE
calculations of the populous East were soon wrenched out of
joint by the leverage of the empty West.

Beyond the Rockies strange affairs were under way, inconceivable to Ottawa's stonemason. He had been in office only a few months when he learned that, on February 7, 1874, the usually law-abiding citizens of Victoria, eight hundred strong, had burst into the Bird Cages, demanding the completion of the railway. They had insulted the British Columbia Legislature, driven the speaker from his chair, and called their night's work the "Rebellion."

This was serious enough to impress even Mackenzie. The news from Victoria could mean only that Canada's hold on the Pacific coast had become exceedingly precarious and might well be broken if it was not soon reinforced by bands of railway steel. The seeds of a still graver crisis had been quietly planted along the banks of the Saskatchewan River by Riel's half-breed race, the Métis. And in Ottawa it appeared that Macdonald, that man of rubber, while stretched thin, was not really broken, as his enemies supposed.

Mackenzie's ears were attuned to abstract theories and the classic symphonies of liberalism. Macdonald's heard the faintest whispers and secret mutterings of common men. He knew that the British Columbians, already talking openly of secession if the railway was delayed, could smash confederation and his lifework at the mountains. Those sounds were disturbing to the patriot. The grumblings of Ontario and Quebec manufacturers against imported American goods, the protests of factory workers against unemployment, were sweet music to the politician.

For reasons of patriotism and politics, then, all these elements of

405

discontent must be mobilized against the government. It was time to bring the discredited policies of the Conservative Party into the open again, to give them a home and habitation. A new name also would help. Thus emerged the most enduring fact of Canadian politics. Macdonald, with his sure sense of semantics, called it the National Policy.

But it must be eased in gradually and urged with discretion, lest its protectionist color disturb the exporting and importing interests, especially the farmers. Macdonald had preached as vigorously as anyone against the heresy of high tariffs; he had fought for reciprocity at the Washington Conference; he still wanted it, if he could get it; if not, he was ready for the alternative of protection even if it might "sin against this or that theory of political economy." In short, as a pragmatist and therefore a typical Canadian, he remained entirely free of consistency, the hobgoblin of little minds, and favored any policy, however inconsistent, if it seemed likely to work.

His mind had been clarified by these years of disaster, though he had not yet opened it to the public. He no longer believed that the Americans would accept reciprocity. Therefore, the alternative of protection must be made to appear better, after all. What all his vague speeches really meant was that the Canadian nation lacked a national economy and it could be built only by tariffs, a railway, and the settlement of the West.

Macdonald worked hard for his National Policy and his own vindication. He could hardly have succeeded, however, without the help of the unfortunate Mackenzie government. It seemed unable to make up its mind on fundamentals and, besides, was powerless to cure a North American depression, that most reliable ally of Canadian opposition leaders.

Brown had been sent to Washington, sublimely confident that he could convert the Americans to something like free trade. All he had secured from President Grant was a draft agreement, reducing certain tariffs, and a presidential message virtually advising the Congress to reject this bargain. Brown's handiwork never escaped from the pigeonhole of the Senate Foreign Relations Committee. Mackenzie was thus left without a workable policy in these hard times, while the business community cried for "Reciprocity of Trade or Reciprocity of Tariffs" and the unemployed for jobs.

The government yielded somewhat to such pressures by raising the tariff in 1874. Then, after a sentimental journey to Britain, Mackenzie remembered that "the principles of Richard Cobden are the principles of civilization" and an expected further tariff increase was canceled. The principles of Cobden and civilization could not rescue a drowning ministry.

Macdonald had risen from obloquy by now, his sins swallowed up in the depression and the obvious failure of the government. He insinuated his National Policy into politics so subtly that the voters, as he intended, could never be sure what it intended. But it sounded good.

He favored a somewhat higher tariff to increase the state's dwindling revenues and only "incidental protection"—not actually higher duties at all but only a "readjustment." And on this formula of the squared circle he was swept back to power in the election of 1878.

The National Policy accompanied him, and with it, as an added dividend, a brief, deceptive return of good times. Protection was immediately unfurled in the government's budget. Customs duties were sharply increased, not for "incidental" but for direct aid to Canadian industry. After that the tariff moved up and down within a pretty narrow range under all succeeding governments. The basic protective principle, core of the National Policy, was never repealed. American restrictions on trade and Macdonald's retaliation have split the North American economy to this day—a reflection and, as Macdonald believed, an essential buttress of the political division.

The other contents of the National Policy were the settlement of the West and the construction of a railway to the Pacific, each being dependent on the other. As a result of Mackenzie's cautious tinkering, the railway was only a few disjointed patches of track in the wilderness. Its completion would be doubtless the most formidable project ever undertaken by four million people anywhere. Nevertheless, Macdonald was resolved to plunge immediately into that gamble.

With one hand he placated the British Columbians, who, after their unsuccessful "Rebellion," appealed direct to Queen Victoria and, that appeal also failing, declared in 1878 that they would leave confederation if the railway was not finished in two years.

With the other hand he directed the organization of the Canadian Pacific Railway.

No business enterprise in America had ever produced a more notable company of men than the first directorate of the C.P.R. At its head was George Stephen, a Canadian and a genius of finance. Its general manager was William Cornelius Van Horne, an American and a genius of organization. James J. Hill, born in Guelph, Ontario, had moved to Red River, then to St. Paul, and made a fortune there in local railway promotions. He had met Donald Smith on a prairie trail after that subtle negotiator had harangued the

Métis crowds at Fort Garry, and these two buccaneers of businesss had formed a highly profitable partnership. It brought them both into Stephen's Canadian Pacific Railway syndicate.

Hill had his own large fish to fry and soon found himself in conflict with the Canadians. Winnipeg, he said, should be the eastern terminus of the C.P.R. From there its traffic would be diverted southward to St. Paul on Hill's own line, the St. Paul, Minneapolis and Manitoba, and thence eastward on other American lines. There was logic in that plan. It would enable the C.P.R. to avoid the profitless barrens north of Lake Superior.

Logic never had any place in Macdonald's calculations. He was not building a railway to make money or to help Jim Hill. He was building "an Imperial highway across the continent of America entirely on British soil." He was opening, in fact, the long-sought Northwest Passage.

Van Horne agreed with him and guaranteed to drive through the cliffs, muskeg, and Pre-Cambrian rubble of the North Shore as he would drive through the Rockies. Unable to halt a plan which he considered crazy—even worse than crazy, unprofitable—Hill soon left the C.P.R. in disgust and built the Great Northern to the Pacific. The lifelong quarrel between him and Van Horne now began, a war of tracks, locomotives, finance, and politics far more costly than the old border wars of arrow and musket.

As Van Horne's railway moved west, the steel tentacles of Hill's Great Northern thrust northward to suck Canadian traffic into the United States. All the way to the coast Van Horne found his enemy forestalling him with these strategic branch lines—into the mines of the Kootenay country in British Columbia, up the eastern slope of the coast range, and finally into Vancouver. The struggle of the boundary was taking a new form. Its weapons were money, management, and imagination, but it was essentially the same old struggle, begun in Talon's time—the struggle to grasp and direct the flow of wealth from the West.

The continental duel between Hill, a Canadian turned American, and Van Horne, an American turned Canadian, lay some years ahead. On Macdonald's return to office the question was whether the C.P.R. could be built at all.

Stephen's syndicate undertook to lay tracks from Ontario to the Pacific within ten years. It was granted $25,000,000 by the government; the steel fragments left by Mackenzie; 25,000,000 acres of land; perpetual exemption from taxes; and a promise that no competing American lines would be allowed to cross the boundary throughout the huge new railway monopoly of the West (a promise soon to be repudiated).

Even with these concessions the scheme had barely got under way before it began to look impossible. So it might have proved but for the many-sided genius of Van Horne.

This Gargantua of the Illinois prairies was the son of an indolent lawyer who had once argued cases with Abe Lincoln. Left with a mother and two sisters to support, young Van Horne delivered telegraph messages, learned the Morse code in his spare time, and soon was managing an American railway. He had become a huge and portly figure, with the square face of his Dutch ancestry, a close-cut black beard, and heavy-lidded stoic eyes. Early in life he proclaimed a philosophy certain to serve him well: "Oh, I eat all I can, I drink all I can, I smoke all I can, and I don't give a damn for anything."

He didn't give a damn for the swamps, muskeg, and solid rock bluffs along the north shore of Lake Superior. He didn't give a damn for the prairie Indians, diverting Chief Crowfoot of the Blackfoot tribe, by conjurer's tricks and the production of little pink rubber balls from his ears. Nor for the financiers and politicians of Montreal and Ottawa, whom he regaled with feasts cooked by his own hands in some dingy bunkhouse, and with the music of his violin while he drank them under the table, beat them at all-night poker and billiards, or painted their portraits as his humor moved him. Yet he was a shy man, as interested in geology and his collection of Chinese porcelain as in railways. He trembled and stuttered on a public platform. When an orchestra in a Paris restaurant took him for Edward Prince of Wales, and played "God Save the King," he fled in boyish embarrassment. It was only for practical affairs that he didn't give a damn.

Among them he didn't give a damn for the daunting pinnacles of the Rockies. Refusing to follow the easy Yellowhead Pass to the northward, as recommended by the great engineer, Sanford Fleming, he struck straight west from Calgary, close to the American border, though he had found no pass through the Selkirks.

Nothing like the prodigy of the C.P.R. had ever been seen on earth before. The Union Pacific had built 1,100 miles of railway by known and relatively comfortable routes, backed by the resources of a great power. Van Horne had to build 2,500 miles with no known passage through the Rockies, backed by four million people who could hardly call themselves a nation yet, by a depleted national treasury, by grudging financiers in London, and mostly by his own faith and Macdonald's. But he didn't give a damn.

He drank, he smoked, he ate (usually ordering two complete meals for himself and informing the London *Times* that his family coat-of-arms was a "Dinner Horne, Pendant, upon a Kitchen Door"); he shuttled from coast to coast by canoe, on horseback, or on foot;

he once drove an engine over a mountain chasm where no engineer would venture; he fed his army of laborers like kings, and systematically shattered all previous records of railway construction.

In his first summer he laid 500 miles of track. In the next summer 800. Along the nightmare stretch of Lake Superior he drove 9,000 men, built two dynamite factories, and spent $700,000 for supplies on a single mile, only to see it sink seven times in the muskeg ooze.

By the first months of 1885 Van Horne had all but mastered the geography of the continent. His railway lay across the prairies and was crawling into the defiles of the Rockies to join its western link, already pushed from the Pacific coast. A gap still remaining north of Lake Superior would soon be closed. And after its prodigious labor the C.P.R. was bankrupt.

Unable to pay his laborers, but hiding his anxiety behind a wooden face and an expensive cigar, Van Horne hurried to Montreal for funds. He found the C.P.R. directors in tears. They had pawned their fortunes, sought aid in London, and vainly appealed to Macdonald for another subsidy. Macdonald's unequaled patience seemed to have run out. Even his alchemy could not extract more gold from a skeptical Parliament. Was the railway, then, to collapse in three disjointed segments a few hundred miles from its goal?

The answer came from an improbable quarter. It came from the United States in the person of Louis Riel. In his march of steel across America Van Horne had encountered more than the eastern muskeg, the gullies of the plains, and the barrier of the mountains. He had collided with the incalculable human stuff of the West.

Many men of note had lately made the same discovery. General George Armstrong Custer, for example, had been lured to destruction by the cunning dummies and empty tepees of an abler soldier named Sitting Bull.

The massacre of the Little Big Horn had started another of those ceaseless Indian migrations over the border. When Sitting Bull and his tribe sought sanctuary on the western Canadian prairie they found it ruled by soldiers of a new kind in red coats, calling themselves the Northwest Mounted Police.

Their army was small, even for those times, a mere 300 men in the vacuum between the Great Lakes and the mountains. But the wily American chief saw at a glance that their commander, a stern, friendly man, Major James F. Macleod, knew his business much better than Custer. An Indian nation driven into exile but still armed, ferocious and numbering four thousand, meekly surrendered to Macleod and a handful of his constables. The terrible Sioux never committed a crime in Canada.

North of the 49th Parallel, the West was in firm Canadian possession without an Indian war, while the United States Army still
grappled with the last remains of native power, conducted its own
massacres, and suffered frequent massacre in return. The contrast
was explained in part by the different attitude of Americans and
Canadians to the law and to life in general, but mainly by the character of the Mounted Police.

This unique band of men had made themselves the Indians'
friends, councilors, and idols. American whisky traders, who had
demoralized the western tribes on both sides of the line with the
unspeakable havoc of drunkenness, poverty, prostitution, and vene-
real disease, had been driven out of Canadian territory.

The old days, the centuries of unchallenged Indian control, the
hundred years of French and English traders, and even the countless
millions of buffalo that had always supported men's lives on the
central plains, were dying. And dying also was the Métis nation,
amalgam of Indian and white.

The Métis of Red River had once been able to mobilize hunting
parties of a thousand men, women and children, disciplined and
deployed like an army, to bring home a million pounds of buffalo
meat and finally to erect their own government at Fort Garry. After
fifteen years of slaughter by the railway builders of Canada and the
United States, the buffalo—undamaged by centuries of Indian hunting—were almost extinct, would number hardly a thousand before
the end of the century. The economic base of the half-breed nation
was gone. The Métis accepted Canadian law in Manitoba or moved
west to the banks of the South Saskatchewan, where their leader,
Gabriel Dumont, conducted at his village of Batoche a government
of sorts, too remote to be questioned by the government at
Ottawa.

The two thousand half-breeds of the Saskatchewan were not left
alone for long. White settlers trickled into a new river town of Prince
Albert. Then came the hated government surveyors, who had precipitated the Red River uprising. As before, the Métis saw their
narrow river farms being redivided into the white man's rectangular
townships, they feared expulsion from their lands, they petitioned
the Canadian government for firm legal titles, and year after year
they were given no satisfaction. Their government of Red River had
lasted only ten months but it had settled the land problem. Perhaps
another such demonstration would settle the same problem on the
Saskatchewan?

Dumont and his council thus brooded at Batoche while far away
in Montana the only man who could hope to revive the Métis nation

was teaching Indian children to read and write at a backwoods Catholic mission.

Riel had traveled far since his brief days of glory. He had been twice elected to the Canadian Parliament by his loyal followers of Red River, had gone secretly to Ottawa and signed the parliamentary register before the government clerks realized that he was a fugitive with a price on his head.

As a scandalized Parliament refused to seat him and made his banishment official for five years, he wandered about the eastern states, preached a French and Catholic prairie state among the French-Canadian immigrants in New England, and even discussed this plan with President Grant, who evidently thought him a little mad.

Mad he undoubtedly was, so mad that his friends smuggled him into an asylum, under a false name, near Quebec City. His madness appealed strongly to Bishop Bourget, of Montreal, the intransigent ultramontane advocate of a French Catholic state in Canada. "You have a mission to fulfill," Bourget wrote to the inmate of the Quebec asylum. This and other letters Riel carried in his pocket for the rest of his life. In them his ruin was assured.

Returning to the American prairies, apparently sane again, he earned a mean living as a woodchopper, a trader, a negotiator between white men and Indians. Now he began to see visions, inherited the miraculous powers of David, and signed himself by that name.

His devout Catholicism, mixed with the superstitions of his Indian ancestors, his heavy brown beard, his ceaseless outpouring of documents, prayers, poems and oratory, his sudden rages, long silences and hysterical laughter, gave him, among the American Métis, the undoubted air of prophecy. His fatal myth, born at Red River and almost forgotten these fourteen years, had come alive again. In their crisis at Batoche, Dumont's half-breeds remembered the messiah of their race.

Riel was no longer celibate; he had married the daughter of a Métis hunter without benefit of clergy, in the western fashion, he had begotten two children, and had become an American citizen, but his mystical powers were said to be stronger than ever. He might rescue his people in Saskatchewan. Dumont resolved to seek him out.

A ride of nearly seven hundred miles brought Dumont to the prophet at his Montana Indian school in June, 1884. Riel realized at once that his divine mission was at hand. Having prayed for guidance and received the desired answer, he set out with his wife and children for Saskatchewan, seeing on the way a vision of himself hanged from a gibbet.

That vision, though accurate, was soon blotted out by his wild welcome in Batoche. Even the English-speaking settlers of nearby Prince Albert rejoiced at his return. They, too, had grievances against the government and Riel perhaps could bring Ottawa to terms.

The affairs of the prairies had always been Macdonald's blind spot. He feared trouble there, as everywhere else, he assured Parliament that the Red River rebellion must not recur, but he expected "the present effervescence to subside." Though he had misjudged Riel, the prophet, and Dumont, the soldier, he decided to take no chances. The Mounted Police were secretly ordered to increase their forces on the Saskatchewan.

That news traveled fast to Batoche by the moccasin telegraph and infuriated the Métis. The government, then, refused to settle the land question, it intended to coerce the law-abiding half-breeds, it had ignored the lesson of Red River, and nothing apparently could change its policy but force.

Riel so far had resisted any overt act. His public speeches were discursive, religious, and mild. Yet the white settlers of Prince Albert rightly began to suspect that beneath his pious air he was meditating violence. In his own mind he was not ready to repeat the Red River adventure; he proposed only a demonstration to bring the government to its senses.

He may have overlooked and certainly refused to face the fact that Saskatchewan was not Red River. He had not rebelled at Fort Garry, for there had been no existing government to oppose. Saskatchewan was under established Canadian authority. Any attack on it would be rebellion. If Riel's deteriorating mind understood that, it had not realized Canada's new power in the West or the meaning of Van Horne's railway.

Thus by anger, by megalomania, and by his visions the prophet was dragged hourly deeper into his people's tragedy and his own.

On March 10, 1885, he ordered ten days of fasting and prayer to invite the will of God. As the Catholic priests of Batoche interpreted it, the will of God was against violence. They refused to bless the provisional government proclaimed by Riel. They threatened to withhold the sacraments from rebels.

The prophet rebuked the clergy as traitors, pulled Bourget's travel-worn letters from his pocket, and on their authority announced that he would perform the Mass himself. "Rome," he cried, "has fallen!"

His people were sorely troubled by this intricate theological dispute. They did not trust their priests less, but their prophet more. When, on March 18, they heard that 500 Mounted Police were coming to the prairies they decided to follow him.

Macdonald had recently moved to settle the land problem by the appointment of an investigating commission. He was too late. Already the Métis of Saskatchewan had seized their rifles, mounted their horses, galloped into Batoche, and demanded that Riel lead them. He was ready for his mission of madness. While Macdonald was telling Parliament that the disturbance out west was temporary and minor, Canada plunged overnight into civil war.

It was to be a minute war of few soldiers, about a hundred dead, some twoscore wounded, but it would finally confirm two continental facts and change the whole course of Canadian politics. The facts were that Van Horne's railway at last had established Canadian power from coast to coast; that the United States had abandoned for good the theory of forcible annexation. The consequences in Canadian politics were the ruin of Macdonald's government (though he would not live to see it); the repeated disaster of his party for the next half century; the triumph of his enemies; and, worst of all, a new antagonism between the two Canadian races.

And so the tragedy of Riel, the Métis, and the nation began at the village of Duck Lake in a spring snowstorm.

Dumont, the last Canadian master of frontier war, the Napoleon of the rebellion as Riel was its Robespierre, had hidden 200 sharpshooters, his entire army, on a hillside. A Mounted Police detachment of some hundred men, approaching in sleighs, found themselves ambushed by an unseen enemy and helpless before a deadly fire. Dumont, his scalp torn by a stray bullet, his eyes blinded by blood, coolly directed the battle, and with the aim of the surest marksman in the West picked off the easy red targets. Riel, on horseback, clutched aloft a wooden crucifix two feet long and prayed for guidance as the police bullets—an obvious miracle— whistled harmlessly by him.

The police, after half an hour of hopeless resistance, were lucky to escape in their sleighs. Dumont ordered his army to pursue and exterminate them. "In the name of God," shrieked the shaken prophet, "let them go! There's been too much bloodshed already."

There were, in fact, twelve policemen dead in the snow and eleven wounded out of ninety-nine; five Métis killed and three wounded out of two hundred. Small casualties, to be sure, but they announced a rebellion.

Riel might clutch his cross and pray, the Métis celebrate their victory with feasting at Duck Lake. There was no drawing back now. Old Tomorrow had another war on his hands. Canada remembered Red River and the murder of young Scott. The militia volunteers of Ontario clamored for action and revenge. The racial heart of Quebec went out to the half-breed French-Canadian Catholics of the West.

A raw Canadian army of 3,000 men was placed under the command of Major General Frederick D. Middleton, a brave, stuffy, and uninspired veteran of jungle warfare in India and New Zealand. He could easily subdue these miserable natives if he could only get at them, but they were half a continent away and no one proposed to repeat Wolseley's appalling overland march if it could be avoided.

It was Van Horne, no soldier but a supreme commander of men, who saw at once the way out of the nation's military dilemma and the threatened ruin of the C.P.R. With two days' notice, he told the government, he would guarantee to carry its troops to Saskatchewan in eleven days. That sounded ridiculous. The C.P.R. had not been finished around Lake Superior. The spring weather was colder than midwinter. No matter, said Van Horne, his promise stood and was accepted.

By bedding down the soldiers in hay-filled flatcars, hauling them by sleigh across the railway gaps, laying tracks on the snow and running locomotives over the ice of frozen rivers, he transported the army to Qu'Appelle, Saskatchewan, in less than eleven days.

Now the dullest man in Ottawa could see the miracle of the C.P.R. It was more than a steel track. It was the custodian of national power. As such it must be completed without delay. Macdonald got his appropriations through Parliament. The railway was rescued on the edge of collapse.

Middleton, however, had no interest in these dull political matters. Foolishly splitting his advance forces into two detachments of some five hundred men each, on either side of the South Saskatchewan, he marched toward Batoche and plunged into an ambush at Fish Creek.

There Dumont and fifty-four Métis, concealed in a gully, firing up at the Canadians against the skyline and chanting the old battle songs of France, taught the British general the old lesson of border war, reinforced by a bullet through his fur cap. His advance was stalled. Ten Canadians had been killed and forty wounded before the Métis withdrew with their four dead and two wounded. Dumont had won his second victory.

The prophet of Batoche meanwhile was establishing the Living

Catholic Apostolic and Vital Church of the New World and informing the frightened women and children of his miraculous discovery that they had nothing to fear from heresy, since hell might last millions of years but not forever.

The old nightmare of Indian massacre reappeared after long absence. The handsome and intelligent Indian chief, Poundmaker, had decided, at long and anxious tribal debate, to join Riel's rebellion and secure justice for his race. Some thousand Crees rode down on the white settlement of Battleford, west of Batoche, drove the inhabitants into the Mounted Police fort, looted the houses, danced in women's stolen gowns, and finally burned the town. Five hundred whites huddled within the palisades for a month, awaiting rescue.

The dozen settlers at Frog Lake, between Battleford and Edmonton, beheld a grisly spectacle on the morning of April 2. A priest celebrating the Mass in the village church found an Indian named Wandering Spirit on his knees before the altar, in a parody of devotion, a rifle grasped in his hand. His face was smeared with yellow war paint. His insolent stare never left the priest's eyes. Chief Big Bear and his braves, crowding the back of the church, watched in silence.

The dauntless priest took no notice of these intruders and quietly closed the service. As the congregation left the church and Big Bear vainly tried to hold the Indians in check, Wandering Spirit fired point-blank at the head of a Hudson's Bay agent. His bullet opened a general massacre. Nine men, women, and children were shot down in as many minutes. Only three of Frog Lake's population escaped. Wandering Spirit finished his work by dancing before the flames of the burned hamlet. He would soon dance again at the end of a rope.

The Mounted Police post of Fort Pitt—a few buildings without a palisade—was under the command of Inspector Francis Jeffrey Dickens, whose father's fiction was hardly more surprising than the adventures of the son.

Young Dickens had been afflicted by nervousness, deafness, an incurable stammer, and a red beard, but not by cowardice. A formidable Indian war party found him, twenty-two policemen, and a crowd of terrified civilians helpless in Fort Pitt. The civilians decided to surrender, on promise of safety. Dickens boldly led his men to a hastily built scow and carried them through the grinding spring ice, half frozen and under heavy fire, to the besieged fort of Battleford.

Middleton had recovered from the ambush of Fish Creek and was moving at last in a three-pronged offensive. He would take Batoche with 900 men. Lieutenant Colonel W. D. Otter, with 400, would relieve Battleford. Major General Bland Strange, with 600, would hold Edmonton in case of an Indian uprising there.

Strange found no serious trouble in the Northwest. Otter's march lifted the siege of Battleford, but when he attacked Poundmaker's Crees at Cut Knife Creek he barely managed to extricate his defeated army after seven hours of fighting.

So far the rebels had won every battle. Yet Dumont, that happy warrior, knew they were losing the war. Five hundred half-breed riflemen and a thousand Indians could not long withstand a nation of four million Canadians, who had twice resisted an American nation much more powerful. Still, by swift guerrilla attacks, he hoped to inflict heavy losses on the enemy. Riel, dreading more bloodshed, rejected this strategy and waited in Batoche for a miracle.

No miracle appeared; instead, only the clumsy, overloaded steamer *Northcote* wallowing laboriously down the shallow Saskatchewan, first and last ship of war to navigate the western prairies. She carried a strange cargo, including a company of Canadian volunteers, Lieutenant Hugh John Macdonald, son of the Canadian Prime Minister, Lieutenant Arthur L. Howard, of the Connecticut National Guard, and the beloved Gatling gun which he had brought all this way to be tested in a real war.

The end of the *Northcote,* despite Middleton's hopeful amphibious strategy, was inglorious. Dumont dropped a ferry cable in front of her, tore off her smokestack, and set her afire. She drifted out of control, stuck on a sandbank, and whistled plaintively for Middleton's assistance.

He was too busy now to answer her appeal. His army had reached the hill above the dusty little town of Batoche and began to destroy it systematically by shellfire. This was not so easy as the British general had supposed. His first advance down the hill was met by such an accurate fire from the invisible Métis gun pits that he ordered a quick retreat. It probably would have turned into a rout but for the Connecticut marksman and his Gatling gun.

No soldiers had ever fought better than Dumont's handful of half-breeds in the whole history of North American war. For four days, short of ammunition, knowing themselves doomed, they held off 900 men, armed with cannon, modern rifles, and the miraculous American machine gun. Their town was leveled behind them. Their wives and children hid in mud caves by the river. Riel, grasping his heavy wooden crucifix, prayed, exhorted, and dashed off a plea for assistance to the United States government. His message could not be taken through the Canadian lines. Chief Poundmaker and his Crees failed to arrive.

Middleton hesitated to attack for fear of heavy casualties. The disgusted Canadian volunteers agreed secretly to end this stalemate for themselves. Ordered to execute a short advance, they charged down the hill, deaf to their general's screams of protest, drove the Métis from the gun pits, and captured the town.

That was the end of the mad civil war, an end assured from the beginning.

Dumont tried to find Riel but he had disappeared somewhere in the confusion. Not to be taken alive, Dumont escaped on his horse and, by a long detour, reached safety in Montana. He did not learn until his arrival there that Riel had walked quietly into Middleton's tent and surrendered.

"How do you do, Mr. Riel? Pray be seated," said Middleton, correct to the last.

Poundmaker, Wandering Spirit, and their braves then appeared. Having first insulted Middleton with delicate irony, they laid down their arms. Only Big Bear remained at large, alone with his eight-year-old son in the northern bush and pursued for weeks by the Mounted Police.

Middleton, a systematic man, now reckoned up the war's casualties. Seventy whites were dead and thirty wounded. Some thirty-five Métis had been killed and eleven wounded. The Canadian government had spent $5,000,000 for its failure to understand the half-breed mind. That was only a first small installment on the ultimate cost to Macdonald's party and to Canada's racial unity.

In the newly built Mounted Police headquarters of a town called Pile o' Bones, but lately rechristened Regina, the trial of Louis Riel, American citizen, frontier statesman, prophet and beholder of visions, was the most remarkable and perhaps the most moving in the record of the North American West.

The stipendiary magistrate, the jury of six white men, and some of the ablest lawyers in Canada beheld a trapped and beaten man. But the visions had not quite left him. If he must die, Riel would die in dignity.

His defense rested entirely on the argument of his lawyers—retained by his friends in Quebec—that he was insane. He would not accept this last humiliation. Again and again he cried out that he was sane, that the stigma of madness must not be inflicted on his wife and children. His chief counsel could not restrain him and threatened to throw up his brief.

It was a pitiable business, this trial, in which all the formalities and real safeguards of British justice, transported across half a continent into a frontier barracks, could not hide the tragedy of doomed man and doomed race. And when the last witness had been heard, when the doctors had argued interminably that the prisoner was sane or insane, when he had delivered his last jumbled speech, madly protesting his sanity and his mission, when he had knelt in the prisoner's box and prayed in French and Latin for a final miracle, the jury retired and returned with a verdict of guilty.

The eyes of the civilized world were on the Regina barracks during those last months of Riel's life. Every avenue of appeal, to the Privy Council in London and to the Queen herself, was exhausted. American opinion was incensed, but the Washington government refused to intervene. Quebec was inflamed by the pending judicial murder of a French-Canadian and Catholic martyr. At a furious mass meeting in Montreal a young politician named Wilfrid Laurier declared that if he had lived on the banks of the Saskatchewan he, too, would have been proud to shoulder his musket with Riel, and in that single speech Laurier had made himself the future master of the nation.

Macdonald had seen enough of rebellion, on the St. Lawrence, on the Red River, and on the Saskatchewan. Whatever the consequences—and they were to be far larger than he dreamed—justice would be enforced. Riel had been judged in fair trial and must die. Perhaps justice, certainly the politics of English-speaking Canada, demanded his death.

He was ready to die. He had written a vain appeal to President Cleveland, denying Canada's legal title to the West and urging the United States to annex it. Fifteen years earlier Riel's government of Red River might have delivered the West to the United States. Now he was a helpless prisoner, convicted of treason, and the Americans had abandoned annexation. He had recanted his mission, confessed his sins to a friendly priest, returned to the Catholic faith, said farewell to his mother (his wife then lying ill at St. Boniface), and written a rambling testament to the Canadian people.

On a crisp November morning he mounted the gallows with firm step, a silver crucifix pressed to his lips, and was muttering the Lord's Prayer as the trap opened. A few nights later his friends carried his stiff and frozen body from a secret hiding place to one of Van Horne's boxcars. Riel traveled to a grave in his native St. Boniface on the railway which had smashed his rebellion and his nation.

Van Horne had no time to meditate long on these things. He was making his ultimate assault on the mountains and his American engineer, Major A. B. Rogers, had found a practicable pass through the Selkirks in the nick of time. Nothing could stop the C.P.R. now.

On November 7, 1885, in Eagle Pass, and at a point called Craigellachie, after the assembly place of Stephen's clan in Scotland, the last spike was driven home by Donald Smith. That spike, said Van Horne, was "just as good an iron one as any there is between Montreal and Vancouver," and no better.

As Van Horne watched critically, "Smith's blow merely turned the head of the spike over. Roadmaster F. P. Brothers yanked the twisted spike out and replaced it with another." Smith's clumsy hands managed to hit the second spike squarely. The bashful Van Horne was called upon for a speech and could only mutter that "the work has been well done in every way."

Well done, indeed. Van Horne's ten-year contract was complete in five. The shores of Canada were joined. The Northwest Passage was open after three centuries of labor.

When the first wood-burning locomotive labored down from the mountains to the sea, it carried a curious freight, including the dreams of countless Canadians from Champlain onward. Now at last, as never until that day, a Canadian nation could be pronounced viable. Like the railway that spanned it, the nation had crossed what appeared to be its final watershed and anchored the boundary for good and all. But there were other daunting watersheds to cross. And the boundary was not quite fixed.

30

Soft Voice, Big Stick

[1855–1904]

T HE YOUNG TWENTIETH CENTURY FOUND A NEW GIANT ON EITHER side of the border. The American was resolved to speak softly and carry a big stick. The Canadian spoke softly also but, as he would soon find, had no stick to carry. Two men could not have been more unlike in look, in character, and in philosophy than Theodore Roosevelt and Wilfrid Laurier. Their collision was inevitable.

Roosevelt's short, burly figure, massive Dutch head and familiar grin, his courage and friendliness, his unquestioning faith in his nation and himself, his assured optimism in human affairs and his determination to improve them, stood as the bridge between the two centuries, ushering out the old and welcoming the new with huge and boyish gusto. In him the American people had reproduced their accurate image, an average American writ large.

Laurier's Old World elegance—the tall, slender body, the plume of white curls, the sensitive and beautiful face, the delicate hands —his immaculate speech, his scholarship, and his air of grandeur were all French. His mind was all Canadian. The accident of birth on the St. Lawrence, among French Canadians who had lived there for nearly three hundred years, had placed him in a limited area, but nature had equipped him with all the native qualities of greatness, and, in addition, a streak of Machiavellian subtlety, a certain polished ruthlessness useful to a master of politics. In any country, large or small, he, like Roosevelt, would have risen to the top. He was born to rise.

Yet the climb had been slow. It began in Riel's Saskatchewan rebellion. No doubt political calculation would have directed that course in any case, but he had rushed to the defense of the French-

421

Canadian and Catholic rebel by sheer racial instinct. A little enclave
of his own people out west had been mistreated by the national
government, their prophet had been sentenced to hang in Regina,
the British conqueror, in the latest incarnation of Macdonald, was
reasserting the conquest. The young Montreal lawyer dared to say
in public that the Métis had a case, that he would have fought with
them on the banks of the Saskatchewan.

Spiritually Laurier's reaction to the rebellion may have been
automatic. Politically it was a master stroke. It made him the spokes-
man and would soon make him the father image of the French-
Canadian people. For some time, however, the future master of
Canada lingered in obscurity, under the restless shadow of Blake,
the Liberal Party's ill-starred leader. While Laurier aroused Parliament now and then with oratory such as it had never heard before
and probably would never hear again, brooded over musty books in
the library or lolled in the House of Commons, his long finger
tracing out the words of an English dictionary (his favorite literature), the Macdonald government was dying.

To Laurier, who succeeded Blake, its death was unconscionably
prolonged, its narrow escapes at the polls unjust and inexplicable.
It was dying, nevertheless, and its quarrel with the French-Canadian race, in the execution of Riel, had inflicted a deep, enduring
wound on the future of the Conservative Party. Only two Conservative governments of brief tenure would be elected in the nearly
sixty years from 1896 onward.

The happy twilight of Macdonald's career did not reveal the
barren road ahead. So long as he lived his government and party
lived with him. He was the institution which the courtly French
Canadian on the opposition benches would become. He hardly
needed to fight any more. His lieutenants could carry the struggle
of Parliament while he capped their arguments with some jaunty
witticism and rested securely on his past triumphs.

Few men seemed to notice that his raillery and the government's
confident exterior covered a growing vacuum of ideas and policies.
That few included one of the greatest of all Canadians—a giant of
tousled red hair and rough-hewn face named John Wesley Dafoe,
who had just arrived from a log schoolroom in Bully's Acre, up the
Ottawa, and would go on to become the nation's leading journalist
and, in time, its conscience. The youthful Dafoe entered the Ottawa
press gallery as a hereditary Conservative. After listening to Macdonald and Laurier in the unequal struggle of debate, he became
the hot-gospeler of liberalism and the chief advocate of free trade
in the economy of North America.

Macdonald, even in old age, had never quite made up his mind on that issue. He had announced the National Policy because he could not wring reciprocity from the United States, but he was always ready to reverse himself if the chance offered. The chance was never offered in his time.

Though the United States had outlived its old feeling of hostility toward Canada and the annexation fever of the sixties and seventies was replaced by solid friendship, the protectionist system designed to restrict trade across the border was not relaxed. If Canada refused political union, why should it be granted, gratis, the benefits of the American market? What mind in Washington could foresee the day, not far off, when Canada would be the United States' largest customer and essential source of foreign supplies?

Senator John Sherman no doubt spoke for a large group of thoughtful Americans when he said, in 1888: "Our whole history since the conquest of Canada by Great Britain in 1763 has been a continuous warning that we cannot be at peace with each other except by political as well as commercial union. . . . This union is one of the events that must inevitably come in the future; it will come by the logic of the situation, and no politician or combination of politicians can prevent it."

Such men did not know Macdonald or Canada. They did not know Laurier either—the Canadian who would attempt commercial union and wreck his government on Canada's fear of resulting political union.

Meanwhile the United States was doing very well behind its tariff walls. Its exports to Canada quadrupled in the last thirty years of the century. It bought hardly more than half as much from Canada and bought mainly raw industrial materials that it could not conveniently produce itself. This adverse trade balance supplied the best argument for Macdonald's tariff retaliation, since, as he said, "we can ring the changes on National Policy, paying the United States in their own coin etc." This he continued to do with a wizard's touch.

Still, remembering Brown's humiliating failure to secure a new trade deal at Washington, Macdonald always kept the door open to any new American proposal. His tariff law permitted the government to remove duties on natural products whenever the United States did the same. Reciprocity thus remained a nostalgic memory in Canada and the National Policy an unavoidable, inferior alternative. Could reciprocity ever be revived? That seemed unlikely, but there were two men who would try to revive it—Laurier in Canada and William Howard Taft in the United States. They would fail.

The inferior alternative of the National Policy, to tell the truth, was not working out exactly as Macdonald had hoped. It could not in a world depression. The railway had been finished, but the West did not fill up. After a brief boom, hard times returned. The farmers, who paid the tariff but as exporters got no protection from it, were growing restive. The Maritimes were prostrate. Nova Scotia was talking of secession from a Canada which divorced it from its natural markets in New England. The provinces were quarreling with the Federal government. A nation not yet twenty years old looked already exhausted.

Macdonald made up his mind, in the midst of Riel's rebellion, to risk one more attempt at a sensible trade bargain in Washington. The expiration of the fisheries agreement arranged at the Washington Conference gave him the chance.

President Cleveland seemed willing to broaden the new fishery negotiations to include trade in general, he encouraged the Canadian government in preliminary private discussions, but when a formal conference opened in 1887 he was quarreling with a protectionist Congress and could offer no change of tariff policy. Fisheries alone would be considered, and even the new agreement on that narrow issue was rejected by the Senate, mainly because it involved free trade in Canadian fish in return for American fishing rights on the Canadian coast.

Protectionism in the United States appeared stronger than ever. A few intellectuals in both countries still agitated for a North American customs union and that imported British oracle, Goldwin Smith, continued to assure Canada that its economic and political future lay inevitably within the United States, but these theories soon encountered the hard facts of American politics, and the brutal McKinley tariff of 1890.

Economic continentalism refused to die, however; the Liberal Party still stood for "unrestricted reciprocity," whatever that might mean, and the Canadian government was in trouble. Having promised to make some dent in the American tariff and failed, Macdonald executed another of his skilled somersaults by denouncing the Liberal pledge of reciprocity as surrender of the nation's political independence. On that issue he decided to stake his last election.

As the old man staggered through the winter campaign of 1891 he saw not only his government but his lifework in peril. "Shall we endanger our possession of the great heritage bequeathed to us by our fathers . . . with the prospect of ultimately becoming a portion of the American Union? . . . as for myself, my course is clear. A British subject I was born—a British subject I will die. With my utmost effort, with my latest breath, will I oppose the veiled treason which attempts by sordid means and mercenary proffers to lure our people from their allegiance."

That might be campaign oratory, but it struck deep and reached the vitals of Canadian life. If the people believed that the issue was Canadian nationality, there could be no doubt of their answer.

It was hard to return a government in these dark and bitter times—impossible, indeed, without Macdonald's three major assets. Above all, he was himself the image and, as it seemed, almost the creator of nationality. He had become less man than myth. Secondly, his opponent, the young Laurier, was little known outside Quebec and his Liberal Party was inwardly split on reciprocity. Blake refused to run because he agreed on this issue with Macdonald, his old enemy, and could offer Laurier nothing but his silence.

Finally, by one of those happy strokes of chance which had saved him so often before, Macdonald carried with him to the hustings a remarkable document, the stolen proof of a pamphlet printed secretly, in only twelve copies, by Edward Farrer, editor of the Toronto *Mail*. In it Farrer, a leading advocate of reciprocity, outlined the steps by which the United States might successfully lure Canada into commercial and then political union. It was not much of a pamphlet, it certainly did not represent the views of Laurier or the Liberal Party, but it was good enough for one election.

These three weapons Macdonald wielded with the last dwindling strength of his nearly seventy-six years. From province to province and town to town he somehow dragged his sick old body, joked as usual, drank, thundered, and in public seemed as good as ever, but the rusty sword had worn out the scabbard. He won his election singlehanded and it killed him. When they took his body back to Kingston, his government and party also were ready for burial. But not his National Policy or his dream.

The verdict of 1891 apparently had destroyed unrestricted reciprocity for all visible time. The gloomy Blake emerged from his silence to agree with Macdonald that the tariff policy of the Liberal Party did mean annexation. Laurier's sensitive fingers quietly dropped that hot political cinder.

Reciprocity was not dead, after all. It was only sleeping and would awaken, at Laurier's touch, exactly twenty years hence to destroy him.

The election appeared accidental at the moment—the accident of Farrer's pamphlet and the last dying prodigy of Old Tomorrow. It was no accident. As Macdonald had known all along, as Laurier would discover too late, the theory of economic continentalism must founder on the fact of political division. The Canadian people voted, as they would vote again on the same issue, against any policy, however sound in economics, which seemed to threaten their national independence. Macdonald had skillfully managed and the Liberals had clumsily tampered with something much more potent than economics—the instincts of a race.

Even Macdonald's skill and his opponents' blunder could postpone the inevitable for only five years. Three successors each tried in vain to replace the Old Tomorrow magic until Tupper was called home from England to perform the final obsequies of the government. It finally floundered into the Manitoba School Question and its end was assured by a cruel paradox.

The Manitoba Legislature established a system of nonsectarian schools; the Catholic Church challenged the provincial statute; the case entered years of complex litigation; the Federal government at last decided to back the church, coerce Manitoba, and thus lay the ghost of Riel by a reconciliation with Quebec.

This was an act of courage. It seemed to be also a subtle stroke of politics. Unfortunately the government had underestimated Laurier and misunderstood his French-Canadian people. Knowing that he could hold Quebec on any policy, he supported the provincial rights of Manitoba and made himself the champion of Protestant English-speaking Canada. As he foresaw, Quebec voted for him because he was its son and idol. He broke the Conservatives' hold on the other provinces because they saw in him a Catholic able to resist the hierarchy and because they were tired of an aged ministry. Seldom had a circle been squared so neatly. This contest of race and religion had an added advantage for the Liberal Party—it submerged the issue of reciprocity and the fatal mistake of 1891. The poll of 1896 carried Laurier triumphantly into office.

The majestic figure in pearl-gray top hat and tail coat towered unchallengeable over Ottawa. His political breach with the church was quickly forgiven. His own people were solidly behind him on any policy he cared to follow. Quebec had never forgotten the hanging at Regina nor forgiven the Conservative Party, which permitted it. That racial anger would linger on for years yet, would repeatedly defeat the Conservatives, elect the Liberals, and yet in his final tragedy would destroy Laurier's power.

Laurier thus could introduce an era of ease and elegance unknown before to the brawling politics of Canada and soon fulfilling —so subtly that it passed unnoticed—the classic dictum of John W.

Dafoe: That power turns any prime minister into an autocrat as surely as a diet of royal jelly turns an ordinary bee into a queen.

Ottawa's beehive buzzed pleasantly and swarmed with many strange inmates destined to leave their several marks on the continental border. The foremost Canadian figure of the future was then a moon-faced college boy named William Lyon Mackenzie King, grandson of Mackenzie the rebel. Young King already had sensed the flavor as he would later gorge upon the substance of royal jelly. At the moment he was receiving his first lessons on the problems of the border from Goldwin Smith, who assured him that they would be solved by nature's laws and political union.

A boy of fourteen, Franklin Delano Roosevelt, lived in the Hudson River aristocracy of Hyde Park and seemed unlikely to rise above it. But the lives of these two youths had a rendezvous with destiny, oddly enough at the St. Lawrence town of Ogdensburg.

Their generation was a long way from power yet.

Meanwhile Laurier was outwardly the antithesis of Macdonald. The earthy, hard-drinking, skeptical Protestant of Scottish blood was replaced by a French-Canadian Catholic of lofty mind, austere habits, and gentle speech.

A second look showed, even in appearance, a curious resemblance between these human opposites. Their lean figures, their mass of curly hair cut in the same fashion, their stylish clothes, and their genial manners were strangely alike.

The likeness was deeper than their friends suspected. It went to the heart of politics. Before he had finished Laurier would be compelled, while always denouncing Macdonald's methods, to imitate them; while always attacking his policies, to follow them; while always deploring the weaknesses of humanity and the dismal side of politics, to accept them.

All that was inevitable. For beneath the surface of politics and the quarrels of election campaigns both these men and all their successors must grapple with exactly the same facts of Canadian life and necessarily reach almost identical conclusions.

Nowhere was that logic so apparent as in the case of the continental boundary and the trade flowing across it.

Unrestricted reciprocity, which had carried the Liberals to defeat in 1891, was quietly dropped because, as Laurier blandly observed, the Canadian people apparently didn't want it. Anyway, Canada no longer required such painful remedies. The world had emerged from a long period of hard times. It was hungry for Canada's raw materials.

Laurier's long reign, therefore, opened in the sunshine of a boom

and the government, of course, claimed most of the credit before it
would begin to influence events. The future looked so bright as the
twentieth century approached that Laurier said it would belong to
Canada. His hope was to be deferred and sometimes mocked but,
long after its author's death, would be substantially vindicated
within his meaning.

The first Liberal budgets altered the emphasis, not the contents
of Canadian trade policy. A final offer of tariff reduction was made
to the United States. As anticipated, it was rejected by the McKinley
government, for the Republicans had promised to fill the American
dinnerpail with the plenty of protectionism and were now contriving the sky-high duties of the Dingley Tariff.

Laurier did not propose to invite another rebuff. There would be,
he said, no more "missions to Washington." Not long ago, he added,
"The market of the great cities of the Union was the only market
we had for any of our products. But, thank Heaven, those days are
past and over now!"

His view would change later. For the moment the government
reduced the Canadian tariff within narrow limits while making
appropriate gestures toward the distant goal of free trade; granted
Britain a substantial tariff preference; and significantly dropped
from the law the long-standing offer of reciprocity to the United
States. With only a slight change, Macdonald's National Policy had
been confirmed by its old enemies because it was more than a
policy—it was a fact of continental life and must remain so as long
as the United States insisted on splitting the continent into two
economic segments. And when the United States finally changed its
mind the change would come too late.

Nevertheless, behind the uninterrupted tariff contest, the American and Canadian economies were being steadily integrated in a
rough, makeshift, and piecemeal fashion. Canada continued to sell
almost half its exports to its neighbor and only a little more to
Britain. The United States was becoming yearly more dependent
on certain raw and semi-raw Canadian materials, like metals and
forest products, especially newsprint. American manufacturers were
breaking a hole through the tariff wall by establishing branch factories north of the border to supply the growing Canadian market,
American capital was investing heavily in Canadian industry.

Such methods enabled the United States to have something like
the best of two possible worlds. It could tap the Canadian products
it required without admitting inconveniently competitive goods. It
could share the Canadian boom without any political responsibility
in a foreign country. The first continental fact of political division

remained and the United States at last was reconciled to it. The second continental fact of natural economic unity was oozing through the artificial tariff barriers.

Full economic sanity in America was a long way off, to be sure, and might never be reached since, in Canadian eyes, it seemed to involve political union and, in America, to imperil prosperity. Political sanity, at least, had dawned.

As the twentieth century opened, memories of the old quarrels were fading. Once the fact of Canadian sovereignty was finally admitted by the United States, the two nations rapidly learned to live as friends. An era of goodwill unique in human history had begun. It was the richest era that either nation had ever known.

Laurier's affairs floated on a flood tide. He had found in William Stevens Fielding, the little gray premier of Nova Scotia, a competent director of the nation's finance; in Clifford Sifton, a young prairie lawyer of iron look and will, perhaps the ablest Canadian organizing brain since Talon. The Prime Minister dwelt in a higher sphere of politics, with a strong aversion to facts and figures. Fielding managed the budget and the tariff. Sifton proceeded to revolutionize the West.

After three hundred years of white man's labor, the West was still virtually unpopulated, a vacuum cut by a lonely line of steel. It would remain empty unless wheat would grow on the semi-arid plains and mature in a brief summer season. That problem had been solved by a little-noted miracle or accident.

In the spring of 1843, Duncan Fife, a farmer living near Peterborough, Ontario, asked his neighbor, George Essen, who was visiting England, to send him some samples of wheat. Essen forgot his promise until he was about to sail for Canada. Observing a foreign grain ship at the Glasgow docks, Essen begged a handful of wheat from her captain and carried it to Peterborough. Fife sowed this seed but only three sprouts appeared. They were enough to change the history of the West. For those sprouts ripened ten days earlier than any wheat ever harvested in Canada, and ten days was the margin between the early frost of the prairies and a mature crop.

Thus arrived on the North American earth—its origin never discovered—the wheat called Red Fife. Crossed with other varieties from all over the world, it produced the early-maturing Marquis strain at the very moment when Canada undertook to populate the West. Fife, the forgotten bush farmer of Ontario, had served his country better than many of its famous statesmen and soldiers. Their policies and conquests might pass. Fife's wheat, and its offspring, would always grow between the Great Lakes and the mountains.

The ensuing wheat boom, by which the Laurier government fleshed the skeleton of Macdonald's transcontinental state, was organized by young Sifton as a single gigantic business. He scoured Britain, Europe, and the United States for immigrants. While he preferred British and American settlers, he regarded "a stalwart European peasant in a sheep-skin coat . . . with a stout wife and half-a-dozen children [as] good quality." European peasants, over sixty thousand of them between 1898 and 1904, poured into the prairies and plowed them. More than twice as many immigrants came from Britain, nearly three times as many from the United States.

This was not only a transatlantic but a major continental migration. The free lands of the United States frontier were now taken up. Land hungry, as always, the American farmer turned north to a virgin frontier, quickly forgot an imaginary political line and became a Canadian. The human current of America, flowing ceaselessly for three centuries, suddenly reversed itself. It had flowed north out of New England into Canada after the British conquest. Then it had turned south as the impoverished Canadians of the nineteenth century sought wealth in the booming United States. Now the tide set northward again. Expatriates came home and with them Americans at the rate of nearly fifty thousand a year—a mere trickle in American measurement, a revolution in Canadian.

The West filled up so fast that the C.P.R. soon could not carry all its grain. The elevators were bursting. The Great Lakes and Atlantic ports were jammed with ships. The farmers' appetite for goods created a new industrial complex in the St. Lawrence Valley. Finally the Laurier government—whose party had attacked Macdonald's C.P.R. as madness—subsidized two more transcontinental railways at far larger cost.

For the first time it dawned on the United States that an almost independent state and a thriving economic system lived on its flank and probably would remain there.

This fact had some disadvantages. It fastened down the northern rim of Manifest Destiny for good unless the United States resorted to war, and that was now unthinkable. Moreover, the Canadians appeared much more difficult to deal with, in their affairs of vital self-interest, than distant and pliable British negotiators had ever been. The United States government deliberately discouraged Canada's increasing independence and much preferred to deal with Ottawa through the easier-going channels of London, where British statesmen had long since recognized American friendship as the first premise of foreign policy.

That shortsighted American view soon passed as the advantages of a strong Canada revealed themselves. People able to manage half the continent in their own way, to exploit its resources for United States' benefit as well as their own, to assist at least in the continent's defense and willing to be good neighbors, offered the United States probably its largest asset outside its own boundaries. Knowledge of that asset grew slowly, would not be complete even half a century hence, but it was growing. Nothing could stop it, or the growth of Canada.

Still, many fag ends of old border disputes remained unsettled as Roosevelt's soft voice boomed through the White House and his big stick appeared in such odd places as the Isthmus of Panama and the seashore of Alaska.

The Maritime fisheries question had dragged on interminably. It had been settled in 1871 but the agreement of the Washington Conference was abrogated by the United States ten years later and Canada began to seize American vessels fishing illegally in its waters. A new agreement was rejected by the Senate in 1888. By this time, however, American fishermen were losing their interest in the old fishing grounds. Anyway, Canada admitted them by a temporary licensing system, renewed year by year. Finally, in 1909, all these tangled legal issues were submitted to the Hague Tribunal, whose compromise judgments resulted three years later in a Permanent Mixed Fisheries Commission able to settle existing and future disputes. The United States' sensible attempt to conserve the seal herds of the North Pacific, outside the territorial waters of Alaska, involved long arguments with other interested nations and was not settled until 1911, when the United States, Britain, Canada, Russia, and Japan agreed to share the sealing industry.

Much more important in an expanding continent was the control of waters running across the Canadian-American boundary. To solve this problem the two nations invented the International Joint Commission of 1909. It was to deal specifically with boundary waters, but by consent any other question could be submitted to it. This extraordinary new instrument—probably the most successful in the record of international relations—was even more important than it looked. It revealed at once, in the unanimous findings of three American and three Canadian members, how disputes could be settled amicably by friends and by the increasing will on both sides to settle them.

Fisheries, sealing regulations, use of boundary waters, and many other matters of less difficulty were adjusted, or on their way to adjustment, before the century was three years old. The big un-

settled issue—far bigger for Canada, Britain, and the Commonwealth than the United States could imagine—was the boundary of
Alaska. Its settlement, apparently a technical question of legal
documents and surveyors' calculations, was to prove a watershed in
the affairs of the British peoples. And on the affairs of North America it would leave an enduring scar.

Theodore Roosevelt was not the first president to interest himself
in the vague boundaries of Seward's northern purchase. He was the
first to decide that they must be fixed—and on American terms.
Since 1821, when Russia tried to close Bering's Sea, Alaska had
remained a secondary point of contention among the Great Powers.
Roosevelt was determined to end this wrangle forthwith.

A treaty of 1824 fixed 54:40 north latitude as the line between
Russian Alaska and the United States' ambitions on the Pacific coast.
That line was inherited by the United States with the title deeds
bought by Seward. What of the line between Alaska and Britain's
interior possessions directly eastward of the Panhandle?

A British-Russian treaty of 1825 attempted to define this
boundary. It began at Prince of Wales Island, followed the Portland
Canal to the 56th Parallel and then "the summit of the n ountains
situated parallel to the coast" to 141° longitude which carried it to
the Arctic Ocean. If the mountain summit proved to be more than
ten marine leagues (about thirty-five miles) from the coast, the
boundary would parallel "the windings of the coast and shall never
exceed the distance of ten marine leagues therefrom."

Though this arbitrary arrangement, like others in America, was
made in ignorance of geography, it caused little trouble until gold
was discovered on the Stikine River, in 1872, and in the Klondike
twenty-four years later. As Alaska and Yukon Territory beside it
evidently contained richer treasure than the old Russian fur trade,
the United States and Canada must determine where their zones of
power, and profit, lay.

The United States controlled the seacoast. The gold rush must
pass through American territory to the Yukon, owned by Canada.
A half dozen Northwest Mounted Police faced, in 1896, the first
wave of gold seekers trickling through the coastal mountains into
Canadian territory and at Ottawa Laurier faced a quarrel with
the United States.

Sifton, Laurier's young minister of the interior, set out next spring
to see the North for himself. He conceived an all-Canadian route
into the Yukon via the Stikine (where Canada had navigation
rights) and a railway from its headwaters, but hoped that the
United States would give Canada a port on the Panhandle coast.

Meanwhile he instructed his police to hold the mountain range because, in the Canadian view, it marked the legal eastern boundary of the Panhandle.

The United States replied that the mountains mentioned in the 1825 treaty did not exist, that the boundary lay at Lake Bennett, thirty-five miles from Dyea. "The difficulty," wrote Sifton, "was that the officers of the United States Government asserted their jurisdiction down to and including the lower half of Lake Bennett, and a military force of the United States Army was being detailed to go to Skagway. This force was gathered at Portland, and in another ten days would have been in possession of the territory down to Lake Bennett, and it would have taken twenty years of negotiating to get them out, in fact I doubt if we would ever have got them out. To prevent the loss of territory I sent secret orders to Major Perry to . . . plant out posts in the Passes just under the Summit, and had them there with a supply of provisions before the other party knew what we were doing. It is a case of possession being ten points in the law, and we intend to hold possession."

A handful of Mounted Police thus watched the rush of '98 tramping through the Chilkoot Pass. The United States charged customs duties or inspection fees, collected in the Alaska ports, on the outfits of foreign miners to protect the lucrative business of Seattle. Canadian business, in Victoria, anxious to share this trade, clamored for reprisals and urged Sifton to close the trails against Americans and American goods. Sifton denounced this proposal as "unprecedented" and "highhanded." He said the American authorities in Alaska were generally co-operative and he pleaded for patience. But obviously Canada and the United States had moved uncomfortably close to a dangerous incident. To forestall it, the line of the boundary must be fixed.

All previous efforts to fix it had failed through twenty years of sporadic negotiation and *ad hoc* arrangements.

In 1898 Canada suggested to the Joint High Commission, then considering other border problems, that the Alaska Panhandle boundary should follow the general curve of the coast, cutting across the heads of the long fiords. This would give Canada a port on Lynn Canal and direct access to the Yukon.

The United States would hear of no such arbitrary arrangement, it stuck to the letter of the old treaty and "the windings of the coast," but it was ready to consider a Canadian port at Pyramid Harbor on a fifty-year lease. Even that compromise brought angry protests from the interested Pacific Coast states, while Canada wanted more than temporary tenure.

Britain (still in charge of Canada's foreign affairs) suggested arbitration. After all, had not President Cleveland recently compelled Britain to arbitrate the boundary of Venezuela and British Guiana?

Besides, there was the matter of the Panama Canal, where Britain had behaved, as it thought, with extreme generosity to the United States. By the Clayton-Bulwer Treaty of 1850 the two nations undertook to build and operate the canal jointly, but by the Hay-Pauncefote Treaty of 1900 Britain (then strained by the South African War) abandoned those rights. Surely, thought London and Ottawa, the United States owed them a little gratitude in Alaska?

Roosevelt felt no such obligation. "Our case," he wrote afterwards, "was ironclad, and the chief need was a mixture of unyielding firmness in essentials and a good-humored courtesy in *everything!*" The Canadians, on the other hand, had come "dangerously near blackmail" in the Yukon when real trouble with the United States "would be death to them." The President, therefore, would consider neither a negotiated compromise nor a settlement by arbitration.

He proposed, instead, a mixed "judicial tribunal" consisting of "six impartial jurists of repute, who shall consider judicially the questions submitted to them, each of whom shall first subscribe an oath that he will impartially consider the arguments and evidence presented to the tribunal, and will decide thereupon according to his true judgment."

Since friendship with the United States was the highest priority in its foreign policy, Britain accepted Roosevelt's proposal in the convention of 1903. Laurier knew at once that these polite arrangements would probably mean another surrender of Canadian interests. The judicial commission, said Sifton, "was agreed to, simply to give effect to a decision which had already, in fact, been made. The proceedings from the American point of view were to be simply a matter of form."

There was no doubt about that from the beginning. Roosevelt had made up his mind to enforce the original boundary definition to the letter, to gain a maximum strip of territory in the Panhandle, and to bar Canada from the coast. "In the principle involved," he said, "there will of course be no compromise."

To make sure of it, he instructed the War Department to send more troops to southern Alaska "as quietly and unostentatiously as possible," and he packed the committee of "impartial jurists" with three Americans who were already committed fully and publicly to his views. They were Elihu Root, Secretary of War, Senator Henry Cabot Lodge, and Senator George Turner, of Washington State.

Only on the assurance that these men would not yield an inch of territory did the Senate ratify an arrangement which looked crudely biased even to John Hay, Secretary of State.

"When," wrote Lodge, "Mr. Hay heard of the three men whom the President had selected he was extremely displeased and protested in the strongest way to the President against Mr. Root, and even more strongly against me, taking the ground that our opinions were already well known, which was also true of Senator Turner."

The Canadian government was simultaneously protesting to London and was blandly assured that "it would be useless to press the United States to withdraw the names put forward." Britain thereupon ratified the agreement without waiting for Canada's consent.

Laurier (who had accepted the mixed tribunal against his own inclinations and a previous promise to Sifton) was furious but powerless. London insisted that no discourtesy to Canada had been intended and was surprised, in the loftiest British manner, at the Canadian objection. Since it had decided to yield to the United States for imperial reasons, far more important than a few acres of Canadian snow and placer gold, the best Britain could do was to appoint two Canadians, Sir Louis Jetté and A. B. Aylesworth, to the British panel of three. The third was the unhappy Lord Alverstone, Lord Chief Justice of England, an eminent jurist but in this assignment inevitably an agent of British policy. And thus the "judicial" settlement got under way in London, with Lodge industriously managing the American and Sifton the Canadian case.

Lodge was being prodded, quite unnecessarily, by his president. On July 16 Roosevelt wrote that the dispute must be settled before the Congress met in November, or otherwise he must recommend appropriate action. The "last chance" of agreement "by the free act of both parties" would soon pass. In Lodge's judgment, however, the Canadian representatives were so "perfectly stupid" that "they seem to fail utterly to see that a disagreement deprives them of their only chance to get out of the matter creditably." Since they could not win against the solid American panel, they should be intelligent enough to pretend that they agreed with the inevitable decision, thus avoiding the stigma of defeat.

Things were not going well in London. On August 30 Lodge had abandoned hope of Canadian intelligence. Would Alverstone prove equally stupid? "Very possibly," said Lodge, Alverstone would vote with the Americans, yet "England is in such mortal terror of Canada that I feel more than doubtful in regard to it!"

Roosevelt was growing doubtful also. He decided to use Mr. Justice Oliver Wendell Holmes as a private messenger to the British government. Holmes was told in a candid letter from the President that, failing agreement, he would ask authority from the Congress "to run the line as we claim it by our own people, without any further regard to the attitude of England and Canada," and would support this enterprise with American troops. Roosevelt added: "If you happen to meet Chamberlain again you are entirely at liberty to tell him what I say, although of course it must be privately and unofficial."

Holmes showed the President's letter to Joseph Chamberlain, the British Colonial Secretary. The British government now realized what it was up against in Washington and, as Roosevelt said later, it "tipped the wink to the Chief Justice," Alverstone.

The President and his impartial jurists would not have been so troubled if they had seen Sifton's private dispatches to Laurier. Sifton knew in advance that he was beaten: "The British Government deliberately decided about a year ago to sacrifice our interests at any cost for the sake of pleasing the United States. All their proceedings since that time were for the sake of inveigling us into a position from which we could not retire. I am bound to say that we have been pretty easy prey, but the result probably would have been the same in any event, as it simply gets down to a very narrow question. The United States would not recede, and England would not take any chances of a quarrel.

"It is, however, the most cold-blooded case of absolutely giving away our interests, without even giving us the excuse of saying we have had a fight for it, which I know of. . . . It may just as well be decided in advance that practically whatever the United States demands from England will be conceded in the long run, and the Canadian people might as well make up their minds to that now."

The method of settlement justified Canada's anger, but anger did not make a case in law. The United States' case, indeed, was so good in law that it hardly required Roosevelt's big stick and soft voice. The Canadian case, while it might be sound in politics and good-neighborliness, was based more on a reasonable interpretation of the 1825 treaty than on its letter.

According to the Canadian view, the old treaty meant that the Panhandle boundary would not run anywhere more than ten marine leagues from the sea and, in common sense, should not follow every sinuosity of the coast. Certainly where an obvious mountain summit existed close to the sea it should form the boundary, as the treaty provided. If that version was accepted, Canada would have a seaport on Lynn Canal and that, in fact, was all it really wanted.

The United States had bought Alaska from Russia and Russia

had never intended to allow any settlement on the coast. Russia had always bottled up the Hudson's Bay Company in the interior and would never yield its position under strong British pressure. Official maps, in Russia and Britain, showed the boundary skirting the coastal inlets and confirming the American case.

Alverstone was too experienced a lawyer to imagine that he was dealing with only a legal case. He knew he was the fulcrum of a contest between two great powers. His Canadian colleagues in the tribunal demanded that he support them. His own government was determined to defeat them. Torn between Canadian and imperial interests, he tried to patch up a compromise. The United States, he suggested, might receive an unbroken coastline if it did not insist on its *lisière* being everywhere thirty-five miles wide and if Canada were given four little islands, supposed to be strategically important, at the mouth of the Portland Canal.

Clearly the possibility of war in the future weighed on some of the minds assembled in London.

The Americans replied that they would withdraw before agreeing to narrow the Panhandle, but in the end accepted the line patiently worked out by the Chief Justice and agreed also to let Canada have two of the worthless islands. Such sops failed to satisfy the Canadians. The Alverstone line, Sifton wrote, was "drawn so far back that the United States gets practically all she seriously contended for." What Canada wanted was a coastal port, and Alverstone could not hope to squeeze that out of the United States in its present humor.

The Canadians, new to international politics, might be surprised at these maneuvers and angry at their own impotence in the solemn charade of London; in actual fact Canada had collided not with a question of contract but with the only Great Power of the continent, and Laurier with a president who intended to exercise that power as he saw fit. In the *réal politique* of power, disguised by ceremonial gestures and "good-humored courtesy in *everything*," what could Canada expect but the loss of a case questionable in law and rejected by both England and the United States regardless of its possible merits?

Few Canadians stopped to realize that they were witnessing, on the Alaska boundary, the emergence of another primary continental fact. Roosevelt might brandish his big stick, he might threaten to run the boundary as he chose, failing an agreement he might pack the jury and even order troops to Alaska, but the United States had actually renounced war against Canada as unthinkable. And this fact was hardly forty years old.

In any case, the United States could not lose the dispute in London. At worst it could only face a stalemate, since its three representatives would not compromise. The two Canadians, at best, could only hope for such a stalemate, provided Alverstone stood with them.

Everything thus depended upon the lonely British jurist—on his sense of politics more than his sense of law. Given the British government's policy of agreement with the United States, at almost any cost, the outcome could not be doubted.

Alverstone voted with the Americans, who accepted his line. The Canadians refused to sign the verdict. The Panhandle, inlets and all, belonged to the United States. Canada's North was isolated from the sea.

Roosevelt at once revealed, in a momentary indiscretion, that the proceedings of London had not been judicial or impartial. The award, he said, was the greatest American diplomatic success in a generation. It was precisely that.

Neither London nor Washington saw then the price that must be paid for a simple deal in power politics.

The price paid by Britain was immediate and massive. By approving the Alaska Boundary Award it had undermined, more than by any previous event, Canada's confidence in the government of the motherland. Canadians' anger was directed at London rather than Washington. They had expected nothing better from the Americans. They had not expected (save for a few insiders like Sifton) what they considered a betrayal by the British.

Yet for Canada there were large gains to be set against the losses. Defeat on the northern boundary stimulated Canadian nationalism even more than the annexation fever of the sixties and seventies on the southern boundary. When Britain clearly would not protect Canada's interests if they conflicted with those of the United States, Canada must protect them itself. And whereas anger against American invaders and raiders had quickly cooled, Canada's new determination to manage its own foreign affairs was permanent. Nothing could now satisfy it but complete autonomy within the Empire. The alternative, if autonomy was refused, must finally be separation. Doubtless autonomy would have been secured anyway in the end. The Alaska award greatly speeded this process and became a leading factor in changing the Empire into the Commonwealth.

The graceful Laurier, smarting under the neighborly tap of Roosevelt's big stick, revealed his immediate bruises and his long thoughts when the verdict on Alaska was announced: "I have often regretted . . . and never more than on the present occasion, that we are living beside a great neighbor who, I believe I can say without being deemed unfriendly to them, are very grasping in their national actions and who are determined on every occasion to get the best in any agreement which they make. I have often regretted also that, while they are a great and powerful nation, we are only a small colony, a growing colony, but still a colony. I have often regretted also that we have not in our hands the treaty-making power which would enable us to dispose of our own affairs. . . . It is important that we should ask the British Parliament for more extensive powers so that if we ever have to deal with matters of a similar nature again, we shall deal with them in our own way, in our own fashion, according to the best light that we have."

That demand staggered the statesmen of London, for did it not mean a constitutional revolution in the Empire? It did, but the revolution was assured without Laurier or Alaska. What was imperial heresy in 1903 would become orthodoxy twenty years later under Laurier's heir. From then on it would be commonplace.

Roosevelt had won his first two foreign adventures, on the Isthmus of Panama and on the passes of the northern gold fields. His nation, too, would pay a price, under his successor, within eight years. According to Dafoe, the Canadian people's anger at the Alaska award was a vital factor in defeating the United States' reciprocity scheme in 1911.

The boundary of Alaska had produced an avoidable and rather absurd quarrel. Happily it was the last quarrel of boundaries between the American neighbors. All the political lines were now complete after three centuries of struggle in war and peace. The two nations had largely mastered the art of living together and sharing the land of the continent. As events would soon show, they had not learned to share its wealth for their joint benefit.

31

Taft's Orphan Child

[1910–1911]

O N MARCH 20, 1910, AN AMERICAN AND A CANADIAN MET PRI-
vately at Albany, New York, for two purposes—to integrate
the economy of North America as the laws of geography
intended; and to save two governments which had suddenly smelled
the whiff of their own decay. Probably neither man at Albany knew
which purpose was the stronger.

President William Howard Taft had inherited the estate of his
mentor, Theodore Roosevelt. It was a rich heritage, including a
prosperous nation, a regnant Republican Party, and the respect of
mankind. But the stout and genial gentleman who appeared at
Albany had found himself suddenly in trouble—worse trouble than
he yet knew.

So far his two enemies were hidden from him. Woodrow Wilson
was as yet only a professor and local politician. Roosevelt had retired to the hunting grounds of big game and the sprawling comfort of his home at Oyster Bay, after wishing his heir and protégé
well.

Lately, however, the supine Democrats had come alarmingly
alive. The Republican Party rumbled with discontent and would
soon split openly under the last blow of Roosevelt's big stick.

The Taft government, in fact, was dying, despite its outer look
of rude health and the obese jollity of its leader. Like most governments, it did not foresee its demise and denied every symptom of
its malady. Taft knew enough, however, to realize that it was a
time for extraordinary remedies. Such a remedy could perhaps be
devised at Albany with the assistance of a distinguished Canadian.

Fielding, Laurier's minister of finance—the quiet, gray little man
from Nova Scotia—had come to Albany in similar circumstances.

His government, for all its surface signs of well-being, also was dying of old age, though no one at Ottawa had detected its senility. The hive of the Queen Bee had never appeared more harmonious and invulnerable. Still, Laurier had detected certain vague intimations of mortality at various by-elections. A powerful group of rebels had challenged him in his own bailiwick of Quebec. Clearly, therefore, some new dish of honey was required to sweeten a rather sour electorate.

Thus Taft and Laurier had hit simultaneously on a joint solution of both economic and political problems. They decided to revive reciprocity.

Contact between them was established by a fortunate accident. The Reverend James A. Macdonald, a clergyman now editing Brown's Toronto *Globe* in the old tradition of free trade, had gone to Washington for a holiday, had met Taft and learned from him that the American government wanted a new trade deal with Canada. Macdonald was so excited by this disclosure that he hurried to Ottawa and reported that "Taft was almost in a panic over what he could do to secure exemption for Canada from the effects of the bill the high-tariff gang are forcing on the country. He wanted to know if I thought Sir Wilfrid would meet him to consider a reciprocity measure. So I am here to find that out."

Laurier was not ready yet to associate himself publicly with his original principles, the cause of his early defeats. He sent Fielding to Albany.

As Macdonald said, Taft had been converted to reciprocity by the Payne-Aldrich tariff law. This remarkable protectionist device equipped the United States with two tariff schedules. By April 1, 1910, the government must apply, besides the ordinary tariff, extra duties of 25 per cent on the goods of any nation which did not admit United States imports at its lowest rates. The supertariff must be levied on Canadian goods, since Canada had not granted to the United States the preference rates applied to Britain.

The Canadian government did not intend to be intimidated by this threat, nor did Taft wish to enforce it. His public already was restive under existing tariffs, the Democrats were attacking them, and if higher barriers were erected against Canadian goods Canada would certainly retaliate in kind. A man of peace, Taft deplored the prospect of a new tariff war with the United States' neighbor and friend. It was avoided for the moment by a technical adjustment of the Canadian tariff, but the old problem of sanity in the distorted trade of North America still remained and Taft's opponents were making the most of it. For the first time since the

Civil War, he judged, the United States was ready to consider a new deal on the border. He was right about his own people. He had misjudged the Canadians.

So had Laurier. In returning to reciprocity he was executing, with customary grace, the second complete reversal of his career. He had advocated reciprocity in the election of 1891 and thus given the Conservative government a last lease of power. Burned once, he avoided the flame for a long time afterward. While the Joint High Commission considering border disputes in 1898 and 1899 had toyed with reciprocity, nothing had come of it, and Laurier apparently was well satisfied with the lack of result.

"We are not," he said complacently, "dependent on the American market now." In 1903 he added: "I have found . . . that the best and most effective way to maintain friendship with our American neighbors is to be absolutely independent of them."

As late as 1907, only three years before the Albany conference, he told the people of England: "If we were to follow the laws of nature and geography between Canada and the United States, the whole trade would flow from south to north and from north to south. We have done everything, by building canals and subsidizing railways, to bring the trade from west to east and from east to west, so as to bring trade into British channels. All this we have done, recognizing the principle of the great advantage of forcing trade within the British Empire. There was a time when we wanted reciprocity with the United States, but our efforts and offers were put aside. We have said good-bye to that trade and we have now put all our hopes in British trade."

This was one of Laurier's smooth oversimplifications. Actually Canada enjoyed a large business with the United States and could not do without it. And Laurier had no intention of confining Canada's trade within the British Empire.

Since the beginning of the century he had consistently fought off the campaign of Joseph Chamberlain and the tariff reformers of Britain to ring the Empire with a picket fence of tariffs in a vast and, as Laurier believed, an impossible British Zollverein. The Chamberlain policy was designed to control not only the trade but the foreign policies of the overseas colonies, to give the Empire a single voice in world affairs, speaking, of course, from London. As a Canadian nationalist—his nationalism heated by the supposed betrayal of the Alaska Boundary Award—Laurier could never agree to any limit on Canada's future autonomy, fiscal or political.

Behind the façade of consistent principle Canada was trying, as always, to make the best of two possible worlds. It wanted all the

markets it could find in the Empire, the United States, and everywhere else for the growing output of its newly established transcontinental economy. Expediency and not theory directed its trading policy then as now—above all, the expediency of domestic
politics.

When Laurier toured the West in the summer of 1910, a drastic
overhaul of the tariff appeared highly expedient. The Canadian
farmers, like their American neighbors, were restive under the
burden of protection, which protected only the Eastern manu-
facturer. Reciprocity would placate this growing rebellion in a
Liberal stronghold, provide a diversion from the rather monotonous
hum of the Ottawa hive, and raise a winning issue for the government. Had not Canada, had not even Macdonald, always sought
reciprocity when it was unobtainable? Now that the United States
had changed its mind after half a century of protectionism, surely
Canadians would welcome this chance and bless the government
that grasped it. Reciprocity would be not only good politics and
good economics but, as a collateral advantage, would bring an
apostate Liberal Party back to its old faith.

Having completed his soundings, Laurier decided to press the
negotiations begun by Fielding at Albany. That old flame of free
trade, which had burned him once, now seemed to offer only a
light in the wilderness of politics and the dark of Laurier's old age.

The benign autocrat of Ottawa had ruled so long and so successfully, he had seen the country grow so rapidly under his policies,
he had become such a personal myth and institution, that he no
longer needed to struggle for power. His sensitive touch was
blunted by ease. Perhaps he did not realize that another flame, the
flame of Canadian nationalism, was as vehement as ever—more
vehement since the Alaska Boundary Award.

Or, if he recognized that growing fact, the passionate nationalist
saw no real conflict between reciprocity and nationalism. On the
contrary, reciprocity would nourish nationalism by increasing the
wealth and strength of Canada through expanded trade. There was
convincing evidence in history for this conclusion. Only in bad
times—as in the annexation movement of 1849—had Canada ever
showed any interest in union with the United States. Prosperity
had always been the surest enemy of annexation. More trade meant
more prosperity. Reciprocity meant more trade. Therefore, reciprocity meant more nationalism.

So ran Laurier's thoughts as Fielding began detailed trade negotiations with the American government in the first days of 1911.
The bargain was easily struck, for Taft had begun to appreciate

the dimensions of his dilemma when the Democrats won the autumn Congressional elections. He must have a reciprocity agreement and was prepared to offer generous terms. On January 26 the deal was completed and announced.

Its broad sweep, reversing nearly half a century of American policy, staggered the public on both sides of the border. The reciprocity agreement of 1854 had been revived almost intact—free trade in the natural products of the farm; low tariffs on secondary products like meat, canned goods, and flour; low tariffs also on many manufactured articles like farm implements, engines, building materials, and lumber.

At Canadian insistence, the deal would be ratified not by treaty but by concurrent legislation at Washington and Ottawa. This arrangement, Laurier thought, would be more acceptable to the Canadian people than a treaty. He had seldom made a worse mistake. With a treaty, binding the United States to low tariffs for a long, fixed period, he might have saved reciprocity. Without it, his policy was doomed.

The first Canadian statesman to see Laurier's blunder was his former righthand man, Clifford Sifton. Though Sifton had quarreled with Laurier and left the government on another issue, he was still a powerful figure in Parliament and country, more powerful than Laurier supposed. He, too, had been an ardent free trader in his youth but had changed his mind, now favored "moderate protection" and, from his bitter experience on the Alaska boundary, strongly distrusted American policy.

Even before the terms of the bargain were announced, Sifton had fired a warning shot across the government's bows. If Canada accepted reciprocity with the Americans, he said, "Must not our trade, our business, our very life, become intermingled so that we shall become dependent on them? What must follow in the natural course of events but political union?" Laurier ignored that shot and strode confidently toward destruction.

Only a political brain as keen as Sifton's could foresee, in the spring of 1911, the ultimate shape of the monster hatched in the innocent hive of Ottawa. As it turned out, the hardheaded man of law and business knew the Canadian people better than did the subtle man of politics.

All the first signs indicated that Sifton was wrong and Laurier right. Reciprocity looked like a sure winner. Even the Conservatives conceded Laurier's latest and greatest triumph.

Robert Borden, the aloof and greatly underestimated Nova Scotian now leading the opposition, could not decide at first whether to support or oppose reciprocity. In his parliamentary caucus, as he later admitted, "The atmosphere . . . was not invigorating; there was the deepest dejection in our Party, and many of our members were convinced that the government's proposals would appeal to the country and would give it another term of office." After all, the Conservative Party, under Macdonald, had repeatedly sought reciprocity and only discovered its dangers when it was refused by the United States. Should it be rejected now when, incredibly enough, it was in Canada's grasp?

Borden's mind, powerful but slow, was made up for him mainly by the mind of the public. Among the nation's leaders, Sifton alone had known from the beginning what the public reaction would be, after the first careless raptures of the government.

As he anticipated, reciprocity soon ignited a fire beyond all economic calculation. The Canadian people might not understand the economics of continental trade. They felt the oldest instinct of their breed, the folk instinct of nationalism, which seemed to be threatened by exposure to the goods, the wealth, the power, and the policies of the United States. A few weeks of consideration convinced many Canadians that reciprocity was only Manifest Destiny in a new guise. And the former guise, a Big Stick across the Alaska boundary, was vivid and raw in Canadian memory.

Still Laurier could not measure the depth of this rebellion outside and inside his own party. His sense of timing for once had deserted him. If he had taken reciprocity to the people in the first weeks of his triumph at Washington, before the shine had been rubbed off it, probably he would have been re-elected and the history of America would have been drastically changed. He saw no reason to hurry. Parliament obviously favored his policy. The country no doubt would approve it. Instead of ramming through his deal with Taft, he allowed Parliament to debate it throughout the spring and he set off blithely in summer for an Empire Conference in London. By then the country's mind had jelled against him.

The opposition of the manufacturing interests to reciprocity had been expected and discounted in advance. No one was surprised when Van Horne re-emerged from private life with a typical announcement. He was "out to bust the damn thing." The C.P.R. had been built for east-west, not north-south, traffic. Laurier had not foreseen, however, as he had every reason to foresee from long experience with him, that Sifton, a Liberal, also was out to bust the damn thing and knew precisely how to do it. Laurier did not foresee either how well Borden had learned the subtler arts of politics and acquired a Machiavellian touch from his enemy. Borden, indeed, had suddenly found what four predecessors since Macdonald had failed to find—a method of exorcising Riel's ghost.

In death, as in life, that uneasy spirit continued to haunt the border. The execution at Regina had alienated Quebec from the Conservative Party. The French-Canadian race had found in Laurier one of its own sons at the nation's summit. Apparently it would never vote for any other leader. But at the summit Laurier could not be merely a French Canadian. He must represent both races and satisfy the English-speaking majority. As a national leader he had settled the Manitoba School Question in favor of English-speaking Protestants, against the will of the Catholic Church, he had brought Canada into the South African War, and lately had undertaken to build a miniature Canadian navy.

His decision in the school question could be forgiven in Quebec, since doubtless it was unavoidable. The South African War had been, in the eyes of the French-Canadian *habitants*, only a British adventure and another conquest of harmless people like themselves. And now what need had Canada for a navy? Obviously it was intended to fight in future British wars.

Laurier had accepted a knighthood from the Queen. Apparently he was yielding in his naval policy to the imperial pressure of her government and the social pressure of the London drawing rooms. He was weakening his policies of Canadian nationalism, deserting the ideals of his race.

These suspicions were ridiculous, as the last tragic chapter of his life would show, six years hence. They were sufficiently strong in 1911 to build a revolt against him in Quebec. It was led by a flaming young prophet of racial mystique, Henri Bourassa, and his able lieutenant, Armand Lavergne. A vague nationalist movement, produced by the South African War, had become a full-fledged political party throughout French Canada. So long as it could find no allies elsewhere it was irritating but harmless to Laurier. The reciprocity issue gave it such allies.

Borden, who was proving himself far more imaginative than he looked behind the dour face and heavy mustache, quickly seized the sudden chance to destroy Laurier among the French Canadians. It would be a tricky and cynical business, of course, and required careful management.

In English-speaking Canada the Conservative Party stood primarily for the British connection. It had fought Laurier's Naval Bill of 1910 on the ground that a purely Canadian navy would strain the links of empire. It had decided, after its first hesitation, to fight reciprocity as the first stage in Canada's annexation to the United States and the Empire's destruction. But it could not win the approaching election without support in Quebec and it could expect none except from Bourassa's Nationalist Party.

Alliance, even as a temporary marriage of convenience or an election liaison between the true-blue Tories of English-speaking Canada and the anti-British Quebec Nationalists, appeared not only immoral and unthinkable but, worse, impossible. Borden arranged it. Such an unnatural combination, of course, could not last long, was unworthy of a statesman of Borden's stature, but it opened his only way to office and the only sure method of killing reciprocity. So he held his nose and made his deal with Bourassa, who would ally himself with anybody, even an outright enemy of his ideals, if that would destroy Laurier, the archenemy.

Thus the catalyst of reciprocity had rearranged the chemical elements of Canadian life into a new and incredible combination. Two opposites, the Conservative and Nationalist Parties, had been united for a brief purpose and, as it turned out, they represented together a majority of the nation.

While this dark witches' brew was maturing in Quebec, the respectable campaign against reciprocity itself—its strategy mainly directed by Sifton, the Liberal—convulsed the English-speaking provinces.

Once he had doubtfully decided to oppose reciprocity, Borden discovered and sincerely believed that it would ruin the nation. To begin with, it would expose the fragile industry of Canada to fatal American competition; would destroy the transcontinental economy built by three centuries of labor and perfected under Macdonald's National Policy. That would be only the first phase of national ruin. Its economy gutted by American goods, its people turned into hewers of wood and drawers of water for the American factories, its British markets lost, Canada perforce must seek admission to the United States, on American terms. And that was precisely what the Americans intended. Reciprocity meant, in short, the end of the Canadian dream.

If the Canadian people could not accept that prophecy entire, at least they could see that reciprocity, as presently devised, would twist the Canadian economy into a new shape. Even if it produced all the benefits claimed by Laurier, there was no guarantee that they would continue. A treaty would have assured those benefits for a term of years, but Laurier, in his most lamentable mistake, had insisted on a mere agreement by concurrent legislation in Washington and Ottawa. At any moment, therefore, the United

States could repeal the bargain, as it had done with reciprocity before.

"Sir," Sifton told Parliament, "we are putting our heads in the noose. . . . These [reciprocity] resolutions, in my judgment, spell retrogression, commercial subordination, the destruction of our national ideals, and displacement from our proud position as the rising hope of the British Empire."

These were not the words of a conniving Conservative politician. They came from the second figure in the Liberal Party, Laurier's former lieutenant and a man who sought no public office. Sifton had cast the bullets for the Conservative Party to fire. His speeches became the opposition's campaign documents, along with Laurier's old speeches against reciprocity.

By this time John Wesley Dafoe, the young Conservative from Bully's Acre, who had turned Liberal on seeing the Macdonald government in its years of decay, had become Sifton's closest associate, as editor of the Winnipeg *Free Press,* and one of the supreme journalists of the world. Sifton owned the *Free Press,* but he did not own and did not try to own its editor. In the most interesting human subplot of the national drama, Sifton crusaded for the defeat of reciprocity. His paper, under Dafoe, was the ringing voice of historic liberalism, the champion of reciprocity, the voice of Laurier. Two great Liberals had disagreed on a public issue. Their private friendship remained unbroken. And Dafoe went on from there to become a primal force in Canadian life when issues greater than reciprocity were at stake.

Borden's decisive allies did not come from Ontario, in the person of Sifton, or Quebec, in the person of Bourassa. They came from the United States. The very men who had revived reciprocity there unwittingly killed it in Canada.

Taft had to push his trade legislation through the Congress. In pushing it he pictured its manifold advantages to the American economy. The Conservatives of Canada shouted that Taft had confirmed their warning—the assets which he claimed in his own country would be Canada's liabilities. Of course, reciprocity would make American industry thrive by giving it the Canadian market and wrecking Canadian industry. The more Taft argued for reciprocity in the United States the more certain was its rejection in Canada.

That fine and luckless president went much further than advocacy. As he saw, too late, the danger of Laurier's defeat, he began to issue warnings and predictions. They were promptly distorted and misunderstood north of the border. Canada, he said, was at the "parting of the ways," meaning that if reciprocity was not achieved now the opportunity would be lost to the United States for the visible future and Canada would contract into a closed system of empire trade.

The "parting of the ways" was a truthful phrase in plain fact. In political semantics it was dangerous, perhaps fatal, when warped in a Canadian election campaign to mean a threat from Washington.

Taft was not content with this damage. He wrote to Roosevelt: "The amount of Canadian products we would take would produce a current of business between western Canada and the United States that would make Canada only an adjunct of the United States. It would transfer all their important business to Chicago and New York, with their bank credits and everything else, and it would greatly increase the demand of Canada for our manufactures. I see this as an argument against Reciprocity made in Canada, and I think it is a good one."

Too good. It was, from the American President, the perfect argument for Laurier's enemies. A "parting of the ways," Canada an "adjunct of the United States"—the humblest stump speaker of the Conservative Party could interpret such phrases as an ultimatum from Washington, another dose of Manifest Destiny, the latest gesture by Roosevelt's Big Stick in the hands of his successor.

Taft little understood the psychology of Canada. The Democratic supporters of reciprocity apparently misunderstood it altogether. Thus Champ Clark, Speaker of the House of Representatives: "I hope to see the day when the American flag will float over every square foot of the British North American possession, clear to the North Pole." No Canadian ear could mistake that echo of Jefferson, Jackson, Clay, and the others who had launched the invasion of 1812, of the Sumners and Chandlers who had claimed Canada as payment for the Alabama Claims.

Laurier could not anticipate the unnatural marriage of British toryism and French-Canadian nationalism. He could not imagine that the American politicians would kill reciprocity, their own child. He should have foreseen, as Sifton had warned him, that the oldest emotions of Canada, once roused by the threat of annexation, even a false threat, would overwhelm all other argument. But he had lived too long in the isolated Ottawa hive; he thought he was giving Canada a chance of a new prosperity and America a chance of economic sanity; he was deceived by the first favorable reaction of Parliament; and, in a final blunder, he allowed passions

to rise and the opposition to consolidate before taking his case to
the people.

Taft pushed reciprocity through the Congress. Laurier could not
push it through Parliament, for Borden was conducting a skillful
filibuster with time on his side. At last Laurier abandoned the attempt and, still confident, called an election. Now began one of
the most angry, confused, and paradoxical campaigns in Canadian
history.

All the magic of Laurier's oratory, his personal legend and his
economic argument could not stem the tide now flowing in English-speaking Canada, where reciprocity was interpreted as meaning annexation and the breakup of the Empire, or in Quebec, where
with highest irony Laurier was represented as the tool of British
imperialism. Even Rudyard Kipling was enlisted in the great cause
to warn Canadians that "It is her own soul that Canada risks today. . . . I see nothing for Canada in Reciprocity except a little
ready money, which she does not need, and a very long repentance."
Against Manifest Destiny, Taft's honest candor, Sifton's cold logic,
Bourassa's racial doctrines, the memories of battles long ago and
the Alaska Boundary Award—the great man of Canada argued in
vain.

He seemed to be caught in a political cabal of peculiarly repulsive cynicism, but it was more than that. He was caught in the
deep current of a history flowing these three hundred years since
his ancestors had first settled on the St. Lawrence—the history of a
people who intended to be themselves, who had always distrusted
the Americans, who had made the border by their own toil and
bloodshed and would defend it, if they could, whenever it seemed
in danger. The border seemed in danger now. There could be
only one answer from Canada.

On September 21, 1911, Canada went soberly to the polls and
rejected the Liberal government. Despite Bourassa's inroads into
Quebec, it was a close thing. The government received 625,096
votes and the combined opposition 669,567. In Parliament Borden
had 133 seats to Laurier's 86 Liberals, almost exactly the former
Liberal majority.

Had reciprocity been defeated or had the people voted only to
dismiss an aged government, and in Quebec to repudiate Laurier's
supposed imperialism? The anguished voice of Dafoe answered
that question with unequaled authority. Allowing for all the contradictions of the election, all its distortion and mean conspiracy,
still, Dafoe wrote, "Canada rejected Reciprocity in pride rather
than fear. . . . Whether the decision was right or wrong, prudent

or rash, vainglorious or self-regarding, it settled for a generation and perhaps for a century all possibility of a mutual agreement for freedom of exchange in trade between these two countries. It is impossible to imagine a recurrence of the favorable conditions which made such an arrangement seem practicable in 1911. When the arrangement fell through, the countries elected for economic war."

After the brief armistice of Woodrow Wilson's low Underwood tariff, Dafoe's judgment, as usual, was fulfilled. Economic war, greedy, impoverishing and insensate, was joined on the border.

There is a queer little sequel to the story of 1911, never printed before now.

President Taft was succeeded in American politics by his abler son, Robert. That dominant figure in the Republican Party was commonly regarded as an unshakable and unrepentant protectionist, an enemy of his father's low-tariff policies. But in 1947, when Canadian-American trade had encountered a new crisis, Senator Taft told this writer in Washington that he favored the removal of all trade barriers between the United States and Canada.

Strangely enough, he had only a vague memory of President Taft's reciprocity agreement, he was surprised to learn its details, but he was convinced that it was sound in principle. He added that he would shortly advocate in the Senate a policy of free trade with Canada, though not with other nations.

Why that announcement was never made the writer does not know. At all events, as Dafoe expected, reciprocity died with the elder Taft and one more futile attempt to revive it would only confirm Dafoe's prediction.

32

The Higher Lunacy

[1911–1937]

AT THE LAST MEETING OF THE LAURIER CABINET ITS YOUNGEST member, William Lyon Mackenzie King, paid no attention to the closing business and the dying gestures of an illustrious regime. He was scribbling a letter and a prophecy to his parents. Someday, he wrote, this dingy chamber would see him again. It was difficult to imagine, in 1911, anything more improbable. But, then, the life of Canada and the struggle of the boundary had never produced a more improbable character than King. When, as an old man, he discovered his youthful letter and read it in tears, his prophecy had been abundantly fulfilled.

More than any of his predecessors, King was the product of the border.

His maternal grandfather, William Lyon Mackenzie, had escaped across the Niagara River in a rowboat, disguised as an old woman, after the fiasco of his rebellion. He had returned briefly with his burlesque "government" to Navy Island, precipitated the American raids of 1838, and almost produced a war between the United States and Britain.

His long American exile had been fertile in children, most of whom died young, in the poverty of a home often without food. Isabel, though her parents often despaired of her life, somehow survived and returned with them to Canada when the rebel was pardoned by his queen. She married John King, son of a British officer who had fought as a loyalist against Mackenzie's scarecrow army. Their son, therefore, was a unique synthesis—with a strong American coloration—of the historic forces that had first produced revolt, then responsible government, and finally a Canadian nation.

Young Billy King—or "Rex," as his family called him—moved to the United States in his college years to study and work at Jane Addams's Hull House, a social settlement in Chicago. It was there that he discovered life, his purpose in it, and the nature of the American people. Now a plump youth of flabby look, ingratiating smile, and inveterate industry, he entered the service of the Laurier government as a labor administrator, soon caught the attention of the queen bee and rose steadily in the Cabinet hive.

The defeat of reciprocity and his own taught him many things. One of them was that free trade with the United States, while an ideal to be admired and advocated in theory, must long remain impossible in fact. Yet better than any Canadian statesman of his time King knew not only the American people but the necessity for American friendship.

At Harvard, as a young teacher, he had encountered briefly a youth of more fortunate circumstances, apparently a darling of fortune but doomed to early physical disaster. His name was Franklin Delano Roosevelt. That chance meeting began the strangest and most fruitful partnership in the history of the border.

Out of office, without prospects, with only $2,000 in the bank, and with an aged mother, a brother, and several other relatives to support, King went back to the United States again, to work for the Rockefeller interests as a negotiator in labor disputes. He learned still more about American society and began to ruminate his own heretical and revolutionary ideas about an ideal society for Canada and the world.

In the meantime the Borden government had begun to raise the Canadian tariff from the ruins of reciprocity, only to find the American tariff falling under the New Liberalism of Woodrow Wilson. This was only a deceptive lull, a mere aberration in a protectionist system, but Borden had little time to consider it, for he was soon catapulted into the First World War—a long, exhausting hemorrhage of Canadian blood and a test of Borden's quality. Both nation and leader proved worthy of that test. But it broke both Laurier and the Conservative Party.

To maintain the ambitious Canadian Army in France, Borden repudiated his Nationalist supporters in Quebec, formed a coalition with English-speaking Liberals and enforced conscription despite the passionate resistance of French Canada, which regarded conscription as a symbol of the English conquest.

Laurier, while supporting the war, refused to join the Union government of 1917 and, in the last crisis of his life, returned by sure instinct to his own people as the protector of their race. That was the end of him as a national leader, but at his death two years later his legend was imperishable.

Borden had fought reciprocity as a threat to the British Empire and Canada's national existence but, like Laurier, he was a nationalist, jealous of his nation's autonomy. After its sacrifices in the war he insisted on its recognition in the peace treaty of Paris. He signed as a member of the British delegation; he made Canada a full-fledged member of the League of Nations; and he vainly tried to modify Wilson's Covenant, by watering down its commitments, in the hope of attracting the support of the American people.

When war and peacemaking were finished, the Liberal Party, as the official enemy of conscription (although most English-speaking Liberal leaders supported it), seemed broken beyond early repair outside Quebec. That general opinion was not shared by the pale, plump scholar who, standing by Laurier and sharing his second defeat, was now committing his private heresies to paper in a ponderous book entitled *Industry and Humanity*. King had watched Borden's retirement and the advent of Arthur Meighen, a fellow student of King's days at Toronto University and now, apparently, the most promising figure in Canada. With sublime confidence King waited for a Conservative collapse and his own elevation. Both expectations were sound.

Chiefly because no attractive alternative was available, but with little hope of recovery, the Liberal Party chose King as its leader in 1919. Nothing could have suited Meighen better. That gaunt, brilliant, and fearless young lawyer from the prairies, with his flashing eloquence and corrosive wit, saw in his opponent only a suet pudding of vague political theory, weak compromise, and pious humbug. Little time need be wasted on such a pale shadow of Laurier and, anyway, Meighen's agenda was full.

He undertook with one hand to raise tariffs against American goods and found complete justification for his lifelong protectionism in the policies of the Harding government, whose "normalcy" included increasing barriers against all imports. If the United States was back to normal after Wilson's tariff aberrations and his own Greek tragedy, so, in Meighen's mind, was Canada. He had refurbished Macdonald's National Policy and was proud of it.

With the other hand Meighen attempted, and with some success, to carry the historic burden of a Canadian prime minister by interpreting the United States to the British Empire. The Imperial Conference of 1921 found him bearding the imperialists of London to demand that the Empire abrogate its alliance with Japan—this solely to satisfy American opinion, for it regarded the alliance as aimed against the United States. Meighen's pressure succeeded. The alliance was abrogated, but with little gratitude from Canada's neighbors. Economic war on the 49th Parallel, foreseen by Dafoe, had been enthusiastically resumed on both sides with the old tariff weapon.

Tariffs, however, were powerless to stop the depression of 1920. Obviously, in the minds of Meighen in Ottawa and Harding in Washington, still higher tariffs were required, and were applied. On a policy of outright and candid protection, of "brick for brick" in the rising customs wall of the border, Meighen went to the country in 1921. King opposed him with a masterpiece of lofty and deliberate confusion. He had learned enough in 1911 never to propose reciprocity again; he said he proposed "freer" not "free" trade; he would somehow reduce the tariff to satisfy an agrarian revolt sweeping the West like a prairie fire and yet keep it high enough to protect the Eastern manufacturers; and by refusing to state his own policy while concentrating his attack on the government, he destroyed Meighen forever.

Destruction was assured in any case by Meighen's inflexible and lonely character, by the usual revulsion against a wartime government, and most of all by Quebec's hatred of the Conservative Party, begun on a Regina gallows and heated, almost to the point of insurrection, by the conscription policy of 1917.

King inherited all of Laurier's shrunken estate. He held Quebec solidly. But he lacked a working majority in Parliament, since the farmers' revolt, called the Progressive Party, had swept the West in protest against high tariffs. No one but a political genius could manage the situation which King now occupied as prime minister. He did not look like a genius. He looked to the public like a pedestrian little man surprised to find himself at the head of a nation, and to Meighen like a contemptible fraud. Nevertheless, in his own way he was a genius and would hold office longer than any other statesman of the English-speaking world.

The adventures of this incredible person constantly and increasingly dragged him back to the border and across it to the scenes of his grandfather's exile and his own youth in the United States.

His first budget, in 1921, showed his stubborn but cautious determination to remove, as fast as possible, what he regarded as the insane economic arrangements of the continent. Every other nation in the world was then embarked on economic insanity, was raising tariffs and lurching toward the Bull Market and the Crash. Canada alone, under King, reduced its tariff, extended the British Preference, and even offered (being sure that the offer would not be accepted) a new reciprocity deal to the United States.

King expected no response from Washington, and certainly did not want reciprocity. Washington was already ushering in the gaudy era and topless towers of the Fordney-McCumber Tariff. Only King's genius of conciliation and postponement, combined with the free-trade drive of the new farmers' party, could resist Canada's impulse to retaliate against American trade restrictions, which threatened to damage and finally devastated the Canadian economy. Somehow King managed to reduce the Canadian tariff gradually in this general climate of protection but toward the end of his first term was talking vaguely of retaliation, if necessary. Dafoe's economic war had reached a dangerous point of international friction.

It was as a North American, however, and a friend of the United States, that King went to the Imperial Conference of 1923. There, as a fledgling, untried empire statesman, he confronted such formidable leaders as Winston Churchill, who were proposing to consolidate the Empire under a single foreign policy. London suddenly discovered, to its amazement, that King was not made of putty, after all. The pressure of the centralizers, the social seductions of the London drawing rooms, and even the personal pleas of the great South African, Jan Smuts, could not move the genial Canadian.

There was nothing to be done about it, since Canada had become unquestionably a nation with autonomous powers in fact, though not yet in law. King wanted them codified but he could wait a little longer—only three years, as it turned out. Meanwhile he must have freedom to deal with Canada's neighbor as he chose.

King quickly completed the structure of Canadian status. Few of his people realized that he was denying and trying to evade the parallel weight of responsibility. He was moving into isolationism. He was moving, in fact, beside his neighbors across the border. Already he had refused to send troops to fight beside Britain against Turkey in 1922. Now he was proclaiming a policy—if it could be called a policy—of "no commitments" abroad. He was behaving like a North American.

In 1923 he carried the affairs of the border and of the Empire into a new phase by ostentatiously declaring Canada's right to make its own foreign treaties. His Quebec lieutenant, Ernest Lapointe, arrived unobtrusively in Washington and, to the horror of the British ambassador, insisted on signing alone a Canadian-American agreement for the protection of the North Pacific halibut fisheries. Ottawa was doing its business for the first time directly with Washington and soon sent its own ambassador there. Slowly broadening down from precedent to precedent, the Empire was becoming a commonwealth. It required only the Balfour Declaration of 1926 and the Statute of Westminster, five years later, to validate its new structure.

Canada had been the unfailing though often unconscious architect of the Third Empire since the Rebellion of 1837. King, in completing the work of Macdonald, Borden and Laurier, was the chief contemporary architect of the Commonwealth.

All this work was implicit in the affairs of the border. They had supplied the ingredients of a Canadian nation in the first place but they could not isolate it from the United States or detach it from Britain. King did not see the end of the Commonwealth process now under way; he gravely misjudged the larger process of the world; but he knew more clearly than any Canadian before him that he must have a free hand to deal with foreign nations in general and his American neighbors in particular.

It was not easy, in the nineteen-twenties, to deal with the American neighbors. They had found the secret of perpetual economic motion by hiving their markets off from the world. They had installed two chickens in every pot and were planning to install two cars in every garage. They exported their goods but would not allow their customers to pay in reciprocal trade, preferring—in the form of unsecured foreign loans—to give their goods, their money, and their labor away, lest repayment impoverish them. When these accents of the higher lunacy were shouted from the White House, from the Capitol, and from the skyscrapers of Wall Street, who could hear the faint protests of the little man in the East Block of Ottawa?

Apparently no one heard him. In the election of 1925 Meighen swept English-speaking Canada on the proposition that low Liberal tariffs were ruining Canada and might well "endanger our nationality." He seemed likely to control the new Parliament, but again he had underestimated King, his own cruel destiny, and the sheer accidents of politics.

After a scandal which would have destroyed any leader less adroit, an open quarrel with the King's representative, and a constitutional issue of his own devising, King clung to office, was returned with a clear majority in 1926, and prepared for easier times.

Instead, he faced the Great Depression. A convulsion of that magnitude was sufficient to give the Conservative Party and a high-tariff policy a new, deceptive flush of life. It would soon reveal more interesting exhibits—among them a crippled and dauntless squire of the Hudson River, King's acquaintance of Harvard days;

a madman with a comedian's mustache in Munich; a gaudy and confident Canadian in Calgary, Alberta.

Richard Bedford Bennett, the new leader of the Conservative Party, out-Meighened Meighen and made Macdonald look like a free trader in a new crusade for tariffs, mainly against the United States. By restraining the movement of goods across the border, by rejecting Washington's "domination," Bennett promised to cure the unemployment of the thirties or "perish in the attempt." By refusing to import he would somehow "blast" his way into world markets and save the nation. And on these assurances a desperate nation elected him in 1930.

Roosevelt was running for the Presidency in 1932 on a traditional Democratic policy of moderate tariffs, sound finance, strict economy, a balanced budget, and other impeccable items of orthodoxy when Bennett assembled in Ottawa a conference designed to set up the Commonwealth in self-contained business. The Canadian's alternating persuasion and threat compelled a doubtful British government to sign a series of agreements which failed to reduce the tariffs between the Commonwealth nations but raised them against all foreigners. This might appear idiotic to the saner minds of the United States but it was hardly surprising. Canada and its Commonwealth partners were merely retaliating, after long delay, against the idiocy of American tariffs. If that involved a final severing of the world's economic jugular, no one seemed to realize it, in Canada anyway, except a little man watching the Ottawa Conference from the gallery.

King knew that the Bennett government was plunging the nation and the Commonwealth into incalculable damage and suspected that he would have to repair it. Bennett soon suspected the same thing and, on Roosevelt's election, arrived in Washington to issue jointly with the President a brave statement proposing "to search for means to increase the exchange of commodities between our two countries." Nothing came of this pledge, since Bennett was imprisoned in his own contrary policies and Roosevelt suddenly turned his back on world trade, sank the London Economic Conference with a torpedo directed by Raymond Moley, and embarked on a policy of outright self-containment bearing the magic letters "NRA."

Sanity had not quite died in the democratic world. Cordell Hull, though humiliated by the President at London, was still in the American Cabinet, still patiently waiting for the NRA, other gimcracks of the same species, and the lapses of Roosevelt's tariff liberalism to pass. In 1934 Hull won his struggle with the passage of the reciprocal trade agreements legislation. The United States was ready to reduce tariffs at last.

So, it appeared, was the repentant Bennett. Negotiations to devise a new Canadian-American trade agreement were almost complete when Bennett went to the country in 1935, though he did not care to reveal his secret somersault to the electors. Inevitably the depression, which had made Bennett, destroyed him and returned the Liberal Party.

King found Bennett's draft agreement awaiting ratification. He seized on it eagerly and, with a few amendments, secured the signature of the American government before the President could change his mind again. Thus began the slow and painful return to sanity in the North American and the world economy. It was too late. Born of depression, the lunatics of Europe and Asia were on the march and could not be turned back.

The governments of the United States, Britain, and Canada continued to deny the inevitable while attempting to halt it by reorganizing the world's trade and thus relieving its tensions.

In 1937 King made a mysterious visit to the White House on his way to a Commonwealth conference in London. He and Roosevelt (now intimates of an improbable sort) agreed on a broad and hopeful tariff deal. It was quickly ratified by the three nations which controlled the largest segment of the world's trade in the historic North Atlantic Triangle. The British Preference system was reduced in Britain and Canada by the agreement of November 17, 1938, and, in return for this concession, the United States reduced its tariffs substantially.

King, as the honest and successful broker between the United States and Britain, regarded the agreement as the largest success of his career so far. "Like Canning," he gloated, "we have done our indispensable part to call into existence a New World to redress the balance of the Old. . . . Each of us sleeps more safely in his bed because of the rapprochement between the world's two greatest democracies, a rapprochement which could not have been effected without the assent and cooperation of Canada."

The rapprochement certainly had occurred and could not have been effected, in terms of commerce anyway, without King's work; for there could be no trade deal between the United States and Britain without the consent of Canada, which had binding agreements with both. Hull saw his long-sought policy of sound economic appeasement beginning to succeed. Its simultaneous counterpart, of questionable soundness, was Chamberlain's policy of political appeasement, recently enforced at Munich.

Both sides of the general appeasement policy were doomed together within twelve months. Meanwhile the new partnership of Roosevelt and King had quietly begun to revise the defenses of North America in case appeasement failed. They had agreed secretly, at the White House meeting in 1937, that American and Canadian officers should undertake joint military planning. Though this was an obvious and necessary step, its premature disclosure shocked the Canadian imperialists, who thought it a betrayal of Britain, and the isolationists, who feared it would involve Canada in the future wars of the United States. When Roosevelt, in the same year, proposed a "quarantine" of aggressors, his nation was equally shocked. Few North Americans, on either side of the border, were thinking straight in those days.

33

Friends, Alive and Dead

[1937–1940]

THOUGH THE WORLD WAS REELING TOWARD ITS SECOND GENERAL war, a new era of good feeling in America had arrived under Roosevelt and King. Their friendship would be needed before long.

The two leaders, each in a different public fashion but with the same political methods, accurately reflected the mood of their peoples.

To Roosevelt, King appeared as an elder statesman of much greater learning, longer experience, and ingratiating ways, to whom secrets could be safely trusted, secrets that could not be trusted to the head of a more powerful state or one less close and friendly. In private character the two were antithetic—Roosevelt gregarious, assertive, gay, careless of facts, uninterested in scholarship, learning by word of mouth and playing brilliantly by ear; King a lonely recluse, when possible, in his farmhouse at Kingsmere, deferential yet ruthless, outwardly simple, inwardly a war of contradictions, in politics a master of intrigue but in private a devout spiritualist who constantly consulted his dead mother, and later would consult the dead Roosevelt.

A rather old-fashioned Victorian like King could not fit into the brawling climate of Washington and the theatricals of the New Deal. He fitted much better into his lonely bachelor's estate north of Ottawa, where he was building, of all things, an amphitheater of synthetic stone ruins at which he gazed by moonlight. Yet few Americans and probably no foreigners were as close to Roosevelt in his last days. The President called him "Mackenzie," a familiarity which no Canadian ever used to the Prime Minister. King, always a little stuffy and aware of his lesser status in the scheme of things, addressed Roosevelt as "Mr. President." Each confessed his secret problems to the other as they were seldom confessed to their cabinets. Those confidences were never betrayed on either side.

Roosevelt regarded King as a kind of political genius, which he was, as an impartial adviser with no ax to grind, and sometimes as a wailing wall. In Roosevelt, King found qualities of grandeur, flair, and stagecraft which he lacked and envied. Many of Roosevelt's policies he dismissed as political claptrap. He was appalled by the NRA, the Blue Eagle parades, and General Hugh Johnson's dead cats. He often shook his head at Roosevelt's economic ignorance—as, for example, when he had asked the President how he proposed to finance his huge budgetary deficits and Roosevelt had replied: "Well, Mackenzie, my family has held French securities since before the Revolution and they're still paying interest, so why can't we do the same?"

It was no use for King, the trained economist, to talk in technical terms with such a man. But King never doubted that his friend was the greatest statesman and most fascinating person of the age—even if, as King once told his friends, Roosevelt secretly would like to annex Canada, as who wouldn't?

Thus complementing each other by their differences, the two men got along famously together and brought their nations into an intimate friendship doubtless without precedent anywhere at any time. That was not the least of their teeming lifeworks.

The cooperation built in small affairs soon made possible a major continental decision. On August 18, 1938, the partners announced the American-Canadian partnership to the world in terms understandable to Hitler, who was currently preparing to partition Czechoslovakia. President and Prime Minister met with ostentatious symbolism to dedicate the Thousand Islands International Bridge and pledge their nations to joint defense.

Roosevelt's brief speech committed the United States by public guarantee, as it was already committed by geography, history, and the Monroe Doctrine, to the protection of Canada. "The Dominion of Canada," he said, "is part of the sisterhood of the British Empire. I give you assurance that the people of the United States will not stand idly by if domination of Canadian soil is threatened by any other empire."

King reciprocated this promise two days later at Woodbridge, Ontario: "We, too, have our obligations as a good, friendly neighbor, and one of them is to see that, at our own instance, our country is made as immune from attack or possible invasion as we can reasonably be expected to make it, and that, should the occasion ever arise, enemy forces should not be able to pursue their way, either by land, sea or air, to the United States across Canadian territory."

Without consulting the American Congress or the Canadian Parliament, the partners had proclaimed, in actual fact, a military alliance, the final issue of three hundred years of struggle along the border.

A year later, almost to the day, this partnership of Roosevelt and King, which had become a partnership of the United States and Canada, was put to the test.

At six o'clock on the morning of September 1, 1939, King was roused by the ring of the telephone beside his bed at Kingsmere. German troops had crossed the Polish border. After a lifetime of pacifism, King, the conciliator, was called upon to lead Canada as the only North American nation in the Second World War.

While he waited for Parliament to assemble and declare war, Roosevelt telephoned him from Washington. Was Canada actually at war? Roosevelt asked. No, said King, it was not. Until Parliament decided to the contrary, Canada was still neutral. "You see," Roosevelt told the advisers around his desk, "I was right!"

Canada being technically neutral, the United States could ship war supplies across the border, despite the existing Neutrality Act. In the hours remaining before Parliament's declaration of war Roosevelt (now a highly fictitious neutral) sold Canada all the munitions the United States could spare. They amounted to little but were invaluable at that time of shortage, especially some training planes which Canada desperately needed. The Roosevelt-King partnership was paying off.

Another year passed in the phony war of Europe, in Dunkirk, and the siege of Britain. By summer, 1940, the Western world would appear in greater peril than at any moment since the Mohammedan invasions. No men understood that better than Roosevelt, writhing in the prison of the Neutrality Act, and King, suddenly asked to perform a miracle in support of Britain. Could Britain hold, or must freedom perish in the Old World and find its last lodgment in a North American island under perpetual siege?

That question was written on the haggard face of King but never uttered even to his cabinet. It was written on the ashen face of Roosevelt as, sitting in his shirt sleeves through the summer heat of Washington, he heard the vain appeals of a falling France and the grim oratory of Winston Churchill.

Events confronted Canada with a special question of its own: If Britain fell, if Europe were overrun, must Canada seek physical survival by abandoning its political independence and joining the United States; was this, then, the end of the old Canadian dream? Not a few Canadians thought so. King had schooled himself against such thoughts. His faculty of self-hypnotism, his power to think only what he wanted to think, now served him well.

The American partners had conferred in April at the White House. King, in retrospect, considered these discussions the beginning of his greatest days. He had made himself, as he believed, the secret link between Roosevelt and Churchill.

Years before, Churchill had called Canada "the linchpin of peace," the magnet drawing Britain and the United States together. That was little more than a vivid phrase when Churchill uttered it. Now King regarded it as a solid and urgent fact. He himself was the linchpin.

Heavy with his sense of mission, he strove to temper Churchill's impatience with the United States' neutrality and pacified Roosevelt when Britain's appeals for help became embarrassing. According to King, these effort mainly prevented a disastrous clash between Washington and London; in proof of which he always carried in his wallet, as too sacred to be placed on any official file, some cables from Churchill thanking him for his intervention.

Until this crisis the British Tory had never taken the Canadian Liberal very seriously, whatever he may have thought of Canada, the free world's linchpin and magnet. King had not appreciated the genius of the young Churchill and had told him frankly, at their first meeting long ago, that Churchill had made an ass of himself in his first speaking tour of Canada. Now the three men under fire, Roosevelt, Churchill and King, began to understand one another. King always claimed to be the essential interpreter of this new friendship.

So far the Washington-Ottawa axis had functioned privately and informally. Toward the end of the ghastly summer of 1940 the partners agreed to confirm their personal agreement by a public act. King was alone at Kingsmere on Friday afternoon, August 16, and when the telephone rang answered it himself. The voice of the President asked him to be at Ogdensburg, New York, next day.

Ogdensburg was well chosen as a symbolic setting for a North American alliance, already operating but never written into binding contract. The Canadians had burned Ogdensburg in the War of 1812. The Fenians had used it as a base of their proposed raids on Canada. How distant, futile, and absurd those events looked in the summer of 1940 when the foundations of the world were cracking! So, no doubt, thought Roosevelt, as his private train carried him into the little St. Lawrence town, and King, as he crossed the river to meet his friend.

They met in the President's car and formalized all the private discussions of these last three years. The Ogdensburg Agreement was scrawled by Roosevelt on the back of an envelope. Again neglecting to secure the consent of the Congress, and giving no advance notice to his people, he had signed a military alliance with a member of the Commonwealth. He had formally repealed, on one of its battlefields, the War of 1812. He had changed the border from a line of division into a line of unity by accepting Canada as a sovereign friend and the United States' only contractual foreign ally. King signed with the same lack of legal authority. It was no time for quibbling. Both men had the unspoken authority of their peoples and the sanction of events.

To agree on joint military planning for North American defense was not difficult, since agreement merely formalized arrangements under way for three years. The real business of Ogdensburg, which continued from the dinner hour until two next morning, was not confined to North America. It covered the whole Atlantic.

Roosevelt had begun the secret negotiations by which he proposed to convey fifty American destroyers to Britain, then at the nadir of its fortunes. The deal was ticklish because it sailed very close to the constitutional limitations of the Presidency, perhaps beyond them, and because Churchill (according to King's account) was being very difficult.

Obviously Roosevelt could not give part of the American Navy away for nothing. For both strategic and political reasons he must present the American people with some immediate and tangible return to justify the bargain. He wanted military bases on British territory in the West Indies and in Newfoundland, then a British colony.

Churchill, having refused to preside at the liquidation of the British Empire, was in no mood to lease even a few bits and pieces of it to a friendly neutral. Could King persuade Churchill? That (according to King) was the real question at Ogdensburg, but it could not be mentioned, of course, in the official communiqué.

King agreed to accept the assignment of the honest broker and undertook to persuade Churchill. Whether King or Britain's need of destroyers in the Battle of the Atlantic convinced Churchill may never be known, but King believed that his intervention was decisive. Later certain distinguished British statesmen would say privately that King had persuaded Churchill to yield too much, but King never regretted it.

Few Canadians realized then what he meant when he told the Canadian Parliament that in the Ogdensburg Agreement "Canada, in liaison between the British Commonwealth and the United States, is fulfilling a manifest destiny." Roosevelt must have smiled on reading those words. His Canadian partner had appropriated an ancient American slogan of hostility to Canada and twisted it into a new meaning of friendship. That spirit, more than the large intrinsic contents of the meeting, was the vital result of Ogdensburg. The partners had sealed, at the most critical moment of modern history, the friendship of North America and the English-speaking world. And Canada's token commission on the deal was a gift of six American destroyers for its own infant navy.

Neither Roosevelt nor King could afford at the moment to explain his work in public. Roosevelt was still the prisoner of his nation's legal neutrality and would not escape it finally without the assistance of Japan, more than a year later. King must bear the criticism of his enemies at home without breaking the secrets of his friends, Roosevelt and Churchill.

The Ogdensburg defense agreement was instantly attacked in the Canadian Parliament by R. B. Hanson, leader of the opposition, as a stunt to re-elect Roosevelt that autumn and as King's latest affront to the British connection. Meighen emerged from his long silence to call the Ogdensburg decisions mere "twilight twitterings" which only diverted Canada from its sovereign purpose, the support of Britain, and from its only reliable defense, the British Navy.

The critics of Ogdensburg thus distorted its whole purpose. It was certainly designed to prepare North America for siege if Britain fell. In the summer of 1940 the leaders of the United States and Canada would have been guilty almost of treason if they had not taken those precautions. The primary purpose, equally clear, was to rescue Britain, within Roosevelt's existing limitations; and the net result was not, as Meighen supposed, to draw Canada further into the American orbit, but to draw the United States, by a treaty with Canada and by the destroyer deal, closer to the whole Commonwealth.

Churchill had no doubts on that score. He quickly relieved the political difficulties inflicted on King by enforced silence. In a rousing public cable from London he thanked the Canadian Prime Minister for "promoting a harmony of sentiment throughout the New World" and concluded: "This deep understanding will be a dominant factor in the rescue of Europe from a relapse into the Dark Ages."

Three other cables from Churchill remained thenceforth in King's wallet, fastened with a silver clasp, and were sometimes shown in confidence to his friends. Their contents proved, said the proud owner, that Churchill at first had underestimated his Canadian friend, was full of contrition for his mistake, and now realized that King had brought America and Britain together at the edge of a serious rift.

This work of reconciliation between the two leaders of the free world King regarded to his dying day as the most important of his life. In 1940, he would add mysteriously, transatlantic friendship had reached a head-on collision. "It was bad," said King, "very very bad!" because Churchill expected more than Roosevelt could grant and Roosevelt had been incensed by Churchill's impatience. Then King would carefully fold Churchill's cables, put them tenderly into his wallet and the wallet into his inner coat pocket as the proof that he had indeed enforced Canada's manifest destiny.

Ogdensburg was not the only occasion when King must suffer in silence to serve the interests of the United States and Britain. Not long afterwards he was attacked for maintaining a Canadian representative in Pétain's French capital of Vichy, for condoning the betrayal of France, and for truckling to the remaining isolationists of Quebec. He could not tell Parliament or people that he had maintained contact with Vichy against his will solely at the request of the American and British governments. As Hull had warned Lord Halifax, British ambassador to Washington, the American government could not keep its observers at the important listening post of Vichy if Canada withdrew and left the United States as the only free nation represented there. Reluctantly King agreed to carry the public load of Pétain. It was part of Canada's burden as the honest broker.

34

Onward from Hyde Park

[1940–1947]

B Y THE SPRING OF 1941 THE IMMEDIATE CRISIS IN OTTAWA WAS
not military but financial. Canada faced imminent bankruptcy. Only the United States could rescue it.

An ancient problem thus appeared in a new and extreme form.
Canada had usually bought more goods in the United States than
it sold there. The resulting deficit was made up by Canada's dollar
surplus in the world market, mainly in Britain. Now Britain could
not pay in dollars for many of its Canadian imports. Yet Canada
must continue to buy hugely in the United States to fuel its war
industries with American coal, oil, steel, and other essentials. Its
supplies of gold and dollars had been steadily shrinking and must
soon run out, thus wrecking its whole war program.

The Canadian government's experts saw this as a problem of
economics. King saw it as a problem of politics and human nature.
He decided to find a political solution in the human nature of his
American partner. Where the Canadian experts had failed for
months in negotiations with the Washington government, King
approached Roosevelt direct at Hyde Park.

The two friends drove about the President's estate in his little
hand-operated car while King explained the crisis in layman's
terms. Roosevelt admitted candidly that he could never understand
the details of foreign exchange, but King insisted that there was
nothing complicated in this situation. Canada needed American
dollars, that was all, to continue its aid to Britain. True, Canada
could raise a few more dollars, and remain effectively in the war
for a few months longer by spending its last gold reserves and
liquidating the small assets held by its investors in the United
States. If they were compelled to do that, King warned, Canadians

would never forgive the United States when they were fighting a war to defend North America as well as Britain.

Roosevelt might not grasp the intricacies of foreign exchange but he instantly grasped the import of King's warning. Why, it was unthinkable, he said, that some financial dispute should endanger the friendship of the North American peoples and weaken the defense against Germany. How could the thing be fixed?

King was ready for that question and primed with a simple answer. The United States, he said, had only to buy Canadian materials and munitions to be supplied to Britain in any case under the Lend-Lease formula and to pay Canada in American dollars. Thus the United States would use Canadian industry to produce essential British supplies, it would roughly balance Canadian-American exchange in dollars and save Canada from economic collapse.

Roosevelt agreed that this was "a swell idea." The partners drove back to his house and wrote the Hyde Park Declaration on a slip of paper. It committed the two nations to King's solution, saved Canada's war effort, buttressed its friendship with the United States, charted a sound policy of Canadian-American trade for the future and, rewritten after the war, was used against the new menace of communism. To the jottings of Hyde Park Roosevelt appended a typical postscript: "Done by Mackenzie and F.D.R. on a grand Sunday in April." The friendship of Roosevelt and King had produced another gigantic dividend.

It was not easy at first to work out the Declaration in practice. When American and Canadian officials fell into technical argument, King telephoned Roosevelt and heard the President shout at his technicians: "This is what I want done! Don't tell me why it can't be done, just do it!" From then on, as long as Roosevelt lived, Canada had plenty of dollars, earned by the production of war supplies. For purposes of war the economics of the American nations had been meshed. For the purposes of peace the wit of man has not yet achieved such a sensible arrangement.

Few Americans understood any better than did their president the dollar crisis of Canada. Some of them still accepted as true the slur of an American statesman who said that Canada demanded "cash on the barrelhead" for every pound of goods shipped to Britain. That slander on his country had infuriated King, but, until the summer of 1941, he had publicly ignored it. Now that the Hyde Park deal was working satisfactorily, he judged the time ripe for an explanation to the American people.

On June 17 he went to New York with Roosevelt's approval and

lashed out at Canada's slanderers. While his speech was worded
with restraint, its meaning was clear to the national radio audience.
Canada, he said, had entered the war not to save others but to save
itself—a calculated reminder to the neutral Americans that they,
too, were in danger, as they would learn in less than six months at
Pearl Harbor. He added that Canada was not demanding payment
from Britain, but was offering its treasure and its sons freely to the
"common cause of freedom"—a cause from which, he intimated, the
United States could not isolate itself.

Then, to show the American people that they were getting their
full money's worth under the Hyde Park Declaration, he translated
Canada's war program into comparable American terms—figures of
enlistment and armament intended to reveal the United States' own
relative weakness.

No more was heard after that of cash on the barrelhead. His
Hyde Park policy thus justified and his critics discredited, Roosevelt congratulated King on a good night's work. These two were
now operating by perfect agreement, almost by telepathy. Pearl
Harbor, ending the United States' technical neutrality, could not
bring the partners personally closer together but it removed the last
barrier between their peoples in the conduct of the war.

Two years later King found himself in urgent need of Roosevelt's friendship.

The Canadian government had reached the low point of its
political fortunes after its overwhelming election victory of 1940.
Public opinion polls showed the electors ready to vote it out at the
next opportunity. The nation was not tired, it had just caught its
second wind and clamored for larger tasks, but it was frustrated by
the stalemate of the war. Its army had been pinned down since
1939 to the drill grounds of Britain. It could not be told that the
hour of action and casualties was fast approaching, that the plans
on foot would soon absorb all its energies. Meanwhile its frustration was taken out on the government.

The Canadians prepared to land with the Americans and British
on Sicily. King demanded that their presence be revealed in the
first British announcement of the new campaign. Canada had a
right to know, he urged, that the days of stalemate and frustration
were over.

The lofty officials of the British War Office said they would
announce only that "British" units had landed with the Americans
under General Eisenhower. King telephoned Roosevelt in a fury.
The Canadian government, King told his partner, could not endure
the reaction of its people if they were insulted and their soldiers
ignored by the intended British communiqué.

Roosevelt, the politician, understood at once that this was a serious affair in the queer politics of Canada, but what could he do? As at Hyde Park, King was ready with an answer: Would Roosevelt instruct his officers in Sicily to include the Canadians by name in their first reports? Roosevelt agreed to do his best, though there was hardly an hour to spare before the Sicily landing. For the first time since Canada's declaration of war, King did not sleep that night. His anguish was relieved next morning. The Canadians' arrival on the battlefield had been announced. Again Roosevelt had not failed his friend.

The President went out of his way in the following month to boost the Prime Minister's political stock. Speaking in Ottawa, after his conference with Churchill in Quebec, Roosevelt informed the Canadian people that King was a "wise and good and gallant gentleman" and concluded, with a typically disarming touch: "My old friend, your course and mine have run so closely and affectionately during these many long years that this meeting adds another link to the chain." It also added—Roosevelt being a Canadian hero much more popular than King—an incalculable number of ballots to the Canadian government's election ledger.

The friendship of the two men and their peoples had reached an unprecedented point of intimacy and warmth. One aspect of King's policy, however, was deliberately designed to checkmate the expansion of American power.

He had decided to persuade the ancient British colony of Newfoundland into the Canadian Confederation. Its colonial position, he believed, could not last long. Its future must lie in Canada or the United States. Since it was garrisoned by American troops, in the bases leased to Roosevelt by Churchill, the danger of its gradual drift into the orbit of the United States was obvious. An American Newfoundland, King feared, would not merely enfilade the St. Lawrence and outflank Canada's Atlantic gateway; in the long run it might well threaten confederation entire. The loss of Newfoundland, the realization that Canada was hemmed in on the east by another giant stride of Manifest Destiny, would inflict a grave, perhaps a fatal, psychic wound on the Canadian people, would make them despair of their long continental labors when they could not hold the most vital strategic point in their natural geography. King's fears may have been excessive, but he held them tenaciously.

His thoughts about Newfoundland could not be uttered aloud, of course. Nor could the people of Newfoundland be pushed into union with Canada. Overt pressure would only antagonize that crusty breed. All King's predecessors from Macdonald onward had tried to attract Newfoundland. All had failed. King, therefore, moved in slow, deceptive stages, insisted that the decision was entirely for the Newfoundlanders to make, planted the idea of union subtly in their minds, and waited patiently for it to grow.

He had found in Joseph Smallwood a resourceful Newfoundland politician and discreetly encouraged this welcome ally. Smallwood's campaign finally produced a plebiscite and a modest majority in favor of union with Canada. On April 1, 1949, a tenth province was added to the Confederation. King had forestalled the United States (as he believed) and completed Canada's boundaries. Concerning them, and little else, King would die happy. He had come to final and friendly terms with Manifest Destiny.

Whether the United States government understood his long thoughts about Newfoundland or not, it did nothing to obstruct his policy and apparently took little interest in the ultimate union. Anyway, it had every reason to trust King's cooperation in virtually all aspects of its own policy.

When, for example, Lord Halifax came to Toronto in 1944 and proposed that the postwar Commonwealth make itself into a titan power with "a common foreign policy, expressed not by a single voice but by the unison of many," King promptly repudiated this eminent representative of Britain. In the titan theory of a few super-states running the world, King said, "lurks the idea of inevitable rivalry between the Great Powers. . . . Our commitments on these great issues must be part of a general scheme, whether they be on a world basis or regional in nature."

He thus rejected the idea of a commonwealth competing for power with the United States in favor of Roosevelt's concept of One World. The former Canadian isolationist had become an outright internationalist and the leading Commonwealth advocate of American postwar ideals. He would soon see the end of the One World, long before the American architects of that dream could accept its collapse, and he would die almost in despair of human prospects. But his partnership with Roosevelt lasted until the senior partner's death in the spring of 1945.

It lasted even beyond that earthly separation. As soon as he could escape his business in Ottawa, King hurried to England, consulted his secret spiritualistic mediums there, and established contact with his dead friend. At first Roosevelt urged King to retire and save his dwindling health; later he changed his mind and decided that King must remain in politics and guide his nation through an approaching storm—or so King reported to his intimates.

King had seen that storm approaching by the spring of 1945.

During the previous winter he had survived the most spectacular and dangerous crisis in the political history of his country. Living for weeks on the lip of personal and, as he thought, of national ruin, or even "anarchy," he had finally held his cabinet and party together by a prodigy of delay, entreaty, threat, and manipulation. He had achieved the apparently impossible by reconciling Quebec to conscription. He had established friendly contact with Roosevelt's successor and gone to the founding conference of the United Nations in San Francisco still dazzled by Roosevelt's One World.

If Harry Truman continued to believe in the dream for some time longer, King abandoned it before the San Francisco conference was a week old. The split between the two worlds, revealed in the drafting of the Charter, might be papered over for the present. King never doubted that it was incurable. From then on the only question in his secret mind was whether the two worlds could live together or, as he was inclined to expect, must collide in mutual destruction.

Roosevelt had died before he could lose his illusions. King was destined to live five years longer and thus to recognize, with an old man's bitterness at the end, that the hopes of his youth, all those utopias he had so often discussed with Roosevelt, were far beyond man's present reach.

The five years were filled with business on the border.

To begin with, there was the case of Igor Gouzenko, who fled from the Russian embassy at Ottawa on September 5, 1945, and revealed the first known Russian spy ring in America. At first King would not believe Gouzenko, suggested that the little cipher clerk was insane, and proposed that he return to the embassy and certain murder. Once convinced, King acted ruthlessly to smash an espionage net extending across the border, and he hurried to Washington to give Truman the facts.

Truman could not substitute for Roosevelt in King's affection. There is no reason to suppose that Truman regarded King as anything more than a friendly old man who knew the art of politics even better than did the master from Missouri. King's first serious business with the new American President was depressing.

After the Russian spy affair King returned to Washington with Clement Attlee, prime minister of Britain, to consider the future of the atomic bomb, then complacently regarded as an American-British-Canadian monopoly. King was shocked to find that Truman, though he had ordered the first bombs to be dropped on Japan, had yet to realize the unprecedented world problems exploded at Hiroshima and Nagasaki. King did not understand them very well either—who did?—but he knew at least that they might well explode civilization itself.

At the Washington discussion he took off his coat and sat down with his assistant, Lester Pearson, to write an announcement by the three heads of state. The resulting statement, signed by Truman, Attlee and King, declared that their three nations, having jointly invented the bomb, proposed to maintain its secret for the good of mankind. The only weakness of this plan was the fact that the Russians already knew the secret and were working industriously on it.

The pious statement of Washington would soon become irrelevant. The conference, nevertheless, had achieved certain intangible results of vast future importance.

It had begun, on the presidential yacht, the process by which Britain and Canada recognized the new world struggle already under way, accepted American leadership but determined to modify, as necessary, the exuberant foreign policy of the United States. That process would continue until the present day under the several successors to Truman, Attlee, and King.

The indestructible Canadian leader had now held office for longer than any other statesman of the English-speaking world. He would soon break Robert Walpole's all-time long-distance record. He was seventy-three years old and he was physically broken. There remained only one more job of work for him on the border.

Canada's wartime dollar crisis, solved by Roosevelt and King at Hyde Park, had returned. Throughout 1947 Douglas Abbott, King's young minister of finance, had watched with a stiff upper lip and a glazed public optimism the hemorrhage of his dollar and gold reserves as Canada bought far more in the American market than it could sell there, could not cover this yawning deficit by dollar earnings in the dislocated world market, and was not an applicant for American charity. National bankruptcy again lay not far ahead.

Disaster could be averted by one of two methods or a combination of both. Canada could seek new American markets, through lower American tariffs—a traditional Liberal policy—or it could restrict the importation of American goods—a Conservative, protectionist policy.

Abbott would later become a dominant figure in Commonwealth politics and in the world economy, but he was then too young and inexperienced to plumb the dark well of King's mind, where such minor stones as a dollar crisis dropped without an echo. Supposing that King was still the same low-tariff Liberal who had gone down to defeat with Laurier in 1911, Abbott decided to sound out the

United States on another reciprocity deal, or something like it. King approved tentatively, as a matter of general principle but without any faith in results at Washington. Besides, all his thoughts were new concentrated on the choice of a successor in this world and on his own arrival in the next, with which he was in constant spiritualistic communication.

Accordingly, a secret mission of Canadian experts began to discuss a drastic tariff reduction with officials of the State Department.

The Americans proved surprisingly enthusiastic. A new reciprocity agreement almost as comprehensive as the old one was quickly outlined on paper. Would the Congress approve it? The American officials could not be sure, but they were ready to fight for their policy on Capitol Hill. The Canadians, in their innocence of American politics, were delighted and hurried home to Ottawa with the good news. It was never clear in these mysterious conversations whether the deal carried the approval of the President or whether he had even seriously considered it.

While his hopeful young men pursued the old will-o'-the-wisp in Washington, King had sailed for Britain to attend—as a kind of overseas uncle to the royal family—the wedding of Princess Elizabeth.

The trip quite distracted King's mind from the trade negotiations. He was frantic at the loss in transit of his housekeeper's trunk and feared that in her anger she would never return to cook his meals at Laurier House. He was humiliated when his own baggage was lost in Paris, and he arrived in Brussels wearing his oldest clothes to meet the Belgian government. His secretaries managed to rent a morning suit for him, his valet slit a starched collar to make it fit, and a sartorial calamity was narrowly avoided. But the old man was failing. He had grown fussy, unpredictable, and at the royal wedding rather pathetically sentimental. He was in no state to govern a nation or to supervise its business in Washington.

Suddenly realizing what his officials were doing there, he roused himself from his lethargy, remembered Laurier's fate in 1911, and canceled the negotiations outright. There would be no reciprocity under him, the man who had gone down to defeat for it thirty-six years earlier.

He had three clear reasons for this complete reversal.

First, he did not believe that the United States Congress would approve a general tariff reduction even if, as he did not expect, the Truman government proposed it. In the light of subsequent events his judgment seems to have been correct. Reciprocity in 1911 had been offered by the United States in a solid, binding agreement.

Reciprocity in 1947 was a gleam in the eyes of a few enthusiastic American and Canadian experts. So it remains at this writing.

Secondly, King believed reciprocity to be politically impossible in Canada. As Dafoe had written, the 1911 decision held for a generation, perhaps a century. Since then Canada had built a huge industrial complex, always sheltered to greater or less degree by Macdonald's National Policy. It had certainly built some pretty exotic and noncompetitive industries during the war boom and the pressures for tariff protection could, therefore, be expected to grow. King would split his government and party if he attempted to revive Laurier's policy. Or so he calculated. In any case, his judgment that protectionist pressure would increase in Canada was fully justified not long afterward.

Third, at a cruel and doubtful moment in Britain's postwar poverty, King—once a rebel and now a royalist—could not bring himself to do anything which, by integrating the Canadian economy more closely with the American, might seem to be a blow at Britain and the ties of the Commonwealth.

These, for King, were reasons enough. He called off the mission to Washington without bothering to explain why. The negotiators came home, baffled. Some members of the Cabinet were angry because they had never understood their devious leader. Yet in this issue his reaction had been simple, instantaneous, and Canadian.

The Canadian nationalist in him feared American economic domination. The loyal citizen of the Commonwealth and personal friend of the royal family was devoted to the British connection, which he, more than any other man, had transformed into complete Canadian autonomy. So reciprocity, as far as the disenchanted free trader was concerned, could not be considered for reasons of politics and of instinct more important than economics. And there was no need to consider it. King remained convinced until the end that the United States would not abandon its protectionist policy.

This did not mean that tariffs could not be moderately and progressively reduced. At the moment when King was rejecting reciprocity the General Agreement on Tariffs and Trade was being completed at Geneva. Its substantial tariff reductions were regarded by King as a huge victory for the cause of world trade, and no nation would benefit from them more than Canada. But in those weeks of mystery and paradox Canada seemed to be undertaking a tariff reduction with one hand and raising its protectionist fence with the other. Actually, it had no alternative.

The dollar shortage was now so alarming that the government perforce restricted American imports by direct (and legally questionable) quotas. Though it promised that they would be temporary, they had a look of permanency to American exporters. Those fears proved groundless. The quotas were removed as soon as Canada's dollar reserves rose, mainly as a result of American tariff reductions under the Geneva agreement.

The supreme paradox now appeared. King undertook to tell his people by radio from London that he was reducing trade barriers while apparently raising them and added that he intended to seek "real reciprocity" with the United States. What could this mean, when he had personally killed the trade talks of Washington? It certainly did not mean that he had changed his mind again. It meant only that Canada would continue to seek a gradual scaling down of tariff walls if the United States would do likewise. It meant very little, but it sounded good. It satisfied the low-tariff wing of Canadian politics without seriously disturbing the protected industries. King had merely achieved, in fact, the inevitable Canadian compromise. Without reciprocity, Canada was moving into freer trade and, on a current of exports and imports massive beyond King's imagination, into its greatest boom.

35

Days of Doubt

[1947–1955]

WHEN THE HERMIT OF KINGSMERE DIED ON JULY 22, 1950, HE left his government, party and nation in good order, under a successor of his own choice. Louis St. Laurent, the new Canadian Prime Minister, was the son of a French-Canadian father and an Irish mother. He came to Ottawa—a short, handsome man of terrier face, brisk speech, courtly manner, and granitic temperament—to do a temporary war job in the Cabinet. He had little interest in politics, and less knowledge of international affairs. But he learned fast.

St. Laurent viewed his problems with a mind much simpler, more incisive, more practical, and less imaginative than King's. As he lacked both King's subtlety and his power of self-deception, he saw the postwar world in clearer terms. As he had never constructed the utopias that filled King's younger years, he suffered less disillusionment when the One World broke in two. And as Russia was the only possible aggressor, St. Laurent wasted no time in lamentation, but proposed an Atlantic alliance before most Western statesmen were ready to support it.

His first real test as an international statesman and as a neighbor of the United States came with Truman's decision to defend South Korea. It was a formidable test for a French-Canadian prime minister, the leader of a race traditionally hostile to all foreign wars. St. Laurent met that test by committing modest Canadian forces to the Korean war and simultaneously to NATO in Europe. By so doing he accepted not only Canada's responsibilities to the United Nations, but the leadership of the United States in the free world.

He held high hopes for that leadership and some doubts, which

478

he did not attempt to disguise, for he was by nature as candid as King was obscure.

So far as relations between Canada and the United States were concerned, he hoped mainly that the American government and people would learn to understand that they now lived beside a nation of some importance. He had not been long in office before he realized that there was little real understanding of Canada south of the border, only a generous friendship and the rather dangerous assumption that his country could be taken for granted.

It had not been in the nature of King to speak these doubts aloud. The more direct St. Laurent saw no reason to suppress them. Repeatedly, when he was invited to speak to American audiences, he warned them that friendship, however openhanded, was not quite enough, that there must be understanding as well, and that Canadians, while flattered by their neighbors' confidence, strongly objected to being taken for granted.

His articulate and brilliant young foreign minister, Lester Pearson, was even more outspoken. Trained in the arts of diplomacy, thoroughly educated in American affairs as ambassador to Washington and in world affairs at the United Nations, Pearson undertook a kind of one-man educational campaign in the United States. A long series of his flashing speeches laid down the fundamentals of Canada's policy in North America.

In brief, Canada had no illusions about its neighbor. It must depend on the United States' power, for it could read a map. It must accept the United States' decisions in great international affairs, but it demanded, as a friend, the right of consultation before decisions affecting it were made. It would remain a loyal friend, but it was not content to be a "camp follower" or "the echo of another's voice."

No sensible American could object to this doctrine, but when Pearson stated the obvious fact that the days of easy and automatic relations between the two countries were finished he produced an explosion of incredulity and anger. In that rather commonplace speech he had been the victim of unfortunate timing. Ignorant of Truman's pending decision, Pearson spoke a few hours before the dismissal of General MacArthur. That the Canadian government should choose a moment of national tumult and strain to lecture a good neighbor seemed incomprehensible to the thoughtful American and ungrateful, unfriendly, and churlish to the thoughtless. Pearson had been trapped by his own little foreign explosion in an unforeseen domestic explosion of huge, though brief proportions.

Nevertheless, what he had said was the plain truth. Until the present era the business of the United States and Canada had almost exclusively concerned them alone—trade, boundary waters, and the like. Now they were both members of a world-wide coalition of defense, and any important international act by either must affect all the other members. Hence, because they were now deeply involved in the world at large, Canadian-American relations could never be so easy and automatic as in the good old days.

Canada's policy toward its neighbor remained what it had always been in fundamentals, since those fundamentals had been laid down, within pretty narrow limits, by history and geography. For Canada a daily working partnership with the United States was not merely desirable, it was essential and a serious quarrel unthinkable. On the other hand, the United States needed the free cooperation of Canada because, if for no other reason, Canada lay directly between it and Russia in the age of air power.

Canada also desired and needed the friendship of Britain. Therefore, the most fundamental of all Canada's foreign policies could never be changed. All Canadian governments must consistently strive to reconcile disagreements between the United States and Britain. Canada must remain the middleman and honest broker of the English-speaking world to preserve itself.

This was a role for which St. Laurent was fitted by a large fund of common sense and Pearson by wide international experience. But never a pleasant, easy role. In practical terms it came down to this: Canada would argue with the United States on world policy where it thought the United States mistaken; it would insist on a friend's right to argue; it would seek to modify American policy when necessary; but it would accept the United States' great decisions if they did not threaten Canada's vital interests.

For several years after St. Laurent won his first election in 1949, the affairs of the border proceeded in perfect harmony. There was no difficulty, for example, in arranging the joint use of Canadian and American forces in the arctic and no friction worth mentioning between American forces and Canadian civilians at various air bases. Economic relations were equally happy in the days of the postwar boom. Canada's good humor was nourished by unexampled prosperity, the discovery of unsuspected resources in minerals and oil, the largest capital investment, in per capita terms, ever known anywhere.

By 1952, however, some of the unpleasant possibilities foreseen by Pearson—conflicts of emphasis rather than principle—had begun to emerge. If the American people did not realize that Canada had become seriously disturbed it was because a Canadian government always grows more silent as its troubles deepen.

Three factors, apparently separate but all interrelated, quietly undermined the ordinary Canadian's confidence in American leadership. By order of importance they were American policy in Asia; American policy in international trade; and those dark, demonic forces called McCarthyism.

Historically, Canada had thought little of Asia until the Second World War. Outside America its memories, its ties of blood, and its economic interests lay across the Atlantic. The attack on Pearl Harbor and the brief presence of Japanese troops in the Aleutian Islands suddenly reminded Canadians that their western coast fronted on Asia. The presence of their troops in Korea convinced them overnight that they would be involved in any great Asiatic war.

Pearson had worried about Western policy in Asia for years before the Communist thrust into Indo-China. Thinking aloud in guarded generalities, he had warned the United States that, to avoid disaster in Asia, it must distinguish between real communism, as an agency of Russian imperialism, and the natural aspirations of native peoples for freedom, sometimes operating under a Communist label. He wondered whether the United States was making that distinction. Like most of his countrymen, he took a dim view of such American protégés as Syngman Rhee and Chiang Kai-shek, and in the spring of 1955 declined to assist the United States in defending certain offshore Chinese islands, though admitting that Canada could not escape any great American war. Viewing events in Asia as a revolution beyond the white man's control, he found reason for hope only in such nations as India, Pakistan, and Japan and in such men as Jawaharlal Nehru.

Canada asserted a friend's prerogative to advise the United States that it was not satisfied with platitudes. It opened its markets to Japanese goods, on the assumption that Japan must trade with the West or seek its survival in the Communist world, and in the hope that the United States would follow the Canadian example.

The Canadian government has often been critical of American policy in Asia, has made no secret of its doubts but, knowing that the United States carries most of the white man's new burdens, it has studiously avoided any breach with its neighbor. For example, it has refused, up to this writing, to consider the recognition of Communist China (though ultimate recognition is regarded as inevitable) lest it offend the American people.

The breach between the United States and Britain in the Indochinese crisis of 1954 found Canadians almost unanimously on

Britain's side—not for reasons of sentiment, but solely because they were as much opposed to intervention as was Sir Winston Churchill. Most of them were appalled by the interventionist speeches of some of President Eisenhower's colleagues. They saw in the strains between Washington and London the oldest nightmare of Canadian life, for a real transatlantic quarrel must tear the whole substance of Canada apart. Thus Eisenhower's refusal to intervene and his apparent reconciliation with Churchill forestalled the danger of new strains between Ottawa and Washington.

Canada, in short, could no more escape its customary acrobat's position on the transatlantic tightrope than it could shuck off its geography and history.

Dominant in all Pearson's reasoning, implicit in the entire history of the continent, explicit in every current problem, was the oldest fact of Canadian life: Other continents and nations conceivably might escape American policies and somehow survive American mistakes, but not Canada. Equipped with the power of hydrogen, as Pearson says, the United States could destroy Canada by a single international blunder—a risk written on the northern map and scrawled across the polar sky by every passing American, Canadian, or Russian plane.

The alternative danger was equally clear, though seldom mentioned: What if the United States, a titan weary under the too great orb of its fate, were to unload its burden and retire within the besieged fortress of America? Or, what if it yielded to the advice of its new isolationists and attempted to construct a new kind of alliance of satellites willing to be coerced in an American imperium?

These fears have long been latent in the Canadian subconscious. They come to the surface only when a lunatic fringe is baying occasionally in Washington. They subside before the sanity of an Eisenhower, a Truman, or a Roosevelt. In times of crisis and tension everywhere they are overmagnified against the record of the past twenty years. The border has been so free of trouble in this generation, so profoundly at peace, that the slightest friction looms in exaggerated dimension. While the nerve of the boundary line may sometimes look taut to a few excited observers on either side, it is healthy and relaxed.

Canada could exert no great influence on Asiatic affairs, but it was not quite powerless. Its middle position seemed to give it an intangible power as the only Commonwealth nation in America and, moreover, a Western nation which the Asiatic peoples had no reason to distrust.

Unlike Britain, Canada had never possessed colonies in Asia, and thus had escaped the price paid for them in native resentment. Unlike the United States, it was too weak to be feared. As the close friend of the United States and Britain, as an American nation which threatened no one, Canada occupied a unique status, in theory at least. The practical question was whether, after its long effort to interpret the United States to Britain and vice versa, Canada should now attempt to interpret the United States to Asia.

That must be a thankless task in the existing climate, but after long thought St. Laurent resolved to make the experiment. In the spring of 1954, as the Indochinese crisis deepened, he flew around the world, ostensibly on a ceremonial tour, his real destination being New Delhi, his real objective a talk with Nehru.

These men, by their own racial origins, were uniquely equipped to work together without prejudice. St. Laurent represented Canada, yet as a French Canadian he could not be suspected of any emotional subservience to Britain. He had also shown a sturdy independence in dealing with the United States. He obviously knew far more than Nehru about the Americans. Moreover, the two men already had become personal friends at the London conference which devised a curious formula to hold the Republic of India within the Commonwealth.

Thus, as an outsider, St. Laurent might be trusted by Nehru in a discussion of American policy where any American statesman would be suspect as a partisan. Certainly the Commonwealth had never been represented in great affairs by such unlikely heads of state as Nehru, the Indian republican, and St. Laurent, the French-Canadian monarchist. In their own persons they symbolized the Commonwealth's diversity, its flexibility, and its hope.

St. Laurent went to India doubtful about some American tactics in Asia but he had no doubt about basic American motives. He was ready to testify publicly, before the Asiatic peoples, in defense of basic American policy. His testimony was delivered in a speech at New Delhi.

St. Laurent assured Asia that the United States had no aggressive intentions anywhere, in particular that its armament of Pakistan offered no danger to India. In support of his verdict he could produce the undeniable exhibit of Canada. If the United States' motives were imperialistic and its policies aggressive, Canada could not long have remained a member of the Commonwealth or survived as a free nation. That argument was valid. But would Asia heed it?

St. Laurent had hardly returned to Ottawa before the tragedy of Indochina moved to the Geneva conference. There Pearson reinforced his leader's testimony by defending the United States' international morals against Communist attack and offering Canada as the best proof that those morals were good.

What effect St. Laurent had on Nehru or Pearson on the Geneva conference may never be known. Apparently their separate missions were largely overlooked in the United States, then distracted by many more exciting matters. Nevertheless, they were a projection across the Atlantic and the Pacific, in modern terms, of Canada's experience as a conciliator on the American boundary. They were the acts of a good neighbor. They did not mean that Canada agreed with everything the United States was doing in Asia. They meant only that if Canada, living in weakness beside the American giant, could trust its real intentions—as often distinguished from some of its statesmen's utterances—those intentions were trustworthy. It was pre-eminently on the North American boundary that they had earned the right to be trusted.

Anyone who knew the history of Canada could see in these vague movements the oscillation of an old pendulum. Historically and instinctively Canadians resist the pressure most felt at any given moment. They resisted the pressure of Britain from the Conquest until they won their complete sovereignty by the Statute of Westminster in 1931. They resist the pressure of the United States whenever it passes a point of tolerance. The center of their gravity has moved perpetually between these pressures to preserve a national balance.

It has been said with some truth that events in the United States and Canadians' distrust of some American policies have pushed Canadians closer to the Commonwealth in recent years and made them appreciate anew the value of a world-wide association which multiplied their own power.

This familiar and oft-repeated movement can never be measured, but the oscillations of the Canadian pendulum are transitory and confined to a narrow range. Behind them the invariable purpose of all Canadian governments is never to separate the United States from the Commonwealth, but to bring them together. The Commonwealth, as Canadians see it, is a cohesive, not a divisive force. Canada is its link with the United States, a kind of central linchpin, as Churchill has called it.

The influence of Canada in these affairs should not be overestimated, but it grows with the nation. It is already greater than it usually appears, being exercised for the most part in private, between a few men in Washington, London, and Ottawa. Canadians' advice carries weight out of proportion to their nation's power simply because they are trusted as honest brokers.

Statesmen like King, St. Laurent, and Pearson symbolize in themselves the inevitable posture of their state. They are middlemen because Canada is a middle-state. That posture can never be easy—as demonstrated, for example, in the truce of Indochina, where Canada is the Western world's representative on the truce commission—but it is unavoidable. It is Canada's lot by the mandate of history and geography.

The current economic frictions between Canada and the United States are another matter entirely, older than the Canadian nation.

After the Second World War, Canada beheld its prewar pattern of trade in ruins. Its British customers lacked dollars for the purchase of Canadian goods—the dollars long used to cover a deficit in Canada's trade with the United States. As a result, Canada needed a greatly expanded American market and secured it through the Geneva trade agreement and the United States' increasing appetite for many kinds of Canadian supplies.

Canada soon found itself selling well over half its exports to its neighbor, and thriving on an almost unbelievable volume of trade. But Canada continued to buy far more than it sold in the United States. It had to carry a huge trading deficit in American dollars. The deficit was covered mainly by American capital investment moving across the border and making the Canadian dollar temporarily the most valuable currency in the world. So long as the investment movement continued, so long as Canada could earn some American dollars in the world market, the deficit could be carried, though it was far too large for comfort. Many Canadians thought, and still think it a dangerous policy to place so many of the nation's eggs in the single American basket.

These fears, often uttered in the Canadian Parliament, were eased by President Eisenhower's clear promise of a reduction in American tariffs. Hardly less than their neighbors, Canadians always liked Ike, even though most of them had long been unofficial Democrats, simply because the Republican Party had so often damaged Canada by its high tariffs. Canada was, therefore, ready to await Eisenhower's reform of American trade policy and to overlook, with only formal protests, the United States' minor breaches of the Geneva agreement.

By 1954, however, when the President postponed any action on trade for a year, to avoid an interparty quarrel in a Congressional election campaign, Canada began to wonder aloud whether the Republican elephant would ever change his tariff spots. At this writing the question remains unanswered. The Canadian government is, therefore, under increasing pressure to raise its own tariffs against the United States and further protect its new industrial complex.

Like all Canadian governments of the past, it will act not according to set principles but quite pragmatically, as the actual trade situation seems to require. Certainly if American tariffs go up, or even if they fail to come down, Canada will be sorely tempted to rectify its trade deficit in the United States by more restrictions on American goods. At the moment it can hardly understand why American industrialists and farmers are demanding more restrictions on Canadian goods when the United States enjoys a huge trading surplus in the Canadian market, when Canada is by far the United States' largest foreign customer, and when American investors own nearly a third of Canadian industry. If Eisenhower cannot convince or subdue the protectionists of his party, if the Canadian deficit is not reduced and the Canadian protectionist pressure continues to rise, the economic warfare of the boundary, foreseen by Dafoe in 1911, could enter another mutually destructive phase.

Tariffs may go up and down as governments and policies change. The St. Lawrence Seaway, its canals and its electrical plants, will remain. The 1954 agreement to construct and use these works jointly opens wider the economic lung of the continent and spills the Atlantic Ocean, uphill, into the Great Lakes.

It also proves that in a clear issue which the two peoples can understand (as they seldom understand the tariff) prudent management of the continent's resources is politically feasible. St. Laurent and Governor Dewey, of New York, turning the first ceremonial sods of this vast project, were carrying forward the task started by Cartier. That task remains, in terms of tariffs, commerce, and the sane use of North American resources, still far from completion, at the daily peril of politicians, pressure groups, and national greed.

McCarthyism, the third item of friction, struck deep into the Canadian mind, for it seemed to deny Canada's basic assumptions about the American character. Rightly or wrongly, many Canadians have regarded the activities of Senator Joseph McCarthy as an attempt to repeal the Bill of Rights and destroy the American Presidency. In a moment of indiscretion C. D. Howe, St. Laurent's right-hand man, an American by birth, cried out in Parliament: "We all abhor McCarthyism!" He was merely saying publicly what millions of Canadians had been saying privately. Senator McCarthy has a substantial body of Canadian supporters, but Parliament, an accurate mirror of the public mind, contains only one member willing to defend him. The defense was greeted with silent contempt. In any case, Canada's fears of McCarthyism waned with the waning of its author and at this writing have ceased to be a serious cause of international friction.

It may be asked what the political enterprises of an American senator from Wisconsin have to do with Canada or Canadian-American relations. Officially, nothing. Unofficially, however, anything which even seems to debase the coinage of American life exacts payment in the coin of Canadian respect.

This, of course, will matter little to Senator McCarthy and those who think with him. Canadian opinion is a matter seldom in the conscious minds of most Americans, though it can sometimes make quite a stir when it happens to catch the headlines. Regarded or disregarded, it must always be an important factor in American foreign policy, since it touches the United States' most important frontier.

The generally slight attention given to Canadian affairs by the American press and the average citizen is an unconscious tribute to the northern neighbor. He is a reliable friend. Unlike many other friends, he makes no trouble, so why worry about him? A passing armed revolution in some remote corner of the world excites American anxiety. Since Canada causes no anxiety to anyone, its current peaceful revolution was hardly discovered in the United States until it had been under way for at least a decade. Canada has seldom made what journalists are pleased to call news. It is being partially discovered at last by the American press, by Hollywood (which customarily sees it as an epic of ice, Indians, and Mounties), and by an annual migration of American tourists (who see the friendly surface but not far beneath it).

Why should Canadians expect Americans to understand them when they have not fully learned to understand themselves? Canada is more than three and a half centuries old by measurement of time; by measurement of national consciousness it is only now emerging from its youth. Its mind still teems with youth's doubts, torsions, and secret conflicts—and with youth's fierce courage, energies, appetites, and dreams.

Considering all its circumstances—the appalling obstacles of its geography and climate, the sparseness and ill-balanced distribution of its people, the clash of its diverse economic zones, above all, its racial split and dual culture—the wonder is not that Canada has matured slowly but that it has survived into manhood. By any measurement it must be judged a successful experiment, carried through against heavy odds.

At all events, Canada has been fully engaged until recent times in the business of survival, with little time left over to look at itself or ponder its nature.

Lately it has begun to ponder, to think furiously of its place in the scheme of things, to exaggerate both its failings and its virtues.

This private national assize has rendered one unmistakable verdict: The Canadian nation has passed its point of no return in our time. It has proved itself viable. The experiment of more than three centuries has produced a state and a society as permanent as anything can be in this kind of world.

Only a Canadian can understand what may be a surprising fact to a foreigner. The Canadian knows, as most foreigners do not know, that until very recent times—perhaps until the beginning of the Second World War—the long future of Canada was in doubt.

Its people were afflicted by a painful inferiority complex before the ancient glories of Britain and the bursting dynamism of the United States. They were haunted by the knowledge of their racial division, discouraged by their relatively slow growth, and uncertain whether their small numbers could ever master the empty half of a continent.

The unspoken question in the Canadian mind was whether a nation so weak could endure and hold a huge northern vacuum in an era of naked power. Must a people thus situated remain a British colony or become an American satellite? Was union with the United States, so long resisted, ultimately inevitable, as so many Americans had always believed from the Revolution onward? Even after Canada had gained all the constitutional machinery of independence those questions lurked deep in its being.

It is impossible to say exactly when they were answered, but they have been answered. The watershed of national life certainly had been crossed by the end of the Second World War.

Canada had fought the First World War as a British colony, for Britain's defense, and ceased to be a colony in the agony of its struggle. It fought the Second as a sovereign state, for its own defense. Its contribution—almost unbelievable in terms of population—made it not a principal but a vital factor in the victory of 1945; so far as Britain was concerned in 1940, an absolutely essential factor. The war of itself revolutionized the Canadian economy and built a major industrial nation. Far more important to Canadians, it made them aware of their own capacities. It proved to their satisfaction that their nation was here to stay.

As the twentieth century dawned, Laurier said it would belong to Canada. That was only an oratorical flourish when Laurier uttered it. Long after his time his prophecy remained a bitter disappointment. But in the sense he intended it has finally been made good during the past decade. If the twentieth century does not belong to Canada, or indeed to any state or group of states, Canada clearly belongs to Canadians.

The acceptance of this fact, not in any constitutional document or public proclamation, but in the mind of the ordinary Canadian, may well be the largest event north of the border since Champlain drove its first stake at Quebec. A vague but undeniable force called Canadianism, for lack of a better word, bestrides the upper slope of America—inarticulate, puzzled, amorphous, incalculable in its outcome, with no visible limits to its future.

The Canadian watershed was not marked in passage as the American watershed was marked by the rebels of Philadelphia. It stands out mountainous in retrospect, and must increasingly influence the future of the whole continent.

The continent, however, remains whole, even while the political, racial, and spiritual separateness of its two peoples becomes increasingly clear. It is made whole by geography, by economic interest, by its common peril, and by that queer unity beginning in hatred and ending in friendship. The boundary that divides it yet laces it together by hidden stitches in a texture entirely North American, unique, *sui generis*.

The principles, attitudes, and living ways of the boundary, if reproduced elsewhere, could mend far more than the fabric of America. They could repair the raveled garment of mankind. Certainly no other system of ideas, whatever the local variations may be, can hope to weld the grinding splinters of a disordered world— except, of course, the opposite system of our enemies. The universal question and the hope of our time, it may be said, is represented by an imaginary line, not one of its 3,986.8 miles defended, running from Fundy to Fuca's Strait.

As Europe could not imprint its image on America, so America cannot print its own on others. At the moment it covers its true face and nature under a false mask. This continent must continue its march in its own fashion, however foreigners regard it. A long march, as it seems to the marchers after 347 years, a march which has carried two peoples out of the palisades of Jamestown and Quebec to the fringes of their continent and, in war, commerce and joint adventure, to the ends of the earth, a march whose furious passage is hardly remembered, whose leaders and followers are buried in lost graves.

Long as the course has been, heavy the baggage, fierce the battles, and wasted most of the bloodshed, that march is only well begun. It has filled hardly a moment in the history of America, a tiny speck of time in the larger march of humankind. But it has left certain blazes beside the trail. Men will mark them, long hence, and pause in wonderment.

Index